THE HISTORY OF GUERNSEY

The Bailiwick's Story

The Family of Islands in the Bailiwick

Guernsey and Lihou; Alderney and Burhou;
Sark and Brecqhou; Herm and Jethou
(of which only Burhou has no resident population)

Apart from the Islands some rocks are also important enough for inclusion in this history

Casquets, Crevichon and Bréhon, Hanois

"Tel est le petit pays qui nous est cher, qui a été cher à nos pères depuis tant de siècles et que nous vous prions de chérir pour l'amour d'eux, pour l'amour de nous et pour votre propre bien. On ne perd rien à l'ideé d'être venu de peuple don't on est fier. On s'en respecte de plus.

Pendant près de sept cent ans, isolés dans la mer, nous avons tenu notre place au soleil, avec des lois, des coutumes, une langue, le tout bien à nous. Prenons soin de les garder et de les passer intactes à ceux qui viendront après nous. Une patrie, qu'elle soit petite ou qu'elle soit grande, est toujours une patrie et les petites ont souvent les meilleures lois et la plus belle histoire."

From *Notre Pays*, written for
Guernsey schoolchildren by
Jurat Peter Roussel (1815–1879)

James Marr

*

THE HISTORY OF GUERNSEY

The Bailiwick's Story

*

With Introductions by

His Excellency The Lieutenant-Governor

and

Air Chief Marshal
Sir Peter de Lacey Le Cheminant, G.B.E., K.C.B., D.F.C.,
Lieutenant-Governor of Guernsey, 1979–1985

and a Foreword by

the late Victor Coysh

Illustrations arranged by

Carel Toms

*

Ad Lesiam Insulam Patriam Meam

Original edition published by
Phillimore & Co. Ltd
London & Chichester

This revised and updated edition published by
The Guernsey Press Company Limited
Braye Road
Vale
Guernsey

ISBN 0-9539166-1-8

Printed and bound in Great Britain by
The Guernsey Press Company Limited,
Guernsey, Channel Islands.

THIS SECOND EDITION OF MY BAILIWICK HISTORY

IS DEDICATED TO

THE TREASURED MEMORY OF

KATHARINE, LADY CLIFFORD (1919–1999)

WHOSE COURAGE FACING CERTAIN DEATH

WAS BEYOND PRAISE

AND WHOSE WARM FRIENDSHIP OVER ELEVEN YEARS

I VALUED IMMEASURABLY

By the same Author

GUERNSEY PEOPLE
wherein, together with its companion

MORE PEOPLE IN GUERNSEY'S STORY
much more is said of persons mentioned but briefly in this History

BAILIWICK BASTIONS
An historic review of the islands' fortifications

BAILIWICK HARBOURS AND LANDING PLACES
The islands' havens' historical growth and anecdotes about them.

GUERNSEY BETWEEN THE WARS: AN ISLANDER RECALLS HIS YOUTH
A collection of glimpses into the inter-war years

CONTENTS

SOURCES OF QUOTATIONS
(Authorized Version where Biblical)

Part Titles
Part I, John XVIII, 38; Part II, Deuteronomy XIX, 14; Part III, Mark XII, 17; Part IV, Mark XIII, 7; Part V, Ephesians IV, 25.

Chapter Headings
Part I, Chapter 1, Genesis I, 1; Part I, Chapter 9, Act of Settlement, 1701; Part III, Chapter 13, Queen Elizabeth I: Motto; Part IV, Chapter 1, Book of Common Prayer: Collect for the Fourth Sunday after Epiphany; Part V, Chapter 14, Psalm CVII, 23; Part V, Chapter 18, Charles Wesley: Hymn, 'Jesu, Lover of my Soul'; Part V, Chapter 21, William Shakespeare: 'Hamlet', Act III, Sc. l; Part V, Chapter 22, 1 Timothy III, 8; Part V, Chapter 25, Benjamin Disraeli: 'Sybil'; Part V, Chapter 26, Old Entrance to Guille-Allès Library.

Text (where not already indicated)

Part I
- Chapter Seven — Book of Common Prayer: Litany
- Chapter Nine — Book of Common Prayer: Catechism
- Chapter Twelve — Book of Common Prayer: Good Friday Collect

Part III
- Chapter Four — Henry Grattan, commenting on the American Revolution
- Chapter Eight — Christopher Hibbert: *Benito Mussolini*
- Chapter Eleven — Lewis Carrol: *Alice in Wonderland*, Ch. 1

Part IV
- Chapter One — (a) Napoleon Bonaparte commenting on Alderney
  (b) W. Walsham How: Hymn *For All the Saints*
  (c) Chateaubriand: *La Monarchie selon la Charte*
  (d) Rabelais: *Gargantua et Pantagruel*, Bk. IV
- Chapter Two — William Shakespeare: *Henry IV, Part I*, Act 5, Sc. 4
- Chapter Three — Book of Common Prayer: Twenty-second Article of Religion
- Chapter Nine — Rudyard Kipling: *Recessional*
- Chapter Twelve — Ruggero Leoncavallo: *I Pagliacci*, Act 2
- Chapter Fourteen — (Section E) — Francis Brett Young: *The Island*

Part V
- Chapter Fourteen — Rudyard Kipling: *A Smuggler's Song*
- Chapter Twenty-four — William Shakespeare: *Twelfth Night*, Act 2, Sc. 3
- Chapter Twenty-six — St. Matthew, XIII, verse 57

LIST OF ILLUSTRATIONS

Colour

Monochrome

PICTORIAL ACKNOWLEDGEMENTS

Colour

The Castel Statue Menhir (Plate 2) and Le Colombier Farmhouse (Plate 3) were photographed by Mr. L. Chester Smith, while the picture of Château à l'Etoc (Plate 5) is the work of Mr. Robin Millard. The remaining photographs (Plates 1, 4 and 6) were taken by myself.

Monochrome

On the religious plane, the Reverend Brother Déodat standing by his Little Chapel (Plate 11) is a *Guernsey Press* photograph, while the pictures of Europe's oldest tomb at Les Fouaillages (Plates 1 and 2) and La Platte Mare burial chamber (Plate 3) were taken by Mr. William Tipping. Illustrating the feudal aspect, the Presentation of the Spurs to H.M. the Queen by La Dame des Eperons (Plate 15) and Mr. Bert Hammond raising the Clameur de Haro in Alderney (Plate 18) are both *Guernsey Press* photographs, as is also that of the sitting of the Anneville Feudal Court (Plate 21), the print of the first-named being kindly supplied by Mrs. J. E. Moullin; the pictures of the Queen as Princess Elizabeth and the Duke of Edinburgh with the Seigneur and Dame of Sark (Plate 19) and also of La Dame de Sercq with her Colombier in the background (Plate 20) were both taken by the late Mr. C. H. Toms; while the Feudal Court of Le Fief Beuval in session (Plate 16) is a Priaulx Library picture. On the political side, the pictures of H.M. the Queen presiding over the Guernsey (Plate 22) and Alderney (Plate 23) States respectively are both *Guernsey Press* photographs. In the military sphere, the photographic reproduction of Terence Cuneo's painting of Major H. W. Le Patourel winning the Victoria Cross at Tebourda (Plate 37) appears by courtesy of the Trustees of the Royal Hampshire Regiment; while that of J. G. Bréhaut's painting, *The Escape from Castle Cornet* (Plate 31) is printed by permission of Miss E. L. Wood of Kirby-le-Soken. The photograph of Burhou's only building, later destroyed by the Germans (Plate 40), was taken by the late Mr. C. H. Toms, that of the King's Birthday Parade (Plate 36) by Mr. C. H. Coker and of Castle Cornet (Plate 32) by Mr. R. Golding. The German troops marching up Le Pollet (Plate 38) were photographed by my uncle, the late Mr. Arthur Machon, while the photographs of the *St. Helier* (the vessel to bring the last shipload of troops away from Dunkirk) (Plate 39) and of the Militia receiving the last Royal Inspection of its career (Plate 35) were both provided by myself. Lastly, in the Socio-Economic field, the Cider Apple Crushing picture (Plate 44) is a Priaulx Library photograph, while that of Cecil Noel's aeroplane, 'The Wee Mite' (Plate 48) is my own.

Irrespective of theme, all other photographs in this book (Plates 4, 5, 6, 7, 8, 9, 10, 12, 13, 14, 17, 24, 25, 26, 27, 28, 29, 30, 33, 34, 41, 42, 43, 45, 46, 47, 49, 50, 51, 52, 53, 54, 55), by far the major contribution, have been provided by Mr. Carel Toms, to whom my debt is immeasurable; the generous scale of his co-operation and of the kindly advice accompanying it being equalled only by the superb degree of his artistry as a photographer. I cannot thank him enough.

PREFACE TO FIRST EDITION

This book having no pretensions to original scholarship, my only excuse for writing it is that for many years the reader entering a bookshop in search of a comprehensive general history of the Bailiwick has done so in vain, even though studies in depth of individual periods or places are available and there has admittedly been no lack of publications of wider coverage containing historical passages interspersed with other material.

I should like to assure Mrs. J. H. Le Patourel of my gratitude to her late distinguished husband for his kindly help and advice regarding mediaeval sequestrations. In addition I should also like to express my heartfelt thanks to Mrs. M. W. Reid, of the Lieutenant-Governor's Office, for her invaluable help with records of past Governors; to Mr. B. G. Jones, then Seneschal of Sark and to Mr. E. G. Couldray, of the States Telecommunications Board, for their conjoint kindness and helpfulness in answering my questions about Sark's original telephone service; to the Reverend Brother Christantian of Les Vauxbelets, for information regarding the social work of Roman Catholic Religious Orders; to the Sister Archivist of Holy Cross Abbey, Stapehill, near Wimborne, for her help in establishing the identity of the Herm monks of the 1880s; to Le Général de Corps d'Armée Guinard, Directeur du Service Historique, Vincennes, for elucidating the precise meaning of 'ars et trousses'; to Mr. A. O. Hamon, President of the Ancient Monuments Committee, for information regarding mediaeval fortifications; to Mr. R. H. Videlo, H.M. Greffier, for his advice about the original deputies in Guernsey and to Mr. W. R. Jones, Clerk to the Alderney States, for similar information regarding his island; to Mr. H. N. Machon, Editor of the *Guernsey Press*, for providing tourist figures; to the staff of the Guille-Allès Library for kindly giving me access to old newspaper files; to the Commandant of the Airport for supplying me with statistics relative thereto; to Mr. Victor Coysh for his generous encouragement and advice as a result of which sundry textual blemishes have been eliminated; to Mr. Hugh Lenfesty who, by unstintingly giving of his time and expertise, enabled me to track down some of the more elusive Feudal Courts; to Mr. G. W. S. Robinson for much-valued help in connection with Jethou; to Dr. S. K. Kellett-Smith, for so kindly providing me with draughts from the virtually inexhaustible well of his knowledge of Herm's history; to the Secrétariat du Syndicat d'Initiative, Tréguier, for so promptly and amply responding to my request for information on St. Tugual; and finally to Mr. A. J. W. McDonald, J.P., late of the Public Record Office, for his help in connection with the 'Glorious Revolution' and especially for his invaluable contribution in identifying a Lieutenant-Governor (Colonel John Legge) hitherto inexplicably omitted from island records.

I should also like to place on record my gratitude to my wife for her invaluable help with proof checking and index compilation.

As it is particularly tiresome when reading a book to come across quotations with no indication of their provenance, a set of three lists is provided after the Table of Contents. The first of these gives the biblical references included in the titles of each part of the book, while the other two give the sources of quotations embodied in chapter headings and incorporated in the text respectively other than those the origin of which is mentioned as an accompaniment to their employment.

Hornchurch JAMES MARR
May 1982

PREFACE TO SECOND EDITION

In preparing this revised edition of my Bailiwick History I set myself a two-fold task. The first was that of updating, so as to take account of the various developments and discoveries of recent years; while the second was the cathartic one of purging away the several blemishes which sullied the first edition, coupled with making amends for its sundry sins of commission and omission. In these endeavours my path was smoothed by the much valued help of a number of Good Samaritans whom I should like sincerely to thank, beginning by assuring Miss Louise de Sausmarez and her sister Mrs. Jennie Lintell of my gratitude to their late father Cecil de Sausmarez, M.B.E., Seigneur du Fief de Sausmarez, for the many fascinating insights into matters relating to his illustrious family which I gained from our long and frequent conversations. I am similarly most grateful to Sir Graham Dorey for his kindly and helpful observations from which I much profited when compiling the tragic account headed 'Daughters of Israel'. I likewise wish to convey to Mrs. Henriette Carré my appreciation of the kindness of her late husband Mr. Hilary Carré in providing the text of the Sark version of Le Clameur de Haro. I am also much indebted to Messrs. Roger Perrot, David Shayer, Bob Burns and John Middlebrook, as well as the late Reverend Brother Christantian and the Reverend John Guille for revelations in the Political, Naval, Archaeological, Theatrical, Educational and Religious fields respectively (in the last-named of which I owe particular thanks to the Reverend G. L. Lugton for the facts concerning latter-day Presbyterianism, to Mr. R. W. Reeve for apprising me regarding Jehovah's Witnesses and to Mrs. J. A. Collas for acquainting me with the fortunes of the Christian Scientists); to Mr. William Bell for permission to quote from his book *I Beg To Report*; to the Reverend Arthur Mignot and Mr. Brian Bonnard but for whom thick darkness would brood yet o'er my knowledge of many Alderney topics; to Dr. H. Tomlinson of the Priaulx Library for particulars of the careers of Saint Guénael and of Jurat Peter Roussel; to Mr. Stuart Falla of Saint Sampson's for details regarding La Garenne d'Anneville, together with Mr. and Mrs. P. Falla of the Vale for putting me in touch with their namesake. I am additionally deeply beholden to Commander Bruce Nicolls, O.B.E., together with Miss Jennifer Cochrane of Sark, Mr. Nigel Jee and Mr. William G. Crampton, Director of the Flag Institute (the last-named a veritable mine of information) for vexillological enlightenment; to J. P. Allez Esq., Chief Customs Officer, for historical data concerning his Department; to Messrs. S. W. Butterworth, Superintendent of Insurance and Frank Bradbrook of Gidea Park, London Borough of Havering, for unravelling the mysteries of Captive Insurance; to Dr. Mark Patton of Trinity College, Carmarthen, University of Wales, for information on megaliths; to Mr. John Bennett of Yatton, Avon, for help with matters telephonic — and to my good friend Mr. Bernard Geffon of Rehovot, Israel, for conducting on my behalf researches at the Yad Washem archives in connection with the three Jewesses from Guernsey butchered in Auschwitz. Last, but by no means least, I owe thanks to Mr. K. H. Tough, H.M. Greffier, for advice regarding Jethou — and finally I am most grateful to my kind cousin Chris Sackett not only for generously shouldering the chore of proof checking but above all for his invaluable support and guidance in promoting the publication of this book. My debt to him is incalculable.

I trust that the book will prove worthy of these benefactions and be found both informative and interesting.

Hornchurch, London Borough of Havering — JAMES MARR
La Saint Michié (Michaelmas) Anno Domini MM, Centuriae Annus Terminalis

INTRODUCTION TO FIRST EDITION

by His Excellency Air Chief Marshal Sir Peter de Lacey le Cheminant, G.B.E., K.C.B., D.F.C.,

Lieutenant-Governor and Commander-in-Chief of the Island of Guernsey and its Dependencies 1979–1985

From: His Excellency Air Chief Marshal Sir Peter Le Cheminant, G.B.E., K.C.B., D.F.C.

TELEPHONE 0481 20002

GOVERNMENT HOUSE,
GUERNSEY,
CHANNEL ISLANDS.

This is without question the most important book on the Bailiwick this century and will, I am sure, be held as the standard work by generations yet to come. I commend it most warmly.

Peter le Cheminant

Air Chief Marshal
Lieutenant-Governor and Commander-in-Chief
of the Island of Guernsey and its Dependencies

INTRODUCTION TO SECOND EDITION

by His Excellency Vice-Admiral
Sir John Coward, K.C.B., D.S.O.,
Lieutenant-Governor and Commander-in-Chief of the Island of Guernsey and its Dependencies

From: His Excellency Vice Admiral Sir John Coward, KCB, DSO.

TELEPHONE:
01481 726666 (OFFICIAL)
01481 720002 (PRIVATE)

GOVERNMENT HOUSE,
GUERNSEY GYI IGH,
CHANNEL ISLANDS.

February 2nd., 2000

I consider that the praise bestowed by Sir Peter Le Cheminant on this book when it originally appeared is now even more richly deserved, thanks to the meticulous revision and extensive updating which characterize this edition. No island home should be without a copy.

FOREWORD TO FIRST EDITION

by the late Victor Coysh

For more than a century students of the Bailiwick's history have awaited such a book as this, for it was in 1876 that F. B. Tupper's celebrated *History of Guernsey and its Bailiwick* was published in the second edition. For years it has been out of print and today copies are both scarce and expensive. Even when obtainable, Tupper's work is a hundred years out of date.

James Marr's Bailiwick History is a piece of writing after my own heart. He deals with his subject in the greatest detail; he writes with style; his book is well illustrated, documented and indexed and its attractive format will certainly appeal to the casual seeker after our history (be he islander or visitor) as much as to the student of the Bailiwick's past.

This history is, in fact, more than a record of our yesterdays, for it tells one a good deal of the contemporary way of life, industries and governmental systems of Guernsey, Alderney and Sark. It copes with today as generously as it deals with prehistory, the uncertainties of the Dark Ages, the adventurous Civil War, the excitement of the Napoleonic conflicts and, certainly not least, the vital years of World War II when, perhaps, the greatest chapter in our history was written: the German Occupation.

This precious volume should have a place in our island schools for this history is something to be proud of and it is proper that young islanders should have a share in it. They ought to be informed of the great days of the past, as they need to be instructed as to how we cope with the present. A scholar, indeed, has written it for scholars of all ages.

While it is true that local historical works have been recently written about a wealth of insular aspects, the Occupation in particular, nothing of the scope of Mr. Marr's work has been attempted for far too long. Moreover, some of the island literature has a weighty quality about it which, to some, could be daunting. On the other hand, James Marr coats the pill of history with an ample measure of sugar!

As a student of Bailiwick history I commend this book to all. It needed to be written. It requires to be read and consulted. Its appearance is most timely. I have read the text and shall do so time and again. It fills a gap in our annals and the author's labours warrant the most loyal support from all with the Bailiwick's interest at heart.

VICTOR COYSH

BIBLIOGRAPHY

Anon, *The Channel Islands or a Peep at our Neighbours* (1847)
Bailey, K. G., *Dachau* (C. I. Marine, 1958)
Bell, W. M., *I Beg To Report* (William M. Bell, 1995)
Blampied, B. G., *Mayday! Mayday!* (Guernsey Press, 1984)
Bunting, M., *The Model Occupation* (Harper-Collins, 1995)
Burns, R. B., *A Field Guide: Archaeological Sites of Guernsey* (Holiday Pak, 1982)
Butler, A., *Lives of the Saints* (Burns and Oates, 1956)
Chapman, W. R., *His Praise in the Islands* (Private Distribution, 1984)
Cliff, W. H., *Jethou* (Guernsey Press, 1960)
Coates, R., *Ancient and Modern Names of the Channel Islands* (Stamford Paul Watkins, 1991)
Cortvriend, V. V., *Isolated Island* (Guernsey Press, 1946)
Coysh, V., *Alderney* (David and Charles, 1974)
Cruickshank, C., *The German Occupation of the Channel Islands* (Oxford University Press and Guernsey Press, 1975)
Crump, F., *The Alderney Cow* (Alderney Society, 1995)
Drake, F., *Thy Son Liveth* (Hodder and Stoughton, 1959)
Eagleston, A. J., *The Channel Islands Under Tudor Government* (Cambridge University Press, 1949)
Everitt, D., *Samaritan of the Islands* (Harrap, 1959)
Ewen, A. H. and de Carteret, A. R., *The Fief of Sark* (Guernsey Press, 1969)
Ewen, A. H. et alii, *Alderney Official Guide* (Guernsey Press, 1961)
Falla, F., *The Silent War* (Leslie Frewin, 1967)
Fleming, P., *Invasion 1940* (Rupert Hart-Davis, 1957)
Fox, J., *Christian Martyrdom* (Sherwood, Jones, 1824)
Froissart, J., *Chroniques* (Everyman, 1927)
Furniss and Booth, *Paul Jacob Naftel* (JAB Publishing, 1991)
Girard, P. J., *Peter Girard's Guernsey* (Guernsey Press, 1986)
Glendinning, A., *Eye on the Past in Guernsey* (Channel Islands Family History Society, 1993)
Harman, N., *Dunkirk: The Necessary Myth* (Hodder and Stoughton, 1980)
Hathaway, S., *Dame of Sark* (Heinemann, 1961)
Hawkes, K., *Sark* (David and Charles, 1977)
Hocart, R. P., *An Island Assembly* (Guernsey Museum, 1989)
Hocart, R. P., *Peter de Havilland* (Société Guernesiaise, 1997)
Hooke, W. D., *The Channel Islands* (Robert Hale, 1953)
Jacob, J., *Annals of Guernsey etc.* (Galignani Press, 1830)
Jee, N., *Guernsey's Natural History* (Guernsey Press, 1972)
Johnston, D. E., *The Channel Islands: An Archaeological Guide* (Phillimore, 1981)
Kalamis, C., *Hidden Treasures of Herm* (Wood of Herm, 1996)
Leale, J., *Report on Five Years of German Occupation* (Guernsey Press, 1945)
Le Huray, C. P., *The Bailiwick of Guernsey* (Hodder and Stoughton, 1952)
Lemprière, R., *Portrait of the Channel Islands* (Robert Hale, 1970)

Le Patourel, J. H., *The Mediaeval Administration of the Channel Islands* (Oxford University Press, 1937)
Lewis, S., *A Topographical Dictionary* (S. Lewis, 1833)
Marshall, M., *Herm: Its Mysteries and Charm* (Guernsey Press, 1958)
Marshall, M., *Hitler Invaded Sark* (Paramount-Lithoprint, 1963)
MacCulloch, E., *Guernsey Folk Lore* (Elliot Stock, 1903)
McCormack, J. A., *The Guernsey House* (Phillimore, 1980)
McCormack, J. A., *Channel Islands Churches* (Phillimore, 1986)
Myhill, M., *Introducing the Channel Islands* (Faber and Faber, 1964)
Ogier, D. M., *Reformation and Society in Guernsey* (Boydell, 1997)
Ovenden, J. & Shayer, D., *The Wreck of the Stella* (Guernsey Museum & Art Gallery, 1999)
Pantcheff, T. X. H., *Alderney: Fortress Island* (Phillimore, 1981)
Pollard, A. F., *Edward VI to Elizabeth* (Longmans Green, 1910)
Ridley, J., *Lord Palmerston* (Constable, 1970)
Robinson, G. W. S., *Guernsey* (David and Charles, 1977)
Scott-Hill, I., *Channel Silver Wings* (Jersey Artists, 1972)
Stevens Cox, J., *Prehistoric Monuments of Guernsey* (Toucan Press, 1976)
Stevens Cox, J., ed., *Channel Islands Anthology No. 1* (Toucan Press, 1972)
Stevens Cox, J., ed., *Channel Islands Anthology No. 2* (Toucan Press, 1975)
Stevens Cox, J., ed., *Guernsey Historical Monographs* (Toucan Press, 1966/79)
Syvret, M. and Stevens, J., *Balleine's History of Jersey* (Phillimore, 1981)
Uttley, J., *The Story of the Channel Islands* (Faber and Faber, 1966)
Venne, R. & Allez, G., *Alderney Annals* (Alderney Society, 1992)
Walker, D., *Bedlam in the Bailiwicks* (Alan Sutton, 1987)
Walker, D., *Task Force Channel Islands* (Alan Sutton, 1989)
Wells, D. H., *History of the Catholic Church in Alderney* (Alderney Society, 1994)
Wilde, J., *Saints Alive* (Steven Banks, *circa* 1987)
Wilson, E., *Railways in Guernsey* (Paramount-Lithoprint, 1974)
Wood, A. and M., *Islands in Danger* (Evans, 1955)
Wood, J., *Herm: Our Island Home* (Robert Hale, 1972)
Dictionary of National Biography (Oxford University Press, 1959)
The Guernsey Farmhouse (Guernsey Society, 1963)
Guernsey Ways (Guernsey Press, 1970)
Nos Iles (Channel Islands Study Group, 1944)
Report of the Committee of the Privy Council on Proposed Reforms in the Channel Islands (H.M.S.O., 1947)
Report of the Royal Commission on the Constitution (H.M.S.O., 1973)
Reviews of the Guernsey Society
Transactions de la Société Guernesiaise

EXPLANATORY NOTES

1. **Guernsey Dry Capacity Measure**

3 Denerels	=	1 Cabot
2 Cabots	=	1 Bushel

2. **Guernsey Land Measurements**

7 Yards	=	1 Running Perch
49 Square Yards	=	1 Perch (Square)
40 Perches (1,960 Square Yards)	=	1 Vergée
20 Vergées	=	1 Bouvée
12 Bouvées	=	1 Carucate

2a. **English Equivalencies**

2.469387755 Vergées	=	1 English Acre
8.1 English Acres	=	1 Bouvée

3. **Weights and Measures**

The 1916 Weights and Measures Law brought Guernsey Avoirdupois Weights into line with those of the United Kingdom, with one Hundredweight consisting of 112 Pounds of 16 Ounces each. Previously the Guernsey Pound had approximated to just under 18 English Ounces (17.92 to be precise), one hundred of which made a Guernsey Hundredweight; while 14 ounces, 10 Drams and 9 Grains Guernsey weight equalled one English Pound.

By the 1989 Weights and Measures Law the use of the traditional Capacity units was discontinued as far as trading is concerned, though retained for the calculation of Rentes. By the same Law Vergées and Perches remain in use for land transfer purposes; but in the realm of Avoirdupois the English Pound, Hundredweight and Ton introduced in 1916 give way to the Kilogram (2.2 pounds), the Quintal of one hundred Kilograms (1.968 Hundredweight) and the Tonne of 1,000 Kilograms (0.98 Ton). This law does not apply to Sark.

4. **Bailiwick Patron Saints** (listed to dispel prevailing misconceptions)

Guernsey — Saint Sampson Alderney — Saint Vignol
Sark — Saint Magloire Herm — Saint Tugual

5. **'Fauna' of the Bailiwick**

The following nicknames traditionally attach to the inhabitants of the Bailiwick's main islands —

Guernsey — Donkeys Alderney — Cows Sark — Crows

PART I

'WHAT IS TRUTH?' —
THE RELIGIOUS ASPECT

Chapter One

'IN THE BEGINNING'

PRIOR TO THE DEATH in November 1980 of its creator (Alan Guppy), readers of the *Guernsey Evening Press* had come to be familiar with a strip cartoon featuring a character known as 'Stone de Croze — The Original Guernseyman'. The conjecture, based on surviving artefacts, is that the genuine Stone de Croze has his counterpart in today's tourist in that he first came to Guernsey as a seasonal visitor — though in his case intent on fishing, together with hunting seals and seabirds — at some point in the late Mesolithic Period (possibly *circa* 6,000 B.C.) by which time primaeval man had developed primitive craft sufficiently seaworthy to permit of a crossing from the mainland — and was followed about 1,000 years later by his Neolithic descendants who settled permanently in the island. Additional credence was lent to these speculations by the 1981 excavations at Les Fouaillages with their evidence of the presence of a tribe of hunters at L'Ancresse *circa* 5,500 B.C.; following on the indications revealed by the 1980 dig of a *circa* 4,500 B.C. farming village in the same vicinity. As far as actual human remains are concerned, however, the oldest yet to come to light might possibly be those the discovery of which at Portinfer was reported in the *Evening Press* of December 8th., 1984, as being that of the incomplete skeleton of a man apparently buried face downwards "which could date back to 2,000 or 3,000 B.C.", its preservation being ascribed to the interment having been in sand rather than soil. Pieces of neolithic pottery lay beneath the *reliquiae*; but unfortunately bone samples taken therefrom were found unsuitable for scientific dating, leaving their age unproven. Be that as it may, information kindly supplied by Mr. Bob Burns, then the Island Archaeology Officer, indicates that osseous fragments of a human nature recovered by Guernsey's pioneer archaeologist, F.C. Lukis, at La Varde and Le Déhus (see Appendix XIII) "must date at least to the early bronze age *circa* 1,800 B.C., if not before". (The Jersey cousin of Stone de Croze, incidentally, had arrived at least a thousand years beforehand, the continued incorporation of the hill range now called Jersey into the mainland long after Guernsey's divorce therefrom — which occurred *circa* 7,400 B.C. — having enabled him to walk there. Indeed at La Cotte de Saint Brelade there is evidence — possibly because of the easier accessibility of these uplands than of the more peripheral ones north-west of them now named Guernsey — of settlement therein as early as the Palaeolithic Age.)

In common with all mankind throughout the ages, Stone de Croze and his descendants experienced the urge to worship. This urge was to lead to the erection of the megaliths which, in Guernsey as elsewhere, provide enduring memorials to our primitive forbears. Indeed, the Bailiwick is particularly rich in these structures, many of which remain to provide the earliest historical evidences in the islands. Thus the religious aspect is a natural starting-point for insular history.

The religious beliefs of Stone de Croze and his contemporaries centred around fertility cults and the dominating deity was the Mother Goddess of Earth. Guernsey has two outstanding monuments to this goddess. These stand in the graveyard of the Castel Church and at the Gateway of Saint Martin's Churchyard respectively and on radio-carbon evidence would both appear to date from *circa* 3,000 B.C. — though the latter was endowed with stronger human resemblances by embellishment wrought many centuries (probably over two millennia) later.

It is noteworthy that this latter statue has for long been popularly known as 'La Gran'mère du Chimquière', and it is an interesting speculation that this might denote a folk memory, with 'Gran'mère' meaning not the homely Granny, but 'The Great Mother' (The Mother Goddess). This folk memory could also account for the fact that La Gran'mère even now has her furtive devotees, who still cling to the superstition that it is 'good luck' to make offerings to her. The present writer saw coins left on La Gran'mère's head in 1969 and a floral chaplet in 1998.

A third ancient statue exists on a much smaller scale in the shape of a three-headed bust at La Pouquelah in the Castel. This, however, is of a much later date than the two already mentioned and was possibly dedicated to a three-headed Celtic god rather than to a goddess. On the other hand, a stone pillar in Sark partly obscured by brambles and standing at the entrance to a field on the left-hand side as one approaches La Coupée, about 750 yards south of La Vaurocque, has vague female resemblances and may perhaps constitute yet another statue-menhir.

A further indication of fertility religion could conceivably be found in the numerous dolmens in the Bailiwick, which are listed in Appendix XIII — and in addition a tomb which, long antedating Minoan Crete and early Sumer, is among the oldest in Europe, dating from *circa* 4,500 B.C., and discovered at L'Ancresse in 1981. This grave, however, is pre-megalithic and it would seem that dolmens proper (such as La Varde, Le Déhus, etc.) date from approximately 4,000 B.C. — see Dr. Patton's assessment below. It is likely that they are the graves of chieftains whose subjects hoped would be able, when placed in the embrace of the Earth Mother, to exert sufficient spiritual power to foster the growth of crops. Strictly speaking, these structures should be called megalithic tombs rather than dolmens (which by definition have but one capstone, the word — deriving from the Bréton 'dol'/table and 'men'/stone — literally meaning 'a table of stone'), but the term is retained here because of its widespread usage. The evidence of food remains in some of these dolmens could well indicate a primitive belief in an after-life, with attendant funeral ceremonial.

It has been conjectured that the large number of burial chambers in Herm (sixteen in its one-half of a square mile) is, by Dr. Mark Patton's analysis outlined below, indicative of a Neolithic population of about 500 and the location of three-quarters of these tombs in elevated positions on Le Grand and Le Petit Monceau suggests the possibility that leading personalities were interred at these high points the better to enable them to keep watch over the fortunes of their descendants — performing a function comparable to that ascribed to Guardian Angels in the Christian tradition. Alderney too had extensive megalithic remains but these were destroyed by British Government building operations designed to create a 'Gibraltar of the Channel' between 1847 and 1860.

Another facet of religious observance is associated with the plain upright structures (as distinct from the aforementioned female statues) listed in Appendix XII and known as Menhirs — from the Bréton 'men'/stone and 'hir'/long — which might have been primitive idols or even primaeval totems to ward off evil and the tradition of erecting which persisted in north-west Europe for almost three millennia — from about 4,850 B.C. to about 2,000 B.C. — as far as Brittany was concerned, though (with one possible exception mentioned below in connection with Le Déhus) only *circa* 3,280 B.C. onwards in Guernsey.

A custom which persisted until the present century could be the vestige of a folk memory indicating the additional possibility of these stones being connected with fertility religion. As fertility cults frequently included a celebration to mark the passing of winter and the accompanying promise of a new spring with further crops, it is not without interest that until recently a 'Guy Fawkes' was regularly burnt at the foot of the Longue Rocque menhir at Les Paysans, St. Pierre-du-Bois. This ceremony could have been the survival of a New Year festival, bearing in mind that the effigy was known not as Guy Fawkes, but as 'Boud'lo' — very likely a corruption of 'Bout de L'an' ('End of the Year') which was March 24th. until 1752.

Finally, the likelihood of these stones being phallic symbols (thus establishing an even closer affinity with fertility cults) must not be overlooked.

La Pierre aux Rats on Herm is, of course, not a menhir, but it replaces one which was wantonly broken up to form part of a granite consignment shipped to England in the 1830s. The present obelisk was built for the convenience of fishermen, who had previously used the menhir as a sea-mark to ascertain their position.

The foregoing assumptions are mostly the traditional ones regarding our megaliths, but the researches of Jersey-born Dr. Mark Patton of the University of Wales (to whom is ascribable the above dating of Menhirs) have led him to arrive at several conclusions at variance therefrom and/or in amplification thereof. Dr. Patton first notes the suggestion of Professor Lord Renfrew that these structures functioned as territorial markers whereby individual clans sought to consolidate their title to one or another area of settlement by invoking the local entombment of their ancestors as proof of the validity of their claim. He then postulated that by estimating the size of the labour force needed for the erection of a tomb and in addition allowing for pregnant women, children and the elderly — plus those involved in food production to sustain the clan — one may calculate the population of the tribe associated with any particular monument. Furthermore, he considers it likely that the very design of the dolmens was such as to exert control over the possession of sacred knowledge in the interests of maintaining 'us'/'them' power relationships in Neolithic society, as the narrowness of the long passages leading to the main chamber would ensure that only initiates or potential initiates had access to the rites therein performed and the gnosis thereby acquired.

In the opinion of Dr. Patton, the first farmers (as distinct from nomadic hunters) arrived in the Bailiwick from the adjacent mainland *circa* 4,500 B.C., bringing with them their domestic cattle, sheep and goats — as well as the seeds from which cereals could be grown. Traces of this immigration are, he feels, provided by Les Fouaillages: a monument representing a population of about 100. The passage grave period ensued, he claims, roughly between 4,250 and 3,830 B.C. and is exemplified by Le Déhus (in which Le Gardien du Tombeau might perhaps incorporate a broken part of a Menhir pre-dating by almost 1,000 years any other in the island — see above — and re-used in the tomb's construction), La Varde, Le Creux es Faies and Le Catioroc, their sizes suggesting that they served as territorial centres for clans 300 to 500 strong; and although the construction of passage graves ceased *circa* 3,250 B.C., many of them continued in use for several centuries. He further avers that the late Neolithic Period (roughly 3,250 B.C. to 2,850 B.C.) also saw the appearance of the statue and plain Menhirs mentioned above as well as new and smaller types of monuments, such as the Cyst above Brenière Bay in Sark — Platte Mare at L'Ancresse and L'Islet's 'Cyst in the Circle' (attendant population about 300). On the religious plane Dr. Patton thinks that during this period a strong belief in the immanence of their ancestors made relatives anxious to share skeletal fragments of their family forebears — and that such Cysts were designed to house treasured ossuaries containing the resultant bone collections.

Dr. Patton considers that the island's megalithic tombs were abandoned between 2,850 and 2,250 B.C. That their abandonment was systematic and deliberate is borne out by the ceremonial deposits at Le Déhus of pottery, human bones and a flat copper dagger in the chamber, the floor of which was then buried beneath a thick deposit of limpet shells — betokening a final offering at the time of closure. At this juncture much smaller monuments were being built, as seen in the small Tourgis Dolmen in Alderney, associated with populations of less than 100 people and thus indicative of a dramatic process of social decentralisation — and the present writer would add that the possibility occurs to him of the culmination of this process of disintegration being seen in the putative depopulation of Guernsey *circa* 1,800 B.C. referred to in Part IV Chapter One.

Chapter Two

THE COMING OF CHRISTIANITY

IT MUST BE BORNE IN MIND at the outset that much of the tradition regarding the conversion of the Bailiwick to Christianity is of a speculative nature, stemming partly from documents dated four centuries after the alleged events. Positive certainty is non-existent.

As part of the Christian resurgence under Theodosius after the pagan régime of Julian the Apostate had ended with his death in 363 A.D. Saint Martin de Tours (*circa* 316–400) initiated in north-western Gaul an evangelistic campaign which probably included the islands in its ambit. The fact that both Guernsey and Jersey contain parish churches dedicated to this saint lends a certain credence to this conjecture. It would seem, however, that the faith sat lightly on such converts as were made and that during the fifth century (with the Empire crumbling under the onslaughts first of Alaric and then of Attila) their connections with their mainland co-religionists — never of more than a tenuous nature — dwindled to intermittent contacts with the wild and ecclesiastically tepid Armoricans after the vestigial Gallo-Roman lands (roughly corresponding to Haute et Basse Normandie) had been infiltrated by heathen Franks under Childeric. Although technically 'co-operating with' the Romanized leader Synagrius, the newcomers assumed an increasingly dominant posture which culminated in outright seizure of power after the defeat of Synagrius at Soissons by Childeric's son Clovis in 486. Thus, while local Christianity may not have died (its survival being inferred by the retention from antiquity in the Town and High Parishes of five dedications of the type approved by Pope Hilary, who reigned from 461 to 468) it most likely wilted! (See also Chapter Ten of this Part.)

Although the Frankish leader, Clovis (466–511), embraced Christianity in 496, his kingdom was split up at his death between his four sons, among whom Childebert was allocated Neustria (Normandy). The savage struggles between Childebert and his brothers led to the devastation and depopulation of Armorica

(Brittany). The residual and impoverished Armorican population consisted of Celts whose links with their cousins in Britain had from the late fourth century onwards been strengthened by a steady migration to their shores of adventurous youth from South Wales and Cornwall. In his magnum opus, *Channel Islands Churches*, Mr. John McCormack has drawn attention to the fact that Saxon onslaughts along the Armorican seaboard had led to the Romans stationing garrisons on the peninsula's coast and adopting a policy of encouraging the advent of such settlers to help in the defence of the area. Extra impetus was given to this well-established pattern of movement by the menace to the Christian Celts of Britain posed by the inexorable western advance of heathen Anglo-Saxon invaders as from the late fifth century, which by the late sixth century had brought them to the Severn — with the upshot that the migrants' numbers swelled to the extent that their destination eventually came to be known as Brittany (the land of the Britons) rather than Armorica. As a corollary of this trend it had long been the practice for peripatetic monks to move to and fro as evangelists among kinsmen on either side of the Channel. Prominent among these roving clerics in the mid sixth century was Saint Sampson, whose Feast Day falls on July 28th. and who is revered in South Wales and Brittany (witness a chapel dedicated to him on the Ile de Bréhat offshore from Tréguier) as well as in Guernsey.

Born in Wales, *circa* 485, to Amon of Dyfed and his wife, Anna of Gwent, young Sampson was dedicated to God while a student in the monastic school at Llantwit in Glamorgan, presided over by the illustrious St. Illtyd, (*c.* 475–525: Festival November 6th.). In early manhood he retired to Caldey Island (offshore from Tenby), where he was later joined by his father, becoming abbot of the island's community on the death of his predecessor, Piro. Subsequently Sampson undertook a missionary journey to Ireland, after which he left Caldey and retired with Amon to the Severn Valley. Before long he was consecrated Bishop by St. Dyfrig (Dubricius) and, following a vision telling him to go overseas, went first to Cornwall — which remained unconquered by the Teutonic hordes until 825 — and where, of the two surviving churches dedicated to him (Golant and South Hill) the former seems likely to be the lineal descendant of the monastery which the saint's younger cousin Henoc, writing as an old man *circa* 620, credits him with founding. (This monastery of Saint Sampson, incidentally, figures prominently in the tragic love story of Tristram and Iseult as recounted by the twelfth century poet Beroul.) Then, after visiting the Scilly Isles, one of which is named after him, he took ship — according to one surmise *circa* 547 — for Armorica: perhaps to escape the 'Mortalitas Magna' (the Great Plague of that year). After his arrival he set up a religious house at Dol and is later said to have helped in the restoration of the rightful prince Judual, who overcame his rival, Conmor, in 555. Sampson then visited Paris where Childerbert nominated him Bishop of Dol, the geographical attribution deriving solely from the monastery which he had founded in that location, no diocesan organisation being known to the Celtic Church at that time. Towards the end of the same year he appears to have embarked on his missionary travels to the Channel Islands (which he may previously have visited briefly when originally en route for Armorica) being said to have established at the point where he landed in Guernsey a wooden chapel in approximately the same position as the present church dedicated to him. From this base he conducted a mission to the islanders whose practice of the faith embraced by their forefathers had long since become adulterated by pagan recidivation. Guernsey's patron saint is probably identical with the 'Samson, peccator, Episcopus' ('Sampson, sinner, Bishop') who signed the Acts of the Council of Paris in 557. He is believed to have died in 565.

St. Sampson is claimed to have had a cousin, St. Magloire (or Maelor: Festival October 24th.), about whom information is of a highly legendary nature. Apparently born to Afrella, the wife of Umbrafel (St. Sampson's paternal uncle), St. Magloire also is thought to have been entrusted in his youth to the care of St. Illtyd; subsequently becoming a monk and a companion to St. Sampson, who is reputed to have ordained him and taken him to Armorica. After many years co-operation with his cousin in missionary labours St. Magloire is deemed to have succeeded him as Bishop of Dol. The story goes that Magloire was visited by the Chieftain of Sark who, in gratitude to the saint for being healed of a skin infection, made a grant to his monks and himself of part of the island. Accordingly, he is stated to have landed in Sark about 565, accompanied by 62 monks, and to have set up a religious house in the valley still called La Moinerie. From here he set about converting the pagans of the surrounding area, presumably crossing to Herm and Jethou where he is credited with building a chapel on the Pierre Percée Reef (then above sea level). Its ruins may have survived as late as 1833 as, in his *Topographical*

Dictionary, published that year, Samuel Lewis mentions "portions of an ancient building, thought to have been a chapel belonging to a hermitage existing here in the sixth century". The tale is also told that Magloire visited Jersey, delivering that island from a 'dragon', in return for which he was granted land there as well. *L'Histoire des Evéques de Coutances* records his death as occurring on October 14th., 575. Local lore holds that he was buried in Sark. What is certain is that a monastery existed in Sark until about 850, when the monks were massacred and the buildings destroyed by marauding Norse pirates.

The career of St. Tugual (alias Tudual, Tutwal, Tugdual: Feast Day, December 1st.) to whom the attractive chapel on Herm is dedicated, is even more steeped in fable than that of St. Magloire. The earliest extant documentary reference to this saint occurs in a register of the churches of the archipelago compiled between 1251 and 1279 which shows Herm's chapel as dedicated to St. Tugual. As this is 700 years after the supposed lifetime of the saint, it is not a great deal to go on. Not even the sex of St. Tugual is certain, as one version of the story refers to a Welsh woman killed by the Saxons whose remains were transferred to Armorica. The main tradition, however, is to the effect that the saint was born in Wales in 490 as the son of Pompeia (Celtic name Coupeia), the sister of Riwal (or Rigwal), paramount chief of the Dumnonii (who inhabited south-western Britain as well as Armorica). Like his contemporary St. Sampson, Tugual is alleged to have been brought up in St. Illtyd's monastery at Llantwit and at some time between 520 and 530 (by which time his cousin, Deroch, had succeeded Riwal) to have crossed to Armorica in the company of his mother and 72 monks. The religious house he set up was known as Lan Pabu ('Lan' denoting church land and 'Pabu' — or 'Father' — being the title accorded to the saint). Several evangelistic journeys ensued and the folk memory of the inclusion in these travels of a visit to Herm might possibly account for the dedication of its chapel — though Tugual's influence is said to have been so considerable in the Armorican area generally that upwards of fifty churches or chapels were named after him. Local folklore in the Côtes du Nord also teaches that about the year 532 his establishment of another monastery (Lan Trecor) led to the growth around it of the city of Tréguier, of which he thus emerges as founder. King Childebert, when visited by Tugual, is said to have confirmed his right to the lands he held and to have had him consecrated bishop, so that Tréguier became a cathedral city. It is supposed that Tugual died in 564. Popular hagiography also credits the saint with being Bishop of Lexovium as well — and even claims that he made a pilgrimage to Rome, where he was elevated to the Papacy as Pope Leo V. (This tale most likely owes much to his appellation 'Pabu' becoming confused with 'Papa' or Pope, while the name 'Leo' is suspiciously similar to the district of Léon, where Lan Pabu was located. How the number 'V' came to be attributed to him, however, is baffling, as two-and-a-half centuries later the famous Leo who crowned Charlemagne was only the third of that name). While in the ninth century Tréguier was being sacked by Norsemen under the Jarl Hasting, the bishop (Gorennan) fled and, taking St. Tugual's body with him, conveyed it to Chartres. Finally it was bruited abroad that during Tréguier's eventual reconstruction a carpenter called Goeder fell from high scaffolding during the rebuilding of the cathedral — but escaped unscathed when his workmates invoked St. Tugual.

The circumstances under which the Celtic Saints came to Alderney have, because of their uncertainty, long given rise to contention; the traditional tale that the island owes its evangelization to Saint Vignal (Latin Vignalis) being one which even as meticulous a researcher and devotee of Alderney as the late Alfred Harry Ewen dismissed with the remark that it "was based on an M.S. misreading, where the reference is intended for Herm". Now, however, thanks to the enquiries pursued by the late Mrs. Jo Wilde, all such confusion is dispelled. The key to this clarification is to be found in Mrs. Wilde's conclusion in her book *Saints Alive* that 'Vignal' (a name unknown to the standard hagiological reference — Butler's *Lives of the Saints*) is simply the Jersey variant of what in French hagiology appears as 'Guénael' or 'Guénault' as twin derivatives from an original 'Winhael': a saint much venerated in Brittany, where — as the son of Laetitia (Lettice), the wife of Count Romelius, Governor of the Armorican Province of Cornouaille under King Meriadec — he is believed to have been born at Ergué-Gabéric, near Quimper, of which parish he is now Patron Saint, with the local church dedicated to him. Further perplexity arises, however, from the frequent identification of Guénael (under the 'Guénault' rendition) with Guénolé. Such a conflation is understandable when the names are so similar and only Guénolé is included in Butler's *Lives of the Saints* — but nevertheless, its unfortunate result has been that much pertaining to the one is ascribed to the other. In point of fact, Guénael (Festival November 3rd.) was the disciple and protégé of Guénolé at Landevennec, of which monastery the pupil succeeded the mentor as Abbot on the latter's death *circa* 538 when Guénael was about 32 years of age. It appears that seven years later (*circa* 545) Guénael/Vignal embarked on missionary work, his wanderings including the Channel Isles where Saint Magloire is stated in the booklet *Early Years of Christianity in Jersey* to have handed Alderney over to his care after they had laboured together in Jersey, Guernsey and Sark. (This booklet, incidentally — as does too Monsieur L. Morvannu in his monograph *Guénolé et Guénael* — also asserts that 'Vignal' was the Jersey version of the saint's name, the etymological sequence from Guénael's primitive form of Winhael being: Winhael — Vendel — Venel — Venal — Vignal). After arriving in Alderney *circa* 575 and spending a few years there reconverting the lapsed inhabitants (who, he sadly reported, were "more interested in might than in right") Guénael is said to have gone to Britain where he is credited with having healed the sick, the legend telling that (as elsewhere in his travels) he gave sight to the blind, hearing to the deaf, mobility to the lame and flexibility to the paralysed. Leaving Britain for Ireland, he eventually returned to his native Cornouaille, where he founded three monasteries before retiring to the island of Groix. According to tradition, he died in the monastery of Blavet *circa* 590. As for Saint Anne, after whom Alderney's town and church are named; the putative pre-Christian worship in Brittany (then Armorica) of a Mother-Goddess called Ana who was habitually depicted with a child in her arms would seem to have nurtured the myth of an Armorican girl — Anne — when pregnant with a child unwanted by her husband Joachim, Seigneur de Moellien, being miraculously transported to Jerusalem where she gave birth to her daughter Mary — who several years later, when "espoused to Joseph" … "was found with child by the Holy Ghost" (Matthew 1, 18). At this point, Anne, by then a widow, is said to have returned home — and a local variant of the 'Christ came to Britain' story immortalised by William Blake's *Jerusalem* asserts that *en route* He visited His grandmother in Armorica! Yet another fable, however, claims that Alderney's Anne was the mother of Saint Sampson and hence the aunt-by-marriage of Saint Guénael's patron Magloire! With its avoidance of anachronism and abstention from any attempt to postulate transportation of the 'magic carpet' type, this latter tale inevitably commands greater credence.

Out of this welter of myth and lore a few reasonable certainties emerge. In the first place, the Christianity established in the Bailiwick in the sixth century (and to which mute witness is borne by the ancient cross-engraven stone unearthed at the Vale Church in 1949 and held by experts to date from this period) was obviously that of the Celtic Church. Secondly, it is clear that it grafted itself on old cults, incorporating pagan rites and customs into its observances. Lastly, two more centuries were to elapse before the Celtic Christian communities were brought within the fold of the Roman Church.

Chapter Three

PRE-REFORMATION CHRISTIANITY

ABOUT THE YEAR 802 Charlemagne commissioned Saint Gervold, Abbot of Fontenelle, to procure confirmation of the islands' subjection to his authority and also a renewed acknowledgment of their ecclesiastical subordination to the Bishop of Coutances, in whose diocese they had been officially included since the sixth century, towards the close of which Romacarus (the then Bishop) is on record as claiming that, following the aforementioned religious revival wrought by the Celtic Saints, he had definitely incorporated the entire archipelago within his See. The uninterrupted continuance of this attachment to organized Christendom must not, however, be taken for granted. From about 925 A.D. the islands and the adjacent Cotentin were so effectively subjugated by pagan Norsemen that the Bishops of Coutances found it prudent for the next century or so to reside in Rouen.

On the other hand evidence of the survival of a (possibly attenuated) institutional Christianity are furnished by the mention of a number of Guernsey churches in a charter of Duke Robert of Normandy (*c.* 1030).

It was not, however, until the appointment to the See of Coutances in 1049 of Bishop Geoffroi de Montbrai, that effective ecclesiastical control could be said to have been established — a control sufficiently strong to make Guernsey in 1055 a suitable place of exile for Duke Richard II's son Mauger (Malgerius: Archbishop of Rouen 1037–1055) who had been unfrocked and banished after falling foul of his powerful nephew Duke William II, who eleven years later conquered England. Featured in the mediaeval Chroniques de Normandie as marrying a Guernesiaise named Gille or Gisla who bore him a son Michael (reputedly a friend of Henry I of England who distinguished himself in the First Crusade) the outcast was later drowned offshore from Barfleur while en route for a (probably surreptitious) return visit to mainland Normandy, his body being buried at Cherbourg. From the time of the assertive Geoffroi onwards the archipelago remained within the jurisdiction of the See of Coutances almost continuously until 1496 in theory and 1569 in fact.

During this lengthy period the authority of the Bishop of Coutances underwent a number of vicissitudes. In the first place, after his loss of Continental Normandy in 1204, King John attached the Channel Isles to the see of Exeter — a transference which was short-lived, being disallowed by Pope Innocent III. A further interruption came in 1378, with the Papal Schism. On the death of Gregory XI the cardinals in Rome elected Urban VI, while those in Avignon elected a rival Pope (Clement VII). This resulted in the Bishop of Coutances (and the Dean of Guernsey) taking the Clementine side. On behalf of Edward III (who acknowledged Urban VI), the Warden (Hugh Calverley) expelled the Clementine Dean, repudiated the Clementine Bishop of Coutances, and placed the islands' churches under the Urbanite Bishop of Nantes. This transference was confirmed in 1399 by the next Urbanite Pope (Boniface IX) and the islands remained within the jurisdiction of Nantes until the end of the Schism in 1417. Towards the end of the same century, however, Henry VII in 1496 prevailed upon Pope Alexander VI to transfer the islands to the diocese of Salisbury — and three years later (in 1499) the same Pope re-transferred them to the see of Winchester. In the event this made little difference, as successive Bishops of Winchester showed no inclination to brave the stormy seas so as to make their authority effective. As, furthermore, they could not speak French, the islands remained *de facto* (if not *de jure*) within the jurisdiction of Coutances until 1569 when Elizabeth I put her foot down and insisted on the islands acknowledging the authority of Winchester. Even so, no Bishop of Winchester visited the islands until the 19th. century.

The power of the Church during the Middle Ages is attested by the considerable landholdings she possessed in Guernsey and her sister islands. In 1030, Duke Robert I assigned the western half of Guernsey to the Monastery of Mont St. Michel, but 12 years later (in 1042) Duke William II (later William the Conqueror) revoked this grant in favour of Ranulf, Vicomte du Bessin, whose support he needed to consolidate his succession in view of his bastardy. The Abbot of Mont St. Michel was compensated by the grant of Sark and Alderney.

A further readjustment at the expense of Mont St. Michel occurred in 1057 when Duke William II granted Alderney and

Sark to the powerful Bishop of Coutances, Geoffroi de Montbrai. Although the Bishops of Coutances retained a substantial part of Alderney for the next three centuries (half of this island and all of Sark being reclaimed by the English Crown in 1093 when Geoffroi took part in an abortive revolt against William Rufus, to whom Duke Robert II had mortgaged Normandy to finance a Crusade), they had difficulty in maintaining control of their area after John's loss of Continental Normandy. This state of affairs is made plain in the document *Status Insulae de Aurineo* (*c.* 1236) seeking to establish definitely the respective rights of Crown and Bishop in Alderney. Nevertheless, the church in Alderney, which had been granted by charter dated 1054 to the Church of Ste. Marie in Cherbourg, was obviously still functioning in 1134 as a charter of that year mentions it as dedicated to Ste. Marie.

Mont St. Michel also suffered in the case of Herm, which had been given to the monastery by Duke Robert I. Here again Duke William II revoked the grant, donating the island to the Augustinian Order of Cherbourg. The Abbot of Mont St. Michel did, however, acquire Jethou from the sea-dog, Restauld, and also Noirmont (in Jersey), which Duke William II gave to the monastery as a partial recompense for the loss of Alderney and Sark.

It is not surprising that successive Abbots of Mont St. Michel persistently sought to recover their fortunes in the islands — and in this they were eventually successful. Bulls issued by Pope Eugene III (1150), Pope Adrian IV (1155), and Pope Alexander III (1178), show that by the second half of the 12th. century the monastery of Mont St. Michel had recovered considerable holdings in Guernsey itself. It may be assumed that these recoveries arose from the desire of Geoffrey of Anjou to win the support of the Church for the claims of his son (later Henry II) to the Dukedom of Normandy and the Kingdom of England. From 1142 onwards Geoffrey was in effective control of Normandy, King Stephen having all his work cut out waging civil war against Geoffrey's wife, Matilda. To avoid alienating the lay landholders, whose military support was wanted in the operations planned against Stephen in England, the Fief St. Michel was carved out of non-arable areas in the western parishes, plus waste land in the Clos du Valle.

Possibly about 1048 Duke William II granted four fiefs in the parish of St. Andrew's to the Church: one to the Bishop of Coutances; the second (Ste. Hélène) to the Abbey of Cormerey,

Tours; the third (La Rue Frairie) to the Abbey de la Croix St. Lenfroy, Evreux; and the fourth to the Abbesse de la Trinité, Caen. The same duke granted a large tract in St. Peter-Port to the Abbey of Marmoutiers.

Land near Saints in St. Martin's, which had originally been allocated by Duke William II to a Prebend of Cherbourg, was granted in 1198 to the Abbey of Blanchelande in the Cotentin by John, Court of Mortain, Lord of the Isles (later King John).

In Sark, also, the church acquired land when in 1162 William de Vernon (whose father had been granted Sark by Henry I) made a donation of land to the Abbey of Montebourg, part of which remained in ecclesiastical hands even after the seizure of the whole of Sark in 1214 by John as a consequence of the de Vernons giving their allegiance to Philip Augustus.

The Middle Ages also saw a number of religious communities establishing their houses in the Bailiwick. The monastery set up on Sark by the original Celtic Christians in the area still called La Moinerie survived until about 850, serving as a school for the children of the nobility of the Cotentin. The inlet at the foot of the valley where the monks built a water-mill to grind their grain is still called Le Port du Moulin.

From the time of William de Vernon's grant in 1162, the Abbey of Montebourg maintained a solitary monk on Sark at what came to be called the Priory of St. Magloire (probably situated near La Moinerie) — originally for the purpose of offering prayer for the souls of the de Vernon family and (after John's dispossession of the de Vernons) for the kings of England. Successive priors were appointed until the abandonment of the island consequent on the devastating French raids of 1372/3.

The Benedictines from Mont St. Michel established on Herm by Duke Robert I (*c.* 1030) stayed for about thirty years until removed by Duke William II as mentioned above. During this time they probably founded the precursor of the present chapel of St. Tugual (which itself is 13th. century), abandoning the chapel on Pierre Percée because of the incursions of the sea. Under the Augustinians of Cherbourg, whom Duke William II installed in their place, a flourishing religious house grew up, the Prior becoming sufficiently powerful to hold his own Court of Assize, with 'judgement of life and limb'. Farming was developed, and grazing rights jealously guarded.

In 1156, the Priory of Notre Dame de Lihou was confirmed to the Benedictines of Mont St. Michel by a Bull of Pope Adrian IV.

This house persisted until the sequestration of alien priories by Henry V in 1414 — and in all probability was then 'farmed out' to its Prior, for as late as 1519 (according to the town church rental) the Prior of Lihou lived in Fountain Street and it was not until 1532 that Jacques Tournier resigned the benefice. The uncertainties attending the whole matter of the sequestration of priories is dealt with in the next chapter. Lihou Priory was doubtless a challenge to the old gods, being built near a collection of dolmens and menhirs — and it is noteworthy that as late as the 16th. century witches meeting at Le Catioroc would shout defiance across the intervening waters, crying, 'Hou! Hou! Marie Li Hou!'

The Benedictines also established a Priory adjoining the church of Saint Michel-du-Valle, on the south side of the graveyard, attached to which one sees a step bearing a most remarkable diaper design heading a flight descending to the road still called 'L'Abbaye'. The researches of Mr. John McCormack have led him to postulate a fascinating conjectural linkage between Priory and Step. It appears that the Casket containing the burial shroud of Our Lord which had been hidden from pagan invaders in Edessa (modern-day Urfa in Turkey) came to light in the mid-sixth century and was placed in a huge cathedral built by the Emperor Justinian to house them, with the Casket's diaper design later becoming a frequent form of decoration on other reliquaries and shrines — such as that of Saint Swithun in Winchester. Spirited away to the Balkans after the sack of Constantinople in 1204, both Shroud and Casket in time came into the hands of the Knights Templar (possibly as collateral security for a loan) but were separated the one from the other when Philippe Le Bel launched his persecution of the Templars in 1307. The Shroud subsequently (1357) was exhibited at Lirey in Burgundy by the nephew of Geoffroy de Charnay, the Preceptor of the Templar Province of Normandy, and thence ended up in Turin. The Casket, however, divorced from the Shroud, seems to have been whisked away with other Temple Treasure, much of which went to Portugal or Scotland. As he was Preceptor of Normandy, the territory of Geoffroy de Charnay (who was soon to be burnt at the stake by Philippe Le Bel) included the Channel Isles, out of the grasp of the French King, and it is therefore credible that the Casket was shipped over to Guernsey and entrusted to the care of the Vale Priory, whence it was afterwards sent to England — most likely to the Templar's House at Templecombe, where a panel, also with a diaper design, was recently found. Mr. McCormack urges the strong possibility that the Prior carved a threshold stone with a diaper design reminiscent of the Casket which he had been privileged to shelter — and incorporated therein a Templar Cross — as a memorial of this episode: and that two-and-a-half centuries later regarded (as was anything ornate) as 'Popish' by the Calvinists, this was cast out and ended up as the top member of a flight of steps! The Priory itself had fallen into decay by 1406 as in that year the sub-warden sought permission to utilize timber from the derelict building to repair Castle Cornet; but some part of the structure must have survived as shown in the print entitled *Vale Church and Priory in 1817* facing page 74 in Edith Carey's *Essays on Guernsey History* published by *La Société Guernesiaise* in 1936 — while as late as 1934 *Ward Lock and Co's Guide* refers to "a small priory of which scanty ruins can be still seen".

During Richard II's reign the Franciscan Cordeliers established a house on the site now occupied by Elizabeth College, with adjacent grounds much more extensive than those now attached to this school. The name, 'Rue des Frères', given to the thoroughfare linking College Road with Upland Road is an evocation of this community. A letter is extant, dated September 20th., 1536, in which the governor reports to Thomas Cromwell that the friars, having refused to take the oath recognising Henry VIII's Headship of the Church, had been shipped over to Normandy, their property becoming forfeit to the Crown.

According to Tupper's *History of Guernsey* (1876) the same order was established in Alderney and Herm. Their stay on Herm would seem to have been of restricted duration — apparently from 1440 to 1458 — at which latter date the hostile attitude of visiting fishermen (there was widespread disenchantment with the mendicant orders in the early 15th. century) led to their decamping to the islets of St. Marcouf, on the east of the Cotentin.

There is a theory (not universally accepted) that the Bailiwick is most likely indebted to these communities for the existence of the famous local cattle, which seem to be the result of crossing the Isigny and Froment du Leon breeds for whose introduction the supporters of this theory claim the religious houses to have been responsible. See Part V, Chapter Three, for fuller details.

Chapter Four

MONASTIC SEQUESTRATIONS

AS MENTIONED in the previous chapter in connection with the Priory of Notre Dame de Lihou, the whole matter of the expropriation of ecclesiastical fiefs is one of considerable perplexity.

In order to prevent alien priories from sending their 'apport' (annual payment) to the mother house in France when England was at war with that country, it was the normal practice in England for these priories and their lands to be 'taken into the King's hand' and restored when the war was over. Such a step was taken by John during his struggle against Philip Augustus, by Edward I during the Gascony War of 1294–8, and by Edward III on the outbreak of the Hundred Years War. In 1414, when the resurgence of the Hundred Years War had led to the priories being 'taken into the King's hand' yet again, parliament petitioned Henry V *not* to restore them, and the king's assent to this request constituted the Act of Seizure. What is problematical is the extent to which these priories were, in fact, 'taken into the King's hand' as far as the Channel Isles were concerned.

Edward III 'took into his hand' all alien priories with an income in excess of forty sols per annum, and it would appear that this measure had at least some applicability to the Channel Isles as well as to England, as in 1343 Brother John Duraunt, the Prior of St. Magloire in Sark, petitioned Edward III for exemption from confiscation on the grounds that his Sark endowments barely supported life.

On the other hand, there is the record of Nicholas Henry in 1392 seeking the permission of his Seigneur, the Abbé de Mont St. Michel, for the erection of the chapel of Notre Dame de Perelle. Obviously, therefore, Edward III's appropriation had not ejected the largest alien ecclesiastical landholder of all. (It must be remembered, however, that Richard II was currently pursuing the policy of pacification which culminated in his marriage to Isabella of France in 1396. Consequently, any neglect on his part to 'take into his hand' alien priories at such a juncture is understandable.)

When one considers Henry V's seizures, it seems at first sight fairly certain that the islands must to some extent have been included (although in strict terminology the Act only applied to England) as Henry VI, when founding Eton College, granted the reversion of Lihou Priory to the Provost of Eton — and by definition an appropriation must precede a reversion. Furthermore, post-1414 documents show that Jean du Gaillard was at that time involved in legal proceedings regarding the tithes of the expropriated Abbey of Blanchelande — not to mention the strong probability that the St. Saviour's section of the fief named after the self-same worthy resulted from his using his influential position as a jurat (between 1448 and 1463) to engineer his acquisition of this part of the (presumably suppressed) Fief de Mont St. Michel. In addition, a royal seizure on the eve of Agincourt may be inferred from the fact that the incumbents of the Parish Churches (until then styled Vicars to indicate their status as subordinate representatives of the great monastic houses such as Mont Saint Michel or Marmoutier which held the advowsons of the island livings) were thenceforth (as Crown appointees) known as Rectors — as indeed (with Crown appointments persisting) they are still called today.

As against this, there is evidence of refugees from the parent house in Cherbourg coming in the late 15th. century to Jersey's Augustinian Priory of L'Islet — which survived until about 1540; and on top of that there is the case of the French Franciscan Friary which, occupying the site of Elizabeth College, was founded in the reign of Richard II and was not 'taken into the King's hand' until 1536.

One suggested solution to this problem is that, after seizure, the kings in many cases may have farmed out the holdings to the religious houses *in situ*, thus ensuring an income for themselves without any physical expulsion of the monks and/or friars. On the other hand, there may have been only a partial and occasional application of the measures to the islands, resulting in a literal fulfilment of the biblical forecast that "one shall be taken and the other left". Bearing all these considerations in mind, the most apt comment on the whole question would seem to necessitate borrowing a Churchillianism — "a riddle, wrapped in a mystery, inside an enigma".

Chapter Five

THE EARLY REFORMATION PERIOD

THE FUNDAMENTAL POSTURE of most Guernseymen to the religious vicissitudes from Henry VIII's break with the Pope to the early years of the reign of Elizabeth I was the result not so much of religious zeal one way or the other, but rather was conditioned by a consideration of their economic and commercial interests. Thus, so long as these interests were not particularly threatened, the islanders in general were quite prepared to trim their sails to the differing winds that blew.

This complaisance is well illustrated in the case of Jacques Amy. Originally ordained as a Roman Catholic priest, he meekly accepted Henry VIII's headship; and in 1547, when appointed rector of St. Saviour's and Dean of Guernsey, was quite prepared to embrace the Evangelical Protestantism of Edward VI, to revert to the Roman Obedience under Mary I, and, when Elizabeth I ascended the throne, to accommodate himself first to the Anglican Via Media and finally to Presbyterianism — an insular Vicar of Bray who contrived to remain Dean continuously from 1547 to 1563.

The circumstances affecting Guernsey's attitude to the Reformation stem largely from local conditions which differed widely from those obtaining in England. It must be remembered that the average Guernseyman was hardly likely to object to the cessation of payments to Rome; that appeals to the Pope were in any case luxuries beyond the means of the islanders; and that from their remote isolation they were indifferent to the 'King's Great Matter' and the succession question. On the other hand, when an important economic interest was involved — the poor relief provided by the popular and highly respected Catholic Confraternities — steps were taken to avoid compliance with the 1547 Chantries Act (which, strictly speaking, applied to all the King's dominions and not just to England) as by its terms these charitable bodies would have ceased to exist. Accepting liturgical change (which until 1552 was not great) was one thing; losing poor relief at the Crown' s behest quite another. (See Part V, Chapter Twenty-one, for details — and one might add as an interesting rider that the stratagem there described emulated a comparable technique of evasion by means of ostensible acquiescence which had been employed a decade earlier in connection with the Henrician ban on pilgrimages. By its Ordinance of July 12th., 1537 prohibiting islanders from going to England as pilgrims — or ships' masters from conveying such persons — the Royal Court seemed to submit to Thomas Cromwell's Injunctions of the previous year disallowing peregrinations of this kind: but in fact linguistic considerations made local shrines and those of France more attractive destinations for devotional journeys and the Ordinance in no way forbade anyone to go to them — or indeed to religious sites even further afield such as Rome or Compostella!)

As far as the closure of the religious houses was concerned, the attitude of the islanders was one of 'deja vu'. When alien priories had been repeatedly 'taken into the King's hand' in time of war from John's reign onwards, the action had made little impact in England (where these priories were comparatively negligible) but the effect of such seizures as had occurred in Guernsey had been considerable — and therefore Henry VIII's depredations were nothing new. Thus most people were indifferent, as the land could still be used the same way, whoever was the owner. Hence, in all probability, the equanimity with which the islanders accepted the 1536 expulsion of the Franciscans already mentioned in Chapter Three of this Part.

Especially crucial to the attitude of the islanders was the question of insular neutrality. Misgiving was widespread lest the religious changes should deprive the islands of the lucrative privileges they enjoyed from the neutrality accorded to the archipelago by a Bull of Sixtus IV in February 1480/81. By this Bull, the islands were treated as neutral in time of war, and all ships and goods were immune from capture within their waters. This arrangement obviously promoted both the prosperity and the safety of the islands, so that the repudiation of papal authority created a most delicate situation, affecting the very roots of insular welfare.

A further marked local characteristic was the pronounced class differentiation displayed in religious allegiance. Because of their basic indifference, the bulk of the population accepted reformed worship, especially when the translation into French of Edward VI's Second Prayer Book in 1553 enabled them to follow the service in their own language. The common people were even more influenced by the religious propaganda of Huguenot refugees from France, carried on as it was in their own tongue and in all probability initiated by Denis le Vair, an ex-Roman Catholic priest who, staying in Guernsey for several years after his arrival as a colporteur in 1548, fled to France on Mary's accession but was there arrested and on August 9th., 1554 most brutally martyred at Rouen. Thanks to these influences Protestantism gradually took root among the rank and file, instead of being no more than a creed imposed from above. In contradistinction the island gentry were more conscious of the benefits of neutrality, having more to lose from its discontinuance, and therefore tended to accept the Henrician and Edwardian reforms with their tongues in their cheeks and to welcome the return to Roman Catholicism under Mary I.

This religious divergence between the classes had tragic consequences in 1556, when Dean Jacques Amy (currently Roman Catholic), as an earnest of his zeal for the old faith to which he had returned, convicted as heretics Catherine Cauchés (of the Saint Martin's family which gave its name to la Rue Cauchés in that parish) and her daughters, Guillemine Gilbert and Perrotine Massey, the latter married to David Jores, a Huguenot pastor who had fled the island. They were condemned by the Royal Court (the Bailiff, Helier Gosselin, having also conformed under Edward VI, being as anxious as Amy to parade his Roman Catholic fervour) and sentenced to be burnt at the stake.

The *auto-da-fé* took place on July 18th., 1556, at a site traditionally thought to be the bottom of Tower Hill — though the knowledgeable island historian, the late Mr. T.F. Priaulx (1906–1996), arguing that the thatched roofs of the adjacent town would preclude so near a conflagration, regarded a more likely location for this and other similar incinerations (such as the famous one involving the three alleged witches, Collette Dumont, Marie Dumont and Isabell Becquet, who went to the stake in 1617) as being Lower Vauvert (then rural and in very truth a 'Green Valley') at the spot nowadays identifiable as that lying at the foot of the Bouillon Steps. As the faggots blazed, Perrotine, "her womb bursting asunder by the vehemency of the flame", gave birth to a baby boy and on the order of Gosselin the child was thrown back into the fire. Justifiably did the Reverend John Fox (1517–1587) remark in his *Christian Martyrdom* that "of all the singular and tragical histories in this book, nothing can be more barbarous, if anything can equal, the inhumanity of this execution". When on trial before the Privy Council nine years later in 1565, the jurats who had tried the case admitted the truth of this account, based on accusations by Catherine's brother, Matthew.

Chapter Six

THE ADVENT OF PRESBYTERIANISM AND THE DIVORCE FROM COUTANCES

ELIZABETH I's ATTEMPTS to arrive at a *via media* with her Acts of Supremacy and Uniformity in 1559 did not go down well with many of the jurats and leading notables in Guernsey — who were, after all, the same people who had condemned Catherine Cauchés and her daughters to death. This disaffection was reported by the governor, Sir Francis Chamberlain, who informed Cecil in 1562 that "the generality here mislike the late alterations in England, so as the queen has few faithful favourers". The significance of this report might be better appreciated if one bears in mind that 'the generality' was the term currently employed to designate the States of Guernsey.

Elizabeth I's dissatisfaction with this state of affairs is shown in a warrant of the same year addressed to the 'Commissioners Ecclesiastical for reforming religion in Guernsey', instructing them "to direct order to our captain or his lieutenant and to the dean and certain of the jurats . . . for the good order of the ecclesiastical government". A token step towards this 'good order' was made in the dismissal of Helier Gosselin as bailiff in the same year (1562). As, however, he was re-elected as jurat, no fundamental effect was produced and leading Protestants continued to report unfavourably on the state of religion in Guernsey.

Prominent among these adverse reports was that of Adrian de Saravia (who later in life was to be one of the translators of the Authorised Version of the Bible). He wrote to Cecil in 1565 that a "seditious gathering led by one of the Jurats went about cursing the Huguenots". The truth of Saravia's allegations was borne out in the 'Articles touching the Jurats of Guernsey' laid before the Privy Council the same year, one paragraph of which states that three jurats in 1564 led an anti-Huguenot riot in St. Peter-Port, 'raging and crying along the street, "Where be these Huguenots? We will have their hearts upon the points of our swords!"' The upshot was that the jurats of Guernsey were summoned before the

Privy Council to answer for their conduct, and in August 1565 seven of them were dismissed from office.

It was now evident to Elizabeth and to the Privy Council that, owing to the non-availability of French-speaking Anglican clergy, the real choice in the Bailiwick was between Roman Catholicism and Calvinism organised by the few Huguenot refugees who were already there. Accordingly an Order-in-Council of August 1565 sanctioned the setting up of a Calvinist Consistory in St. Peter-Port. It should not, however, be overlooked that sentiment hostile to religious innovation persisted in many parts of the island. As late as 1572, besides Saint Saviour's (where the incumbent was the notorious ecclesiastical trimmer Jacques Amy) the livings of Saint Sampson's, the Vale, Saint Andrew's and the Castel — which, added to Saint Saviour's, amounted to half the island's parishes — were also held by ex-Roman Catholic priests who, though outwardly conforming, were with some justification described by Saravia as "still in heart and affection Papists". The last-named of these (Guillaume Pacquet of the Castel) was in May 1589 the witness to a Will of decidedly Romish complexion, the testator invoking Holy Mary and the Saints and bequeathing a legacy to the church. Two years previously — in June 1567 — his eponym Nicolas Pacquet admitted before the Royal Court that he had said Mass in several places; as did too another cleric in the person of Jean Mourain. The fact that these celebrations attracted congregations is significant, as is also Saravia's report that, outside the Town, ministers of the reformed faith were jeered at and pelted with dirt. It was possibly with this state of affairs in mind that the 1565 Order-in-Council required the rural parishes to observe the Anglican rite as translated into French by François Philippe in 1553 (and to the essential Catholicity of which Walsingham in 1571 drew the attention of Henri, duc d'Anjou — the brother of Charles IX of France and the future Henri III — during the abortive marriage negotiations between him and Elizabeth I). In the event, however, as the sullenly conforming priests died off, sheer lack of suitable clergy made it impossible to enforce this order. By contrast, a fresh influx in July 1585 of Huguenot ministers (accompanied by le Prince de Condé) fleeing the renewed persecution in France ordained by an Edict stemming from the Treaty of Namours finally ensured the triumph of Presbyterianism which earlier the same year had been seriously embarrassed by a dearth of pastors, whose numbers had dwindled to two. The hold of Geneva was consolidated with merciless thoroughness. The historian Edith Carey (1864–1935), citing a reference which has proved so elusive as to be unknown to *La Bibliothèque Nationale* in Paris (an article entitled *Coligni* by one Turgin in *La France Illustrée*), held that over 400 Roman Catholics fled to Herm and were slaughtered after the terms under which they yielded had been repudiated. (The whole claim may well be no more than a mistaken inference from the widespread unearthing of bones when many dolmens were demolished in the 19th. century to be shipped to England as granite.) Nevertheless, be the Herm story true or false, what is undeniable is that the 1597 Michaelmas Chief Pleas forbade all pilgrimages on pain of a sixty sou fine for the first offence and punishment at the Court's discretion thereafter; while the same court four years later gave holders of "idols, papistical books and other superstitious things" until November 1st. to surrender them, failing which a fine of twenty ecus would be incurred. Likewise the 1611 Easter Chief Pleas warned "all idolatrous and superstitious people" who "still have not renounced the Pope, the Mass... and the abominations of the said Antichrist" that they will be "diligently searched out and brought before the Court to receive condign punishment for such grievous faults". Fifty percent of receipts from fines went to those laying information against all such heinous sinners — who by 1611 had apparently persisted in their waywardness for almost half a century! That the threat of 'condign punishment' was no idle one becomes apparent when one considers the fate of Charles Halouvrys who, in retribution for "having been at the Mass and on pilgrimage in the country of Normandy" was on July 27th., 1572 sentenced to be placed in the deep and unwholesome 'profonde fosse' at Castle cornet "with irons on his feet and on bread and water", to pay a fine of £6-13s.-4d. (= 10 marks) and on release to acknowledge his fault before the congregation in Saint Pierre-Port Church on one Sunday and that in Saint Sampson's Church on the next.

Although, in the end, the illogicality was appreciated of territories under a Protestant Crown forming part of a French Roman Catholic diocese, the strange thing is that in the early stages of the Reformation, this anomaly was not so keenly felt as to prevent a compromise from being acceptable. Such a compromise was reached in 1542 when Henry VIII, through Paget (his ambassador in Paris), demanded that the Bishop of Coutances should not exercise jurisdiction in the name 'of the Bishop of Rome whom some call Pope', but in that of the Crown.

In response to this demand the bishop was sufficiently pliable to be able to devise a formula which satisfied both his conscience and Henry's susceptibilities — and thus continued to exercise his *de facto* jurisdiction until 1569.

Tolerance of this paradox stemmed largely from territorial aspirations, it being feared that a formal separation of the islands from the Diocese of Coutances might impair the title of the Crown to the Duchy of Normandy. This attitude 350 years after John's expulsion is less extraordinary than might appear at first sight when it is recalled that the Huguenots were very strong in Normandy (even to the extent of humiliating the Bishop of Coutances, driving him out of his own cathedral city, sitting on a donkey facing the tail) and at one time made an unofficial offer of it to Elizabeth I.

Even a petition to the Privy Council from the Protestant party in Guernsey (*c.* 1565) recommends that "As long as the Queen holds the isles governed by the laws of Normandy spiritual and temporal, Her Majesty is not out of possession of the Duchy, but may by the laws, usages and customs of Normandy maintain just claim and title to the Duchy".

Possibly these territorial considerations explain why the Crown even went so far as to endorse this strange arrangement by Orders-in-Council. Thus in 1550 (Edward VI's reign) an Order-in-Council directed that the bishop should continue to have ecclesiastical jurisdiction in all things not repugnant or contrary to the king's laws, orders and proceedings. Elizabeth I herself, by another Order-in-Council dated 1565, instructed insular officials to see that all dues and sums of money as had previously been paid to the bishop should continue to be paid to him or his officers.

On the other hand, Elizabeth I's acceptance of a Calvinist discipline in the islands posed the problem of reconciling this fact with ecclesiastical allegiance to the Bishop of Coutances. She sought to resolve this contradiction by claiming that the Huguenots were to all intents and purposes the established church in Coutances and that their doctrines accorded in essentials with those of the Anglican Church. Thus the 1565 Order-in-Council authorising the insular Presbyterian establishment started by saying that "the Queen's most excellent Majesty understandeth that the Isles of Jersey and Guernsey have anciently depended on the Diocese of Coutance [*sic*] and that there be certain churches in the same Diocese well reformed, agreeably throughout in doctrine as it is set forth in this Realm".

The extraordinary situation resulting from this exercise in ecclesiastical dialectics might have continued indefinitely had not the Bishop of Coutances over-reached himself. Thinking to take advantage of the position guaranteed to him by the 1565 Order-in-Council, the bishop took proceedings in the Royal Court of Guernsey against Dean After, claiming possession of the deanery and the dean's benefices on the grounds that he had not been canonically instituted by the bishop, nor paid his fees. To this, Dean After (an advanced reformer) retorted that he would not recognise the bishop's claims unless he took the oath of allegiance to the queen and renounced papal authority. The matter was referred to the Privy Council, which, of course, found the bishop's attempt to interfere with the queen's ecclesiastical appointments absolutely intolerable. The upshot was the Order-in-Council of 1569 finally separating the islands from Coutances and placing them under the jurisdiction of the Bishop of Winchester — a jurisdiction which persists to the present day.

Chapter Seven

THE CALVINIST EPOCH

IN 1563 THE HUGUENOT REFUGEE, Nicholas Baudouin, who had already set up a Presbyterian organisation in the Town church of St. Peter-Port, obtained the permission of Sir Francis Chamberlain, the governor (who was himself a Roman Catholic) for the election of Elders and Deacons and the formation of a Consistory.

The Order-in-Council of 1565 foreshadowed a triumphant Presbyterianism. As has been seen, the stipulation in the Order that the 'Residue of the Parishes' should adhere to the Anglican rite was eventually disregarded. So, too, were the Bishop of Winchester's injunctions requiring the parishes outside St. Peter-Port to use the Book of Common Prayer. Instead, a complete Presbyterian system of church government was set up, and in 1569 the Synod drew up a set of articles called *Police et Discipline Ecclésiastique.* In June 1576 this document was officially adopted by the full Synod and became the regular system of church government — indeed, it was even grafted on to the insular constitution and tacitly accepted by the Crown.

The responsible Anglican authorities did nothing to combat this Presbyterian tide. Dean After was himself a strong Calvinist and actively connived in Geneva practices: far from asserting his authority as dean, he sat on the Synod on an equality with the other incumbents. As for Robert Horne, the Bishop of Winchester, he also held Puritan views and made no attempt to obstruct the march of Presbyterianism in the islands. Indeed, in 1575, when the Guernsey Colloque appealed to him over the intransigence of Elie Bonamy, a person of Catholic sympathies, he did not take the opportunity of exercising any authority, but merely wrote back signifying his approval of the Colloque's attitude.

In these circumstances, the Presbyterian Establishment was prepared to recognise the Bishop of Winchester as a nominal superior provided he abstained from any active interference. Thus the Synods of 1567 and 1568 sent him polite greetings, while that of 1569 presented him with a copy of *Police et Discipline*. Furthermore, up to 1575 incumbents were instituted by him after taking the oath of canonical obedience. However, as soon as the bishop attempted to make his authority at all effective, this immediately proved to be a cause of severe contention. Trouble arose out of an Order-in-Council of 1581, which provided that probate and the administration of the revenues of vacant benefices should be ordered by the Bishop of Winchester. In the light of this, the bishop appointed the procureur, Louis de Vic, as his commissary to deal with wills and other ecclesiastical business. Outraged by this episcopal intrusion into their Presbyterian establishment, the ministers in 1582 brought trumped-up charges against de Vic.

Although himself an ardent Calvinist, this shameful exhibition of 'malice and all uncharitableness' was too much for the governor, Sir Thomas Leighton, and he stood by de Vic, asking Walsingham to deal with the matter — which ended with de Vic being vindicated. Upon de Vic's acquittal, Nicholas Baudouin (the 'founder' of Guernsey Calvinism), professing fear for his life, sailed for England in 1583, and, on the recommendation of Walsingham, took a living in Jersey in 1584. The following year (1585) three other ministers, after a search of their houses ordered by Leighton, also left for Jersey. This led to a violent quarrel between the Colloques of the two islands, which refused to meet in Synod until 1597 — twelve years later.

The Calvinist system was based on the absolute equality of each minister and each congregation with each other. The organisation consisted of an equal federation of parish churches, where each parish was governed by a Consistory (Consistoire), made up of Elders (Anciens) and Deacons (Diacres), meeting under the presidency of the incumbent. It met every Sunday. Above this came the Colloque, representing all the parishes of the Bailiwick (though the adherence of the Sark and Alderney parishes was spasmodic) and met at least quarterly but frequently more often. The governor or his deputy presided (creating yet another religious paradox as until 1570 the governor was a Roman Catholic) and each parish was represented by its incumbent and one Elder. Lastly the Synod consisted of the Colloques of Guernsey and Jersey meeting initially annually, but subsequently biennially.

The appointment of ecclesiastical officials in this system was complicated. By the *Police et Discipline* adopted by the Synod of

1576 the governor nominated a candidate for the ministry. The Colloque examined him, and, if satisfied, endorsed his nomination, seconding him to the vacant living. The parishioners also examined him and accepted or rejected the candidate. In any case of disagreement the matter was settled by the governor and the Colloque after hearing the disputants. This system replaced institution by the Bishop of Winchester, which was discontinued in 1575. However, by the revised *Police et Discipline* of 1597, candidates were presented to the governor *after* approval by the Colloque and submission to the parish — i.e., the governor's power of nomination was reduced to that of veto on the choice of the Colloque.

Elders (anciens) were selected by the Consistoire (advised by two or three jurats), submitted to the governor for approval, and then brought before the congregation concerned for the appointment to be confirmed or rejected. Elders were responsible for enforcing church discipline on members. Their fellow officers, the deacons (diacres), came to office by the same path. These latter were in charge of finance, collecting and disbursing relief for the poor.

The church discipline enforced by the elders was formidable, shot through with repressive and killjoy regulations, with — for example — a fine of eighteen sous attaching to 'dancing and dissolute songs' (1567 Michaelmas Chief Pleas). Everybody had to attend church twice on Sundays and at least one member from each family the weekday services, which were held twice a week in St. Peter-Port and once a week elsewhere. The tolling of a passing bell, candles around a bier, prayers for the dead — and anything else smacking of 'Popish superstition' — was utterly banned. Attendance was compulsory at the quarterly communion services. Furthermore, the flock were catechised annually and failure to display sufficient knowledge was penalised by excommunication — and even possibly civil penalties.

The most rigid standards of conduct of life generally were enforced and the system did not shrink from inquisitorial and denunciatory methods of an almost '1984-ish' intensity. Elders were enjoined to visit every family and to enquire from their servants and the neighbours as to their life and character. A favourite punishment was for anyone revealed by these investigations as an offender to be made to sit on the penitents' bench facing the congregation during the Sunday service, wearing the white sheet of penitence, bare-headed and bare-footed. Then, with a burning torch in one hand and a Bible in the other, the victim had to confess his or her fault, express regret, promise never to offend again, acknowledge the justice of the punishment — and then listen to a scathing sermon designed to make the humiliation complete.

The remarkable thing is that, despite the draconian nature of the régime's measures to curb unseemly exuberance and to promote a 'godly discipline', they did not always prove effective — witness the complaint made in September 1633 by the ministers of the country parishes about young men running amok of a Saturday evening and so indulging in debaucheries and revelries as to become incapable of attending the 'exercises de piété' when Sunday dawned.

Not only marriages, but even betrothals, had to take place in the presence of a minister or elder — and once entered into could not be broken off without the consent of the Consistoire or Colloque. In 1600, Marie Robilliard of St. Pierre-du-Bois did manage, after a two-year defiance, to obtain the agreement of the Colloque to the cancellation of her betrothal to Roger Langlois, so that she could marry Jacques Martel — but only after both of them had undergone the rigours of the 'white sheet of penitence' procedure.

When, in 1565, Helier de Carteret was engaged in his original colonisation of Sark, the services of Cosmé Brévint were recruited as minister in the temple set up in an outbuilding of Le Manoir. Brévint was of Norman birth and came to Sark from Switzerland to which (as a Huguenot) he had fled to avoid persecution. Thanks to his forceful character, both Sark and its church rapidly gained great esteem — a potent factor in cementing the sense of identity of a new community with diverse origins. So great, indeed, was Brévint's prestige that as early as 1570 Sark was chosen as the venue for the fifth Synod of the churches of the archipelago.

There was, however, another side to the coin. Brévint adopted an aggressively independent attitude towards the Guernsey Colloque, whose meetings he avoided on the plea that the Sark Consistoire had not yet decided whether to attach itself to the Guernsey or Jersey Colloque. His consistently overbearing demeanour eventually led the elder of his church (Thomas Roo) to appeal to the Guernsey Colloque to discipline him. This body censured him in 1601, but by sheer force of personality he retained his incumbency until his death in 1605.

After Cosmé's death, a few unsatisfactory stop-gap appointments were followed by that of his son, Elie Brévint, who was presented to the Guernsey Colloque in 1612 and ministered to the Serquiais until his death in 1674, thus prolonging Presbyterianism in Sark long after it had been superseded by Anglicanism in the other islands.

The Presbyterian hold on Alderney was less firm than in the other islands, largely owing to the opposition of John Chamberlain who, although a Roman Catholic, had nevertheless contrived to obtain a Patent from the Crown in 1584 whereby he was granted Alderney as a fief, much as Helier de Carteret had been granted Sark 19 years previously. Yet, despite the hostility of John's brother and successor, William Chamberlain, which (according to a 1607 complaint of the islanders) included withholding any ministerial stipend for 16 years and seizing the tithes and parsonage house, the Calvinists persisted in a stubborn loyalty to their dour faith. Thus for many years the Alderney elders contributed to the cost of training the son of a member of the Huguenot colony in Southampton at the Calvinist Training School for the ministry attached to that colony. The trainee in question was Simon Maçon, who took up his pastoral duties in the island in the year 1607, after the salary dispute with Chamberlain had been settled.

It was during Maçon's ministry that the name of the church (and of the eponymous town) was changed from St. Mary to St. Anne. It is possible that this reflected the somewhat wary attitude towards the Virgin which was (and still is) one of the main characteristics of Calvinism.

It is remotely possible that Herm remained an 'odd man out' in a Calvinist archipelago. In his notebook, Elie Brévint of Sark refers to 'des beaux-pères [priests?] d'Herm' seen in Jersey in 1619 by one Perrin la Broque and also states that "en la dite île dans l'hermitage y a une petite table de pierre [altar?]." Almost incredibly, this enigmatic evidence has led to the suggestion that the island contained a monastery housing Roman Catholic scions of survivors from the onslaught postulated by Edith Carey.

The Calvinist régime coincided with the witch-hunting frenzy of the 16th and 17th centuries. There was no doubt some foundation for many of the accusations in that the fears and aspirations of simple people were played on by unscrupulous opponents of the Church who organised Devil-worship characterized by revolting ritual and mocking parodies of the Sacraments. The fury that was unleashed upon these wayward simpletons was, however, barbaric in the extreme. The extent of the campaign against witchcraft may be gauged from the fact that during the century 1550–1650 there were 100 accused of witchcraft, of whom 18 were burned, 27 hanged, strangled and burnt, 32 banished, and two flogged and banished. Furthermore, savage tortures were used to obtain confessions. These were administered in the Tour Beauregard (Mignot Plateau) and involved the victims being suspended by their thumbs which had previously been tied behind their backs.

Amice de Carteret, when Bailiff of Guernsey, was an especially ardent witch-hunter. During his period of office alone (1601–1631) 34 witches were burnt and 24 banished out of the 77 who were tried by him.

Not even the normally placid Sark escaped the fever. Jean Nicole of La Sablonnerie was banished for practising the Black Art in 1620, and in 1627 his wife, Rachel Alexandre was taken to St. Peter-Port and burnt as a sorceress. On the credit side, the Calvinists did try to wean people away from Satanism by sponsoring education, setting up additional schools to supplement those already in existence.

As a matter of interest it may be noted that the last witch-craft trial in Guernsey took place in 1914. The accused (Mrs. Aimée Henrietta Lake) was sentenced to eight days' imprisonment for disorderly conduct. A certain frisson may perhaps attach to the revelation that by a macabre coincidence Mrs. Lake's maiden name of Queripel had also been the surname of one Alechette of Saint Andrew's who in 1598 had been burnt at the stake as a witch!

Chapter Eight

THE EROSION OF CALVINISM

ALTHOUGH HE TEMPORISED at the outset of his reign, James I, true to his maxim, 'No Bishop, No King', sought to eradicate Presbyterianism in the Channel Isles. By playing on the ambitions of individual clerics, he ultimately succeeded in achieving his objective in Jersey, but he failed in Guernsey.

In 1613, a letter from the King-in-Council was sent to both Bailiwicks, stating that James was determined to establish religious uniformity in all his dominions and therefore intended to introduce Anglicanism into the islands as opportunity offered. Only Jersey, however (where religious disputes had already developed between the Colloque and the Anglican governor, Sir John Peyton), obeyed the direct order to send representatives of both sides to state their case before the Privy Council in a 'mini Hampton Court Conference'.

In Guernsey, the receipt of the letter led to a closing of the ranks so as to deny the king the kind of opportunity he was seizing in Jersey, both Church and State combining in a steady resistance to any attempt to infiltrate the Calvinist system. This resistance was aided by the fact that the governor, Lord Carew, was an indifferent absentee, while his deputy (the Bailiff Amice de Carteret) was a dyed-in-the-wool Presbyterian.

A possible opportunity for exploiting dissension in the Anglican interest arose when a parishioner named Le Page, who had been excommunicated by his Consistoire, appealed to the Court of Arches, which summoned the incumbent of the parish to appear before it. The States of Guernsey (which to a large extent had membership interlocking with that of the Colloque) regarding the summons as an infringement of insular autonomy, instructed the minister to go to London, but to refuse to recognise the competence of the Court when he got to England.

Once in London, however, the minister found himself in a weak position, as the king himself took a personal interest in the case, and he was only able to return to Guernsey temporarily on parole pending a further visit to London. After his return to Guernsey, the States instructed the minister to disregard this requirement, whereupon the Court of Arches notified the Colloque that it had excommunicated him.

Again the States and the Colloque put on a united front, the former protesting that Guernsey had its own church establishment not subject to any other jurisdiction; while the latter authorised the minister to continue in his living and sent a capable and persuasive young man, named Jean de la Marche, to London to appeal directly to the king. James accorded two interviews to this emissary and as a result decided to permit the Guernsey Presbyterian system to continue, as the arguments advanced by de la Marche had convinced him of the islanders' strong attachment to Calvinism and of the consequent folly of alienating the loyalties of an outpost so near a potentially hostile France.

The eradication of the Presbyterian system in Jersey was not fully completed until 1620, when an Anglican dean was finally installed. According to Peter Heylyn's *Survey of the Estate of the two Islands of Guernsey and Jersey* (1656), Buckingham, as the chief minister of James I and subsequently of Charles I, meant to deal firmly with Guernsey after Jersey was settled. These plans, however, remained unfulfilled because of the distractions caused by the breach with Spain in 1624, followed by the war with France and the Ile de Ré expedition of 1627 — a war which not only increased Guernsey's importance as a frontier fortress, but was, moreover, fought in alliance with the islanders' Huguenot co-religionists.

In the years 1635–1637, Archbishop Laud took a hand in the matter of Guernsey's Presbyterianism. In the first of these years, he established scholarships at Oxford (Exeter, Jesus and Pembroke) for Channel Islanders in theological training, with the obvious object of encouraging them to study in an Anglican atmosphere, instead of the Calvinist ambience of Saumur or Geneva. He followed this up in November 1636 by notifying the governor of Guernsey, Lord Danby, of his intention to order an episcopal visitation on the report of which he would take action — and required Danby's co-operation "that both islands may go alike and that Guernsey as well as the other may conform to the Church of England".

Danby replied the following April with a memorandum deprecating on grounds of political expediency any attempt to change the Guernsey ecclesiastical system, regarding such a step as one which the islanders would interpret as an attack on their independent status as well as an affront to their beliefs — and which therefore would provoke unanimous resistance. The Edinburgh riots following Laud's attempt to foist an Anglican liturgy on another Presbyterian community gave point to Danby's warning and left neither Laud nor Charles much time to worry about the Church in remote Guernsey. Finally, the ensuing Bishops' Wars and the Civil Wars guaranteed Presbyterianism's survival in the Bailiwick.

Guernsey's adherence to the Cromwellian side in the Civil Wars caused the island's establishment to regard the Restoration with anxiety. Bearing in mind the assurance of the Declaration of Breda regarding 'liberty for tender consciences', as well as the fact that Charles II owed his restoration in large measure to Presbyterian support in Britain, the Guernsey authorities hoped for the best and made humble submission.

Although Charles II stood by the Declaration of Breda, renewing insular charters and privileges and granting a general amnesty to erstwhile royalist opponents, the sands were nevertheless running out for Presbyterianism in Guernsey. The 1662 version of the Book of Common Prayer was translated into French by a Jerseyman, the Rev. Jean Durel, and Charles ordered that it should be used in Channel Isles churches. This was followed up by the Bishop of Winchester in 1663 appointing John de Sausmarez as Dean of Guernsey, while at the same time a body of troops was sent to the island to repress any resistance to the introduction of Anglicanism. De Sausmarez joined battle with the Presbyterian organisation, threatening the use of these troops and employing the authority of the Royal Court to compel submission. Opposing him was a Presbyterian divine, Thomas le Marchant, who was only silenced by being imprisoned in Castle Cornet and later in the Tower of London for two years. Other recalcitrant clergy were removed from their livings, though some later conformed. An example of the latter is Dr. John Morehead of St. Saviour's, who was suspended in 1663, then went to England, where he overcame his scruples and returned in 1664 as Anglican rector of the same parish. By contrast, Daniel Perchard, who had been ejected from the living of Saint Pierre-du-Bois, ultimately obtained from Charles II a dispensation dated August 12th., 1672, permitting those "of the persuasion commonly called Presbyterian" to assemble in his house for "their Publick worship and devotion". It could therefore be argued that, enjoying as it did this toleration, Guernsey's Presbyterianism resembled old soldiers in never officially dying — but it is nevertheless clear that like the self-same old soldiers it did eventually fade away. It must be said, however, that although de Sausmarez had won, Guernsey only grudgingly adhered to Anglicanism. The outward structure was secured, but the mode of worship in the island's churches remained largely unaltered.

The transition to Anglicanism in Alderney was more peacefully effected. Charles II granted the island to three Jersey royalists — Edward and James de Carteret, and Clement Le Coureur; but these three gentlemen almost immediately transferred their rights to Sir George Carteret, who became the governor of Alderney, the administration of which was now divorced from that of Guernsey.

Sir George appointed a poacher-turned-gamekeeper as Lieutenant Governor, in the person of Captain Nicholas Ling, former parliamentary governor and now an ardent royalist. Under his wing, the Rev. Elie Picot, who in 1654 had succeeded Simon Maçon as Alderney's Calvinist minister, was reappointed in 1662 on the death of Sir George's nominee, the Rev. W. J. Germain. Putting to good use his tact and popularity, Elie Picot accomplished the transition to Anglicanism in the island, where he remained as incumbent until his death in 1696.

The Restoration brought the reinstatement of Sir Philippe de Carteret as Seigneur of Sark, but no immediate attempt was made to extend Anglicanism to the island, as Sir Philippe felt that the special status of Elie Brévint (who had been appointed by his grandfather as far back as 1612) precluded any change as long as he lived. Sir Philippe died in 1663 and was succeeded by his 11-year-old son (also named Philippe) whose minority status enabled Brévint to continue his dominance. Philippe came of age in 1671, and the death of Elie Brévint in 1674 finally paved the way for setting up the Anglican system in the island, where Presbyterianism had lingered longer than anywhere else in the archipelago. Philippe appointed as incumbent Moise Benoist, a Frenchman who had been ordained as an Anglican priest by the Bishop of Winchester. Thus at last Sark became part of the See of Winchester and the occasion was marked by Dame Anne Dumaresq, the Seigneur's mother, presenting a chalice to the island church. Adherence to Anglicanism for long remained perfunctory, however, the vicar (Rev. J. L. V. Cachemaille) writing as late as 1874 that most incumbents, including himself, had come from a Presbyterian background and only conformed in greater or less degree to the rites of the Church of England.

Chapter Nine

'BY LAW ESTABLISHED': THE ANGLICAN SETTLEMENT

DEAN DE SAUSMAREZ may well have achieved the 'outward and visible sign' of a re-established Anglicanism, but of the 'inward and spiritual grace' of espousal of Anglican doctrine there was little evidence.

It is true that the parochial clergy resumed the title of rector, while the elders and deacons were renamed churchwardens, and services were conducted more or less according to the Book of Common Prayer — but it took another 150 years before Anglican beliefs came to be embraced by the congregations generally.

Indeed, for the next one-and-a-half to two centuries, the reaction of the insular Calvinists to their enforced 'conversion' was to adopt a policy of passive resistance to the religious changes which they deeply resented. Thus the sign of the Cross was omitted in baptisms, and the baptismal fonts which had been banished by the Huguenots were only restored on the specific orders of the Bishop of Winchester after his visit to the island as late as 1829. Similarly, the Calvinist tradition of four communions a year persisted right down to the 1850s, while the communion tables were left in the side chapels to which the Presbyterians had relegated them, not being restored to their traditional position in the chancel until about the same time. Finally, as no bishop visited the archipelago until 1818, there were no confirmation services, so that the Anglican requirement of this rite as a pre-condition of communion was ignored. Instead the Presbyterian system of examination of potential communicants by the Consistoire was retained, with the rector and churchwardens making up an unofficial Consistoire for this purpose.

The post-Napoleonic War arrival of English settlers, attracted by improved communications and the low cost of living, resuscitated the Anglican Church from the zombie-like existence which had been its lot since 1663. Under the patronage of Admiral Lord de Saumarez the church of St. James the Less was built to provide worship in the English tongue for these settlers. On its completion in 1818, Dr. Fisher, Bishop of Salisbury, came over to consecrate the church, thus providing the island with its first episcopal visit since the Reformation. Thanks to this visit, confirmations were also administered for the first time since the break with Coutances. It would seem, however, that the Bishop of Winchester still deemed it imprudent to visit this intractable part of his diocese (he was in any case old and ailing), and another 11 years were to pass before Dr. Sumner became the first Bishop of Winchester to visit the Bailiwick since its transference to his See in 1569 (or 1499 according to taste).

Anglicanism's firmer hold in the 19th. century was further attested by the erection of St. John's church in 1836, St. Matthew's (Cobo) in 1852, St. Stephen's in 1864, and St. Barnabas' in 1874. On the other hand, the persistence of Calvinistic leanings is witnessed by the building of Holy Trinity in 1789, to ensure the continued proclamation of a strictly Protestant doctrine within the Anglican fold. At first only a 'proprietary chapel', it was consecrated as an Anglican church in 1846.

The 20th. century, however, although witnessing the opening of Saint Mary's at L'Islet in 1912, later saw the closure of Saint Barnabas in 1927 and of Saint James the Less in 1965: and it must also be recorded that — for good or for ill, according to one's theological understanding — both Guernsey's representatives on the General Synod of the Church of England voted on November 11th., 1992, in favour of female ordination to the priesthood. It remains to be seen whether or not this development will have in the Bailiwick disruptive consequences within the Anglican fold comparable to those experienced in England. The first Guernsey-woman to go through a form of ordination pursuant to this was Mrs. Linda Le Vasseur, who did so on June 30th., 1996. Thereafter, Mrs. Le Vasseur's official position became that of a non-stipendiary assistant curate to the Rector of the Castel. Nearly two years later, however, in March 1998, the Guernsey Deanery Synod voted in favour of allowing women to be appointed as incumbents of island livings, with the proviso that no woman would be imposed on any parish opposed to female ordination. States approval of this vote was given the following May.

A similar immigration into Alderney led to the construction of the existing church of St. Anne, which was consecrated by the Bishop of Winchester in 1850. The old one had become inadequate, despite the addition to it of an aisle and north chapel in 1761. It is also possible that the influence of the newcomers lay behind Alderney's emergence as a vestiarian pioneer in the Bailiwick; John Jacob reporting in regard thereto in his *Annals* (1830) that "the Minister wears a surplice in this island, which is not used in any other part of the Deanery".

Likewise in Herm (which was devoid of inhabitants at the time of the Restoration) it was a population influx which brought the Anglican Church to the island. The spiritual needs of the labourers recruited to work Herm's quarries in the early 19th. century led to the appointment in 1838 of the Rev. Henry Benwell as chaplain of the island — and to the renovation of the ancient chapel of St. Tugual.

In Sark, a dispute arose over the status and tenure of office of the island's incumbent. Starting in 1752, the dispute was not finally ended until five years later. In that year, the Seigneur, Daniel Le Pelley, died, leaving as heir his son, Pierre, who was a minor. His widow, Elizabeth Le Pelley, acted as Dame during her son's minority. From the time of Helier de Carteret onwards, it had been the custom for the Seigneur to appoint the minister, subject to the approval first of the Colloque and subsequently of the Dean of Guernsey. In this tradition, shortly before his death, Daniel Le Pelley had appointed to the Sark living the Reverend Jacques Levrier — ordained December 29th., 1751 — whose posthumous daughter Marie (born to his wife Magdelaine Jachau on November 11th., 1752) subsequently became the wife of René Martineau, from 1774 to 1780 and again from 1789 to 1816 Rector of Saint Sampson's and Vicar of the Vale in which latter Parish Church her memorial tablet is still to be seen. Not long surviving his appointment and dying well before Marie's birth, poor Jacques was succeeded by his brother (or cousin?) Pierre whose sacerdotal qualifications are problematic (possibly a pastor of L'Eglise Reformée de France whose lack of episcopal ordination was winked at) and to whom Elizabeth Le Pelley soon afterwards took such exception that she summarily dismissed him.

Supported by his congregation, Levrier refused to leave, whereupon La Dame locked both pastor and flock out of the out-building at Le Manoir which did service as a church. As a result of this, the inhabitants (who had to cross over to Guernsey to get married) complained to the dean, who thereupon summoned La Dame to attend his Court to justify her actions on pain of excommunication. La Dame, however, refused to go, maintaining that the minister was the personal chaplain of the Seigneur and held office at the Seigneur's pleasure.

In 1755, Pierre Le Pelley came of age, and, faced with the dean's threat of excommunication if no services were held, invited François Guillaume Durand, Rector of Saint Sampson's and Vicar of the Vale, to cross to Sark to officiate. During this service, Levrier rushed in and raised the Clameur de Haro, which automatically brought the whole matter within the jurisdiction of the Royal Court of Guernsey. The Royal Court ruled that Levrier was in the right, on the grounds that the Seigneur had the right of appointment, but not of dismissal. The incumbent's victory, however, proved to be a pyrrhic one, as in 1756 the Seigneur, egged on by his mother, prevailed upon the Seneschal to issue an order to Levrier to quit Sark for causing a public mischief. Two years later the outcast was inducted to the twin livings of the Forest and Torteval in Guernsey, but in 1765 he betook himself to the New World and was never again seen in the Bailiwick — though he surprisingly retained for over thirty years his Guernsey livings, of which he was not deprived until June 22nd., 1796.

The conflict finally ended with the appointment in 1757 of the Rev. Cayeux Deschamps by the Bishop of Winchester — an appointment accepted by the Seigneur. However, the vexed question of the Seigneur's power to dismiss the incumbent was left in the air: though later it came to be accepted that, while the Seigneur has the right to nominate the vicar, the nomination must be approved by the Bishop of Winchester and the incumbent cannot be removed save through discipline under the Dean of Guernsey.

The present Anglican church in Sark exists as a result of the reactions in 1818 of the Seigneur, Pierre Le Pelley (son of the previous Pierre), to the strictures of Dr. John Fisher, Bishop of Salisbury (who had visited the island while in Guernsey for the consecration of Saint James the Less) in which he called urgently for more commodious provision to replace the unsatisfactory and cramped out-building at Le Manoir used since 1565. Much embarrassed, Pierre reluctantly obtained from the Church Building Society a grant of £500 towards the construction of a Church on land which he made available for the purpose. He himself contributed £200 towards building costs and raised a further £150 by selling private pews to the Forty Tenants for a down-payment followed in each case by an annual rent — a charge which, incidentally, continues to this day, making Sark one of the few places in the British Isles where pew-rents survive. Eventually, the foundation stone was laid in 1820 and the building, dedicated to St. Peter, was licensed for divine service in 1821 by the Bishop of Winchester, who consecrated it on his first visit to the Channel Isles in 1829. Some years later, during his exclusion from Oxford between 1843 and 1846, Dr. Edward Bouverie Pusey, the Tractarian leader, conducted services in Sark for the first time in English — and also inaugurated the use of surplices in the Sark church.

Chapter Ten

THE ANCIENT PARISH CHURCHES — AND OTHERS

THE VICTORY of Dean John de Sausmarez led to the parish churches coming to be (like Winchester Cathedral in Bernard Shaw's *St. Joan*) 'temporarily in the hands of the Anglican heresy'. Precisely how ancient are the churches is difficult to establish with accuracy — though Mr. John McCormack, in his deeply researched *Channel Islands' Churches*, has advanced exceptionally well-informed estimates of their successive constructional periods.

At some time towards the end of the reign of Elizabeth I (or early in the reign of James I) an unknown author produced a manuscript entitled *Dédicase des Eglises de l'Ile de Guernesey*. This publication, which purported to give the precise dates of the building or consecration of every parish church, is utterly spurious — a veritable 'documentary Piltdown Man'. Its bogus nature becomes obvious on two counts. In the first place, the document assigns dates from the 12th to 14th centuries for the consecration of the churches, beginning with the mnemonic 1111 for St. Sampson's (as mentioned in *The Toilers of the Sea* — Hugo too was duped) and ending with 1312 for St. Peter-Port. The oldest extant copy of the *Dédicase* is included among the registers of St. Saviour's church, to which building the date 1154 is given. Yet St. Saviour's is specifically mentioned in a Charter of 1030, whereby Duke Robert I granted it and three other Guernsey churches to the Abbé de Mont St. Michel. Secondly, the rites described for the alleged 12th.-century consecrations are distinctly post-Reformation, with a complete absence of Ave Marias, invocation of the saints, and prayers for the dead. The amazing thing is the widespread credulity which has been accorded to this forgery during the three-and-a-half centuries or so since it was first foisted on a gullible public — a credulity which in some quarters persists to the present day.

Although Robert I's Charter makes it clear that churches stood on or near the present sites as early as the eleventh century, many were modified structurally after this period, several of them being architecturally metamorphosed in the process. For example, extensive restoration work became necessary at the Town Church and at Saint Sampson's in the wake of the damage wrought by a particularly savage raid launched by the French in 1294, some of the ravages of which were still in evidence ten years later. However, Mr. McCormack has become convinced by his researches that to regard this onslaught as having inflicted such wholesale destruction on the island's places of worship generally that they had to be completely rebuilt in the early fourteenth century (as was previously thought to be the case) is to postulate a gross exaggeration.

On the other hand, it must not be overlooked that Mr. McCormack's investigations also reveal that, in the face of perennial threats from a hostile France following King John's loss of continental Normandy in 1204, the Abbots of Mont Saint Michel, Saint Martin de Marmoutiers and Blanchelande (on whose shoulders fell the bulk of the cost of church upkeep) took good care, as and when maintenance became necessary, to replace the original wooden roofs with the stone-vaulted ones which to this day are so prominent a feature of these buildings.

One of the parish churches — Torteval — is, of course, relatively modern. The old church had become ruinous and was demolished in 1818, after which the present structure was erected to replace it. This nineteenth century edifice, however, does possess Guernsey' s oldest church bell, dated 1432 and dedicated (as was the original church itself) to the Virgin. The Castel Church is similarly dedicated, with its immediate southern neighbour honouring the Holy Saviour (le Saint Sauveur), while the church in the parish adjoining Torteval shares with that of the Town a dedication to Saint Peter. This group comprises half the island's parish churches, all of which comply with the ruling restricting dedications to Our Saviour, Mary His Mother, John His Precursor, Peter His Apostle and Lawrence His Deacon, made by Hope Hilary, who reigned from 461 to 467. The persistence of these ancient dedications, originating in a papal edict issued six hundred years before the erection of the churches to which they apply (plus the fact that the entire Hilary quintet is to be found in Jersey) suggests the — probably attenuated — survival (despite the adverse circumstances mentioned in Chapter Two of this Part) of a local Christian presence during the fifth century, following an initial late fourth century evangelization and preceding the mid-sixth century arrival of the Celtic Saints.

In the approaches to these churches, it is still possible in some cases to trace residual portions of the ancient paths along which worshippers in the Middle Ages wended their way to their devotions — that leading to Saint Andrew's Church from la Rue de la Boullierie being particularly well defined, as too is the pretty track descending to Sous l'Eglise from Saint Saviour's Church so as to pass le Fief Jean du Gaillard Feudal Court. In his book, *Peter Girard's Guernsey*, this well-known islander asserted that these old tracks constituted 'sanctuary paths' (comparable to those named 'Perquages' in Jersey) which 'radiated out at least from the churches of the higher parishes' and along which offenders 'in trouble with the law ... could make their way safely to the sea coast', where they had the chance of avoiding arrest by leaving the island. As far as the Castel is concerned, Mr. Girard in Chapter 2 of the same book mapped no less than three 'escape routes' connecting the Parish Church with the coast — the first ending at that part of Vazon Bay adjacent to le Crocq, the second near the spot where 'Martello' Tower Number 12 now stands, and the third at Cobo. Similarly Mr. Nigel Jee, writing on *Guernsey's Green Lanes* in the 1987 *Shell Guide to the Channel Islands* traces a route (part of which is still known as 'Le Chemin de l'Eglise') connecting the Church of Saint Pierre-du-Bois with 'Le Prévôté' — whence one may remark that a somewhat perilous embarkation could presumably be made at the adjacent Havre de Bon Repos. It is, incidentally, interesting to note that the Assize Rolls of 1299 reveal the identity of one offender against the law who took advantage of such facilities. The person concerned was a woman with the Christian name of Emmerion (no surname recorded) who, admitting the theft of wool from Guillaume Melege, fled to the Town Church whence she used the sanctuary path — in this case obviously a very short one — to gain access to the sea and leave the island.

Although it is not a parish church, this is a convenient point at which to consider the history of La Chapelle Sainte Appoline at Perelle. In 1392, Nicholas Henry of La Perelle returned safely with his ships after service with the English Navy and he obtained the consent of his Seigneur (the Abbé de Mont St. Michel) to the endowment of a chapel in thanksgiving for his deliverance from the defeat the French had inflicted on the English fleet shortly after he had left it. Because of the 1279 Statute of Mortmain (aimed at preventing the accumulation of property by the clergy) the consent of the Abbé was subject to the sanction of the King, seeing that

Henry's proposal would create an item of real estate to be placed in the hands of the church. Richard II gave his permission in a Charter of 1394.

Richard's Charter authorised Nicholas Henry to build the Chapel of Notre Dame de la Perelle for the purpose of maintaining a chaplain to say Mass daily in perpetuity for Henry and his wife, Philippa, for their souls after their deaths, and for the souls of all their ancestors and benefactors and those of Christian people generally.

An Act of the Royal Court (Plaids d'Héritage) of 1452, refers to the Chapel of Notre Dame de la Perelle called the Chapelle Sainte Appoline. It was then in the hands of the founder's grandson and 40 years later, when the Guille family had acquired the entire Henry property, the advowson of the Chaplaincy was sold to the Seigneur of Anneville.

Since then the property has changed hands several times. Urged by Sir Edgar MacCulloch, the States of Guernsey acquired it in 1873 when the old chapel was being used as a stable — such as housed at birth the Master to whose glory it was built.

After it had been the focal point for an annual Anglican pilgrimage for some time, plans were made in the early 1970s for the restoration of this ancient shrine as a Chapel of Unity for the promotion of Ecumenicism in Guernsey. These plans came to fruition in October 1978 when, with restoration completed and some ancient wall murals revealed, the chapel was consecrated for this purpose in a ceremony jointly conducted by Anglican, Roman Catholic and Nonconformist clergy. As Sainte Appoline is the patron saint of dentists (her martyrdom having involved the crushing of her jaw) members of this sadistic profession far and wide were circularised in search of their financial support for this venture.

Despite the fact that it is neither ancient, nor a parish church, the small chapel of Christ the Healer at La Monnaie, St. Andrew's, nevertheless deserves a mention in any treatment of the religious aspect of island history. During the autumn of 1955 the Rev. Frank Drake, who had been brought to a state of intense spiritual awareness as a result of his son Robin's long and painful terminal illness, had a mental vision of a tiny church with a square tower in the chicken-run behind his house. As a result of this experience he persuaded his friend, Clifford Moullin, an architect, to design a miniature church, although he had no money to pay for it. Six months later, Fr. Drake was told of a local donor who was prepared to defray all construction costs, on condition of remaining anonymous. Accordingly, the work was put in hand, the builder being Marcel Flouquet. The construction is of pink and blue Guernsey granite — the pink, because of its rarity, being fetched, with special permission from the seashore.

On May 9th., 1957, the chapel was dedicated to Christ the Healer by the Bishop of Winchester. Prayers are said daily for the sick whose names are deposited in a box in the porch.

Chapter Eleven

ECCLESIASTICAL ADMINISTRATION

HISTORICAL EVOLUTION has produced two main peculiarities attaching to ecclesiastical administration in the Bailiwick. The first of these involves the Dean and his Court, while the second is concerned with the individual parishes.

The retention of the islands in the diocese of Coutances after their political separation from Continental Normandy in 1204 led to friction between the king's Courts in the islands and the bishop's Court on the Norman mainland. The king complained that pleas were being heard in the bishop's Court that ought to come before his own — and furthermore claimed that the Papacy had granted to the islanders the privilege that they should not be cited out of the islands even for ecclesiastical causes.

Matters came to a head in 1377 when the bishop cited some islanders to appear before his Court at Coutances. The warden, Sir Hugh Calverley, supported the islanders' privilege of not being tried outside the islands, and the bishop countered this by making the Dean of Guernsey the special commissary of the bishop. As a result the dean's Court was empowered to deal with matters which normally would have gone before the bishop's Court — with the consequence that the dean's Court developed an importance of unusual magnitude. These extraordinary powers came into the hands of the Anglican dean in 1663 — a fact which is symbolised by the seal of the deanery which, bearing the portrait of Charles II enthroned with the Town Church in the background, bears the motto, 'Restauratus restauro' ('Being restored, I restore').

The net results of this historical legacy have been of great significance. In the first place, the dean has come to combine the rôles of rural dean, archdeacon, chancellor and bishop's commissary (in which capacity he has from of old been inducted with the possession of a stall in St. Peter-Port church, even when he is the incumbent of another parish). Secondly, his Court has been empowered to grant faculties, issue marriage licences, hold visitations, suspend clergy, license curates, institute incumbents and grant probate — powers it retains to the present day. The Dean's Court is composed of himself as judge and nine assessors (the rectors of the other nine ancient parishes); there are also the vice-dean and surrogate, the registrar and surrogate, two proctors, advocates and an apparitor.

The peculiarities attaching to parish administration stem partly from the expropriation of alien priories and partly from the Grand Coutumier de Normandie.

As a result of the expropriation of alien priories the rectors of the ancient parishes came to hold Crown appointments — a state of affairs which is still with us. Furthermore, there has been no Guernsey legislation comparable to the 1919 Enabling Act in England whereby Parochial Church Councils came into existence. Instead all executive power is vested in the rectors and churchwardens.

By the Grand Coutumier de Normandie (the ancient customary law of the Duchy) parishioners from time immemorial were required to keep their churches and rectories in good repair. Nowadays this obligation devolves on all parishioners, regardless of creed. The resultant responsibilities resting on the shoulders of parishioners were — and are — twofold. The first concerns 'La Cure', consisting of the rectory and adjacent land appertaining to it, in respect of which the parishioners have to keep the buildings in repair, and the rectory habitable — though they are not responsible for interior decoration. The second concerns the church, where parishioners are responsible for the structure, the windows, the weather-cock, and bells, the upkeep of the churchyard, and half the caretaker's wages — but not the interior of the church. To defray the expenses of church and cure, there have been throughout the ages two sources of revenue. The first is the Trésor, which consists of income accruing from rentes and other investments. The other comes from contributions made by the parishioners, raised from antiquity by levying a parochial rate. (See Appendix XVIII).

Up to 1369, the parishioners were responsible for two-thirds of the upkeep costs of church and cure, the remaining one-third being the responsibility of one or other of the Abbots of Mont St. Michel, Marmoutiers, and Blanchelande — an arrangement which as early as 1303 was described as 'an ancient custom'. Persistent attempts by the abbots to avoid payment led to an agreement in 1369 whereby they assigned to the Trésors various rentes in perpetuity on condition of a final release from their liabilities.

During the century of Presbyterianism, Trésor income was frequently diverted to other uses. This flagrant malversation was ended by an Order-in-Council of 1662 which ordered that these monies should be 'restored to their ancient primary use'.

The officers in charge of the Trésor were called Trésoriers and later 'les Curateurs du Trésor' (churchwardens). From of old, their accounts have had to be approved by the bishop's nominee (first the Prior of the Vale, and subsequently the dean), and presented to the parishioners. The custom of holding parish meetings to audit the Trésorier's accounts was well established as far back as 1368.

Until the mid-19th. century, churchwardens called parish meetings of Chefs de Famille which considered both secular and ecclesiastical matters. Since then, the ecclesiastical side has been kept separate, with the sole exception of an application for money from the proceeds of the Occupiers' Rate which is made to the Royal Court through the parish constables (who are normally responsible for secular parish administration only).

The permission of the Royal Court for the rate to be levied is known as a Rémède (See Appendix XVIII) and is granted only after close scrutiny by the Royal Court, which sees itself as the protector of the interests of all ratepayers (many of whom are not Anglicans). Furthermore, all monies received must be spent as stipulated in the Rémède. Rémède income is handled by the peoples' wardens, while that accruing to the Trésor (which is nowadays small and inadequate) is handled by the rector's wardens.

These arrangements are not applicable to the 'ecclesiastical parishes' carved out of the ancient parishes of St. Peter-Port and the Castel in the 19th. century. They have to be maintained by the efforts of their congregations — who, in addition, must play their part towards the upkeep of the parish church proper through their contributions to the parochial rate authorised by the Rémède.

(It is not without interest, however, that reference to Appendix XVIII reveals that in 1988 one such spiritual enclave — Saint Matthew's, Cobo — was subsidised by the Castel ratepayers to the tune of £1,800, the relevant subvention appearing among the items covering parochial 'Secular Needs'.)

Chapter Twelve

OTHER RELIGIOUS DEVELOPMENTS

THE CLOSING YEARS of the 18th. century saw two non-Anglican creeds establishing themselves in the Bailiwick for the first time since the overthrow of Presbyterianism at the Restoration. First in chronological order came Methodism, and secondly, Roman Catholicism.

The Methodist movement first reached Guernsey in 1785 when islanders who had been involved in the Newfoundland cod fisheries returned home, bringing their newly-acquired faith with them. Already in 1783 Methodist soldiers among the garrison in Jersey had appealed to Wesley for a preacher as all worship in the island was in French. Thus in 1784 Wesley had sent over a bilingual preacher, Robert Carr Brackenbury, in response to this request. Brackenbury decided to take advantage of the situation in Guernsey and accordingly sent over Jean de Quetteville, one of his most able Jersey converts. Thanks to the disgruntlement of the Guernesiais with the Anglican imposition, de Quetteville found a fertile soil for the spread of his teachings. Mon Plaisir, the house of Henry de Jersey, became the headquarters of the movement.

In March 1787 another preacher, Adam Clarke, already established in Guernsey, introduced Methodism into Alderney. Undeterred by the threat of the Governor, John Le Mesurier, that he would transport him to the Casquets, Clarke landed secretly after being conveyed by smugglers in a night crossing, scrambling ashore at first light across the rocks at Hannaine Bay. He took shelter in the house in La Venelle Jehannet nowadays known as 'La Maison Jeanette', but then the abode of Pierre and Elizabeth Barbenson — and here within a few hours he delivered his first sermon, one version of local folklore holding that either then or subsequently he made use of the open window above the front door to serve as a pulpit.

During the same year John Wesley himself (now aged 84) visited the Bailiwick. In Guernsey he was enthusiastically welcomed, and preached to large numbers at Mon Plaisir, at the

Assembly Rooms (now the Guille-Allès Library), and in the open air. His visit had a profound influence, and as more and more bilingual converts were made, so the movement gained momentum.

En route for Guernsey, Wesley, on the evening of August 14th., 1787, had been forced by threatening weather to put in at Alderney where, after sleeping overnight at the 'Diver's Inn', he preached on the nearby beach the next morning before resuming his journey. His visit gave a boost to the efforts of Adam Clarke, and a chapel was built in 1790, to be followed by the present Methodist church in 1852.

The ensuing years saw persecution and an attempt was made to banish de Quetteville from Guernsey. This failed, as it was not regarded favourably by the bailiff, William Le Marchant — and, indeed, the persecution served to strengthen the movement, the influence of which spread with the building of the first chapel in Rue Le Marchant in 1789. Thirty-one others followed in the next 120 years. Methodism had become a force to be reckoned with. As time went on, however, (and especially in the years following the Second World War) its fortunes waned: a decline reflected in the fact that of the thirty-two places of worship established by this sect between 1789 and 1909, no fewer than fourteen structures had ceased to function as such by 1986 — with even more closures ensuing in April 1990 when the Methodist churches of the Forest, Saint Saviour's and Saint Pierre-du-Bois decided "to combine forces, using the Forest building as a base". This downward trend was yet again in evidence in 1995 when the sheer inability of the dwindling band of Wesley's disciples to maintain Ebenezer Church in Brock Road (the listed status of which debarred its envisaged replacement by a specially designed edifice with lower upkeep costs) led to its being closed and left to deteriorate, with all Methodist activity in Saint Peter-Port (apart from that in Le Bouet) concentrated in Salem Chapel in Vauvert, thereby reducing to two only the eight buildings in the island's capital in which this denomination had operated during the inter-war years.

In both Guernsey and Alderney, trouble arose as the strict Sabbatarianism of the Methodists led to their refusal to participate in the Sunday drills of the Militia. In Guernsey, when it was found that the passive resistance of the Methodists could not be overcome by abuse, nor imprisonment, nor threats of banishment, Sunday parades were abolished in 1798. In Alderney, on the other hand, the Methodists were eventually permitted to form a company of their own number, which drilled extra hours on weekdays. In 1797, this unit was dubbed 'L'Armée de Gédeon' by the island's Governor Peter Le Mesurier — possibly out of admiration for the courage of their convictions displayed by its members, the force commanded by Gideon (Judges Ch. 7) though small, having been of superb quality, consisting as it did of God's elect. Realising the compliment implied by this nickname, the 'Gideonites' accepted it with pride and enthusiasm.

Wesley did not visit Sark, as Adam Clarke had informed him that not a single family in the island understood English, but in 1789 Jean de Quetteville turned his attention to this island, preaching in the kitchen of Clos à Jaon, the property of Thomas Mollet. One of his audience, Jean Vaudin, the tenant of La Ville Roussel (who was described by de Quetteville as 'illitré et croyant aux sorciers') offered a site adjoining his house for a chapel. Called Ebenezer chapel, the building was completed in 1796. Methodism took a strong hold in Sark and the chapel became a centre for formulating hostile action against the Seigneur and for planning strong opposition in the Chief Pleas to the levying of impôts for defraying some of the expenses of the Anglican church. The Methodist chapel was moved to its present site in 1925.

The triumph of Methodism paved the way for the advent of many other nonconformist bodies during the 19th. century, thus bringing about the present situation whereby practically every sect is represented in the Bailiwick. In this connection a branch of the Religious Society of Friends ('Quakers') — a sect of Christian complexion but deaf to Saint Athanasius' call to "worship one God in Trinity and Trinity in Unity" and hence doctrinally divorced from Trinitarian Christianity — had in fact already been established by Claude Gay of Barking in 1776; and it is sad that to one of its members (Thomas Gallienne) belongs the unenviable distinction of being the last Guernseyman to suffer physically for his religious faith, being subjected to ill-usage and imprisonment early in 1800 because of his refusal to perform military service. The year following the building of the afore-mentioned first Methodist Chapel in la Rue le Marchant in 1789 saw the construction at the other end of La Rue du Manoir of Bethel Chapel (now demolished) by the disciples of the schismatic Calvinist variant of Methodism propagated by George Whitefield (1714–1770) which, denying Wesley's Arminian emphasis on the universal availability of salvation, restricted it to the Elect. In 1810 the first Congregationalist Chapel (known as Bethsda and destined later to be transformed into the erstwhile Lyric Cinema) was erected in

New Street, while the Baptists made their initial appearance with the building of Bethanie Chapel at La Fosse in 1827. The Brethren arrived in 1835, opening in Torteval the Chapel which they called Le Douit d'Israel (now converted to housing). Then came the turn of Presbyterianism, extinct in the Bailiwick since Elie Brévint's death in 1674. In 1852 the initial success of the efforts to revive it made by William Turnbull (an immigrant from Scotland) was signalized by an inaugural service conducted by the Reverend James Don in the town's Temperance Hall on October 17th. of that year. In 1855 the congregation moved to the building now known as Clifton Court — and finally, on September 16th., 1897 (six years after Turnbull's death) came the dedication of the present church in the Grange built on a plot bought four years previously, the vacated Clifton premises shortly afterwards becoming the island's first telephone exchange. The next arrival was the Salvation Army, which first 'went into action' on August 7th., 1881; while the Pentecostalists initiated their mission in 1911 — though they do not seem to have acquired any building until 1934 when they purchased Delancey Chapel (now converted into flats) from the Methodists. Lastly, yet another dissenting Sect (the Zion Christian Fellowship) came into existence in 1988 and acquired Carmel Chapel in Saint Saviour's in 1992. In addition, it is convenient to note at this point two other religious bodies to be found in Guernsey, each of which derives its beliefs from the New Testament and reveres Jesus of Nazareth but neither of which worships Him as divine — and so are perhaps best defined as quasi-Christian — in the shape of Jehovah's Witnesses who, meeting weekly (the German Occupation apart) in various hired halls from 1926 onwards, opened their Kingdom Hall in Victoria Avenue, Saint Sampson's, in 1974; and the Christian Science Society (so named in 1989 after being fully operational in the island as the Church of Christ, Scientist, from 1906 though initially present two years earlier) which moved between 1959 and 1963 to purpose-built premises in Forest Lane from the base in Vauvert which it had occupied since 1920.

Before the arrival of some of its adherents during the French Revolution, Roman Catholicism had been utterly obliterated in the islands. Irrespective of the validity of the speculation claiming that a few Roman Catholics still survived in Herm in 1619, it is certain that no members of this faith remained in the Bailiwick by the end of the 17th. century. The repercussions in Guernsey of the Glorious Revolution had finally eliminated any Roman Catholic element in the population. In September 1687, James II had appointed Colonel John Legge, a Roman Catholic, as Lieutenant-Governor under Governor Viscount Hatton — and had sent over Irish troops and officers of the same faith, together with their chaplains, to form a large part of the garrison.

In 1688 the Island leaders and the senior Protestant officer in the garrison jointly planned a coup, to take place on the day when it was this officer's turn to take command of Castle Cornet. When the appointed day arrived, the commander of the Town Militia at the head of his men seized and disarmed any Roman Catholic officers or soldiers to be found in St. Peter-Port. At the same time, the garrison was paraded at the castle, and at a pre-arranged signal the Protestant troops, with loaded muskets, moved forward and swung to face their Roman Catholic comrades, intimidating them to lay down their arms. Legge was taken into custody. Guernsey was now safe for William III, and the Roman Catholic soldiery was removed.

Just over a century later, the excesses of the French Revolution led to members of the self-same faith being received in Guernsey with the utmost sympathy. The States of Guernsey even had temporary houses built to accommodate them. The influx started in 1792 when many French priests fled to the Channel Isles because they would not take the oath demanded by 'The Civil Constitution of the Clergy' — the refusal to do which brought 225 of their fellow clerics to the guillotine in September the same year. The Jacobin Terror of the following year drove thousands of Roman Catholic laity to seek refuge as well. On December 27th. of that year, Sir James Saumarez arrived in Guernsey with five warships and ten transports of exiles. Among the refugees to arrive in Guernsey during this period was François René de Chateaubriand, who was sick to the point of death when brought ashore in September 1792, but who was nursed back to health by a fisherman's family.

The first Roman Catholic place of worship to exist in Guernsey since the Reformation was a primitive chapel in a store in Le Bordage. The officiating priest was the Abbé Coulon, who had been chaplain to Marie Antoinette. He stayed until 1796. During his incumbency, Guernsey was visited by Father Mathew de Grucy, a Jerseyman who was among the first converts to Roman Catholicism in the Channel Isles. Later de Grucy went to La Vendée and in 1797 was arrested and condemned to be shot at Nantes as a 'returned émigré' despite the fact that he was, of course, a British subject.

In 1803 the chapel in Le Bordage was replaced by another larger building on the site later to be occupied by St. Barnabas Anglican Church. This remained the sole Roman Catholic place of worship until 1828 when the Reverend Father André Navet (regarded as the founder of modern-day Roman Catholicism in the island) acquired a building plot in Burnt Lane where he erected a new chapel which was consecrated on September 13th., 1829, by the Right Reverend Robert Gradwell, Roman Catholic Bishop of Leeds. Then called la Chapelle de Sainte Marie, but now known as Notre Dame de la Rosaire, it was reconstructed in 1962 as a most delightful church with a ceiling resembling the interior of an upturned boat. Finally in 1846 the site was obtained at the top of Cordier Hill where arose St. Joseph's Church, designed by Augustus Welby Northmore Pugin. It was opened and dedicated by Cardinal Nicholas Patrick Stephen Wiseman in 1851. Roman Catholicism had become finally established in insular life, an outstanding convert being the famous Egyptologist Sir Peter Le Page Renouf, whose remains lie in Saint Joseph's crypt beside those of Father Navet.

In Alderney a large proportion of the workforce imported into the island in connection with the British Government's fortification scheme consisted of Irish Roman Catholics and accordingly a Roman Catholic church was established at Crabby in 1848. This was destroyed during the German occupation and the existing church of SS Anne and Mary Magdalene was built to replace it between 1953 and 1958. Its basement forms a social centre for the use of the island community.

During the last century, Roman Catholic religious orders have been prominent in educational and medical work in the Bailiwick. First on the scene were the Sisters of Mercy who, coming from Brighton, set up first an infant, and later an elementary school at Cordier Hill near St. Joseph's church in 1868. They were followed by the Sisters of Notre Dame des Chênes, who set up elementary schools for boys and girls in Burnt Lane in 1874. In the July of the same year, some of the Sisters of Mercy from Cordier Hill went to Alderney to engage in educational and medical work.

In 1882 a group of Carthusian monks took up residence in Herm, possibly seeing in that peaceful island a refuge well suited to the eremitic life. (Incidentally, although the idea is widespread that these monks were Trappists, it is nevertheless entirely erroneous, the only members of this order to set foot in the island being a small advance party which arrived in February 1881 but left again in May when the main body's settlement plans were abandoned as all attempts to negotiate a lease had failed.) Although they left again in 1884 to go to the great Charterhouse at Parkminster in Sussex, these brothers left an enduring memorial of their stay in the hundreds of Monterey pines, cypresses and gum trees which they planted, and some of which (the remnant surviving the October 1987 hurricane) still adorn the island.

In 1902 the Sisters of the Sacred Heart of Jesus established a Girls' Secondary School at Blanchelande near Moulin Huet which for many years remained a prominent feature of Guernsey's educational life. Although they left in 1956 the school survived, being taken over by the Sisters of Mercy who came back from Alderney. In 1993, however, the Order withdrew, placing the premises on the market. In an effort to preserve the school, the teaching staff, as a temporary expedient and independently of the nuns, came to an accommodation with the States which enabled them to continue their work at the former Girls' Grammar School in Rosaire Avenue — and did so with gratifying results, the number of pupils in attendance at the outset of the venture having quadrupled by 1995. This had grown to 220 by autumn 1997 when the 1999 move to Les Vauxbelets (see below) was announced.

A major impetus to the activities of these religious orders came in 1904, making it an *annus mirabilis* as far as their work in the island was concerned. The policy pursued by the Government returned at that year's General Election in France led to the expulsion of all religious orders from that country, as a result of which several of them came to Guernsey. Les Filles de Sainte Marie de la Présentation arrived and founded primary schools at La Chaumière in the Castel and at Saint Magloire, L'Islet. Their establishments at L'Islet and La Chaumière were under the supervision of the Salesians, who likewise arrived in 1904 and devoted themselves to mission work among the French-speaking population until their departure after the Second World War. La Chaumière continued to be used for worship after educational work there had ceased, but the church there (Saint Francis) eventually closed in December 1985. The life of the school at Saint Magloire ended in 1972, though it continued to be used as place of worship for nearly twenty years, Mass still being said there until 1991. Les Soeurs de la Présentation also set up a school for French girls at Les Côtils which survived until 1941, when the exigencies of the German Occupation led to its conversion to a nursing home run by the States in co-operation with the Sisters, in which capacity it remained until 1984. The nuns remained until 1993 when, announcing their intention of leaving the island, they placed the property on the market. *Pro tempore*, part of the accommodation continued to be used by the Board of Health as a geriatric day centre; and at this juncture a purchaser emerged in the shape of Les Côtils Project Trust — an interdenominational body formed with the aim of developing the estate as an international ecumenical centre for retreats, healing and counselling, and which finally acquired it in May 1994. Les Côtils Christian Centre's first Warden, the Reverend Martyn Cripps (who a year later was replaced by a Manager with comparable responsibilities) was appointed the following August.

The same year (1904) also saw the arrival of the De La Salle Christian Brothers, who acquired property at Vimiera and Les Vauxbelets — the latter on a 'fee farm' basis. The house at Vimiera was used as a training centre for Novices to the Order until 1945. It was eventually sold in 1972. Les Vauxbelets has known many vicissitudes. It provided a boys' secondary school from 1906 to 1953 and in addition an agricultural school from 1907 to 1926, a French secondary school from 1908–24, and a training college for Novices to the Order (supplementing Vimiera) from 1905 to 1939. After playing host to a 'Centre de Rencontres Scolaires Internationales' since 1966, Les Vauxbelets assumed control thereof in 1971 and, operating as Les Vauxbelets Language School, had by 1994 provided tuition for over 35,000 students. Late in 1996, however, staffing difficulties led to its closure in 1998 being reluctantly envisaged. Fortunately it was at this juncture that a benign providence secured the preservation of the property's educational heritage achieved by agreements reached in 1997 for the move thereto in 1999 of Blanchelande College from its previously mentioned temporary home in Rosaire Avenue. It was poignant, however, that the August after Blanchelande had settled in at the end of the 1999 Easter Holidays should have seen the death of the Reverend Brother Christantian who since 1958 had striven to stave off the dereliction threatening Les Vauxbelets following the 1953 closure of the College and whose efforts had finally been crowned with success by this arrangement with Blanchelande which flowed from his initiative. During the 'twenties and 'thirties of this century Frère Déodat (1878–1951) built at Les Vauxbelets the miniature replica of Notre Dame de Lourdes, which has become one of Guernsey's main tourist attractions. It survived a major threat to its existence at the end of

1977, when the discovery of the imminent danger of subsidence was followed by a flood of donations enabling under-pinning and restoration work to be put in hand.

Last of the religious orders to arrive were the Hospitaller Sisters of the Sacred Heart, who in 1919 set up at Le Platon, Clifton, the Nursing and Geriatric Home which is still in operation.

Glancing back at this somewhat fulsome catalogue, the writer thinks it is as well to state that he is an Anglican.

One final word. A current religious development of considerable importance is that of Ecumenicism and it is gratifying to be able to conclude this chapter by noting that the Bailiwick of Guernsey has not been by-passed by the ecumenical spirit which happily has replaced the sectarian antagonisms of the past — witness the account given to the present writer by a Baptist minister of a trip he took to Sark in the company of the Roman Catholic rural dean with the object of their conducting a joint service in that island's Anglican church. In 1978 (as seen already in the preceding Chapter Ten) this trend received concrete expression in the consecration of Ste. Appoline's Chapel as an ecumenical shrine — and in 1994 it was further emphasized by the establishment of Les Côtils Ecumenical Centre mentioned earlier in this chapter. In a still wider context — that of charitable relations with 'Jews, Turks, Infidels and Hereticks' — it was the Guernseyman, the Rev. James Parkes (1896–1981), who from the inter-war years onwards was foremost in pioneering a Christian-Jewish rapprochement by promoting through study a fuller and more sympathetic understanding between Christ's followers and His nation.

PART II

'NEIGHBOUR'S LANDMARK' — THE FEUDAL ASPECT

Chapter One

ORIGINS AND EARLY VICISSITUDES

THERE IS NO OTHER TERRITORY under the Crown where the inheritances of feudalism still play as large a part as they do in the Bailiwick of Guernsey. Feudalism was for long woven into the very fabric of the life of the islands and its legacies continue to permeate both governmental and economic activity. Hence this aspect of insular historical development is of prime importance.

The institution of feudalism in the Bailiwick was by way of reaction to hostile incursions. Although the Cotentin and the Channel Isles were officially added to the domains of the Duke of Normandy by William Longsword's acquisition in 933 of 'the land of the Brétons by the sea coast' (the phrase of the chronicler Flodoard), nearly a century was to elapse before ducal control became effective. Indeed, the depredations of sea raiders were so considerable as to persuade the Bishops of Coutances to reside in Rouen — as has already been seen. Furthermore, the Vicomtes of the outlying areas (Cotentin, Bessin and Avranchin) themselves retained their pagan warlike ways, continuing to speak Norse rather than French, defying the ducal authority and (very probably) conniving in the piratical attacks of the sea-raiders for the sake of a share in the booty.

The persistence of these perils eventually led Duke Richard II in 1020 to divide Guernsey diagonally into two halves, granting the south and east to Néel, Vicomte of the Cotentin, and the west to Anchetel, Vicomte of the Bessin. (The Clos du Valle was a separate island and apparently wasteland.) By this action, Duke Richard killed two birds with one stone. In the first place, he gave these powerful subordinates a vested interest in resisting attacks on the island, while, secondly, by giving them half each, he prevented either of them using Guernsey as an offshore base for launching a rebellion against himself.

In order to attract settlers to make good the depopulation resulting from repeated piratical incursions, Richard and his successors offered specially attractive terms to the settlers, to the nature of which there are a number of pointers. During the Middle Ages villein cultivators in Guernsey were frequently called 'Les Hôtes du Roi', and an 'hôte' is mentioned in the Charter (*c.* 1050) whereby Duke William II gave lands in Guernsey to the Abbey of Marmoutiers. In this connection it is noteworthy that in Continental Normandy 'hôtes' (i.e., 'guests') were peasants attracted to newly cleared land by a 'Contrat de Défrichement' (Land Reclamation Contract) giving them a tenure and a personal status above that of serfs. Thus the system that developed in Guernsey was one of feudalism without serfdom, the only obligations devolving upon the peasantry being trivial services and modest payments in kind.

In 1030, ten years after Duke Richard II's grant, Anchetel was deprived of his fief by Duke Robert I because of traitorous alliance with the Count of Brittany. To mark the conclusion of peace with the count (at Mont St. Michel) Robert transferred the holding to the Abbé du Mont St. Michel. In 1042, however, Duke William II, soliciting the support of the powerful Vicomte du Bessin to consolidate his succession as his father's illegitimate son, returned western Guernsey to Anchetel's son, Ranulf, giving Sark and Alderney to Mont St. Michel in lieu. Fifteen years later, however — in 1057 — William, again in search of strong support, re-transferred Sark and Alderney to the warlike Geoffroi de Montbrai, Bishop of Coutances, compensating Mont St. Michel with the fief of Noirmont in Jersey.

As for Néel of the Cotentin, although he had forfeited his fief for rebellion after being defeated by William at the Battle of Val-ès-Dunes in 1047 — the battle which finally established William's authority — he was reconciled with William in 1054 and his fief was later restored to him. Thus, by the time of the conquest of England, the two fiefs had returned to the families of the original holders.

Chapter Two

DEVELOPMENTS IN THE FIEF DU BESSIN

THE FIEF DU BESSIN, consisting of the Vingtaine de L'Epine and the parishes of the Castel, St. Saviour's and St. Pierre-du-Bois, became known as Fief Le Comte in 1120 when Ranulf, Vicomte du Bessin, was created Earl of Chester. This name it still retains. At some indeterminate date in the early 12th. century, the fief was split into sub-fiefs, consisting of the Fief Rozel, which went to the Rozel family, the Fief Longue, given to the Wake family (who held land at Longues, near Bayeux), the Fief Suart, which went to the Suhart family, and finally, the Fief Sotuas, given to a cadet branch of the Magneville (Mandeville) family from Sottevast.

In the civil war between Matilda and Stephen, Matilda's husband, Geoffrey of Anjou, seized Normandy and was crowned at Rouen in 1144. In the course of the struggle he came into possession of the whole of Guernsey as a result of two developments. Firstly, Roger, Vicomte of the Cotentin, had been killed (1138), fighting for Stephen, and had left no heir. Secondly, Ranulf, Earl of Chester, 'whose hand, like Ishmael's, was against every man', had sided at times with Stephen, thus rendering his Norman fiefs forfeit. To advance the interests of his son Henry (later Henry II of England), Geoffrey needed both to win the support of the Church, and also to consolidate the military strength of Normandy in preparation for an attack on England — and the action he took in these circumstances may be inferred from two Papal Bulls. In 1150 a Bull of Pope Eugène III confirmed the Monastery of Mont St. Michel in ownership of 'whatever you possess in the island'. A further Bull of Pope Adrian IV in 1155 spoke more specifically of the monastery holding a quarter of the whole island.

It thus emerges that by 1155 Mont St. Michel had recovered half the territory in the Fief du Bessin taken from it by Duke William II in 1042. It is probable that Geoffrey made this restitution around 1150 (he died in 1151) both to win the support of the Church for the claims of Henry (to whom he handed over the Duchy in 1150), and as reparation for the damages suffered in 1138 by Mont St. Michel itself in the course of the fighting. However, to avoid alienating the powerful lords whose support was needed for the projected invasion of England, the area granted by Geoffrey to Mont St. Michel as its fief consisted of scattered non-arable wasteland. It was this which was inspected in 1156 by the Abbé, Robert de Torigny, when he came over to Guernsey to survey his monastery's new acquisitions.

The administrative stability of Henry II's Angevin Empire promoted a great trade expansion which in its turn created the demand for increased agricultural output. This demand encouraged the clearance of wastelands and woods — a process known as 'essarting' (from the French *essarter* — 'to clear'). Many such clearances took place in the Fief St. Michel: witness the place-name 'L'Essart', which still survives in two locations in this fief. As a result two sub-fiefs were created — the Fief de la Couture and the Fief Huit Bouvées — both titles indicative of agricultural development. At the same time a number of peripheral areas on the fief were sub-infeudated to the Priory of Lihou, eventually coming to be known as the Fief of the Priory of Lihou.

In March 1153 an event took place affecting the destiny of the Fief Le Comte. As a manoeuvre preceding the Treaty of Wallingford, Henry made an agreement at Devizes with the treacherously opportunist Earl of Chester to let bygones be bygones and to restore the earl to his Norman lands (including the Fief Le Comte in Guernsey). This bargain, however, came to nothing as the earl died in December 1153 and his heir (Hugh) was only six years of age. The fief thus reverted to Henry as Duke of Normandy and he made it over to Hugh Wake (who already held the sub-fief called Fief Longue). Never again was Fief Le Comte in the hands of the Earls of Chester. Shortly afterwards Wake founded the Abbey of Longues, to which he donated the sub-fief, though, of course, remaining Seigneur of Fief Le Comte as a whole.

John's loss of Continental Normandy in 1204 posed Seigneurs with the awkward dilemma of declaring for John and losing their Norman lands or for Philip Augustus and losing their lands in England and the Channel Isles. Roger Suhart declared for Philip and hence his sub-fief (Fief Suart) escheated to the Crown. Half of it was handed on to the local family of Revel, thus creating the Fief Reveaux. After some beating about the bush, Baudouin Wake (Hugh Wake's grandson) made his submission to John in 1210 and thus retained Fief Le Comte — although, of course, he lost his lands in mainland Normandy. The fief passed to his son, Hugh Wake, on his death in 1213 and in 1239, to raise funds to go on a Crusade, Hugh sold the fief to Baudouin de Ver for half a knight's fee and an annual payment of £6 sterling. The Extente of 1248 names Robert de Ver (Baudouin's son) as Seigneur of Fief Le Comte.

The next 40 years saw a sustained attempt by the Monastery of Mont St. Michel to gain possession of Fief Le Comte. The attempt started in 1253 with the death of Robert de Ver. As his heir, Baudouin de Ver, was only 17, he was made the ward of Hugh Bigot. Previously in 1248 Henry III had granted to his favourite, Sir William de Cheny (and his wife, Felicia) the Fief Anneville, which had escheated to the Crown in 1204 as the previous holders had declared for Philip Augustus. Shortly after Robert de Ver's death the same Sir William de Cheny leased the Fief Le Comte from Hugh Bigot during Baudouin de Ver's minority — and then promptly sub-let it to the Abbé de Mont St. Michel, who thought that he thus had the chance of regaining the whole of the Fief du Bessin taken from the monastery by Duke William II in 1042. The monastic memory was obviously a long one. In 1257, however, Baudouin came of age and in 1262 he sold the fief to Sir William de Cheny. The Abbé immediately challenged the legality of this sale, invoking the 1030 Charter of Duke Robert I, but suppressing any evidence of Geoffrey of Anjou's grant in 1150 of half the original Fief du Bessin. (This suppression probably accounts for the lack of specific documentary evidence of Geoffrey's grant available today.)

Sir William de Cheny died in 1265, and the litigation was adjourned until his heir, Nicholas, came of age. Meanwhile his mother, Felicia, energetically pursued her claims. In face of this determination, the Abbé, in 1270, promised Hugh de Trubleville (subwarden of the Isles) half of the fief if judgement went in his favour. To quote Tupper, "The priest having a bad cause, bribed the judge to cheat the widow". In the event the bribe came to nothing as de Trubleville gave up his post before the case was heard and the fief was entrusted to Robert de Meleches. He, too, died, *c.* 1274, and in 1283 the bailiff took the fief into the king's hands. The dispute, however, still dragged on until at last in 1289 Nicholas de Cheny succeeded in establishing his title to the fief, the Abbé abandoning his claims.

During the ensuing centuries the ownership of Fief Le Comte

has changed hands several times. After being in the de Cheny family for two centuries, it passed to Robert Willoughby de Broke by his marriage with Anne de Cheny. In 1509 de Broke sold it to Nicholas Fouaschin of St. Pierre-du-Bois. Fouaschin later settled in Southampton and Anglicised his name to Fashion. In 1630 his descendant, George Fashion, disposed of the fief to Peter Priaulx. It remained in the Priaulx family until 1722 when it was bought by Eleazar Le Marchant, whose descendants held it to the present century.

Fief St. Michel remained in the hands of the monastery until ecclesiastical seizures brought it into the possession of the Crown, which still retains it. The reversion of the Priory of Lihou, however, was granted in 1443 by Henry VI to the Provost of Eton.

The vicissitudes of the sub-fiefs of Fief Le Comte are many. In the first place, the development of wasteland on the borders of the Sub-Fief Longue led to the emergence of three further sub-fiefs — the Fief des Mauconvenants, the Fief d'Illaire, and the Fief des Trois Vattiaux. Similar developments on the half of the sub-fief Suart retained by the Crown when the other half was given to the Revel family led to the emergence of the Fief de Gohiers, the Fief de la Bouvèe Marquand, the Fief Dieu le Voye, the Fief Au Roux, and the Fief de la Pomare. Furthermore, on the main Fief Le Comte yet more agricultural development led to the emergence of sub-fiefs bearing place-names (e.g., Fief Groignet, Fief Carteret), and others with the names of the holders (e.g., Fief Granté, Fief de la Court, Fief Videclin).

Other sub-fiefs owe their existence to land sales from the parent Fief Le Comte. Thus the Fief de St. Georges was created by the sale of this area as a sub-fief by George Fashion in 1629, while the Fief Au Coq derives from sales to the Le Cocq family in the 16th. or 17th. century. Similar land disposals by the Abbots of Mont St. Michel before seizure by the Crown account for sub-fiefs contiguous to the present Fief St. Michel, notably the Fief Saumarez and the Fief Jean du Galliard.

Chapter Three

DEVELOPMENTS IN THE FIEF DU COTENTIN

DURING THE PERIOD after the Battle of Val ès Dunes (1047), when Néel de St. Sauveur was in disgrace, Duke William II made important changes in the allocation of sub-fiefs which Néel had to endorse as part of the price of his return to favour. In particular, William created six ecclesiastical fiefs, four in St. Andrew's parish, and one each in St. Peter-Port and St. Martin's. In St. Andrew's the Fief St. Hélène was given to the Abbey of Cormery, Tours, the Fief de la Rue Frairie to the Abbey de la Croix St. Leufroy, Evreux, the Fief de la Trinité to the Abbesse de la Trinité, Caen — and a fourth fief to the Bishop of Coutances. In St. Peter-Port a fief was granted to the Abbey of Marmoutiers and in St. Martin's one near Saints to a Prebend of Cherbourg.

The subsequent history of the Fief du Cotentin derives from the time between 1144 and 1150 when the whole island was in the hands of Geoffrey of Anjou. While wasteland in the Fief du Bessin was being enfeoffed for the benefit of Mont St. Michel, that in the Fief du Cotentin was retained by Geoffrey and consequently under his son became Fief Le Roi. Thus, for example, the whole of the Forest parish (the name was deserved in the 12th. century) is Fief Le Roi. Furthermore, no new Seigneur of the entire fief was appointed (in contrast with the Wake family in the case of the Fief du Bessin), so that the Fief du Cotentin ceased to exist as a feudal unit and became a mere geographical expression. For this reason it is more convenient to consider developments in this area parish by parish.

In St. Andrew's the wasteland in the north of the parish became Fief Le Roi on enfeoffment and from it the Fief Rohais was carved out in favour of Rohesia, the wife of Eudes, who was Vicomte of the Cotentin between 1092 and 1104. Other fiefs in the parish dating back to the 11th and 12th centuries are the Fief Mauxmarquis (named after the Malmarchy family), the Fief Au Fay (named after a Norman family from D'Auffai, a town between Rouen and Dieppe) and the Fief Burons.

The Fief Au Fay was held by payment of a pair of silver spurs and the Fief Burons by payment of a pair of gilded spurs. During the 16th. century these two fiefs were combined as the Fief des Eperons, held on payment of a pair of silver-gilt spurs. This duty was rendered to Elizabeth II on her visits to Guernsey in 1957 and 1978.

As far as ecclesiastical fiefs in St. Andrew's are concerned, in 1292 the Abbey of Cormery sold St. Hélène to Guillaume de St. Remy, the then Bailiff of Guernsey, and this fief has been in lay hands ever since. The other ecclesiastical fiefs in the parish were most probably taken into the king's hand by Henry V in 1414.

In St. Martin's parish the peripheral land was waste and so became Fief Le Roi. Elsewhere the fertile land had from antiquity been cultivated as open fields. On this the feudal system was superimposed and the fragmented nature of the holdings in this area still reflects the ancient strip cultivation. These fiefs now possess the names of local families to whom they were allocated after escheating to the Crown from the original Norman holders in 1204. Thus we have the Fief des Bruniaux, given to the Brunel family mentioned in the 1274 'Complaints of the Islanders'; the Fief Au Marchant, associated with the Le Marchant family, the Fief Hailla, held by the Hailla family, the Fief Massy Gros (from the Massy family), and the Fief Beauvoir, made over to the Beauvoir family. The Hailla, Massy and Beauvoir families, incidentally, are all mentioned in the Extente of 1331. Finally, there is the Fief de Sausmarez, which was originally the Fief de Barneville (a Cotentin family from the port of the same name who opted for John in 1204). The French menace thereafter added the Jerbourg Headland (with the responsibility for maintaining the castle there) to the holding of this family. The fief passed to the de Sausmarez family by marriage in 1250.

Other fiefs of St. Martin's are associated with defence or the Church. The holders of those associated with defence had the responsibility of keeping a watch on the coast — hence their name 'velleresses' (from *veiller* — 'to keep watch'). They are two in number: the Fief de la Velleresse de la Fallaize, and the Fief de la Velleresse de Fermaine. The ecclesiastical fief of Blanchelande, given to the Cotentin Abbey of the same name by John, Count of Mortain (later King John) in 1198 when he transferred to it the lands given by Duke William II to the Cherbourg Prebend; reverted to the Crown in 1414, but in 1563 was sold by the Crown to Nicholas Carey, whose family have retained it since.

Apart from a few properties in the Franc Fief de St. Martin, the whole of St. Peter-Port is now Fief Le Roi. While much of this stems from the enfeoffment of waste, some areas result from escheats. Of these the most important are the Fief de Rozel, formerly held by the Cotentin family de Rosel and which passed to the Crown in 1204; and the ecclesiastical fief granted by Duke William II to the Abbey of Marmoutiers, which was taken into the king's hand in 1414.

The marshy nature of much of St. Sampson's parish rendered it wasteland and hence it became Fief Le Roi when enfeoffed between 1144 and 1150. The De Vaugrat and Brunaiux fiefs in the detached part of the parish are military fiefs and hence may derive from creations by Geoffrey of Anjou about 1150, when he was developing military potential for his projected invasion of England.

A prominent fief in this parish is that of Anneville which, having escheated to the Crown, was granted by Henry III to Sir William de Cheny in 1248. When the de Cheny family became Seigneurs of Fief Le Comte they established their Seigneurie at Anneville and so the idea grew that Anneville was in some way a paramount fief — an idea without justification. Bought by the Fouaschin (or Fashion) family from the de Chenys in 1509, it passed by marriage into the hands of the Andros family in 1663 and remained with this family until its purchase by Mr. Cyril Northcote Parkinson (of *Parkinson's Law* fame) who also held the Fief Mauxmarquis in St. Andrew's and the Fief de Beauvoir in St. Martin's. In 1984, however, Professor Parkinson, while retaining the two latter fiefs, sold Anneville (together with its dependencies of Fauville and la Croûte Bouilleuse) to Mr. and Mrs. Kevin Lycett. Professor Parkinson finally left Guernsey for the Isle of Man in the summer of 1986. On June 4th., 1994, Anneville's 7½ vergée Garenne, where seigneurs of old exercised their exclusive rabbit-hunting entitlement, was leased for ten years at a peppercorn rent to la Société Guernesiaise by Mr. Stuart Falla in order to promote its preservation as a nature reserve. It had been divorced from the rest of Fief since 1902 when the Andros family sold it for fern growing purposes to Mr. C.A. Smith of the Caledonian Nursery, from whose successor (Mr. John de Putron) Mr. Falla bought it in 1984.

Lastly, St. Sampson's parish includes the interesting Franc Fief au Gallicien, which was carved out of Fief Le Roi and the tenants freed from all dues by Edward IV as a reward for their help when as Earl of March he fled to Guernsey after the Rout of Ludford on October 13th., 1459 during the Wars of the Roses.

The parish of Torteval presents very special problems. Although on the evidence of the Charters of Dukes Richard II and William II this parish was in the Fief du Cotentin, many of its fiefs overlap into St. Pierre-du-Bois, which was part of the Fief du Bessin. An analysis of the fiefs of the area sheds some light on this problem.

The original Fief Au Cannely (granted to a Cherbourg family and thus, naturally, within the territory of the Fief du Cotentin) has been replaced by the following fiefs as a result of marriage settlements and partages:

Fief Guillot Justice	Fief Robert de Viq (or de Ver)
Fief Janin Besnard	Fief Jean de Gaillard
Fief Thomas Blondel	Fief La Cour Ricart
Fief Bouvée Duquemin	Fief Canteraine

Only the first of these is wholly within modern Torteval. The next four are in both Torteval and St. Pierre-du-Bois, the sixth is in Torteval, St. Pierre-du-Bois and St. Saviour's, the seventh is in St. Pierre-du-Bois only, and the last is in St. Pierre-du-Bois and St. Saviour's.

Among these succession fiefs of the Fief Au Cannely, the Fief Robert de Viq was sold to the de Cheny family (Seigneurs of Fief Le Comte) about 1315. It was because the de Ver family had previously been Seigneurs of Fief Le Comte that the confusion arose whereby this fief is often called Fief Robert de Ver.

Another fief in the area is the Fief Beuval. This was originally called the Fief de l'Espesse, after the Cotentin family of that name to whom the original grant was made. Its area was therefore obviously within the Fief du Cotentin and yet is now entirely within St. Pierre-du-Bois (which was part of the Fief du Bessin). In this connection it is worth noting that the l'Espesse family died out *c.* 1270 and that the fief came into the hands of the de Cheny family before 1331.

The Fief de Pleinmont was originally granted *c.* 1040 to the Monastery of Mont St. Michel by the brother of Néel, Vicomte of the Cotentin, and was thus originally within the Fief du Cotentin. Although it passed for a time to the Le Boutillier family, it escheated to King John in 1204 and was then restored to Mont St.

Michel. It is wholly within Torteval. So, too, is the Fief Au Colletin, which was originally granted to a Cotentin family of that name.

On the other hand, wholly within St. Pierre-du-Bois is the Fief La Corvée ès Corbinets, which, originally held by a family from the southern Cotentin, escheated to the Crown in 1204 and was then granted to the Monastery of Mont St. Michel.

From the analysis in the preceding paragraphs a solution to the perplexing overlapping of parish boundaries emerges. In the first place it is plain that the modern parish boundaries differ from those of the 11th and 12th centuries. Indeed, the evidence of the fiefs is that Torteval's boundaries were originally the Forest parish in the east, the valley below St. Peter's Church in the north, and the coast to the south and west. It would appear that the modern boundaries date from 13th.-century 'essarting' which would naturally increase tithe revenues, the destination of which was determined by parish boundaries.

The likelihood is that the Prior of Mont St. Michel (who collected all revenues accruing to the parish of St. Pierre-du-Bois) used his possession of the Corbinets fief to incorporate that fief (in the area adjacent to the Forest parish) into St. Pierre-du-Bois. A further loss of territory by Torteval occurred as a result of the acquisition by the Seigneurs of Fief Le Comte of the Fief Beuval and the Fief Robert de Viq (or de Ver) which led to the absorption of these areas also into St. Pierre-du-Bois (and hence into the parent Fief du Bessin). The modern boundaries of Torteval would emerge from these transfers and would account for the present-day overlapping.

A final point of interest is that the section of the Fief Jean du Gaillard in St. Saviour's was a holding of this family distinct from its portion of the parent Fief Au Cannely. It was most likely acquired by the du Gaillard family in the early 15th. century from the erstwhile Mont St. Michel lands after they had been seized by the Crown. The whole du Gaillard fief passed to the Crown in the early 16th. century for lack of an heir within the required seven degrees of kinship. The Crown holds it still.

Chapter Four

GENERAL CHARACTERISTICS OF FIEF EVOLUTION

CONSIDERING THE EVOLUTION of Guernsey's fiefs as a whole, an historical pattern emerges, showing that the development of the system would seem to fall into three main phases.

The first phase comes with the original grant of the two parent fiefs about 1020, followed by the grant of sub-fiefs to Norman knights. These knightly holdings, together with the ecclesiastical grants of Duke William II within the Fief du Cotentin, were all allocated before William's death in 1087 and in nearly all cases the seigneurs were absentees.

Geoffrey of Anjou's ascendancy in Normandy dominates the second phase, which was marked by the extension of enfeoffed land to include erstwhile waste areas — and which led to the emergence of fief holders who were resident in the island (especially in the previous Fief du Cotentin).

The third phase arose from the escheats to the Crown of lands whose seigneurs declared for Philip Augustus after 1204. This led to further land passing into the hands of local families — though much was retained by the Crown as Fief Le Roi or granted to Mont St. Michel.

The final upshot was that the distinction between the Fief du Bessin and the Fief du Cotentin lost all meaning with, for example, the de Cheny family becoming owners of fiefs in all parts of the island. As a result the fiefs became merely a form of land-holding, no longer bearing the names of their seigneurs, but of the locality where they were situated — and delimited by landmark stones, most of which have disappeared, though one of those marking the boundary of le Fief Rozel is still to be seen in La Charroterie. Already by 1248 the distribution of fiefs was much as at present — save for the escheats to the Crown of ecclesiastical fiefs, all of which the Crown still holds apart from the Fief Saumarez and the Fief de Blanchelande.

The transference from absentee seigneurs to local ones militated against the interests of the peasantry, as the resident seigneurs were far more concerned with exacting their dues than with ensuring protection and security for their tenants.

Chapter Five

THE EVOLUTION OF THE FIEFS IN THE OTHER ISLANDS

WHEN DUKE RICHARD II made his grants in Guernsey in 1020 to the Vicomtes of the Bessin and the Cotentin, he retained Sark as part of the ducal domain, but his descendant, Duke William II, in 1042 granted the island (together with Alderney) as a fief to the Abbey of Mont St. Michel in compensation for lands lost in Guernsey.

In 1057, however, Duke William II revoked this grant, transferring the fief of Sark (and of Alderney) to Geoffroi de Montbrai, Bishop of Coutances. Geoffroi's tenure lasted until 1093, when he was deprived of his fiefs for his part in a revolt against William Rufus of England (to whom Duke Robert II had mortgaged the Duchy), and Sark thereby reverted to the ducal domain.

On the evidence of Charters showing Sark in the possession of his son early in the 12th. century, it is justifiable to assume that the island was included in the extensive grants made to Richard de Reviers by Henry I soon after 1100. On de Revier's death in 1107 his son, William de Vernon, became Seigneur of Sark and divided the island into sub-fiefs, the tenants of which were liable for the supply of boats for the conveyance of the seigneur's wheat to Normandy. These tenants were in all probability the 'hospites' or 'hôtes' whose presence in Sark is mentioned in a contemporary charter — an indication that on this island, as in Guernsey, a system evolved of feudalism without serfdom.

About 1160 — he died in 1162 — William de Vernon granted land in Sark to the Abbey of Montebourg, on condition of its maintaining a monk on the island for the purpose of saying masses for the souls of himself and his family. On the evidence of the Charter making this grant, it also appears that William de Vernon had sub-infeudated Brecqhou to Alain de Vinchelez, Seigneur of the Fief Vinchelez in Jersey. This probably resulted from a marriage settlement.

In 1192 William's son, Richard de Vernon, gave his allegiance to Philip Augustus for the sake of his Norman lands, when John, during the absence on Crusade of Richard Coeur de Lion, agreed to hand over Upper Normandy to the French king. Consequently when Richard Coeur de Lion returned in 1194 the Crown seized Sark as the escheat of a traitor — but within two years John was reconciled with his brother (who appointed him the first 'Lord of the Isles'), and Richard de Vernon was reinstated in his fief. However, when Richard de Vernon again declared for Philip Augustus on John's loss of Continental Normandy, the island escheated to the Crown once more and became Fief Le Roi. It retained this status for the next 150 years and the five sub-fiefs (on the evidence of the Assize Rolls of 1309) still survived. Sark's exposed position, once the Hundred Years' War had started, made life on the island most perilous and after devastating French raids in 1372 and 1373 it was temporarily abandoned. Feudalism in Sark had temporarily lapsed.

Like Sark, Alderney remained a ducal domain until 1042 when (again like Sark) it was granted as a fief to the Abbey of Mont St. Michel. Once more (as in the case of Sark) it was transferred from Mont St. Michel to Geoffroi de Montbrai, Bishop of Coutances, in 1057. Geoffroi, however, did not suffer such dire consequences as in the case of Sark following his revolt against William Rufus, but managed to retain a foothold in the island. The document, *Status Insulae de Aurinea* (*c.* 1236), shows his successors as holding half the island, which is stated to be divided into two equal parts, with the bishop possessing a water-mill and the king a windmill — one of the earliest references to windmills in western Europe.

In the meanwhile, in 1190, the Crown had granted the fief of Alderney to Guillaume l'Ingeniour, who thus became seigneur. (This was probably one of Richard Coeur de Lion's money-raising expedients before setting off on the Third Crusade.) The fief was, however, sold back to the Crown in 1238 by the sons of Guillaume l'Ingeniour.

The outbreak of the Hundred Years War nullified the holdings in Alderney of the Bishops of Coutances, and although the Treaty of Brétigny (1360) expressly restored to the bishop his rights in the island, the re-award never became effective. Instead in 1376 Edward Portman, a merchant of Salisbury, became Seigneur of the Fief on payment to the Crown of £20 a year — but the holding was not retained for long and Alderney reverted to the Crown, in whose hands it remained until 1584.

Herm was granted to the Abbey of Mont St. Michel by Duke Robert I about 1030, but about 1062 Duke William II transferred the island to the Augustinian Order of Cherbourg. This Order was obviously still in possession of Herm in 1298 as there is a record of the trial for theft in that year of a certain Jean Charnethous before the Abbot's Court. The island reverted to the Crown, however, when these monks were expelled by Henry V in 1414 prior to the campaign which culminated in Agincourt — and although it has been argued that the appointment in 1480 of Jean Guyffart of Cherbourg as incumbent of Herm implies their possible return thither after the end of the Hundred Years' War in 1453, it must be remembered that this cleric's Augustinian connections were tenuous at best and even such a shadowy presence of that Order, as his tenure of the living may be held to suggest, eventually lapsed with the Reformation. Thereafter Herm retained its status as a Crown holding until its purchase by the States of Guernsey in December 1946.

Between 1035–40 the sea adventurer, Restauld (who seems to have obtained Jethou from Duke Robert I in return for war services) donated the island to the Abbey of Mont St. Michel, in whose hands it remained until it was taken into the king's hand — possibly by Henry V in 1414. The island remains in the hands of the Crown to this day.

Chapter Six

THE STRATA OF FEUDAL SOCIETY AND THEIR OBLIGATIONS

FROM 1144, when Geoffrey of Anjou was crowned Duke of Normandy, the escheat to him of the Fief du Cotentin led to the existence of extensive ducal domain in Guernsey — which under his son, Henry II, became Fief Le Roi. This Fief Le Roi was directly administered by a 'Vicomte of the Islands' to whom the dukes farmed out any revenue accruing. In addition, the Vicomte acted as the duke's personal representative in his capacity as overlord of the other fiefs. As a result, however, of John's loss of Continental Normandy in 1204, the Vicomte of the Islands was replaced by wardens and/or 'Lords of the Isles', who made an annual payment to the Exchequer and in return had the revenues due to the king farmed out to them.

Beneath the duke or king as overlord there were three kinds of holdings. Foremost were those of Suitors — the Seigneurs of Fiefs. The highest rank of seigneur was entitled to the symbol of a dove-cote — a partly reconstructed one is still to be seen at Le Colombier Farm at Torteval — while the next rank was allowed a 'Tourelle' attached to the house and the lowest rank was symbolised by pigeon-holes cut in the gables. Secondly, came the holdings of Villeins on Fief Le Roi, who enjoyed the status and privileges of 'hôtes' already mentioned. Lastly there were the holdings of Villeins on Seigneurial Fiefs, where once again the status and privileges of 'hôtes' applied.

A number of obligations devolved upon seigneurs. Although no Guernsey fief was large enough to impose the duty of knight service on its holder, all seigneurs had to pay an annual relief (or rente) in Livres Tournois (which, incidentally, is technically still the case), and all seigneurs had to pay suit of service in the king's Feudal Court — as they are still required to do at the Cour de Chefs Plaids. In addition to the obligations of money payment and allegiance, some fiefs were held on petty serjeanty — the obligation of rendering a service 'amounting to half a mark or less'. The

Seigneur of Anneville, for example, had to keep under strict guard any prisoner of the king, convicted of a minor offence. A similar obligation devolved upon the Seigneurs of Rohais and La Rue Frairie. Other fiefs carried alternative forms of petty serjeanty, involving the obligation of performing duties whenever the king was in residence. The Seigneur of the Fief de Sausmarez, for example, still has to perform the office of cup-bearer to the monarch (an obligation which was discharged when George V was in Guernsey in 1921). Similarly, the Seigneur of the Fief des Eperons has to provide a pair of spurs — as was done when Elizabeth II was in the island both in 1957 and in 1978.

As far as Villein Holders on Fief Le Roi were concerned, their main obligation was to pay 'the King's Farm' (a general payment in lieu of servile obligations, which also came to be known as 'Chef Rente') of two sols per Bouvée throughout the island. The only exceptions consisted of a few holdings in St. Sampson's where four sols per Bouvée were payable. It is worth noting that this payment did not only relieve the villeins of servile obligations, but also guaranteed political liberties under local law.

In addition to 'the King's Farm' a number of supplementary obligations devolved upon villein tenants. The first of these was Champart, which consisted of every twelfth sheaf of grain or bundle of flax. This was later commuted to a cash 'equivalent de champart' and in this form the obligation persisted until its abolition in 1942. Secondly came a payment known as Poulage, whereby two hens per annum had (and in some cases a cash equivalent still has) to be paid in respect of every inhabited house. The payment of Mêlage was one of one bushel and two denerals (one and one-third bushels) of oats per Bouvée under this crop, whereas Brassage was a money payment of two deniers per Bouvée held, irrespective of land use. Lastly came Pannage, which was another money payment — this time of one denier per pig.

In addition to the above, by their very status villeins incurred a miscellany of further obligations, involving both services and payments. The labour services themselves were not onerous. Villeins were obliged to carry the king's Champart to one of his granges (located at the 'King's Barn' at La Plaiderie which for many years housed the Royal Court and also the building now called 'The Granary Club', situated in Grange Road), and had to appoint one of their number a granger to look after it there. He in his turn had to account to the king's receiver for the money realised on the sale of the grain. As well as this, villeins incurred the obligation of Corvée (labour on road maintenance and/or coast protection), but there was no week work nor boon work. Such holdings as were retained in the king's name were cultivated by hired labour.

By the obligation of Multure villeins were compelled to grind their grain at the king's mills (whence the eponymous village derives its name) at a 'rate of multure' of one-sixteenth the value of the corn. Sometimes, however, the corn was ground by private millers to whom the king had 'farmed out' this privilege.

A further obligation was that of Éperquerie. This word originally meant a drying place for conger — as the place-name in Sark bears testimony. After 1204, however, King John made 'éperquerie' a right of pre-emption: i.e., he claimed the right of buying the conger, in preference to anybody else, at a special rate. Thus villeins fishing for conger were obliged, between Easter and Michaelmas, to sell their catch to the king, though in practice they sold it to a nominee (usually the warden) to whom the king had 'farmed out' this source of income. An associated obligation required that the catch be later taken to one of the Royal 'Saleries' or 'Salting Points' for the curing process to be completed — a service for which payment in cash or in kind was due. Tenants sought to evade these obligations by catching fish other than conger, to the detriment of the royal revenue. In 1288 Edward I regularised the matter by permitting the villeins to fish for herring or mackerel provided they paid to him or his nominee two deniers for every hundred fish caught between Easter and Michaelmas. During the Black Death of 1348–50 Edward III temporarily remitted these 'rents', admitting that because of the catastrophic rate of mortality among fishermen they could not be obtained "without the impoverishing and excessive oppression of those fishermen still left".

Stray animals were impounded by the king's officers and could only be reclaimed on payment of a fine called Werp, failing which the animals became the king's property.

The last of the villeins' obligations was that of paying Congé. Deriving from the French *Droit de Mutation*, this was (and still, though now accruing to the States) a payment to the lord by his tenant when land is sold, amounting to one-thirteenth of the sale price. Hence it is sometimes referred to as the 'triezeième'.

Villeins on seigneurial fiefs had to pay chef rente to their seigneurs, and also owed dues such as Champart and Poulage, much as villeins on Fief Le Roi owed them to the king. Likewise

Congé was payable to the seigneur when property was sold. (In several parts of Guernsey this is still the case, though since 1985 all such payments have been diverted to the States via the Crown — see Chapter Nine ensuing.)

In Sark the villein tenants of the five sub-fiefs had the additional duty of supplying boats for the conveyance of the seigneur's wheat to Normandy — an obligation which naturally lapsed after 1204.

Chapter Seven

THE ADMINISTRATION OF FEUDALISM

THE WIDE EXTENT of the Fief Le Roi in Guernsey made it necessary for it to be sub-divided for ease of administration into areas called Bordages, in each of which an official known as a Bordier was responsible for collecting the king's dues. Each such bordier had to account to the king's receiver for money income and to the granger for income in kind. In return for these services he received a house with its adjacent land, known as a Borde (but, sometimes, confusingly, a Bordage) and also the right to attend the dinner held thrice yearly to mark the meetings of the Cour de Chefs Plaids — the king's Feudal Court. This right the bordiers relinquished in the mid-19th. century as a *quid pro quo* for being excused their duties.

The years since the Second World War have seen a major change in the administration of the Fief Le Roi. In 1947 the Crown relinquished the revenues derived from the royal holdings to the States of Guernsey, in consideration of that body meeting the cost of the salary of the Lieutenant-Governor and associated charges. In 1974 Fief Le Roi yielded £310,000, from which £119,000 was needed for the Lieutenant Governor's salary and emoluments, his house expenses and staff salaries, the annual cost of the prison, and the cost of keeping Guernsey prisoners in gaols in the United Kingdom.

In all fiefs, seigneurial as well as royal, records have been kept throughout the ages known as Livres de Perchage. These give details of all tenants on a fief and of their respective holdings: information vital to a seigneur to enable him to be sure of receiving all his dues. The Livre de Perchage for each fief is compiled by a 'Douzaine' of 12 tenants of the fief appointed by the seigneur and sworn in by the Royal Court. The interval between successive revisions is supposed to be 20 years, but in practice has often been greater than this. Livres de Perchage regarding tenancies of Fief Le Roi are compiled for each parish by the Parish Douzaine — the parochial governing body. Expenses are defrayed by a small levy on tenants, supplemented by a contribution from parochial rates and sometimes also by the proceeds of selling copies to tenants. The custom of compiling these records is of extreme antiquity and may perhaps have inspired the Domesday Book in England. Copies as far back as 1470 are still extant.

An obviously essential concomitant in the structure of feudal administration is a system of Courts. Historically, three types of such Feudal Courts have been in evidence in Guernsey, two of which still survive. Appendix XIII lists those still to be seen.

The first type — which disappeared with John's loss of Continental Normandy — was the Ducal Court. Up to 1204 Guernsey was regularly visited by justices from Normandy, who held sessions which besides administering justice also constituted the Duke's Feudal Court at which suitors had to render homage.

The first of the surviving types is the Royal Court in one of its aspects. From 1204 onwards the wardens representing the king were progressively authorised to hold local courts. From this development there grew the Cour de Chefs Plaids, meeting at Hilary (later Christmas), Easter, and Michaelmas. This became, inter alia, the King's Feudal Court, presided over by the king's bailiff. To this Court seigneurs had (and still have) to pay suit. The wardens (later governors) attended (and are still summoned to attend), but the suit was (and is) paid to the Bailiff.

On rare occasions extraordinary sessions of this Court are convened for the performance of the Ceremony of Homage to the reigning monarch in his or her capacity as successor to the Dukes of Normandy. The extreme rarity of such occasions is inescapable by the very fact of the sovereign's personal presence being essential for the enactment of the ceremony. Paradoxically, the first recorded ceremony of this kind in connection with a Guernsey suitor was held in a context divorced from any assembly of the Cour de Chefs Plaids. This involved one only of Guernsey's seigneurs and took place in 1637, when Sir Amias Andros, Seigneur of the Fief de Sausmarez, paid homage to Charles I in Whitehall Palace.

The ceremony has been performed three times in Guernsey — to George V in 1921, and to Elizabeth II in 1957 and 1978. In 1921 the seigneur of Sark took part in the ceremony in Guernsey, but on the other two occasions separate ceremonies were held in Sark itself.

In 1957 the Ceremony of Homage took place at an

extraordinary meeting of the Cour de Chefs Plaids held in St. George's Hall (now, alas! no more). First came the Bailiff's Procession, which entered the hall preceded by the Usher of the Royal Court, and consisted of the Parish Constables carrying their bâtons, the Advocates, the Greffier, the Procureur de la Reine, the Comptroller de la Reine, the Jurats (walking two by two), the Sergent, and, lastly, the Bailiff in his ceremonial robes. After a fanfare of trumpets, the Queen's Procession, which consisted of Her Majesty and Prince Philip, and the Royal Suite, entered the hall preceded by the Sheriff with drawn sword. As the Queen entered the Sheriff cried out, 'Sa Majesté et Son Altesse Royale'. After the Greffier had said the Lord's Prayer, he read the roll, and each member of the Court of Chief Pleas answered to his or her name, rising and bowing as this was done. The Bailiff then read the loyal address and presented it on bended knee to the Queen, who then rose and replied. The Seigneur of the Fief de Sausmarez, as the paramount seigneur of the island, was then called by the Greffier, and he mounted the platform, escorted by the Lieutenant-Governor and the Bailiff, and approached the Queen. He then bowed and knelt in front of her and all the other seigneurs and dames who owed homage stood up in their places. With his hands held between those of the Queen the Seigneur de Sausmarez then spoke the words of homage to which she gave reply. The Greffier then called the Seigneur des Eperons, and he ascended the platform carrying a crimson and gold cushion on which were the pair of silver-gilt spurs owed by him as his feudal due. The Seigneur then addressed the Queen, stating that he wished to discharge his service and to offer the spurs which he owed for his fief. Then on bended knee he offered the spurs to the Queen, who touched them as a token of acceptance. The Seigneur then rose and withdrew. The proceedings closed with the Greffier reading the grace.

A ceremony on similar lines was held in 1978, when the Cour de Chefs Plaids convened at Beau Séjour Leisure Centre for the purpose. The obligation of the Seigneur de Sausmarez, as hereditary third Butler to the Sovereign, of performing the office of cup-bearer to the Monarch, was carried out in 1921, but was remitted in 1957 and in 1978.

The second surviving type of Feudal Court consists of the Fief Courts, the seigneur of each fief having originally had the right to hold a court for the ordering of his domain, together with the power to punish offenders. A Court of this kind was presided over by the Seneschal (the seigneur's bailiff). The other officials were the Vavasseurs, who acted as assessors, a Greffier, to keep the records, and a Prévôt, to execute the orders of the Court. Tenants of the fief had to attend to render homage on pain of temporary 'saisie' of their holdings.

These Courts ordered the affairs of the estate and gave judgements in disputes between tenants or between tenant and seigneur. In many instances they had criminal jurisdiction and some Fief Courts even had gallow rights. The seigneur had the duty of providing the Court officials with a dinner at his expense.

Several of these Courts still meet in picturesque settings such as that of the Cour du Fief Beuval at Les Sages, St. Pierre-du-Bois, with a stone table flanked by stone seats — all in the open air. Now, however, tenants are no longer obliged to attend, and the main business consists of reports on changes of tenancy made by the Vavasseurs. This was important, as it provided a check on the seigneur having, in fact, received all the 'triezeièmes' due to him by way of Congé. The seigneur's duty to provide a dinner persists and is the high point of the day.

The *Guernsey Weekly Press* of November 28th., 1974 gave a fascinating account of a meeting on November 20th. of the Court of the Fief de Sausmarez at which the main point of interest was that the seigneur had in the course of 1973 received £10,076 by way of Congé. An income of this size from a fief of 379 vergées (about a quarter of a square mile) is eloquent testimony to the continued significance of feudalism in Guernsey in the very recent past.

Chapter Eight

FEUDAL LEGACIES

A NUMBER OF FEUDAL LEGACIES still exert considerable influence in the Bailiwick in connection with the administration of justice, inheritance, the conveyance of real estate and the nature of land-holding. Their variety is such that in the interests of clarity the several legacies will be considered in separate sections of this chapter.

A. — Appeal to Caesar

The turbulence accompanying the decline of the Roman Empire led many a small landowner in the Rhine borderlands to seek protection from a powerful neighbour, thus establishing a patron and client relationship known as the Patrocinium. The supplicant would solicit this protection by surrendering his land to his protector, receiving it back as a mere Precarium, whereby he was reduced to the status of a lessee devoid of rights, but, thanks to the code of the Patrocinium, able to rely on his Patron's sense of honour as his safeguard. This system was adopted and adapted in Gaul by the incoming Visigoths, who developed from it the concepts of feudal homage and fealty and of the ties between lord and vassal. The Franks in their turn took over the Visigoth version and later passed it on to the Norse settlers in Normandy.

The type of feudalism established in the Bailiwick by the Normans thus had its roots in Roman practice and codes of conduct and it is not beyond the bounds of possibility that other strands of Roman tradition were also woven into the fabric of the system.

One such Roman practice was the right of any citizen to appeal directly to Caesar for the redress of any injury, as did St. Paul (*Acts* XXV, 11, 12): and in any case such an idea is inherent in the patron/client relationship of the Patrocinium. A tradition such as this stemming from the Romans may perhaps account for that most picturesque (and practical) of feudal vestiges — *the Clameur de Haro* which by its very wording is an appeal to the prince for help when one is being subjected to injury. In this connection it may be significant that some authorities think that the word 'Haro' is of German (i.e., Visigoth) derivation, meaning 'Come here'. The word, in fact, is not unknown to the English language, although it is now obsolete. *The New English Dictionary on Historical Principles* provides the definition: 'Haro — A cry of distress or alarm, a call for succour. To cry — (on any one) — to denounce a person's doings. Obsolete since about 1600.' It then gives a number of examples such as: '*c.* 1480 Towneley Mysteries, "Oute, haro, out, out, harkyn to this horne" '; or again 'Caxton — Reynard (1481), "I crye out haroe on them that so falsely haue belyed me".'

Irrespective of whether or not these derivative speculations have any substance, the *Clameur de Haro* is certainly of extreme antiquity, the custom having been prevalent in Neustria long before the arrival of the Norsemen — a fact which dispels the facile notion that 'Haro' is a contraction of 'Ha Rollo', invoking the first Duke of Normandy. In her autobiography the late Dame de Sercq put forward the thesis that in ancient Normandy anybody who suffered assault or trespass could shout 'Haro' three times, thus compelling anyone who heard to come to his help. She added that if the wrongdoer escaped the cry was repeated throughout the Duchy until the culprit was arrested. Thus every citizen became a constable and escape was rendered most difficult. Arising from this, it is, incidentally, interesting to note that yet another dictionary (*The Waverley*) shows the English word 'harass' as coming from 'the Old French "harer" ("to set a dog on")' — to which it also links 'the Norman French "Haro!" ("A cry to assemble a crowd")'.

Although the *Clameur de Haro* was abolished in Continental Normandy in 1583, it still survives in insular Normandy as, considerations of romantic survivals apart, it provides a speedy and efficient method of obtaining redress. If a person thinks that he is being wronged by encroachment or infringement of his rights, he calls upon his adversary to desist. If this requirement is not met he kneels on the ground and in front of two witnesses cries out, 'Haro! Haro! Haro! À l'aide mon Prince, on me fait tort!' He then recites the Lord's Prayer in French. Within 24 hours he must lodge at the Greffe his protest which has been drawn up in writing in the presence of the bailiff, or the lieutenant-bailiff, or at least two jurats. The Clameur is tantamount to an injunction and the action complained of must stop at once as the royal protection has been invoked, so that failure to desist involves liability to prosecution for breach of the peace and contempt of the queen's authority. When the case comes to Court the prosecution is carried on by the Crown — as the aid of the prince has been invoked. Whoever loses the case is mulcted in a fine, as raising the *Clameur* frivolously is regarded as being as blameworthy as the commission of a tort. In Alderney this remedy is available in matters pertaining both to persons and to property, but in the rest of the Bailiwick in those relating to property only.

In Sark the formula employed for raising the *Clameur* differs from the Guernsey usage. In this island the complainant, who may act on his own behalf or for somebody else, must bare his head and in the presence of two witnesses cry out, "Haro! Haro! Haro!' Au non de Dieu et de la Reine, quittez ce travail-là à l'instance de ... qui vous en depossède." ("Haro! Haro! Haro! In the name of God and of the Queen, leave this work on the demand of ... who prevents you."). Details of the dispute must be registered at the Sark Greffe and a deposit of 10 livres tournois made. If the Court disallows the complaint, this deposit is forfeit. The *Clameur* is used sparingly by the Serquiais and La Dame de Sercq stated in her autobiography that it had been raised only twice since her birth in 1884. It was, however, raised in 1985 in a boundary dispute between Mary Collins and Norman Wackley and again in 1993 by Mr. Paul Amorgie of Stocks Hotel in protest against building operations by his neighbour, Mr. John Cubbon, on land adjoining the hotel's swimming pool and dining room and hence, he claimed, detrimental to his interests.

In recent years the *Clameur* has been raised in Alderney in June 1970 and in Guernsey on August 26th., 1975 as a protest against a giant crane overhanging a shop in the Pollet, allegedly to the detriment of the establishment's trading prospects. Passing tourists stood around dumb-founded. The most unusual occurrence of a Guernseyman raising the *Clameur* outside the island took place in November 1978, when Mr. Ronald Payne raised it outside the Law Courts in London, alleging that the divorce which his wife had obtained in England was illegal as, their marriage having been contracted in Guernsey, they could only be divorced there on the grounds that, by the terms of Elizabeth I's Charter of 1560, any attempt by an outside Court to supersede the Guernsey Court's jurisdiction over islanders constitutes an action in derogation of the Bailiwick's legal autonomy.

B. — Preserving Naboth's Vineyard

The smallness of Guernsey holdings has made it essential throughout the ages to employ precautions against fragmentation, as such a process would before long produce units so lilliputian as to be ruinous to an agricultural economy. Accordingly two legal safeguards were evolved, one of which has now been abolished, while the other survives.

The first of these safeguards was *le droit de Préciput*, whereby the eldest son of a deceased parent could apply to the douzeniers of the parish in which his late parents' property was located for his 'préciput' or eldership. This was his right of claiming a specified inheritance over and above his normal share and varying from 14 to 22 perches according to the extent of the realty left by the deceased (and in practice including the family house) before his brothers and sisters were taken into account and without prejudice to his rights in the distribution of the remainder of the estate. The corollary of this right was the eldest son's obligation to take the entire 'enclos' in which his designated portion was located, so that besides deciding on the extent of the 'préciput', the douzeniers placed a value on 'le restant de l'enclos', at which price the eldest son had to compensate his co-heirs in respect of this residual area. The douzeniers would then embody their action in a 'préciput report' which, incorporated in the 'partage' (or testamentary allocation) would constitute the eldest son's title to his inheritance.

As the whole point of the arrangement was to keep farming land intact, the law did not allow the eldest son to raise his préciput if his late parents' estate was situated within the boundaries of the town (as distinct from the parish) of St. Peter-Port. To obviate any disputes as to the exact limits of this zone, the St. Peter-Port constables, in compliance with an Ordinance of the Royal Court, set up in 1700 the 'Barrière de la Ville', stones still to be seen in the Pollet, Smith Street, Fountain Street, near the Town Church and at the top of Tower Hill Steps. Although the official boundaries of the town (and thus of the area in which préciput did not apply) were extended in 1840, these monuments to the limits of the mediaeval town survive.

Modern circumstances having deprived Préciput of its *raison d'être*, it was abolished in Guernsey in 1954. In Alderney it was disallowed by implication in the Alderney Land and Property Law of 1949 and in any case the practice in that island had lapsed by desuetude. As for Sark, prior to the 1999 introduction of inheritance by will recounted in Chapter Thirteen of Part III there obtained a dispensation approximating to Préciput, with succession confined to the eldest son (or daughter failing sons) so as to secure the indivisibility of the Quarantaine Holdings stipulated by the Letters Patent of 1611 — see Chapter Ten of this Part.

The surviving legal safeguard against fragmentation is the right of 'Retrait Lignager' (or, simply, 'Retraite' — and possibly deriving from Mosaic Law: see Leviticus XXV, 25) whereby the near relatives of the vendor of a property may retrieve it by paying the purchase price to the buyer within 40 days (Sark) or a period which, originally a year and a day, was reduced by Order-in-Council in 1924 to one calendar month (Guernsey). In the case of inherited property, this right is limited to male relatives of the original owner, but if the property was purchased by the vendors, then relatives of either sex may claim a Retraite. A specific instance of the exercise of this right occurred in March 1987 when a property in La Couture Water Lanes known as Le Jardin de la Fontaine was reclaimed from its purchaser (Mr. David Winn) by Mrs. Loni Stevenson in her capacity as daughter of the vendor (Mr. Carl-Otto Johann Moller). An enraged Mr. Winn protested vehemently — but to no avail!

C. — 'Money in Bricks and Mortar'

The influence of feudalism is particularly apparent in connection with the nature of the ownership and valuation of real estate. Because of feudal tenure 'freehold' in the sense attached to the word in the United Kingdom is non-existent in Guernsey. When land changes hands, the buyer does not actually acquire the land itself. This he 'holds of' the seigneur of the fief in which it is located, as the seigneur in his turn 'holds it of' the queen. What the purchaser does acquire are the rights and obligations attached to the land. Nevertheless the term 'freehold' *is* used, though with an implication consonant with feudalism. In this sense the word indicates land free of 'rente' — which may mean either feudal dues or an obligation in some ways akin to those of a mortgagee in the United Kingdom.

This peculiar connotation of 'freehold' may be better appreciated when it is explained that property is valued notionally in quarters of wheat, the cash equivalent of which has varied from £20 to £25, but is now usually the latter. Thus the vendor of a property may make an arrangement with the buyer to 'sell it in quarters'. If the price sought by the vendor were (say) £20,000, he would 'place eight hundred quarters' upon the property and the purchaser would undertake to pay a 'rente' at an agreed rate of interest on these 'quarters'. If the 'rente' were £2 per annum per quarter, this would be the equivalent of 8 per cent. per annum interest on what amounts in practice to a loan.

Despite the fact that he has in practice advanced a loan, the vendor is not in the position of a mortgager in that he does not enjoy the right to claim repayment of capital — i.e., he cannot foreclose. The purchaser, by contrast, may make capital repayments at will (which the vendor is compelled to accept) by redeeming one or more of the 'quarters' placed on the property at their cash value (£25 each). 'Rente' naturally ceases to be payable in respect of redeemed 'quarters'. In the event of his bankruptcy, however, the purchaser's unredeemed 'quarters' have a prior claim over all other liabilities.

The vendor for his part will receive his 'rentes' periodically (in this example amounting to £1,600 per annum) and his 'rentes' or 'quarters' count as real property and would be included in any calculation of the value of his estate in the event of his death. While he lives he may sell all or some of these 'quarters' to a third party, to whom the 'rente' attached would now become payable. Thus his position is in many ways comparable to that of the holder of undated loan stock in the United Kingdom. It is pertinent to note, however, that the phenomenal rise in house prices during and after the 1960s associated with the establishment in the island of the "Finance Industry" militated against the practicability of the property transactions of this nature, although making such arrangements remained a perfectly legal (albeit unusual) method of conducting real estate business.

D. — Fee Farms: An Eighteenth-Century Footnote

The expression 'Fee Farm' denotes a feudal derivative form of land-holding which is the nearest approximation in Guernsey to leasehold in the United Kingdom. Land held 'by fee farm' is situated on Fief Le Roi and, prior to the 18th. century, consisted largely of waste or marsh. The Crown had been in the habit of letting such areas on a short-term basis, but this was unsatisfactory, as it gave no tenant any incentive to spend capital on improving and draining these grazing areas.

With the object of rectifying this unsatisfactory state of affairs, the lieutenant governor, Lieutenant-General Richard Sutton, petitioned the Crown in 1737 for permission to grant leases 'for and during the term of sixty-one years, renewable every one and twenty years at a fine certain of three years value of the Reserved Rent'. The resultant Order-in-Council creating such leases was registered in Guernsey in the same year.

This system gives far greater security of tenure to tenants, seeing that the title is almost as good as in more orthodox forms of land-holding. Furthermore, providing the annual rent is paid, plus the renewal fine of three times the annual rent, there is virtually no risk of misappropriation, while at the expiry of the 61 years a new lease may be drafted with identical terms and conditions. Finally, there is no bar to the holder of the lease alienating all or part of the land involved. Consequently, this system has promoted considerable improvements in the areas affected, resulting in major enhancements in their market value. Well-known examples of fee-farm leases are the islands of Jethou and Lihou. The latter of these leases was acquired late in 1994 by the States' Board of Administration from the last private tenant (the Honourable Robin Sandbach Borwick) who some time previously had put it on the market. In February 1996 the new lessee announced plans for converting the islet into a centre for environmental education and field studies, with overriding priority given to its conservation as a habitat for plants, birds and marine wild life, as well as to the preservation of the Priory ruins. As for the former, approval by the States on July 28th., 1994 of a recommendation put forward the previous June 20th. by the Advisory and Finance Committee resulted in the States of Guernsey, with effect from May 26th., 1995, assuming the rôle of "Head Tenant", holding Jethou directly of the Crown much as Sark is held directly of the Crown by its Seigneur (see Chapter Ten of this Part). Consequent upon this innovation the status of the erstwhile Joint Tenants — Messrs Peter Ogden and Philip Hulme, enjoying (by virtue of a deed executed on November 5th., 1984) security of tenure until May 25th., 2007 — was altered to that of Sub-Tenants, holding the islet of the Head Tenant much as in Sark a Quarantaine Tenant holds his/her land of the Seigneur.

Chapter Nine

THE SURVIVAL OF FEUDALISM: REPRIEVE AT THE SCAFFOLD

THE REMARKABLE TENACITY of Guernsey's feudalism was once again exemplified by a series of developments in the second half of the 1970s. The course of events commenced in November 1974 when the States' Advisory and Finance Committee issued a report denouncing feudal dues, on the grounds that they amounted to a quasi-tax being levied on property-owners without any authorisation by the legislature.

The report accordingly recommended that the Privy Council be asked to grant exemption from compensation in respect of the 34 fiefs held by the Crown, on the understanding that the loss of the annual income derived from Crown Fiefs would not affect the lieutenant-governor's salary and associated disbursements amounting to £119,000. The committee acknowledged that this income 'would have to be substantially replaced' from other sources — presumably taxation. The committee further recommended that the 20 seigneurs of the 48 fiefs not in the hands of the Crown should retain their titles and be paid £50,000 compensation between them for the loss of their rights.

Bearing in mind that a week previous to the publication of this report it had been revealed that on the Fief de Sausmarez alone £10,076 had been yielded by Congé during 1973, it is not surprising that the island's seigneurs described as 'derisory' an offer of £50,000 among 20 of them as a 'once-for-all' quittance. Thus in the same Billet d'Etat which gave details of the proposals of the committee, the Seigneur de Sausmarez, on behalf of all the seigneurs, stated that they rejected the report's contentions that feudal dues were anachronistic; and that, in any case, £50,000 was far from being 'fair and adequate' compensation for the loss of revenue from holdings with a joint capital value in the region of £1,250,000.

On December 19th., 1974 the States approved a sursis proposal whereby a final decision was deferred pending an investigation and report by the Advisory and Finance Committee on the total annual loss of States' revenue which the abolition of Congé would entail — together with proposals as to how this loss could best be recouped.

Early in 1976 the Advisory and Finance Committee published its report arising out of the 1974 sursis resolution; reiterating its recommendation that feudal dues should be abolished and stating that although the discontinuance of feudal revenue on Crown Fiefs (£374,351 in 1974–5) would be a factor influencing budget decisions, it did not necessarily follow that any taxation increases would ensue. The committee did, however, admit that the possibility of recouping the losses on waived feudal income by an increase in stamp duty would receive its attention if the proposals for the abolition of dues were approved by the States.

The upshot was that on February 25th., 1976 the States voted by an overwhelming majority that the retention of feudal dues in a modern society cannot be justified, resolving to request the Bailiff to ascertain Her Majesty's pleasure with regard to the implementation of the proposals for their abolition, together with the removal of the obligation to obtain formal leave from the seigneurs to purchase properties on their fiefs. The Bailiff was further requested to convey an assurance that the resultant loss of income by the States would not cause the States in any way to fail in their responsibility for maintaining the salaries and establishment of the lieutenant-governor, together with the salaries of the bailiff, deputy-bailiff and the law officers of the Crown. Lastly the States reiterated that compensation should be paid by the States to the private seigneurs (who would retain their titles) the aggregate amount of which would not exceed £50,000.

The following day Deputy Cecil de Sausmarez, in his capacity as Seneschal of the Court of Seigneurs, announced that a meeting of the Court would be held to discuss the decision of the States, after which it was "quite possible" that there would be an appeal to the Judicial Committee of the Privy Council against the ban on feudal dues.

An attempt to reconcile the opposing interests by an amendment to the effect that the abolition of Congé should apply only to the first £15,000 of the purchase price in any transaction was rejected by the States with a majority of 26 votes to 17 on October 28th., 1976, the decision of the previous February being confirmed. Also confirmed was the decision to pay to private seigneurs compensation up to £50,000.

This final determination was followed by legislation in the form of a Projet de Loi entitled 'The Feudal Dues (Guernsey) Law, 1977' which was approved by the States with a majority of

38 to 11 at its November 1977 meeting.

The issue of the confirmatory Order-in-Council (which had been anticipated during the early months of 1978), was, however, delayed as a result of a decision by the island seigneurs to petition the Queen-in-Council to withhold any such Order pending a reinvestigation of the adequacy of the proposed compensation for the loss of income from feudal dues. This petition was successful, the promulgation of a confirmatory Order-in-Council being refused in April 1979 on the grounds that the arbitrarily fixed sum of £50,000 compared so unfavourably with the level of income accruing to seigneurs and dames from feudal dues as to appear as confiscatory. This income level had been £98,000 in 1978 and £671,000 over the decade ending with 1978. The 1977 Projet le Loi was accordingly referred back to the States — a most unusual occurrence.

In September 1979 an extraordinary volte-face followed on this reference back to the States of the 1977 Projet de Loi, with the Advisory and Finance Committee now coming round to the opinion that the retention of feudal dues would be quite tenable provided all the proceeds eventually benefited the public purse! Accordingly the States approved revised proposals whereby the seigneurs and dames should between them receive an annual payment of £50,000 a year for five years by way of compensation, with any income from Congé above that figure accruing to the Crown. After the end of the five-year period all Congé income from private fiefs (estimated at £100,000 per annum) would accrue to the Crown together with the income from the Crown fiefs themselves (£619,000 for the year ending April 5th., 1979). The fact that under the 1947 arrangement described in paragraph 2 of Chapter 7 such income is relinquished by the Crown in favour of the States was invoked as justification for this reversal of attitudes whereby dues continue to be paid and Guernsey's feudalism was thus apparently reprieved at the very foot of the scaffold! Subsequent experience, however, indicated that while feudal dues had survived and feudal courts still occasionally convened (such as that of Fief Le Comte late in 1987), the system as a whole had withered to a derisory shadow of its former self so insubstantial that fiefs came to be bought outside the island by total strangers to Guernsey interested only in gaining the social eminence attaching to the title of Seigneur — witness the spate of such sales during 1987 and 1988 which saw the Seigneuries of Anneville, Fief de Mauxmarquis and Fief au Marchand being put up for auction in England and acquired by purchasers of but nebulous identity.

Chapter Ten

SARK: A QUINTESSENTIAL FEUDALISM

FEUDALISM IS of the very essence of life in Sark, and to this day permeates the entire administrative and social structure of the island. Yet it is a feudalism born out of its time, being established in Sark when it was already in its death throes elsewhere. Nevertheless, it has proved remarkably tenacious and capable of adapting itself to the needs of the present day, so that Sark provides a phenomenon of never-failing interest not only to the historian, but also to the student of politics and to the sociologist.

In 1563 Elizabeth I was involved in war with France in support of the Huguenots, and the campaign was going badly. This prompted anxiety about the security of the Channel Isles, and especially of Sark which, rendered vulnerable by its periodic desertion since 1373, had already been occupied by the French between 1549 and 1553, and again for a short while between 1560 and 1562. It was naturally feared that the occupation of Sark by a determined enemy could threaten the entire archipelago. At this juncture Helier de Carteret who, as Seigneur of the Fief of St. Ouen in Jersey, had his own reasons for wishing to forestall any further French adventures, approached the Commissioners whom Elizabeth I had appointed to realise Church property for the financing of defence. To these Commissioners Helier proposed that he should be granted Sark as an adjunct to his Fief of St. Ouen, in return for which he would, at his own expense, establish a settlement on the island and guarantee its defence.

The Commissioners were so impressed by the prospect of Sark being defended at no cost to the Crown that, after gaining the consent of Sir Francis Chamberlain, the Governor of Guernsey — who was officially responsible for Sark — they granted to Helier and his heirs in perpetuity the island of Sark as an adjunct to St. Ouen, in return for an annual payment of fifty sols tournois to the Crown Receiver in Guernsey. Accordingly, in 1564 Helier de Carteret made a reconnaissance of Sark, sowing some wheat on ground he cleared. The resulting crop being satisfactory, he and his wife, Margaret, in the spring of 1565 led a party of pioneers to lay the foundations of a settlement.

In the summer of the same year de Carteret visited London and strengthened his position by obtaining Letters Patent from Elizabeth I confirming the Commissioners' grant. These Letters stipulated that Helier was required to arrange for Sark to be permanently occupied by 40 men for its defence — and this had to be done within two years, failing which Helier would incur a penalty of ten pounds. If after another six months the 40 men were not settled, a further penalty of £20 would be incurred — and should yet another six months elapse without the settlement reaching 40, a forfeit of £40 would apply. Further delay beyond that would entail the lapse of the grant. Provided, however, that the 40 men were settled, Helier was granted Sark with all its appurtenances to dispose of as he wished 'for ever for the twentieth part of a Knight's Fee, and by paying for the same annually on the Feast of the Archangel St. Michael to Us, Our Heirs and successors, fifty sols of good and lawful money'. A final clause debarred Helier and his heirs from alienating the estate without the express permission of the Crown.

Helier de Carteret's friend, Nicholas Gosselin (son of the notorious Helier Gosselin prominent in the burning of Catherine Cauchés, her two daughters and her newly born grandson), had been largely instrumental in obtaining the acquiescence of Sir Francis Chamberlain to the original grant Helier had received from the Commissioners. In recognition of this valuable service de Carteret made over to him as a sub-fief the area known as Beauregard. Furthermore, he gave Gosselin the unique right of 'chasse' over his sub-fief — but the grant was conditional on Gosselin supplying four men for the defence of the island, and on his paying an annual rental of 50 shillings (thus exactly covering Helier's commitment to the Crown).

To make up the remaining 35 armed men he needed to meet the terms of the Letters Patent of 1565, Helier de Carteret divided up the rest of Sark into 35 holdings varying in extent from 10 to 40 vergées. To these holdings he attracted settlers by issuing Letters under his own seal guaranteeing complete security of tenure. Besides stipulating that each holding was conditional upon the supply of one man armed with a musket and ammunition for the defence of the island, the Letters issued by Helier also required the payment of an annual rente of one cabot of wheat for each arable vergée (bearing in mind that part of each holding consisted of côtils — cliff slopes — for sheep runs) as well as the building and maintenance of a house on the holding, and the planting and upkeep of dividing hedges.

Having by these attractive terms induced young married couples to settle on the island and found a community bound together by Calvinistic zeal under the spiritual guidance of Cosmé Brévint, Helier returned to London in 1572 and reported to Elizabeth I the successful fulfilment of his commission under the Letters Patent of 1565. He so impressed the queen that in appreciation of his services Elizabeth I created the Island of Sark as a Fief Haubert in its own right, independent of St. Ouen, and granted it to Helier and his heirs in perpetuity at an annual payment of fifty sols tournois to the Queen's Receiver in Guernsey. She also gave Helier six pieces of ordnance from the Tower of London. At the Seigneurie one of these is still to be seen, inscribed, 'Don de Sa Majesté la Royne Elizabeth au Seigneur de Sercq A.D. 1572'.

In her autobiography the late Dame de Sercq remarked that none of the privileges granted to Helier de Carteret has ever been annulled, and although some have fallen into abeyance, they are nevertheless capable of enforcement at any time. A review of developments since Helier de Carteret's death reveals how this preservation has been achieved.

Elizabeth's Charter of 1565 had entitled Helier de Carteret to exercise his authority as Seigneur and to administer the island's affairs through a Fief Court, at which his tenants would have to pay suit. This practice was continued after his death by his son, Philippe, and from this Court arose Les Chefs Plaids, so beginning the evolution which resulted in its development into the island legislature. During the Seigneurship of Philippe's son (also called Philippe) an important decision was made regarding the composition of this Fief Court cum Legislative Assembly. An Ordinance was passed in January 1606 (new style) that only the Chefs de Famille of the original 40 holdings would be eligible to participate in the proceedings of Les Chefs Plaids. Hence arose the term 'Maisons de la Quarantaine' to distinguish these original properties from other houses which had been built later to accommodate the younger generation.

In the years since Helier de Carteret's death two problems had arisen. In the first place, the practice had grown up, and become widespread, of raising mortgages on many of the island's holdings. The burden of such mortgage liabilities threatened the capacity of tenants to derive an adequate income from their holdings — and also to meet their seigneurial dues. Secondly, several tenants had taken to selling part of their holdings to other quarantaine holders. This practice was one which could be potentially ruinous to the economic welfare of the island, as it might result in some holdings becoming so small as to be incapable of supporting the holder. Above all, both the mortgage and land-sale developments put in jeopardy the seigneur's ability to maintain 40 men-at-arms in permanent residence.

Alarmed by the undesirable possibilities inherent in these practices, Sir Philippe de Carteret approached James I and the upshot was the Letters Patent of 1611 which provided that the raising of any 'incumbrancy' on a holding was forbidden — and that no holdings could be 'partable or parted', but were to remain indivisible and had to pass intact to the direct heir. The Letters did permit tenants, however, to sell their holdings as intact units providing the buyer was capable of fulfilling the obligations attached to the property, including providing an armed man for defence. Sales such as these, however, could only be made subject to the Congé (consent) of the seigneur, to whom 'Triezeième' (one-thirteenth of the purchase price) then became payable. These terms created Sark's unique form of land tenure and to the present day remain the basis of the island's law of property.

Sir Philippe de Carteret's support for the royalists in the Civil wars led parliament in 1642 to confiscate his Fief of Sark and the revenues attaching thereto. A pro-parliamentary garrison was installed in the island, and the authority of the seigneur vested in the Juge. In addition the Letters Patent of 1611 were ignored and tenements dismembered and mortgaged, to the ultimate harm of the island community.

Sir Philippe died in 1643 and his son (also Sir Philippe) was formally reinstated in the Fief of Sark by the Royal Court of Guernsey in 1660, whereafter the fief remained in the hands of the de Carteret dynasty until 1720, when a series of changes of ownership was started. In 1720 the seigneur, Lord George Carteret, with royal permission, sold the fief to Colonel John Johnson, to whom he was heavily in debt. Three years later Johnson died, and the fief was bought by James Milner, who died in 1730. Pending royal permission to sell the fief, Milner's nephew-in-law, Joseph Wilcock, Bishop of Gloucester, became temporary seigneur, but later in the same year he disposed of the fief to Susanne Le Pelley (widow of Nicholas Le Pelley), and a line of Le

Pelley seigneurs was initiated that was to last until 1852.

The fifth Le Pelley seigneur, Pierre Le Pelley, had to contend with a sustained attack on his feudal rights which began in 1796 and was not finally settled until 1812. The dispute centred around the seigneur's milling monopoly (Droit de Multure) and also the Corvée obligations of the tenants. Trouble started when Thomas de Carteret, tenant of La Forge, erected in 1796 a windmill of his own and refused to demolish it when required to do so by the seigneur. De Carteret was then arrested and appeared before the Guernsey Royal Court, which ruled however, that he *was* entitled to possess a mill for his own use, but *not* for the use of anybody else. In the next year (1797) the seigneur's mill was partly burnt down; no culprits could be discovered, and soon afterwards a second private mill was erected in Little Sark.

As for Corvée obligations, these had been imposed by an Ordinance of 1585 when Philippe de Carteret (son of Helier) was seigneur and required of the tenants two days' labour per annum on the roads. This state of affairs was increasingly resented by the poorer tenants who were obliged to give their labour in person, while the richer ones employed substitutes; and a meeting of Chief Pleas in 1803 voted for making road upkeep the responsibility of contiguous house-holders — but the resolution was nullified for want of seigneurial approval. At this, the disgruntled tenants of Great Sark refused to work on the roads of Little Sark — and vice versa; and both refused to work on La Coupée on the grounds that it was not a 'Grand Chemin' within the meaning of the 1585 Ordinance. It was not until 1812 that the confrontation ended with the tenants finally agreeing to work on La Coupée on condition that the seigneur made a contribution towards the cost of the operation.

In the mid-19th. century the Le Pelleys lost heavily on unsuccessful silver-mining ventures, and in 1852 Pierre Le Pelley was forced to seek Crown permission to sell. The buyer was Mrs. Marie Collings (née Allaire) from whom the present seigneur is descended.

During the 'reign' of the late Dame de Sercq, Corvée was finally abolished in 1951 in favour of a household levy. Nevertheless, most of the attributes of a mediaeval manor remain, with the seigneur flying his personal standard, enjoying his Droit de Colombier, collecting his feudal dues, and paying his annual £2.50 to the Crown for his Fief Haubert. Despite the fracas of 1796/7 the present writer in 1961 saw a notice at La Seigneurie regarding charges for the grinding of grain. Sark remains a bastion of feudalism unique in the world.

In 1957 the survival of this feudal bastion was emphasised by the Ceremony of Homage which took place in Sark for the first time in history. As the Queen entered the Chief Pleas the Prévôt announced loudly, 'Sa Majesté la Reine et Son Altesse Royale'. After calling upon the Greffier to read the opening prayer and the Roll Call, the Queen received a Loyal Address, presented on bended knee by the Seneschal. After the Queen's reply, the moment came for La Dame de Sercq to render homage. She approached the Queen, making three obeisances, and knelt at her feet, holding out her hands palm to palm. The Queen enclosed La Dame's hands in her own while La Dame said, 'Ma Souveraine Dame, je Vous rends Homage lige et Vous serai foyale et loyale contre tous'. Her Majesty replied, 'Nous vous acceptons Advouant tous vos légitimes droits et possession relevant de cette tenure de Nous, sauf pareillement à tous Nos Droits de Régalite'. La Dame de Sercq then rose and curtsied, backed to her seat, and curtsied again, before sitting. The Queen then rose and said, 'Greffier, kindly read the closing prayer', whereupon the Greffier recited the Gloria in French. Then, escorted by the Seneschal, with La Dame de Sercq accompanying Prince Philip, the Queen left the building. Homage was rendered by the present seigneur in a similar ceremony in 1978.

No consideration of feudalism in Sark is complete without reference being made to Brecqhou. As the grant made in 1563 by the Queen's Commissioners to Helier de Carteret embraced not only Sark but 'all the other Isles adjacent to it', it seemed obvious that the award included Brecqhou. In fact, this islet had from about 1160 until 1363 been appurtenant to the Fief Vinchelez in Jersey. In 1323 Nicholas de Cheny had purchased Fief Vinchelez and passed it on to his son, Guillaume. On the death of Guillaume in 1363 the fief had been divided between his two daughters, Brecqhou passing to his daughter, Jeanne, the wife of Denis Le Marchant of Guernsey — hence the name Ile aux Marchants which is sometimes given to it. The Commissioners seem to have taken no cognisance of the islet's ownership by the Le Marchant family. Maybe they did not know or maybe they considered that the lapse of 190 years had extinguished that family's title by sheer desuetude. In any case, the Le Marchant family's long-standing rights were ignored.

The support given by the de Carterets to the royal cause during the Civil War put them in a very strong position after the Restoration, especially as George Carteret, Treasurer of the Navy, was a favourite of Charles II. It might have been this consideration which finally decided the Le Marchants to end any assertion of their rights. In 1681 Dame Rachel, the widow of James Le Marchant, together with her son, Sir William Le Marchant, formally renounced all claims to the Isle of Brecqhou in favour of Sir Philippe de Carteret and his heirs. However, the grant of 1563 and the Le Marchant family's renunciation of title in 1681 notwithstanding, the islet's constitutional position vis-à-vis Sark was questioned in a court action brought in 1996 against the Seigneur (with the Crown later emerging as co-defendant — as was subsequently confirmed by the withdrawal of the plaintiffs' objection thereto) by the joint tenants David and Frederick Barclay, who sought reimbursement of the Treizeième (amounting to £179,487) paid on the purchase price of the lease, their claim based on a denial that Brecqhou is integral to the Fief Haubert with the consequent contention that the latter's inheritance laws are inapplicable therein, thus leaving any lessee with untrammelled discretion in regard to the holding's bequeathal. This dispute was finally settled, thanks to the January 2000 decision of the Bailiff of Guernsey in the case of de Carteret versus Surcouf. By this judgement the Bailiff overturned the finding of the Seneschal's Court disallowing long leases on realty and ruled that a widow should continue to enjoy the lease on the bulk of his tenement granted to her by her husband before his death, thereby establishing the validity of long leases on Sark property. This dictum, coupled with the 1999 legislation by Chief Pleas permitting inheritance by will, enabled Brecqhou's tenants to bequeath their holding as they wished, prompting them to discontinue the action which they had brought in 1996.

In 1835 the seigneur, Pierre Le Pelley, had bought the tenement of La Moinerie de Haut (thus permitting an extension of the grounds of La Seigneurie). As this was a quarantaine holding, its possession entitled the seigneur to an additional seat on Chief Pleas over and above his own.

In 1929 the late Dame de Sercq sold the lease of Brecqhou to Mr. Angelo Clarke and transferred to him the seat in Chief Pleas attached to La Moinerie de Haut. It is by virtue of the same arrangement that subsequent tenants of Brecqhou have also been accounted quarantaine holders.

Chapter Eleven

ALDERNEY: FEUDALISM IN DECAY

PROMINENT AMONG THE REASONS why feudalism in Sark survived and became embedded in the life-style of the island is the essential unity which bound the community together. Not only were most of the settlers of Jersey provenance, but they shared in common the adventure of colonising a wilderness, while social cohesion was fostered by a common, fervent Calvinism.

None of these conditions applied in Alderney; indeed the conditions which did obtain were of the opposite extreme. The seigneur was a 'foreigner' from England in an island which had long been settled, while the community was split by bickering between a Roman Catholic seigneur and Calvinistic islanders. As feudalism can never survive a persistently disaffected peasantry, it is not surprising that in Alderney's case it withered to the point where its existence was merely theoretical.

Alderney's feudal phase occurred during what may fittingly be called the Chamberlain Era. Despite the adherence of the Chamberlain family to Roman Catholicism, Elizabeth I on her accession had retained Sir Leonard Chamberlain as Governor of Guernsey — and had also allowed his son, Francis, to succeed after his death in 1561. In a similar placatory vein, Sir Leonard's third son, John Chamberlain, received a Patent in 1584 whereby he was granted the Isle of Alderney in fee simple for an initial payment of £20 and an annual due of £13 6s. 8d. A further condition was that he should settle at least forty of Her Majesty's subjects in the island — which had allegedly been laid waste. This requirement might have been inspired by the grant made to Helier de Carteret in Sark, but it ignored the fact that, far from being waste, Alderney had a settled population of about seven hundred — with whom Chamberlain was at loggerheads before a year was out because of the islanders' resentment at the high-handed manner in which he tried to exploit to the full the potentialities of the island.

Because of Alderney's importance as a 'gateway to the

Channel' (it was, after all, from 'Aurigny's Isle' that Macaulay would have us believe came the first tidings of the approach of the Spanish Armada three years later) the Privy Council was most alarmed by reports of unrest among the population. It therefore ordered Sir Thomas Leighton, the Protestant Governor of Guernsey, to intervene. On Leighton's recommendation, a set of Ordinances was drawn up defining the respective rights of the seigneur and the people. Although these Ordinances served as a model for all subsequent grants of the isle as a fief, yet the contrast with seigneur/people concord in Sark is pointed in the extreme.

In 1590 John Chamberlain was in sore straits because of his failure to fulfil the contract he had made with the Earl of Essex to provide him with supplies for his expedition to aid the Huguenots in Normandy. This embarrassment led him in 1591 to sell to the earl his rights in Alderney for £1,000 — but the Earl of Essex, for his part, at the same time granted a lease of the island to John's younger brother, William.

The Earl of Essex thus became the absentee seigneur, entitled to the income deriving from feudal dues, with William Chamberlain on the spot as deputy seigneur enjoying a virtual free hand in the management of the island. Despite the earl's execution for treason in 1601, James I, three years later (1604), restored all his late father's property to his son, Robert (the Earl of Essex of Civil War fame), so that the Essex/Chamberlain arrangement continued.

William was soon embroiled in disputes with the independently-minded inhabitants, whose wont it was vigorously to oppose anybody set in authority over them from outside their midst. So acrimonious did their relationships become that in 1607 the islanders presented to the Royal Commission in Guernsey a Petition of Complaint against him. In this Petition they alleged that Chamberlain had encroached on their common lands; had seized all tithes, together with the Parsonage House (which he had allowed to fall into ruin), and, ever since 1591, had withheld any salary for a minister, thus reducing Alderney to an 'unchristian and barbarous estate'.

The Royal Commissioners in Guernsey acknowledged that these complaints were well-founded and sent over delegates to impose a settlement, whereby Chamberlain's property was delimited to the tip of the island east of a line between Corblets Bay and the Grand Fort (now called Essex Castle), plus the island of Burhou. In addition, he was ordered to pay a salary of £20 a year to a minister. In 1608 William Chamberlain died, and the lease passed to his son, who was also named William. In 1620 he (and Alderney) acquired a new overlord as the Earl of Essex made over the rentes of the island to a Sir William Essex. This Sir William was no relation of the earl, but merely the nephew of a friend of his father. He was a profligate and heavily in debt, and the earl's action has all the appearance of a quixotic gesture. Sir William took to styling himself 'Governor of Alderney' but no patent was issued to him, nor is there any evidence of his visiting the island. He died in 1642 and the island reverted to the Earl of Essex, who himself died in 1646, leaving no issue.

In the meanwhile William Chamberlain II had died, and the lease passed to his cousin, John Colles, who in 1640 made it over to his brother, William Colles, for £200. William Colles died *c.* 1642.

By now the Civil War had supervened and the occupation of Alderney by a parliamentary force ended the travesty of feudalism which had dragged on since 1584. The Restoration was to see the appointment by Charles II of a new 'seigneur', but the persistent intransigence of the inhabitants meant that such 'feudalism' as was thereby re-established was of so attenuated a form as not to deserve the name. Developments after the Civil War are therefore more appropriately considered in the context of political history.

PART III

'RENDER UNTO CAESAR' — THE POLITICAL ASPECT

Chapter One

ROMAN AND NORMAN ADMINISTRATION BEFORE 1204

THE BAILIWICK'S political development is so closely intertwined in a Gordian Knot with the feudal structure from which it emerged that it is virtually impossible to separate the two. Hence any division between them such as is made in this book is a purely arbitrary device to aid presentation. It is inevitable, therefore, that the close correlation between the two should repeatedly obtrude itself. What is more, largely because of the feudal provenance of the Bailiwick's political institutions, a further Gordian Knot unites their development in an interlocking fashion, with the executive functions of government coming to be performed by committees of a legislature which itself grew out of a feudal judiciary — and right up to the middle of the 20th century was so enmeshed with it that both organs had their most influential members in common.

Under the Roman Empire the Bailiwick of Guernsey formed part of the administrative unit based on Constantia (Coutances). This was a sub-division of the Province of Gallia Lugudensis Secunda, whose capital was at Rotomagus (Rouen). Although excavations carried out in Alderney by Baron Anatole von Hugel as long ago as 1889 and 1890 had established the presence there of an extensive late second century A.D. Gallo-Roman settlement, details of his finds were neither widely published nor investigated at the time, with von Hugel himself, writing about his site, referring to it dismissively as the 'Longy rubbish pit'. It is hardly surprising, therefore, that until the early 1980s the conventional wisdom held that, with the possible exception of Alderney's Nunnery, there was little indication that the archipelago (whose inhabitants, together with those of the Cotentin, the Romans called 'Unelli') was either colonised or garrisoned. The Roman coins, tiles and pottery which had been unearthed from time to time were regarded as connoting not so much Roman settlement as the visits of tax-collectors and traders from Constantia — plus perhaps (as has been seen) missionaries sent by Saint Martin de

Tours. The amphorae of garum found on the sea-bed of the Little Russel by Mr. Richard Keen in 1977 (see Part V, Chapter Fourteen) could be accommodated within this hypothesis, as could also — though at a pinch and much less convincingly — the Roman ship discovered by the same diver at the entrance to the Town Harbour on Christmas Day 1982 and brought to the surface in 1985. Subsequent developments, however, gave considerable pause to anyone inclined to be dogmatic about these traditional assumptions. The existence of a hypocaust underneath the Castel Church established by Mr. John McCormack's investigations in 1984 strongly suggests the likelihood that a Castellum stood on this militarily dominating site; while remarkably persuasive evidence of an imperial presence in the islands is provided by the Roman buildings which came to light in the excavations at La Plaiderie conducted during the same year by Mr. R.B. Burns, who regarded them (considered in conjunction with the ship) as representing a major 'way-station' in the passage between Reginca (Saint Malo) and Clausentum (Southampton) operating during the period *circa* 150 to *circa* 400 A.D. These events of 1984 were followed twelve years later by the emergence of further corroborative testimony when second century artefacts of the she-wolf's brood described by the Archaeology Section of La Société Guernesiaise in that organization's Autumn 1996 Newsletter as "indicating a substantial Roman presence in the area" were unearthed the previous January by a 'dig' beneath the Bonded Store on the west side of Church Square. What is more, it is significant that an echo of Roman farming estates or Villas is to be found in many local place-names, such as Ville-au-Roi, Ville Amphrey or Anneville (Guernsey) as well as Grève de la Ville and La Ville Roussel (Sark).

The Roman names for these imperial outposts may be deduced from the *Antonine Itinerary*, a gazetteer of the Empire associated variously with the Emperors Antoninus Pius (138–161), Marcus Aurelius Antonius (161–180), and Antoninus Caracalla (211–218); a maritime appendix to which lists the islands 'in the seas washing Gaul and Britannia'. From this source the conjecture originally made in 1749 by the Reverend Isaac Vallant (who that year took up the island living) to the effect that Alderney was Riduna has been accorded general acceptance, despite an anonymous objection to it advanced in the mid-nineteenth century, based on the surmise that it was Thanet (known to the Ancient Britons as Ruithina) which the Romans called by this name. As for the opinion expressed by William Camden in his 'Britannica' (1586) in favour of Arica or Aurica, a derivation of Orniacum (which at first sight seems to have a greater affinity with Aurigny), it must be remembered that 'Arica' occurs in one transcript only of the Itinerary out of the twenty regarded by cognoscenti as possessing any worthwhile claims to validity.

Sarnia (or — more probably — Sargia) was in all probability Sark and *not* Guernsey as is popularly (but most likely erroneously) supposed — an *idée fixe* resulting from centuries of naïve acceptance of an unsupported assertion made by William Camden in 1586. The identification of Sark with Sarnia/Sargia finds support in the report that the Frankish King Childebert donated 'Sargia' and 'Besargia' to Sampson of Dol (c. 552–8). The prefix 'Be-' denotes a diminutive and consequently the names have been associated with Great and Little Sark (or more likely with Sark and Brecqhou). Furthermore, by linguistic derivation one gets the sequence Sargia — Serquay — Sercq — Serk — Sark.

Both Henoc (writing *c.* 620) and Baldric (1120) tell of St. Sampson travelling from Neustria to Armorica by way of 'Lesia and Angia, "islands of the sea"'. As there is a 'Lisia' in the *Antonine Itinerary* and as, moreover, there is a ninth-century reference to Geroaldus being sent to 'an island called Augia, which ... lies near the Cotentin', it would seem that Guernsey is the former and Jersey the latter — 'Angia/Augia' being corruptions of the 'Andium' featured in the *Itinerary*. It is on the assumption of the accuracy of identifying Lisia with Guernsey that the dedication of this book is based.

(Although not strictly relevant to a history of the Guernsey Bailiwick, it may nevertheless be interesting to note that as regards 'Caesarea', popularly attributed to Jersey — and latterly thought possibly to pertain to Chausey or the Minquiers — Dr. S. K. Kellett-Smith has put forward the intriguing suggestion — in despite of Jacquetta Hawkes's dictum that whatever Caesarea denoted, it certainly did not denote Jersey — that this was an additional appellation given to Andium by a chieftain of the Unelli in accordance with the custom mentioned by Suetonius whereby client rulers called their leading cities after Augustus — the chieftain in this case naming his largest island after the emperor for lack of a city. However, Dr. Richard Coates of Sussex University — see Bibliography — dissents from this view, considering that through a series of scribal rationalisations as successive generations repeatedly copied the *Itinerary* 'Sargia' in some cases became 'Saria', thence 'Seria', followed by 'Ceseria' and finally 'Caesarea' which, far from designating Jersey, should apparently refer to Sark!)

When one comes to Herm, its proximity to Guernsey, so similar to Barsa's juxtaposition with Lisia in the *Itinerary*, leads to the tentative (and very shaky) identification of the one with the other. A more convincing theory stems from the statement in the biography of St. Helier that Childebert donated to St. Sampson 'Sargia, Besargia, Rima and Angia'. On these grounds it can be argued that Roman Herm was 'Rima' — a name omitted from the *Antonine Itinerary* because of the island's unimportance. Moreover, the word 'Rima' meant 'open and bare' — which aptly described Herm before 19th. century afforestation — and so did 'erimus' in low Latin. From Erimus the mediaeval name of Erm or Arme is rather obviously derived: and from Erm to Herm is a mere matter of aspiration. On the basis of this assumption Barsa would, of course, have been some other island 'in Mare Oceano Quod Gallias et Britannias interluit' — perhaps (as the word means 'circular and dome shaped') neighbouring Jethou. In contrast to the Rima theory, however, Dr. Richard Coates' deep researches convinced him that this island's name derives from the *Antonine Itinerary's* 'Sarmia' (not 'Sarnia) by the linguistic mutations Sarmia — Sermia — Serm — Herm.

The defeat at Soissons in 486 of 'the local Caesar' Syagrius by Clovis of the Merovingian dynasty of Salian Franks ended the last vestige of Roman rule in Gaul and ultimately brought about the emergence therein of the two Frankish kingdoms of Neustria and Austrasia, the former of which (as the researches of the late Alfred Harry Ewen revealed) embraced the Channel Isles. This is borne out by the exile in 577 by the Neustrian King Chilperic of Praetextatus (who had offended his Queen Fredegonde) to Jersey, as a place which, though remote, was under Neustrian rule. The Merovingians, however, became increasingly effete and in 751 they were overthrown by the *coup d'état* of Pepin the Short who established the Carolingian dynasty. Meanwhile, the migratory movements across the Channel of Britons, some of whom (as seen in the careers of the Celtic Saints) included the archipelago in their itinerary, had led to intermittent and tenuous connections developing between the islands and the Bréton realm which, coincident with the Merovingian decline, grew up in Armorica. This Armorican régime became a considerable kingdom when in 867, by the Treaty of Compeigne, the Carolingian King Charles the Bald granted to the Bréton King Saloman the whole of the Cotentin, thereby bringing the islands within the grantee's dominions in theory — though hardly in reality, beset as they were at the time by the depredations of the Norsemen (see Part IV, Chapter One). Then, in 911, by the Treaty of Saint-Clair-sur-Epte, Ganga-Hrolf (popularly known as Rollo), one of these Scandinavian despoilers, was ceded land in the vicinity of Rouen by the Frankish King Charles the Simple, thereby founding the Duchy of Normandy — and in 933 Rudolf, the son of Charles, enlarged the Duchy's territory by granting to Rollo's son, William Longsword, "the land of the Brétons by the sea-coast" (i.e. the Cotentin and the Avranchin), with the upshot that the islands' status of being technically appendages of Brittany was replaced by their incorporation into the Duchy of Normandy; though it must be said that Rouen's control over the archipelago remained largely a legal fiction for the better part of a century, not becoming effective until the latter part of the rule of Duke Richard II, who wore the Ducal Coronet from 996 to 1026. Thereafter they became in very truth an integral part of the Duchy and were administered on the feudal basis examined in Part II of this book. The especially favourable terms accorded to the feudal 'hôtes' in the 11th. century inaugurated the 'customs' which were to form the basis of the autonomy which the islands were later to wrest from monarchs such as the first three Edwards intent on subordinating them to centralised control emanating from London.

Prior to Duke William II's conquest of England (and for about a century thereafter) the archipelago as a whole was administered by a Seneschal of Normandy, who appointed a deputy (the Vicomte of the Islands) to act for him on the spot. Visiting justices from Normandy dispensed the duke's laws. The conquest of England by Duke William II did not make any difference to the status of the islands as part of Normandy — whose dukes by no means always coincided with the kings of England. Thus, on the death of Duke William II in 1087, his son, Robert, became Duke Robert II of Normandy, while his other son, William Rufus, became King of England, and it was not until six years after Rufus was killed that, by his defeat of Robert in 1106 at Tenchebrai, his other brother, now King Henry I of England, became Duke of Normandy as well, with the rightful duke being incarcerated in Cardiff Castle until his death.

On Henry's death, while Stephen reigned precariously in England, turmoil ensued in Normandy until Geoffrey of Anjou established himself as duke, being crowned in 1144. In 1150 (the year before Geoffrey died) he was replaced on the ducal throne by his son, Henry, who four years later, by the terms of the Treaty of Wallingford, became King of England also on the death of Stephen. Only after 1154 did English monarchs and Norman dukes permanently coincide.

The period of divorce from the English monarchy after Geoffrey's installation in Rouen was an especially important one for the Bailiwick of Guernsey. In the first place, the fact that he had the whole of Guernsey in his hands after the death of Roger of the Cotentin and the forfeiture of his Norman lands by Ranulf of Chester, enabled Geoffrey to re-allocate land-holdings in the island and to institute the system of the general payment — later to be called the 'King's Farm' — which not only carried exemption from servile obligations, but also guaranteed political liberties under local law. Thus the islanders' entitlement to trial in their own courts and their immunity from arbitrary exactions stem from Duke Geoffrey's time.

Secondly, the probability is that from the same period dates their exemption from military service outside the islands except 'that they will go with the Duke of Normandy, if need be, when he goes in person to recover England'. As Professor Le Patourel has pointed out, such a proviso would only be of relevance at the time Geoffrey was planning an invasion of England in support of his son's claim to the English throne.

Finally, the increase in the ducal holdings in the island inaugurated by Geoffrey increased the importance of the Guernsey Ducal Court and led to Guernsey having a deputy of its own responsible to the Seneschal of Normandy, instead of sharing one with Jersey.

While Richard Coeur de Lion was king and duke he made his brother, John, 'Lord of the Isles' at some date between 1195 and 1198, thus, for the first time, giving the archipelago an administration as a distinct entity. John became responsible for the government and defence of the islands, and in return enjoyed the revenues that otherwise would have accrued to the duke. When John succeeded his brother the turbulence of the Cotentin nobles led him to seek to separate the control of the islands from that of mainland Normandy and to that end he created Pierre de Préaux Lord of the Isles (1200). It was this same Pierre de Préaux who was to surrender to Philip Augustus at Rouen in 1204, but to 'forget' to include the islands in the terms of submission.

To conclude this chapter a potentially confused situation may perhaps be somewhat clarified by 'parallel' tabulations of Norman dukes and English kings.

Dukes of Normandy		Kings of England	
Rollo	911–931		
William I (Longsword)	931–942		
Richard I (The Fearless)	942–996		
Richard II (The Good)	996–1026		
Richard III	1026–1027		
Robert I (The Devil)	1027–1035		
William II (The Bastard)	1035–1087	= William I	1066–1087
Robert II (Curthose)	1087–1106	William II (Rufus)	1087–1100
Henry I (Beauclerk)	1106–1135	= Henry I (Beauclerk)	1100–1135
Fighting,	1135–1144	Stephen	1135–1154
Geoffrey	1144–1150		
Henry II	1150–1189	= Henry II	1154–1189
Richard IV	1189–1199	= Richard I	1189–1199
John	1199–1204	= John	1199–1215

Chapter Two

POLITICAL ADMINISTRATION UNDER JOHN AND HENRY III (1204–1272)

AN ARTICLE by Geoffrey Weston in *The Times* of January 25th., 1973, said that the addresses given by Mr. Geoffrey Rippon to the States of Jersey and Guernsey on the E.E.C. terms which had been offered to the Channel Isles amounted to 'a constitutional rarity, possibly unique, which served to underline the special status of the islands and their relationship to the United Kingdom'. The article went on to say, 'Never having been either a colony or a part of the United Kingdom and with ancient insular traditions of their own, the Channel Islands can claim to be fundamentally different from any other territory in the world'.

The recurring interest of the political history of the Bailiwick from 1204 onwards pivots around the twin foci of the evolution of its internal governmental apparatus on the one hand, and on the other the developments whereby was forged the 'special status' emphasised in the above-mentioned article. These two themes intermingle and react on each other throughout the Bailiwick's story.

During the period of débâcle on the Norman mainland Guernsey was in chaos, rent by factional feuds, not only between rival claimants for properties, but also between the supporters of John and those of Philip Augustus (whose myrmidons were ejected after temporarily overrunning the islands). His defeat brought it home to John that the situation of St. Peter-Port roadstead on the main route to his remaining possessions in Gascony made vital the security of the Channel Isles. Consequently, although the islanders after their initial ambivalence ultimately threw in their lot with him — doubtless influenced by local leaders who saw a chance of gaining independence from their feudal superiors on the Norman mainland — John took no chances but, after seizing hostages from the principal local families, initiated the building of fortifications (especially Castle Cornet and Le Château des Marais) and instituted a system of 'Wardens of the Isles', responsible to him for the safety and good government of the archipelago. He retained the hostages until 1214, when they were released as a reward for the help given by the islanders in the recapture of Sark which had earlier been taken by Eustace the Monk for Philip Augustus. Having regained Sark, John dispossessed Richard de Vernon, who had sided with the French king.

Having decided that the islands, although of insignificant size, were nevertheless worth retaining, John adopted the device of treating them as a possession of the king of England, *but separate and distinct from his Kingdom of England.* In this way their relationship with England became (and has remained) comparable to that between Hanover and the United Kingdom in the period 1714 to 1837 — a principality united with another in the person of the prince only. In line with this initial decision, the general policy pursued by John and Henry III was to maintain as far as possible the *status quo ante bellum*, regarding the Channel Isles as part of the royal domain *outside the realm* and as such to be administered by a warden as a 'royal peculiar'. In this connection it is significant that the islands at times shared a warden with Gascony — witness the Prince Edward who was both Lord of Aquitaine and Lord of the Isles from 1254 to 1275.

There were two types of such wardens appointed by John and Henry III. Firstly there were those to whom the islands were granted in fee for life. They were styled 'Lords of the Isles', and, accepting the liabilities as well as the assets pertaining to their office, enjoyed the status and powers of the Duke of Normandy. As a result, the king alienated a considerable part of his dominion over the islands when he appointed a 'Lord of the Isles'. Apart from Pierre de Préaux, who was appointed in 1200 and who was dismissed after his capitulation at Rouen, John appointed no Lords of the Isles. Henry III, however, appointed Henry de Trubleville between 1234 and 1239 and his son, the Prince Edward, from 1254 until his (Henry's) death in 1272. The second type of warden consisted of those who were simply entrusted with the custody of the islands during the royal pleasure — hence their title of 'Custos' (or 'Warden'). They were essentially the king's agents or 'Bailiffs' in the islands.

Wardens of both types were responsible for a multiplicity of duties, exercising the royal authority in all spheres, military, judicial and administrative. Thus their duties involved not only keeping fortifications in good repair and commanding the garrison, but also acting as the king's bailiff, both in the collection of royal revenues and in the implementation of the king's orders. (The latter required marked tact as the islanders could always threaten to transfer their allegiance to France if their 'laws and customs' were not respected.) In addition the wardens were responsible for administering justice on the king's behalf, including taking the triennial assizes according to Norman law which hitherto has been done by visiting justices from Normandy. To this responsibility was later added that of holding Royal Courts distinct from the assizes.

In 1254 Henry III, realising the extreme improbability of Normandy ever being regained, annexed the islands to the Crown of England, but this did not materially alter their status of appertaining to the Crown but not to the Realm. He then handed them over to his heir for the rest of his life, creating him 'Lord of the Isles'. Five years later — in 1259 — Henry finally abandoned the title of Duke of Normandy, but the islands continued to be administered as though he were still duke.

Towards the end of the reign of Henry III appeared the document, *Copie des franchises que le roi degleterre a en Guernerie et que les hommes de Guernerie ont*. This document states that in consideration of the general payment ('farm') made by the inhabitants, they should enjoy the twin privileges of being judged by 12 jurats without going out of the island except for appeal, and of having all amercements assessed by these jurats. Officers known as jurats also appear in Alderney, where the King's Court was held by a Prévôt appointed by the warden, but where judgement was rendered by seven jurats: and in Sark, where the Court consisted of a Prévôt and six jurats.

The participation of local jurats in both assizes and ordinary courts assured the safeguarding of the laws and customs of the islands — and hence insular autonomy. The jurats therefore were obviously a cardinal factor in insular self-assertion, so that it is pertinent to enquire as to their origins, but unfortunately the evidence is confusing.

In 1248 the warden, Drew de Barentin, was ordered to enquire into the usages of the islands and to have these set down in writing for reference should disputes arise between the warden and the islanders. The resultant enquiry revealed that John 'instituted twelve sworn coroners to keep the pleas and rights pertaining to the Crown'. It is likely, however, that in doing this John adapted an earlier institution to new needs. The free election by the people of judges and magistrates chosen from among themselves is of great antiquity and was a right claimed by the Celtic Gauls who provided some of the earliest settlers in the islands. Another suggestion that John might have made use of an existing institution (despite the doubts cast thereon by the silence regarding jurats of a Charter of 1179 recording a Court action) comes from Jurat T. F. de Havilland, who, writing in 1841, expressed the opinion that regular courts were established in the archipelago in the time of Duke William II (mid-11th. century) and that it was then that jurats came into existence.

Yet one more clue is provided in the ancient document, *Le Précepte d'Assize* (1441), which says that the jurats replaced 'four knights'. It is true that in Normandy the baillis were bound in some cases to consult four knights, and it is noteworthy that in 1201 Pierre de Préaux was ordered to take 'a reasonable aid' from the islands, 'by view of four lawful knights'. Jurat T. F. de Havilland, however, in his treatment of the subject referred to above, was most sceptical about the four knights on the grounds that the islands were of insufficient importance to warrant the appointment of four knights to deal with minor local disputes — and he pointed out that *Le Précepte d'Assize* is most vague as to when the alleged change from four knights to 12 jurats took place. (It was, by contrast, far more precise in withholding from the Court the right to inflict punishment in cases of treason or crimes against the Bailiff or any Jurat while in office — the power of pronouncing sentence in such cases being reserved to the Sovereign).

H. Marett Godfray, in his *L'Origine des Jurés-Justiciers dans les Iles de la Manche*, puts forward the idea that the jurats originally were recruited from the 'optimes patriae' of the parishes to form a permanent jury of presentment for the whole island (as distinct from comparable parochial bodies). In this connection it is perhaps significant that the *Shorter Oxford English Dictionary* defines 'Jurat' as 'one sworn to give information about the crimes committed in his neighbourhood'.

It would appear, considering the cacophony of discordant theories, that all that may be said without fear of contradiction was said by Mr. T. F. Priaulx in an article in Volume XXIX, No. 1, of the *Guernsey Society Review* — 'The office of Jurat is a very ancient one. It has been in existence for such a long time that no one can say with certainty when it was instituted'.

Chapter Three

THE RÉGIME OF OTTO DE GRANDISON (1275–1341)

IN AN ADDRESS to the Guernsey Society in October 1970, Jurat Jean Le Pelley remarked that when asked about his nationality an Englishman replies, 'I'm English' a Frenchman, 'Je suis français', but the Guernseyman says, 'Me? I'm Guernsey'; and he went on to say that the Guernseyman 'wraps his island around himself as his mark of identity'. This sense of strong insular identity was forged during the period now about to be considered — a period characterized by an overlord intent upon exploitation and kings intent upon centralisation.

The kings were Edward I, who attempted to apply to the islands the policy of extinguishing local privileges which he employed in England, Scotland and Wales; followed by his son and grandson (Edward II and Edward III), who sought to continue this policy until the attempts were finally frustrated. The method adopted by these monarchs was twofold — first they attempted to place the islands under the authority of the English Judiciary, and, secondly, they challenged the continuance of local rights by the issue of Quo Warranto Writs.

The overlord was Otto de Grandison, a Burgundian knight who had won Edward I's favour, becoming first the king's secretary and then the Seneschal of Gascony. In 1275 Edward I appointed Otto Warden, and in 1277 made him Lord of the Isles. Apart from the period 1294–8 (when Edward took the islands into his own hands because of the war with France over Gascony) Otto remained Lord of the Isles until his death in 1328. The grant of his office was regarded by both king and recipient as a means of providing this royal favourite with an income, which Otto sought to ensure by instituting an oppressive and extortionate régime. Otto only visited the islands once (1323) and in his perpetual absence the administration was of necessity adapted, with sub-wardens carrying out executive functions and bailiffs (who first appeared at this time) the judicial ones. It was around this emergent official the bailiff (together with the jurats) that was centred the resistance of the islanders to Otto's depredations and one result of the struggle was the establishment of the bailiff as the foremost authority in the island. It is therefore pertinent to investigate the evolution of this pivotal figure in insular administration.

During Otto's first tenure of office (1275–94) his subordinates were indiscriminately described as 'bailiffs', 'wardens' or 'sub-wardens' — but during his second period as Lord of the Isles (1298–1328) 'bailiffs' came to mean officers concerned with the courts, whose authority was limited to one island, while 'wardens' or 'sub-wardens' designated those who held Otto's authority in all the islands in commission.

Guillaume de St. Remi (who was slain in the French raid of 1294) became in 1292 the first holder of the office to receive a Royal Patent and from 1299 onwards it is possible to trace a succession of bailiffs who were purely judicial officers, recognisably the predecessors of the bailiffs of today — while the growing status of these bailiffs is well exemplified in the affair of Gerard d'Oron.

In 1321 Gerard d'Oron (Otto's nephew) was appointed as sub-warden and, finding the islands in open revolt against his uncle's extortionate rule, withdrew to Sark. Later, however, he returned to Guernsey and attempted to unseat the bailiff (John Le Marchant), whereupon the bailiff and the Court threw him into jail. Two years later (1323) the jurats pleaded before Edward II's visiting judges that Gerard's credentials were invalid as his letters of appointment failed to stipulate that his administration was to be 'according to the laws and customs of the island'. Nothing could show more clearly than does this confrontation how local grievances were finding a focus in the bailiff and jurats of the Court. Moreover, the affair makes it clear that the bailiff now had a distinct identity — so distinct, indeed, that he, as the representative of the judicial authority of the Lord of the Isles, had thrown the representative of his administrative authority (and his nephew to boot) into prison.

The crystallisation of the bailiff's position is also indicated in the history of the official seals of the islands. In 1279 Edward I sent a common seal to the 'bailiffs of Jersey and Guernsey'. As its use was envisaged in both islands, it was obviously intended for the administrative officer — the sub-warden. In 1304, however, two slightly dissimilar seals were issued by the king — one for each major island, consisting in each case of the royal arms as they were from Richard Coeur de Lion to Edward III (three golden lions —

sometimes called leopards — passant-guardant palewise on a red ground) but with the Guernsey one surmounted by a sprig. Thus the judicial authority of the Lord of the Isles was now delegated to two units. Such a step was both inevitable and irreversible because of the sub-warden's inability to attend court meetings in four islands and also to be versed in local legal idiosyncrasies. Thus the separate Bailiwicks of Jersey and Guernsey came into being — with Prévôts deputising for the Bailiff of Guernsey in the courts of Alderney and Sark.

A device tried five years previously (in 1291) might have prevented this development from taking place. In that year Alderney and Sark were farmed out to Ralph, son of Odo, who called himself 'Bailiff of Sark and Alderney' — but this experiment of a joint separate bailiwick was unsuccessful, with the consequence that these islands were included in the Bailiwick of Guernsey in 1304.

Once Otto was installed in office both monarch and overlord saw in the manipulation of the judiciary a means of attaining their ambitions — that of the king to centralise and that of de Grandison to exploit. Thus they combined in pursuing a policy which eventuated in a series of General Eyres which was to prove a most potent threat to local autonomy. Edward I and his two successors saw in the infiltration and ultimate domination by English judges of the judiciary in the islands a possible means of annexing them to the Realm (as distinct from the Crown) of England. This prospect arose from the fact that the courts were the main legislative authority in the early 14th. century, so that once English jurisdiction had been established in the archipelago's courts, the islands would become virtually as much part of England as the Isle of Wight. Furthermore, as mediaeval legislation often appeared to forbid something when in reality it meant that the activity in question could not be indulged in without a licence that had to be paid for, it followed that court rulings constituted an ideal means of raising money time and time again — which was exactly what Otto required of the islands.

As an initial measure the scope of the local assizes, which had been held since the loss of Continental Normandy, was progressively widened during Otto's first tenure of office (1275–94), their commissions being extended to cover 'all pleas'. As a further step periodical Commissions of Inquiry were instituted, charged with establishing the 'extente' of the king's holdings in the islands (and also those of lay and ecclesiastical fiefs), as well as investigating the conduct of the administration and hearing complaints.

These preliminaries paved the way for combining both the assizes and the inquiry commissions into a General Eyre, at first employing local justices who were subservient to Otto de Grandison and later on replacing them with English judges. Such General Eyres were entrusted with the three-fold function of enquiring into royal lands and rights, of hearing the complaints of the islanders (the erstwhile functions of the inquiry commissions) and, in addition, taking the assizes and 'all other pleas'. Thus an essentially English institution was foisted on the islanders, largely at the instigation of Otto and his subordinates who stood to gain thereby as the enormous sums paid in fines were remitted to de Grandison and *not* to the royal exchequer. What it boiled down to therefore, was that men who had a financial interest in insular exploitation proposed that an eyre should be held, had themselves or their underlings appointed as justices — and then enjoyed the execution of their own judgements. In these circumstances it is hardly surprising that the islanders felt that they were being subjected to an intolerable imposition and protested that their 'laws and customs' were being disregarded.

The sufferings of the islands during the Gascony War of 1294–8, when devastating French raids had wrought terrible havoc, provided a cynical excuse for holding the First General Eyre of 1299, ostensibly as a tidying-up operation. In view of the fact that even before the outbreak of war there had been complaints about the oppressive conduct of Guillaume de St. Remy (Otto's sub-warden), this First General Eyre required the islanders to set down their 'laws and customs' in writing — but only gave the Guernesiais a fortnight in which to do so, demonstrating clearly that the gesture was nothing but a hollow mockery. Furthermore, as the Court was presided over by the Prior of Wenlock, a cousin of Otto de Grandison, it is not surprising that any complaints against officials were quickly dismissed.

The Second General Eyre of 1304 was essentially an occasion for straining the law in Otto's favour with a view to extracting every possible penny from the inhabitants. For almost every action somebody would be fined. If the accused were convicted, he would obviously be fined — and if he were not convicted, then his accuser (possibly a jury of presentment) would be fined for false accusation.

The Third General Eyre in 1309 dealt with a number of Quo

Warranto Writs — i.e., writs requiring the islanders to explain and prove by what warrant they claimed their rights and privileges. Edward II was obviously trying to apply to the islands the device whereby his father had successfully curtailed local privileges in England. In face of intense resentment the matter was adjourned to the Court of King's Bench, where it hung fire.

The Fourth General Eyre, in 1320, was the upshot of a petition to the king in which the islanders complained of extortion, imprisonment without trial, and other tyrannical acts by Otto's officials. This time the bench was occupied by local magnates and for once the participation of the jurats in the proceedings was not made farcical by their being overawed by English judges in league with Otto. Some of Otto's officials were fined and ordered to return property that they had fraudulently acquired, and judgement was delivered that the ancient 'laws and customs' should be enjoyed by the islanders. Furthermore, one of Otto's most notorious henchmen, Gautier de la Salle, was condemned and hanged. As this is Guernsey's outstanding 'cause célèbre', it deserves further attention.

Many years previously, early in 1304, a group of officials, prominent among whom was Ranulph Gautier (an ex-Bailiff and the probable builder of La Tourgand — see Part IV, Chapter Three) set out for the Priory of Lihou Island to arrest Thomas Le Rouvet (hailing from Les Rouvêts in Saint Pierre-du-Bois) who had murdered one of the monks, Brother Jean del Espin. Le Rouvet resisted arrest and in the ensuing skirmish was killed by Ranulph Gautier, who thereupon sought sanctuary in Saint Sampson's Church and subsequently secured a guaranteed immunity from prosecution for homicide by abjuring the island (i.e. undertaking to quit it, never to return unless pardoned by the King). Gautier was in fact granted such a pardon by Edward I the following March and on the strength of this returned to Guernsey where, incurring the enmity of de Grandison's subordinates by leading resistance to their depredations, he was (as testified by his nephew, Gerard Philippe, in a petition to the King) held in Castle Cornet by Gautier de la Salle and there tortured and finally done to death by de la Salle and a number of accomplices. De la Salle's accomplices escaped, but he himself was apprehended and, following sentence, was hanged at the Courtil de Gibet in St. Andrew's after having halted to make his last confession at the spot still known as the 'Bailiff's Cross' — not because he had at any time been bailiff in the modern sense of the word, but because in the early 14th. century any official of the Lord of the Isles was frequently so designated. His 'villa' (or holding), called 'La Petite Ville', was forfeit to the Crown as the estate of a felon, and is to this day known as 'La Ville au Roi'. (Needless to say, the whole farrago about a well and silver cups hidden in a rick to incriminate the well's owner, so beloved of raconteurs, is utterly without foundation.)

The Fourth Eyre's championing of insular 'laws and customs' was naturally displeasing to Otto de Grandison, especially as it was followed by a petition from the islanders for his dismissal. When the Gerard d'Oron affair followed hard upon the heels of the 1320 Eyre, Otto decided that his personal intervention was called for, and in 1323 he paid his one and only visit to his 'estate'. It is hardly surprising, therefore, that in the same year the Fifth General Eyre quashed the Fourth's judgement and was deaf to the jurats' plea that Gerard d'Oron's appointment was invalid for lack of instructions to rule according to local 'laws and customs'.

This *volte face* caused general alarm, from the seigneurs fearing for their holdings to the common people enduring fines and petty acts of oppression — while all the inhabitants resented their traditional rights being regarded as a franchise to which they had to show a title. Otto's death in 1328 failed to allay these fears. The upshot was that when Edward III's judges arrived in 1331 to hold the Sixth General Eyre they were met at St. Peter-Port by a crowd 500 strong led by the joint wardens (Pierre Bernard de Pynsole and Laurens de Gaillard), plus 21 other prominent personages — all of whom, with their fingers firmly planted on the popular pulse, were sworn to resist every attack on local liberties. When these spokesmen protested that 'their customs belonged to them alone, that the king had no right to modify them or impose new ones: and that they were ready to defend them with their lives', the riotous crowd backed them up with shouted threats and cries of 'Oui, Oui, Oui'.

Despite this defiance (which cost the two wardens their appointments) the judges once again produced Quo Warranto Writs challenging island liberties in general. The protests of the demonstrators were more formally re-stated in Court by the dictum, 'Dominus Rex Angliae nichil habet in Insula hic nisi statum Ducis' ('The Lord King of England has no status in this island save that of Duke'). Consequently the matter was adjourned to the Court of King's Bench — an action which, the islanders complained, was itself an infringement of their ancient rights.

Furthermore, they argued in a special petition in 1333 that they had no need to answer the writs as English statutes only bound those who held of the king as tenants of his Crown, whereas they (an ancient cantlet of the Duchy of Normandy) held of the king as their duke. This protest was reinforced by the action of the Abbé de Mont St. Michel — the largest landholder in Guernsey — who challenged the competence of the Court of King's Bench to hear cases from the Channel Isles, as island custom prescribed that pleas should be determined in the island of their origin, by their own jurats.

This contention was still unresolved when the Hundred Years War broke out. There is a widespread impression that nothing much occurred between the start of this conflict in 1337 and the Battle of Sluys in 1340. In fact 'nothing much' consisted of a two-year enemy occupation of Guernsey, Sark and Alderney. Once the islands had been recovered, Edward III decided that because of their strategic value it behoved him to be conciliatory — especially as the French remained in occupation of Castle Cornet until 1345. The upshot was Edward III's Charter of 1341, by which he finally abandoned all attempts to subject the islands to centralised control:

> Considering how faithfully the beloved men of our Isles have ever maintained their loyalty towards the Kings of England, and how much they have suffered in defence of their Islands and of our rights and honour, we concede for ourselves and our heirs that they hold and retain all privileges, immunities and customs granted by our forebears or of other legal competency and that they enjoy them freely without molestation by ourselves, our heirs and our officers.

No more General Eyres were ever held. Not only was Otto dead, but his system with him — a fact which remains true despite the extraordinary spectacle of a statue of this most hated figure in island history being accorded a prominent position outside the banking premises in Helvitia Court on the South Esplanade. The islanders were free — as indeed they still are. 'Me? I'm Guernsey!'

Chapter Four

THE PERIOD OF POLITICAL ADOLESCENCE (1341–1481)

BORN AS the unlooked-for progeny of military defeat in 1204, Guernsey's political life had, throughout a perilous childhood, survived the attempts of the monarchy to stifle it with Eyres and writs and those of the warden to bleed it to death by exactions. Its survival secured for the nonce by Edward III's Charter, it was now to enter upon its adolescence and the definitive development of the institutions which were to characterize its maturity. It was not an adolescence devoid of menace. Apart from physical attacks by the French during the Hundred Years War, there were two occasions during the period when all the islands came near to sharing the fate of Joseph when his brothers sold him to the Ishmaelites — and were thus in danger of joining Les Iles Chausey as mere adjuncts of France.

The first of these threats arose when, in pursuance of his efforts to achieve a permanent peace with France (which was finally agreed in the autumn of 1396) Richard II undertook to marry Isabella, the seven-year-old daughter of Charles VI. As part of the bargain Charles pressed for the surrender of the Channel Isles as an integral part of Normandy. The wedding took place in the November of the same year, but in the event this clause was not included in the marriage settlement. It was, however, a close shave.

The second danger came about in 1463. Jersey having already been seized in 1461 by French forces under her cousin — and most likely with her connivance (she seeing in the islands a refuge for Lancastrian hopes after her defeat at Towton) — Margaret of Anjou in 1463 offered the archipelago to Louis XI in return for aid to the Lancastrian cause. As she had made a similar offer concerning Calais to get support for her Northumberland expedition of the previous year, Louis regarded both offers as chancy speculations in futures. In the event, Jersey was re-taken in 1468 and the offer came to nothing, Margaret herself being finally defeated and taken prisoner by Edward IV at Tewkesbury in 1471.

Neither threat to the islands' continued independence having materialised, Guernsey by 1482 had reached a stage in her political development where the institutions of government were recognisably akin to those of today, with its own governor representing the Crown; its own fully-established court system, and its own legislative organ in the form of the States. The evolution whereby this result was achieved has now to be investigated.

During this adolescent period the seeds of self-government were to be found in the fact that the islands had their own customary law, the very existence of which necessitated a separate administration to apply it. The opportunity for these seeds to germinate was provided by the slackening of royal control arising from the pre-occupations of the Hundred Years War. Centuries later, in a much larger island, there was a dictum that 'England's difficulty is Ireland's opportunity'. A very similar situation applied in the case of the Channel Isles in the 14th and 15th centuries where, taking advantage of 'England's difficulty', the islanders converted the royal institutions to their own use for the attainment of their own objectives.

It is interesting to note that growth towards self-government occurred despite the neglect of any attempt to overthrow the previous institutions and replace them with others geared to the requirements of autonomy. On the contrary, the administration remained feudal, with the islanders taking no active part in their own government in their own right. None of the feudal obligations was repudiated and no attempt was made to replace any of them by special administrative arrangements of the islanders' own devising. In this context, Professor Le Patourel has pointed out that it was the possession of their ancient customary laws by the islanders that was the *fons et origo* of their constitutional development towards autonomy, enabling them as it did to argue that they were not bound by English statutes. The instrument whereby this argument was transmitted into the fact of autonomy was to be found in the institutions employed to protect and administer that law.

Summing up, therefore, it may be said that it was by adapting existing institutions and by laying more stress on the duties of officials towards their fellow-islanders than on their duties towards the king, that royal administration was gradually converted into insular self-government. It is this process of institutional adaptation which now has to be considered.

The perils of the Hundred Years War gave the wardens little

time for anything apart from their military functions, obliging them to delegate other administrative duties. Thus the status of the Receiver (the lineal predecessor of the modern Comptroller du Roi) was raised, and he became the official responsible for rendering accounts to the Exchequer.

The discontinuance of the General Eyre after 1331 led to the warden being given power to exercise full jurisdiction in all causes 'in accordance with the laws of the islands'. This power, however, was not exercised by the warden himself, the convention having become firmly established that the Bailiff should preside over Courts in Guernsey and the Prévôts in Alderney and Sark. In this connection it should be noted that the bailiff was 'the King's Bailiff' and held the Court in the king's name — and not the warden's. He was not, strictly speaking, a judge, but directed the procedure of the Courts and pronounced judgement as found by the jurats, who rendered all judgements and assessed all fines. The bailiff was responsible for executing their findings.

The bailiff presided over several types of Courts. First came Les Plaids Vicomtaux (or Plaids d'Héritage), a court which was held fortnightly and dealt with cases involving real estate. Secondly came La Cour Mobilière, which was held weekly and dealt with cases involving chattels, debts, and trespass. The third court was La Cour des Etrangers, which was held daily (if necessary) for the purpose of administering the Law Merchant. The most important of all, however, was La Cour des Chefs Plaids held (then as now) at Christmas, Easter and Michaelmas. It was the most solemn form of the court — and indeed, the King's Feudal Court, which all Seigneurs of Fiefs had to attend to pay suit of service. The Receiver and the Bordiers were also obliged to attend.

It was this Feudal Court which became the instrument *par excellence* for the attainment of independence. Its potentiality as an emergent legislature had already been apparent in 1323 when the justices at the Fifth General Eyre had commanded that their ordinances should be read out annually at the Michaelmas Chief Pleas. In this Court the jurats declared and interpreted the law, and in so doing made law, but on the other hand, it was held that the law ultimately resided in the community which might refuse to sanction the jurats' interpretation.

It must be remembered that the general outlook in the Middle Ages was that legislation (which in those days was, in any case, exceptional) should be the act of the prince with the consent of the people. It might therefore originate in a petition by the people. Hence the earliest legislation took the form of a petition to the king in the name of the bailiff, the jurats and 'the community', the royal assent being expressed in Letters Patent. The earliest example known to us of such a legislative process is found in a petition of the year 1305 for the right to levy a toll on shipping to finance repairs to St. Peter-Port jetty. The presence of the Seigneurs of the Fiefs at the Cour des Chefs Plaids led to their taking an active part in the proceedings, being consulted as educated people on matters of law, and adding the weight of their opinions to the judgements of the jurats.

This participation in the work of the Court of Chief Pleas by the seigneurs proved to be of incalculable significance. During the 15th. century the authority assumed by the bailiff and jurats to lead and speak for the community, coupled with their practice of consulting the leading members of insular society, gradually led to the development of the States, which gave institutional form to the previous vague 'consent of the community'. The rectors of the parishes attended this enlarged version of Chief Pleas (for that is what it was) at an early date, forming as they did the chief, if not the only, educated element in the community at large. It is possible that it was their presence which gave rise to the name 'Les États', as the gathering represented the various estates (also 'états') of society — gentry (jurats), clergy (rectors), and the 'Third Estate' (the constables of parishes, whose attendance had also become customary).

Although doubtless convened on previous occasions (as, for example, in 1429, when there assembled an embryonic States prototype, the precise composition of which is uncertain), the earliest gathering of this nature of which a record survives took place in 1481, when the purpose of the meeting was the discussion of dealings with the French. Thus the outcome was that by the end of the 'adolescent period' the States consisted of the bailiff, the jurats, the rectors and the constables of the parishes (the heads of parochial administration). This body was by no means as yet a separate legislature in its own right, the rectors and constables merely being summoned to advise the Court, which either petitioned the king for any legislation that might be needed or, in some cases of lesser importance, issued ordinances having the force of law. It must be emphasised that it was the Court, and not the States, which issued such Ordinances.

Chapter Five

THE ATTAINMENT OF POLITICAL PERSONALITY (1481–1560)

THE CHANNEL ISLES had suffered repeatedly during the Hundred Years War, while the Wars of the Roses had led indirectly to a French occupation of Jersey and even to an offer to sell the archipelago to France. Piracy added to these tribulations, and the trouble became so acute as to lead to island traders complaining to Pope Sixtus IV about the extent of piratical molestation.

The upshot was that just over two years before his death in 1483, Edward IV obtained from Pope Sixtus IV a Bull of Neutrality, forbidding on pain of excommunication and interdict any attack on ships, persons or goods in the islands or in the sea surrounding them. It ordered that the islands should be treated as neutral in time of war and that all ships and goods should be immune from capture within their seas 'as far as the sight of man goes'. In addition the Bull pronounced 'a sentence of anathema and eternal damnation with confiscation of goods on all who shall land in the islands to burn, plunder and murder the inhabitants, or shall carry out such crimes within sight of the islands as far as human eye shall reach'. This declaration of neutrality was ordered to be posted on the cathedrals of Canterbury, London, Salisbury, Nantes, St. Pol de Leon, Tréguier, and the church of St. Peter-Port (clearly indicating, incidentally, that at the time St. Peter-Port must have been the principal town in the archipelago). The Bull was enthusiastically accepted, not only in the islands, but also in France, where both Charles VIII and the Duke of Brittany had it proclaimed in the ports of their dominions: and this special status was enforced by the courts both of France and of the Isles.

(It is interesting, however, to mention in passing that, enthusiastically accepted though this Bull was, proof of its failure completely to eradicate piracy in local waters is furnished by a macabre episode in Guernsey's history early in the reign of Elizabeth I. In 1565 a pirate ship — the *John* of Sandwich — was wrecked off the island's coast and its captain, Richard Higgins, together with some of his crew, was captured and the whole party imprisoned in Castle Cornet while the Queen's pleasure in the matter was sought. When this became known the following year it was to the effect that, some of those arrested having been deceived into thinking that they had embarked on a purely commercial voyage, only 'the most culpable' were to be executed, while the rest were to be sent to London to sue for pardon. Higgins being obviously 'the most culpable', he was taken in November 1566 to Saint Martin's Point and there hanged from a gibbet situated where the light and fog signal now stands, with his dangling body subsequently left as an object lesson for other marauders. The joys of *schadenfreude* were vouchsafed to spectators assembled on the flat stretch of turf amid the rocks still to be seen below the Idle Rocks Hotel.)

Although sometimes breached, this privilege of neutrality, the Reformation notwithstanding, continued in force for two centuries. Thus in 1586 William Camden wrote, 'Here is alwaies a continual truce, as it were; and lawfull it is for Frenchman and others, how hot soever the warre is, to have repaire hither too and fro without danger, and to maintain entercourse of trafficke in security'. This status consolidated the feeling of a distinct insular identity and thus produced a further strengthening of local autonomy.

At the time Henry VII came to the throne, the Lordship of the Isles was in the hands of the Countess of Warwick, Anne de Beauchamp, but effectively authority was exercised by Sir Richard Harliston whom, despite his Yorkist affinities, Henry confirmed in the office of 'Captain-in-Chief of the Islands of Jersey, Guernsey, Sark and Alderney', which Edward IV had granted him by patent of January 13th., 1473. Before long, however, Harliston was attainted for joining the Earl of Lincoln in Lambert Simnel's Rising, in connection with which he had already attempted to establish himself as Lord of the Isles under the protection of France and the Duchess of Burgundy, only to find his design thwarted by the resistance of the Jersey seigneurs. Astonishingly, Henry pardoned him late in 1486, but he had already been deprived of his office of Captain-in-Chief. (He was finally attainted yet again in 1494 as a supporter of Perkin Warbeck and eventually died in exile.)

After Harliston's treason Henry persuaded the Countess of Warwick to renounce the Lordship of the Isles and so ended an appointment first held by John as Count of Mortain 300 years previously. With this anachronism out of the way the king now decided on establishing distinct government for the two Bailiwicks. It is true that in a sense Guernsey had had a governor of its own since 1478, when Sir John Dichefield was appointed 'Captain of Guernsey'. Sir John had been succeeded by Sir Edward Brampton in 1482, and he in his turn by Thomas Rydley in 1484, and Edmund Weston in 1485. All four, however, had been subordinate to Harliston as 'Captain-in-Chief'. What Henry now did was to appoint for each Bailiwick a separate governor directly responsible to him. In Guernsey Edmund Weston, who since 1485 had been the 'Keeper' as Harliston's subordinate in the island, now became 'Captain of Guernsey' directly under the Crown. After him, in 1488, came John Apris. Thus for the first time Guernsey indisputably had its own direct representative of the monarch.

By a quirk of fate it was Henry's individual gubernatorial appointment in Jersey which was destined indirectly to exert a profound influence on Guernsey's political evolution. The atrocious behaviour of the governor concerned, Matthew Baker, so alienated public sympathy in that island as to lead its people to make complaint to the king. As a result Baker was eventually dismissed and the 'many and divers grievances doleances and complaints' brought to his notice caused Henry to issue a Writ of the Privy Seal in 1494, followed by an Order-in-Council in 1495. These two Orders constitute a Code of Regulations for the conduct of the Administration which, although primarily arising out of a dispute in Jersey, was, in fact, applied to Guernsey as well.

In the first place the Code of Henry VII (as it came to be known) aimed at ensuring adequate defence measures, requiring a day's corvée per inhabitant on fortifications and calling on seigneurs to help in the defence of the island. Secondly, the Code included measures to protect the population from arbitrary encroachments on their ancient rights and liberties. The governor was forbidden to imprison anybody on his own authority except for treason: likewise he was debarred from interfering in the proceedings of the Royal Court. In addition he was required to allow free movement to and from the island, subject to his receiving prior notification. Furthermore, the bailiff was to be nominated by the king without gubernatorial interference and neither the governor nor the jurats were to levy taxes, save by royal consent. Should any dispute arise between the governor and the jurats, it was to be referred to the Privy Council. Lastly, the Code provided against misconduct by the insular authorities or infringement of the king's rights. Thus jurats were to take an oath on assuming office and were to keep a signed record of the Acts of the Court — and, what is more, they were to be deprived of their office if it were not well and loyally executed. The Island Seal was only to be used in the presence of seven jurats, parish constables were to be elected in a regular manner, and the king's right to levy customs was safeguarded. The importance of this Code can hardly be exaggerated, as it was the spirit animating it which was to prove the basis of all future constitutional development in the islands.

Definitive recognition of an individual political personality attaching to Guernsey came in 1560, with the Charter of Elizabeth I. Previous Charters given by Richard II, Edward IV, Henry VII, Henry VIII, and Edward VI, had applied to the archipelago generally, but that of Elizabeth I applied specifically to Guernsey, a separate one concerning Jersey being granted two years later. Besides reiterating the freedom from 'all tolls, exactions or dues' in 'all towns, markets and ports of the realm of England' conceded to the islanders by Richard II and subsequent monarchs, the Elizabethan Charter particularly acknowledged Guernsey's neutral status by expressly authorising trading with all persons, even the enemy, in time of war; besides confirming the jurisdiction of the Royal Court in all causes arising in the island; and laying down the right of the Guernesiais not to be cited by writs or processes issuing out of English courts, but to have all matters heard and determined in the island.

A neutral territory, with its own governor pledged to uphold its own laws administered in its own courts to which alone its inhabitants were answerable, the Bailiwick of Guernsey had now acquired a fully individual political personality. Its adolescence over, it entered upon its manhood.

Chapter Six

THE RULE OF THE SAINTS (1561–1689)

THIS PERIOD of the 16th. and 17th. centuries is of the greatest importance in Guernsey's political development as it saw many of the modern institutions of government taking shape, with constitutional developments accompanying repeated disputes between the islanders (in effect the island gentry) and the governors. Furthermore, from this period onwards Guernsey's system of government embarked on the intimate relationship with the sovereign and the Privy Council which has characterized it ever since. Thus to this day legislation takes the form of Orders-in-Council (though mostly originating in the island) — a relic of the conciliar government which was ubiquitous throughout the monarch's domains in Tudor times.

For the greater part of the period the Presbyterian Establishment held sway in the Bailiwick and its influence, far from being confined to the spiritual sphere, so pervaded the secular one as to exert considerable influence on the course of political development. Not only was the membership of the Colloque to a large extent identical with that of the States, consisting as it did of the governor, bailiff, jurats, ministers and elders of the churches; but in addition the ecclesiastical organisation became so powerful that it bade fair to supplant the civil administration — and it was strong enough in the latter part of the period to ensure that Guernsey should declare for parliament in the Civil War.

At the head of the administration stood the governor (often referred to as the captain), who was appointed by the sovereign and exercised vice-regal powers, being especially charged with protecting the Bailiwick from invasion and obtaining intelligence about French dispositions for the monarch. He was also responsible for the civil administration, taking the Crown revenues of every kind, paying the expenses of government out of them, and keeping the rest as his salary — and although such an arrangement inevitably made for friction between him and the people on fiscal questions, he was nevertheless supposed to keep the inhabitants of the Bailiwick contented.

Ranged against the governor was the Royal Court which, thanks to the powers and prestige it had accumulated during the previous period, had become the chief organ of administration. The bailiff at its head was appointed by the monarch, but effectively by the governor (despite the terms of Henry VII's Code) — a fact that was to prove a fruitful cause of dispute. The jurats on the other hand (who by Henry's Code could be dismissed by the Crown for misconduct) were judges both of law and of fact. As the decisions of the Royal Court were final except for an appeal to the sovereign, and as, furthermore, Guernseymen were notoriously litigious, there was a continuous flood of appeals to the Privy Council.

Halfway through this period the bailiff, Amice de Carteret, who was appointed in 1601, swept away many obsolete customs that had accumulated around the Court since the Middle Ages, codifying the laws and reorganising procedures. To ease the pressures on the jurats, de Carteret in 1608 introduced the system of dividing the jurats into three sets of four to deal with minor cases. The first quartet served from Christmas to Easter, the second from Easter to Michaelmas, and the third from Michaelmas to Christmas. This system persists to the present day, with the bailiff (or Deputy Bailiff) and the four jurats of the term constituting the Ordinary Court and the Contract court. All 12 jurats are of course on the bench when the Full Court sits.

Although still summoned primarily to advise the Court, the States (often at this time referred to as the Generality) during the 16th. and 17th. centuries increasingly came to be regarded as the proper body to deal with the more important matters and in particular passing ordinances to meet sudden emergencies (such as precautions against bringing the plague from Southampton). It was also its function to represent the island in any exceptional dealings with the English government, and to defend insular liberties against English encroachments. Lastly, it came to be recognised as the appropriate organ for imposing taxes (mostly to finance armaments); or to pay for the expenses of sending delegates to London to represent the views of the islanders before the Privy Council; or to pay for students preparing for the Ministry at Saumur or Geneva.

Paradoxically, even though it temporarily overshadowed the civil government, the formidable Calvinist church organisation was largely instrumental in advancing the standing and importance of the States. This stemmed from the considerable contribution

RELIGIOUS

1. The dig at Les Fouaillages, L'Ancresse. In foreground — entrance to the tomb older than the Pyramids.

2. Les Fouaillages (*c.* 4500 B.C.).

3. La Platte Mare Burial Chamber (*c.* 3000 B.C.).

4. La Gran'mère du Chimquière (*c.* 3000 B.C.).

5. (*above*) St Tugual's Chapel, Herm (pre-1251).

6. (*left*) Parish Church of St Peter-Port (earliest part pre-1048).

7. (*opposite above*) Ruins of Priory of St. Mary, Lihou Island (pre-1156).

8. (*opposite below*) Chapel of Ste. Appoline (1392).

9. (*left*) Christianized Menhir, St Saviour's.

10. (*below*) The Wesley Stone (1787)

11. (*opposite above*) Frère Déodat an[d] his Little Chapel (*c.* 1935).

12. (*opposite below*) Chapel of Christ the Healer (1957).

13. Burning of Catherine Cauchés, her daughters and grandson (1556).

14. Feudal Court of Fief La Cour.

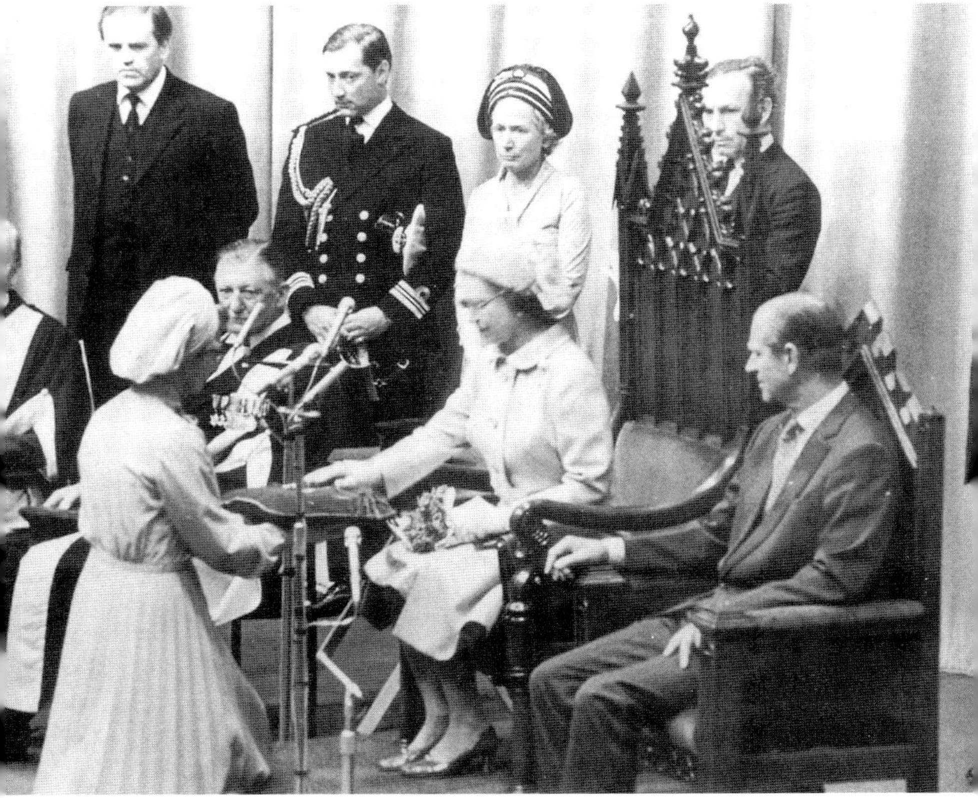

15. Court of Chief Pleas: La Dame des Eperons renders homage to H.M. the Queen (1978).

6. (*above*) Feudal Court of Le Fief Beuval in session (inter-war years).

7. (*right*) Le Colombier at Torteval.

18. (*above*) Mr. Bert Hammond raising the Clameur de Haro in Alderney (1956).

19. (*left*) H.R.H. the Princess Elizabeth and H.R.H. the Duke of Edinburgh with the Seigneur and Dame of Sark (1949).

20. (*left*) La Dame de Sercq with the Colombier symbolizing her authority.

21. (*below*) Feudal Court of Anneville and Fauville in session (1980).

POLITICAL

2. (*opposite above*) H.M. The Queen presiding over the States of Guernsey (1957).

3. (*opposite below*) H.M. The Queen presiding over the States of Alderney (1957).

4. (*above*) The induction of Vice-Admiral Sir Charles Mills as Lieutenant-Governor (1969).

5. (*right*) The Royal Court House: Seat of Guernsey's Government.

26. (*left*) Local Government: Constables' Office, St Peter-Port.

27. (*below left*) Local Government: Miniature Bâtons to symbolize Constables' authority.

28. (*below right*) Local Government: Official limits of the Town in 1700.

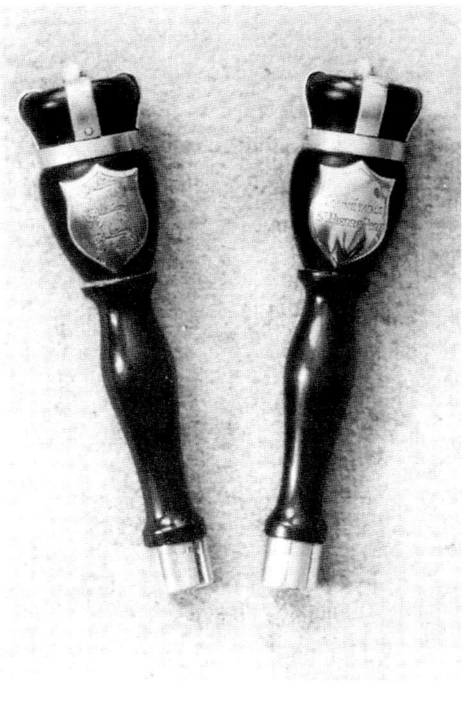

made to the political education of Guernseymen by the 'Discipline ecclésiastique', whose Consistoires and Colloque accustomed them to the discussion of public affairs.

Nevertheless, the States as yet performed very little legislative work (although this body in 1581 did help prepare the legal code approved by Elizabeth I the following year as 'L'Approbation des Lois'). Legislation was still overwhelmingly by royal order, the monarch frequently acting *proprio motu*. Thus early in the 17th. century, when the States of both Bailiwicks were still practically identical, the Bailiff of Jersey in a submission to the Privy Council, summarised their functions as follows:

> Cette assemblée se fait quand il est question de pourvoir à la place vacante de quelqu'un des jurés de la cour, ou bien quand il est question d'envoyer vers le Roi pour les affaires publiques de l'île, ou quand il est question de pourvoir à la sureté du pays quand il est menacé de quelque danger, ou quand il est question de lever quelque argent pour la necessité publique.

The competence of the assembly obviously remained markedly restricted.

Turning from political trends in general to public affairs in particular, one finds the outset of the period characterized by severe constitutional disputes over the financing of defence. In the early years of the reign of Elizabeth I the war with France in support of the Huguenot insurgents gave rise to considerable anxiety about the defence of Guernsey and the vital St. Peter-Port roadstead — despite the Bailiwick's neutral status. The governor, Sir Francis Chamberlain, submitted alarming reports about the island's defence capacity, emphasising that normal corvée obligations were insufficient for putting in hand extensive refortifications and that the island revenues could not raise the money needed. In these circumstances advantage was taken of an Act of Edward VI, which gave the Crown the right to all chantries, obits and minor religious foundations, and accordingly a Commission was appointed in 1561 consisting of the captain, the bailiff and the jurats, charged with realising such property to defray defence costs.

Most of the jurats were Catholics (and had been implicated in the burning of Catherine Cauchés and her daughters) and were therefore ill-disposed towards any diversion of chantry funds to government defence works. They consequently adopted an obstructive and hostile attitude which led the Privy Council to make use of the powers implicit in Henry VII's Code, as a dispute between the governor and jurats obviously existed. Thus in 1565 the bailiff and the jurats were summoned to London. They were collectively fined £1,000 for having spent some of the money which had been collected in lawsuits against the governor concerning the rights of the Crown — and seven jurats were dismissed. Their involvement both in the execution of Catherine Cauchés and her daughters, and also in the street fray against the Huguenots in 1564, were taken into account by the Privy Council in reaching its decision.

Although the new jurats were more amenable, Elizabeth I was still dissatisfied as to the safety of the Island, and in 1567 a Royal Commission was appointed to go thoroughly into defence. It reported that, besides encouraging the neglect of fortifications, Guernsey's neutrality had also sapped the morale of the population — 'They trustid altogethere to the Pope's Bulls and other placetts obtayned of the French'. It added that as a consequence the inhabitants were ill-armed and ill-prepared, so that 200 soldiers could take the island. The Commissioners ended by recommending the sale of church bells to raise defence funds.

Chamberlain's attempts to increase revenue by strictly enforcing the collection of Crown dues led eventually to a constitutional dispute between himself as governor and the Royal Court. Trouble arose when, on behalf of the Farmers of the Revenue, the Procureur de la Reine took proceedings against the dean for encroaching on Crown Rights. At this the Court (hand-in-glove with the dean) confiscated the document regarding the ancient precedent on which the Crown's case rested: whereupon the Procureur refused to go on and left the Court, rendering it incapable of acting for lack of the presence of the Queen's Officers. The Court reacted to this by imprisoning the Procureur for contempt, and demanding a new one. It also appointed representatives to go to the Privy Council, but two of these were members of the Fortifications Commission and Chamberlain imprisoned them to stop them leaving Guernsey until the defence works were completed.

There was now a complete constitutional deadlock, with the Court refusing to sit for lack of a Procureur and the governor insisting that the existing Procureur be recognised and the case against the dean prosecuted. In these circumstances Chamberlain begged the Privy Council to appoint a Commission of Inquiry, and the upshot was that the Procureur was directed to resign 'voluntarily' and the governor to appoint a new one: while the Court for its part was ordered never again to refuse justice. A further — and more lasting — result was that the report of the Inquiry Commission led to the Orders-in-Council of 1569, which contained two important regulations for the future conduct of Guernsey's government. In the first place the governor was forbidden to imprison anyone henceforth except for military or revenue causes; while, secondly, it was laid down that any future dispute between the governor and the bailiff and/or jurats should be considered in conference between them, with the proviso that failing agreement within forty days, anyone who wished could appeal to the Privy Council.

Sir Francis Chamberlain died in 1570 and his successor, Sir Thomas Leighton, addressed himself anew to the defence problem, only eventually to find that he, too, became embroiled in confrontations on the issue of royal revenue, the nature of local law and the status of neutrality. Leighton's policy was to finance refortification by levying a duty on all goods (foreign or not) arriving in foreign ships. He obtained a Royal Warrant in 1571 to authorise his adopting this course of action, and the Privy Council upheld him despite the protests of the merchants.

Although Leighton as an ardent Puritan was more in tune with the Calvinist Establishment than his Roman Catholic predecessor, and consequently enjoyed an initial honeymoon period, he was to find that religious accord was to avail him little when the Guernesiais felt that their ancient privileges were under threat. Trouble flared up in 1578 with popular disturbances which obliged the bailiff and jurats to take refuge in Castle Cornet. As a result they applied to the Privy Council for a Commission 'to bring the people to better obedience'. At the same time some Guernsey people appeared before the Privy Council alleging that they were wronged touching their Liberties and the Administration of Justice. Accordingly a Royal Commission was appointed (including Leighton in its membership) to investigate 'defects touching the jurisdiction of the Bailiff and Jurats'.

When the Commission arrived in Guernsey in September 1579, the bailiff and the jurats joined forces with the complainants to blame Leighton for all disaffection. It was obvious that the bailiff and jurats had persuaded the complainants that a joint attack on the governor might lead to a reduction in the dues he levied. What is more, the Commissioners' inquiry only served to increase the disorder in the island, one of them (John Hammond) even encouraging the malcontents, so that Leighton was driven to ask the Privy Council to insist that 'more respect be had of Her Majesty and Her Officers'.

The Privy Council replied with two Orders-in-Council (1580) forbidding the bailiff and jurats and the inhabitants to 'intermeddle in anything touching Her Majesty's rights, revenues or privileges'. These Orders, however, had no effect. Not only did the disorders continue, but the Royal Court imprisoned the Farmers of the Revenue. Leighton reported that many people refused to pay their feudal dues to the Crown unless their obligations were 'proved true by Guernsey witnesses and they perjure themselves to acquit one another'. Leighton regarded the chief instigators of the trouble as the bailiff (William de Beauvoir), his brother (a jurat), and Nicholas Martin (another jurat), and warned that if they were not removed the garrison would have to be kept permanently on a war footing 'to repress these mutinies'. Accordingly in 1581 these three were arrested and taken before the Privy Council, where they were persuaded to resign 'voluntarily'.

Considering the fracas as a whole, it seems that the complaints against Leighton were compiled on the simple principle of listing all grievances of every description and blaming the governor for the lot. Many of them related to taxation and royal dues, while others alleged misgovernment and tyranny, imprisoning men without orders of the Court, and compelling Guernseymen to take ship against pirates in defiance of their privilege exempting them from service outside the island. It is true that Leighton had been a strict and careful administrator who husbanded the Queen's revenues, getting in all he could, and reviving lapsed feudal dues. As for service against pirates, Leighton claimed that he had only used volunteers and that the complaints arose from such action putting a stop to trade with the pirates. It would appear that basically the disturbances stemmed from distress caused by the decline of trade resulting from the Wars of Religion in France, and also from foreign resentment at alleged unfair treatment in Guernsey. Hence (possibly) the anxiety to trade with the pirates — strange conduct from God-fearing Calvinists.

Prominent among the causes of the popular discontent which had bedevilled Leighton was a feeling of dissatisfaction with the Royal Court because of the indefinite and fluid state of the law. Because of this in 1581 the Privy Council ordered the Royal Court and the Procureur to draw up a report as to the laws, customs and usages of the Isle of Guernsey to the extent that they differed from

Le Grand Coutumier de Normandie from ancient times observed in the island. To do this was a difficult task which could only have been performed adequately by a body of jurists, and, except for the bailiff and the Procureur it is unlikely that any of the Court (or for that matter of the States who were also consulted) had received any legal education. Nevertheless, the task was completed and the resulting compilation, as approved by Elizabeth I in 1582, forms the frequently cited 'Approbation des Lois, Coutumes et Usages de l'Ile de Guernsey'.

It was intended that this document should form a Code of Law for Guernsey, but the intention never took effect, as the Rev. Thomas Le Marchant, an evicted Calvinist minister, demonstrated in 1660 in his 'Remarques et Animadversions sur l'Approbation des Lois'. In time of war there was always the danger of a real clash between the necessities of defence and the terms of the island's charters, so that in such circumstances the governor was likely to find a serious constitutional question on his hands. It was in such circumstances that Leighton was again to find himself in trouble — this time over the issue of insular neutrality.

The occasion for the dispute occurred in 1586 when the governor seized four French ships in St. Peter-Port, believing them to have Spanish goods on board. The Royal Court immediately declared the seizure invalid on the grounds of Guernsey's neutrality. Leighton, however, declined to release the ships, and the Court appealed to the Privy Council — which upheld its ruling and instructed Leighton that no such arrest should again be made to the prejudice of the island's privileges. Leighton now complained to the Privy Council that the bailiff (who was none other than his own nephew, Thomas Wigmore) and the jurats had taken advantage of this dispute to levy slanderous charges of tyranny against him — and as a result the bailiff and jurats were summoned to London in 1587. To present the case for the governor the queen's Procureur (Louis de Vic) also went to London, where, the accused having hired two men to murder him, he was attacked in Westminster, and left for dead, but recovered. The upshot was that the bailiff and the jurats were consigned to the Marshalsea, de Vic's chief assailant was set in the pillory in Guernsey, and de Vic himself was appointed as the new bailiff. Leighton was vindicated and triumphant.

Although Leighton had ultimately emerged triumphant in his confrontations with the local Establishment, the experience of the clashes wrought a change in the political atmosphere which became particularly noticeable after the death of Elizabeth I, and the accession of James I, with a definite disposition manifesting itself to seek every opportunity to reduce the power of the governor and to increase that of the bailiff and the Royal Court. Thus Leighton's concluding years as governor (he held office until 1610) again saw his position challenged. What is more, on this occasion, circumstances favoured a more assertive attitude on the part of the local hierarchy, the time being opportune to press for concessions, as peace had been concluded with Spain, and the French Wars of Religion were over, so that the islands' importance as frontier fortresses was reduced. Consequently, the governor's paramountcy over the island authorities was no longer an urgent necessity, with the result that the Privy Council was increasingly reluctant to coerce the islanders to accept such supremacy. The outcome was that two petitions were forwarded to the king — one in 1604 and the other in 1607 — the nature of which shows that the Guernsey gentry was becoming conscious of itself as a political force, with the result that it was anxious to curtail the governor's prerogatives so as to acquire for itself a larger share in the government of the Bailiwick.

The petition forwarded to James I in 1604 requested that the bailiff and king's officers might be appointed by the king and not by the governor. Strictly speaking, this was already provided for in Henry VII's Code (though the provision had been honoured more in the breach than in the observance), but the request added the rider that the candidates for these posts should be elected by the States, the king appointing those so elected. It also asked that 'the ancient use and authority of assembling the States for ordering the principal affairs of the island' might be re-established. (This, of course, boiled down to asking that the States should meet more often and discuss a wider range of business.) Lastly, the petitioners prayed that the Royal Court should not be denied the ancient right of inspecting Castle Cornet to see that it was in a proper state of defence. Castle Cornet, of course, was the residence of the governor.

An Order-in-Council of 1605 dealt with this petition, refusing the first request and simply ignoring the rider — which the Privy Council presumably regarded as too audacious a concept to merit consideration. The second request was allowed without specifying what was involved in 'ordering the principal affairs of the island', while on the third point the Privy Council confined itself to expressing its confidence that the governor would, in fact, admit island leaders when requested. The decisions of the Privy Council were seen as far from satisfactory by the islanders. The next step clearly exemplified the profound nature of the influence exerted in the political sphere by the Calvinist ecclesiastical organisation. In June 1606 representatives of the States of both Jersey and Guernsey met in St. Peter-Port and jointly agreed to petition the king that the two Bailiwicks should have a Provincial States General — a suggestion obviously inspired by the Presbyterian Synod of the two Colloques which was the supreme authority in religious matters for the entire archipelago. The meeting also agreed to ask that appeals should no longer go to the Privy Council but should be heard by a Court of Appeal appointed by the States. This suggestion was three-and-a-half centuries before its time. It was obvious that there was a desire common to both Bailiwicks to be possessed of fuller self-governing powers.

Accordingly a petition listing all grievances was finally sent to James I in 1607. The evident intensity of insular dissatisfaction led the Privy Council to appoint another Commission, whose recommendations were embodied in the Order-in-Council of 1608. This Order-in-Council restricted the power of the governors and enhanced the position of the Royal Court and of the States, ruling *inter alia* that in future the Jurats should be elected by an assembly comprising the Bailiff, the Jurats and the Constables and Douzeniers of each Parish — and thereby originating the States of Election, the membership of which was later in the seventeenth century extended to include the parochial Rectors, or Ministers as they were then called (1631) and the Procureur du Roi (1671). (Prior to this — as recounted by Viscount Hatton, Governor of Guernsey 1670–1706 — a new Jurat had been chosen whenever a vacancy occurred by the votes of worshippers which their respective Constables recorded as they left their parish churches after divine service — though this expression of *vox populi* only became effective when confirmed by the Royal Court, to which the Constables were required to report the church door poll results). The governor's prerogative was circumscribed by his being required to consult the Royal Court before taking action previously regarded as unquestionably within his competence. In his concluding months in office Leighton was suffering the fate of Ozymandias.

The advanced status thus achieved by the island authorities was well exemplified in 1629, during the war with France in support of the Huguenots at La Rochelle. In response to repeated indignant representations the Privy Council eventually assured the

Guernsey spokesmen that Lord Danby's project for applying martial law should be limited to the soldiers of the garrison and would not be extended to the civil population as originally intended.

The next political confrontation was not one between governor and islanders, but between rival local magnates. When Charles I hoisted his standard at Nottingham, the entrenched rule of the Saints in Guernsey made inevitable the Bailiwick's adherence to the cause of his enemies, the self-styled 'Bien Affectionés', who branded royalists as 'Refractaires'. Among the few royalists was Jean de Quetteville, who had been bailiff since 1631. At the instigation of Pierre de Beauvoir, Sieur des Granges, he was deprived of his office and placed under arrest in 1643 for conniving in the exploit of George Carteret (he anglicized his name to avoid embarrassment in the Royal Navy), who managed to run the blockade and get supplies through to the Lieutenant-Governor, Sir Peter Osborne, who was besieged in Castle Cornet, which he was holding for the king. The senior jurat, Jean Bonamy, was then sworn in as Juge Delégué, 'pendant l'absence de Jeane Quetteville, Ecuyer, Bailli'. As de Quetteville was under arrest (he was subsequently imprisoned for a time in England) 'pendant l'absence' was apt to be of indefinite duration.

On Christmas Eve 1644 Pierre de Beauvoir, Sieur des Granges, was sworn in as bailiff on his return from London, where he had been nominated for the post by the Earl of Warwick, whom parliament had appointed as 'Governor of Guernsey' in place of the royalist, Sir Peter Osborne, who had succeeded Lord Danby on the latter's death the previous January.

In February 1647, however, Jean de Quetteville, showing considerable spirit, returned to Guernsey and claimed that he alone had the right to perform the duties of bailiff. He proceeded to convene the States a number of times as a display of his rightful authority — despite the vociferous opposition raised by de Beauvoir on each occasion. In these circumstances Lieutenant-Colonel Robert Russell, parliament's lieutenant-governor, persuaded the Court in March to declare that the office of bailiff should be regarded as vacant until the differences between the rival claimants had been settled. In the meantime Jean Careye was sworn in as Juge Delégué, and each rival bailiff found himself barred from the Court over which he claimed the exclusive entitlement to preside. At this juncture Pierre de Beauvoir indignantly declined to hand over the Seal of the Bailiwick to the Juge Delégué, and as he had strong support in his refusal, parliament appointed four M.P.s to investigate the whole matter. The upshot was de Beauvoir's confirmation in the office of bailiff, signalised by his presiding over a sitting of the Court early in December. Not long afterwards Jean de Quetteville died.

Pierre de Beauvoir's tenure of office did not in the event remain secure. Parliament deposed him in 1651, reappointed him in 1652, and then removed him again in 1653, when an Order of Parliament required that the office of bailiff be held by each of the jurats in turn for a month at a time. This arrangement lasted until 1656 when de Beauvoir was again reinstated and held office until the Restoration. In 1660 he retired and Josué Gosselin was sworn in as Juge Delégué pending the arrival in 1661 of Amais Andros, who, as Charles II's nominee, was installed as bailiff in May. The States, much discomfited by the Restoration, appealed to Sir Henry de Vic (Guernsey's greatest Cavalier who, beyond the island's shores, had consistently supported the Royalist cause at considerable cost to himself) to seek from the Sovereign 'indemnity and oblivion' regarding their misdeeds. This he did so persuasively that Charles not only granted a general pardon to his father's enemies (even including de Beauvoir therein) but also renewed the Bailiwick's ancient privileges and charters.

* * * * *

The rule of the Saints was to have an epilogue, which proved to be epochally terminative. As has already been seen, although Calvinism's body might have been mouldering in the grave after Dean de Sausmarez's imposition of Anglicanism, its soul went marching on. Indeed, it proved to be a soul sufficiently powerful to ensure, by the overthrow of Colonel John Legge, that the Roman Catholic father-in-law of the Calvinist William III would not find refuge in Guernsey as his brother had done in Jersey 40 years previously.

William III's single-minded dedication to his struggle to save his native Holland from Louis XIV left no room for any considerations of gratitude for this support of his cause to impede the vigour of his war-effort. He had no intention of allowing 'Frenchmen and others, how hot soever the warre is, to repair hither too and fro without danger' and therefore unilaterally repudiated the status of neutrality which for so long had given security to the archipelago. He did this by Order-in-Council of August 8th., 1689 which, although apologetic in tone and with the superficial appearance of being provisional, nevertheless effectively put a stop to the local franchise which had been a major formative influence on island development for over two centuries. The legacy of the Saints had indeed brought about the end of an era.

> His Majesty in Council is this day pleased to declare that (being at this time strictly obliged in his treaties with his allies and confederates to prohibit in all his dominions all trade and commerce whatsoever with France) he does not think it fit or expedient to dispense with the execution of this said order in this present and extraordinary juncture of time; yet, it is not the intention of His Majesty in any manner whatsoever to revoke or infringe upon any privileges that may have been granted by his royal predecessors to the inhabitants of the said island of Guernsey.

Chapter Seven

THE RIP VAN WINKLE CENTURY (1689–1820)

APART FROM an indignant and exasperated protest at its outset the period of 131 years from the abrogation of neutrality to the accession of George IV was for the most part one of unspectacular but steady political consolidation rather than of any marked advance. Little attempt was made by the British government to interfere in Guernsey's affairs over these years, the governors frequently being absentees and their lieutenants often ineffective. The 18th.-century struggles with France were mainly carried on in remote theatres of operations such as the Rhine or Danube basins or even in India and North America as part of the great tussle for Empire; and although these struggles in their later stages necessitated the fortification of the islands of which the "Martello" towers still serve as reminders, the great Whig and Tory potentates in London were not greatly concerned with remote and possibly barbarous islands, and so were content to let them be.

Internally, the Bailiwick's government remained an oligarchy of the leading families, with common interests and often linked by marriage. They were sufficiently efficient and public-spirited to avoid any cause for popular unrest. Furthermore, the oligarchy was self-perpetuating as the jurats were elected by the States whom they themselves dominated.

The outcry at the beginning of the period was largely a by-product of the repudiation of neutrality. William III's fight against Louis XIV necessitated the garrisoning of Guernsey and the patrolling of its sea approaches by the Royal Navy — and the discontent arose from the friction between the soldiers of the garrison and the local population.

Full details of this dispute have only recently come to light as the result of the appearance of a hitherto unrecorded pamphlet which circumstantial and internal evidence indicates as being dated December 1690 or January 1691 (new style). Called *The Complaint of the Inhabitants of the Island of Guernsey*, a reproduction of the pamphlet was published by Dr. G. Stevens

Cox in an *Historical Monograph* — an invaluable contribution to the study of island history. The people of Guernsey seem to have made two complaints, the first of which was referred by the Privy Council to Viscount Hatton (the governor) for action, while the second was dealt with by an Order-in-Council.

In their first complaint, dated August 6th., 1689, the Guernsey leaders alleged 'that they were compelled to raise a general tax to provide quarters for such officers and soldiers as cannot be lodged in public houses, and among them, for divers inhabitants who have enlisted as soldiers, and have habitations of their own; also that they were much oppressed by the soldiers not paying their landlords at the removal of quarters'.

When this complaint was passed to him by the Privy Council, Viscount Hatton on August 24th., 1689 directed that no more islanders were to be recruited and that those already recruited were to be discharged as soon as possible, and meantime were to lodge with their own families; that five sols per week billeting money should be paid to householders upon whom soldiers were quartered; and lastly that commissioned officers were to pay for their quarters out of their own pockets, with the right of complaint to the bailiff and jurats if they felt that they were overcharged.

The second complaint alleges that the circumstances giving rise to it stem from a failure to obey Hatton's instructions and contains several points of interest. In the first place it claims that for 18 months the officers of the garrison, under threat of quartering troops without payment, compelled the Royal Court to supply money at the rate of 13 sols tournois to the shilling sterling, passing on the money to the troops at the normal rate of 12 sols to the shilling. To this the complainants add that they have not so far complained of the exactions of the officers or of the burden of taxes to pay for fortifications for fear that news of any rupture between the garrison and the inhabitants might have encouraged the French to invade. (This looks suspiciously like the traditional Channel Islanders' ploy of uttering a veiled threat to throw in their lot with the French if their grievances were not remedied.)

The document goes on to say that the burden by long continuance having become insupportable, the authorities solicited the officers to have money brought over in specie from England, or to obtain it from merchants on bills of exchange. Furthermore the complaint avers that the intransigence of the officers led to the summoning of 'the three Estates of the Island', which assembly resolved 'that no more money should be raised by any publick Tax for the satisfying of these Exhorbitant demands of the Officers'. (This evidence that, once again, the States were summoned when an emergency arose, is indicative of the increasing significance of this body in the rôle of watchdog over the public welfare.)

The pamphlet goes on to allege that the officers, by threatening that the troops would mutiny if they were not adequately provided for, prevailed upon the lieutenant-governor to authorise their placing the troops upon free quarters. What is more, they did this in a violent fashion, on one occasion firing into a house and breaking down the door so as to intimidate the owner into providing three shillings a week besides food. An additional complaint was that the officers sent drummers and trumpeters outside the Cohu (i.e., the Court) with orders to create such a noise as to render proceedings impossible. A final grievance was that murders and robberies had been committed by the soldiery but that the officers removed the culprits from the jurisdiction of the Court, promising to punish them, but in fact setting them free. Furthermore, the non-availability of Castle Cornet meant that there was no prison for other offenders either.

The pamphlet concludes by asking for reimbursement of the monies handed over; for fuller accommodation for troops in Castle Cornet and in Vale Castle; and for the provision by the Crown of a civil prison.

The Privy Council dealt with these grievances by an Order-in-Council of February 1691 (new style). The Order directed in the first place that if the officers in future needed ready money for the subsistence of the troops, they were in respect thereof to give bills of exchange upon the regimental paymaster at the rate of 12 sols to the shilling. Secondly, it stipulated that soldiers were to be tried by court martial only for breaches of military discipline — any breach of the peace coming within the jurisdiction of the civil court. Thirdly, it was laid down that billeting arrangements be regulated by the civilian authorities, with no interference from military officers, save only the quarters of commissioned officers, which were to be settled by the governor or lieutenant-governor. Lastly, the Order directed that the governor was to arbitrate in any case of dispute between the soldiery and the inhabitants, reporting his actions to the Privy Council.

It will be noted that nothing was said about the reimbursement of any monies. As for the provision of a civilian prison at Crown expense, the matter hung fire for over a century before definitive action was taken. This was in 1799, when a petition from the

States to the King in Council proposed financing the construction of a prison by a general tax of sixpence per quarter of Wheate Rente, on the understanding that the subsequent cost of upkeep and payment of the staff would be the responsibility of the Crown. The upshot was that after some confusion over the choice of site, a decision was made in 1807 in favour of the location in New Street which remained in use until the move to Les Nicolles, Saint Sampson's, in 1989. The prison was accordingly constructed between 1811 and 1815 at a cost of £11,000. On completion, it was handed over to the Crown.

After the 1690 tumult and shouting had died, political life settled down to the long sleep which characterized the 18th. century (which, however, was far from devoid of incident in other directions), interrupted only by rare somnambulant stirrings. Thus, in 1709 the Customs Commissioners sought to impose their rules on insular trade, but this attempt to infringe the Bailiwick's autonomy was successfully resisted. In similar vein, in the second decade of the 18th. century Guernsey triumphed over the protests of the Southampton merchants and secured confirmation of her ancient right to bring her produce and manufactures freely into England. Furthermore, a significant step in constitutional evolution was taken in mid-century. The better to resist the unwarranted claim of the Lieutenant-Governor (Sir John Mylne) that he had the right to veto sentences imposed by the Court, as well as strengthen both a renewed protest over quarters for troops (the Seven Years War this time) and also opposition to a British Government attempt to control shipping leaving the island, a momentous course of action was taken on February 21st., 1758, with a lengthy note being circularised to all Parish Constables forewarning them of a States' Assembly the following March 3rd., itemizing minutely the matters for deliberation and requiring them to ascertain the views thereon of their respective Douzaines in advance of the meeting. Although notifications of forthcoming sessions of the States had been sent out occasionally since 1739 they had been no more than brief summaries of the subjects to be considered by the Assembly, so that the extensive missive of February 1758, with its detailed specification of the topics to be discussed, may be regarded as substantially the first Billet d'Etat of the genre known to-day, its issue initiating a procedure which by now has long been institutionalised.

A lively political episode occurred during William Le Marchant's tenure as bailiff (1771–1800), when allegations were made that he had exceeded his powers in deciding legal cases and other matters without consulting the jurats. These accusations, coupled with Le Marchant's bad-tempered and sometimes violent behaviour, gave rise to a long-standing quarrel which even led to a duel between the Procureur, Thomas de Sausmarez, and the bailiff's son, Robert. In 1776, after Le Marchant had threatened Jurat Pierre de Jersey with a knife in open court, 10 jurats petitioned George III to be allowed to resign. After they had been re-elected, an Order-in-Council commanded the bailiff to swear them in. Although four remained obdurate, the other six eventually agreed to return to the Bench. The experience, which was tantamount to a reproof from the king, would seem to have had some salutary effect upon Le Marchant, who displayed a sufficient sense of fair play to save the Methodist leader, Jean de Quetteville from banishment in 1788 — as has already been seen in Part I. Just how far the leopard had in fact changed its spots, however, may perhaps be more accurately inferred from Le Marchant's gratuitous declamations that same year against the opponents of the autocratic pretensions of his Jersey counterpart, William Charles Lemprière.

Towards the end of the sleepy century two developments of some significance occurred, indicative of the steady consolidation which had been achieved. The first was that the enhanced status of the Bailiwick's administration was symbolised by the construction in 1799 of the present Royal Court House as a fitting seat of government. It was financed partly from the sale of the old Plaiderie, partly from taxation, and partly from the proceeds of a States Lottery. The second development occurred in 1801 when, on the Home Secretary being relieved of responsibility for the colonies, he retained the responsibilities he had exercised since 1782 in respect of relations between the Crown and the Channel Isles, in deference to the special status enjoyed by the islands which set them apart from mere colonies.

Chapter Eight

FROM OLIGARCHY TO DEMOCRACY (1820–1940)

THE MAIN TREND of political development up to the point so far reached has been found in the increasingly successful efforts by the Guernsey authorities to assert their right to self-government saving only their fealty to the monarch. This right had been confirmed by the triumphant resistance to the pretentions of Sir John Mylne in the middle of the 18th. century (see last Chapter) with the result that the prerogatives of the Governor had been sufficiently curtailed to give virtual *carte blanche* to the Bailiff and the Court (or its *doppelgänger* the States) in the conduct of the Bailiwick's affairs — a power that (save for Sir William Napier's fulminations in the mid-nineteenth century) was never again to be challenged. From now on the centre of interest becomes the progressive democratization of the administration — a progress at first slow to the point of imperceptibility but later gaining momentum until by the outbreak of the Second World War directly or indirectly elected elements had come to dominate all the Bailiwick's governing bodies with the exception of Sark and the partial exception of Alderney (where property-owners were disproportionately reflected in the composition of the States of that island).

At first the only representative element in the States was provided by the parish constables, elected on a restricted franchise rather for their parochial duties than as potential representatives of the parishioners in the island assembly. Nevertheless, their presence in the States created a useful connection between parochial and island affairs, knitting the community together and providing the States with members possessed of an intimate knowledge of 'grass roots' feeling in the parishes.

Gradually a more public conception of government evolved, whereby its function was no longer seen as confined to keeping order and preventing political injustice, but rather as involving the obligation to take account of social and economic injustice as well, so that it had the duty of regulating conditions of life, providing social services and assuming a liability for the welfare of the people. In its turn this rôle of watchdog in the public interest led to an ever-increasing competence being claimed by the States, whereby they came to insist on their right to make representations when an Order-in Council (or any Act of Parliament transmitted thereby) was deemed as in any way endangering the welfare of the Bailiwick.

Thus from the beginning of the 20th century the infusion of directly-elected representatives into the legislature accompanied not only an ever-increasing spate of legislation concerned with social provision, but also the development of a conventional acknowledgement that consultation with the States was an essential preliminary to any Act of Parliament likely to have applicability to the Bailiwick. Indeed (if one may anticipate beyond the period under consideration) one view regarding these enactments, put forward in a joint memorandum by a group of Alderney residents to the Royal Commission on the Constitution, is that, as legislative power is vested in the sovereign, such Acts derive their force from the Order-in-Council transmitting them, rather than from the authority of parliament itself (paragraph 1458 of the Kilbrandon Report). Whatever the merits of this view, it is true to say that no Act of Parliament has any validity within the Bailiwick until registered by the Royal Court.

The nature of the Acts of Parliament involved is invariably such that they have a bearing on matters of mutual concern to the United Kingdom government and to the Islands — as, for example, the Merchant Shipping Acts and the Wireless Telegraphy Act. Of particular interest in this category was the Act defining the national status of Channel Islanders. This was the British Nationality Act of 1948, which provided that 'a citizen of the United Kingdom and Colonies may, if on the ground of his connection with the Channel Islands he so desires, be known as a Citizen of the United Kingdom, Islands and Colonies'. This provision was included in the Act thanks to its advocacy by Lord Justice du Parcq (1880–1949), a Jerseyman and a Lord of Appeal in Ordinary. (Unfortunately the new — 1981 — Nationality Bill lacks such definitive clarity, merely including islanders in the vague 'umbrella' term, 'British citizen'. The Home Office, however, emphasises that this imprecision will not undermine the special status of Channel Islanders. Time will tell.)

In line with these general tendencies, the rôle of the governor has progressively assumed a more constitutional complexion analogous to that of the monarch whom he represents. This transition had already received an impetus many years prior to the period under review when on December 30th., 1672 lightning struck the magazine in Castle Cornet, causing an explosion which killed the wife and mother of the governor, Viscount Hatton, and obliging him to quit the castle for St. Peter-Port. By this accident of history the monarch's representative came to live among the islanders for whom he was responsible, rather than in splendid isolation in an offshore fortification. Official residences since 1672 have included (*inter alia*) Havilland Hall and the building now called *Old Government House* hotel — with the present dwelling in Queen's Road coming into use after the First World War. This development naturally led in the end to a more intimate relationship and greater rapport with the island authorities.

As time went on the office of governor became a sinecure. Some of the holders were engaged in various duties that kept them away, while others were unwilling to bury themselves far from their estates or the pleasures of London. The governor often had a lieutenant to assist him, and when he was not present in the Bailiwick the lieutenant exercised all his powers. The logic of this arrangement was to dispense with the governor entirely, leaving the lieutenant-governor to carry out the functions he had been performing in any case. Guernsey's last governor was Sir William Keppel, who died in 1834. Since 1835 lieutenant-governors have invariably been appointed.

[In modern times the lieutenant-governor has been received in audience by the sovereign before taking up his appointment — normally of five years' duration — and has become largely a figurehead who represents the monarch on official occasions. Passports are issued in his name, and, possessing a voice but no vote, he has the right to attend the States as a 'privileged spectator'. As has been seen in considering feudal history, the responsibility for his salary and emoluments has since 1947 been assumed by the States in exchange for the Crown revenues in the island. The constitutional status of the lieutenant-governor is well exemplified by the order of proceedings when he is sworn in. He presents his royal warrant to the bailiff, the Court and the States, and takes an oath swearing to maintain and protect the privileges, liberties and ancient customs of the inhabitants. Only when the oath has been taken does the cry go up, 'Dieu sauve la Reine!'.

In mid-1999 — again anticipating a later period — the selection of personnel for this position became a vexed issue. Traditionally each Lieutenant-Governor has assumed office following a Royal appointment based on the recommendation by the Privy Council of a high ranking officer in the Armed Forces, but the Blair administration proposed to replace this arrangement by one whereby upon a vacancy occurring, the post would be publicly advertised as open to either sex and a choice then be made between the applicants. Ostensibly such a change would merely extend the gubernatorial candidature beyond the Services (though how a civilian office holder could operate as "Commander-in-Chief" — part of the Lieutenant-Governor's mandate — awaits explanation) but it was nevertheless feared in the islands that the result would be to make the Lieutenant-Governor a nominee of the British Government — and thus its political subordinate — rather than a non-political person appointed by the Monarch, whose direct representative he had hitherto been. Considerable anxiety was therefore felt lest the installation of a functionary subservient to it might open the door for inference in (and possibly eventual dominance over) insular domestic affairs by a Whitehall Executive which by disdainfully 'leaking' its proposals to the Press before consulting the authorities in either Bailiwick had so infringed accepted constitutional usage as to augur ill for future mutual trust and confidence in relationships between the islands and the United Kingdom.]

Dramatic evidence of a political re-awakening after the prolonged somnambulance of the 18th. century is provided by the career of Daniel de Lisle Brock, who, as bailiff from 1821 to 1842, rapidly acquired a well-deserved reputation as the champion of the Bailiwick's 'liberté' — its charters and privileges upon which depended its survival as a political entity. He was foremost in putting up stubborn resistance to any attempt by British ministers to over-ride these rights, or by the British parliament to interfere with them. Even before his appointment as Bailiff, Brock had already had experience as a protector of the Bailiwick's privileges. During the Napoleonic Wars, while serving as a jurat, he went to London to protest before the Privy Council against attempts to impress islanders for the Royal Navy. Although confronted with as formidable an opponent as Lord St. Vincent, he had, with the support of Lord de Saumarez, succeeded in carrying the day.

With the coming of peace, further trouble arose as a result of the enactment of the Corn Laws prohibiting the import of grain into the United Kingdom as long as the price of British grain was not in excess of £4 a quarter. Immediately following his appointment as bailiff, Brock launched a campaign against the attitude of the British government which construed the Act as applying to the Channel Isles as well as to the United Kingdom. Once again Brock was triumphant, successfully demonstrating that this claim was in derogation of the islands' status as free ports.

In 1830/1 another crisis arose involving the export of grain from the islands. The islanders were accused of bringing into England more grain than they could have grown themselves, and the British Customs demanded a duty on it. Brock led a joint deputation from both Bailiwicks which proved the falsity of the accusations and vindicated the islands' rights in respect of this valuable trade.

The right of islanders to be tried only in their own courts was defended by Brock in 1832. A St. Pancras beadle (one John Capes) had been arrested in Guernsey for dumping paupers on the island and, when the St. Pancras Council obtained from the King's Bench a writ under the Habeas Corpus Act, Guernsey's deputy sheriff ignored it as inapplicable to the Bailiwick. Matters came to a head when the tipstaff whom the Lord Chief Justice, disregarding Guernsey's rights, had sent to arrest the deputy sheriff, was himself taken into custody. Brock thereupon led an embassy from Guernsey to London to lodge a protest — and yet again emerged victorious.

Brock died on September 24th., 1842, and his funeral was the occasion for a spectacular display of esteem. It was a semi-State affair and literally thousands of people lined the funeral route. He is commemorated by a plaque affixed to a 13-foot menhir at St. Sampson's harbour, the construction of which was commenced during his term as bailiff.

In the year of Brock's death Major-General Sir William Napier was installed as lieutenant-governor and his period of office (1842–1848) came near to disaster, due to his insistence on regarding the bailiff and jurats as ignorant civilians, whose powers could easily be over-ridden by his military authority and prestige as the queen's representative. His over-bearing demeanour soon led to a clash when he saw fit to expel a Frenchman (Isidore Le Conte) from Guernsey on his own account, without deigning to refer to the island authorities. The upshot was a tense interview between Napier and the bailiff (Jean Guille), made even tenser by the lieutenant-governor's refusal to enter into any discussion with the bailiff while the jurats were present. Not surprisingly, the interview was inconclusive and relationships between Napier and the Royal Court became extremely strained.

Napier's next action constituted a deliberate defiance of Guernsey Law, in that he took it upon himself to issue a free pardon to a soldier (Private Thomas Fossey) whom the Royal Court had sent to prison for assault. This high-handed arbitrariness led to a petition to Queen Victoria, over which the Home Secretary, Sir James Graham, failed to take decisive action. Then came the bombshell. In May 1844 a force of 600 men was landed at St. Peter-Port from troop transports 'to quell the island's insurrection', Napier alleging that there was a conspiracy afoot against his life. Over 12,000 infuriated islanders gathered at a protest meeting on the New Ground (now Cambridge Park) to consider the statement that 'imputations have been recently thrown upon the loyalty of the inhabitants of the islands', and General Sir Thomas Saumarez was chosen to carry a loyal address across the Channel to the queen.

In August 1846, at the suggestion of Sir George Grey (the new Home Secretary) Queen Victoria herself took a hand in the dispute, paying a surprise visit to Guernsey accompanied by Albert, Prince Consort. She pointedly snubbed Napier, refusing to receive him on her yacht. The following day the queen landed and, as the first reigning monarch ever to visit Guernsey, was accorded a tumultuous reception which made the loyalty of the islanders plain for all to see: La Petite Marche was re-named Queen's Road in her honour, with the ensuing thoroughfare of La Pierre Percée being also re-named as 'Prince Albert's Road'; and to commemorate the visit, the Victoria Tower, designed by William Colling, was built by Matthieu and Jacques Tostevin in 1848.

(From a perusal of family papers, Mr. Cecil de Sausmarez in 1982 aired the likelihood of the fracas stemming in part from General Napier, even prior to his arrival in the island, being already predisposed against the bailiff. This prejudice, it is suggested, resulted from an unfortunate confrontation between Jean Guille — then a jurat — and General Napier's predecessor and erstwhile patron — Major-General Henry Bailey: lieutenant-governor 1816/21 — which had occurred over the period November 1818 to February 1819. Taking exception to remarks made by this jurat in the course of a States' debate on November 25th., 1818 when he criticised as excessive the level of expenditure on the Militia now the Napoleonic Wars were over, Bailey deprived Guille of his colonelcy in the force's North Regiment. Alleging that this action by the lieutenant-governor, penalising him in his military capacity for what he had said in his administrative one, infringed the privileges of the States, Guille declined to acknowledge the validity of his demotion, and this clash of wills persisted until the following February when the Home Secretary — Lord Sidmouth — resolved it by an Order-in-Council requiring Guille on the one hand to withdraw his refusal to accept his dismissal and General Bailey on the other to reinstate him.)

Whatever the validity of these speculations, Napier's tenure of office survived the queen's visit by just over a year. Then Sir George Grey, who found his rudeness intolerable, persuaded the prime minister (the Duke of Wellington) to replace him by Major-General John Bell, who healed all wounds by his kindliness and courtesy. Nevertheless, Napier's adverse comments (coupled with a campaign of agitation in Jersey led by Abraham Le Cras) led to the appointment in 1846 of a Royal Commission to investigate the Criminal Law in these islands which appeared on the one hand to be run by oligarchic cliques claiming excessive independence, and on the other to be populated by inhabitants so litigious that their flood of appeals to the Crown had been a major factor leading to the creation of the Judicial Committee of the Privy Council in 1833.

The Royal Commission of 1846 found that the Royal Court did what it saw fit in the individual case before it, considering itself competent not only to deal according to its discretion with any case not covered by the text-books, but also to vary the rules laid down in the books as it thought necessary. In this connection the Commissioners reported:

> According to the theory of the Guernsey constitution, the Jurats may on one day, sitting in the Court of Chief Pleas, make an Ordonnance without the consent of Your Majesty, against the will of the functionary representing the Crown in the island, and without consulting the body of the States, and on the next day, sitting as a Court of Justice, they may proceed to put their own construction on it and to execute the law of their own making, without their decisions in any matter of criminal law being capable of review by any superior authority.

The paradox was that the people of Guernsey seemed to be content with a situation where the jurats (as the late A. J. Eagleston put it) 'were more like a circle of Kings of the Homeric Age handing down the dooms which they had received from Zeus than the judges of a modern state administering an organized system of statute or customary law'. Even the Commissioners had to admit that powers so unlimited appeared to be little abused. In view of the general acceptance of this paradox, it is hardly surprising that a further century was to elapse before steps were taken to curtail the discretionary and legislative functions of the jurats and the Royal Court.

In fact, a modest political reform had already been achieved before the investigations of the Royal Commission ever started. This had resulted from a complaint by the Parish of Saint Peter-Port that, were current proposals to be implemented, the traditional tax system (whereby it found only one-third of any sum to be raised, with the rest coming from the Country Parishes) would be replaced by a uniform levy throughout the island (a method already used tentatively — and on a strictly ad hoc basis — to pay both for the erection of the Prison and also for Doyle's road schemes) with the outcome that the Town Parish — whose property owners possessed the lion's share of Guernsey's wealth — would be called upon to provide some two-thirds of the total tax receipts and yet would remain with no greater representation in the States than the other nine Parishes which between them would, under such a revision, contribute only one-third.

After repeated failures to effect reform, success came in 1844, facilitated in the first place by the division of Saint Peter-Port into four components called Cantons (each under a Cantonal Douzaine with minor administrative responsibilities, as subsidiaries to the Parish's Central Douzaine operating in a supervisory and co-ordinating capacity) and secondly by discontinuing the Parish Constables' automatic membership of the States in favour of a system whereby delegates (who could be either Constables or Douzeniers) were sent to individual sittings of the States from the various Douzaines. Then, by ruling that the Cantonal Douzaines of Saint Peter-Port should each send one delegate and the Central Douzaine two, making a total of six for the Parish, while the Douzaines of the other nine Parishes were to send one delegate each (Loi relative à la Réforme des Etats, 1844) more accurately proportional numbers were devised for the only representative element in the States. It must be borne in mind, however, that this element was only indirectly representative and was chosen on a narrow franchise.

Up to three years prior to this reform of the States, the franchise for the election of constables and douzeniers had been even narrower, being restricted to Chefs de Famille. In 1841, however, it had been extended to include taxpayers (all of whom, in the context of the contemporary tax system, were of necessity property-owners). Indeed, it was not until early in the 20th century that the suffrage for Douzaine Elections was extended to 'the *occupiers* of premises of which the assessed rental value for rateable purposes is not less than £14 per annum, the *proprietors* of premises assessed below £14 per annum, and the proprietors or tenants who let or sub-let premises furnished or in apartments'. (1946 Privy Council Committee Report.)

It is impossible to pretend that these cautious reforms of the franchise and of the States brought about any fundamental change in the island's political structure, which remained as essentially oligarchic as it had been previously for almost the entire remainder of the 19th. century. Indeed, it was not until 1899 that the principle of *direct representation* of the electorate was first acknowledged in Guernsey's governmental system, by the enlargement of the membership of the States to include nine 'Deputés du peuple'.

To be eligible to seek election as a deputy a candidate had to be a British subject or 'admis par la Cour Royale habitant de cette Ile' — and he also had to be a parochial taxpayer. The entire island was regarded as a multi-member constituency returning all nine deputies. Elections were to take place every three years with the franchise restricted to ratepayers ('Chefs de Famille'). Those elected would be the nine who received 'the plurality of votes' (i.e., the largest number, the second largest number, and so on, down to the ninth largest number; those with even fewer votes being unsuccessful). In the same year the Comptroller de la Reine was given a vote in the States, the Procureur de la Reine having had one since that body's first emergence.

No further steps towards increased democratization were taken until 1920, when the climate of opinion engendered by the First World War led to the number of deputies being enlarged to 18, with differential representation accorded to the five districts into which the island was divided, as follows:

No. 1	District (St. Peter-Port)	8
No. 2	District (St. Sampson and the Vale)	5
No. 3	District (St. Martin and St. Andrew)	2
No. 4	District (Castel, St. Saviour, Forest)	2
No. 5	District (St. Pierre-du-Bois and Torteval)	1

These deputies were elected for a period of three years on what was in theory a universal adult suffrage. In practice, however, while the parish constables were under an obligation to place the names of ratepayers upon the electoral register, non-ratepayers had to apply each year to the constables for registration — and women who were non-ratepayers had to be over 30 to be eligible to register. The result was that, effectively, ratepayers predominated among the voters. Thus, for example, the 1946 Privy Council Committee found that of the 9,156 on the register in 1945 (the last year in which elections under this system occurred) 6,835 were ratepayers, and only 2,321 non-ratepayers, who had made the requisite application. Only 2,600 actually voted in 1945.

Nevertheless, to vote is one thing, and to have the right to do so is another — and it is manifestly true that during these inter-war years no-one who was sufficiently politically conscious to take the necessary trouble to register was denied the vote, so that the system may fairly be described as a democratic one. Furthermore, as a result of these changes the composition of the States of Deliberation in the inter-war period was made up in such a way that the directly and indirectly elected members outnumbered the appointed ones by 45 to 13: a balance with far greater pretensions to democracy than may be said for the British parliament, with its vast numbers of unelected members of the House of Lords. This composition was as follows:

The bailiff — a Crown appointment
The two law officers — also Crown appointments
Ten rectors — Crown appointments
Twelve jurats — elected for life by the States of Election
Fifteen delegates from Douzaines
Eighteen peoples' deputies

Jurats (and also the Prévôt du Roi — the chief executive officer of the Royal Court) were elected by the States of Election, which was composed as above except that the 10 parish constables and all 180 douzeniers sat instead of a mere 15 delegates, giving a total membership of 243, as against one of 58 for the States of Deliberation.

With a more democratic atmosphere prevailing, it was inevitable that the accompanying proliferation of administrative functions would lead to the growth of a bureaucracy. Even before the First World War the growing consciousness by the States of responsibility to the community led to the setting up of centralised control, through Committees of the States, of functions which, where they had not been neglected entirely, had been the responsibility of the parishes — or even of the feudal fiefs. (It may here be mentioned in passing that Committees of this nature, as permanent institutions, had originated with the appointment of a few such groups in the early nineteenth century to supervise road construction, coastal protection and finance; following eighteenth century experimentation whereby temporary ones had been set up with purely specific — and transient — responsibilities.) This development ran counter to the normal course of events where bureaucracies derive their authority from the Crown or its representative. In the case of Guernsey (and, incidentally, Jersey, too) the Civil Service is answerable to the Legislature rather than the Executive, and is thus under the immediate control of these Committees — a legacy of the triumph of bailiff over governor in the 17th. century.

Experience during the First World War, coupled with the greater complexity of affairs thereafter, brought a further extension of this form of government. A professional island police force was created in 1920 under the administration of such a Committee, taking over the day-to-day police duties of the parish constables who, although not deprived of their powers, came to be seldom, if ever, called upon to exercise them.

During the inter-war years this administrative system spread its tentacles further and further with, *inter alia*, a Finance Committee, an Education Council, a Board of Health, a Hospital Committee, a Telephone Department, and a Water Board. It was under the aegis of the last-named that the reservoir was constructed at St. Saviour's shortly after the Second World War.

After an initial review, this chapter at its outset considered the career of Daniel de Lisle Brock as a champion of Guernsey's freedom. The seriousness with which one should take the warning of John Philpot Curran that 'the condition upon which God hath given liberty to man is eternal vigilance' is illustrated by the fact that it will end with an account of yet another episode which posed a threat to the Bailiwick's autonomy. The threat arose in 1923 when the British government put forward a demand to both Bailiwicks for an 'annual contribution to the Imperial Exchequer' towards the cost of Imperial defence.

This demand provoked considerable bitterness, not only because of the excessive amount asked for (£600,000 per annum), but also as the contribution from the Irish Free State had been cancelled; and, finally, because it was in any case unconstitutional and contrary to the Islands' Charters, in that the imposition by the

United Kingdom government of an annual charge would amount to the imposition of taxation, in derogation of the islands' fiscal autonomy. After attempting joint action with Jersey (which, unfortunately, came to nothing at this stage) the bailiff, Sir Havilland de Sausmarez, on behalf of the States, eventually offered £220,000 as a 'final free gift' — but the offer was not even acknowledged by the British government.

In 1926, following the publication of the Report of the Privy Council Committee appointed to deal with the question (which suggested that Guernsey should make a reduced contribution of £75,000 per annum) the States of Jersey and Guernsey acted in close concert, insisting that any contributions were to be seen as a 'once-for-all gift'. This intransigent united front yielded dividends and the case was settled in 1927 when the British Treasury accepted the 'gifts' and when agreement was made between the British government and the Islands on the prevention of 'tax dodging' by persons resident and companies registered in the two Bailiwicks. In the event this agreement was never implemented (hence the rise thirty odd years later of the 'Finance Industry') but nevertheless the outcome of the Imperial Contribution Question had important results, for its resolution clarified yet again the independence of the islands and ushered in more friendly and co-operative relationships with the United Kingdom than ever before.

['*Historia magistra vitae*'. Frequently, however, her pupils prove loath to heed her lessons: a reluctance well demonstrated in 1984 — this chapter's third post-Liberation digression — when the British Government revived this contentious issue by suggesting that the Channel Islands should consider making annual payments "towards the cost of defence expenditure and of international representation". A public meeting held at Beau Séjour having revealed a large majority opposed to any such subvention being provided, the Advisory and Finance Committee recommended in November 1985 that any moral obligation to help pay for insular defence and foreign representation (such as there is) could be discharged without the Bailiwick's constitutional position being compromised if the States were to assume responsibility for the upkeep of the Alderney breakwater (see Part IV, Chapter Ten); contribute towards maintaining the Royal Navy Port Head-quarters at Castle Cornet ; hand over to the United Kingdom the fees paid for locally-issued Passports ; and defray the cost of Guernsey's representation at such international fora as the Court of Human Rights. The annual expense of implementing these recommendations would not, it was (perhaps optimistically) thought, greatly exceed £600,000 — about £11 per head of population — and there would be no question of regular remittances to the British Exchequer which might in time come to be regarded by the recipient as an inherent entitlement, in derogation of the Bailiwick's autonomy. In January 1986 the British Government accepted in principle Guernsey's offer voluntarily to render aid in this way, at the same time categorically stipulating that in shouldering such an undertaking the islanders would not by one whit jeopardise the continuance of the traditional relationship between the Bailiwick and the United Kingdom. After detailed discussions on arranging the transfer of responsibilities, full formal acceptance followed in 1987. The Castle Cornet Port Headquarters responsibilities lapsed in 1994, thereby partly offsetting the maintenance costs of Alderney's Breakwater which proved to be much greater than originally estimated — so much so that in 1997 Guernsey's Board of Administration proposed economising by surrendering the structure to Neptune as his plaything, while building a cheaper and shorter mole in its lee. Vehement opposition to this project voiced by the States of Alderney led to a Guernsey-Alderney Joint Consultative Council being set up and also to the appointment of a Panel of Inquiry (the impartiality of which was guaranteed by a predominantly Jersey membership) charged to go into the whole matter and then to submit its recommendations to the Council, which in its turn was required to report to the States' Board of Administration. To the Panel of Inquiry a petition was presented early in 1998 bearing 2,656 signatures and strongly objecting to the proposed new short breakwater. In August of the same year the Panel recommended the retention of the existing breakwater, not only because of its environmental and historical importance, but also on the grounds that its disappearance would entail the loss of two-thirds of the available sheltered anchorage in Braye Bay, while the accumulated detritus resulting from allowing it to crumble away would pose a major hazard to shipping. To reinforce this advice the Panel added that its calculations revealed that, far from saving money, the projected new mole would involve an annual expenditure of £950,000 whereas the maintenance cost of the existing structure (given the adoption of more efficient methods employing the latest technology) would come to rather less than £500,000 per annum. Thus matters stand as this book goes to print, with further enquiries and discussion continuing.]

Chapter Nine

POLITICAL DEVELOPMENTS SINCE THE SECOND WORLD WAR

DURING THE GERMAN OCCUPATION from 1940 to 1945 the Bailiff and the States remained the official government of the Bailiwick, but delegated their powers to a Controlling Committee of eight members under the presidency first of H.M. Procureur, Major Ambrose J. Sherwill, and later of Jurat John Leale.

The trauma of the Occupation led to the question of political reform looming large after the Liberation — witness the report in the *Daily Telegraph* of August 7th., 1945, that a Petition containing over 2,000 signatures had been addressed to the King denouncing both the Controlling Committee and the States as 'unrepresentative and undemocratic' and asking that, pending a full investigation, each of these bodies should be suspended and a Commission appointed by the King-in-Council to conduct Guernsey's affairs. The need for a response to such disenchantment with the status quo was obviously urgent and in January 1946 the States of Guernsey adopted Reform proposals which formed the basis of an enquiry by a Privy Council Committee under Viscount Samuel during the September of the same year. The suggestions contained in this Committee's report considerably influenced the nature of the Reform (Guernsey) Laws, 1948 to 1963, from which all subsequent political arrangements derived. This series of Reform Laws affected the States of Deliberation, the States of Election and the Judiciary.

As far as the Legislature was concerned, the States of Deliberation became the Bailiwick's Legislature and the umbilical cord connecting it with the Royal Court as its parent was finally severed in that the Jurats as such ceased to be members of the States. They were replaced by 12 Conseillers (though Article 2 of the 1948 Law specifically stated that a Jurat was not debarred from seeking election as a Conseiller). Furthermore, in conformity with the policy of separating the Legislature from the Judiciary, the States assumed the powers hitherto exercised by the Royal Court of issuing Ordinances enjoying the force of law provided they did not impose taxation or alter existing written or customary law — powers which, it will be recalled, had been looked at askance by the Royal Commission of 1846 a century previously. Such Ordinances are known as 'Ordinances of the States'. An example of some years ago was the Order forbidding smoking on omnibuses. The Reforms do, however, permit the Royal Court to continue to exercise residual legislative functions in regard to Defence Regulations and the Rules of Procedure in the Court, by the issue of 'Orders of the Royal Court', an example of which is given in a subsequent paragraph.

It should perhaps be explained that, Ordinances of either kind apart, legislation stems from the enactment of *Resolutions* (which may be defined metaphorically as the butterflies that, nurtured by States' approval, emerge from the chrysalis composed of all the items contained in any session's agenda — known as *Le Billet d'Etat*. For inclusion in a Billet d'Etat (the first of which to specify in detail the topics to be discussed was issued on February 21st., 1758 — see Chapter Seven of this Part) an item must be submitted either by the Bailiff, or the President of a States' Committee, or originate in an initiative (called *un Requête*), sponsored by at least seven members of the States of Deliberation. To pass into law a Resolution has to be presented to the States embodied in *un Projet de Loi* (comparable to a Bill in the United Kingdom). If accorded majority support the Projet is submitted to the Queen-in-Council and later becomes law with the registration by the Royal Court of a confirmatory Order-in-Council. Should such confirmation be withheld (as happens on extremely rare occasions) the proposed legislation is still-born.

While the Rectors of the parish churches lost their seats in the States of Deliberation, the Law Officers of the Crown (H.M. Procureur and H.M. Comptroller) were permitted to retain theirs for the purpose of speaking, but were deprived of their votes.

The 18 Douzaine Delegates sent to each sitting of the States of Deliberation were replaced by a system whereby each of the ten Douzaines (Saint Peter-Port's Cantonal Douzaines having been abolished) chose a Douzaine Representative for a whole year. As for the Deputies, they now came to be elected for a three-year term on a universal franchise based on a residence qualification and were increased in number to 33 to represent the ten parishes as follows:

Saint Peter-Port, 13; Saint Sampson's, 4; The Vale, 5; The Castel, 3; Saint Saviour's, 1; Saint Pierre-du-Bois, 1; Torteval, 1; The Forest, 1; Saint Martin's, 3; and Saint Andrew's, 1.

In addition, by the States of Guernsey (Representation of Alderney) Law, 1949, the membership of the States became swelled by two Alderney Representatives appointed by the States of Alderney.

The net result of the foregoing was that the pre-1994 States of Deliberation resolved itself into:

Three Crown appointees (the Bailiff and the Law Officers),
Twenty-four indirectly elected members
(12 Conseillers, 10 Douzaine Representatives and
2 Alderney Representatives),
Thirty-three directly-elected members (the Deputies).

Thus the directly representative element constituted a majority of the States, with 33 members out of sixty. In effect this boiled down to 33 out of 58, because of the Law Officers not being able to vote. However, although these reforms had rendered the franchise universal, subsequent experience revealed that many islanders disfranchised themselves by failing to complete the form necessary for inclusion in the Electoral Roll, which in 1996 contained a mere 27,110 names out of a total of 45,000 eligible for inscription — i.e. only 60.2% of the population of voting age. Many horses (or perhaps one should say donkeys) when led to the water, plainly refused to drink!

At the time of the Reforms the functions of the States of Election were to elect persons to the offices of Jurat, Conseiller and H.M. Sheriff, but the practice of electing the last-named was discontinued in 1960 while Conseillers were elected by this body for the last time in 1991 (see below). By the terms of the Royal Court of Guernsey (Miscellaneous Reform Provisions) Law, 1950, Jurats serve until attaining the age of seventy but may, at the discretion of the Court, remain in office up to the age of seventy-five. There survived no sex, religious or occupational barriers to the assumption of this office, the previous requirements that Jurats should be persons of the male sex 'qui se conforment à la religion reformée' and who were neither brewers nor publicans, having been abolished by the same law. (Thirty-seven years were to elapse, however, before a 'cliff-hanging' series of three ballots on

October 30th., 1985 at last produced the requisite absolute majority in the States of Election whereby Mrs. Dorothy Winifred Le Pelley, the widow of Il Cavaliere Jean le Pelley — who had himself held this high office — became the first woman to be elected to the bench.) As for Conseillers, they were elected for a six-year term, half of them falling due for election (or re-election) every three years.

In October 1976 the States of Deliberation resolved that the ten Parish Rectors should be excluded from the States of Election as far as the election of Conseillers was concerned, on the grounds of their being unrepresentative Crown appointees who are often strangers to the island, having little knowledge of candidates for election: the self-same grounds, incidentally, which seventeen years later led to a further resolution adopted in March 1993 whereby only Rectors with at least one year's residence in Guernsey could sit in that body. As, furthermore, Alderney representatives only participated in the election of Conseillers, it followed that the composition of the States of Election varied according to whether Jurats or Conseillers were being elected. Thus for the election of Conseillers the States of Election had a membership of 84, consisting of the Bailiff, 12 Jurats, the 12 Conseillers, H.M. Procureur, H.M. Comptroller, 33 Peoples' Deputies, 20 Douzaine Representatives (two per parish) and four Alderney representatives. On the other hand, for the election of Jurats the membership of the body was approximately 104, made up of the Bailiff, the 12 Jurats, the 12 Conseillers (until April 30th., 2000) H.M. Procureur, H.M. Comptroller, 33 Peoples' Deputies, the residentially qualified Rectors (maximum 10) and one Douzaine Representative per parish plus a further 24 Douzaine Representatives (10 for Saint Peter-Port, four for the Vale, three each for Saint Sampson's, the Castel and Saint Martin's and one for Saint Andrew's). However, in the context of a reform embodied in two Projets de Loi approved by the States of Guernsey and Alderney early in 1993, the 1991 meeting of the States of Election became the last one where Conseillers were elected, so that the above variations in its composition thereafter ceased to exist. This reform ruled that Conseillers who otherwise would have held office until 1997 would only do so until April 30th., 1994; their resignations making way for a system whereby the office of Conseiller would be held only by such persons as had been elected thereto by popular vote as expressed in special Conseiller elections to be held in Guernsey and Alderney in March 1994 and thereafter triennially in the same month, those so elected assuming office for a six-year term from the ensuing May 1st. It was also ruled that, in the first instance only, the six Conseillers commanding the fewest votes would resign after three years, so as to facilitate the election thereafter of half the Bench of Conseillers every three years. By the same reform the General Election of Deputies was scheduled as from 1994 to occur triennially in April, with successful candidates taking their seats the following May 1st. The strength of the States' directly representative element thus rose to 45 while that of the indirectly elected one fell to 12 — but at the time of writing the survival of these arrangements is already doomed, consequent upon the States voting in February 1998 in favour of the total abolition of the office of Conseiller with effect from April 30th., 2000 and thereby promoting the triumph of an historically heedless revisionism over inherited tradition; the Conseillers having functioned as the lineal descendents of the Jurats, the *optimates patriae* around whom Guernsey's nascent legislature had originally emerged.

In the sphere of the Judiciary an Order of the Royal Court of June 1964 made the Bailiff the sole judge of law, the Jurats in criminal cases assuming a function comparable to that of an English jury, save that majority verdicts are permissible. In civil cases, however, the Jurats give their individual decisions in open Court. Contracts are passed by the Court as described in the case of Alderney in Chapter Thirteen. The responsibility devolving on the Bailiff as sole Judge of the Law (with the corollary that only a fully qualified lawyer may exercise his functions) made impossible the continuance of the old system whereby he was replaced by a Jurat acting as Juge Délegué in the event of his involuntary absence. Provision for such a contingency was made five years later by the creation in 1969 of the office of Deputy Bailiff, the holder of which assists the Bailiff generally and may act on his behalf in all judicial matters save that of Judge in the undermentioned Court of Appeal.

The Court of Appeal (Guernsey) Law, 1961, set up a Court of Appeal in the Bailiwick with both criminal and civil jurisdiction. The option of ultimate appeal to the Judicial Committee of the Privy Council is preserved, it being specifically stated that "nothing in this law shall affect ... the jurisdiction of Her Majesty in Council". In the same realm of appeal, an additional and simple mechanism providing facilities for the review of any action by a States' Department alleged to be unjust, oppressive or improperly discriminatory, was brought into existence by the Administrative

Decisions (Review) (Guernsey) Law of April 1987, which set up a Review Board before which complaints of this nature could be brought in cases where no tribunal or court is available to the complainant or where it would not be reasonable to expect the aggrieved to use such recourse. Yet another recourse for aggrieved islanders came into existence in May 1999 as a result of a Court of Appeal ruling by virtue of which the Royal Court acquired both the right to review decisions made under the law and also to control any excess or abuse of power by States' Committees — thereby becoming available to any islander for the investigation of complaints made against any such Committee.

To complete the picture of Guernsey's constitutional arrangements, mention must be made of the main officials involved in legislative and judicial work. The Clerk of the States and of the Royal Court is H.M. Greffier, who heads a department that may perhaps be described as a combined Secretariat and Record Office. He is also a Registrar for the purpose of solemnizing marriages. H.M. Prévôt (or Sheriff) whose office derives from that of Sergent de L'Epée in ancient Normandy, has since 1960 been appointed by the States' Appointments Board (though previously he was elected by the States of Election) and besides being the Governor of the Prison, is the Chief Executive Officer of the Court. In addition he performs duties in connection with the States, including attendance on the Lieutenant-Governor when His Excellency is present in the Assembly. Lastly comes H.M. Sergent, who is appointed by the Crown and is the process server of the Royal Court and of subordinate courts.

In conclusion it must be noted that there is no division of labour in the legal profession comparable to that in England between barristers and solicitors, both of whose functions are performed by Advocates. An Ordinance of the Royal Court of 1867 permitted the existence of the *Corps des Ecrivains*, limited to eight members, all of whom were authorized to give legal advice and to prepare conveyances, bonds and other similar documents. In 1914 the Royal Court resolved that no more Ecrivains should be admitted but that those still practising would be allowed to continue. The last of these (Mr. Herbert Ogier) retired at the end of 1971, thus bringing to an end the Corps des Ecrivains after a century's existence.

One last word. It is only prudent to add that as the 20th century nears its end in this autumn of the year 2000 their examination of the entrails prompts the political haruspices to foresee yet more changes in the offing.

Chapter Ten

THE BAILIWICK'S FLAGS

THE PRECEDING CHAPTER having examined post-war political developments in general, a natural thought sequence leads on to the consideration of one such development in particular which is plain for all to see — the Guernsey flag in its present design. Although so familiar as to be taken for granted, this frequent sight is in fact the end product of a history beset with bewilderment, even if it were for many years generally (though before 1936 with questionable justification) considered to be Saint George's Cross. Precisely when the Dragon-slayer's emblem was first used as Guernsey's standard is a contentious issue, starting with the assertion made in *Flags of The World* (a recognised vexillological *vade-mecum*) that "its use in the island is attested as far back as 1406". On investigation, however, this claim seems to be based on F.B. Tupper's reference in his *Chronicles of Castle Cornet* to the raid on Jersey of October 7th., 1406, led conjointly by the Castilian corsair Pero Nino and the Bréton knight Hector de Pontbriant, during the course of which (as recounted by the eminent Jersey historian G.R. Balleine) Nino, on espying a white flag with Saint George's Cross held aloft among the defenders, called to Pontbriant, "While yon flag flies they will never own themselves defeated". This said, why a recorded appearance of the standard in Jersey in 1406 should be construed as establishing its contemporaneous use as the flag of Guernsey is far from clear; unless (remembering that Edward, Duke of York, was Warden of **all** the Isles at the time) one assumes that the flag was common to both Jersey and Guernsey — as, apparently, did Sir Havilland de Sausmarez, who, looking into the matter in 1935, concluded (*inter alia*) that Saint George's Cross "would have been flown IN THE CHANNEL ISLANDS" (i.e. not just in Guernsey) "as the flag of England, probably from at the latest, the middle of the 14th. century". (In this Connection, incidentally, one may note that Jersey adopted Saint Patrick's Cross as late as *circa* 1841.)

Moving on to the 16th. century, one finds the late Jurat Jean le

Pelley (1899–1982) commenting that a French captain in 1523 excused himself for seizing a Guernsey ship (The *Jehan*: Captain Phelipot le Marinier) and thereby infringing the insular neutrality ordained by Pope Sixtus IV, by pleading that she flew naught save 'des bandières où estoit les croix rouges' — i.e. the normal English banner; and le Pelley deduced from this incident that at the time the island lacked any flag of its own (compare Sir Havilland de Sausmarez above) — whereas the reputable vexillographer Commander Bruce Nicolls, O.B.E. (of whom more anon) regards it as indicative that by then Saint George's Cross was the *de facto* Guernsey flag. Each interpretation is obviously no more than conjectural — and even in the comparatively recent past the evidence available is contradictory. Thus while Jonathan Duncan in his well-known *History of Guernsey* (1841) refers to the Cross of Saint George as the island's flag, pictures of Queen Victoria's visit (1846) or the foundation of the Town Harbour (1853) barely portray it, though White Ensigns abound and it is interesting that his researches led the late Major S. Carey Curtis to conclude (not altogether correctly) that the legal use of this standard dates only from 1906. In that year the two Bailiwicks were seeking permission to display Arms derived from their respective seals, as a result of which a considerable correspondence ensued between the Bailiff, the Lieutenant-Governor and the Home Office. In the course of this correspondence a letter written in January 1907 from the Lieutenant-Governor to the Bailiff was mistakenly interpreted as signifying Edward VII's sanction for 'Saint George's Flag' to be that of Guernsey (although in fact only the requested Coat of Arms had been authorized) and its consequent registration as the island's 'Pavillon Officiel' was recorded in *Le Recueil d'Ordonnances*, Tome V.

Although it persisted for almost thirty years, a practice of such dubious legality as flying a flag devoid of proper authorization was obviously undesirable and in 1935 steps were at last taken to regularize the matter. A States' Investigatory Committee advocated a flag with the Guernsey Arms superimposed on Saint George's Cross (comparable to that of Alderney described below) but in deference to the wishes of Bailiff Victor Carey a request was made — and granted by Edward VIII in 1936 — that the unadorned Cross should be officially sanctioned. This confirmation as the island's flag of one identical with that of England caused confusion at functions such as the Commonwealth Games, thereby emphasising how Guernsey was bereft of any specific expression of its identity — and growing dissatisfaction with this lack of any flag conveying a precise and unique distinction led to the appointment in September 1983 of a Flag Investigation Committee. This Committee, adapting and simplifying a design submitted by the afore-mentioned Commander Nicolls, proposed combining Saint George's Cross with the Gold Cross featured on the gonfalon awarded by Pope Alexander II to Duke William II (the Conqueror) to bless his invasion of England, thereby symbolising Guernsey's Norman identity as well as its links with the English (and subsequently British) Crown: and pending authorization the resultant standard — blazoned 'Argent a Cross Gules thereon a Guernsey Cross (being a representation of the Cross on the banner of William of Normandy) Gold' — was flown (unofficially) for the first time on February 15th., 1985.

This flag, however, shares with its predecessor the drawback that it may only be used on land as Guernsey, enjoying no internationally accorded status as an independent country, does not qualify for recognition of its flag on the high seas. Technically, therefore, Guernsey vessels are British registered and as such are required by the 1894 Merchant Shipping Act to fly the Red Ensign. In these circumstances the Flag Committee advised taking advantage of a proviso in the 1894 Act whereby a Special Ensign may be flown under the authority of a Royal Warrant — and it advocated that application be made for a warrant authorizing the use by Guernsey ships of the Red Ensign embellished with the Conqueror's Gold Cross — blazoned 'Gules in the Canton the flag of the United Kingdom of Great Britain and Northern Ireland and in the fly a Guernsey Cross (being a representation of the Cross on the banner of William of Normandy) Gold' — thereby remaining legal while at the same time satisfying the desire to be distinctive. It transpired, however, that, though permitted anywhere on vessels privately owned by Guernsey residents who are British subjects, for commercial vessels flying this "Guernsey Ensign" would be restricted to adjacent waters — defined as those between Cap de la Hague and Les Roches Douvres — beyond which (allegedly to escape the odium attaching to flags of convenience: an unconvincing argument) the Red Ensign would be required as of yore. These complications notwithstanding, the States approved the Flag Committee's recommendations in March 1985, after which both designs were submitted to Her Majesty the Queen, seeking her consent plus the issue of the requisite Warrant in regard to the marine ensign. Both consent and Warrant were granted on May 1st., 1985.

Finally, while still on the subject of flags, this would seem an appropriate point at which to take note of those appertaining to other parts of the Bailiwick — starting with Alderney, where the same epistolary misinterpretation which had issued in the Cross of Saint George being registered as the 'Pavillon Officiel' of Guernsey in 1907 led to its simultaneous adoption by the Aurigniais, though in their case with the island seal mentioned below in Chapter Thirteen of this Part as being granted in 1745 ('Vert, a Lion Rampant Imperially Crowned Or, holding in its Dexter Paw a sprig of Broom Proper') superimposed on the Cross at its intersection. Over three decades were to elapse before Sark too flew its own flag, consisting of the Cross of Saint George with the Arms of the Duchy of Normandy ('Gules, Two Lions Passant Guardant Or') occupying the first quarter. This flag was originally commissioned by the late Dame de Sercq; a record being preserved of a memorandum from La Dame dated March 10th., 1938, asking the late H.J. Pitt Esq., the noted heraldist and vexillologist, of Hilperton Road, Trowbridge, Wiltshire, to draw a flag — and this is supplemented by a photostat of a drawing by H.J. Pitt resembling to-day's flag and dated March 15th., 1938. Initially envisaged as the 'banner of dominion' of the Seigneurie of Sark (i.e. the régime, not the dwelling) and hence by derivation regarded as the personal standard of the Seigneur, it has now, with the sanction of accepted custom and practice, been transferred to the Island of Sark as its official flag — the distinction between arms of dominion and those of state or territory having practically vanished in modern times. Meanwhile the Seigneur at the moment (2000) awaits a new standard based on his family coat of arms. Moving from Sark to its appanage, it is interesting to note that the late Leonard Matchan during his tenancy of Brecqhou (1966–1987) flew in that islet by permission of La Dame and her successor a flag with the Coat of Arms granted to him by the Lord Lion King of Arms ('Two Seagulls, a Wave and Three Trefoils') incorporated into what was then the Seigneurial Standard, though now the Flag of Sark. Lastly one comes to Herm, to which Eve Devereux in the 1992 edition of her *Book of World Flags* assigns a flag 'based on the cross of Saint George' with 'the island arms (featuring dolphins and monks) in the top left-hand corner'. The 'island arms' alluded to are clearly those designed in 1952 by the Reverend S.T. Percival which J.H.B. Bedells, in an article sub-titled *A Problem in Pseudo-Heraldry* in the October 1965 issue of *Coat of Arms* says may be blazoned 'Azure on a Bend Or between

Two Dolphins embowed Argent Three Monks Cowled and Habited Sable'. Unknown to the College of Arms (as personal enquiry there revealed) these bearings (even if originally intended as Arms of Dominion) in strict legality merely constitute an unofficial presumption by an individual, Herm's subordination to the jurisdiction of Guernsey depriving it of any title to armigerity. Nevertheless the widespread display of this device on notice boards throughout the island and as a letter-head on the White House Hotel stationery has been tolerated for many years — and information provided by Mr. William G. Crampton, Director of the Flag Institute, indicates that in 1983, on the basis of this prolonged acceptance, he suggested to Major A.G. Wood as appropriate 'a flag on the same lines as those of Sark and Brecqhou, with the charges from his Arms in the canton of a Cross of Saint George". He adds that he understood that quotations for having such a flag made were being sought and concludes, "After that vexillology took over and the design has been published in several books and charts as 'the flag of Herm'". One might also remark that the difference between seeking quotations and actually hoisting colours may account for the fact that nobody yet approached by the present writer has seen this standard, any more than he has himself.

Chapter Eleven

CONSTITUTIONAL RELATIONSHIPS WITH THE UNITED KINGDOM

IN APRIL 1969 a Royal Commission on the Constitution was appointed to consider, *inter alia*, whether any changes were desirable in the constitutional relationships between the United Kingdom on the one hand, and the Channel Islands and the Isle of Man on the other. The Commission issued its Report (popularly known as the Kilbrandon Report) in October 1973.

In this Report the Commission stated that, being neither part of the United Kingdom nor Colonies, the Channel Isles are dependencies of the Crown (paragraph 1347) with the United Kingdom responsible for defence and foreign relationships (paragraph 1363). It observed that these relationships are feeling the strain of modern developments as international agreements made by the United Kingdom were capable of being seen by the Islands as impinging on matters hitherto regarded as purely domestic. Hence constitutional relationships required investigation anew because of the possibility that such international agreements might call for the application to the Islands of policies to which they were opposed (paragraph 1374).

The Report quoted the States of Guernsey as saying that the Island's link with the United Kingdom and the rest of the Commonwealth is through the sovereign as latter-day successor of the Dukes of Normandy (paragraph 1349). It also stated that the members of the Commission were told in all the Islands that the loyalty of the people was to the sovereign and not to any United Kingdom government. Nevertheless, it was accepted that, because of the growing complexity of affairs and improved means of communication, practical links with the United Kingdom governments are strong and tending to increase (paragraph 1465). In this connection the States of Guernsey had expressed disapproval of any formal agreement giving statutory effect to constitutional conventions (such as had been urged by the States of Jersey). It was felt that the Island did not want to replace centuries of mutual trust and respect by such an instrument, which would rob the United Kingdom/Guernsey relationship of the flexibility whereby adjustments and innovations can be made to meet new developments. Guernsey was prepared to accept the United Kingdom's assurances of not seeking to legislate on any matter infringing insular autonomy (paragraph 1414).

Some British government departments, however, did not entirely favour any such unqualified assurances as Guernsey had indicated its willingness to accept. When questioned by the Royal Commission the Home Office and the Foreign and Commonwealth Office both said that the geographical proximity of the Islands made it desirable that their institutions should not differ beyond recognition from those of the United Kingdom, so as to ensure the presentation to the rest of the world of a coherent pattern enshrining common broad principles (paragraph 1431). The same departments also held that the inter-related nature of the economies of the United Kingdom and of the Islands necessitated compatibility of legislation to prevent commercial practices developing detrimental to the economic well-being of the British Islands as a whole (paragraph 1432). In the light of these considerations the departments were insistent in their view that so long as the United Kingdom government was responsible for the Islands' external relationships, it was essential for the United Kingdom to have residual power to legislate, if need be, even on matters domestic to the Islands (paragraph 1433).

In its actual recommendations, the Commission came out against any formal legislation dividing responsibility between the United Kingdom government and the Island authorities, feeling that such legislation would be difficult to draft and in any case would very likely be unacceptable in the international field (paragraph 1494). It therefore urged as a general principle that the counterpart of the United Kingdom's obligation to respect local autonomy was an obligation on the part of the Islands to co-operate with the United Kingdom in the exercise of its international responsibilities (paragraph 1498). In the final analysis the Commission was convinced that in the event of irreconcilable conflicts of views arising, the United Kingdom government has and should retain the right to decide — and that Parliament has and should retain the right in the last resort to legislate — for the Islands. Indeed, the Commission came to the conclusion that legally Parliament has the paramount power to legislate for the Islands in any circumstances, even though it might be regarded as improper for it to do so (paragraph 1472).

In paragraph 1499 of its Report the Commission enumerated a number of areas of political activity where it suggested that the United Kingdom has paramount powers which it should be free to exercise. The first of these was defence (in regard to which it may be remarked parenthetically that the United Kingdom's freedom of exercise was of little avail to the Islands in the Second World War). Secondly, the Commission mentioned matters common to British people throughout the world, where uniformity of policy is essential throughout Her Majesty's territories; such as the Royal Style and Titles and questions of nationality and citizenship. In its next consideration the Commission indulged in a flight of fancy, stipulating the United Kingdom's freedom to exercise paramount power where the ultimate good government of the Islands was involved — such as the right of intervention to preserve law and order in the event of grave internal disruption. (Possibly General Napier's Shade was hovering over the Commissioners' deliberations at this point.) In connection with international commitments the Commission stressed that any insular claim for exclusion from any international agreement should be reasonable. In particular, no exemption from agreement as to any line of conduct could be tolerated were it to prevent the United Kingdom's participation in that agreement. Lastly, the Commission emphasised the United Kingdom's right to take steps to protect its own domestic interests, such as preventing commercial arrangements damaging to the United Kingdom's economy.

On the other hand, the Commission obviously favoured marked restraint by the United Kingdom in the assertion of the paramountcy imputed to it, stressing in paragraphs 1473, 1498 and 1502 of its Report that parliament should be no more ready than in the past to interfere in the domestic affairs of the Islands, that the Islands have a right to respect for their autonomy, and that the United Kingdom government and parliament ought to be very slow to impose their will on the Islands. It goes without saying that from the Islands' standpoint these paragraphs are of crucial importance.

In another part of its Report the Royal Commission noted an increase in recent years in the number of contentious matters which have not been easily resolved through informal channels of communication. It felt that this difficulty of resolution sprang from the growing complexity of domestic administration and greater international involvement in affairs formerly seen as purely domestic. In paragraph 1517 of its report, therefore, it recommended the setting up of a 'Council of the Islands' to be composed of a chairman and two independent members appointed by the Crown, six representatives of the United Kingdom government and six of the Islands, to be served by an independent secretariat. In paragraphs 1520 and 1523 the Report suggested that the Council should be responsible for considering matters referred to it by any of the governments concerned; for keeping under review relations between the United Kingdom and the Islands; for considering appeals against any United Kingdom government action disliked by any Island; and, lastly, for advising the appropriate Committee of the Privy Council in the event of any petition to the Crown by an aggrieved Island. The Royal Commission further suggested that the Council of the Islands should be empowered to appoint sub-committees to consider particular matters or matters of concern to one Island only.

As far as the status of the Islands as tax havens is concerned, the Commission felt (paragraph 1535) that the situation flowed from the accepted constitutional position and that it was a matter for good sense and co-operation between the United Kingdom and the Island governments to ensure that tax losses to the United Kingdom Exchequer are kept to a minimum.

Obviously one could not expect the Islanders to react with unreserved enthusiasm to all the recommendations of the Commission. In an article in the *Guardian* of February 28th., 1974, Edward Owen remarked that not all Channel Islanders are happy about the conclusion that Westminster has an ultimate paramount power to legislate for the Islands. The article quoted Deputy Cecil de Sausmarez (the Seigneur of the Fief de Sausmarez) as saying that he considered the Report went too far in claiming that the 'United Kingdom Government' is responsible for the 'good government' of the Islands. Instead, he felt that the Commission should have referred to 'The Crown', as the islands' link has always been with the Crown and not with Westminster. Furthermore, Deputy de Sausmarez regretted the Report's failure to reaffirm Mr. Geoffrey Rippon's promise during the E.E.C. negotiations that if the terms offered to the Islands were unacceptable they could opt for complete independence. He added that he believed that full independence should stay on the table as a permanent option in case the E.E.C. or any future similar body should ever threaten the Islands' vital interests.

Time went by without any steps being taken to implement any

of the recommendations of the Kilbrandon Report; yet the investigatory visit of the Commissioners which preceded its publication was to have a bizarre sequel.

This occurred in the spring of 1978 when (partly at the instigation of an organisation called the Guernsey Reform Group) the British Labour Party sent two emissaries in the persons of the backbench M.P.s Mr. John Cartwright and Mr. Arthur Latham to inquire into insular government with a view to making suggestions to their Party for advancing the 'democratization' of what Mr. Cartwright was later to describe in a newspaper article as 'this rather odd corner of the British Isles' in which 'the Labour Party should take a much closer interest' and whose political complexion he likened to that of 'a prosperous market town dominated by Tories masquerading as Independents' — a simile which, drawn by a person of his outlook, can hardly be construed as an expression of unstinted admiration.

However one may interpret the terms of a Report whose compilers seem to have been inspired by St. Paul's example of being all things to all men, one is hard put to it to perceive any corollary whereby an individual British political party is authorised to arrogate to itself the right to stipulate to an autonomous community how it should conduct its own domestic affairs — quite irrespective of the intrinsic merits or demerits of such measures as may be envisaged. Yet it was 'the finding of the Kilbrandon Commission that the United Kingdom parliament has ultimate responsibility for the good government of the islands', which Mr. Cartwright invoked in correspondence with the present writer as justification for the activities of Mr. Latham and himself in regard to what he went on to define in the same letter as 'off-shore dependencies'.

Subsequent experience, however, was to reveal the Cartwright/Latham attitude as positively benign when contrasted with that voiced as from the mid-1980s in the fulminations of Mr. George Foulkes, M.P. (also, incidentally, a Labour Party politician) who, obsessed by the delusion that the fiscal independence of the two Bailiwicks posed a grievous threat to the entire British economy, called repeatedly for their incorporation into the United Kingdom — an aspiration far removed from the constitutional circumspection of Kilbrandon and which in its immoderation provided the theme of the pseudonymous 'Desmond Walker's' brilliant satires in his novels *Bedlam in the Bailiwicks* (1987) and *Task Force Channel Islands* (1989). Completely ignoring such jocular sallies, however, this particular leopard showed no signs of changing its spots with the passage of the years. Addressing a meeting at the Duke of Richmond Hotel in December 1995 yet another Labour politician — the Right Honourable Roy Hattersley (from April 1997 Lord Hattersley) — expressed his party's 'general disapproval' of tax havens and, finding it 'reprehensible' that the freedom of islanders to go and settle in the United Kingdom is not matched by unrestricted movement in the opposite direction, deplored the enjoyment by the two Bailiwicks of 'some of the benefits of British Citizenship' without their making 'a full contribution to British society'. It would seem that such major contributions as the carnage of the First World War entailing the sacrifice of 7% of the manhood of an island whose sons, strictly speaking, were under no obligation to fight beyond its shores; and the service in H.M. Forces during the Second World War (all as volunteers) of 17% of the Bailiwick's population — not to mention the monetary assistance or its equivalent extended to the United Kingdom in 1927 and 1987 — had all failed to impinge upon this Privy Councillor's consciousness! Be that as it may, in January 1998, eight months after his party's assumption of office, Lord Hattersley's comminatory remarks were followed by action decried by the then Bailiff, Sir Graham Dorey, as 'a profound breach of constitutional convention' likely to 'impact detrimentally upon reciprocal respect' between the Bailiwick and the United Kingdom. The conduct of which Sir Graham complained was seen in the Blair administration's discourteous neglect of any prior consultation with the respective insular authorities before announcing in the House of Commons its unilateral initiation of a review of financial regulations in the Channel Islands and the Isle of Man — behaviour tantamount to making a governmental decree involving the islands and completely at variance with hitherto accepted practice congruent with the United Kingdom's obligation to respect local autonomy as emphasised in the Kilbrandon Report. Sad to say, the 'atmosphere of suspicion' which Sir Graham felt had been created by this churlishness was intensified rather than diminished by the contemptuously dismissive attitude to traditional proprieties later displayed by the Home Secretary's brusque declaration that 'it would have been false to have implied that we were going to consult widely with the islands on whether to have a review'.

With the persistence of so ill-disposed a posture on the part of the Blair administration, the continuance of the 'centuries of mutual trust and respect' to which Guernsey had alluded in its submission to the Kilbrandon Commission came to be seen as increasingly problematical, prompting Advocate St. John Robilliard, at a conference on the archipelago's relationships with the United Kingdom and the European Union which was held in Jersey during November 1998 to voice the fear that the islands' advantages might be eroded away — and consequently to urge that Guernsey and Jersey should seek a greater degree of independence than that inherent in their autonomy. Similar misgivings were expressed during the same autumn by an eminent Bailiwick resident — the distinguished Parliamentarian Sir Edward du Cann — who, writing in the 1998 *Alderney Society Bulletin* and perceiving that 'if we retain our deferential subservience to the current official view in the United Kingdom ... we face the prospect that our finance industries ... will certainly be at risk', asked, 'Why should we not seek independence within the British Commonwealth?' The perturbation engendered by the British Government's animus (intensified by its niggardly reimbursement demands precipitating the curtailment of reciprocal health provision to the detriment of the islands' tourist industry and coupled with the apprehension relative to the European Union considered in Chapter Twenty-four of Part V) was reflected in the foundation at about the same time of a pressure group operating as the Campaign for an Independent Guernsey and calling for the Bailiwick to seek to exchange its status of a Crown Dependency for that of an independent member of the Commonwealth, retaining the Queen as its Head of State in her capacity as the latter day successor to the ancient Dukes of Normandy. Admittedly early reactions to the launch of this campaign failed to accord it majority support — but it would seem that this public tepidity merely reflected widespread confidence in the historic Guernsey/United Kingdom relationship being respected by Brussels and honoured by Westminster. However, the possibility that such trust could be misplaced manifested itself in November 1999 in the shape of the veiled threat to Guernsey's fiscal autonomy made by a governmental answer to a question in the House of Lords to the effect that an Order-in-Council confirming a Projet de Loi modifying the island's tax regulations in a way displeasing to the European Union could not be guaranteed. Alerted by this malign revelation, Lord Lamont, speaking in each Bailiwick, warned that both Jersey and Guernsey should consider independence 'a practical possibility'; while in Jersey Senator Pierre Horsfall agreed that such a step could no longer be ruled out — coincident with Advocate R.A. Perrot in Guernsey writing in similar vein to the Editor of the *Press and Star*. A point of crisis had clearly been reached, with insular suspicion of the United Kingdom's bona fides accentuated by anxiety over the constitutional implications of 'new-style' gubernatorial appointments already mentioned in Chapter Eight of this Part.

'"Curiouser and curiouser," said Alice.'

Chapter Twelve

PARISH ADMINISTRATION

IN CONSIDERING the genesis of Guernsey's parochial administration a fact of great significance is that the dividing line between the Fief du Cotentin and the Fief du Bessin, into which Duke Richard II divided Guernsey, *c.* 1020, coincides with the present-day parish boundaries from the Braye du Valle to St. Pierre-du-Bois. This coincidence enhances the indications that the parishes existed in the 11th. century, as is further proved by the names of churches in Norman Charters of the period. Furthermore, the boundaries of the sub-fiefs (as shown in the Livres de Perchage) always follow parish boundaries, save in the case of Torteval, which, as has been seen, lost territory to St. Pierre-du-Bois in the 13th. century. The generality of this coincidence of fief divisions with parish boundaries indicates the great antiquity of the parish units, which on this evidence must have pre-dated the effective Norman organisation of the island inaugurated by Geoffrey de Montbrai after his appointment to the See of Coutances in 1049.

It would seem that these ancient ecclesiastical parishes originated as agricultural (and hence social) units. The term 'villa' was employed in Latin documents when referring to a parish, and this in itself is indicative of an agricultural unit (a Roman farming estate). Thus the parish was not only an ecclesiastical, but also a 'natural' unit, easily capable of adaptation into an important unit of secular administration.

This emergence of the parish as an administrative unit of consequence was greatly stimulated by the General Eyres of the 14th. century — largely because they required each parish to provide an Harèle, or Jury of Presentment. In this connection it should perhaps be explained that a Jury of Presentment was a company of men sworn to render a true answer upon facts or matters within their own knowledge, for which reason they were summoned from the neighbourhood to which the question submitted to them related, or in which the person lived as to whose conduct the investigation was held. They would be asked questions such as, 'What are the customs of your area?'; 'What rights has the King in your area?'; 'Name all the landowners in your area and say now much land each has'; 'Name all the persons in your area whom you suspect of...'; 'Does Guillaume or Jean have the greater right to Le Clos à L'Essart?' The importance of the information thus obtained can be gauged by remembering that the Extentes drawn up by the Sixth General Eyre in 1331 were based on the testimony of such 'harèles'. These parish spokesmen (who were often summoned against their will) sometimes did not reveal all they knew, and there is evidence of the itinerant justices fining the parishes for these concealments — to which the 'communities of the parishes' (possibly embryonic parochial administrations) responded by appointing attorneys to sue in the King's Court for the rescinding of these fines.

The responsibility for forming the parish into a police unit also very likely rests with the General Eyres, in view of the fact that they imposed on the parishes the duties of pursuing malefactors, keeping watch at night, keeping prisoners in custody and seeing that suspects in sanctuary did not escape from the church.

This imposition of police duties on the parishes by the General Eyres of the 14th. century very likely brought about the origin of the office of parish constable — the lynch-pin of parochial administration. It is most probable that the holders of this office were included among the members of the States as from the first emergence of that body — and (as has been seen) they so remained until 1844.

Despite the antiquity of this office, however, the first documentary mention of parish constables is dated February 1438, and deals with the action to be taken by them should any stranger arrive in the Island without lodging. Other early references occur in Henry VII's Order-in-Council of 1495 (which, *inter alia*, required that these officials should be elected in a regular manner) and in a ruling of the Royal Court of 1535 instructing parish constables to ensure compliance with its regulations regarding road upkeep. However, the first reference in the official records housed at the Greffe is as late as 1570, taking the form of an insistence by the Royal Court that the constables must see to the implementation of the ordinances passed by that body.

An Order-in-Council of 1846 describes the constableship as 'a laborious and responsible office' which is 'compulsory upon all qualified persons'; and to this day the acceptance of the office is obligatory on anyone duly nominated, seconded and elected.

The 'laborious and responsible' nature of the appointment meant that through the years the office was often assumed with reluctance, which was made even more pronounced by the foreboding that, once elected, one would be kept in office for an inordinate length of time. The anxiety to remove the prospect of the treadmill in perpetuity led in 1778 to a 'requête' from the parishes to the Royal Court for a legal limit on the period of office. This supplication elicited a new ordinance whereby the constables' term of office was not to be more than three years, but need not be more than one year, after which a new election became permissible if demanded by a meeting of the Chefs de Famille of any parish. This regulation still stands.

The distaste with which the office was regarded became manifest yet again in 1799, when there was a complaint by the Law Officers of the Crown that constables delayed taking the oath after an election so as to postpone as long as possible (and, it was hoped, *sine die*) the assumption of their duties. This led to a Court Ordinance that any constable-elect was to appear in court for swearing-in as soon as summoned, subject to a fine of £100 — a vast sum in those days. In this connection it is interesting to note that, referring to the election of constables, Article 61 of 'The Reform (Guernsey) Law, 1948' states — 'After any election every successful candidate shall take an oath of office before the Royal Court *at the instance of the Law Officers of the Crown or either of them*, and after taking of such oath the validity of the election shall not be further subject to question'.

A regulation of 1801 required one constable per parish to attend the Court of Chief Pleas to facilitate the promulgation and execution of laws and ordinances. Although this custom still persists, constables are nowadays excused further attendance as soon as they have made their reports.

The 1846 Order-in-Council referred to above describes the fourfold duties of constables as presiding over meetings of the parish douzaine, keeping the parish records, acting as parish treasurer, and assuming police responsibilities. It was the last-named of these functions which constituted the original (and for many years the primary) responsibility of parish constables. Documentary evidence is extant of their being authorised in 1581 to search for stolen property in suspected premises, provided they were in the company of two men of means. However, this surveillance by the affluent does not seem still to have been insisted on in 1661, when the constables' police functions were further strengthened, in that victims of theft were recommended by the Royal Court to apply to the parish constables, whose authority to make house searches was reaffirmed.

The responsibilities shouldered by the constables were slowly but profoundly modified between the years 1838 and 1920 — a period which saw the gradual emergence of a professional island constabulary. In the first of these years public disquiet at increasing crime in St. Peter-Port led to the douzaine of that parish instituting a system of conscripting 12 unpaid auxiliaries (each compelled to serve for a year) as reinforcements for the parish constables. By 1853 law enforcement problems associated with the growth of the town resulted in the St. Peter-Port douzaine appointing four uniformed salaried assistant constables. As a consequence of further population expansion the number of these 'assistants' was increased to six in 1870, and 12 in 1902. (Incidentally, the last surviving member of the St. Peter-Port parochial constabulary, P.C. No. 6 — later sergeant — Frederick George Le Poidevin — obit. Christmas Day 1952 — is remembered with considerable affection by the present writer, whose great-uncle he was.) In the year 1896 similar problems in other parishes caused the Vale, St. Sampson's and St. Martin's to emulate St. Peter-Port by appointing their own paid uniformed assistants, numbering two, two and one respectively. The need for a force covering the entire island was highlighted by the 1914 war emergency, though such a body was initially regarded as a purely temporary measure for the duration of hostilities only. Thus in 1915, a salaried island constabulary was created, consisting of an inspector, two sergeants, two corporals, and 11 constables, supplemented by six further constables seconded from the St. Peter-Port force. The following four years witnessed the extraordinary spectacle of a fascinating variety of policing devices, consisting of the Temporary Island Force, the St. Peter-Port police, the uniformed officers of the Vale, St. Sampson's and St. Martin's — and lastly the parish constables operating the honorary system of antiquity. Experience soon indicated that in the interests of justice, law enforcement and efficiency, such a plethora of policing provision was impracticable. After due deliberation in the States in 1919 the upshot was the Projet de Loi entitled 'Loi ayant rapport à la Police Saleriée de l'ile entière' which was registered in January 1920 and whereby the present Island Police Force was constituted under the control of a Committee of the States.

Parochial police vanished from the scene. As a result of this evolution the police functions of the parish constables waned to the point of being little more than a legal fiction. Nevertheless, miniature bâtons still provide their symbol of office.

The practice throughout the years has been for each parish to elect two constables. The 'senior' constable assumes the more active rôle, while his 'junior' counterpart (who was elected a year later) is largely in the position of an apprentice, ready to assume the responsibilities of his 'senior' when the latter retires after two years as constable. In this way continuity in office is assured. In the country parishes the constables usually retire after two years, one as a 'junior', and one as a 'senior; but in St. Peter-Port it is customary for both constables to serve their full three years under the 1778 Ordinance — and then to seek re-election, so that they frequently remain at their posts for many years. Another contrast between St. Peter-Port and the other parishes is that in the former the constables are normally elected from among the members of the douzaine, whereas in the latter it is usual to seek election as a douzenier *after* serving two years as constable.

During the 19th. century constables had to see that hedges, walls, ditches and banks were kept in good order, that pumps, wells and fountains were looked after, and roads kept clean and repaired. Only constables could number houses, and they also had to keep a register of those under police supervision in their parish. Most of these tasks are now performed by various States Committees — Guernsey has been no exception to the trend whereby erstwhile local government functions have been lost to the central administration.

In the early years of the 19th. century the constables of St. Peter-Port entered the lists as the champions of their ill-used parishioners. In 1810 and 1811, in order to finance road works, the Royal Court tried to impose taxes on the parishioners without their consent and ordered the constables to advance the money. Parish meetings were hurriedly assembled in defence of parochial rights, and as a result the constables were charged with disobedience to the Royal Court and were jailed. The matter was referred to the Privy Council, whose decision was in favour of the parishioners on the grounds that although the Court could order repairs to be made, it could not originate any new work, and had no power to levy taxes on the inhabitants without their consent.

Nowadays the constables' duties are almost entirely clerical. They preside over meetings of the douzaine, keep the minutes and deal with the correspondence. They issue shot gun, liquor and Sunday trading licences. They also collect the parochial taxation based on the Cadastre (the register of the annual value of real property). The amount to be collected is sanctioned by a ratepayers' meeting and is authorised by the issue of a 'Rémède' by the Royal Court (see Appendix XVIII). Ratepayers have the option of further objection to the Royal Court while the 'Rémède' is being considered. In addition, the constables, in conjunction with their douzaines, issue documents known as 'Bornéments' when application is made for any building development or alteration within 30 feet of a road. In this connection their concern is limited to the *alignment* of the building and does not include the type of development, which is under the control of yet another Committee of the States — the Island Development Committee. In their capacity as treasurers the constables make any payments which are necessary on behalf of their parishes — and their accounts have to be audited and presented to a parish meeting of ratepayers prior to their retirement from office.

In considering the constables, reference has occasionally been made to the douzaine — the name given to the governing body of each parish. The very name, evocative of 'twelve good men and true', suggests that this ancient body might well have evolved from the 14th.-century Juries of Presentment summoned by the General Eyres; or possibly from the contemporary 'communities of the parishes' which sued in the King's Court for the rescinding of collective fines imposed on the parishes.

It is also possible, however, that these parochial bodies might have arisen in conscious or unconscious imitation of the douzaines responsible for drawing up Livres de Perchage in the feudal fiefs — and in this connection it is significant that as late as 1785 the St. Peter-Port douzaine still referred to itself as the 'Douzaine of Fief Le Roi' and when reprimanded by the Royal Court for this practice, pleaded that it had 'always' done so.

Until 1844 douzeniers were elected for life, with sons frequently following their fathers. Hence they tended to form a parochial conservative oligarchy. This tendency was reinforced by the fact that under a Royal Court Ordinance of 1621 (which was reaffirmed in 1841) douzeniers, to be eligible for office, had to hold real property to the value of 30 quarters of wheat rente (£600) in St. Peter-Port, and to the value of 10 quarters of wheat rente (£200) in the other parishes. On top of this the narrowness of the franchise also served to maintain the olympian status of the douzaine. The above-mentioned 1621 ordinance restricted the suffrage to the owners of real property to the value of at least five quarters of wheat rente (£100). There was a modest extension in 1841 to include all taxpayers: and even up to the Second World War ownership or occupancy of property was essential to the enjoyment of the franchise.

Under the 1948 Reform Law, anybody on the voters' list is now eligible for the office of douzenier for his parish of residence. Service on the douzaine is no longer compulsory, the candidate having to sign a declaration of willingness to serve. Under the same Reform Law douzeniers are now elected for six years, with two retiring each year. A retiring douzenier may, if he so wishes, seek re-election. The franchise now includes all residents of the parish on the Electoral Roll for the election of States deputies. Finally, by the same Reform Law the four Cantonal douzaines in St. Peter-Port, which came into existence in 1844 as a device for giving the town greater representation in the States, were abolished.

Previously douzaines had the duty of assessing the value of property for taxation purposes, as well as administering the laws of Préciput (which have already been considered). A very early function, for which they are still responsible, was the compilation of Livres de Perchage for Crown Fiefs in their parishes. Nowadays they keep surveillance over banks, walls, douits, drinking troughs, and streams, as well as having to see that hedges are trimmed and quarries fenced.

Despite its name, the St. Peter-Port douzaine is 20 strong, but two of its members are also the parish constables, whereas in the other parishes the constables are not members of the douzaine. Outside St. Peter-Port all the douzaines are 12 in number, apart from that of the Vale parish, which has 16 members, four of whom represent the Vingtaine de l'Epine.

Douzaine meetings, which are held in private, are convened by the parish constables. The senior constable presides, while his junior keeps the minutes. The longest-serving douzenier is the dean (or doyen) of the douzaine, with the douzenier with second-longest service as the vice-dean. It is the dean who recites the opening and closing prayers at each meeting. He is the key-man and sets the tone of the whole douzaine. Attendance is compulsory, any defaulting douzenier incurring a fine of 5p, which goes to a fund to buy wreaths for deceased local worthies.

The douzaine prepares the parochial budget for submission to the ratepayers at the Easter parish meeting. If this budget is agreed the constables apply to the Royal Court for a Rémède to levy the appropriate tax on realty in the parish. Furthermore, before any States meeting, each douzaine is furnished with a copy of the Billet d'Etat. The douzaine considers the agenda and forms opinions on its proposals. However, the douzaine representative in the States is not bound by these opinions, though he will, of course, bear them in mind.

The tenfold functions of a modern Douzenier were summed up with great clarity on placards which the Vale Douzaine, with commendable initiative, displayed in June 1984. They were shown to embrace: attendance at all meetings convened by the Constables for the general welfare of the Parish; attendance at Douzaine Meetings held prior to States' Meetings to discuss the Billet d'Etat with the parochial Deputies as well as considering other parish business; reporting to the Constables any complaints from parishioners where remedial action is needed; looking after the particular interests of one of the Parochial Cantons; carrying out twice a year the inspection of hedges and watercourses in the Parish; making site visits for the issue of Bornéments; staffing polling stations for elections; serving when required as members of certain States' Committees; attendance at the States of Election for the elections of Jurats; serving when required as Douzaine Representatives in the States.

This mention of the Vale Douzaine calls to mind arrangements ancillary to local government and unique to the neighbourhood which exist in le Clos du Valle and reflect the strong *esprit de corps* of the vicinity nurtured by its prolonged separation from the rest of Guernsey prior to the reclamation of la Braye du Valle in 1806. Thus it is that although (as its name suggests) L'Ancresse Common is available to all islanders for pleasure and recreation, grazing rights thereon attach solely to the residents of the erstwhile islet — les Habitants du Clos du Valle — some of whom also enjoy furze-cutting and quarrying entitlements on designated plots. The creation of the Golf Course in 1890 brought about the loss of some of these allotments and the families concerned still receive annual financial compensation for the deprivation then suffered. To les Habitants also is restricted the franchise for electing the five-member L'Ancresse Commons Council (two of whom must be Vale Douzeniers) serving for five years and charged with the regulation and supervision of the use of the Common by a series of Ordinances of the Royal Court from 1839 onwards and culminating in that of 1932 under the terms of which the Council now operates. This body (which, incidentally, is answerable annually to a meeting open to all Habitants, any one of whom is thereby given an opportunity to make representations or voice grievances) nowadays finds one of the most intractable problems confronting it to be that of resisting the persistent intrusions of the motor-car on the pleasant expanse of greensward bordering a magnificent bay for the protection of which it is accountable. One of its responsibilities however — the control of race meetings — has been in abeyance since 1994 as a result of the Guernsey Race Organizers' decision reached early that year to suspend such events (dating back to 1830) because of an insufficiency of thoroughbred horses in the island.

Before leaving the subject of parish administration, mention must be made of Les Procureurs des Pauvres, who inherit another historical office, dating possibly from the attempts of the Calvinist Establishment to provide poor relief in the face of 16th.-century inflation. A system then came into being (and persisted up to the First World War) whereby money for the relief of the indigent was raised by each parish, being collected by 'Collecteurs des Pauvres', who handed the proceeds to the 'Procureur des Pauvres' of the parish concerned and also helped him in caring for the poor.

After the end of the First World War the office of Collecteur des Pauvres was abolished, but the Procureurs des Pauvres were retained, becoming answerable to the States' Poor Law Authority, although still elected on a parish basis. Thus to this day each parish has two Procureurs des Pauvres, a senior and a junior. In St. Peter-Port they are helped by Overseers of the Poor, who are also elected and unpaid. It is usual for a person intending to embark on a career in parochial politics to seek election as Procureur des Pauvres, as this appointment tends to be regarded as the first step in such a career.

Chapter Thirteen

ALDERNEY: 'HEREDITARY GOVERNORS' TO STATES' PRESIDENTS

AT THE RESTORATION, Charles II granted Alderney to three Jersey royalists, Edward and James de Carteret and Clement Le Couteur, for an annual rent of 13 shillings. In the autumn of the same year (1660) they sold their rights to Sir George Carteret, who became governor of Alderney. The government of the island was divorced from that of Guernsey, any mention of Alderney being expressly omitted from the Letters Patent issued to Lord Hatton on his belated appointment as governor of Guernsey in 1664.

Technically, Sir George Carteret held Alderney of the Crown as a feudal fief of which he was seigneur, and the same applied to his successors. However, the attitude of the islanders, plus the fact that the governmental institutions referred to later in this chapter were already well developed, meant that no seigneur and tenant relationship comparable to that of Sark was practicable. By contrast, any attempt even to make use of the title of seigneur was likely, in the Alderney atmosphere, to provoke intense resentment — as one of the governors (John Le Mesurier) found when he tried to do so in the early 19th. century.

In such circumstances the title of 'Governor' became current, and although such a designation, strictly speaking, was a local conceit, with Privy Council papers (as was pointed out by the late Mr. Maurice Ouseley, sometime Secretary of the Guernsey Society) invariably referring to the 'Governors' as 'Fee Farmers', yet the fact remains that it was used for more than one-and-a-half centuries, and can be represented as both appropriate — in view of Alderney's removal from the jurisdiction of the governor of Guernsey — and also the only one that was practicable, bearing in mind the *realpolitick* of the situation.

Both Sir George Carteret and Captain Nicholas Ling (the erstwhile parliamentary governor of the island whom Sir George had confirmed as his lieutenant) died in 1679. In 1682 Sir George's widow sold the residue of the Patent to Sir Edmund Andros

(Seigneur of the Guernsey Fief de Sausmarez) for £200. Sir Edmund, however, voluntarily resigned his rights to the Crown, in consideration of which a fresh Patent was issued in 1683 farming Alderney to him and his heirs for 99 years at an annual rent of £13 6s. 8d.

Sir Edmund died without issue in 1713, leaving Alderney to his nephew, George Andros, despite the opposition to rule by a Guernseyman from an influential section of the Alderney population, led by Thomas Le Cocq, who had become the island judge in 1704. The following year (1714), however, George Andros also died, and after the death of his two daughters (his immediate heirs) the island passed in 1721 to his sister, Anne, wife of John Le Mesurier. So started the 'reign' of the Le Mesurier dynasty, which lasted for more than a century.

Experience was to prove that the dictum, 'Uneasy lies the head that wears a Crown' was one which applied most fittingly to the Le Mesurier line of governors. On Anne Le Mesurier's death in 1729, her son, Henry, became hereditary governor, but the feud with the Le Cocq faction continued unabated until 1738 when Thomas Le Cocq was suspended from exercising his functions as judge on account of alleged irregularities. He nevertheless retained the office until his death in 1760, his duties being performed meanwhile by Juges-Délégués.

In 1736, while still at loggerheads with Le Cocq, Henry had founded Braye Harbour by constructing the 'New Pier' (now known as the 'Old Jetty'), but in 1744, 'worn out with feuds', he exchanged his patent in Alderney with his younger brother, John, for lands in Guernsey. At the outset of John's Governorship the Alderney Court petitioned for — and obtained from George II in May 1745 — a Seal distinct from that awarded to Guernsey by Edward I in 1279 and depicting a Crowned Lion Rampant with the device surrounded by the words, 'Sigillum Curiae Insulae Origny 1745'. (The sprig held by the Lion, incidentally, was added *circa* 1793, thereby putting the finishing touches to what was to become Alderney's Armorial Bearings, which — with 'Curiae' and '1745' removed — was ultimately — December 20th., 1993 — so registered by the College of Arms and defined as 'Vert, a lion rampant imperially crowned Or, holding in its dexter paw a sprig of broom proper'.) The truculence induced by this boost to the Court's morale boded ill for the new Governor, who in his turn had such difficulties with 'the people, wreckers and pirates by habit and tradition' that in September 1747, in the wake of an altercation with the Le Cocq faction involving firearms, he fled to Guernsey, fearing for his life. The Guernsey Royal Court extended its protection to him, confirming his title of governor and forbidding the States of Alderney to assemble in his absence.

Privateering ventures during the Seven Years War provided an outlet for the 'lawless and insubordinate islanders', who consequently ceased to give serious trouble to John Le Mesurier. Furthermore, the profits yielded by these activities brought such a boom to Alderney that in 1763 John exchanged his Patent for a new grant of 99 years. He enlarged the old family residence, which now became Government House, the new family dwelling becoming Les Mouriaux House, built in 1779. In 1767 he added the clock tower to the old church (it is now all that remains of it), and in 1770 provided the island with its first Court House, the Court having previously met in the open air. Finally, in 1790, the governor endowed the town of St. Anne with a school.

John Le Mesurier died in 1793 and was succeeded by his son, Peter, who had already acted as lieutenant-governor for 20 years. However, when Peter also died in 1803 he left a troubled inheritance to his son, John, who fell foul of the Alderney jurats by assuming the title of seigneur. Four jurats refused to pass a contract in which he was so designated and John's appeal to the Privy Council to enforce recognition of his title was rejected in 1814. In the meantime vigorous action to suppress smuggling taken by the British government in 1808 had brought distress to Alderney — and this was later made worse by the removal of the garrison after Waterloo. The financial burdens on the governor became so onerous that in 1823 John wrote to the Treasury offering to surrender his grant of the island on payment of suitable compensation. In 1824 the British Treasury offered £700 per annum for the rest of the lease (i.e., until 1862). John accepted this offer and surrendered the island in 1825.

With the cessation of the hereditary governorship, the government of Alderney became vested in the Crown, represented by the lieutenant-governor of Guernsey. Alderney's tenuous connection with the rest of the Bailiwick of Guernsey was strengthened, with an ultimate veto being possessed by the larger island.

Attention now needs to be turned to the Institutions of Government which operated under the sway of the hereditary governors — and also to their subsequent development. Right up to the outbreak of the war in 1939 Alderney's political institutions were fourfold, consisting of the Douzaine, the Court, the Court of Chief Pleas, and the States.

The douzaine was the oldest of these bodies and operated as an assembly of 12 heads of families responsible for government at a parochial level, especially the administration of agricultural land, the collection of *vraic* (seaweed) and the marking of boundaries. Its marked resemblance to the Council of Elders of primitive societies indicates the likelihood of its going back to the earliest periods of Alderney's history, when the island was under the joint control of the Crown and of the Bishop of Coutances. Its members were elected by the ratepayers for a period of six years, two retiring annually. They were eligible for re-election, and served until the age of seventy. The senior douzenier (as in Guernsey) was known as the dean, and was chairman of all douzaine meetings. The Procureur du Roi (a Crown appointment) was ex-officio a member of this body.

The Court dated back at least to the 13th. century and probably earlier, as the document 'Status Insulae de Aurineo' (*c.* 1236) shows that the Island Court of six jurats under a Prévôt was already well established by that time. It consisted of the judge, the six jurats, the Procureur du Roi, the Greffier, the Sheriff and the Sergent.

The title of 'Juge' (the lineal descendant of the mediaeval Prévôt) derived from his duty to pronounce the judgement of the Court. The actual term 'Juge' is not found until 1612; so that it would appear that the previous designation of 'Prévôt' survived until the end of the 16th. century. The judge was a Crown appointment.

To qualify for election as jurat a candidate had to be a ratepayer with property assessed at more than 20 quarters of wheat rente (£400), so that the office tended to be hereditary from the 17th. century onwards. The office was an honorary one held until the age of 70, and no legal qualifications were necessary. Jurats were elected by ratepayers with a qualifying age of 20 for men and 21 for women. As married women could not hold property, they could not be ratepayers and so were disfranchised, the female voters being confined to spinsters and widows.

All other members of the Court were Crown appointees. They consisted of the Procureur du Roi (the Crown prosecutor); the Greffier (who, as well as being clerk of the court, was also clerk of the States and registrar for the Island); the Sheriff and the Sergent (with duties comparable to those of their counterparts in Guernsey as already noted in Chapter Nine).

The Alderney Court performed both legislative and judicial functions, issuing ordinances having the force of law and playing an essential part in the passing of contracts. Conveyances and bonds securing loans were presented to the Court, the parties stating that they understood the terms, and the seller or borrower giving an assurance that the appropriate consideration had been received. The transaction was then legalised by the document being signed, not by the contracting parties, but by the judge and two jurats. In the judicial sphere, the Alderney Court's powers in criminal cases were limited to the imposition of imprisonment not exceeding one month and fines not exceeding £10. More serious cases were committed for trial before the Royal Court of Guernsey. In civil cases, however, the Court possessed unlimited competence.

The Court of Chief Pleas had the same composition as the ordinary Court, with the addition of 12 members of the douzaine, and the four constables. The constables were elected every three years by the Chief Pleas itself at its January sitting.

The main concern of this Court (which met twice a year — in January and at Michaelmas) was with matters of public interest, such as laws for trapping vermin and road tax questions. It also considered petitions from members of the public, any one of whom was entitled to address it to voice any complaint he or she might wish to make.

The attributes of this organ clearly indicate its feudal origins as a Fief Court in which suit was paid to the Prévôt (later judge) representing the Crown by the more substantial tenants (the jurats) and those of humbler station (the douzeniers), while facilities were available to any churl to solicit the protection of his lord should he be in any way aggrieved.

As in Guernsey, the States of Alderney evolved as an afforcement of the Court. It consisted of the governor of the island (after 1825 the lieutenant-governor of Guernsey) who either attended or was represented at all meetings; the judge, six jurats, four douzeniers, one douzenier-delegate, the Procureur du Roi, the Greffier, the Sheriff and the Sergent — plus (as from 1923, when they were introduced by a 'Réforme des Etats') three peoples' deputies who held office for three years, being eligible for re-election and retiring at the age of seventy.

The franchise for the election of the deputies embraced all males who had attained the age of 20, and all females of 21 and above, provided they were British subjects and possessed a three-year residence qualification; whereas the four douzeniers to attend the States were elected annually by the ratepayers only. These four douzeniers, incidentally, expressed their own opinions in the deliberations of the States — in contrast to the douzenier-delegate who was appointed by the douzaine to voice its opinion as a body in the Assembly.

Representation in the States was thus weighted heavily in favour of property-owners, who directly or indirectly elected 11 members (six jurats, four douzeniers, and one douzenier-delegate) as against three deputies elected on a popular vote. The functions of the States included finance, the collection of import duties, the allocation of grants for the maintenance of public services, and any general matter concerning the administration of the island. The legislative process approximated to that of Guernsey, consisting of the enactment of Projets de Loi which were ultimately embodied in Orders-in-Council and registered in the Courts of Alderney and Guernsey.

The whole of this governmental structure was demolished by the arrival of the German occupying forces, immediately prior to which virtually the entire population of the island was evacuated to the United Kingdom. During these sad years, however, Alderney was noteworthy in operating a Government in Exile, which succeeded in maintaining the integrity of the insular community. A Voluntary Relief Committee, composed exclusively of Alderney people, was set up in London, elected by a postcard vote to all adult Alderney evacuees. As subsequent postcard votes were taken whenever required for special purposes, the Committee was enabled to be apprised of the opinions of all Alderney refugees and to obtain their approval of its actions. In addition, the members of the Alderney States were on several occasions similarly consulted by post, and their approval obtained for measures recommended by the Committee. It is no exaggeration to say that this experiment in the administration of an exiled community is unique in British constitutional experience.

It is hard to believe, however, that the Relief Committee could possibly have foreseen the extent of the devastation which was to confront the population of Alderney on its return at the end of 1945 — and which made it clear that recovery was beyond the island's unaided resources. For three years the United Kingdom government gave advice and financial assistance, and Home Office officials co-operated in the administration of the island so as to get it on its feet again.

At the end of the period of emergency first aid, Alderney was given the alternative of British or Guernsey control, in order to ensure a minimum of social services. In these circumstances Alderney agreed that Guernsey should assume complete responsibility for its finances; and at the same time undertake the administration of police, education, social services, public health, roads, airport, and water supply — on the basis that Alderney would be taxed on the Guernsey scale. As a result income tax came to Alderney for the first time in its history. Thus under the impulse of cruel necessity, Alderney assented to an arrangement which curtailed its independence and meant that Guernsey laws on social services would apply to the island: and furthermore, that the States of Alderney were precluded from enacting any legislation involving additional expenditure without the sanction of Guernsey — so that the Alderney budget came to require Guernsey approval.

As the result of the recommendations of a Privy Council Committee, the States enacted the Government of Alderney Law, 1948, which now regulates the island's constitution. Under this law the douzaine and the Court of Chief Pleas were abolished, their existence making for an excessively overpowering structure for so small a community. The public's erstwhile right to address the Chief Pleas to voice any grievance was replaced by a comparable right to address the States on two occasions each year. Confusingly, these occasions are still misnamed 'Chief Pleas'.

The same law inaugurated a complete separation of powers as between the Legislature and the Judiciary. The Court, shorn of its legislative functions, consists of a chairman and six jurats, who are no longer elected, but appointed by the Crown. On the other hand, the States of Alderney form the Legislature and consist of an elected president and 12 (originally nine) elected members of equal status. The president was elected at a separate presidential election and held office for three years — as did also States' members. Licensed victuallers are no longer debarred from becoming either jurats or members of the States and no one is required to take an oath inconsistent with his or her religious beliefs. Although under this law States' members served for a three year term, a system was operated whereby one-third of their number was elected annually in December, resulting in a measure of constituent fluidity attaching to the legislature; but in 1996, with a view to ensuring greater stability in the composition both of the States and of its component committees, an amendment was adopted to take effect in January 1997 arranging for half the membership to be elected biennially in December to serve for forty-eight months, with the States' President being elected quadrennially during one of the intervening years.

As far as the franchise is concerned, all sex and property qualifications were abolished, all men and women of 20 years of age and over who have been resident in Alderney for 12 months on October 15th. of any year being entitled to vote in the elections for that year. Similarly, any adult qualified by three years' residence is entitled to stand for election.

Island administration is carried on by some half-dozen Standing Committees of the States. These committees are assisted by the Clerk of the States, who is secretary to all the committees and clerk to the court as well.

Lastly, to protect Alderney's interests, the States of Alderney nominates two of its members to attend the Guernsey States of Deliberation.

The passage of the years has naturally been accompanied by the growth of aspirations for some modification of Alderney's tutelage — and also by some controversy over the application of the post-war constitution. To both these topics attention needs to be directed before concluding this chapter. When shortly after the war, Guernsey assumed responsibility for Alderney's finances, it was anticipated that the larger island would bear an annual £20,000 deficit on its ward's behalf. In the event, however, Alderney for several years cost Guernsey nothing, as its contribution towards Guernsey's tax revenue (*c.* £200,000 per annum) adequately counterbalanced all expenditure incurred, despite heavy spending on the school, roadworks, airport and hospital. Indeed, the pace of Alderney's recovery was such that by 1955 it was in a position to resume responsibility for water-supply and roads; while in 1971 it had its own police again.

In these circumstances the necessity of sending proposals to the Guernsey States for approval was increasingly resented as an affront to Alderney's dignity. Thus, while recognising the value of constant telephonic communication between related departments in the two islands, Alderney manifested a growing hankering for the 'status quo ante bellum' and the States' president declared publicly his Island's desire for something approaching the pre-1948 situation, comparable to that in Sark, 'where we can run our own affairs under the benign eye of Guernsey'.

Furthermore, it was argued that Guernsey's guardianship cost

Alderney thousands of pounds a year for administration and services, plus further fees for the collection of Guernsey taxes — and moreover that Alderney's economic reliance on tourism and wealthy settlers rendered highly undesirable the taxation levels inseparable from the expensive health and other social services stemming from the policies pursued in Guernsey.

This discontent found successful expression in December 1972 when the vehement opposition of the two Alderney representatives won sufficient support in the States of Deliberation to obtain a vote exonerating Alderney from having to impose the increases in spirit and tobacco duties which were being applied to Guernsey. For the first time since the Liberation Alderney had been able to assert the right to maintain its own scale of duties independent of the larger island. Nevertheless, this widespread restiveness did not mean that Alderney was entirely able to dispense with the Guernsey connection. This was made evident in December 1974 when the Guernsey States voted in favour of granting the request of the States of Alderney that the Guernsey Board of Health should administer the Mignot Memorial Hospital in consultation with the Alderney Health and Welfare Committee. What is more, as time went by, the burden of the expenses already mentioned as stemming from Guernsey policies grew increasingly onerous and crisis point was reached with the abrupt cessation of the substantial contribution to Alderney's element in the Guernsey Income Tax yield made by forty-five wealthy residents, who, as 'Lloyd's Names', lost their money in the insurance giant's near collapse. This woeful occurrence was prominent among the factors productive of so marked a decline in the revenue notionally accredited to the island that a renewal of Guernsey's intervention in its affairs comparable to that of the immediate post-war period seemed inevitable — and as a result of the deliberations of a special committee appointed in 1994 to review financial arrangements between the two islands, the decision was reached that their respective tax receipts and expenditure therefrom be administered thenceforth as a single common entity, as was the original intent in 1948.

Turning to the constitutional question, there was nothing in the letter of the 1948 Government of Alderney Law which precluded any person who had been appointed as a jurat from seeking election to the States — despite the fact that to do so could be construed as alien to the spirit of the law which established a separation as between the Legislature and the Judiciary.

The contradiction inherent in this situation became apparent in 1970 when Mr. George Baron, who was already President of the States, accepted appointment as a jurat, subsequently declining to vacate either post. Mr. Baron's action led to a resolution being passed by the Alderney States in January 1971 'that a Member of the States should not also hold the office of Jurat'. Later, after further consideration and in the light of correspondence between the Alderney authorities and the Home Office, a passage was drafted intended to form part of legislation generally amending the parent Government of Alderney Law. The passage reads: 'That a Jurat shall not be eligible as from the date of the next election after the law comes into operation for the presidency or membership of the States'. It was approved by the States in September 1974, but it was not until September 11th., 1975 that the legislation embodying this ineligibility came into force, when the Alderney Court registered the Government of Alderney (Amendment) Law, 1975. Accordingly, Mr. George Baron announced that, not intending to resign his warrant as jurat, he would not seek re-election to the presidency of the States in the December 1975 election. He did, however, return to this office in 1994.

Chapter Fourteen

'SEMPER EADEM': POLITICAL EVOLUTION IN SARK

THE STORY of the evolution of Sark's three political organs (the Court, the Chief Pleas and the Douzaine) resolves itself into a survey of the vicissitudes attending the Court's development from the original Fief Court established by Helier de Carteret; the emergence of the Chief Pleas (an enlarged version of this Fief Court to hear the pleas of the inhabitants) as the island legislature; and the growth of the Douzaine as a local executive body.

As Sark had been granted as a fief by the Crown to Helier de Carteret, he was entitled as seigneur to administer the affairs of his holding through a Fief Court. Furthermore, the Letters Patent of 1565 had given him the specific right to issue contracts under his seal having the same validity as if they had been passed in the Royal Court of Jersey or Guernsey. Accordingly, Helier disregarded a summons to attend the Guernsey Chief Pleas in 1571 to pay suit for his holding; and the elevation of Sark into an independent Fief Haubert in 1572 encouraged him to conceive of an even more exalted status for the island as a 'Little Jersey', with its own Judiciary and officials on an equal footing with those of Jersey and Guernsey.

Helier felt that his opportunity had come in September 1578 when the Royal Commission arrived in Guernsey in connection with the disaffection in that island recounted in Chapter Six. Alarmed lest the Commissioners should recommend that Sark's anomalous position in relation to Guernsey should be resolved by placing the island more firmly under Guernsey's control, the Serquiais petitioned Philippe de Carteret (who was acting as *locum tenens* for his father) to establish an independent Island Administration based on the Jersey model. Seeing fate as playing into his hands, Helier advised Philippe to accede to this request, with the result that on October 27th., 1579 he called a meeting of all tenants and inhabitants at Le Manoir. This meeting decided unanimously to set up an Island Court on the model of Jersey's, consisting of a bailiff and 12 jurats, to administer Sark's affairs. It also chose various officials to assist the Court — a Procureur, a sergent de l'Epée, a sergent ordinaire, a connétable, two vingteniers and two assistants. In all a good half of the total male population of the island was involved in the establishment of this 'Little Jersey'.

The new Court first met on November 5th., 1579 and subsequent meetings occurred at approximately monthly intervals, dealing with such matters as crop damage, unpaid debts, and non-attendance at church. It also ruled that the corpus of Jersey Law as it had existed at the time of Helier de Carteret's original colonisation should be adopted as the Law of Sark.

As soon as Sir Thomas Leighton had finally emerged triumphant from his confrontation with the Guernsey leaders (see Chapter Six) and had installed his nephew, Thomas Wigmore, as bailiff, the Guernsey Royal Court ordered Helier de Carteret to show by what authority a Court of Justice had been set up in Sark. Helier ignored this summons and died before anything more could be done — but his heir, Philippe de Carteret, played into the hands of the Guernsey authorities by refusing to pay Première Saisine (the sum payable by a tenant-in-chief to his feudal overlord on entering into his succession). The Guernsey Royal Court profited of this to take drastic action. On May 28th., 1582 the Procureur laid a formal complaint against Philippe for setting up a Court of Justice without authority in the Bailiwick of Guernsey — and the bailiff and four jurats were sent to Sark to investigate the complaint.

On arrival the Guernsey party ordered Philip Messervy (Philippe de Carteret's deputy) to muster the defence force. When less than 40 assembled the Guernsey bailiff declared Sark forfeit to the Crown. He impounded the records of the Sark Court and arrested the Sark bailiff and two Sark jurats, taking them back to Guernsey. The two jurats were later allowed to return to Sark, but only on condition of abstaining from any judicial function; whilst the Sark bailiff (Edouard de Carteret) was imprisoned in Castle Cornet and, although released two months afterwards, was never allowed to go back to Sark, having to stay in Guernsey until his death in 1601. Finally, the Sark Establishment dethroned, the Guernsey Court sent the Prévôt and the Comptroller to Sark, formally to proclaim saisine of the island and its revenue.

In his plight, Philippe de Carteret appealed to the Privy Council, whose decision was embodied in an Order-in-Council of April 24th., 1583. By this Order Philippe was permitted to inherit the fief on payment of £40 as a token 'Première Saisine'.

Furthermore, the Guernsey Court was instructed to set up a new Sark Court consisting of five jurats (elected by popular vote of the inhabitants), the senior one acting as juge — but this Court's competence was to be limited to civil cases, all criminal cases having to be referred to the Royal Court of Guernsey. It was thus clear that the Order-in-Council unequivocally established Sark's subordination to Guernsey. The dream of any independent 'Little Jersey' was shattered. Nevertheless, Philippe de Carteret continued to exercise his authority as seigneur through his original Fief Court and this new Court ordained by the 1583 Order-in-Council never assembled during his lifetime.

Philippe de Carteret died in 1594, leaving an heir (also Philippe) of 10 years of age. Accordingly the boy's uncle, Amice de Carteret, acted as seigneur during his nephew's minority. As a gesture of goodwill towards Sir Thomas Leighton, Amice immediately arranged for the formal installation of the new Court which had been ordained by Order-in-Council 11 years previously. The ceremony occurred on July 16th., 1594, when five jurats were elected and sworn in, with Robert Slowley (who had received most votes) being appointed as juge.

Things now settled down for nearly half a century until Sir Philippe de Carteret's adherence to the royalist cause led to parliament confiscating the Fief of Sark in 1642, vesting the authority of the seigneur in the juge, Jean Le Gros — a worthy whose family now became dominant in the Island, its position being further strengthened in 1649 by the marriage of Jean junior to Anne Brévint, the daughter of the formidable minister. The upshot was that the Le Gros faction was able to run the Island according to its wishes and exploited the situation to its own advantage. Ignoring the Letters Patent of 1611 (see Part II, Chapter Ten), tenements were dismembered, mortgages contracted, and new houses built — all by the authority of the Court under the thumb of Le Gros.

Sir Philippe de Carteret died in 1643, and although his son (again Sir Philippe) was reinstated at the Restoration, he, too, died in 1663; so that the minority of his heir (yet another Philippe) enabled the Le Gros faction to continue its domination of the island, still employing the Court as the instrument of its designs. When, however, he came of age in 1671 the young Philippe sought to assert his authority as seigneur and obtained an Order-in-Council *suspending* the Sark Court on the grounds that the jurats refused to take the oath of allegiance and supremacy in the

Anglican form required by the royal grant of pardon in 1661. Because of the prestige of the minister (Elie Brévint) further action was precluded as long as he lived, but after his death in 1674 Philippe obtained another Order-in-Council (May 19th., 1675) whereby the Royal Court of Guernsey was instructed to *abolish* the Sark Court in its existing form, replacing it with one consisting of nominees of the seigneur.

It is this Court instituted by the Order-in-Council of 1675 and installed on July 15th. of the same year, which has persisted unchanged to the present day. It consists of a Seneschal, with a Prévôt and Greffier as Court officers. As all are appointed by the seigneur, this Court was largely a reversion to the Fief Court originally established by Helier de Carteret and denies the inhabitants any voice in the selection of their Judiciary. The Seneschal became invested with the same powers as the juge and jurats of the earlier Court, enjoying universal competence in civil cases, but in criminal cases having his competence restricted to fines up to £50 sterling, or imprisonment to a maximum of one month — with cases calling for higher penalties having to be remitted to the Royal Court of Guernsey.

Despite the fact that, once appointed, he cannot be dismissed by the seigneur, the Seneschal originally had to contend with the suspicion that, as the seigneur's nominee, he would not be impartial in any case where the seigneur was involved. These suspicions were finally allayed during the time when William Frederick Collings was seigneur (1882–1927). This seigneur's bizarre behaviour brought him several times before the Seneschal's Court on such charges as assault and battery, abusive language, and breaking windows. The Seneschal (Thomas Godfray) did not hesitate to impose upon his seigneur the appropriate penalties for his misdemeanours.

The time has now come to consider the metamorphosis whereby a judicial organ — Le Cour des Chefs Plaids — became Sark's Legislature. The birth of this assembly to regulate the affairs of the fief took place on November 5th., 1579 when (as has already been seen) the Court of Bailiff and Jurats appointed a few days previously met for the first time — and issued an ordinance requiring everyone to ring his pigs. Its midwife, however, may be regarded as the meeting summoned by Philippe de Carteret on October 27th., 1579, which decided on the creation of this original Court of Chief Pleas — and it is noteworthy that this meeting was essentially an enlargement of Helier de Carteret's original Fief

Court, in that in this instance all tenants attended as participants and not merely to pay suit for their holdings. Thus, although in the Court which it set up no distinction was made between judicial and legislative functions, nevertheless this inaugural meeting served as a precedent for establishing the right of the inhabitants to take part in the administration of the Island, assembling, *inter alia*, to hear the pleas of the islanders. This tradition was maintained in the revised Court of 1583/94 where legislative business was conducted in the sessions attended by the inhabitants; so that in Sark, as in Guernsey, the nascent legislature consisted of an afforcement of a Court of Justice.

A distinction between the judicial and emergent legislative functions of this Court was made by the Order-in-Council of 1583 (implemented in 1594) in that it referred only to the jurats in connection with the administration of justice, but required 'the consent of the Seigneur of the said Island and of the generality of the inhabitants' for the making of 'such Ordinances as they may find expedient and necessary from time to time for the regulation of public order in the said Island'. It was in this way that the legislative Chief Pleas, which included 'the generality of the inhabitants', came to be a distinct entity from the Court in its judicial capacity, consisting solely of juge and jurats. The same Order-in-Council ordered the convening of Chief Pleas 'three times a year, namely at about the first Wednesday after the twenty-ninth day of September, the first Wednesday after the fifteenth day of January and the first Wednesday after Easter Day'.

Originally all adult male members of the population participated on equal terms in Chief Pleas, but as time went by a new generation of younger sons arose who were accommodated in additional houses built on the family holdings, but who were under no obligation to form part of the island defence force. Accordingly, a meeting of Chief Pleas on January 23rd., 1605 (new style) passed an ordinance to the effect that only the tenants of the original tenements would have a voice as Chefs de Famille in future proceedings — and the term, 'Maisons de la Quarantaine' came into use to differentiate the original 40 tenements to whose holders membership of Chief Pleas was now restricted.

Despite the replacement by the Seneschal's Court of the Court of Juge and Jurat in 1676, the latter in its legislative persona survived with the Seneschal, by virtue of his office presiding over its meetings as the juge (and previously the bailiff) had done before him — it being understood, however, that only the seigneur (and not the presiding Seneschal) could convene Chief Pleas.

At the beginning of the present century the fiscal attractions of Sark began to lure immigrants whose arrival progressively diversified the character of the island community and radically changed the personnel of the Quarantaine Holdings (who alone constituted Chief Pleas) in that the holdings became concentrated in a small number of individuals. Thus by the end of the First World War the situation had been reached whereby the Baker family held nine tenements, the Godfray family five, and the seigneur three, while ten were in the hands of non-islanders, resulting in a tight oligarchy with the bulk of the population being deprived of any adequate representation in the body that determined their destinies. This led to the Sark Reform Law, approved by Order-in-Council of June 20th., 1922, whereby 12 people's deputies were to be added to the membership of Chief Pleas, elected by all men over 20 and all women over thirty.

Apart from the people's deputies, members of Chief Pleas enjoy a vote in respect of their Quarantaine holdings only and not in respect of their personal status. Thus the seigneur, like everyone else, has as many votes as he has holdings (currently two). After a vote has been taken on any subject (by roll-call) the Seneschal asks the seigneur or his representative for his approval and, this once given by word of mouth, the matter is concluded. The ordinances of Chief Pleas technically are subject to the approval of the Guernsey Royal Court — but this is never withheld. Conversely, Guernsey legislation is applicable to Sark only if ratified by Chief Pleas. Such ratification has not been accorded to the Guernsey income tax laws. Not until 1977 was it accorded to the divorce law, so that prior to that the Serquiais were free of income tax, but bound to their spouses. If inheritance is involved, they still were as late as 1999, though in August that year the Seigneur announced that proposals were anticipated for the enactment by Chief Pleas of a Sark Divorce Law as a corollary of the modifications to the island's inheritance laws examined below. A particularly interesting example of the denial of ratification (motivated by resentment at the threat to the island's autonomy posed by the encroachment of European Community legislation, regarding which it was resolved that the Seigneur should protest to the Lieutenant-Governor) was provided in January 1993 by the refusal to ratify three Projects de Loi implementing Community regulations regarding military exercises, the Organization for Economic Co-operation and Development and the European Bank for Reconstruction and Development. Chief Pleas further emphasized its disquiet by requiring the European Affairs Committee to nominate a member to attend future inter-island meetings the better to monitor developments concerning the Community so as to clarify Sark's position in relation thereto.

A further Sark Reform Law was confirmed by Order-in-Council in 1951. Prior to its enactment, if the seigneur refused his approval of the vote of Chief Pleas, the matter was referred to the Royal Court of Guernsey, with a final appeal to the Privy Council. By the 1951 law, the seigneur's veto becomes null and void if Chief Pleas re-approve an ordinance within 21 days thereof. In addition, the provisions for the election of peoples' deputies were reaffirmed, as they had not been fully implemented after the 1922 law. Finally, Corvée was abolished in favour of a household levy, and the seigneur was given the right to apply at any time for help from the Guernsey police force.

From the time of its inception, married women Quarantaine holders were debarred from participation in Chief Pleas, though a husband could sit and vote in respect of his wife's holding. In practice an exception had been made in the case of the late Dame de Sercq (whose husband was legally the seigneur) and the 1951 law removed this anomaly by granting both voice and vote to married women holders of one of 'The Forties'. Further legislation approved by Chief Pleas in November 1974 — and confirmed by Order-in-Council in June 1975 — gave all married women in Sark rights broadly equivalent to those of wives in the rest of the Bailiwick. As a result a married woman now enjoys some entitlement in the disposal of personal movable property, one-third of which may be disposed freely if she has children, the other two-thirds going to surviving spouse and children respectively. If she has no children, or is a widow, she may dispose of half her personal movable property, with her surviving spouse (or children as the case may be) being entitled to the other half. Only if she is both a widow and childless may she freely dispose of all her personal movables. However, a married woman is not able to dispose of real estate, as to do so would conflict with Sark's inheritance laws stemming from the Letters Patent of 1611 (see Part II, Chapter Ten). Similar concern, incidentally, was manifested for the sanctity of these laws in January 1977 when Chief Pleas voted to acknowledge divorces obtained elsewhere, except where they affected inheritance rights — though the approaching discontinuance of this exception was foreshadowed in August 1999 with the imminent expectation announced by the Seigneur of the enactment of a Sark Divorce Law congruent with the modification of the Fief Haubert's inheritance laws considered in the next paragraph. While alive a married woman may take employment or run a business, enjoying the resultant earnings in her own name.

Prior to this, however, Chief Pleas, little realizing the possible consequences of so doing, had in 1971 accepted the European Convention on Human Rights — and the chickens thereby hatched ultimately came home to roost in September 1998, ushering in an episode pregnant with profound implications for Sark's constitutional arrangements. Forebodings of such an unwelcome return of the poultry were reflected in a petition signed by 61% of Sark's adult population and submitted in December 1997 to the European Commission asking that the island's feudal way of life be left undisturbed and changed only by the Serquiais themselves should they so desire (see also Part V, Chapter Twenty-four). That the petitioners' fears were well founded became apparent the following September when a Law Reform Report submitted by the Chief Pleas General Purposes and Advisory Committee pointed out that the Human Rights Convention was infringed by the Fief Haubert's inheritance laws with their application of the ruling laid down in the Letters Patent of August 12th., 1611, obtained from James I by Sir Philippe de Carteret (see Part II, Chapter Ten) that 'no lands or tenements lying or being within the said Isle of Sark or any parts thereof shall or ought to be partable or parted amongst any sonnes and daughters .... but shall, from time to time, descend and come wholy (*sic*) and directly to the eldest son and other heirs of the sonne'. The Report therefore recommended that the rule of male primogeniture be abolished so as to enable realty to be devolved by will — with the proviso that the indivisibility of tenements be preserved. It was also recommended that in the case of a tenant dying intestate title to the tenement would vest in the eldest child regardless of sex. No change of legislation was suggested regarding leaseholds, personalty, Seigneurial Rights and corporate ownership of realty. After a period of nervous uncertainty the upshot was that at the 1999 Easter Chief Pleas the Seigneur revealed a set of proposals which had emerged from discussion with the Home Office, the aim of which was so to modify the 388-year-old inheritance laws as to reconcile them with the preservation of

Sark's feudal life-style. It was felt that this could be done by minimising change while complying with Human Rights requirements to the extent that male preference would disappear as would also age preference save in cases of intestacy, a limited disposition of property would be ensured and current rights protected. Thus under these proposals — which were eventually approved at an extraordinary meeting of Chief Pleas held in June 1999 — holders of tenements and freeholders become entitled to dispose of their holdings by will (with the proviso that their indivisibility must be preserved) to descendants of their choice or, failing any such, to anyone with Sark residential qualifications: but in the case of anyone dying intestate the applicable principle is to be that of primogeniture devoid of any sex discrimination. An entirely distinct — and unwelcome — additional consequence of Sark's adherence to the Human Rights Convention became apparent in July 2000 when the likelihood of the island's traditional property tax conflicting with the Convention's requirements led to the reluctant recommendation that it be replaced by the long-shunned levy of an Income Tax. (See Part V, Chapter Twenty-three). Turmoil in Chief Pleas ensued.

To complete this review of Sark's political arrangements, consideration must be given to the officers and the douzaine of the fief. The Court appointed under the Order-in-Council of April 24th., 1583 and sworn in on July 16th., 1594, included a Greffier, a Prévôt, a vingtenier and a connétable. These four appointments persist to this day.

The Greffier is nominated by the seigneur and, although he may resign, he cannot be dismissed. He attends the Chief Pleas, but votes only if he is one of the Quarantaine holders. He writes up the minutes of Chief Pleas and also keeps a record of all cases brought before the Court.

The Prévôt is nominated like the Greffier and has the same position in Chief Pleas. He has to act as Queen's Attorney in case of need, has to make distraint in cases of debt and has to see that the Seneschal's verdicts in Court are executed; he also acts as gaoler and must at need take prisoners to the Royal Court of Guernsey. He inspects public houses and liquor imported.

Day-to-day administration is entrusted to the vingtenier and the connétable. The vingtenier is appointed by Michaelmas Chief Pleas and he becomes connétable one year later, holding each office for a year. The connétable (but not the vingtenier) sits in Chief Pleas, but does not vote unless he is a Quarantaine holder.

These two officers are conjointly charged with maintaining the peace and arresting for crime. Since the January 1970 Chief Pleas they have been helped by a full-time policeman from Guernsey (as permitted by the 1951 Reform Law). In addition the connétable is responsible for road repairs and he levies the taxes authorised by Chief Pleas.

The Court and officials appointed on October 27th., 1579 included two 'assistants'. From this nucleus the douzaine has developed. The 12 douzaine members are elected annually by Chief Pleas, forming a committee of that Assembly which, under the chairmanship of the Seneschal, advises the connétable in assessing the amounts due from each taxpayer. In this connection the traditional tax is levied on property, and the amount is fixed year by year. The greatest yield, however, comes from Impôts on goods such as tobacco and alcohol, while another major source of revenue is the landing tax imposed on strangers, plus the tonnage tax on the ships bringing them to Sark. Sark also receives from Guernsey one-eightieth of the revenue the latter obtains from import duties on liquor and tobacco, as a good deal of these dutiable goods are consumed in Sark by visitors.

Finally, Chief Pleas elect triennially Overseers of Poor Relief (for which a special tax is levied), but these officers merely carry out the decisions of Chief Pleas which discusses individual cases.

This chapter was entitled, in part, 'Semper Eadem'. Bearing in mind that the introduction of deputies into Chief Pleas constitutes in effect a reversion to the pre-1605 situation when a voice in that body was not confined to Quarantaine holders; this smallest of Her Majesty's self-governing territories may be said (with the sole exception of the replacement of juge and jurats by the Seneschal) to have retained practically intact the organs established in the reign of her illustrious eponym, whose motto has indeed been most scrupulously honoured.

PART IV

'WARS AND RUMOURS' — THE NAVAL AND MILITARY ASPECT

Chapter One

'IN THE MIDST OF SO MANY AND GREAT DANGERS'

FROM ITS POSITION as an outpost of the Roman Empire, by way of its function as 'le bouclier d'Angleterre' during the centuries of Anglo-French conflict, culminating in its rôle as a well-nigh impregnable bastion of Hitler's 'Festung Europa', it has been the fate of the Bailiwick of Guernsey for a great part of its career to find itself where 'the strife is fierce, the warfare long'. Throughout a history characterized by perennial suspense and fear, the Bailiwick has suffered recurrent invasions and occupations, not to mention devastating raids. It is small wonder, therefore, that the islanders came to be steeped in a martial tradition, adopting an enthusiastic and die-hard patriotic attitude of being 'plus royaliste que le roi'. Thus in the Second World War (as was revealed by the then Bailiff, Sir Graham Dorey, in a statement made in January 1993) despite the curtailment of recruitment resulting from enemy occupation only ten months after its outbreak, more than 7,500 of the Bailiwick's sons and daughters — over 17% of the 1939 population — served in H.M. Forces, while Elizabeth College alone (a school at that time about 150 strong) provided the Services with no fewer than 130 officers, in addition to other ranks.

Just how far back go the alarums and excursions to which the Bailiwick has been subjected is a moot point as the extent to which the vulnerability of the islands invited attack in the remote past can only be a matter of conjecture. One such supposition is connected with the indications revealed by pollen analysis coupled with radio-carbon dating at La Grande Mare of a total cessation early in the second millennium before Christ of all agricultural activity — with no sign apparent of any resumption thereof until that discernible at Le Tranquesous and associated with Iron Age material of *circa* 500 B.C. The theory has been advanced that, when considered in conjunction with the absence from Les Fouaillages of any artefacts later than 1,800 B.C., this hiatus strongly suggests the likelihood of a complete depopulation of

Guernsey during this prolonged period, possibly as a result of devastating sea-raids by migrants from Eastern Europe. Many centuries later — indeed, within the Christian era — a case of particular interest arises with the mute evidence of archaeology posing what may aptly be termed 'a Roman conundrum'.

The source of this perplexity is a building standing on the seashore at Longy Bay in Alderney which soldiers during the Napoleonic wars dubbed 'The Nunnery' because of its isolated position. On the basis of the large fragments of Roman tile embedded in its walls, as well as the 'herring-bone' work which is still visible, Sir Thomas Kendrick in his *Archaeology of the Channel Islands* (1928), stated that 'there is a reasonable likelihood that it is a late Roman fort, perhaps a part of the defences of the Saxon Shore, and built in the latter half of the fourth century A.D.'. This analysis by Kendrick led to a widespread belief that the Nunnery was a Roman naval base and signal station, part of a system of intercommunicating forts designed to sustain the Roman fleet in its patrols against pirates and Teutonic invaders. This belief was strengthened by Roman coins and pottery found in the vicinity, as well as the discovery in 1929 of bolts, rivets and charred fragments, presumably from burnt boats.

In an article in the *Guernsey Evening Press* in 1966, however, Lieutenant-Colonel C. S. Durtnell (who had excavated at the site while stationed in Alderney in 1929) expressed the opinion that the building was erected on top of a Roman kitchen midden, which obviously precludes Roman construction. He therefore inclined to the view that the Nunnery dates only from the Hundred Years War, by which time the builders would have been unaware of a midden beneath the foundations. Lieutenant-Colonel Durtnell's misgivings are shared by Mr. D. E. Johnston of Southampton University who, in the Alderney Society's *Bulletin* for December 1971, claimed that no written evidence goes further back than about 1540, and that the curtain walls and bastions could well be mediaeval. In this connection it is noteworthy that Kendrick admitted that the presence of tile and herring-bone work in the walls was not conclusive evidence, as such features could have been Norman as easily as Roman — but in his book, *The Channel Islands: An Archaeological Guide* (written in 1981), Mr. Johnston relented to the extent of conceding that comparison with the signal stations of Goldsborough, Scarborough and Huntcliff on the Yorkshire coast 'supports a Roman date for the single entrance, gently rounded corners and functionally insignificant bastions'.

Shortly after the appearance of the first edition of this history, however, further complications arose when excavations near Cherbourg revealed that a fort there dated about 365 was of the same pattern as the Nunnery, thereby prompting the surmise that the pair might represent the two forts mentioned in contemporary documents as Grannono and Grannona.

If an archaeological ignoramus may venture to obtrude himself, the present writer feels that these disputes about the age of this particular structure do not seem to be especially relevant to the underlying question of Roman fortification in the area, as such a concentration on one building tends to divert attention from vital associated considerations. To begin with, not only was Longy Alderney's only port until the 18th. century (indeed, the remains of the old pier are still visible), but it was also the island's main settlement until it was gradually rendered untenable by progressive inundations of sand. Moreover, it was undoubtedly a centre of habitation in Roman times — witness the coins and pottery (not to mention the midden) found in its locality. Now, we know from such examples as Pevensey and Portchester that Roman forts of the Saxon Shore were at times adapted in Norman and later periods for contemporary defence needs — and it is arguable that the same could well be true of the Nunnery, which Durtnell himself admitted was a fortification at Alderney's most vital point: hardly the kind of location to be neglected by Roman military efficiency. Furthermore, Alderney's position at the mouth of the English Channel would evidently have rendered it an ideal naval base for operations against sea raiders making for Brittany or the Biscay coast. Bearing these various reflections in mind the present writer must say that, while the Nunnery itself may not be of Roman construction, it does not seem that this consideration alone justifies jumping to the conclusion that no Roman defence establishment existed in the vicinity.

It must of course be admitted that, whatever may be the truth about the Nunnery, the Bailiwick does not, in fact, seem to have been greatly troubled by the Frankish invaders against whom such a fortification would have been built. This comparative immunity owed much to the fact that these land-based incursions (which culminated in the victory of the Frankish leader, Clovis, over the Roman general, Syagrius, in 486) were largely spent before they reached this remote area. Consequently, although the chaos of the mainland was reflected in island life, it was largely a matter of sheltering refugees and of suffering occasional raids, such as that which appeared to have been made on Sark towards the end of the fifth century by a band of Visigoths, evidence for which consists of an excavated hoard of coins of the period minted in south-west France (then under Visigoth control).

Veritable trials came to the Bailiwick with the Vikings, whose sea-borne operations placed the islands in the front line, experiencing the familiar pattern of the long boats, the burning homesteads and fleeing inhabitants put to the sword. The earliest Viking raider of note was the Jarl Hasting who, during the middle and latter years of the ninth century, made incursions into France, Spain and England, besides attacking the Islands. His attempt to invade England was defeated by Alfred The Great during a four-year struggle between 893 and 897, but long before that he had left his terrible mark on the Islands and the neighbouring Cotentin, which was almost reduced to a desert. About 850 a marauding band under his leadership pillaged the monastery in Sark, set up by St. Magloire in the sixth century, destroying the buildings and massacring the inhabitants. The Jersey poet, Robert Wace (1100–1175), who became a Prebend at Bayeux and was attached to Henry II's Anglo-Norman Court, describes a raid by Jarl Hasting in his 'Roman de Rou' ('Romance of Rollo').

De sa gent e de sa contree
en plusiers lieux part le ruine
ke firent la gent Sarrazine
en Aureni, en Guernesi,
en Sairc, en Erm, en Gersi.

In 860 Harold the Fair Haired became King of Norway at the age of 10, and reigned for 70 years until in 930 (three years before his death) he divided his kingdom among his sons, with the eldest (Eric Bloodaxe) as overlord. In the early years of his reign he set out to subjugate his turbulent nominal underlings — the Jarls. He succeeded in doing so in 872 and this subjugation, together with Harold's repression of free-booting, caused many of the Jarls to seek their fortunes elsewhere and so stimulated Viking migration to Iceland, Scotland, the Orkneys, the Shetlands — and Eastern Normandy, which the Norse leader, Rollo (who, according to Icelandic sources, may be identified as Ganga-Hrolf, son of Rognvald, Jarl of Moer), wrested from Charles the Simple by the Treaty of St. Clair-sur-Epte in 911.

One of the sons of Harold the Fair Haired was the Jarl Godefroy, prominent in Guernsey lore as Geoffroi le Grand

Sarrazin ('Sarrazin' being the name given to sea raiders in general). The Castel parish takes its name from the castle which he is alleged to have built on the site of the present church, most likely to dominate the western half of the island, over which Le Grand Sarrazin seems to have established a local hegemony late in the ninth or early in the tenth century. However, in the light of the discovery made in 1984 by Mr. John McCormack of a hypocaust beneath the church, indicating that the site was occupied by a (maybe military) Roman building; the possibility emerges that the tradition associating such a castle with this Norseman might reflect an anachronistic folk memory of a fortification within the Saxon Shore system already mentioned in connection with Alderney's Nunnery.

A rather shadowy figure who could have been the last of the Viking sea dogs is found in the person of Jethou's 'Admiral Restauld', commemorated in the name of an inn which met the gaze of visitors when, during the tenancy of Group Captain W. Hedley Cliff, D.S.O., access to this island was available. Evidence of this adventurer's possession of Jethou is found in an undated charter in which Restauld, described as 'one-time shipmaster of the Duke Robert', donated the island to the Abbé de Mont St. Michel, stating that he himself intended to become a monk. 'The Devil is sick, the Devil a Monk would be'. The Duke Robert of the charter was almost certainly Duke Robert I.

A clue as to Restauld's identity exists in another charter whereby Duke Richard II (996–1026) founded and endowed the Priory of Héauville and also gave lands in the vicinity to the Abbey of Marmoutier at Tours, stating that some of the land donated was the property of Restauld. On this evidence Restauld emerges as a substantial landowner early in the 11th. century — a status at that time invariably synonymous with being a warrior of eminence.

The likelihood therefore is that Restauld was a leading pirate among the Norse community established around Cap La Hague, which was not brought under the control of the Dukes of Normandy until the early 11th. century. From this area he would have been in a highly strategic position at the entrance to the Race of Alderney. The probability is that Duke Robert I (The Devil: 1027–1035) was helped by Restauld when storms dispersed his naval expedition against Canute in 1030 (and maybe also in his subsequent campaign against the Duke of Brittany) and — about 1034 — gave Jethou to him for services rendered. The gift would have been very welcome, considering Jethou's usefulness to such a pirate leader who already controlled the eastern side of the Race of Alderney, for, with ships based on this island as well as in the Héauville vicinity, he would be able effectively to close the passage of the Race. Restauld probably donated Jethou to Mont St. Michel about 1055, when his life was drawing to its close — presumably in the hope of thereby atoning for his misdeeds and averting the terrors of hell-fire; but also possibly as a ploy to promote a corrody giving security in his declining years.

The series of Viking attacks left a permanent legacy in the very names of the islands: the suffix 'ey' or 'y' (Guernsey, Aurigny, Alderney) being the Norse designation for a larger island, while the suffix 'ou' (Brecqhou, Burhou, Jethou) was used by them to indicate smaller ones.

Chapter Two

FROM ROUEN TO BRÉTIGNY: THE TRIBULATIONS OF THE EARLY MIDDLE AGES

A FEW YEARS AGO the story was current of the burly schoolmaster who, confronting for the first time a notoriously troublesome class, called out the toughest boy he saw as soon as he entered the room, knocked him down and announced, 'That's what you get for doing *nothing* — now try doing *something*!'

The need for similar deterrent tactics was apparently felt by King John after the loss of Continental Normandy resulting from the capitulation at Rouen in 1204 — though the present-day presumption is that the Plantagenet prince was probably better placed than the pugilistic pedagogue to plead provocation. The researches of Doctor Wendy Stevenson have shown that in the course of his campaign against John, Philip Augustus secured possession of the Channel Isles at least once and possibly twice; and also that their recovery by the English king stemmed from particularly vigorous military efforts, inspired by his realisation of the enhanced economic and strategic importance of the archipelago once mainland Normandy was lost. The likelihood appears to be that the islands originally fell to the French king after the Rouen capitulation in the summer of 1204 (being held on his behalf by a castellan named Romerel), and were regained by John (probably in September 1205) who for the purpose made use of the services of Eustace, the renegade monk turned sea-dog, who sailed with 30 ships supplied by the English king (to whom he had sworn fealty after quarrelling with the Count of Boulogne, whose Seneschal he had previously been). Eustace so harried and pillaged the islands that contemporary accounts held that 'nought was left to burn'. Philip Augustus, however, seems to have returned to the attack round about Christmas and once again to have seized the islands. In April 1206 John dispatched to the archipelago 275 sailors in five galleys and three large ships and writs issued to the Wardens of Jersey and Guernsey in May of the same year suggest that by then he had effected its recovery —

possibly to the accompaniment of yet further rampage.

Dr. Stevenson has also revealed that, fearful for their large estates on the mainland, no less than 14 fief holders in the Bailiwick chose allegiance to the French Royal House and so lost their property in the islands. (These were Sampson d'Anneville; Seigneur du Baard; Richard de Martinwast; Richard le Boulanger; Seigneur de Fortescue; Robert Legat; Ralph de Lemmyng; Seigneur de Mautalent; Jean Perles; Seigneur de Rosel; Roger Suart; Seigneur du Fief de la Velleresse de Fermaine; Guillaume de Wereville [all Guernsey]. Richard de Vernon [Sark]). In the words of the Rolls of the 1309 Assizes:

> '... lord John the King after his said second conquest of these islands ... disinherited all the Normans living in France or Normandy ... and ... the said lord King John died in seisin of these their tenements which he had not already given away.'

After this defiance it is hardly surprising that John, determined to show beyond doubt who was master, seized leading inhabitants as hostages (see Part III, Chapter Two). That done and feeling that the islanders would now be sufficiently cowed to recognise that 'the better part of valour is discretion', he appointed Hasculf de Suligny as Warden of Jersey and Philippe d'Aubigny as Warden of Guernsey and Alderney. In the fall of 1212, following John's attempts to recover a debt of 20 marks — attempts in which the royal creditor showed unusual restraint, even allowing the ex-monk to retain seisin of his Norfolk lands pending settlement — Eustace deserted to Philip Augustus with five of John's galleys and once more seized the archipelago. Although he was repulsed from the larger islands, he managed to hold Sark, which he garrisoned with a force of his followers and retained for the next two years. It was not until the autumn of 1214 that Sark was recaptured by Philippe d'Aubigny and, as a reward for the part played by the islanders in this action, John released his hostages.

Although restored to favour the following spring by a monarch desperate for any support he could find in the tense situation preceding Runnymede, the freebooter once more played a lone hand, constantly with an eye to the main chance. This he evidently saw in renewed support for the Capetians after the invasion of England by the Prince Louis in May 1216. Thus, profiting from the absence of Philippe d'Aubigny (who had gone to John's support during his struggle with the barons after Magna Carta) Eustace the Monk yet again attacked the islands, this time capturing them for the French king (or ostensibly so) and holding them until after John's death. Eustace was subsequently employed to ferry across reinforcements in support of Louis who, after the death of John in October 1216, was now attempting to wrest the Crown from his nine-year-old successor, Henry. In the course of these operations Eustace was intercepted and, at the ensuing Battle of Sandwich, defeated by d'Aubigny, who had him beheaded on his own quarter-deck.

This reverse off Sandwich, coupled with the French defeat at Lincoln, led to the abandonment of Louis's attempts and peace was concluded by the Treaty of Lambeth (or Kingston) in September 1217. Clause 8 of this Treaty reads:

> 'Concerning the Isles. The Lord Louis shall send letters to the brethren of Eustace the Monk, ordering them to give them back to the Lord Henry of England, and if they surrender them not, the Lord Louis will compel them to do so.'

Thus liberated from the depredations of Eustace and his confrères, the islands were to enjoy reasonable tranquillity for the next three-quarters of a century, their possession by the English Crown implicitly recognised by Louis IX in the Treaty of Paris of 1259, as a *quid pro quo* for Henry III's abandonment of all claims to the title of Duke of Normandy.

This period of respite, however, was to be followed by atrocious sufferings which had their roots in the policy of ousting the English from Gascony pursued by Philip the Fair on his accession to the French throne in 1285. Taking advantage of a series of outrages perpetrated by English and Gascon sailors in the Channel, culminating in an English success in a regular battle fought off Saint-Mahé, Philip summoned Edward I, as Duke of Aquitaine, to answer for what had happened before his Court in Paris. Edward tried to hedge, seeking alternative arrangements whereby justice might be done to the injured parties, but Philip persuaded Edward's representative, Edmund of Cornwall, to surrender all English fortresses in Gascony pending a satisfactory settlement, with the understanding that they would subsequently be returned. Thus early in 1294 Gascony was occupied by the French — whereupon Philip immediately disowned his agreement. Infuriated by this breach of faith, Edward I declared war at Whitsun, thereby initiating a turn of events which, putting the archipelago in the forefront of the battle-line, was to prove disastrous for Guernsey.

In July of the same year the French, under Jean d'Harcourt and Mathieu de Montmorency, launched a devastating attack, the worst on record. Although Castle Cornet withstood the onslaught, a quarter of the population was slaughtered, and St. Peter-Port set ablaze, with the pier and shipping destroyed. In other parts of the island houses, cottages, mills and crops were burned, and animals killed. The churches of Saint Peter-Port and Saint Sampson's suffered severely, with priests here and elsewhere being put to the sword, and vestments, holy vessels and crucifixes spat upon and smashed. Women and girls were torn from the sanctuaries, ravished, killed, or carried away. It is interesting to note that one of the slain was the Bailiff, Guillaume de Saint Remi, who was also (inter alia) Seigneur du Fief Mauxmarquis in Saint Andrew's and was probably killed while fleeing thence towards the Town; the site of his death providing an alternative — and perhaps more credible — reason for the name of the Cross at the summit of Le Vauquiédor than that associated with Gautier de la Salle's last confession already alluded to in Part III, Chapter Three. (Particularly intriguing, however — albeit less dramatic — is the suggestion of Mr. Arthur Klein that the famous stone originated as no more than one defining the boundary between Fief de la Haule and Fief Mauxmarquis.)

It was a long time before the island was able to get over the widespread looting and plundering of this raid, the more so as subsidiary attacks followed before recovery could be completed. As a result, the above-mentioned churches were still heaps of ruins ten years after the attack (see part I, Chapter Ten); and the first known example of local legislation is connected with a toll on shipping to finance repairs to St. Peter-Port jetty in 1305 (see Part III, Chapter Four).

A third of a century later, events in far away Scotland were destined to have their repercussions in the Bailiwick of Guernsey. On the death of Robert the Bruce in 1329, the Scottish throne passed to his five-year-old son, David, in whose infancy the Balliol faction saw an opportunity to recoup its fortunes. Accordingly, they sailed from the Humber with the tacit support of Edward III and defeated David's forces under the Earl of Mar at Dupplin Moor in 1332, with the result that Edward Balliol was crowned king at Scone. Soon afterwards, however, Balliol was driven from Scotland again and fled to Edward III who, now coming out openly in his support, marched north, took Berwick-on-Tweed, and defeated David's supporters at Halidon Hill in 1333. Edward

Balliol was replaced on the throne as the puppet of Edward III, who was recognized as Lord Paramount of Scotland. David Bruce (by now nine years of age) sought asylum in France from Philip IV; and once there, the boy-king in exile plotted revenge, encouraged by his royal host, who still pursued the traditional policy followed by his uncle, Philip the Fair, of seeking the ejection of the English from Gascony.

Scope for such revenge was offered by the Channel Isles, whose vulnerability had been demonstrated at the turn of the century and whose defences had further decayed owing to their neglect by the rapacious henchmen of Otto de Grandison up to his death in 1328. Although Otto's successor as Warden, Jean de Roches, had attempted to make good this neglect, he was hampered by lack of funds (Otto having sucked the islands dry); and, furthermore, he reported that Alderney was incapable of being defended, while Sark's lack of landing facilities made it immune from attack, so that it stood in no need of defence.

The plums being ripe for the picking, young David (now 12), aided by the French, sailed in 1336 for the islands, where his forces were reported to have committed 'arson, murder and diverse other atrocities'. Not surprisingly in view of their lack of defence, the worst damage occurred in Alderney and Sark. David's forces were not, however, able to establish themselves and withdrew to France. The following year (1337) the Islands suffered yet more raids, when they were harassed by French privateers in a series of hit-and-run operations. Open war was now imminent.

The outbreak of the Hundred Years War once more placed the Bailiwick in immediate peril, and yet again 'England's buckler' bore the initial brunt of enemy action. When war began in 1338 the French under Admiral Nicolas Béhuchet attacked the islands. On September 8th. Sir Symon de Goldingham surrendered Castle Cornet, whereupon Guernsey, Sark and Alderney were occupied, the last-named being looted mercilessly. The administration of the islands was then handed over by the French king to Robert Bertram, Marshal of France. Tradition holds that an 87-strong underground movement in St. Martin's rose against the enemy at La Mare Mado, but the Guernseymen were defeated and, retreating to Petit Port, embarked for Jersey, finding refuge at St. Ouen's.

Edward III's naval victory at Sluys in 1340 robbed the French of control of the Channel and enabled a relief force led by Walter de Weston (the Sub-Warden under Thomas Ferrers) to liberate the islands in the autumn of the same year after a two-year enemy occupation. De Weston was unable, however, to subdue Castle Cornet, which the French continued to hold until 1345, when it was finally retaken by Godfrey de Harcourt.

Although Guernsey was now clear of the foe, Jerbourg Castle had been reduced to a ruinous state, while St. Peter-Port had suffered so greatly that Edward Ill, as a precaution against any possible repetition, ordered that it should be enclosed by a protective wall. Apart, however, from the discovery in 1982 of a ditch adjacent to the putative wall and containing fourteenth century artefacts, evidence of this order being obeyed is scanty.

Meanwhile, in 1343, the French, under Prince Luis de la Cerda (the son of Alphonso V of Aragon, who, educated in France, had taken service under the French Crown), had easily overcome the puny garrison of one armed man and six archers allocated to the defence of Sark, and again occupied the island, not being dislodged until 1347. A twelvemonth later came the Black Death (which was particularly virulent throughout the archipelago, whence the infection is thought to have been carried by ship to England*) its terrible ravages occasioning a lull in hostilities for the next few years.

Edward III's victory at Crecy in 1346, followed by his occupation of Calais and the ensuing bubonic plague provided a temporary respite from attack, but in 1356 another French force staged a yet further overthrow of the defences of Castle Cornet. After some time the enemy was driven out by a force consisting largely of Jerseymen led by Sir Reginald de Carteret of St. Ouen's and the bailiff of Jersey, Ralph Lemprière. In the course of this relief operation, however, an incident occurred which unfortunately aroused intense inter-insular bad blood. During the siege of the castle an eminent Guernseyman, Guillaume le Feyvre, was executed for treason by the Jerseymen, whereupon the executed man's widow instituted proceedings in the Guernsey Court, which found those responsible guilty of wrongful execution and sentenced them to banishment. De Carteret and Lemprière stood by their men, and in consequence found themselves arrested and thrown into a dungeon in the very fortress they had taken, languishing there for two years until pardoned by the king on the strength of their services in recovering the castle.

---

*See page 100 of *The Black Death* by Philip Ziegler (Folio Society, 1997).

Considerable ill-feeling was thus aroused between the two major islands, echoes of which were still to be heard until recent times. Some would say that since 1905 it has regularly come to the surface in the annual tussle (inaugurated that year) for the 'Muratti' football cup.

In 1360 the Islands at last gained relief from their troubles when by the Treaty of Brétigny the French abandoned all claims to the Channel Isles, the English in return recognising the rights in the Islands of the Bishop of Coutances.

Chapter Three

MEDIAEVAL FORTIFICATIONS

THE EXIGENCIES of the Hundred Years War naturally focussed attention on Guernsey's fortifications and led to their renovation and extension the better to parry the constant threats posed by an enemy whose coastline was near enough to be clearly visible on most days. With the building of the Vale Castle (the oldest part of which most likely dates from the early 15th. century) the mediaeval defence pattern was completed. This is therefore an appropriate point at which to consider these dispositions.

The urgent need to protect St. Peter-Port's invaluable roadstead led King John to embark on the building of Castle Cornet in 1206. Work continued until 1256, with the most important period of construction falling in the years 1224–26, when Geoffrey de Lucy was Warden of the Isles. The castle's vital position made it the chief objective of French attacks on the archipelago and also the centre of insular resistance. As has been seen in the previous chapter, the French twice succeeded in occupying it during the earlier stages of the Hundred Years War.

Before the separation of the governments of Jersey and Guernsey by Henry VII (see Part III, Chapter Five), Castle Cornet most likely served as the main seat of government for the archipelago as a whole. After the separation it was the residence of the governors of Guernsey until 1672 (see Part III, Chapter Eight). The castle served as a fortress throughout the centuries until 1945, when its German garrison surrendered to the British liberation forces. The present writer clearly recalls salutes being fired by its guns during the inter-war years.

Le Château des Marais (or 'Ivy Castle'), surrounded by a moat and wherein was located the chapel of Notre Dame des Marais, guards the northerly approaches to St. Peter-Port. It is mentioned as already in existence in a document of 1244. The findings of Mr. Kenneth Barton, who directed excavations on the site in 1975 and 1977, indicate that the original mound was of volcanic origin. It appears that late in the 12th. century a bank was raised and a ringwork formed for defensive purposes. (It is interesting to note that this must have been *before* John's loss of Continental Normandy in 1204, which gives rise to speculations as to the nature of the threat prompting this fortification.) Drainage problems created by the slope of the interior of the site from north to south led to the interior being in-filled in the late 13th. century and the site was then reoccupied as a defence work during the era of French raids until the middle of the 14th. century. In this connection, the evidence of the pottery found in the vicinity indicates that the bailey was raised above the level of the surrounding marsh on a clay platform, *c.* 1250–1275. No further military use was made of the site (which was given over to farming) for many centuries, and it was not until the late 18th. century that the French threat resulting from the War of American Independence led to the present outer walls and the magazine being built. The foundations of these walls, however, are mediaeval. Similarly, although the present ditch surrounding the mound is the result of late 18th.-century re-excavation, the indications are that a previous one had existed in the Middle Ages. After the Napoleonic Wars were over the site again reverted to farmland, with a cottage being built on the outer perimeter. In the Second World War the Germans again used the site for military purposes, erecting the bunker which is still to be seen adjoining the magazine.

Because the offshore position of Castle Cornet made it inaccessible to the Guernsey population in an emergency, the construction of Jerbourg Castle was started about 1309, and was finished in the early years of Edward III's reign, the fortification being treated as a royal castle to be garrisoned by the Warden. In 1330 Edward Ill committed the castle to the charge of Matthew de Sausmarez. His commission ordered that 'men of the commonalty of the said island shall be received there with their goods and chattels'. In other words, these defences across the Jerbourg headland would be the last ditch in the event of invasion. Shortly afterwards the castle functioned in precisely this way, when the French invaded and occupied Guernsey from 1338 to 1340. As a result of this invasion the castle suffered acutely, and was in a state of ruin by 1350.

Despite this ruination successive Seigneurs de Sausmarez remained ex officio castellans, as Mr. Matthew de Sausmarez was reminded in 1811, when he was warned by the lieutenant-governor (Sir John Doyle) that he was expected to take command of Jerbourg Castle in the event of an invasion. This tradition lingers, and although nothing now remains of the castle beyond a hummock which is allegedly the site of the keep, the Seigneur of the Fief de Sausmarez to this day retains among his titles that of Chatelain de Jerbourg.

The French occupation of Castle Cornet from 1338–45 manifested the urgent need for additional defences on the Guernsey mainland, with the result that (as has been seen) an order was issued by Edward III that the somewhat derelict fortress of Jerbourg should be supplemented by a wall around St. Peter-Port. Although evidence for such a wall is largely conjectural, a letter of 1357 from the bailiff and jurats to the Lord Chancellor refers to the construction of La Tour Beauregard, which, guarding the southern approaches to the town, came to be a subsidiary to Castle Cornet and under the same command. By the end of the 16th century, however, this castle 's usefulness had declined to the point at which it was considered of little value and some of its land was sold in 1597. Nothing of the building now remains, and the sole reminder of its existence is found in the name of the incline giving access to its site — Tower Hill. Its counterpart to the north of the Town — La Tourgand, sited near to-day's Thomas de la Rue Public House but demolished in the 18th. century — was of somewhat earlier construction, the researches of Mr. George Brammall indicating that its builder was most likely Ranulph Gautier, for whose murder *circa* 1305 Gautier de la Salle was hanged in 1320 (see Part III, Chapter Three).

One reads in Edith Carey's *Essays on Guernsey History* that the Vale Castle (Le Château de Saint Michel) was featured in the apocryphal *Dédicase des Eglises* with a constructional date of 966 assigned to it. Equally spurious is the oft-repeated tale that this fortification was built in 1030 by Duke Robert I (The Devil) after his fleet had sheltered from a storm in L'Ancresse Bay. In contrast to these romances of the 'fond thing vainly invented' category, Ferdinand Brock Tupper, in his famous *History of Guernsey* (1854) cautiously conjectured that 'Some portion of the Vale Castle is thought to be the work of the Normans, though certainly not so ancient as the tenth century'. However, Mr. R. B. Burns indicated in his *Archaeological Field Guide* that excavations carried out in 1980 suggest that (apart from a Hill Fort which would seem to have crowned this eminence during the Iron Age) 'the first military presence here occurred as late as *circa* 1400' — an estimate which he later defined more explicitly as the period 1410–1440, though Mr. K. J. Barton regarded 1450 as the earliest possible date. Mr. Burns went on to say that the same investigation also revealed that the walls and drum towers seen today are largely the result of eighteenth century reconstruction, though he considers that the fine gateway, despite the mediaeval implications of a portcullis, embodies Tudor work.

Three other ancient fortifications deserve mention which, although on structural evidence mediaeval, do not have the dates of their construction recorded in any extant document. They are Hougue à la Perre, Le Château de Rocquaine (Fort Grey) and Fort Pezerie. All three are mentioned as already of antiquity in a report of May 28th., 1680 addressed to 'the Honourable George Legge, Lieutenant-Governor of his Majesties Ordinance', by Captain Richard Leake, Master Gunner of England. In addition they are included in the Phillips Report (now in the British Museum) which has an illustration showing Fort Grey as a small mediaeval castle, as well as a less detailed one of Pezerie.

Chapter Four

LA DÉSCENTE DES ARAGOUSAIS AND THE LATER MIDDLE AGES

THE RENEWAL of fighting in the Hundred Years War in 1369 brought a vivid personality into Guernsey's story as the central figure in an action renowned in local minstrelsy. This colourful character was Owen of Wales, a soldier of fortune in the French service, who claimed to be the rightful heir of the Princes of Wales. Although the contemporary chronicler, Jean Froissart (*c.* 1337–*c.* 1404), states that he was the son of Aymon or Edmund, a Welsh prince wrongfully put to death by Edward III, his true father seems to have been Thomas ap Rhodri (*c.* 1295–1363), a nephew of Llywelyn ap Gruffydd — which would have meant that Owen, as the illustrious Llywelyn's great-nephew, was indeed consanguineous with the Welsh princely line.

Born *c.* 1330, Owen appears to have entered the service of Philip VI of France while still quite young, earning for himself, as 'Yevain de Galles', an outstanding reputation as a mercenary leader. Although he came to England in 1365 to take possession of his late father's manor of Tatsfield in Surrey, he returned to France in 1366 — and was deprived of his estates in England for adhering to the king's enemies when Charles V repudiated the Treaty of Brétigny in 1369.

Owen having spoken much at the French Court about his hereditary claims as lineal successor of Llywelyn, Charles V conceived the idea of exploiting his pretensions by utilising them to foment a diversionary insurrection in Wales. With this in mind, a fleet set out from Harfleur in 1370, preceded by a notable proclamation setting out Owen's claims — but it came to nothing, being forced back by bad weather. Two years elapsed until all was again in readiness, so that it was not until May 1372 that another expedition set sail, this time with the intention of joining forces with a Spanish fleet (sent by the Castilian King Enrique II, who was indebted to Charles V for his throne) in the vicinity of the Channel Isles for a combined assault on the Welsh coast. It was the failure of this Spanish force to arrive at the rendezvous which caused the attack to be diverted against Guernsey.

Owen landed at Vazon Bay (most likely on June 15th., 1372) at the head of a force which, according to Froissart, was 4,000 strong, the invasion traditionally held to have been witnessed by Jean Le Tocq of La Hougette, who is credited with raising the alarm. Against him Edmund (or Aymon) Rose, the Sub-Warden under Walter Huwet, Warden of the Isles, was able to muster 800, consisting mostly of the local Militia (see Chapter Eleven) reinforced by some 80 English men-at-arms and archers who had been sent over from St. Sauveur-le-Vicomte as a precautionary measure when news of Owen's preparations had first reached English ears. The outnumbered defenders were gradually forced back, finally giving battle on the plateau where Elizabeth College and the adjacent streets are now located — an area which, until the mid-19th. century, was known as 'La Bataille', and which still contains a passageway by the name of Battle Lane. Part of the hillslope to the north of the plateau is still called La Rouge Rue, because, so the story goes, it ran red with the blood of the wounded carried there for shelter. Froissart says that the Guernseymen left 400 dead on the field before they yielded, withdrawing into the town and the defences of La Tour Beauregard.

Meanwhile Owen's ships had sailed round the island intending to attack St. Peter-Port from the sea, but this project was frustrated thanks to the protection of the sea approaches afforded by Castle Cornet, to which they therefore laid siege. Besides the defending forces invested in Castle Cornet, tradition postulated another centre of resistance at the Vale Castle (at that time probably no more than a Hill Fort) where Rose himself is said to have held out:

Mais Aymon Rose retranché
Au puissant Château de l'Archange,
Dit qu'Il serait avant tranché
Que de se rendre à gent estrange.

During these sieges, probably to find payment for his men, Owen sent pillaging parties to Jersey and Sark, and they laid waste many farmsteads. Indeed, for Sark this raid was to prove the beginning of the end. Meanwhile, Castle Cornet was proving well-nigh impregnable, Owen finding it to be 'strong and well purveyed with good artyllary, so that it was not easy for it to be wonne'.

Thus Owen still had failed to take it when he was recalled by the French king, with orders to go to Santander to arrange a joint Franco-Spanish attack on La Rochelle. He therefore lifted the siege and departed.

Half a dozen years later Owen met his death. That he was considered a serious menace to England is suggested by the circumstances of his assassination (obviously with English connivance) while he was besieging Mortain-sur-Mer in 1378. His assailant was a 'hit-man' named John Lamb who, as related by Froissart, 'came out of England by the borders of Wales' and made use of his knowledge of Welsh to worm his way into his victim's confidence.

The Guernsey ballad recording this incursion is called 'La Déscent des Aragousais', suggesting an assault by Aragonese. There are two possible explanations for this apparent discrepancy. In the first place, as has been seen, Owen's operation was planned in collusion with Spanish forces with which he intended to link up to the north-west of Guernsey. It is not impossible, therefore, that a Spanish liaison contingent might have been included in the force which sailed from Harfleur — and its presence among the invaders (some of its members perhaps being taken prisoner) could have created the impression that the enemy were Aragonese. Secondly, the turmoil of the Hundred Years War provided ample opportunity for Spanish and Algerian pirates to plunder when and where they chose. Thus 'Aragonese' might have come to be a generic term for brutal and murderous attacks as a whole.

The year after La Déscente des Aragousais the English were being besieged in Brest by Bertrand du Guesclin, Constable of France. Wearying of the prolonged inactivity involved, du Guesclin decided to entrust the operation to his subordinates and sailed for the islands in search of more active pursuits. After subduing Jersey and taking hostages there, he continued to Guernsey and Sark. While in Guernsey he wrought considerable damage and collected a ransom. In Sark he caused such devastation, hard on the heels of Owen's depredations of the previous year, as to induce such few inhabitants as survived the 1372 onslaught to quit the island. It has long been assumed to have remained abandoned for nearly two hundred years, a haunt for pirates and smugglers. Thus the 1374 accounts of Thomas de Beauchamp, Warden of Guernsey, record that owing to the devastation by the French, no income had been received from Sark, and that no income was likely to be received in the immediate future, apart from the catching of rabbits. Similarly, the 1376 accounts of Thomas of Appleby, the King's Receiver and Approvator, included an item of 25 sols for the hire of a boat sent to Sark to collect rabbits for the king's customary dinner to Chief Pleas — expenditure that would have been unnecessary had the island been peopled. It might be added that, even if bereft of any permanent population, the occasional presence of the ruffians postulated by the premise mentioned above — and to whose villainy Sir Arthur Conan Doyle devotes a long chapter in his novel *Sir Nigel* — could account for a prominent element in Sark's folklore which stems from this period and reflects an act of revenge by Cinque Port mariners resentful of the wrecking activities of the resident brigands, who are thought to have lured ships to their doom by displaying false lights. The story goes that the island was taken by attackers who obtained permission to bury a passenger who had died at sea; and thereupon brought ashore a coffin filled with arms which were used to overpower the knavish inhabitants.

(In this context, incidentally, it is only fair to remark that, as against the traditional assumptions, his investigations have led Mr. John McCormack to doubt any prolonged depopulation of Sark, arguing that not only does architectural evidence show Le Manoir to be a fifteenth century construction, while signs indicating habitation in the same century are provided by L'Ecluse and La Moinerie; but also that on examination the accounts of Thomas Guille, H.M. mid-fifteenth century Receiver-General, belie any notion of an empty Sark in his day. These accounts for the years 1450 and 1451, falling as they do in the very middle of the alleged depopulation period, show that Sark was at the time 'put out to farm' — i.e. let to a tenant or lessee — and yielded an income of 63 Crowns from the 'farmer' or lessee. Moreover, the same accounts reveal that in 1450 the amount due from Sark's lessee was reduced by 12 Crowns because he had had to pay that sum to the Duke of Brittany for a safe conduct, the need for which implies that there must have been Serquiais then trading with some such Bréton port as Saint Malo. Furthermore, the 'farmer' or lessee in 1451 is named in Guille's accounts as William Richard, signifying the continued presence of a family which had been prominent in Sark's life at least as far back as 1274 — well before du Guesclin's onslaught — when Geoffrey Richard had held one of the sub-fiefs into which William de Vernon had divided the island in 1107. Because of these considerations, Mr. McCormack, while accepting that the devastating attack of 1373 might well have led Sark's population to forsake the island temporarily, denies that their absence was a lengthy one. Persuasive though he is, one is nevertheless compelled to observe that even when due weight is given to Mr. McCormack's views, it is indisputable that the French on their arrival in 1549 — see the next Chapter — found Sark deserted! Mr. McCormack implicitly admits that this is true, but shuns going into the question as to how long such had been the case prior to the French invasion — which after all was almost a hundred years after Thomas Guille had drawn up his accounts!)

Yet another attack came in 1380 when the French under Admiral de Vienne over-ran and occupied Jersey and also captured Castle Cornet once more. They were, however, soon driven out by a force organised by the Warden of the Isles, Sir Hugh Calverley, described as one 'who slept not on his business', and whose record of service went back almost as far as Crécy.

The islands were now to enjoy a reprieve lasting half a century, with the war dwindling down to a series of uneasy truces following on the deaths of both Charles V and du Guesclin in 1380. Thereafter each contestant was beset with internal troubles, with Burgundy and Armagnac struggling for supremacy in a France on whose throne sat the idiot king, Charles VI; while England had to contend first with the Peasants' Revolt, and later with the internal dissensions confronting Henry IV, who was seldom free from rebellion by the supporters of the cousin whose crown he had seized. Henry V's victory at Agincourt brought increased security and the renewed fighting after his death engendered offensive action, with three Guernsey ships (*La Pitié, La Marie* and *La Trinité*) participating in the blockade of Mont St. Michel in 1425. However, the period of French resurgence initiated by Jeanne d'Arc saw further raids, culminating in the major incursion on the morrow of the English débâcle at Châtillon mentioned in the *Paston Letters* (Botoner to John Paston, June 8th., 1454):

> The Frenchmen hafe be afore the Isles of Gersey and Guernsey, and a grate many of hem, and VC (500), be taken and slayn by men of the seyd trew Isles.

The end of The Hundred Years War did not prove to be any guarantee against molestation for the islands, and in 1461 Jersey was occupied by the Count de Maulevrier, Grand Seneschal of Normandy, possibly in the Lancastrian interest (see Part III, Chapter Four). The French were driven out in 1468 by Sir Richard Harliston, who had picked up forces in Guernsey en route. In the same year Edward IV granted a Charter to Guernsey confirming its liberties, in which he stated

> how valiantly manfully and steadfastedly the said peoples and communities of the said islands of Guernsey, Sark and Alderney have stood out for us and our progenitors, and what great dangers and losses they have sustained for the safety of the same islands, and for the recapture of our Castle of Mont Orgueil.

It would seem that Edward was unaware of the depopulation of Sark — a state of ignorance which, if Mr. McCormack is right in his conclusions outlined above, would have been amply justified.

The turbulence of the Middle Ages was at last brought to an end by the Bull of Neutrality obtained from Pope Sixtus IV by Edward IV in 1480/1 (see Part III, Chapter Five). Two centuries of almost complete immunity from external dangers were to ensue.

Chapter Five

BELLIGERENCE IN NEUTRALITY: ALDERNEY AND SARK

ALTHOUGH THE NEUTRAL STATUS of the archipelago (apart from the minor infractions now to be considered) was honoured on both sides of the Channel, the Tudors nevertheless deemed it prudent to act on the maxim of Vegetius, 'Qui desiderat pacem, praeparet bellum', with the somewhat ironical result that the period of peace saw the overhaul of the Islands' defences with almost continuous building and rebuilding of the castles. The Tudors were also influenced in their decision by the usefulness of the islands as centres for the collection of military intelligence, so that defence works were pushed ahead in spite of the sustained opposition of the islanders (already considered at length in Part III, Chapter Six) who 'trustid altogethere to the Pope's Bulls and other placetts obtayned of the French'. The first application of this policy was the enhancement of Castle Cornet's defences by the captain, Sir Peter Mewtis, who in 1545 arranged for the construction of a bastion and artillery emplacement, appropriately called the Mewtis Bulwark. (Included in its armament, incidentally, was a falcon inscribed, 'Tomas Owen made this Pese for the Yel of Garnse Vhan Ser Peter Mevtas was Governer and Captayn. Anno Dni 1550.' Removed a century later — most likely by the Parliamentarian Governor, Colonel John Bingham, in 1652 — this cannon after many wanderings was in 1920 sent from the Woolwich Rotunda Museum of Artillery to Plymouth, Massachusetts, to mark the tercentenary of the arrival of the *Mayflower*'. Thence, with President Reagan's compliments conveyed by telegram, it was returned to Guernsey in October 1985 and re-installed in its presumed original site — whence it was transferred in 1997 to the Museum depicting the Castle's history which was opened that year in the erstwhile barrack block to be seen on the right when the Outer Bailey is reached after passing through the Entrance Gateway.)

By far the most important defence project, however, resulted from the decision of the Privy Council to build a strong castle above Longy Harbour in Alderney, so as to dominate the approaches through the Race. Work on this was begun in the last year of Henry VIII's reign (1547) and was vigorously pushed forward by the Protector Somerset after Edward VI's accession. To undertake it a labour force 200 strong, supplemented by a garrison of 200 troops, was sent to the island under the command of Captain Robert Turberville, who was given the title of Marshal of Alderney. The fall of Somerset in 1549 caused a lull in the building programme, but work was resumed in 1550 and continued spasmodically for the next four years. Resenting the influx of labourers and soldiers and especially Turbeville's attempts to exercise some authority over them, the Aurigniais complained to the Privy Council — and this complaint, coupled with the reversal of policy after the accession of Mary I, led to the abandonment of the project in 1554.

This Tudor castle was demolished in the 1840s to make way for the building now called Fort Essex — a name deriving from the completely erroneous notion, current from 1770 onwards, that the original fortification had been the work of the Earl of Essex, who held the lease of the island 37 years after all work on the stronghold had been discontinued.

In 1558 the people of Alderney had reason to regret their agitation for the withdrawal of the garrison. In the summer of that year a French soldier of fortune, Captain Malesart, with a crew of volunteers from Cherbourg, swooped on the defenceless island, collected all the cattle and booty he could carry, and returned whence he had come to auction his acquisitions on the quayside. Encouraged by his success, Malesart returned with yet larger forces, and made another unopposed landing, but withdrew hastily when the English fleet was sighted. Eventually thinking the coast was clear Malesart came back for the third time — but a force dispatched by the Captain of Guernsey, Sir Leonard Chamberlain, captured his whole expedition and Malesart was sent as a prisoner to the Tower of London.

Further threats emerged during the reign of Elizabeth I. In 1563 the Virgin Queen's intervention in the French wars of Religion (ostensibly to bolster the Huguenot cause but in reality as a first step in a bid to regain Calais, lost five years earlier under Mary I) came to nothing when her forces surrendered on July 28th. — ironically just before the arrival of reinforcements under Lord Clinton. This defeat, as recounted by the late Professor

Albert Frederick Pollard, quoting the *Hatfield MSS I:227*, 'was followed by months of alarm ... in the Channel Islands'. Nearly thirty years later, the 1588 dispersal of the Armada notwithstanding, the Spanish menace loomed anew as the dependence of Philip II of the French Holy League was such that had it succeeded in preventing Henri of Navarre from ascending the Throne after the assassination in 1589 of Henri III, France would have been completely dominated by Spain to England's (and the Channel Isles') dire peril. Elizabeth therefore sent two expeditionary forces to Brittany under Sir John Norris, initially between the Spring of 1591 and the Autumn of 1592 and subsequently between September 1593 and November 1594, when the saving of Brest by the expulsion of the Spaniards from Crozon was no mean factor in enabling Henri of Navarre triumphantly to assert himself as Henri IV to the discomfiture of Spain. A wreck was discovered off Alderney in 1991 and the fact that it contained a bottle bearing the date mark 1586 led to its being provisionally identified with the pinnace *Makeshift* which (as documents in the Public Record Office disclose) foundered in these waters in 1592 while carrying dispatches from Lord Burghley to Norris. Deductions based on an examination of the vessel's rudder after its retrieval, however, call this presumption into question, suggesting that the sunken craft was apparently much larger than the *Makeshift* — probably measuring 51½ feet long with a beam of 20 feet — which, constructed during the reign of Elizabeth I of timbers thought to come from trees in south-eastern England, most likely functioned as a supply ship provisioning Norris' expedition. It is noteworthy that, whereas the other famous Tudor relic, the *Mary Rose*, was part-salvaged after sinking, this one remained totally undisturbed over the years, to the enhancement of its potential as a source of valuable historical information.

Many years later during the Period of Neutrality (1627) Alderney once again stood in peril when a French invasion was threatened. The Privy Council reacted by sending munitions to William Chamberlain for the defence of the Island, but they were not needed as the invasion fleet was destroyed by Sir Peter Osborne (the Lieutenant-Governor of Guernsey under Lord Danby as Governor).

Attention now needs to be turned to Sark which François Rabelais would have us believe had by the early sixteenth century become a base for the operations of formidable pirates, by reason of whose presence he described it as 'Ile des forfants, des larrons, des brigands, des meurtriers et assassineurs. Ils sont pires que les Canibales.' It is not without interest, however, that Mr. John McCormack, in his efforts mentioned in the last Chapter to disprove the depopulation of Sark and its subsequent use by brigands, argues that this outburst was no more than a Frenchman's hyperbolical reaction to the bellicosity of the islanders (their neutrality notwithstanding) in time of war between France and England. Be that as it may, this bellicosity — piratical or not — having demonstrated Sark's potentialities as a base for harrying shipping in the neighbouring waters, Henri II of France decided that its seizure would strike a useful counter-blow against the English fortification of the other islands — with the added advantage that its uninhabited condition (for such was indeed the case in 1549) would mean that its occupation would not constitute any overt act of war to impede the delicate negotiations then being conducted for the conclusion of the peace which was formally proclaimed the following March 29th., ending three years of Anglo-French conflict with English acceptance of French dominance in Scotland and the return to France of Boulogne, seized six years earlier during the previous hostilities.

In pursuance of this decision a fleet of 11 galleys and 12 supply ships sailing from Havre de Grace under Leon Strozzi, Prior of Capua, reinforced by another flotilla from St. Malo under Captain Puolain, Baron de la Garde, landed in Sark in July 1549 a force 200 strong recruited largely from convicts, occupying the island without meeting any opposition. As a next step, after having been reinforced by a further 200 men from St. Malo under his brother, the commander of the occupation force, Captain François Bruel, set about consolidating his position with triple defence works. Le Grand Fort was constructed to cover the landing places at l'Eperquerie and La Banquette in the north, while Le Château de Quénevêts was erected on the headland dominating the approach to Dixcart Bay — and finally a third fort was built at Vermondaye in Little Sark to cover the approach across La Coupée.

Bruel's main worry was the retention of his convict garrison, which desertions had reduced to 90 by 1551, when he left Sark to the care of his brother, himself assuming command of the garrison at Granville.

Although the English government did not regard Sark's occupation by the French as serious enough to justify any operation to evict them which would constitute an act of war against France, Thomas Compton, the Lieutenant-Governor of

Guernsey under Sir Leonard Chamberlain, saw an opportunity in 1553 of achieving this result without open hostilities. Taking advantage of the fortuitous arrival in Guernsey waters of Adrian Crole (a Flemish corsair sailing under Letters of Marque issued by the admiral of the Emperor Charles V) Compton suggested to this adventurer that an attempt should be made on Sark, offering unofficially to supply four pilots. Crole fell in with this proposal, and on September 7th., 1553 he landed on Sark, overcame the depleted and unenthusiastic garrison and took possession of the island. (It is worth noting that the 'Arms in Coffin' version of this attack — beloved of raconteurs — is utterly mythical, originating in an error on the part of Sir Walter Raleigh who, in his treatise *A Discourse of War* anachronistically ascribed the 1553 expulsion of the French to the ruse oft told in island folklore and in all probability employed nearly two centuries earlier by Cinque Port seamen in their avenging onslaught referred to in the preceding chapter).

Leaving a holding force of 50 men on Sark, Crole went to London and reported his capture to the ambassador of the Emperor Charles V, only to find that Charles was so little impressed by this new addition to his vast dominions as to instruct his ambassador to negotiate the island's transfer to the English for a cash payment. However, Mary I's preoccupation with domestic religious issues, coupled with a reluctance to antagonise the French, led to the failure of these negotiations — and Charles therefore ordered Crole to abandon the island after removing the ordnance and demolishing the forts, paying him 1,200 livres as reimbursement for expenses. Crole accordingly returned to Sark and removed some of the ordnance; but left in haste on the arrival of a body of men sent by the Captain of Jersey to demolish the forts, mistakenly taking them for superior enemy forces. On his way home he sold some of the equipment he had removed to Turberville in Alderney.

Thus Sark once again remained uninhabited until 1560, when the Seigneur of Glatigny submitted a proposal to the French king that he should be granted the island in perpetuity in return for establishing a resident settlement. Charles IX agreed to this and granted him a lease of the island, after which a small settlement was established by some of his tenants. In 1562, however, the outbreak of war between England and France led the seigneur to order his settlers to return to Normandy as their exposed position made them too vulnerable to attack.

By now Sark's years of neglect were rapidly drawing to a close. Within two years of Glatigny's departure, Helier de Carteret was to make his reconnaissance, prior to setting up his colony on the island the following year and establishing the régime which persists to the present day. The better part of four centuries was to elapse before hostile forces again set foot on the island.

Chapter Six

THE CIVIL WAR

IN THE CHANNEL ISLES the Civil War was not primarily concerned with the constitutional struggle between king and parliament (to which with their autonomous status, both Bailiwicks tended to be indifferent), but rather reflected the desire to redress local grievances or to further personal feuds.

The latter consideration was especially noteworthy in Jersey, where a party had gradually coalesced representing other local families who resented the monopoly of the important offices in the island held by the de Carteret clan, whose paterfamilias, Sir Philippe de Carteret, besides being bailiff was also lieutenant-governor under Sir Thomas Jermyn as governor, as well as being Seigneur of Sark. This opposition group dignified its supporters as 'Les Bien Affectionés', stigmatising the de Carteret entourage as 'Les Refractaires'.

In Guernsey on the other hand, local grievances loomed large in determining the island's attitude to the struggle. The *bête noire* of the Guernesiais was Sir Peter Osborne (father of the famous Dorothy) who since 1621 had been lieutenant-governor under his brother-in-law, Lord Danby, as governor, and who had also been granted the governorship in reversion on Danby's death. As a staunch Anglican, Sir Peter had already become estranged on religious grounds from the island's Calvinist Establishment. This tension had been enhanced in 1636 and 1637 by Laud's declared intention of ordering an episcopal visitation preparatory to taking steps to ensure 'that Guernsey as well as the other may conform to the Church of England' (see Part I, Chapter Eight). Hence Guernsey's support for the parliamentary cause was pre-eminently the result of the island's Calvinism.

In addition to this religious consideration, trouble had arisen on military grounds. In 1627 Osborne had brought 200 men to Guernsey to strengthen the defences against France during the Ile de Ré fiasco (when, as seen in the last chapter, his vigorous action had saved Alderney from invasion). Reinforcements had been added in 1629, and Charles I's chronic impecuniosity had led to the islanders being obliged to raise large sums for the upkeep of Castle Cornet and the payment of this garrison. In 1628 Osborne had further alienated the inhabitants by attempting to impose martial law so as to enforce this contribution. To make matters worse, the widespread resentment over this financial burden and the manner of its imposition was compounded when, because of the same shortage of money, Charles I took no action over the request to ransom a crew of Guernseymen who had been sold into slavery by Algerian pirates.

This tension reached its dénouement in March 1643 when parliament appointed Pierre de Beauvoir, together with his brother-in-law, Pierre Carey and James de Havilland, as leaders of the twelve commissioners deputed to act on its behalf; the royalist bailiff, Jean de Quetteville, having been arrested and deposed (see Part III, Chapter Six). Sir Peter Osborne from his fastness in Castle Cornet rejected de Beauvoir's call to submit, and on March 11th. he fired his guns into the town, carefully avoiding damage to de Quetteville's property. The Civil War in Guernsey had begun.

Meanwhile in Jersey Sir Philippe de Carteret was forced to abandon his original policy of neutrality by the activities of his nephew-cum-son-in-law, George Carteret, who, as a senior officer in the Royal Navy (where he had dropped the French-sounding 'de' as an embarrassment) made use of the island as a base for harrying parliamentary shipping. As a result of this fighting broke out, with Les Bien Affectionés besieging Sir Philippe in Elizabeth Castle, and his wife in Mont Orgueil. Sir Philippe, however, died in August 1643 and on November 19th. George landed in Jersey at the head of a force assembled in St. Malo and relieved the two castles. Henceforward Jersey was held for the king, with George Carteret as bailiff and lieutenant-governor.

George and his cousin, Philippe (son of the late Sir Philippe) now set about preparing plans for the relief of Osborne in Castle Cornet as well as for the recovery of Philippe's fief of Sark which, true to its Calvinist tradition, had aligned itself with Guernsey, whence a small garrison had been despatched to hold it.

While these events were taking place in Jersey, the royalists in Guernsey had staged a coup. Some time before Captain Bowden, commanding *The Bramble* under a parliamentary commission, had sailed his ship from Guernsey to Dartmouth where Prince Maurice had persuaded him to change sides. He then returned to Guernsey under his new allegiance (and, according to Tupper, in a new ship, *The George*) in order to attempt the capture of Lieutenant-Colonel Robert Russell (the parliamentary lieutenant-governor under the parliamentary governor, the Earl of Warwick), together with the three leading commissioners, de Beauvoir, Carey and de Havilland. On arrival Bowden contacted the three commissioners through an agent and on October 21st., 1643 persuaded them to come aboard his ship in Fermain Bay for a conference. Taking them prisoner, he set sail for Jersey in the hope of repeating his stratagem. Unfortunately for him Russell had smelt a rat, and, avoiding Bowden's trap himself, had sent a fast ship to Jersey to warn Les Bien Affectionés.

Being thus frustrated in Jersey, Bowden returned to Guernsey where Osborne forced him to hand over his prisoners, who were consigned, first to the deepest dungeon in the castle, but later to an upper dungeon in the Carey tower. Here the captives, cutting through to the cell beneath, found some flax which they twisted into ropes, and with the aid of these got away on December 3rd. at low tide through a window to the rocks below — within minutes of the arrival from England of the royal writ for their execution. Fired at by the castle guns, they scrambled over the rocks with the cannon balls bouncing around them, and at last reached St. Peter-Port where they received a rapturous welcome from the congregation which poured out of the evening service at the Town church to greet them.

At the time of the escape of the three commissioners the news of George Carteret's seizure of Jersey provoked the immediate Guernsey reaction of sending an officer, Pierre le Febure, to Alderney with orders to drive out all Papists and put the island in a state of defence against the royalists in Jersey. The island Militia (see Chapter Thirteen) was organised for this purpose, and Alderney was held in the parliamentary interests until the Restoration.

In January 1644 (new style) Lord Danby died, and Sir Peter Osborne, under the terms of the reversion granted 23 years previously, became governor of Guernsey, though his writ did not of course run beyond Castle Cornet — where at a later stage (Spring 1646) he had to contend with a mutiny occasioned by his striking one of his gunners with the flat of his sword.

Meanwhile, in Guernsey itself, the imposition on August 30th., 1643, at Russell's behest, of a special tax to finance the Roundhead war effort had provoked extensive resentment and opposition to it coalesced around Pierre Priaulx, Seigneur du Fief Le Comte, its most outspoken critic. Together with several associates (Antoine Grymes, Michel de Rozel and Gabriel du Perrier) Priaulx was apprehended some time later and appeared before a Tribunal convened on January 26th., 1643/4, where Pierre Girart testified against him that, before witnesses in the house of Richard Robin, he had disavowed his oath of loyalty to Parliament as a bad oath for which he asked God's pardon. His goods, together with those of de Rozel, were sequestered on February 2nd., the hands of their adversaries having been strengthened by a new development which had now supervened. Shortly before the sitting of the Tribunal which had tried Priaulx and his friends a Parliamentary flotilla arrived on January 10th., and — a short break in February apart — remained until the following summer, being especially in evidence on April 24th., when the States authorized a forced loan to defray the cost of its maintenance. Its presence in island waters induced the disaffected to temporize for the nonce: hence, presumably, the lack of support for Sir Peter Osborne's attempt in mid-February (when the Parliamentary ships were temporarily absent) to bring about the reduction of Guernsey by four men-of-war under the Earl of Marlborough — a venture which came to nothing, with Marlborough tamely withdrawing to Jersey in face of the 'obduracy of the people' when a threat was made to fire on the boat which, under a flag of truce, carried his envoy with a demand for submission.

Later in the same year (May) George Carteret's plans to attempt the recovery of Sark came to fruition. An expedition was launched consisting of about one hundred men in four boats: two under the command of Captain Lane with orders to land at l'Eperquerie, while the other two under Captain Chamberlain were to land in Dixcart Bay. Chamberlain's party (the minor detachment) took the parliamentary garrison by surprise, seized the captain in his bed, and made the male population prisoners. In the morning, however, a party of women, seeing the smallness of Chamberlain's force, crossed to Little Sark and lit beacons and fired cannon to attract the attention of a parliamentary frigate (part of the flotilla stationed off Guernsey) cruising in the Russel. At this juncture Chamberlain found to his dismay that the main invading force under Lane, overcome by the rough crossing, had been frightened off by the three-man guard at l'Eperquerie and had returned to Jersey. In these circumstances a landing party from the frigate had no difficulty in overcoming Chamberlain's small contingent, all of whom were taken prisoner and carried off to Guernsey — where Chamberlain languished in close confinement for two and a quarter years until he managed to escape to France.

Although the Parliamentarians had been successful in Sark, difficulties still confronted the Roundhead Establishment in Guernsey where, the sanctions incurred by Priaulx and de Rozel notwithstanding, the departure during the summer of 1644 of the cat of the Parliamentary flotilla emboldened the Royalist mice to play once more and a resurgence of discontent ultimately led to a number of parishes entering into a pledge whereby should one of them be provoked to take up arms, the others would come to its help. At this juncture (Autumn 1644) Russell, goaded by the outright refusal of Saint Saviour's 'John Hampden' (the Parish Constable, Leonard Blondel) to pay his levy, dispatched a punitive expedition into the western parishes. Jonathan Duncan in his well-known *History of Guernsey* records that two parishioners of Saint Saviour's were killed and the infuriated neighbourhood, led by Jacques Guille of Saint George in the Castel, rose *en masse*, seized two pieces of cannon and compelled Russell by articles which he signed on November 22nd., to behave constitutionally and to reimburse Blondel for any losses incurred by him. Despite these assurances, however, the situation remained tense and the undaunted Pierre Priaulx, still staunch for the King, became involved in a plot to seize Jerbourg Castle and the Vale Castle in December 1644 coincident with a general uprising against Guernsey's Parliamentarian Establishment which Osborne sought to encourage by letters promising a full pardon, release from all indebtedness, religious toleration and freedom from being 'molested or disquieted in any sort'. In the event this attempt came to nothing as a result of the indiscretions of Pierre Priaulx' associate Richard Robin who, while in his cups, betrayed both the identities of the insurgents and their plans. Yet even after this setback Royalist activity persisted and as late as May 13th., 1645, the States were sufficiently alarmed to order the parochial authorities to do all possible to search out trouble-makers. As a result a further seven 'Refractaires' were eventually arrested and resistance was finally crushed by the arrival later that month of another Parliamentary squadron. Pierre Priaulx, who had fled the island after Richard Robin's disclosures, was eventually permitted to return, subject to the payment of a heavy forfeit to ransom his goods — and then, by a cruel quirk of fate, was in April 1650 killed by a cannon-ball fired by his fellow-Royalists in Castle Cornet.

(While on this topic of Royalist resistance and before dropping it, mention must be made of Pierre de Beauvoir's nephew James le Marchant who, blood ties notwithstanding, is credited by both F. B. Tupper and Edith Carey in their respective historical works as having been so recklessly daring in supporting the Stuarts as to be compelled to flee for dear life to France. One hesitates to gainsay such eminent authorities, but the fact is that a perusal of *Les Acts des Etats* and Pierre le Roy's Diary reveals that this worthy was a prominent participant in the island's Roundhead administration during the whole of the Civil War and the ensuing Commonwealth period. One of the Parliamentary Commissioners appointed in March 1642/3, he was made Receiver in November 1648 — in which year he was among those described as 'of known worth and fidelity to the Parliament' — and was sworn in as Jurat in November 1649. His departure for France in November 1653 coincided with his involvement in a lawsuit against Jean Bonamy and may well have been occasioned thereby. He was, however, back in Guernsey the following February, serving his term as Bailiff under the rotation system then prevailing — and serving again as such in January 1654/5. Furthermore, his presence as a Jurat is subsequently recorded at every States meeting throughout the Commonwealth period. Hardly the curriculum vitae of a dedicated Royalist!)

The failure of the aforementioned uprisings as well as of the royalist attempt on Sark meant that the only part of Sir Peter Osborne's governorate over which he had effective control remained confined to Castle Cornet, his ability to hold which was dependent on the support and supplies he received from George Carteret in Jersey. Unfortunately relations between the two men were strained so that Carteret only grudgingly supplied Osborne at irregular intervals. This bad rapport between the two leaders meant that Sir Peter's days were numbered when Charles, Prince of Wales, arrived in Jersey in April 1646, after having been driven out of the West of England by Fairfax. George Carteret (who had been knighted in 1645) enjoyed tremendous prestige with the young prince, and he cogently argued the case for the recall of Osborne — with the upshot that later in the year Sir Peter, while technically remaining Governor, relinquished effective command to Sir Baldwin Wake as his Lieutenant-Governor (a face-saving arrangement) and withdrew to Saint Malo where he spent the next three years organising the dispatch of supplies to the Royalists both in Jersey and in the Castle. He died on March 11th., 1653/4.

In 1648, while Charles was a prisoner in the Isle of Wight, Sir George Carteret mounted another expedition to recover Sark for his cousin (whom Prince Charles, while in Jersey, had knighted on his royal father's behalf). A tremendous storm, however, caused the operation to be abandoned.

Carteret's plan to invade Guernsey the same year was also foiled. His relations with Sir Baldwin Wake were little better than those he had had with his predecessor, and Wake refused to allow him to enter Castle Cornet with more than six men. Any invasion of Guernsey was thus obviously out of the question, though St. Peter-Port continued to suffer grievously from the repeated bombardments to which it was subjected.

After Charles I's execution Carteret had Charles II proclaimed in Jersey — the last remnant of the royal dominions. Later the same year he entertained Charles II, who stayed in Jersey until his departure for Scotland in February 1650 (new style). During the king's stay Carteret once again exerted his influence with his royal master with the result that Wake followed in the footsteps of Osborne, to be succeeded as royalist Lieutenant-Governor of Guernsey in command of Castle Cornet by Colonel Sir Roger Burgess, with Henry, Lord Percy, as absentee Governor.

After Charles II's defeat at Worcester, parliament despatched Colonel James Heane in command of an expedition to reduce Jersey. Admiral Robert Blake was ordered to accompany him 'to give his best advice and assistance for its reduction' (September 20th., 1651). Heane's forces made landfall on October 22nd. at La Pulente, the first ashore being a detachment of Guernseymen led by Major Harrison — who, sad to relate, subsequently proved to be incorrigible looters. The island was rapidly over-run, but Carteret held out in the fastness of Elizabeth Castle until 15 December, when (with permission so to do received from Charles in Paris) he surrendered after obtaining terms whereby he was allowed to keep his property and go to France — where he took service under Louis XIV. Carteret failed, however, in his attempt to obtain the return of Sark to his cousin Philippe on payment of a penalty — and parliament retained control of the fief with Captain Nicholas Ling (and, from 1656, when Ling went to Alderney, Captain Richard Winne) in command.

Parliamentary control of Jersey made the position of Burgess in Castle Cornet impossible, and on December 19th., 1651 this last royalist stronghold surrendered after sustaining a siege of eight years and nine months. Colonel Burgess and his garrison of 55 men marched out with the honours of war; Burgess himself being granted an indemnity of £1,500 as an acknowledgement of the humane way in which he had treated some parliamentary prisoners whom he had captured in an earlier abortive attack on the fortress. The Civil War in Guernsey was over — though the victors (providing an object lesson of utter ruthlessness towards all opponents by incarcerating the prominent Leveller John Lilburne in Castle Cornet) were to repay the island's support for the Parliamentarian cause by showing so scant a respect for its autonomy that in 1653 the Cromwellian Protectorate's foundation document (the Instrument of Government) included it among the places chosen to send members to the Westminster Parliament. In the event the Guernesiais contrived to avoid conforming to this requirement with its implication of political absorption into England; but three years later (in 1656) they faced a further threat to their ancient privileges when, in derogation thereof — and despite protests by the Bailiff and Court supplemented by several manifestations of armed resistance — two attempts were made to infringe the Bailiwick's neutral status by pressing its sons into the Commonwealth Navy. After such experiences it was surely of little consolation to reflect that the Lady Protectress from September 1658 until May 1659 (Dorothy Mauger, wife of Richard Cromwell) was reputedly — albeit rather distantly — of Channel Island stock.

Chapter Seven

THE PRIVATEERING ERA

THE 18th.-CENTURY FRANCO-BRITISH TUSSLE for commercial and imperial dominance, which resulted in repeated wars between the two rivals from the Glorious Revolution until Waterloo, provided plentiful opportunities for privateers from the Bailiwick of Guernsey to display their daring and their skilled seamanship. The excellence of St. Peter-Port's harbour and roadstead made Guernsey an ideal base, and islanders of all classes participated in the ventures.

Although privateering has been confused with piracy, any automatic mutual identification is unjustifiable as a privateer (until the abolition of the practice in 1856) was a legally-recognised and fully-accredited combatant operating on behalf of the country whose flag he flew — and holding credentials consisting of a Letter of Marque issued by the sovereign of the state for which he fought, the format of which was along the lines shown in Appendix XVI.

Despite this distinction between privateering and piracy, however, it must be admitted that the dividing line between the two pursuits was very thin — and it was not unknown for a privateer to step over it from time to time. The temptation to do so was strong as French-speaking crews of Channel Islanders, flying the French flag and attacking British ships, could easily be mistaken by their victims for what they purported to be. Thus piratical and privateering activities could be intermingled as (according to her autobiography) seems to have been the case with the late Dame de Sercq's great-great-grandfather, Jean Allaire, who — like Restauld before him — is said to have used Jethou as the base for his illicit operations; whereby, as it happened, he amassed the fortune which enabled his daughter to purchase the seigneurie of Sark. (If, incidentally, this sea-dog's reputed use of Jethou did, in fact, occur, it must have been either with the connivance of or in despite of its tenant, Phillip de Quesnel, as Allaire himself did not acquire the lease of the island until 1822, seven years after Waterloo, and rather late in the day for privateering.)

While privateering was of enormous profitability, it must not be forgotten that it also had its debit side, quite apart from the perils directly incurred. In the first place, the demand for crews constituted a serious drain on man-power, a factor which was particularly serious in Sark, where several tenements fell into decay for lack of tenants. Secondly, participation in this activity also brought smallpox to the Bailiwick, three major outbreaks of which (in 1695, 1705 and 1731) caused a heavy death-toll, which again was especially serious for the smaller islands. Especially relevant in connection with the adverse aspects of these forays are the findings published in the 1986 *Transactions* of La Société Guernesiaise of the late Reverend Canon James Peter Caplin Priaulx Raban, T.D. (1918–1996), whose island affinity was emphasised by his last Christian name. This investigator's researches revealed that the War of the Spanish Succession produced a 30% failure rate of privateers that took no prizes to offset the costly initial outlay involved in equipping craft for action; while an even greater failure rate of 45% was experienced during the War of the Austrian Succession. It is also noteworthy that this latter conflict, considered in conjunction with the ensuing Seven Years War, brought the loss of some one hundred and thirty trading and sixty privateering ships — a reflection which prompted the learned cleric to observe:

> 'Much attention has been given to the profits from privateering, little has been focussed on their shipping losses and the considerable number of their seamen who were incarcerated in filthy prisons for prolonged periods.'

Strictly speaking, the privateering era proper dates from William III's repudiation of the archipelago's neutral status, coupled with the opportunities afforded by the War of the League of Augsburg. Nevertheless, small-scale ventures were not unknown prior to this. Indeed, as early as 1598 — a century before the abrogation of the Bull of Neutrality — Elizabeth I, enraged by Henry IV's conclusion of peace with Philip of Spain at Vervins, issued a Letter of Marque to Jean Briard to attack French shipping with his vessel, *La Colombe*. Again, in 1667, when to Charles II's surprise Louis XIV sided with the Dutch against him, John Tupper had operated as a privateer, his achievements earning an accolade from the governor, Colonel Sir Jonathan Atkins:

> How bravelie the men of St. Martyn's have behaved themselves at sea. They have brought in a prize of sixty Ton, of Amsterdam, laden with wine, tobacco, figs and rosin.

Moreover, there was more significance to this operation than the valour of the mariners, as the French had hoped that Guernsey, with its Calvinist traditions and its resentment over the imposition of Anglicanism, could prove to be a British Achilles heel, rallying around General Lambert (who was a political prisoner in Castle Cornet) in revolt against the Crown. Tupper's exploits demonstrated unequivocally that any such hopes were doomed to disappointment.

These episodes, however, may be regarded as no more than curtain-raisers, and privateering activity started in earnest in 1692, with the Battle of Cap La Hogue, where James II on the Cotentin cliffs watched the destruction of the French fleet on which depended his hopes of regaining his throne. In connection with this action John Tupper (the eponymous son of the aforementioned) by his exploits won the award of a massive gold medal and chain presented to him by William III and Mary II in recognition of his signal services on the eve of the engagement. It fell out that Tupper, commanding the *Monmouth Galley*, was crossing from Guernsey to England when, thanks to a temporary lifting of the prevailing fog, he espied the French fleet under Admiral Tourville. Making with all haste to Saint Helen's in the Isle of Wight, he alerted Admiral Russell regarding the enemy's presence in the Channel — thereby providing intelligence which led to this famous victory. In the battle itself Tupper gained further distinction, destroying four French ships as they tried to escape through the Race of Alderney and thus earning a public citation. After this battle, the striking power of the French Navy reduced to negligible proportions, Guernsey ventures proliferated, and by the end of the war in 1697 some 30 Guernsey privateers were in operation.

During the War of the Spanish Succession the Guernsey privateers put their knowledge of the French coastal areas and its reefs to the service of the Grand Alliance, to which they made a considerable contribution by disrupting the French coastal trade on which, in the absence of good roads, the French economy largely depended. Convoys were ambushed and rivers and roadsteads raided. By the end of the war (1713) Guernsey had 115 privateers in action which, thanks to boarding operations with small arms and cutlasses, brought in 608 prizes to a total value of £100,000.

The outbreak of the Seven Years War (1756) brought the men of Alderney into the fray, with ships fitted out by the governor, John Le Mesurier, basing their operations on the new harbour at Braye. This wild life so appealed to the Aurigniais that in ever-increasing numbers they forsook their traditional agriculture for the sea. The massive profits gained brought Alderney unprecedented prosperity, so much so that when the war ended in 1763 John Le Mesurier (who previously had found the intractable islanders well-nigh insupportable) now exchanged his Patent for a new grant of 99 years.

These Alderney exploits did not mean that the men of Guernsey were idle in this struggle, as a monument in the Town church testifies:

> Sacred to the memory of Captain Nicholas le Messurier, Commander of the Private Ship of War the Bellona of 20 guns, belonging to this island, who being on a cruise, in the night of the twelfth of February 1759, fell in with a large French East India ship, and in the morning by dawn of day gallantly attacked and engaged her, but about an hour after was unfortunately slain. The Privateer being greatly shatter'd in her Masts and Rigging, having several shots betwixt wind and water, and many Men killed and wounded, was obliged to sheer off, after having greatly shattered the Enemy. He was a Native of this Island. Born on the 18th. of May, in the year 1731, and always behav'd like a brave and diligent Officer; to whose memory the Owners of the Privateer have erected this Monument out of gratitude for his good Services.

When in the year 1778 France entered the lists on the side of the colonists in the American Revolution, the governor of Cherbourg (General Dumouriez) reported on the menace of the Channel Isles privateers, stating:

> These two islands are the despair of France, at the breaking out of each war, through their remarkably active privateers. The habit of encountering the dangers of the sea renders the natives very brave.

It was obvious that even the ranks of Tuscany could scarce forbear to cheer.

The islanders rapidly justified the Cherbourg governor's warning. After their apprenticeship in the Seven Years War, the Alderney privateers now really came into their own. In 1779 alone

John Le Mesurier's ship, the *Resolution*, carrying 20 guns and a crew of 100, brought in prizes to the value of £134,589. By 1782 the Alderney fleet was eight strong, with total prize money for that year coming to £212,381. At the same time from Guernsey the three ships operated by John Tupper (the great-nephew of John Tupper of Cap La Hogue) collected nearly £60,000 in prizes; while John Henry's *Alarm*, a lugger carrying fourteen guns and a crew of fifty-six, brought in seven prizes with a gross value of £38,500. By the time peace came with the Treaty of Versailles in 1783, the total value in prizes came to over £900,000. Although the French struck back with an abortive attack in 1779, followed by an invasion of Jersey in 1781, when they were driven out thanks to the gallant leadership of Major Francis Peirson, who tragically fell in the hour of victory, Guernsey and her sister isles were lucky enough to escape unscathed.

With the coming of the French Revolutionary War the assistance rendered by the privateers to the Royal Navy was so valuable as to lead that indefatigable commentator, Edmund Burke, to declare that the Islands were entitled to be reckoned 'One of the Naval Powers of the world'. War broke out in 1793 and the journals of Elisha Dobrée, a douzenier of St. Peter-Port, records that during the following April alone no fewer than seven prizes were brought into the harbour. By 1800 the prize money brought into Guernsey since the outbreak of war came to nearly £1,000,000, and in that year a further 35 ships were fitted out, which were destined to bring in another million. The opportunities open to the privateers became even wider with the entry into the struggle of the U.S.A. as Napoleon's ally in 1812 — and they lost no time in seizing them. One American ship alone, taken on her way back from the Indies, was worth £60,000.

When peace finally came in 1815 with Napoleon's defeat at Waterloo, the audacity of Guernsey's seamen had brought to the island prosperity as never known before. There was, however, to be no further repetition. The privateering era had come to an end.

Chapter Eight

ILLUSTRIOUS WARRIORS AFLOAT AND ASHORE

TWO BRANCHES of a prominent Guernsey family trace their origin to the Fief de Samarès in Jersey ('Samarès' meaning 'marsh-land'). One branch of this family takes the name 'de Sausmarez'; while the other omits the second 's'. Both these sections of the 'Marsh People' have distinguished connections with the Royal Navy.

The outbreak of the War of Jenkins' Ear against Spain in 1739 saw two brothers (Philip and Thomas) who, though born bearing the second 's', dropped both it and the prefix on joining the Royal Navy, picked for service in the squadron under Admiral George Anson, who in 1740 was sent off to harry the enemy's galleons. They returned with Anson in the *Centurion* (of which Philip was first lieutenant) in 1744, after having circumnavigated the globe, capturing the *Manila Galleon* and seizing treasure worth £600,000 en route. The brothers' share of the prize money enabled their family to buy back the Fief de Sausmarez from the Andros family, who had held it for over two centuries.

In September 1746 Philip was given command of H.M.S. *Nottingham* of 60 guns. On October 14th., 1747, during the War of the Austrian Succession, in an action off Brest, Philip attempted to stay the flight of the *Intrépide* and the *Tonnant*, and was killed by almost the last shot fired. He was 37 years of age. He left his memento in the uniform chosen by George II for naval officers — a uniform which he had designed. A monument was erected to him in Westminster Abbey.

The French Revolutionary and Napoleonic Wars brought glory to Guernsey's undoubted greatest naval hero who, until the Germans razed it in 1943, was commemorated by an obelisk in Delancey Park inscribed:

> To James, First Baron de Saumarez of Guernsey, G.C.B., K.B., D.C.L., Admiral of the Red and General of Marines. B 1757 D 1836. This Memorial was erected as a tribute of admiration by his fellow countrymen, 1877.

James Saumarez (from the branch of the family without the second 's' and the nephew of Philip) entered the Navy as a Midshipman in 1770 at the age of thirteen and, while a junior officer, served in H.M.S. *Victory*. He first caused island hearts to swell with pride in Spring 1793 when, with the rank of Captain in command of H.M.S. *Crescent* (the crew of which was composed almost entirely of Guernseymen) he captured the French frigate *La Réunion* (36 guns) off Cherbourg. For this exploit he was knighted. Christmastide of the same year saw Sir James engaged in a daring errand of mercy. On the 27th. of the month he commanded five warships which escorted into Guernsey ten transports of Roman Catholic refugees from the Jacobin Terror (see Part I, Chapter Twelve).

In 1794 a plan to invade the archipelago and put paid to the privateers was drawn up by Lazare Carnot, the Committee of Public Safety's 'Organizer of Victory'. In November 1974 when a photostat of the original plan was presented to him, the late Cecil de Sausmarez, Seigneur du Fief de Sausmarez, stated that he believed that the invasion plan for February 1794 was put off, but that it was set in motion the following June. What is certain is that on Sunday June 8th., 1794 a most exciting naval action was fought off the west coast of Guernsey. What happened is described in the next paragraph.

Sir James Saumarez, commanding a squadron consisting of his own ship (H.M.S. *Crescent*) accompanied by H.M.S. *Druid* (Captain Joseph Ellison) and H.M.S. *Eurydice* (Captain Francis Cole) had sailed from Plymouth the previous evening under orders to escort to Guernsey what his ship's log records as four small craft, comprising the lugger *Valiant* under Lieutenant Baker, plus two other luggers and a cutter (though the orders given to Saumarez before departure — which may of course have been changed — had been to escort the five cargo vessels *Valiant*, *Dolphin*, *Cockchafer*, *Active* and *Prestwood*) — and after arrival to reconnoitre the strength of enemy naval forces in the Saint Malo area, where intelligence reports suggested that a force of 20,000 was assembled for an invasion of the archipelago. When about half way between Les Casquets and L'Ancresse and positioned N.N.W. of Guernsey, he sighted five French frigates S.E. of him, so that his effective force was three to five. This soon became two to five, for H.M.S. *Eurydice* was only a slow sailer and Sir James therefore ordered her to head S.S.W. towards Les Hanois in order to make for Saint Peter-Port via the south coast. Meanwhile,

Crescent and *Druid* continued on their original course (S.S.E.) so as to shelter *Eurydice* by luring the French to draw up to them. This stratagem succeeded and when, at about six nautical miles N.N.W. of Grand Havre, they came within range, Saumarez ordered a turn to the S.W. and crowded on sail towards Les Hanois in the wake of *Eurydice*, now far enough ahead to be out of danger. With the enemy hot in pursuit and with his depleted force completely out-gunned, Sir James ordered *Druid* to continue S.W. to Les Hanois and safety, while he turned *Crescent* to confront and delay the foe to facilitate the escape of *Druid* — and for the next half-hour he contrived by daring and skilful seamanship to avoid serious damage to his ship despite the intense barrage of fire to which she was subjected, so monopolising the enemy's attention that the small craft which he had been escorting managed to slip away unnoticed and sail back to Plymouth. Obviously this unequal struggle could not be sustained indefinitely and, to evade defeat and capture, Saumarez headed S.S.E. towards the headland of Houmet de la Nicole about four nautical miles distant which is now (but then not yet) graced by Fort Houmet. Fear of the shore batteries and of the hazardous rock-strewn coastal approaches induced the French to hold off, convinced in any case that their opponent intended to run his craft aground rather than strike his colours. To their astonishment, however, *Crescent* was neither beached nor did she come to grief in the offshore shallows, but achieved the seemingly impossible by suddenly veering to larboard after passing through an apparently unnavigable gap in the rocks — a feat accomplished thanks to the intimate knowledge of local waters possessed by Jean Breton of Saint Saviour's, a Guernsey pilot whose request for a lift home had been granted by Sir James (to whom he was already known) shortly before leaving Plymouth. Thereafter, sailing in reef-infested waters even if protected by the shore batteries, *Crescent* tacked N.E. against the wind, rounded le Clos du Valle and finally reached Saint Peter-Port roadstead to rejoin *Druid* and *Eurydice*, all three snug under the guns of Castle Cornet. The story goes that as they fled through their needle's eye Saumarez asked Breton if he was sure of his sea-marks and received the reply, "Quite sure, Sir, for there is your house and my house in line" — but it must be said that reconnaissance around Breton's house at Les Jenemies strongly suggests that the account is apocryphal, intervening higher ground between there and Saumarez Park precluding a simultaneous sighting of the two dwellings.

The extensive researches into this engagement conducted by Mr. David Shayer led to him too to doubt the 'two houses' story and also to believe that the near-miraculous escape which so astounded the French was made through the passage separating Les Grunes de Nord-Ouest from La Suzanne (about two nautical miles N.N.W. of the Houmet headland) which was rendered negotiable by the fact that the tide was rising at the time. He furthermore concluded that *Crescent* then headed straight towards Les Pecqueries and emphasised that the subsequent perilous manoeuvring N.E. towards L'Ancresse amid a vast array of treacherous rocks was safely executed solely because of the superb navigational skills displayed by Breton and his anonymous fellow pilot, whose joint contributions to ensuring the ship's survival was praised by Saumarez in a letter to his brother written six days later.

After distinguishing himself at Cape St. Vincent in 1797 and serving as Nelson's second-in-command at the Nile in 1798, Sir James in the summer of 1801 (the year in which he was appointed Rear-Admiral) won a resounding victory in a battle fought with an amalgamated French and Spanish squadron in the Gut of Gibraltar. In recognition of this he was later voted the Thanks of the British Parliament — and added lustre was lent to the proceedings on October 30th., 1801 in that no less a person than the great Viscount Nelson (sitting in the House of Lords during the respite of the Peace of Amiens) devoted his maiden speech to describing the engagement when seconding the motion 'That the Thanks of this House be given to Rear-Admiral Sir James Saumarez, K.B., for his gallant and distinguished conduct in the Action with the Combined Fleets of the Enemy off Algeziras, on the 12th. and 13th. of July last'. The renewal of the war after the Peace of Amiens saw the islands in imminent danger, with Napoleon fulminating against them because of their privateering exploits and stating, 'France can no longer tolerate this nest of brigands and assassins'. In these circumstances Saumarez in 1803 assumed command in Guernsey waters of a squadron based on St. Peter-Port with orders to defend the islands and also to co-operate with Cornwallis (patrolling off Ushant) in blockading the enemy fleet under Genteaume in Brest. The efficiency with which he discharged these duties played an important part in frustrating Napoleon's plans to invade, not only the Channel Isles, but Britain as well. While engaged in these operations de Saumarez destroyed a flotilla of enemy gunboats due to sail from Granville to the invasion assembly point at Boulogne.

After this assignment in his native seas, Sir James in March 1808 was given command of a squadron sent to the Baltic, originally to support the Swedes against the Danes and Russians. He maintained control of the Baltic for five years and by affording to the Russians (now Britain's allies) communications by sea (which were, of course, denied to the French) he helped to bring about Napoleon's débâcle of 1812. In recognition of his services he was presented by the Crown Prince of Sweden with a diamond sword valued at £2,000, and his memory is revered in Sweden to this day. (A special visit to Guernsey by a Swedish warship was made in his honour in 1910, followed by another in 1936 to mark the centenary of his death.) On his return from the Baltic he was made a full admiral.

Retiring in 1827, he was raised to the peerage in 1831 and died in 1836 at his country house in Saumarez Park. His funeral at the Castel church (in whose graveyard he is buried) was attended by an enormous concourse.

On September 4th., 1975, a commemorative plaque to de Saumarez was unveiled in Gothenburg City Hall in the presence of H.M. the King of Sweden and Earl Mountbatten of Burma.

An additional Guernsey sailor of renown was Admiral Thomas Le Marchant Gosselin (1765–1857) who in 1808, during the Peninsular Campaign, with the rank of Captain, convoyed to the Tagus an expeditionary force together with its commander, the Jerseymen Lieutenant-General Sir Harry Burrard, Baronet; and later (in January 1809) covered the Corunna evacuation of Sir John Moore's troops — a service for which he (like Saumarez before him) was voted the Thanks of the British Parliament. Yet another was Rear-Admiral Sir Thomas Mansell, K.C.H. (1777–1858), who was credited with the capture of no fewer than 170 enemy vessels between 1808 and 1814.

By an unhappy quirk of fate the year 1812 which, with the retreat from Moscow, witnessed Saumarez' efforts in the Baltic reaping their reward, also saw two of Guernsey's outstanding sons meet their deaths in action.

The first of these was General John Gaspard Le Marchant, who was born in 1765 and was a member of the family whose ancestral home was La Haye du Puits in the Castel. Entering the army in 1783 at the age of 18, Le Marchant later evolved a plan for the introduction of a sword exercise throughout the service, which earned him promotion to lieutenant-colonel. His main contribution to military immortality, however, was the establishment of the

Royal Military College, plans for which he submitted to the Duke of York (commander-in-chief) in 1799. This was eventually founded in 1802 and Le Marchant became its first lieutenant-governor. Originally there was a senior department at High Wycombe and a junior one at Great Marlow, though both were later moved to Sandhurst.

After holding this office for nine years Le Marchant was promoted to major-general and given command of a brigade of heavy cavalry in the Peninsula. Here, on July 22nd., 1812 General Le Marchant led a charge of 800 horse against over 5,000 infantry at Salamanca. Although the enemy was scattered and 1,500 prisoners taken, Le Marchant was shot and died immediately. In recognition of his invaluable services a monument to his memory was set up in St. Paul's Cathedral, and a pension of £1,200 settled on his family.

The second casualty of 1812 was Sir Isaac Brock (the brother of Daniel de Lisle Brock, whose career was examined in Part III, Chapter Eight), who is invariably acclaimed as Guernsey's greatest soldier. Born in 1769, Brock entered the army in 1785 at the age of 15, and after distinguishing himself in Holland in 1799, and being second-in-command of the land forces in Nelson's attack on Copenhagen in 1801, he was sent to Canada in 1802, with the rank of colonel

In 1805 he returned to Guernsey but, when relations with the U.S.A. deteriorated in 1806, was hurriedly recalled to Canada. Given command over Upper Canada in 1810 Brock, through the respect he won from them, established his ascendancy over the Indian tribes under the leadership of the Shawnee warrior, Tecumseh.

When war broke out in 1812 Brock, now a major-general, in his capacity as Governor of Upper Canada, was responsible for a frontier of 1,300 miles with scarcely as many men. Nevertheless, he took the offensive and marched to capture Detroit (August 16th., 1812), thus uniting behind him both British and French Canadians as well as retaining the support of the Indians. For these services he was knighted on October 10th., 1812, but three days later, on October 13th., he fell in a skirmish at Queenstown Heights, near Niagara Falls.

Nowadays these Heights are graced by a tall monument in his honour, and he is also commemorated by Brock University in Ontario. In London a monument to him is to be seen in St. Paul's Cathedral, while Guernsey has the Brock Memorial chapel in the

Town Church, besides having two roads named after him and a plaque outside the premises of Boots the Chemists, recalling that he once lived in the building.

Neither Le Marchant nor Brock was, however, the first Guernseyman to attain the rank of Major-General. This distinction falls to Major-General John Tupper, Commander-in-Chief of the Royal Marines (1727–1795) who during the Seven Years War, as a Captain, participated in Hawke's victory at Quiberon Bay in 1757; while during the War of American Independence he fought as a Major at Bunker's Hill (where he was wounded) in 1775 and (as a Lieutenant-Colonel) commanded the Marine contingent under Rodney at the Battle of the Saints in 1782. He died in 1795 of grief at the loss of his only son.

In conclusion it should be noted that although the remainder of the nineteenth century following Napoleon's defeat saw few military exploits involving Guernseymen, its last thirteen months were marked by the emergence of two further soldiers of valour in the persons of the Old Intermedian Corporal (later Lieutenant) George Edward Nurse of the Royal Artillery and of the Old Elizabethan Captain (later General Sir) Lewis Stratford Tollemarch Halliday of the Royal Marine Light Infantry. Each of these won the Victoria Cross: the former on December 15th., 1899 and the latter on June 24th., 1900 — just six months before the century drew to a close. Defying withering Afrikaner fire, Nurse participated in the retrieval of two artillery pieces which had been abandoned at the battle of Colenso in the South African conflict, while Halliday achieved glory during the Boxer rising in China when he led a sortie to drive away the foe menacing the British Legation in Peking, persisting in the foray even after being seriously wounded.

Chapter Nine

THE EMBATTLED ISLE — AND DISCONCERTING ALLIES

THE THREAT FROM FRANCE during the American Revolution dating from the French entry into the struggle on the side of the colonists on the morrow of Saratoga led to a spate of fortifications in Guernsey — especially after the abortive enemy attack on Jersey in 1779 had emphasised the urgency of the need. An even stronger impetus to the work (which had already been started) was given by the actual French invasion of Jersey two years later in 1781.

Besides the erection around the island of a ring of fifteen so-called but misnamed 'Martello' towers (Guernsey's only towers deserving this appellation being those built later at Forts Grey, Sausmarez and Houmet), the period is noteworthy for the construction of Fort George, which, commenced in 1780, was to become the hub of Guernsey's defensive system. Ironically, this stronghold's first blooding (in 1783) involved no alien foe, but stemmed from a mutiny in its own garrison, the 104th. Regiment. Disaffected by newly-arrived ex-servicemen from the 83rd. Foot, and unappeased after six days' congé to come and go at will, the troops on March 24th. fired on their officers, forcing them to flee — but capitulated, outnumbered, when the lieutenant-governor (Lieutenant-Colonel P. A. Irving) moved against them at the head of the Militia and the 18th. Regiment.

The existence of Fort George meant that from the American Revolution until the Second World War a battalion of the regular army was habitually stationed in Guernsey. Although Fort George by itself could not house a full battalion, its accommodation was supplemented by that provided in the numerous Alderney forts, the barracks at Jerbourg, and Icart, and Forts Houmet, Richmond, and Le Marchant. As time went by the population became so accustomed to the garrison that the presence of the troops became part of Guernsey's way of life, a major event in the island's year being what was by a previous generation called 'La Grande Mourtre' — the ceremony of Trooping the Colour at the

1. (*above*) Le Trepied Dolmen, Le Catioroc, St Saviour's (*c.* 4000 B.C.).

2. (*left*) Statue Menhir, Castel Churchyard (*c.* 3000 B.C.).

3. (*above*) Le Colombier Farmhouse with pigeonnier (c.1570).

4. (*left*) Philippe de Carteret's tunnel to Creux Harbour, Sark (1588).

5. Alderney: Château à l'Etoc (mid-19th century).

3. Candie Gardens. Part of Osmond de Beauvoir Priaulx's benefactions (1871)

Belvedere Field presided over by the lieutenant-governor on the occasion of the monarch's official birthday, and culminating in a march past ending at noon precisely when the 21-gun royal salute boomed out from Castle Cornet. This tradition came to an end in June 1940 when, in face of the occupation menace, the British government withdrew all military establishments and equipment, and declared the entire archipelago an open town.

Although built to withstand Britannia's foes, Fort George received its baptism of fire from her friends when, on June 5th., 1944, the R.C.A.F. launched a very thorough attack, rendering the citadel untenable as well as the barracks and the sergeants' mess. The officers' quarters also suffered badly, some of them being reduced to heaps of rubble. Fort George had been neutralised. The Germans sought to camouflage the size of their losses by scattering their interments among several cemeteries. Despite these precautions, however, the most casual glance at the fort cemetery shows the number of German deaths in a five-year tenancy to be many times those of the British (who, of course, succumbed to natural mortality) during the half-century between the opening of this necropolis in 1894 and the withdrawal of the garrison in 1939. Its defence potential being obviously inadequate for modern needs, Fort George, its military glories departed, now provides the site for a housing estate. "Lo, all our pomp of yesterday is one with Nineveh and Tyre!"

It is by contrast pleasant to record that Fort George's minor contemporaries (the demolition of three of them apart) have been spared comparable obliteration and still grace the island's shores. Particularly noteworthy among the twelve survivors is the Tower at Rousse which, after being attractively refurbished, now houses a set of human models providing an evocative portrayal of living conditions for the Militiamen on duty within its confines; while on display outside are examples of armament in use during the thirty-eight year period between Saratoga and Waterloo — the whole ensemble constituting a tasteful and appealing exhibition.

Returning after this digression from the post-Hitler age to that of Napoleon, the year which stands out as an historical landmark is 1803, when Admiral Saumarez' squadron was based on St. Peter-Port and when the invasion peril was such as to prompt the drawing up of a major defence plan by the newly-arrived Sir John Doyle (lieutenant-governor, 1803–1816). This embraced the entire coastline from La Salerie in an anti-clockwise direction to Fermain Bay, the defence of St. Peter-Port being left to Castle Cornet and the still uncompleted Fort George. Doyle planned that every vantage point on the low-lying coast from La Salerie to Grand Havre was to be used to accommodate a battery of guns, while similar gun emplacements were to be erected between Grand Havre and Grandes Rocques — whose fortifications were to be supplemented by a powder magazine. Further down the west coast parapets were to be thrown up at Houmet and L'Erée and battery sites constructed, while the ancient Rocquaine Castle (Fort Grey) was to be repaired and guns placed at strategic points on the rising ground above the bay. Finally, to complete these western defences, the old castle at Pezeries was to be repaired, the parapet strengthened, and a powder magazine installed.

Although one would have thought the unscalability of the cliffs from Pleinmont to Petit Bôt to be such as to provide automatic defence, Doyle was taking no chances, and insisted on the erection of watch houses at the high points of La Prévoté, Les Tielles, Mont Herault, and Pleinmont. Thereafter three vulnerable bays remained — Petit Bôt, Saints and Fermain. In each case Doyle had stone ramparts built at least 12 feet in height, supplemented by trenches and parapets.

In all cases the constables of the parish concerned, assisted by a jurat, were responsible for the execution of the plan. They were enabled to discharge their obligations thanks to their possession of the power of Corvée — made more palatable by the fact that a flat rate of 1s. 6d. (7½p.) was paid for each and every man, cart, ox and horse.

Having dealt with primary defence, Doyle later turned his attention to its major ancillary — communications. Having studied William Gardner's famous 1787 six-inch map of the island, he realised the inadequacy of the road system for the rapid movement of troops and guns to any threatened part of the coast. In 1812, therefore, he drove two new roads through the island — from St. Peter-Port to Vazon and from St. Peter-Port to L'Erée. These roads set the pattern for Guernsey's present network. To finance this work, Doyle first of all drained La Braye du Valle in 1806 and sold the reclaimed land for £5,000. In this fashion he killed two birds with one stone, for, by uniting the Clos du Valle with St. Sampson's, he removed any possibility of the northern islet being used by an invading force as a base for further attack.

With all these achievements to his credit, it is small wonder that Sir John is revered as Guernsey's greatest lieutenant-governor, his memory honoured by a road, a fort, and a column at Jerbourg which, although destroyed by the Germans, has now been replaced by a commemorative obelisk.

A few years before Sir John Doyle assumed office, his predecessor, Sir Hew Dalrymple, was confronted with a particularly ticklish variant of the not unfamiliar problem of the embarrassing guest (and on this occasion an involuntary one as well) an account of which will provide an interesting anecdote with which to end this chapter. The difficulty arose in the year 1799 when a Russian force fighting side-by-side with the British in Holland sustained a defeat and had to be evacuated. The Bill of Rights precluding their landing in the United Kingdom, they were quartered in the Channel Isles awaiting the breaking of the ice to enable them to return through the Baltic to Russia. Six thousand were quartered in Guernsey in barracks at Delancey, as well as at L'Ancresse and the Vale Castle.

Although General Sedmoratzky and his officers, in honour of Czar Paul's birthday, staged a grand ball at the Assembly Rooms, where the principal inhabitants and the officers of the garrison were entertained, trouble arose with the soldiery following the deaths of several hundreds of a fever contracted in the Dutch marshes, the victims being buried in a field near the Vale Castle — though later, when this field was sold, the bodies were exhumed and some of them were re-buried in an enclosure adjoining the Castle itself, the vestiges of which are still to be seen on the left-hand side as one ascends the slope to the main gateway. The demoralised survivors took to drinking raw spirits and their conduct deteriorated alarmingly. One soldier was committed for rape, but was acquitted on the grounds of insufficient evidence; while another, caught stealing vegetables on a farm, was fired at and wounded by the farmer.

The evidence regarding the identity of this farmer is conflicting. The fact that in 1801 the States compensated John Le Poidevin of St. Sampson's for imprisonment at the instance of the Russian commander has led to the assumption that he it was who shot the marauder. On the other hand, the hurried departure from the island at this juncture of William Ogier of Duvaux Farm suggests his involvement in the episode — and thereby hangs another tale. Whatever his motives, Ogier betook himself to the New World where he was later joined by several fellow islanders. In 1807 the whole group linked up with another party led by Thomas Sarchet who the previous year had sailed from Guernsey and settled at Cambridge in Ohio (which had become one of the United States in

1803). In the year 1810 the State of Ohio created a new county around Cambridge, and, at the suggestion of Jacob Gomber, named it in honour of these settlers. Guernsey County had come into existence.

Irrespective of who fired on the thief, however, the incident incensed the whole Slav force and it was feared that the Russians might revenge themselves on the inhabitants generally. With only a small garrison of regular troops available in the island, it needed all the tact and conciliation of which Sir Hew was capable, as well as the efforts of General Sedmoratzky, to prevent an ugly situation from developing. When the Russians eventually embarked, the guns of Castle Cornet were kept loaded and ready to prevent any re-landing — and the whole population of the island heaved a sigh of relief.

Chapter Ten

THE GIBRALTAR OF THE CHANNEL

IN THE EARLY 1840s a number of factors resulted in tense relationships between the United Kingdom and France. In the first place, by the bombardment of Acre in 1840, followed by the 1841 Convention of the Straits debarring foreign warships from the Dardenelles while Turkey was at peace, Palmerston's aggressiveness had humbled Louis Philippe in that it checked his aspirations to establish control of the eastern Mediterranean through his protégé, Mehemet Ali. On top of this the prospect of Louis Philippe's son, le Duc de Montpensier, marrying the Princess Fernanda, sister of the Spanish Queen Isabella, was also alarming as Isabella's proposed spouse, the Duke of Cadiz, being commonly supposed to be impotent, the ultimate outcome seemed likely to be the old bogey of a union of the French and Spanish Crowns.

Although the visit of Queen Victoria to Louis Philippe at Château d'Eu arranged by the Foreign Secretary, Lord Aberdeen, in 1845, seemed to smooth things over, establishing as it did the original Entente Cordiale, the accord was of short duration as, despite Louis Philippe's assurances that Montpensier would not marry Fernanda until Isabella had borne a child, the two marriages in fact took place almost simultaneously in 1846.

Of particular moment to the Bailiwick of Guernsey was the fact that a constant background to these strained relations was provided by the spectacle of extensive defence installations being constructed at Cherbourg, including a great naval harbour with several forts to protect it.

The upshot of this latent hostility was that in 1842 the Peel/Aberdeen administration resolved to counter the French threat to British security implicit in the Cherbourg fortifications by converting nearby Alderney into 'the Gibraltar of the Channel': supplementing Guernsey's forts Richmond, Houmet, Le Marchant, and Doyle which the atmosphere of mutual distrust had already brought into existence — and to which, a number of years later, under the impulse of the same wariness, the Brehon Tower in the

Little Russel, with its five 18-pounder cannon manned by 35 gunners, was to be added in 1856, the Franco-British alliance in the Crimean War notwithstanding.

Although in 1844 Peel's government approved the construction of a breakwater to screen Braye Bay from the Atlantic seas, the project hung fire for a time in the more relaxed climate attending the Entente Cordiale of Château d'Eu. However, the Montpensier/Fernanda marriage coupled with the return to the Foreign Office of the imperious Palmerston in Lord John Russell's Ministry of 1846, led to work being put in hand in 1847, with a plan to create a harbour of 168 vergées, enclosed by one mole extending north-east from Grosnez Point and another built out from Roselle Point towards its fellow. Although work went ahead with the Grosnez mole, that on the other was postponed, and in 1852 Lord Derby's Ministry decided that it would be better to build the second mole from Château à l'Etoc, as in this way the area enclosed would be increased to 375 vergées. In the event, however, this project was never implemented.

Nevertheless, spurred on by the uncertainties of the 1848 Revolution and Louis Napoleon's *coup d'état* three years later, work on the western arm went ahead, despite the fact that (according to local report) experienced Alderney pilots were sceptical in the extreme about its ability to withstand the onslaught of Atlantic gales. It consisted of a masonry wall superimposed on a rubble mound and was finally completed in 1864, having reached a length of 4,680 feet. Work was facilitated by the railway which had been laid to Grosnez Point from Mannez Quarry, whence it brought stone to be used in the operation.

On August 9th., 1854 Queen Victoria and the Prince Consort arrived to inspect the work. The Guernsey artist, Paul Naftel, was commissioned to paint the scene — and the old Rue de Grosnez in St. Anne's was promptly re-named Victoria Street (though the fort commanding the naval base was only named Fort Albert after the Prince Consort's death by way of commemoration). A further visit of inspection was made by the royal couple on August 8th., 1857.

Work on the breakwater had barely been finished when any misgivings as to its feasibility were rapidly justified. Within six months of completion in 1864 two huge breaches were torn in the mole by winter gales. These were repaired during the following summer, but from then onwards winter damage proved to be continual — a fact which is hardly surprising when one considers the exposed position of the breakwater, directly facing the open

Atlantic. By this time serious doubts had already been expressed as to the justification of the entire scheme. In 1858 evidence submitted to the Select Committee on Harbours of Refuge by Captain Christopher Claxton, R.N., had claimed that the whole base could hardly hold seven ships — and he had added that the defences of the base were so under-manned that the French, had they a mind, could take it before sufficient reinforcements could arrive.

By 1872, when the economy-minded Gladstone was at Downing Street, many aspects of the situation had radically changed. To begin with, not only had the potential enemy of a quarter of a century earlier been the ally of the Crimean War, but it had also subsequently been utterly defeated and humbled by Bismarck. Furthermore, to the Treasury's dismay, the cost of construction of the breakwater had much exceeded the original estimate — and when the expenses of the perpetual repairs were taken into account, the total outlay on the mole since 1847 had amounted to £1,250,000.

The outcome of these considerations was the appointment the same year of a Select Committee of the House of Lords to investigate the entire project and to make recommendations as to whether the breakwater should be maintained, destroyed, or merely allowed to decay through neglect. The initial reaction of this Committee was to express profound doubts as to the value of the anchorage, feeling that had the benefit of hindsight been available in 1847, work would never have been started. An Alderney deputation, however, pleaded that, as the British government had built the breakwater to suit its own convenience, and as, furthermore, the old anchorage had thereby been spoilt, the mole should be maintained, since otherwise the island would be denied any adequate harbour, to the ruination of its economy. As a result of these representations, the Committee recommended that the mole should be maintained 'temporarily'. Maintenance still continues.

The experience of a further quarter of a century, however, led to the feeling that a shorter breakwater would suffice to protect Alderney's small commercial harbour. Accordingly the far (and most buffeted) end of the mole was abandoned to the tender mercies of Poseidon and degenerated into a sunken reef extending 1,800 feet beyond the maintained section, thus creating a hazard which is given a wide berth by shipping entering or leaving the harbour. The preservation of the remaining length of 2,850 feet was originally the responsibility of the British Admiralty, whence it was later transferred to the British Department of the Environment and finally became that of the States of Guernsey in 1987. It involves repeated trips from Mannez Quarry to the breakwater by a string of trucks, hauled by a diesel locomotive, laden with huge blocks of stone which are tipped on the seaward side of the mole to break the force of the waves. As has been seen in Part III, Chapter Eight, acute financial embarrassment ensued ten years after the assumption by the States of responsibility for this Labour of Sisyphus — so much so that the abandonment of the breakwater was considered together with the construction of a shorter jetty in its lee. As has also been seen, however, the continued maintenance of the existing structure was recommended by a Panel of Inquiry set up to examine the matter.

The 'Channel Gibraltar' actually operated as a naval base on one occasion only. This was in 1901, when the Channel Fleet used the anchorage during summer manoeuvres. To provide one anchorage used by part only of the fleet on a single occasion at an expenditure of over £1 ¼ million must surely be unique in naval annals.

To anyone in an aircraft flying over Alderney the breakwater (even in its truncated form) provides the outstanding spectacle; but once one has landed, the overwhelming impression is of the island as a heavily-fortified bastion. This impression derives from the chain of forts, built as a complement to the naval base, stretching from La Clonque in the west along the north coast as far as Fort Essex in the south-east, and constructed between the years 1847 and 1861. Only the south-western part of the coastline is free of such forts, as here the steepness of the cliffs was considered to be sufficient protection. These forts were designed by Captain W. F. D. Jervois (later Lieutenant-General Sir W. F. D. Jervois), whose taste in military architecture ran to the mediaeval pattern rather than that normally associated with the 19th. century. Thus embellishments abound, such as arrow slots, machicolations, battlements and moats.

The kingpin in the chain was Fort Albert, as its position on Mont Touraille commanded the approaches to the naval harbour itself, above which it still looms like a fairy-tale castle. This fort was primarily intended as a main artillery position and it mounted no less than 16 heavy guns, a number which was later reduced when more modern six-inch guns were installed. These guns were used, *inter alia*, for the training of the Royal Alderney Militia

Artillery (see Chapter XIII). Until the withdrawal of the military garrison in 1929, Fort Albert was used as Alderney's military headquarters.

Fort Tourgis, commanding potential hostile landings in Clonque and Saline Bays, mounted 16 heavy guns, while its junior partners nearby (Forts Platte Saline and Doyle) mounted five 68-pounders and two eight-inch guns respectively. The building of this fort displaced a seamark on La Rocque Tourgis, invaluable for the navigation of the perilous Swinge. This was replaced by the still-surviving whitewashed stone cone beside the fort.

Fort Clonque was intended to command the Swinge approaches, its design rendering it almost invisible from the sea. It mounted one 68-pounder, four 64-pounders, and one eight-inch gun.

Fort Grosnez, adjacent to the breakwater, was specifically designed for its defence and consequently was heavily armed, with 14 guns in eight batteries. As with many of the other forts, it was manned by the Royal Garrison Artillery.

Château à l'Etoc was designed to command any possible landings at Saye Bay or Corblets Bay and included seven well-armed batteries. On the other side of Corblets Bay its companion, Fort Corblets, was built on the site of an earlier battery (La Grande Corblette) which had mounted two nine-pounders. The fort itself mounted six guns, including 64-pounders.

Two forts of minor importance were Fort Les Hommeaux Florains and Fort Quesnard. The former covers a rocky approach little likely to be used by an enemy and thus mounted only two 32-pounders and one 64-pounder gun; while the latter, commanding the forbidding area of the meeting point of the Swinge and the Race, boasted only four 8-inch guns. Indeed, the only fort in the vicinity covering an even remotely possible landing place (the rock-strewn Grounard Bay) is Fort Houmet Herbé, which housed three 64-pounders.

The far more tempting landing place at Longy was covered by Fort Essex, coupled with the fort on Raz Island. The former, with its neighbouring batteries, carried three eight-inch guns and a howitzer, besides a 64-pounder, while the latter had four 64-pounders in two batteries.

The total constructional cost of these forts and batteries was £260,000 — to which the cost of the armament installed has, of course, to be added. Bearing in mind the much greater purchasing power of money a century ago, the Gibraltar of the Channel was certainly a shockingly expensive white elephant.

Quite apart from the exorbitant cost of the implementation of this grandiose defence scheme, it also exerted incalculable influence on the life of Alderney itself. The local population was utterly insufficient to enable the work to be carried out, with the result that a large immigrant force had to be employed, bringing the population from little more than 1,000 in 1841 to one of 4,932 in 1861, dropping back to 1,350 in 1891.

Less than half these immigrants were of Channel Isles origin, a very large number coming from Ireland, in search of a refuge from the Great Hunger which assailed that unhappy land during the 1840s. Many of the newcomers settled in Alderney and intermarried with the islanders, with the result that by the end of the century the native-born inhabitants were outnumbered by the English-speaking immigrants. The immediate outcome of this shift of the balance of the population was that the island patois rapidly fell into disuse, so that Alderney became the most anglicised of all the islands. Furthermore, the large Irish element in the influx brought Roman Catholicism back to Alderney for the first time since the departure of the Chamberlains (see Part II, Chapter Eleven). The English element stimulated the construction of the present Anglican church of St. Anne to cater for the needs of the increased population.

Yet another result was the spate of house-building which was triggered off by the need to provide accommodation for the immigrants. The main developments were at Neuve Rue (New Street), and at the area near the harbour appropriately named New Town, the nucleus of which was provided by the erection of a group of workmen's cottages.

Lastly, but by no means least, a most unfortunate by-product of the defence operations was the obliteration of almost the whole of Alderney's rich heritage of memorials of the Megalithic period (see Part I, Chapter One). Despite the efforts of Guernsey's pioneer archaeologist, Frederick Corbin Lukis (1788–1871), to preserve some sort of record for posterity, a very large number of burial chambers, cists and even whole cemeteries were destroyed before any adequate examination could be undertaken or records compiled. Vandalism on this scale was a high price to pay for such material prosperity as Alderney may have derived from this ill-starred attempt to create a second Gibraltar. On the credit side of the account, however, it is pleasant to record some latter-day benefits deriving from Jervois' creations in that since the Liberation a restored Fort Clonque has been adapted to provide holiday accommodation; a refurbished Château à l'Etoc (like Fort Essex before it) has been divided into attractive flats; and Fort Corblets has been converted to create a charming residence — while the quality of the island's environment is likely to be yet further enhanced by major renovation at Fort Quesnard and the extensive redevelopment planned for Fort Houmet Herbé.

Chapter Eleven

THE ROYAL GUERNSEY MILITIA

THE FACT THAT THE BAILIWICK was spared invasion during the American and French Revolutionary Wars largely arose from the enemy's appreciation that it would be a tough nut to crack. Prominent among the factors contributing to this formidable reputation were the island Militias, described by the governor of Cherbourg in the Report mentioned in a previous chapter as 'well-disciplined' and 'excellent marksmen'.

When precisely the Guernsey Militia emerged is shrouded in the mists of antiquity. Although one hypothesis conjectures that the force may have originated in an order issued in 1203 by King John to the island Seigneurs requiring them to muster levies for insular defence against Philip Augustus (see Chapter Two of this Part), the subsequent defection of fourteen of these magnates suggests that compliance with this order was unlikely — and moreover the degree of uncertainty regarding its beginning is emphasised by the existence of two opposed opinions concerning the obligations of the islanders to perform military service prior to the 14th. century. On the one hand, Ralph Durand held that this obligation is of immemorial antiquity and that their 'laws and customs' only exempted the islanders from military service outside the islands; while on the other, Professor J. H. Le Patourel held that such exemptions were absolute, applying internally as well as externally, and maintained that this privilege was indeed claimed at the 1248 Enquiry — 'except that they will go with the Duke of Normandy, if need be, when he goes in person to recover England'. Clearly Durand's interpretation could accommodate the King John theory (irrespective of its implausibility on other grounds), whereas Le Patourel's could not.

Irrespective of the comparative merits of these rival views, it is clear that the logic of events in the time of increasing tension that culminated in the outbreak of the Hundred Years War led to a series of steps involving the islanders making a contribution to their own defence. To begin with, it is evident that some rudimentary contribution was being made as early as 1330 from the accounts submitted that year by the warden, Jean de Roches, as they included an item for expenditure on wine given to Guernseymen who kept watch in Castle Cornet against sea-raiders. Five years later (in 1335) while Henry de Ferrers and William of Montacute were wardens, de Roches was ordered to array the men of the islands and to take such measures as he thought fit for their defence. Finally, in 1337, on the morrow of David Bruce's raid (see Chapter Two of this Part) the warden, Thomas Ferrers, was commanded to organise levies in thousands, hundreds and twenties, to arm them, and to lead them, if necessary, to repel such hostile attacks as were being made at the time by French privateers.

The first explicit mention of any obligation on the part of the islanders to participate in insular defence comes after Guernsey's liberation from the French occupation of 1338–1340 when, during Thomas Hampton's period of office as warden (1341–1343), he was ordered to assign places in Jerbourg Castle and to compel Guernseymen to defend these places, providing them with victuals. A further indication of the same trend of compulsion comes in 1357 when the jurats petitioned Edward III that all who resided or held lands in Guernsey should be compelled to find men for the defence of the island. The peace brought by the Treaty of Brétigny in 1360 made the matter one of far less urgency, but in 1370, the year after the Treaty's repudiation, Edward III ordered the islanders to remain in the islands and to hold themselves ready to defend them from attack.

While these incidents obviously represent successive steps in the evolution of the Militia, it is unlikely that any permanent and organised force existed until the 15th. century. Thus the array that resisted Owen of Wales in 1372 (see Chapter Four of this Part) most likely consisted of feudal levies maintained by the seigneurs — as the terms of the above-mentioned jurats' petition of 1357 would seem to suggest. It was most likely from these feudal levies that the Militia proper slowly grew. It was with the gradual decline of feudal administration which accompanied the emergence of the States that the island forces came to be organised on a parish basis, followed by a combination of parish companies into regional battalions. Thus arose a 'citizen army', service in which, without pay or uniform, became compulsory.

The oldest extant ordinance relating to the Guernsey Militia is dated 1546. It orders that all male inhabitants, on their allegiance, should obey their captains. Captains of the various parishes are required to see that all 'haquebuttes, ars et trousses' (arquebuses, bows and quivers) are in good order, 'les boulvars' (earthworks) properly constructed, and munitions always ready. Another ordinance of 1549 enacts that 'the Bailiff should have the survey over all the town parish and should cause bulwarks to be erected wherever required'. He was also authorised 'to inspect every townsman's haquebutte and to furnish one, with all its appurtenances, to such as had none, fining each defaulter four sols and one denier per day'. The same authority was vested in the captains of the country parishes (who frequently were also the parish constables) and they were given the power of requisitioning horses and vehicles for the transport of cannon and munitions.

After the Civil War the Militia consisted of 13 companies, four drawn from St. Peter-Port and nine from the other parishes. These were formed into one body and commanded by the lieutenant-governor. As has been seen (Part I, Chapter Twelve) the town companies played a significant part in securing Guernsey's adherence to the cause of William and Mary in the Glorious Revolution.

In 1719, as a by-product of Stanhope's assertive foreign policy against the attempts of Philip V of Spain and his minister, Alberoni, to re-establish Spanish power after the Treaty of Utrecht, the regular army garrison was withdrawn from Guernsey for service elsewhere, the defence of the island devolving entirely upon the Militia. In the event, no enemy attack was launched against its shores.

By 1755 the Guernsey Militia had become a force of 54 officers and nearly 2,000 N.C.O.s and men, divided into three regiments in which the island's leading families were proud to serve. In the July of the same year two companies of artillery were formed to man the coast batteries — a number later increased to four. The outbreak of the Seven Years War the following year found the Militia's morale high, all ranks ready to mount night-watches around the coast, to man the guns, and to keep themselves ready by intensive drill, prepared at all times to turn out at a moment's notice. The island's pride in the 'amateur army' was shown in 1761 when a large area above the town, known as the New Ground (now Cambridge Park) was acquired as a drill ground for the town regiment. (It is interesting to note parenthetically that not only did the New Ground later come to be put to additional use as a fashionable promenade for the gentry, but also that in 1795 the avenue on its southern fringe provided the setting for one of the last — but, as appears below, certainly not the last of all — duels to be fought in Guernsey: an *affaire d'honneur* involving Doctor

James Taylor and Major Byng, each of the garrison regiment, the latter of whom was shot through the skull. During the present writer's youth still to be discerned was the incision 'Byng 1796' carved in the Major's memory the following year on the bark of a nearby tree which has since, alas, been felled, the site of this *rencontre au pistolet* now being marked by a commemorative stone. In this same context of duelling one might add that a less distressing outcome attended both a previous encounter in October 1790 when the Comptroller, Thomas de Sausmarez, crossed swords with Jurat Robert Porret le Marchant and a subsequent one which *La Gazette de Guernsey* records as having occurred near L'Hyvreuse on October 17th., 1840 when Lieutenant Herbert of the Devonshire Regiment twice exchanged shots with Mr. John de Sainte Croix. On the first occasion de Sausmarez spared the life of his defeated adversary, while on the second mutual inaccuracy of aim resulted in neither participant being injured.)

During the American Revolutionary War the artillery companies were embodied as a regiment of field artillery, and a fourth regiment of infantry was formed. The perilous position of the archipelago in this war and the French Revolutionary War that followed hard on its heels led to the inauguration of regular Sunday drills — which, however, were discontinued in 1798 under Methodist pressure (see Part I, Chapter Twelve).

In 1780, with the idea that the sight of red coats would convince any approaching enemy that he was confronted with soldiers of the line, the Royal Court passed an ordinance compelling Militiamen to provide themselves with military uniforms. The parish douzaines, however, protested vigorously on behalf of the unpaid amateur soldiers, most of whom could not afford such finery. They pointed out that, unlike the English Militia, which was paid and clothed by the British government and subject to military law, 'the Militia of this island are volunteers, being simply a citizen Militia; which receives no pay, recognises no power save the civil power, but who, after the example of their forefathers, are ready to fight against every enemy who may assail their persons or properties'. In spite of these protests the ordinance was not repealed — but neither was it enforced, and in 1782 the problem was solved by the British government undertaking to supply all necessary clothing and equipment. It continued to do so until 1928.

The Militia's heyday came with the 19th. century. At its beginning the force numbered 3,158 all ranks, besides 450 boys, who were regularly drilled. Apart from the Guernsey Light

Dragoons, four field batteries of artillery and the coast artillery, there were four infantry regiments organised on a regional basis. They were the 1st. East (Town) Regiment, the 2nd. North Regiment, known as 'le Régiment Vert' from its green facings, the 3rd. South Regiment or 'Régiment Bleu', and the 4th. West Regiment or 'Régiment Noir'. Despite the erosion of the French threat as the century wore on, as late as 1872 there were still an artillery regiment of two garrison batteries and two field batteries, plus four infantry regiments of eight companies each. In the early years of the century — between 1800 and 1820 — there were several independent corps on the establishment of the island Militia: the 'Fermain Battery Corps', the 'Marine Corps', and the 'Pioneer Corps'. After Waterloo, however, these corps were disbanded and absorbed into the Militia proper.

In 1830 an aide-de-camp to the sovereign was appointed for the Guernsey Militia, and in 1831 the proud title of Royal Guernsey Militia was conferred upon the force (as also on the other Militias of the archipelago) by William IV to mark the 50th. anniversary of the expulsion of de Rullecourt's forces from Jersey (see Chapter Seven of this Part).

In 1873 the Royal Guernsey Militia was reorganised on the basis of one artillery and three infantry regiments, with an adjutant and permanent staff from the regular army being appointed to each regiment, their pay being met by the British government. The States provided quarters for the staffs and storage for guns, arms and clothes, in the town and country arsenals. In addition an annual contingent grant was made to each regiment, including the maintenance of a band.

Although the outcome could not possibly be foreseen at the time, an unfortunate contretemps was in fact to result from this reorganisation. It occurred in May 1899 when a revolt broke out in the North Regiment, where the regular adjutant appointed under the 1873 arrangement was Captain John Beville Pym of the Royal Marines. While probably an efficient officer, Pym was a tactless man who failed to appreciate the difference between paid regular volunteer soldiers and unpaid conscript quarrymen and labourers unenthusiastically parading after a hard day's work. Punishing breaches of the military code by fines, he showed his contempt for the men on parade by abusive language which was keenly resented. The upshot was a refusal to drill which, starting with a few men, spread rapidly until only one man presented himself and was drilled alone by a regular staff sergeant in the presence of his C.O. (Colonel Leale), and the inevitable Pym.

The ringleaders were arrested and tried by the Royal Court, which was responsible for the final enforcement of discipline in the Militia. Some 40 men were sentenced to a month's solitary confinement, to the accompaniment of demonstrations outside the prison and the Court House as well as in the vicinity of Baubigny arsenal. To avoid further demonstrations on release, the prisoners were discharged the evening before their term of imprisonment was up. They left their clothes behind, however, and called for them *en masse* the next morning. A crowd quickly gathered, and the 'martyrs' marched back to St. Sampson's in a triumphal procession, being welcomed at their destination by blasts from the siren of a ship in the harbour.

Under cover of the further Militia reorganisation referred to in the next paragraph, Captain Pym was quietly removed, and the trouble was smoothed over. The incident, however, was far from forgotten and 'Pas Pour Pym' was still a family saying by the older generation in the northern parishes at the time of the present writer's childhood.

The reorganisation which served as a cloak for Pym's departure emanated from a Projet de Loi passed by the States in 1899 as a result of which the Militia was run much on the lines of the territorial force in England, save that service was compulsory. Under these arrangements every able-bodied man between 17 and 35, unless exempted by law, was liable for service with the colours for five embodied trainings, after which he passed into the first reserve until the age of 45 and then into the second reserve until the age of sixty. Recruiting was undertaken by the island authorities, who annually drew up lists of all liable to serve. Only a sufficient number of recruits to fill vacancies was taken each year and men called upon might either volunteer or submit to a ballot. There were, in fact, always more volunteers than vacancies.

The Militia was now embodied during training, officers and men being subject to the Army Act when embodied and when in uniform. Each unit was trained for 11 days and recruits for 21 days, the training taking place in a special encampment designed for the purpose at Les Beaucamps in the Castel parish. The training period (during which officers and men were paid) began early in August (with recruits called up first) and lasted until mid-October. The system, which became very popular, cost the States £4,000 per annum, including pay and allowances, rations, contingent expenses, and the upkeep of the brigade band.

Chapter Twelve

THE R.G.L.I. AND THE FALL OF THE CURTAIN

ALTHOUGH THE FIRST WORLD WAR was to bring its supreme test to the Militia (metamorphosed into the Royal Guernsey Light Infantry), a casual visitor to the islands at the time would have noticed few overt signs of the Bailiwick's involvement in the struggle. In contrast to the feverish activity characterising the Napoleonic Wars the only indication of any departure from normality immediately evident to the onlooker would have been the acute shortage of manpower, with women (as in the United Kingdom) now proving their worth — and from July 1917 onwards the presence near Castle Cornet of a French air base under the command of Enseigne de Vaisseau Le Cour Grandmaison, followed (as from March 1918) by Enseigne de Vaisseau Flandrin, comprising 12 (later 16) seaplanes maintained in four hangars built on the Model Yacht Pond site and ordered to seek and attack enemy submarines: orders so executed, incidentally, that four aviators won La Croix de Guerre, which was also awarded in the autumn of 1918 to the Station as a whole in recognition of 25 attacks on enemy submarines and the discovery of three minefields between August 1917 and August 1918. In addition to this the newcomer might also have noticed the unfamiliar feature of a detachment of the South Staffordshire Regiment stationed on Herm as a precaution against enemy submarines landing spies and saboteurs to operate from that island which was now empty as a result of the internment of the tenant, Prince Blücher, as an enemy alien, despite his opposition to German policies and the service of his two sons as officers in the Royal Guernsey Militia.

Had this hypothetical visitor formed any judgement based on the impressions gained by such superficial observations, however, he would have been most grievously misled, for, as far as the toll taken of the Bailiwick's sons was concerned, the impact of the conflict was nothing short of catastrophic. As a gesture of patriotism in the British Empire's hour of need, the States at the outbreak of the war enacted legislation relinquishing for the duration of hostilities the ancient right of freedom from military service outside the islands, save to help the duke to re-conquer England. For the first time in history a Guernsey force, as distinct from individual Guernseymen, was to fight overseas. The response to this 'self-denying ordinance' was phenomenal, with no fewer than 7,000 out of a total population of 40,000 serving in the war — about 400 volunteering for the Royal Navy and the rest for various military units.

The initial arrangement was for Guernsey companies to be attached to battalions of the regular army — and especially to the Royal Irish Regiment when the Irish troubles adversely affected its recruitment. After a time, however, an Army Council suggestion was made for the formation of a joint Jersey/Guernsey battalion — a suggestion which, needless to say, elicited no enthusiastic response in either Bailiwick. Indeed, only an utter lack of knowledge of the islands could explain such advocacy of a union of Montague and Capulet. The upshot of the unacceptability of the Army Council's recommendation was that, on the advice of the lieutenant-governor, General Sir Reginald Hart, it was decided in 1916 to transform the Royal Guernsey Militia (which had been mobilised at the outbreak of hostilities) into a service unit to be called the Royal Guernsey Light Infantry, including men from Alderney and Sark, with a First Battalion to serve overseas and a Second Battalion for home service and reserve. In the same year the States waived the ancient right of the Militia to be employed for home defence only.

After its initial training, the R.G.L.I. went into action at Passchendaele and then took part in the advance with tanks at Cambrai, being entrusted with holding the apex of the captured salient by Mesnières. Counter-attacked by the Germans and outnumbered twenty to one, they withdrew, but twice fought back to the key village of Rue Vertes. Finally, after suffering 600 casualties in two days, they were ordered to cover their brigade's withdrawal. The fighting qualities of the R.G.L.I. in this action won universal admiration. General Sir Beauvoir de Lisle, commanding the 29th. Division, wrote to the Bailiff of Guernsey: 'I want to convey to the Guernsey authorities my very high appreciation of the valuable services rendered by the R.G.L.I. in the battle of Cambrai. Theirs was a wonderful performance'.

Five months later, in April 1918, the battalion, its Cambrai losses made good by replenishments from the reserve, was thrown in to plug the great gap driven in the British line by Ludendorff's offensive towards the Channel ports. In the ensuing Battle of the Lys, from April 10th. to 14th., they fought a bitter withdrawal action under a hail of machine-gun, mortar and artillery fire, with the enemy making his supreme effort of the war. When the Australians relieved the R.G.L.I. at Merriss, fewer than one hundred were left. As this remnant marched to entrain for duty at G.H.Q. the divisional band played them on their way. The widespread mourning which this carnage produced in the Bailiwick was tempered by pride and the list of one thousand dead on the Island war memorial testifies eloquently to the fact that the Royal Guernsey Militia, in its guise as the Royal Guernsey Light Infantry, emerged from the holocaust of 1914–1918 with its past unsullied and its glory enhanced. The last survivor of this valiant battalion — the 97-year-old Chelsea Pensioner Albert Alexandre, Ordre de la Légion d'honneur — figured prominently in both London and Ypres (where he was presented to H.M. The Queen) in the ceremonies held during November 1998 to mark the eightieth anniversary of the Armistice.

After the Armistice the Militia was re-established on its pre-war footing, but in 1928 it suffered a severe blow as the British government, the Imperial Contribution dispute settled, decided to economise by withdrawing financial support. In this situation the States of Guernsey resolved to pay for a small force manned on a voluntary basis. The outcome was a fine 'mini-army' with magnificent *esprit de corps* and maintaining a band which made a splendid showing at king's birthday parades, and at Sunday concerts at Candie Gardens — not to mention the George V Jubilee celebrations in 1935. In that year, too, the force was inspected by royalty for the last time when it provided the guard of honour on the occasion of the visit of the Prince of Wales (later King Edward VIII, and subsequently Duke of Windsor).

When war once again broke out in September 1939 the regular army garrison was withdrawn, and, as in 1719, the defence of Guernsey was left entirely in the hands of the Militia. In February 1940, however, wishing to avoid any repetition of the atrocious casualties which had resulted in the previous conflict from concentrating the island's manpower in one battalion, the States decided to disband the force, urging its members to enlist in various units of the British army. This they did, their numbers swelled by other young men who had not belonged to the Militia, to such effect that 17% of the population served in the forces — all as volunteers. These included not only Brigadier Herbert Wallace Le Patourel — obit 1979 — who as Major Le Patourel was to win the Victoria Cross at Tebourba, Tunisia, on December 3rd., 1942 (see Appendix XVII); but also a young man concerning whom Ares had decreed that to Lord de Saumarez and Sir Isaac Brock as the Bailiwick's greatest warriors on sea and land respectively, there would now be added their peer of the air. Subsequent to his emergence from valorous empyreal exploits during and after the conflict as Air Chief Marshal Sir Peter de Lacey Le Cheminant, G.B.E., K.C.B., D.F.C. and indisputably Guernsey's greatest airman, the career of this intrepid islander — who kindly provided the Introduction to this book's first edition — reached a fitting culmination in his appointment in 1979 to represent his Sovereign in his natal isle as Lieutenant-Governor and Commander-in-Chief of the Island of Guernsey and its Dependencies. The wisdom of this disbandment and dispersal policy is vindicated by the Second World War's casualty lists. As against the appalling carnage suffered by the R.G.L.I. in the First World War, the fallen in the Second numbered: Guernsey, 221; Alderney, 18; and Sark one.

After the war it was seriously debated whether to revive the Militia. A Committee of the States investigated the matter, and in its report in 1951 it advised against re-establishment, largely on the grounds of expense. Thus, sadly, this ancient force came to an end after six centuries of continuous existence. All that remains is its silver and uniforms in the Militia Museum at Castle Cornet, and its colours adorning some of the parish churches. 'E finita la commedia.'

Chapter Thirteen

THE MILITIAS OF ALDERNEY AND SARK

THE ORIGINS of the Alderney Militia are obscure, but, as in the case of Guernsey, its emergence would appear to have been the outcome of the exigencies of the Hundred Years War. Its martial ardour, however, does not seem to have been particularly conspicuous, judging by the ease with which Captain Malesart indulged in his depredations of 1558 — as already seen in Chapter Five. Indeed, so unremarkable was its career that there is little by way of concrete evidence for its activities until as late as the Civil War when, at the end of 1643, the force was overhauled by Pierre le Febure for the defence of Alderney against the royalists — as noted in Chapter Six of this Part.

Yet another century was to elapse before the Alderney Militia again emerged from its coy seclusion. As 'Hereditary Governors' the Le Mesuriers considered themselves responsible for the command of the force, which towards the end of the 18th. century was stated by Peter Le Mesurier in correspondence with the War office to be 217 strong. For most of the previous century, however, arrangements for the island's defence appear to have been remarkably casual, considerable reliance being placed on the womenfolk who, while the men worked, watched from beacon towers, ready to light fires to signal across to Guernsey should any attack be launched. It was said that during the War of the Spanish Succession a French invading force turned back when its commander saw the cliffs lined with red coats — which were, in fact, the red skirts of the women.

In 1777, however, Peter Le Mesurier, as 'lieutenant-governor' deputising for his aged parent, John Le Mesurier, set about reorganising the Island Militia on an efficient basis, making service and drills compulsory for all men between 16 and 60 years of age. The British government helped by supplying 200 stands of arms, and, four years later — in 1781 — uniforms (hitherto worn only by officers at their own expense) were adopted for all ranks. In his above-mentioned correspondence, Peter Le Mesurier claimed to have spent £500 out of his own pocket on barracks and other contingent expenses associated with this reorganisation. As has been seen in Part I, Chapter Twelve, this new-found efficiency was threatened by Methodist sabbatarianism at the beginning of the French Revolutionary War — but Peter solved the problem by the establishment of the separate 'Armée de Gédéon'.

In common with the Militias of the other islands, that of Alderney was made royal in 1831, but by 1850 its strength was down to 150, of whom 100 were infantry, and the remainder artillerymen. The infantry was disbanded in 1882, but the Royal Alderney Militia Artillery survived until 1929, when it was abolished following the British government's refusal to continue providing financial support.

The Sark Militia was essentially an enlargement of the Quarantaine Defence Force, its creation as such arising out of the invasion dangers accompanying the 18th.-century struggles with France. The nucleus of such a force had emerged by 1730, when Robert Slowley (who was also Prévôt in the island court) acted as Captain of the Militia under the ultimate command of the Governor in Guernsey. Later, in 1744, while the War of the Austrian Succession was being waged, the watch duties, which hitherto had been the sole responsibility of the Quarantaine tenants, were enforced on all male inhabitants between the ages of 16 and sixty. By this ordinance the strength of the Militia was brought up to one hundred.

During the Napoleonic Wars, when a small detachment from the regular garrison stationed in Guernsey was housed in specially-built barracks in Little Sark, the Militia was re-equipped, and all able-bodied males were again enrolled to take their share of the watch duties.

The heyday of the Royal Sark Militia (this force, too, having shared in the honour bestowed on the archipelago's Militias by William IV in 1831) came during the years between 1853 and 1882 when the Reverend William Thomas Collings was seigneur. Despite his clerical status, this seigneur took his military duties very seriously. Taking his cue from the British government's extensive fortification programme in Alderney, he was convinced that in the event of Franco-British hostilities, Sark's strategic significance would be considerable. Accordingly, arrayed in the full uniform of a lieutenant-colonel, and girt with a sword, he insisted on parades and shooting practices being held at regular intervals. The ardour of this warrior-priest was displayed almost as soon as he became seigneur, one of his first acts being to persuade Chief Pleas to appoint a paid quartermaster to look after the weapons and equipment housed in the arsenal (October 5th., 1853).

The next seigneur, William Frederick Collings, although he had been forced by his father to serve as adjutant, did not share his parent's military zeal. As a consequence the Royal Sark Militia — rapidly degenerated to the point where a visiting journalist described it in 1887 as 'seven dozen pairs of boots'. Thereafter it simply withered away, finally disappearing from the Army List in 1900. The men of Sark, however, in common with their Alderney comrades, served with distinction with the R.G.L.I. during the First World War — and individually in the British army in the Second one.

Chapter Fourteen

THE SECOND WORLD WAR

THE SECOND WORLD WAR, involving as it did the most prolonged period of suffering resulting from hostilities known to the islands' experience, has prompted the publication of a substantial number of memoirs and investigations, besides an official history, and a West End play (not to mention a wildly inaccurate and misleading flight of fancy screened in a television series during the winter of 1977/8). Inevitably, therefore, any attempt to condense such a plethora of material within the confines of a single chapter (even a long one) presents considerable difficulties, to alleviate which it will be seen that the device has been adopted of subdividing the presentation into separate sections corresponding to the various facets of this traumatic episode in the history of the Bailiwick. Accordingly the account commences with:

A — The Storm Breaks

The illusion that the Bailiwick of Guernsey (and, indeed, the entire archipelago) was a peaceful harbour of refuge from the ravages of war was rudely shattered during the summer of 1940 when the victorious German army cut through France like a hot knife through butter, bringing it by mid-June to the coast of the Cotentin Peninsula. After a brief and half-hearted flirtation with the idea of defending the islands, the British government finally decided on June 19th. to demilitarise them, declaring the group an Open Town. A Sea Transport Officer was appointed to organise evacuation, and after some confusion adequate shipping was provided for the purpose. In all, 23,000 people (over half the population of Guernsey) were thus evacuated to the United Kingdom.

Arrangements worked far less smoothly in Alderney which at the time was out of telephonic touch with the rest of the world as the security embargo placed on wireless communication precluded the use of the radio-telephone link with Guernsey. Because of an unhappy sequence of misunderstandings no ships were sent to the island, the inhabitants of which were seemingly left to their unenviable fate only eight miles from an enemy-occupied coast. On June 21st. Judge Frederick French sent a message to the Trinity House ship *Vestal* (which was engaged in removing all lighthouse-keepers in Channel Island waters) requesting help. He then called a meeting of the island population, where total evacuation was reluctantly agreed. The *Vestal* passed the message to another ship in mid-Channel, asking her captain to telephone the Admiralty on arrival in Britain. Later, on arrival in Guernsey, the captain of the *Vestal* informed Major Ambrose Sherwill of the plight of Alderney — but Sherwill's request to the Sea Transport Officer for shipping to be sent to the island was refused as the risk was considered excessive, Alderney being within range of enemy artillery. Sherwill then telephoned the Ministry of Shipping in England, and the upshot was that six small cargo boats arrived in Alderney at 0440 hours on Sunday, June 23rd., and sailed again by 0800 hours, taking to England virtually the entire population, with 502 men, 529 women and 401 children — 1,432 persons in all — being evacuated. (It must regretfully be added, however, that a deplorable sequel to this hurried departure was the plundering of many vacated premises by salvage teams sent from Guernsey and especially by one of the few remaining residents — a chiropodist named James Alfred Rutter — who was later imprisoned for looting on a grand scale.)

No such contretemps occurred in Sark where, under the persuasive influence of La Dame, practically the whole population elected to stay.

The British government having omitted to inform the Germans of the demilitarisation decision, the enemy assumed that the islands would have to be taken by assault, and a signal was accordingly dispatched on June 20th. from Naval High Command in Berlin directing an operation by 'units of naval assault parties already in northern France'. The directive added that 'army and air support will be arranged in co-operation with the local commanders of these armed services'. A further signal, 'The capture of the British Channel Islands is necessary and urgent', was sent the same day.

After evacuation had been completed, the usual British attitude of not bothering about things until they happen had led to the resumption of the normal mailboat services between Southampton and the islands. Thus it was that on the evening of Friday, June

28th., 1940 the S.S. *Isle of Sark* was in St. Peter-Port harbour together with several cargo ships on which tomatoes were being loaded from a queue of waiting lorries. Suddenly nine Heinkel IIIs dive-bombed the harbour and strafed the line of lorries — and then went on to machine-gun haymakers in the fields, an ambulance taking wounded to hospital, and even the St. Peter-Port lifeboat, which was at sea. Against this onslaught the only defence consisted of the light anti-aircraft guns on the *Isle of Sark*. Besides the wounded, 29 were killed in this 'probing' raid to test the defences. Their names are now listed on a memorial tablet set into the wall between Saint Julian's Pier and the Queen Elizabeth II Marina Car Park.

At the time of this attack the S.S. *Courier* was *en route* from Alderney to Guernsey, carrying salvaged stores and the few people who had stayed on in Alderney, plus a salvage team which had been sent there by Major Sherwill. In addition the ship carried most of Alderney's pig population. Off St. Sampson's harbour the *Courier* was machine-gunned, 11 on board being wounded, but fortunately was not hit when bombed. The captain beached the ship, but on Saturday, June 29th. she was refloated and took her cargo to England, where she rendered valuable service throughout the war.

In the light of the air-raid the British government decided to publicise the demilitarisation of the archipelago, which was announced on the B.B.C. nine o'clock news the same evening. The German monitoring service having missed this announcement, an inter-service conference was called in Paris the following day — Saturday, June 29th. — to make detailed operational plans for a landing. While the conference was in session its members heard of the demilitarisation from a Reuter message, the news being subsequently confirmed by the United States Embassy in Berlin. Thus on Sunday, June 30th. a reconnaissance aircraft piloted by Captain Liebe-Pieteritz landed at La Villiaze airport just after noon, and soon left again, to be followed between 1800 and 1900 hours by four Junkers 52 transport planes. Inspector Sculpher, the head of the Island police, handed a letter to Major Albrecht Lanz stating that the island had 'no armed forces of any description'. The German occupation had begun.

B — Major Ambrose Sherwill

Two days after the decision to demilitarise the islands — on June 21st. — the States of Guernsey voted in favour of delegating all its powers and functions for the duration of the emergency to a Controlling Committee of eight members, each of whom was to be responsible for one aspect of administration. The chosen president of this committee was H.M. Procureur, Major Ambrose Sherwill (who nine years later was to become Sir Ambrose Sherwill, C.B.E., Bailiff of Guernsey). Thus, although the bailiff, Mr. (later Sir) Victor Carey, had, on the withdrawal of the military incumbent, Major-General J.R.M. Minshull-Ford, been appointed as lieutenant-governor representing the Crown, Sherwill emerged as the virtual 'king of Guernsey' on whose shoulders fell the responsibility of dealing with the Germans. In doing this his task was somewhat eased by the fact that his soldierly bearing and magnificent First World War record (he had won the M.C. for outstanding gallantry) evoked the respect of Major-Doktor Albrecht Lanz, the German commandant, and also of his chief of staff, Dr. Maass — who spoke fluent English.

Sherwill was soon to need — and imperil — his standing of esteem with the German authorities, as a result of military operations of which he naturally had no fore-knowledge.

Between Sunday, July 7th. and Wednesday, July 10th. Lieutenant Hubert Nicolle, a Guernseyman serving with the Hampshire Regiment, successfully completed an espionage assignment in preparation for commando raid 'Ambassador' (see Section C ensuing). The submarine which took Nicolle away landed two more Guernsey subalterns, Lieutenant Philip Martel of the Hampshire Regiment and Lieutenant Desmond Mulholland of the D.C.L.I., with orders to conduct further espionage and to guide the 'Ambassador' commandos when they arrived. The postponement of the raid meant that Martel and Mulholland found no submarine at their rendezvous at Le Jaonnet on Friday, July 12th.; and on Sunday, July 14th. (when the raid did occur) the section of the raiding party which saw the spies' torch flashes (about which, because of an oversight, they had not been informed) mistook them for enemy signals and immediately withdrew. Martel and Mulholland were stranded, and although C.Q.M.S. Stanley Ferbrache of the Hampshire Regiment was sent over to contact them and bring them back, by the time he landed in the small hours of Sunday, August 4th., he was too late and had to content himself with gathering intelligence, before being taken off again in the early morning of August 6th.

In the meantime Martel and Mulholland had been on the run. After failing to get away in a fishing boat which they stole at

Perelle, they made a hazardous trip to Sark on the same ship as a group of German officers, but found escape from that island to be impossible. Deciding to give themselves up, they went to Sherwill's house early one morning and sought his aid. To save the two subalterns from being shot as spies, Sherwill took a course of action which placed his own life in jeopardy. With the aid of a friend, Donald Bisset, he stole from the Town arsenal two Militia uniforms whose buttons were replaced by British army ones by Mrs. Dawes, the wife of the arsenal caretaker. He then produced the two young men, duly arrayed in uniform, before Dr. Maass and, when one of them admitted to Maass how long they had been on the island, muttered to them under cover of offering cigarettes, 'You bloody fools — just rank, name and number'. After prolonged interrogation in Dinard, the Germans eventually accepted Martel and Mulholland's story that they had landed in uniform and took civilian clothes from an empty house. They were treated as prisoners of war and Sherwill heard nothing more.

Despite his courageous help to Martel and Mulholland, Sherwill believed that the survival of the islands (which had been left by the United Kingdom to fare as best they could) depended on keeping good relations with the Germans. He also sought to allay the anxieties of Channel Island refugees in Britain. With the first object in mind, Sherwill in a speech to the first meeting of the States after the commencement of the Occupation (August 8th., 1940) expressed the hope that the Occupation would be a model to the world, and that after it was over it would be possible to say, 'We were civilians and we behaved as such in the strictest sense in accordance with the usages of war'. As for his second aim, in order to reassure the refugees in the United Kingdom Sherwill asked the Germans to arrange a Red Cross message system and, when this request was refused, recorded a speech which was broadcast by Bremen radio, referring to the 'correct and kindly attitude' of the Germans and their respect for the islanders' loyalty to the British Crown.

Sherwill's good relations policy apparently sank to the most craven sycophancy when on July 31st., 1940 the Royal Court at his instigation issued an ordinance making criticism of the Germans a criminal offence — with retrospective application to the beginning of the Occupation. There was, however, more to this move than meets the eye. Sherwill had found two Germans about to arrest Mr. H. H. Collins, the manager of Le Riche's stores, who had reproved a shop assistant for leaving a local customer to serve a

German; and fearing that Collins, a sick man, would never survive imprisonment, he offered to obtain the retrospective legislation if the Germans would permit trial by the Royal Court. The bargain was struck, and Collins was tried immediately after the issue of the ordinance — and acquitted. The ordinance was never again invoked.

Sherwill's efforts to establish a *modus vivendi* with the occupying forces were destined yet again to be embarrassed by the presence of British spies to whom, at the dictates of patriotism, he extended help despite the danger to himself. This time he was to pay dearly for his quixotic conduct. After his successful venture in July, Hubert Nicolle was sent back on another fact-finding mission, this time accompanied by another Guernsey subaltern in the Hampshire Regiment, Lieutenant James Symes, both of whom landed at Petit Port at 0300 hours on September 4th., 1940. On returning to Petit Port on the night of September 6th., when they were supposed to be picked up, they found that no M.T.B. appeared. The same thing happened on the following two nights. A further scheme to escape from Bordeaux harbour with the connivance of Captain Fred Noyon was frustrated by a German order concentrating all fishing craft in St. Peter-Port following the escape to England of a party of eight men on Friday, September 6th.

Nicolle and Symes were now forced to seek shelter with relatives and friends, but to avoid compromising them too much they spent a great deal of their time hiding in Elizabeth College cricket pavilion, where they were helped by the groundsman, William Allen. Towards the end of September an attempt to rescue the two young men came to nothing when Captain John Parker, landing at La Corbière in an attempt to contact them, was unfortunate enough to run straight into the arms of a German A.A. detachment, and was taken prisoner. Luckily for him, he was in uniform.

By now Major Sherwill had learned of the presence of the two spies through Hubert Nicolle's father, Emile Nicolle, who was the Secretary of the Controlling Committee. A cat-and-mouse game now ensued between him and the Germans, who had been made suspicious by the Parker affair. With the consent of the newly-appointed commander-in-chief, Colonel Graf von Schmettow, the Guernsey commandant, Major Bandelow, hinted to Sherwill that British soldiers were in hiding and promised that if they gave themselves up they would be treated as prisoners of war. Sherwill contrived to have the time limit extended to October 21st. (so as to give the two subalterns the maximum chance of escape in the meanwhile) and followed this up with a letter to Bandelow published in the *Evening Press*, the crucial part of which was: 'I have noted that you intend to arrange with me a time limit within which any personnel of the British Armed Forces in hiding in the island (*if such there be*) must surrender, and that if this direction is complied with, such personnel will be treated as prisoners of war and no measures will be taken against any of their relatives'. By the words in parenthesis Sherwill laid himself open to the charge of deliberately misleading the Germans. While these negotiations were in progress, Nicolle's uncle, Captain Frank Nicolle, discovered in his capacity as assistant harbour master that a stock of battle-dress had been stored in the harbour sheds and forgotten. Wearing the two uniforms thus stolen by Frank Nicolle, the two subalterns gave themselves up on October 21st., after further escape attempts had failed.

The question now was whether the Germans would keep their word. When Bandelow and Schmettow on the one hand, and Colonel Schumacher (the Feldkommandant) on the other, reported developments to their respective superiors, Count Brockdorf and General Schreiber, Brockdorf agreed that the amnesty promised had to be honoured. Schreiber, however, demanded that an example should be made of the two subalterns and their helpers to strike terror into anyone should further British agents operate in the islands or France. While a decision was pending all who had sheltered Symes and Nicolle — and who had been identified by the German counterintelligence — were dispatched to solitary confinement in the Cherche Midi prison in Paris, where Louis Symes (James Symes' father) was later found dead in his cell. The Germans claimed it was suicide, but it could well have been murder. To Sherwill's protests the Germans replied that their promise had been won by a trick as Sherwill had pretended not to know that the spies were in the island. Such were the consequences of 'if such there be'. He was not surprised when he, too, was arrested and also placed in solitary confinement in the Cherche Midi. The prisoners were saved by Graf von Schmettow's sense of military honour. Together with Colonel Schumacher and Major Bandelow, he asked to be relieved of his post if the amnesty promise were not kept. He followed this up by a personal appeal to Count Brockdorf, who in his turn contacted Admiral Canaris, Chief of Counter-Intelligence. On the orders of Canaris, the show trial in Paris was abandoned and the prisoners released.

Because of his part in the Symes-Nicolle affair, the Germans deposed Sherwill, who was thus obliged to retire into private life, supporting his family as best he could. In July 1942 he was allowed to resume his functions as Procureur on the death of Mr. G. J. P. Ridgway, but the Germans would not permit his reinstatement as President of the Controlling Committee.

After the Germans discovered the help given by Mrs. Pittard to the commandos who raided Sark in Operation 'Basalt' in October 1942 (see Section C to follow) they decided in January 1943 to deport all former officers of the British forces. The deportations took place in February 1943 and although those in official positions were excused, the exemption did not extend to Sherwill, whose part in the matter of Nicolle and Symes had never been forgotten. His wife and children were spared, thanks to the gallantry of Baron von und zu Aufsess, the Chief of Administration, who took the courageous risk of ignoring the orders of his superiors in their cases.

Sherwill spent the rest of the war in Laufen Internment Camp where, in his capacity as British 'Camp Senior' he contrived by his representations to the Camp Commandant to secure the transfer thither of the Jerseyman, Stanley Green, who was in Buchenwald.

C — Commando Raids

During the course of the Second World War, six commando raids were launched at various points in the Bailiwick of Guernsey, in addition to one other raid on Jersey.

The first raid was 'Operation Ambassador', which took place on the night of July 13/14th., 1940. It was in preparation for this raid that Hubert Nicolle came over on his first espionage assignment, while Martel's and Mulholland's ill-fated venture was supposed to be its vanguard. Indeed, the failure of the raiders to establish the planned contact with the two spies typified the tragi-farcical incompetence of the entire operation.

The plan was to launch a four-pronged attack. The first (which Mulholland was supposed to direct) was to be at La Moye Point, with the object of attacking La Villiaze airport. Martel was intended to direct another at Petit Bôt, planned to provide support for the airport attack. A third incursion at Petit Port was charged with creating a diversion and preventing German reinforcements from reaching the airport — while yet another diversionary party with similar responsibilities was to land at Vazon. In the event, the main party destined for the airport lost its way and landed in either Sark or Herm — nobody knows. Two other parties withdrew under the mistaken impression that the torch being flashed by Martel and Mulholland betokened an alerted enemy. Only the Vazon party landed — but did so at Petit Port, led by Lieutenant-Colonel John Durnford Slater. They constructed a road block at Jerbourg and withdrew. The dinghy taking them back to their main craft sank, so that the three non-swimmers in the group had to be left behind to be taken prisoner. So ended what Churchill himself called a 'silly fiasco'.

Between early September and early October 1942 three commando raids were staged in quick succession, each of them featuring Major Geoffrey Appleyard, D.S.O., M.C., who was acquainted with the Bailiwick from pre-war holidays (and whose sister, Joan Joyce — alias 'Jenny' — as Mrs. 'Peter' Wood, was later to become 'Lady of Herm'). The intrepid Dane, Anders Lassen, V.C., M.C., also took part.

The first of the trio, 'Operation Dryad', attacked the Casquets on the night of September 2nd./3rd., taking prisoner the seven Germans who were manning the lighthouse, as well as capturing code books. (No small interest, incidentally, attaches to the fact that all involved in this assault on the Casquets benefited greatly from the intimate knowledge of local waters possessed by the dashing Aurigniais Captain John Lewis 'Bonnie' Newton, D.S.C., Croix de Guerre, whose participation therein was supplementary to his activities in collusion with the Special Operations Executive where he posed as a Cornish fisherman discharged with ignominy from the Royal Navy in order to cover his exploits smuggling into and out of France British and Allied agents collaborating with the Resistance; and preliminary to subsequent hazardous ventures on which he embarked in the Mediterranean.)

The second raid, 'Operation Branford', took place on September 7th., and consisted of a reconnaissance of Burhou, which was found to be deserted.

The third raid was to have widespread repercussions. It was an attack on Sark — 'Operation Basalt' — carried out on the night of October 3rd./4th. Landing on the Hog's Back, the commandos broke into La Jaspellerie, where Mrs. Frances Pittard, the widow of Dr. M. Pittard, provided them with a map of Sark and a copy of the *Guernsey Evening Press*, containing news of the deportations (see Section D following) which were thus known about in England for the first time. She also told them what she knew about gun sitings and directed them to the Dixcart hotel annexe, where she knew a party of German engineers to be sleeping. The annexe was attacked and prisoners taken, but on the way back to the boat four of them attempted to escape and were initially tied up — but when they again tried to escape, the commandos shot at them, killing one. This incident led to the Germans ordering the chaining of 1,376 prisoners taken at Dieppe, to which the British responded by chaining 1,376 German prisoners in Canada. This was followed by Hitler's order of October 18th., that captured commandos were not to be treated as prisoners-of-war, but 'slaughtered to the last man'. Mrs. Pittard had to endure 11 weeks' imprisonment for the aid she had given to the raiders.

On the night of February 27/28th., 1943 'Operation Huckaback' was launched against Herm. Led by Captain Porteous, V.C., its mission was to establish that artillery could be landed on the Shell beach to provide supporting fire for any assault on Guernsey. The commandos ascertained that the beach was not mined by the nerve-racking process of walking up and down it. They failed to take any prisoners, as there were no Germans on the island at the time.

The last commando raid — 'Operation Hardtack 7' — occurred in two parts. The first part, on the night of December 25/26th., 1943, led by Lieutenant McGonigal, landed in Sark at Derrible Point, but withdrew as it could not get across the neck of land connecting the Point with the rest of the island. A second attack on the night of December 27/28th. landed on the Hog's Back, but ended tragically as the party stumbled into a minefield. Two were killed, and, the Germans being alerted by the noise, the rest (all of whom, save one, were wounded) had to withdraw hurriedly, being very fortunate to get back to their boats.

D — Island Madness

After the invasion of the U.S.S.R., Hitler ordered the construction of the Atlantic Wall to make Germany secure in the west while the bulk of her forces were engaged in the east. In this defence project the Channel Isles loomed large, as Hitler had an obsession with them, being convinced that a British attempt at recapture was imminent for two reasons. The first of these was that, in face of an uninterrupted succession of German triumphs, Britain badly needed a prestige victory; while in the second place, the British (who, once in, would stay — witness Malta) would use the islands' airfields to attack Brest and other U-boat bases.

Thus, deaf to the objections of Field-Marshal von Witzleben, commander-in-chief in the west (whose chief of staff, General Hilpert, deplored what he described as 'Inselwahn' — 'Island Madness'), Hitler issued a directive on October 20th., 1941 — 'The permanent fortifying of the Channel Islands to convert them into an impregnable fortress must be pressed forward at maximum speed'.

The Fuehrer's instructions were carried out with extreme thoroughness. A complete division was brought in, under Major-General Mueller (who became commander-in-chief) until there were over 36,000 men in the archipelago. In addition, extensive fortifications with tremendous fire-power were constructed (among which the vast Mirus Battery in St. Pierre-du-Bois was outstanding), plus enormous tunnels for storing ammunition and large underground hospitals — the Guernsey one having 600 beds. To service the gun emplacements a railway was laid from St. Peter-Port right round the east, north and west coasts, as far as L'Erée. The west coast section, however, was soon pulled up again. In all, one-twelfth of the entire Atlantic Wall fortifications system was concentrated in the Channel Isles. Thanks to Hitler's intuition, therefore, considerable fighting strength was diverted from the main fronts. The most intensive resistance movement could never have done more to hold down enemy forces than was achieved by the bee in Adolf Hitler's bonnet.

A deplorable adjunct to the vast fortification programme was the employment of thousands of Organisation Todt slave labourers from a whole variety of nations: French, Spanish republicans, seized in France after its fall, Poles, Czechs, Belgians, Dutch, Algerians, Moroccans — and Russians captured on the eastern front. These poor wretches, clothed in rags and housed in atrocious conditions, were fed a starvation diet, and on Sundays were to be seen near the St. Peter-Port sewer outflow, desperately trying to catch the fish attracted by the effluent. For those caught trying to escape, 'Le Paradis' in the Vale was used as a prison and punishment centre. The screams of the inmates subjected to the attentions of the brutal sadist in charge could be heard throughout the neighbourhood.

Particular attention was paid to Alderney, which became a huge unsinkable battleship. It had six batteries of heavy guns, controlled by a central fire system, but each also with independent electrical power, so that any one could carry on firing even if the rest were silenced.

The labour force in Alderney included 'political prisoners' and was housed in the only concentration camps on British soil: the living hells of Norderney, Borkum, Helgoland, and Sylt. The victims' purgatory at the hands of such lagerfuehrer as Maximilian List, Heinrich Evers and Adam Adler is commemorated by the memorial in English, French, Spanish, Hebrew and Russian at Saye (near Norderney's site) — a memorial which was visited in 1974 by 55 survivors of the horror from many parts of Europe. On the occasion of this visit, Dr. Boucher, Président de l'Association Nationale des Deportées, internées et Familles des Disparus, spoke of having to go for three days at a stretch without food. Marc Shasier stated that a specially-constructed tunnel was designed for the extermination of the slave workers in case of rebellion or invasion by the Allies. He also recalled how he had seen thousands die under atrocious conditions and spoke of systematic killing in cases of what was considered unruly behaviour, adding that of the Russians alone 687 thus died of over-work, beatings and starvation. (It is true that these figures were disputed in 1981 in his book *Alderney: Fortress Island* by Major Theodore X.H. Pantcheff, who conducted a post-Liberation investigation on behalf of the Judge Advocate General and who estimated that the total death-toll from ill-treatment and malnutrition came to 389. His findings, however, were contradicted by those given in the M119 reports relative to the years 1944 and 1945 released by the Ministry of Defence in November 1996 which averred that 'many times this number died' — and also revealed that some were brought to a slow and agonising end by crucifixion, with one impaled victim having buckets of cold water repeatedly thrown over him by his murderers until death mercifully supervened.)

One of these unfortunates, known only by his prisoner number of 178284 as no record of his name survives, was a French priest who volunteered to take the place of a younger fellow-prisoner sentenced to death — an offer which was accepted. Requiem aeternam dona ei Domine et lux perpetua luceat ei. Among those who survived was Juan Dalmau, a Spanish republican, who spent 18 months in Alderney in 1943 and 1944. Describing an incident when he was working as a diver repairing the anti-submarine boom at Braye Harbour entrance, he said that he became aware of not being alone. All around him were the remains of prisoners who had been thrown into the water when they collapsed at their work. Beside cleanly-picked skeletons, there were bodies half eaten by the very crabs and lobsters which were caught and fed to the labour force. In addition there were more recent arrivals swollen to superhuman size by the expansion within them of putrefying gases.

The evil things which happened in Alderney are most poignantly hinted at in a single phrase from a letter written by a French woman conscripted to act as cook in a camp — 'Aurigny, île du silence, du cauchemar et de l'épouvante' ('Alderney, isle of silence, of nightmare and of terror'). It is abhorrent to reflect that though Adler and Evers were tried and punished by the French, not a single brute responsible for these atrocities (even when identified, his conduct investigated and a report thereon submitted) was brought to justice by the British after victory was won — possibly because doing so would have involved the embarrassment of revealing in the sensitive immediate post-war period that there had been Concentration Camps on British soil.

A further distressing accompaniment to 'Island Madness' (though mercifully nowhere near as draconian as the treatment meted out to slave workers and political prisoners) was the deportation to Germany of all residents born outside the archipelago. This was decided by Hitler personally at the time of his directive of October 20th., 1941, concerning the fortification of the isles — but was not implemented until a year later, the first contingent leaving on September 24th., 1942.

The Fuehrer originally threatened to deport residents born in the United Kingdom as a reprisal against British seizure of German nationals in Iran — but confusion in the transmission of orders led to the threat not being implemented at the time. His insistence on definite numbers (1,200 from Jersey and 800 from Guernsey) suggests that he may have wanted specified numbers of British people as pawns in a bargain, such as an exchange for interned Germans: although the immediate cause of the 1942 deportations was Hitler's pique on discovering the muddle of the previous year. Especially in view of this pique the Fuehrer's direct order had to be obeyed at once without demur — as the Feldkommandant (Colonel Knackfuss) discovered when he attempted to protest against it.

Those who stayed did all they could to give a good send-off to the deportees with gifts they could ill spare, as well as providing hot meals and hot soup at the harbour — but in the long run the deportees fared better than those left behind as far as food was concerned. Single men were sent to Laufen, while men with families, and single women went to Wurzach and Biberach.

Children were well cared for, and those who volunteered for work in the neighbouring farms were well treated by the Bavarian farmers. One of the deportees was Frank Stroobant, who had the unique experience of being the only civilian in a party otherwise consisting of British and American servicemen conducted by the Germans to Katyn to view the mass graves containing the remains of several thousands of Polish officers of whose massacre the Russians and the Germans mutually accused each other.

Further deportations took place in February 1943 as a result of the German decision to deport all ex-officers in the British forces, following on 'Operation Basalt', described in the previous section.

Right up to 'D'-Day Hitler's obsession with the Channel Isles remained unabated. He was incapable of realising that this group of unsinkable battleships would as little deter an Allied invasion of the Continent as the Scilly Isles, if heavily fortified, would have deterred a German invasion of Britain, had Germany possessed the necessary naval and air supremacy. Thus on March 3rd., 1944 the islands were declared 'Fortresses' on a priority level for supplies with Cherbourg, Dunkirk and Le Havre; while as late as May 2nd., 1944, misgivings about island defences were aired at a high-level conference on the likely objectives for an Allied landing.

E — 'In Defeat, Defiance'

It is obvious that in the restricted confines of Guernsey it was impossible to set up any organised resistance movement such as that of Marshal Tito in Jugoslavia with its vast mountain redoubts from which to operate. All the more honour is therefore due to those who, alone or in small groups, attempted opposition to the enemy war effort and of whom it may be said

"— that certain men
Uncouth, untutored, of our island brood
... Loved freedom better than their lives".

A magnificent early example of defiance of the foe was set by Sir Abraham Lainé who, when on October 23rd., 1940, the Royal Court (mistakenly imagining that there were no Jews in the island) decided to placate the Germans by registering their anti-Jewish measures, 'openly and categorically refused his assent' — the sole Jurat so to do. Truly a man 'sans peur et sans reproche'.

The Guernsey population as a whole had one outstanding

opportunity to demonstrate its loyalties — and the opportunity was seized upon avidly. It was the 'Charybdis' funeral. On October 25th., 1943 the 5,450-ton cruiser, H.M.S. *Charybdis* was sunk in an action between the Channel Isles and Ushant. Between November 13th. and 15th. 21 bodies in an advanced state of decomposition were washed ashore on Guernsey's west coast. The Germans decided that these bodies should be buried with full military honours, and accordingly a few officers and a firing party were detailed to parade for this purpose at the Foulon cemetery on November 17th.

On arrival at the cemetery the German party was taken completely by surprise. Seeing this as a unique opportunity for a demonstration of their feelings, 5,000 islanders (over 21 per cent. of the post-evacuation and post-deportation population of 23,181) presented themselves at the cemetery, business houses having closed to release their employees for the occasion. The German guard of honour was utterly swamped. Besides the people, there were the wreaths — 900 of them — which had used up every flower available in the island, bearing inscriptions such as 'They died that we may be free'.

Following this exhibition of public feeling, the Germans banned civilian attendance at British servicemen's funerals, as well as expressions of sympathy or newspaper mention. To this day a special 'Charybdis' memorial service takes place annually, attended by the lieutenant-governor and a detachment from the existing ship of the same name, not to mention hundreds of islanders.

Turning from public demonstration to actual resistance, probably the first man in Guernsey systematically to undertake such activity was William Symes, the cousin of James Symes, to whom, before giving himself up (see Section B) James had passed the information he had obtained, asking him to get it back to England. William ran *The Dive* in Fountain Street — a pub frequented by sailors from ships which brought supplies from France. Through resistance workers among them, he smuggled out James's information and subsequent messages to a British agent in Spain. The French resistance called him 'Sandeman Bill', from the well-known brand name displayed outside the pub.

Eventually one of the messages was intercepted and Symes was arrested. Despite continual interrogation and maltreatment at the Cherche Midi, he denied any knowledge of the messages, and so avoided betraying any of his collaborators. Sentenced to imprisonment for the rest of the war, he was sent to Compiègne and later to Roumainville: the 'hostage' prison from which inmates were selected for shooting as reprisals. From Roumainville William Symes was sent to Buchenwald in a cattle truck whose hundred occupants, because of an escape attempt, were forced to undress and heap all their clothes on one side, after which they travelled naked for four days with no means of sanitation.

Symes owed his release from Buchenwald to a near miracle. He risked writing a postcard to his wife (who had been evacuated to Taunton before the Occupation) and smuggled it out among the postcards which French prisoners, at rare intervals, were allowed to send to their families. By an incredible freak it was delivered in England, where its receipt led to an official demand from the British to the German government for Symes to be moved to conditions more befitting a British subject — with the result that he was transferred to Laufen.

A stand which, though it achieved nothing, was nevertheless very plucky, was made in October 1941 by Mrs. Winifred Green, a waitress at the *Royal* hotel. Nettled by a foreign employee in the same hotel who, as a fervent admirer of Hitler, offered her some rice pudding on condition of her saying 'Heil Hitler', Mrs. Green replied, 'To hell with Hitler for a rice pudding — and one made of skimmed milk at that!' Retribution was swift. At 10.30 hours on October 13th., 1941 Mrs. Green was arrested and at 11.00 hours she was court-martialled and sentenced to six months imprisonment at Caen.

After a fortnight in Guernsey prison, Mrs. Green was taken to Granville where she spent five days in a cell with some prostitutes who treated her with much kindness, showing her how to make a straw palliasse comfortable. Once arrived at Caen, the indefatigable Mrs. Green risked further punishment by embroidering a sheet with the legend, 'Heil Churchill, R.A.F., "V"'. Eventually a letter reached the prison authorities from her husband, pointing out that his wife had had no defence at her court-martial. Surprisingly, this plea won a response, and the last few weeks of Mrs. Green's sentence were remitted. Complete with her embroidered sheet the defiant Mrs. Green returned to Guernsey and her work at the *Royal* hotel, where she was thereafter known as 'Mrs. Churchill'.

In 1942 moral indignation springing from sheer compassion led yet another Guernseywoman into making a defiant gesture which in her case brought terrible reprisals. The great-hearted lady in question was Miss Marie Ozanne who, as a dedicated Salvationist, had already in 1941 been involved in a brush with the Kommandantur arising out of her refusal to doff her uniform in compliance with its orders. She now followed up this stand on principle by courageously protesting to the Germans about their maltreatment of slave labourers and paid for her audacity by being incarcerated at Paradis in the Vale — the aforementioned House of Correction for Organization Todt workers. From the Occupation Diary kept by the Reverend Douglas Ord (who was then the Minister at the Methodist Church in Brock Road which was subsequently known as Ebenezer and later still closed down) one learns that here she was so cruelly tortured that her screams could be heard for a terrifyingly long way. Previously hardly robust and thenceforth a broken woman, brave Marie died at the age of 37 on February 25th., 1943, a few months after emerging from the clutches of her tormentors; the cause of death being recorded as appendicular abscess and peritonitis.

By the autumn of 1944 the food situation in Guernsey had become desperate (see next section), and already on September 18th. a directive from German headquarters had threatened a complete stopping of rations to the civilian population. There was widespread feeling that everything depended on getting the facts to London, so as to persuade the British government to relax the blockade to the extent of allowing Red Cross supplies to come through. At this juncture Captain Fred Noyon volunteered to attempt to escape to England to acquaint London with the facts. Noyon was supplied with statistics from every States Department, which were rapidly collected, thanks to the initiative of Deputy C. H. Cross.

On Friday, November 3rd. Noyon, accompanied by his friend, William Enticott, made his way to his boat, the *Littlewood* (for which he had accumulated eight cans of petrol, acquired by bartering fish) in St. Sampson's harbour, ostensibly to go fishing. After obtaining his fishing permit, Noyon dissuaded the German Customs officer who should have accompanied them by saying that he was going to put out his net and then proceed to St. Peter-Port for repairs to his engine pump, returning the next day. Not relishing walking back from St. Peter-Port to St. Sampson's, the Customs officer returned ashore. Thus left unsupervised, Noyon and Enticott put out their net and then carried on, pretending to be looking for longnose. When a drizzle sprang up they made for the Channel, hoisting sail as soon as it was dark.

At 2200 hours they were picked up by an American submarine

chaser and taken to Cherbourg where Noyon handed over his valuable papers, while Enticott, who had driven a lorry for the Germans, gave details of their guns and defences. Noyon reached London on November 12th., his information confirming the British government in its decision independently reached on November 7th. to allow Red Cross supplies into the islands, in the light of the report it had received from Cherbourg after Noyon's arrival there.

Another daring escape was made in January 1945 by two brothers, John and Thomas Le Page, together with a Frenchman called Xavier Jolivet, the instigator of the exploit being the French Consul, Monsieur Louis Lambert. Monsieur Lambert was anxious to acquaint Paris with the urgent need of French prisoners-of-war for Red Cross parcels. He also wished to transmit to the Allies the information on German naval constructions and minefields which he had obtained from Jolivet (who had worked for the German navy in St. Peter-Port) in return for which he had promised to help him escape back to France. With these objectives in mind, Lambert approached the Le Page brothers, and on their agreeing to make the attempt as soon as there was a misty day, he entrusted them with a sealed box containing his information — weighted so as to sink at once in the event of interception. In the meanwhile his accomplice, Jolivet, accustomed the Germans to permit him to accompany fishermen by representing himself as skilled in that pursuit and handing over to them part of his alleged catch (often, in fact, bought by Lambert).

The misty day having arrived, Jolivet, followed by the Le Page brothers, went to the guard room at the Albert pier. Jolivet managed to get himself assigned to the Le Page's boat, the brothers feigning reluctance to take him so as to divert suspicion. At the last moment Jolivet excused himself and went to the men's lavatory adjoining the Prince Consort's statue. Here Lambert, who was awaiting him, handed over further documents and last minute news of German operational plans, including the projected raid on Granville mentioned in the next section. Jolivet returned with the papers in a fisherman's bag over his shoulder and the boat sailed — ostensibly to pick up lobster pots south of Jethou. Under cover of the mist they turned north between Herm and Sark, and were 10 miles north of the latter island when, to their dismay, the sun came out — but they remained undetected.

At 1100 hours the following day Lambert saw a 'plane fly across to Guernsey, circle the island and fly back again to France

— the signal he had asked for should the three men reach France in safety. The testimony of the Le Page brothers reassured London that Red Cross supplies were, in fact, going intact to the civilian population, so that they were allowed to continue.

Action of a highly controversial nature, but claimed by those involved to constitute resistance, culminated in the sensational trial late in April 1942 by the Feldkommandant's Court of eighteen policemen, together with one civilian, all of whom were charged either with burgling from German Army Stores or with subsequently receiving therefrom, in full knowledge of their being stolen, items comprising fresh and tinned meats, German sausages, tins of butter, lard, sacks of grain and logs for heating. After all save one (who was acquitted) had received sentences ranging from four weeks' imprisonment to 4½ years hard labour, ten of the accused faced a second trial on June 1st. before the Royal Court charged with the theft of butter, beans, tomatoes, cooking oil, wines and spirits, from civilian stores. Again found guilty, they had further sentences imposed on them to run concurrently with the German ones. Writing after the war, one of the convicted group (Mr. Kingston George Bailey) understandably sought to exculpate his co-accused and himself by maintaining that their forays aimed at sabotaging the German war effort and furthermore asserting that they acted as latter-day Robin Hoods, robbing the rich to succour the poor, to whom he claimed that they passed on the bulk of what they had purloined. Suffice it to say that, irrespective of whether or not this plea be deemed valid (and relevant here is the failure of a post-war appeal by the surviving accused to the Judicial Committee of the Privy Council to be vindicated on these grounds), Mr. Bailey's conduct certainly did not merit the sadistic treatment meted out to him, with subjection to an ever-increasing scale of brutality for the next three years until his sufferings reached their climax with incarceration at the dreadful Dachau Concentration Camp — a prolonged purgatory which he vividly described in his harrowing book named after that terrible terrestrial hell. Equally unjustifiable was the persistent vicious ill usage amounting to calculated torture inflicted on several of his associates, one of whom (Herbert Percival Smith) was killed by his evil gaolers' deliberate and sustained malefactions; while unremitting cruelty and savagery had brought others (notably Messrs. Jack Harper, Frank Tuck and Frederick Short) so low that the advancing Americans arrived just in time to snatch them from the jaws of death. One might also add that, regarding the rejection by the Judicial Committee of the Privy Council of the survivors' appeal for exoneration, it is significant that in his book, *I Beg to Report* (a minutely detailed account of the Police Force during the Occupation) Mr. William M. Bell remarks:

> 'Many people held the view that the British Judicial System was just not equipped to deal with the situation which arose in Guernsey during the German Occupation. As a result, seventeen members of the Island Police Force were in their view and that of many other people, denied natural justice.'

The most sustained and widespread subversive activity carried on in the entire Occupation was the publication of a daily news-sheet giving the B.B.C. nine o'clock news bulletin plus a summary of the 0800 news on the day of issue. The news-sheet, which appeared regularly from May 1942 to February 1944 under the title of 'G.U.N.S.' (Guernsey Underground News Service) was the brainchild of Charles Machon, a linotype operator on the *Star* newspaper. He was helped by Frank Falla, assistant editor of the *Star*, Cyril Duquemin, a greenhouse worker and near neighbour, and two carpenters, Ernest Legg and Joseph Gillingham.

In June 1942 Hitler's 'Island Madness' led to a decree that all wireless sets should be confiscated, so as to prevent the islanders from receiving instructions from the B.B.C. when the British launched what the Fuhrer regarded as their inevitable assault on the archipelago. The deadline for surrendering sets was June 20th. This development reinforced Machon's determination to publish his news-sheet, which he had started the previous month for the benefit of those who were too poor to own wireless sets.

As many as one hundred copies a day were turned out on thin tomato-packing paper, averaging 780 words a time. One appeared daily on the bailiff's desk, disappearing mysteriously after he had read it. Another was placed in a pre-arranged book in the Priaulx library, where those in the secret could consult it. Three were sent to Sark, taken by passengers who hid them behind hat-bands or in the heel of a shoe as a precaution against being stripped and searched at the harbour barrier. In Sark they were further distributed by Mr. C. F. Wakley, the carrier, and Hubert Lanyon, the baker, helped by Mr. W. K. B. Giffard (who worked in Lanyon's bakery), and the Rev. E. A. Tardiff, the Methodist minister.

Betrayed by an Irishman named Peter Doyle in whom he had confided — possibly because this person's marriage to the

Alderney Greffier's niece lent him an aura of trustworthiness — Machon (and Duquemin too) was on February 11th., 1944 arrested by the Gehemie Feldpolizei who found his typewriter and past copies of 'G.U.N.S.' in his house. Cruelly beaten up and further ill-used by being placed in an overcoat before a red-hot stove and then thrown naked into an icy cell, Machon was finally threatened that his 74-year-old mother, Mrs. Mary Ann Machon, would be sent to Germany if he did not talk. When his mother fell ill with shock Machon was incredibly allowed to visit her, guarded by an English-speaking German officer, who doubled the time allowed and informed Mrs. Machon that her son was a hero.

Legg and Gillingham were next rounded up, and finally, on April 3rd., 1944, Falla was placed under arrest. On April 26th., they were tried and Machon was sentenced to two years and four months, Duquemin one year and eleven months, Legg one year and ten months, Falla one year and four months, and Gillingham ten months. These terms were meaningless as any commitment of six months or more involved leaving Guernsey, and once in Germany all sentences became *sine die*.

By the time of the trial Machon was already wretchedly ill, the effects of his maltreatment exacerbated by the refusal of his captors to allow him the special food essential to his ulcerated stomach. The severities of prison life in Potsdam rapidly took their toll, and Charles Machon died on October 26th., 1944. Joseph Gillingham, too, was far from robust and although he survived the ten months to which he had been sentenced, his stamina could not stand up to the extended rigours and brutal treatment which followed a point-blank refusal to release him, and he also succumbed in prison. Thus died two very gallant Guernseymen.

The other three survived by a hair's breadth. When the Americans liberated them from their prison at Naumberg on Saale, Legg was emaciated and limping from injuries received from being hurled down a flight of stone steps, while Falla, who had not even been allowed an aspirin when ill with pneumonia, was considered by his liberators to have only a fortnight to live. Only devoted and skilled nursing by the Americans pulled him through.

The only member of the network to escape the horrors of imprisonment in Germany was Hubert Lanyon. The Geheime Feldpolizei grilled him mercilessly, beating him unconscious with brutal blows and knocking out two of his teeth in an effort to discover the names of his helpers. He staunchly refused to divulge anything or to incriminate anybody else, maintaining that he had merely read a copy of 'G.U.N.S.' which he had come across. At his trial he received a sentence of six months, reduced to four on appeal, and so was not sent to the Continent.

So much for resistance activity within the Bailiwick: but it would be churlish to end this Section without paying tribute to the heroism displayed beyond its bounds by the underground operations of the Guernseywoman Mrs. Alice Brouard who, caught in France by the onrush of the German forces in 1940, year after year risked unspeakable torture and the firing squad by sheltering in her flat at 25, Rue de Madrid, Paris, a succession of airmen (mostly American) who, shot down in combat, made use of it as a staging post on the escape route to freedom, sometimes staying there for weeks on end. Twice did she escape discovery by the Gestapo by no more than a hairbreadth and her exploits in providing refuge for (*inter alia*) no less than eighteen American airmen earned this courageous woman a commendation accompanied by a Silver Laurel Leaf from His Majesty King George VI in 1946, followed by the award in 1947 of the Medal of Freedom of the U.S.A. — the highest of all American civilian decorations and comparable to the British George Cross.

F — 'Daughters of Israel'

An especially grim feature of the Occupation was that from Guernsey too there trod the Via Dolorosa to extermination sundry hapless members of what in its Good Friday Collect the Book of Common Prayer (1928 version) calls 'thine ancient people the Jews'. It is hardly surprising, therefore, that the circumstances attending the island's involvement in this evil pogrom have given rise to much heart-searching issuing in various assertions — some understandably of an emotive nature — which have appeared in print over the years. It is thus of cardinal importance that the facts of the matter be made known and an accurate record of these appalling events be provided.

Two of the Jewesses slain in this vile massacre were of modest means, working at the Castel Hospital where the elder — Auguste Spitz — was employed as a cleaner earning 15s. (75p.) a week plus keep and the younger — Theresia Steiner — as a nurse earning £48-10s. (£48.50) per annum, also plus keep. Each hailed from Vienna, where the former was born on August 25th., 1901 and the latter on April 22nd., 1916 — and consequent upon the absorption of Austria into the Third Reich by the 1938 Anchluss, each woman was of German nationality. It appears that their troubles commenced on June 4th., 1940 when, on the instructions of the Lieutenant-Governor's Office, they were interned as enemy aliens. Three weeks later — on June 25th. — they were released, together with 26 others, on the instruction of Colonel Frederick Brusson, Secretary to the Lieutenant-Governor, His Excellency having by then left the island.

Five days after the internees' release the Germans arrived and once their administrative régime was fully established the Feldkommandant required the Island Authorities to provide him with lists of all aliens — regardless of race or religion — resident in Guernsey as on June 1st., 1940. Theresia Steiner and August Spitz (plus also Marianne Grunfeld of subsequent tragic mention) were naturally included in these lists which contained over 400 names — in several cases of people who had taken refuge in England after that date. (Prominent among those then safe in England, incidentally, was *malgré lui* — the universally admired Doctor William John Montague who, with scrupulous fidelity to his Hippocratic Oath and disregarding the dire consequences for him as a Jew of so doing, had decided to remain by his patients' side in Guernsey, but had been tricked into going on a purportedly brief visit to London to seek guidance on further civilian evacuation practicalities. He was, of course, not allowed to return and his fate thereafter is a mystery. The General Medical Council admits that it is 'unable to trace any record of him after 1944' — but as the Medical Register for 1944 is inaccurate, showing him as still in Guernsey, the fact is that no record of him is traceable after 1940!). During the Autumn Doctor Brosch of the Feldkommandantur required the Police Inspector (Mr. William Robert Sculpher) to inform all Germans and Italians (the former including four Austrians) to attend for interview at the Feldkommandantur, Grange Lodge, at 3 p.m. on October 21st. — again regardless of race or religion. Theresia Steiner and Auguste Spitz were among the 33 persons warned to attend.

Three more days passed and then, on October 24th., the Germans published in the local press their Order relating to measures against Jews, which required anyone who professed or had professed Judaism to register with the Inspector of Police. Four persons came forward and registered, including Auguste Spitz and Theresia Steiner. The other two were Mesdames Elda

Brouard (née Bauer in Florence) and Elisobet Duquemin (née Fink in Vienna), each of whom was a British subject by marriage, the former being a widow.

In November 1940 the President of the Controlling Committee (in which capacity Jurat John Leale was acting pending his official appointment thereto the following January) was asked by the Germans for details of the nationality of any Jews living in the Bailiwick and whether they included any of American nationality. Again Theresia Steiner and Auguste Spitz were included in the return and described as German. Two months later — in January 1941 — the Police Inspector was required by the Germans to provide a list of Jews in Guernsey and to state whether there were any male Jews or Jewish children under the age of 16. Once more Auguste Spitz and Theresia Steiner were included in the list, the Inspector also reporting that there were no male Jews or Jewish children resident in the island.

Matters took a decidedly sinister turn on March 17th., 1941, when Doctor Reffler of the Feldkommandantur wrote to the Bailiff (who, in accordance with the provisions of the Hague Convention, operated as the channel of communication between the Occupying Power and the Island Administration) ordering that the cards of all Jews in the Foreigners' Card Index be marked with a capital 'J' in red. This instruction was passed on to Inspector Sculpher on March 19th. and on March 21st. the Inspector reported that it had been complied with as far as foreign Jews were concerned but that the cards of Mesdames Brouard and Duquemin had remained unmarked. (Incidentally, these two ladies, in common with all residents born outside the island, were subsequently deported to internment, whence they returned safely after the defeat of Germany. Mrs. Duquemin later went to live in Warwickshire). Bailiff Victor Carey sent the Inspector's Report to the Feldkommandantur on March 22nd., with a forwarding letter the quotation of which has figured prominently in controversial treatments of this poignant episode in island history.

After the endorsement of the cards of die Frauleinnen Spitz und Steiner a year elapsed until, as the terrible outcome of the whole sequence of events, the two women on April 20th., 1942 (Hitler's birthday, incidentally) received orders to report at the Town Harbour the next day and there board a ship bound for France. Reports vary as to their reaction to these orders. While Mrs. Duquemin, when interviewed after the war, maintained that when she saw them on the eve of their departure they were very distressed, Mrs. Whale, their hospital's Assistant Matron recalled that they left the island in good heart, fondly imagining that they were to rejoin their kith and kin — and indeed, so trustingly naïve was Theresia Steiner in this respect that a few days prior to their departure she went of her own accord to the Kommandantur to solicit official aid in expediting a family reunion! Whatever their mood when sailing, however, the harsh fact is that, as shown in the Yad Washem archives, on July 20th., at Drancy Concentration Camp near Paris, these two victims were herded into Convoy Number 8 which on July 23rd. reached Auschwitz, where they were slaughtered soon after arrival.

A like gruesome fate befell Pani Marianne Grunfeld, a Polish Diplomate in Horticulture, University of Reading, employed at Duvaux Farm in Saint Sampson's and hailing from Silesia, having been born on December 5th., 1912, in the town of Katowice, which at that time was included in the German Empire of Kaiser Wilhelm II but was later awarded to Poland by the vote of the 1921 Plebiscite. Her facial appearance being Slavonic rather than Semitic and hence hoping to escape detection, she did not accompany Auguste Spitz and Theresia Steiner in coming forward to register as Jewish with the Inspector of Police on October 24th., 1940. As a result officialdom remained unaware of her existence for quite a time, though, as both the list of aliens handed to the Feldkommandant early in the Occupation and also the identification registries compiled the following autumn included her place of birth and nationality as declared by her, anyone intent on so doing (such as a zealous anti-semitic German official) could have picked her out as potentially Jewish. This reflection renders the assertion of her fellow employees that she was betrayed by a malicious anonymous informant as incapable of categorical confirmation as it is of outright refutation. The sad fact is that, whether maliciously betrayed or ferreted out by a Jew-baiting registry scrutineer, Marianne's Hebraic identity was discovered one way or the other and the attempt on April 18th., 1942, of her employer (Edward Ogier) to save her by a personal appeal at the Feldkommandantur availed nothing, with the consequence that she was included in the 824 victims (of whom only fourteen survived) who were transported to Auschwitz in the same convoy as her two co-religionists from Guernsey and she too met her death on July 23rd., 1942.

Verily did these three daughters of Israel have ample cause to weep, as David had exhorted their forebears to do when lamenting the death of Saul (II Samuel 1, 24). Requiem aeternam dona eis Domine et lux perpetua luceat eis.

G — Darkness and Dawn

The front page of the *Daily Telegraph* of June 7th., 1944 carried a map of the invasion area. Arrows pointed towards the Channel Isles with the caption, 'Allied Paratroops reported here'. This report was, of course, false, and in fact the 11 months following the Normandy landings were to be the worst period of the war for the beleaguered islanders.

The over-riding problem was food. Admiral Krancke, commanding German Naval Group West, proposed that, to enable the islands to hold out as long as possible, any islanders not working for the Germans should be shipped to Granville — but by the time this proposal had been authorised, Granville had fallen to the Americans. The result of this failure to transport the population to the Continent was a directive from Supreme Headquarters dated September 18th., 1944 and signed by General Keitel, that civilian rations were to be reduced to 'the barest survival level'. If this did not suffice, the civilian population had to be 'pushed over to the enemy' — apparently to be segregated in one corner of each island, giving the British the chance of removing them, sending food, or letting them starve.

Starve they nearly did. On September 22nd. an American ship approached Guernsey from Diélette flying a white flag of parley. The American Staff Major from S.H.A.E.F. asked if the Germans were aware that their position was hopeless, to which von Schmettow replied by Morse signal that he was fully informed about the war situation and did not intend discussing terms with the Americans. The starvation siege was on.

Life became completely primitive, with people going to bed soon after midday because there was nothing left to eat, and they had insufficient energy to go on working. A shortage of fuel compounded the misery, making it almost impossible to keep warm or to cook what little food there was. Thefts became common as hunger brought desperation, and people took weapons to bed with them to deal with prowlers — such as the knobkerries taken upstairs every night by Dr. Symons, the Guernsey health officer.

The information taken out by Captain Fred Noyon, who reached London on November 12th., together with the telephone call to the International Red Cross which Victor Carey, the bailiff, was permitted by the Germans to make on November 7th., and in which he stressed the desperate nature of the situation, reinforced Churchill's independent decision of the self-same November 7th. to allow Red Cross supplies into the islands. Thus it was that, after an utterly dismal Christmas, the Red Cross ship *Vega* reached Guernsey on December 27th., carrying New Zealand and Canadian Red Cross supplies. In all the *Vega* paid five visits, thanks to the reassurances as to the recipients of its cargoes given to the British government by the Le Page brothers, and these calls alone saved the population from downright starvation. Even with the Red Cross parcels, a situation of near-starvation persisted for the rest of the war.

Their extraordinary sense of military honour meant that the Germans were punctilious about touching nothing from the parcels — one soldier even refusing the offer of a few cigarettes on the grounds that they had come from the *Vega*. Thereafter the lot of the German troops was worse than that of the civilians, rummaging in dustbins, parading to search for limpets, or combing the hedgerows for berries and nettles to boil and eat. This scrupulosity characterising the majority did not, however, restrain a minority of hunger-maddened members of the Wehrmacht who took to extensive theft from homes and farms, often resorting to violence — and in some cases murder — when discovered.

After liberation, evidence of the astonishing discipline of the Germans came to light in Sark. The troops had been so weak from lack of food that they had been seen collapsing when walking up Harbour Hill — yet a store of three month's food supplies was found in the girls' school, kept intact for any last-ditch stand.

At the end of February 1945 Graf von Schmettow was removed as being 'too magnanimous' over civilian rations, and was replaced by Vice-Admiral Huffmeier, a fanatical Nazi, who was determined to hold on, come what may. Schmettow's stock had sunk so low that his life was spared thanks only to the influence of his uncle, von Rundstedt. Despite the fact that it had been planned by Schmettow, Huffmeier's prestige received a fillip from the successful German raid on Granville on March 8th., which wrought considerable damage to installations, 'liberated' between 30 and 40 German prisoners, and brought back 26 American prisoners of war. The vice-admiral left no doubt about his intentions, when on the occasion of Hitler's birthday (April 20th.) he addressed the troops in the *Regal* (later *Odeon*) cinema in

Upland Road. So impassioned was his call for a fight to the end that even the anti-Nazis among the officers were impressed. Not so the rank and file, however, who grumbled at losing their last miserable consolation of three cigarettes a day.

In these circumstances, the more prudent and realistic among the leading German officers decided that the removal of this fervent disciple of the Fuehrer was essential. On April 23rd., Baron von Aufsess who, fearing for his life, had tried, but failed, to escape to the Allies in France, entered into a plot to assassinate Huffmeier with Baron von Helldorf, who had been Schmettow's Chief of Staff. Aufsess told Helldorf that Huffmeier always went to the officers' mess in Castle Carey each day at 0900 hours to take a glass of milk — and was always alone. It was agreed that Helldorf would take advantage of this opportunity to kill Huffmeier, take his place, and agree surrender with the Allies. However, the vice-admiral smelt a rat and on April 28th. Helldorf was exiled to Herm. It had been the hope of Aufsess and Helldorf to carry out their plans with the support of some Georgians serving in the German army who had planned to mutiny — but once again Huffmeier's suspicions were aroused, and the Georgians were sent to Alderney. Leading what was obviously a charmed life, the vice-admiral also escaped unscathed from Monsieur Lambert's plot for an attractive woman to lure him to a spot where he could be seized by some Alsatians in the German garrison, chloroformed and taken to England.

So Huffmeier stayed at the helm and remained as intransigent as ever, as the captain of the *Vega* discovered when the Red Cross ship arrived in St. Peter-Port just after Hitler's death — and received a peremptory order to fly her flag at half-mast. Not long after this Huffmeier replied to the surrender demand of an Allied ship off Alderney with the signal — 'You're wasting your time!' Even as late as May 6th. he went to Jersey to send off yet another commando raid on Granville — and was only stopped at the last minute by direct orders from Admiral Doenitz. Back in Guernsey on May 7th., but still unsubdued, this Nazi last-ditcher reprimanded Jurat John Leale (president of the Controlling Committee) for permitting Union Jacks to be flown — and indicated that any attempt by the Allies at a landing would be resisted, irrespective of what the consequences might be in civilian casualties.

Suddenly, on May 8th., Huffmeier changed his mind — possibly on direct orders from Admiral Doenitz, or possibly for fear of widespread mutiny among his forces. Accordingly at 1400 hours that day Brigadier A. E. Snow, commanding 'Operation Nest Egg', made rendezvous four miles off Guernsey on H.M.S. *Bulldog* (escorted by H.M.S. *Beagle*) with Kapitän-Leutnant Arnim Zimmermann, who said he was authorised to receive armistice terms for consideration by Huffmeier. When Snow answered that he would be sent back with an instrument of instant surrender, Zimmermann accepted this document, but said that unless the British ships moved away from Guernsey's shores, Admiral Huffmeier would regard their presence as a 'provocative act'. To this Snow's rejoinder was that if Huffmeier opened fire, he would hang him — but *Bulldog* and *Beagle* withdrew just the same. At midnight, however, Zimmermann returned with Major-General Heine, who had Huffmeier's authority to sign an unconditional surrender. After details had been arranged, he signed eight copies at 0715 hours on May 9th.

Shortly afterwards British troops, part of a force under Colonels Power and Stoneman, landed to a delirious welcome. The late Ralph Durand remarked that 'an island which had been rendered an impregnable fortress, garrisoned by thousands of soldiers and with a reserve of 16,000 tons of ammunition, was occupied by an advance party of one British officer and 25 men'. The long ordeal was over.

H — Good and Faithful Servants

On December 12th., 1945 *The Times* published details of honours granted by the king in recognition of Occupation services. This list is especially interesting for its omissions. That the bailiff (Victor Carey) and the president of the Controlling Committee (Jurat John Leale) should be granted knighthoods was to be expected — but that the original president of the Committee, whose patriotism had cost him both his post and his liberty, should only receive a C.B.E. is hard to understand, even though this neglect was made good four years later after Sherwill had himself become bailiff.

Even more significant is the fact that those who suffered acutely (and even died) as a result of their behaving in the way which Churchill exhorted the people of Great Britain to behave in the event of an enemy landing ('You can always take one with you') are conspicuous in this Honours List by their absence. No posthumous award for Charles Machon, Joseph Gillingham or

Marie Ozanne, and no acknowledgement of the courage of William Symes, Frank Falla, Cyril Duquemin, Ernest Legg, Hubert Lanyon, Captain Fred Noyon, or John and Thomas Le Page. The contrast with the adulation showered on members of the Resistance in neighbouring France is startling. Some insight regarding such omissions may perhaps be gained from a telling passage in his 'Report on Five Years of German Occupation', made by Jurat Leale on May 23., 1945, in which he said — 'Guernsey was, in fact, an impossible place in which to indulge in underground activities. Any attempt on these lines brought retribution on the population and it was generally realised that getting other people into trouble is a doubtful way of displaying one's patriotism'.

Such a statement makes it hard to resist the conclusion that the efforts of these brave people were resented more than admired, on the grounds that they might have imperilled the maintenance of 'correct relations' between the island authorities and the Occupying Power. One, of course, can do nothing but sympathise with Leale's assertion that 'It's easy to talk big when you have no responsibilities on your shoulders'; and it is hardly reasonable to blame Victor Carey for his oft-quoted notice in *La Gazette Officielle* of July 8th., 1941, offering a reward of £25 for information leading to the conviction of anyone marking in any place the letter 'V' or any words calculated to offend the German authorities. The relevant truth is that Carey was then old beyond his years and no longer fully alert — as may be judged from the fact that although Churchill's government was formed seven weeks before the Occupation, and wireless sets were not confiscated until June 1942, he was nevertheless surprised to be visited by Herbert Morrison after the Liberation, saying he did not realise that Socialists were in the British government. On the other hand, however, elsewhere in his account of his stewardship, Leale stated frankly — 'One of our main functions was to soften the impact of German orders when they were harsh'. Consequently he made no bones about the fact that 'we espoused the Hague Convention "for better, for worse, for richer, for poorer, in sickness and in health" ' — while, towards the end of his speech he claimed, 'Our behaviour gave them no cause for severity'.

In the light of such statements, not to mention the failure of the same speech to include any recognition of the heroism of the 'underground', it is difficult to avoid suspecting that although an order to submit was implicit in the British Government's demilitarisation decision, such submissiveness was at times carried to questionable extremes and that the civil authorities discharged their obligations with a punctilio verging on the obsequious. That widespread resistance in a small place like Guernsey was impracticable will readily be conceded and, of course, most people are not heroes; but it must surely be a rare phenomenon to shun one's heroes and to regard them askance, arguing (as did Sir John Leale in 1955 during the conversation with the authors of *Islands in Danger* recorded on page 302 of that book) that 'it might be difficult for a Government which is a signatory to the Hague Convention to recommend Honours for those who broke the Convention'. Indeed, far from justifying the denial of Honours, such a remark merely prompts the reflection that, as the legally constituted Government of France had entered into an Armistice with Germany, General de Gaulle and his entourage could also be held to have broken the Hague Convention — but this did not preclude them from being honoured once victory was won! The upshot is that pondering on what Sir John said (and discounting as based on no more than uncorroborated hearsay the reference to him in the M119 files released by the Ministry of Defence in November 1996 as 'an evil influence and considered to be pro-German') leads one to conclude that in order to see his scathingly dismissive comment in perspective it should be borne in mind that the outlook thereby revealed was not confined to him alone — witness Sir Victor Carey's frank post-war admission that 'the one thing I was keen about was that there shouldn't be any sort of resistance movement'.

(As an incidental rider to these observations on the stance of the Establishment — and while on the topic of attitudes — it may be remarked parenthetically that in regard to the deportment of the people in general during the Occupation, Guernsey has never been populated exclusively by saints and of course there were women who consorted with Germans — with a minority of such conjugalities genuine love-matches; of course there were malicious persons informing on those who kept secret wireless sets or painted 'V' signs or — in all probability — on poor Marianne Grunfeld; and of course nest-feathering by catering for German requirements to the detriment of islanders' needs was not unknown — as exemplified by the case of the grower whose horticultural activities were investigated after the Liberation by the incorruptible Sir Abraham Lainé and whose protestations of innocence sounded decidedly hollow when it emerged that his pre-war bank balance of

£340 in the red had been transmuted into one of £70,000 in the black! That a quantity of linen should be thus soiled was inevitable, but its post-war laundering was sufficiently discreet to ensure the avoidance of serious overt public scandal.)

A magnificent example of dignity in defeat was provided in Sark by La Dame, who made a point of never going to the Germans, but always insisting on their coming to her. Far from appealing to the Hague Convention, she simply dominated the Germans (whose language she spoke fluently), using such remarks as: 'But you can't do that, I won't allow it', or, 'Oh dear, no, that's not the way the British do things; in Britain we never shout' — and (during the starvation siege), 'You haven't got an Army, you've only got a pack of thieves and beggars'.

When starvation faced the island before the *Vega's* first visit, La Dame organised her own 'commando raid' on the enemy food depot at the Island Hall, aided by William Baker and Philip Le Feuvre. A hole was bored through the floorboards of the hall (underneath which it was possible to crawl). Thus a cartload of grain was taken to La Seigneurie mill by Le Feuvre, ground into flour and distributed in small parcels by Hubert Lanyon, the baker. La Dame followed this up by issuing a secret order to all households to bring part of their potato reserve to La Seigneurie where it would be hidden from German eyes. By these two measures many Sark families were saved from starvation during the cruellest winter of the war.

Mrs. Hathaway's absolute ascendancy was manifest immediately after the Liberation when, seeing no British troops were instantly available, La Dame 'took over' the defeated German garrison, supervising their clearing up the island and disposing of land mines. Considering her consistently spirited attitude, one cannot avoid reflecting on the fact that La Dame's name, too, was absent from the Occupation Honours List!

PART V

'MEMBERS ONE OF ANOTHER' — THE ECONOMIC AND SOCIAL ASPECT

Chapter One

'DONKEY LIFE STYLE'

THE CONCLUDING PART of the Bailiwick's history will unavoidably be a long one, so that it might prove helpful to start with a short chapter by way of a general introduction to the theme.

The Guernseyman has sometimes been accused of adopting a mercenary approach to life, to the detriment of both his awareness of his social responsibilities and of his appreciation of the cultural and artistic aspects of his environment. If this accusation means that he is acutely conscious of the problems of earning a living, then it may be answered by saying that such awareness has *had* to be acute to enable him to survive in a small island with limited natural resources where, until comparatively recent times, he has had to wrest his living as best he could from the soil and the sea with all its attendant hazards — not to mention the perennial dangers of being raided and despoiled. To develop 'an eye for the main chance' under such historical influences is practically inevitable; and it must not be forgotten that the same influences have also produced the virtues of diligence and thrift (as well as the stubborn persistence which has earned the nickname of 'donkey') — and these, too, are prominent characteristics of the islanders.

The consequence is that through the centuries the Guernseyman has turned his hand to almost everything, with certain occupations emerging as distinct landmarks. From mediaeval times until the 16th. century a subsistence agriculture was supplemented by the fish trade and the wine traffic, with Saint Peter-Port roadstead operating as a vital link on the route to England from Gascony. The 17th. century was characterised by the knitting of woollen garments, succeeded in the 18th. century by privateering and smuggling. Shipbuilding, quarrying and cattle-farming were predominant in the 19th. century, while the 20th. century saw the rise of market-gardening ('growing'), a lucrative tourist industry, the provision of tax-haven facilities and the rise of the 'finance industry' as the dominant feature of the island's economy. All have been grist to the mill and indicate the ingenuity and adaptability which have been the keynotes of the Bailiwick's economic history, while the attitude of sturdy independence thus engendered has coloured its social and cultural development.

Chapter Two

ARABLE AGRICULTURE

THE CULTIVATION of the earth is obviously *the* fundamental economic activity, as without food man would perish — and therefore in the Bailiwick of Guernsey as elsewhere it has been pursued from the earliest settlers, though for many centuries only on a subsistence basis. It should be noted that, despite the repute of Guernsey's agricultural produce, her soil is not intrinsically more fertile than that of England. It is derived from the weathering of gneiss and granite, overlain with loam, a few patches of valley gravel and a wide scattering of dune sands, the soil so formed having been enriched by generations of manuring with cow dung and *vraic* (seaweed), the one grave deficiency being a lack of lime. In more recent times artificial fertilisation and steam sterilisation have further increased the productivity of the soil. Climatic factors have also been advantageous, with rainfall averaging 37 inches per annum, a high annual total of sunshine (usually exceeding 1,800 hours), and an equable temperature with a mean of 50 deg. F. (10 deg. C.).

In Guernsey hamlets growing around an original Celtic pattern of scattered homesteads became (under Norman influence) agricultural nuclei with attendant open-field systems plus common pasture. In addition, however, intensive cultivation also has roots going far back into the island's history. The smallness of the area, a plentiful water supply, and a network of lanes, led to closer settlement with the workable land between the dwellings intensively cultivated. This trend was reinforced by the division of the land into very small fields — a consequence of the inheritance laws where, despite the 'préciput' of the eldest son, younger children would acquire small plots of land with the proceeds of their compensation for 'le restant de l'enclos', or where parents while still alive would deliberately create additional 'enclos' on their property to safeguard the expectations of their younger sons and daughters. The influence of the resulting personal ownership encouraged the emergence of a spirit of independence and an untiring capacity for work still evident today. The increase in the number of small landowners was first strongly in evidence in the latter half of the 13th. century, when the peasants were encouraged to enclose their sub-divisions of the big estates by the increasing cultivation of parsnips (a crop suitable to island soils) which was exempt from Champart.

A more typical open-field development occurred in Sark, where the Assize Roll of 1309 shows agriculture as the main activity, with conger fishing and the collection of rabbit skins as important subsidiaries. When Helier de Carteret's colonists arrived in 1565 they noted the absence of hedges in the island — a clear indication that during the Middle Ages the fertile plateau had been cultivated on the open-field system. It is probable that the arable zone extended from L'Eperquerie southwards, in the area of which a part is still known as 'Les Camps' ('Les Champs'), with the nucleated village on the site of St. Magloire's old monastery. The rest of the island was most likely held in common as pasture.

Similarly, in another area also known as 'Les Camps' (in St. Martin's parish in Guernsey) the fragmented nature of the present-day feudal holdings (as mentioned in Part II, Chapter Three) points strongly to mediaeval strip cultivation in the context of an open-field system — the plural noun 'camps' originally denoting such strips, though later coming by extension to be also applied loosely to the Open Fields wherein they lay. Here and elsewhere where open-field cultivation was practised the year fell into two periods, known as Mession and Banon. At the time of Mession (roughly from Easter to Michaelmas) cattle had to be tethered for the better protection of growing crops; but in the Banon season, which lasted approximately from Michaelmas to Easter, cattle could roam freely under the supervision of an official called a Messier who was responsible, *inter alia*, for seeing that they did not enter upon the occasional enclosed areas (known as Clos or Clôtures). Indeed, as time went by, the very existence of Banon (which survived until 1717) encouraged ever increasing numbers of landowners to protect their holdings from encroachment by other people's cattle by enclosing them with the earth banks (Fossés) which persist to this day as a feature of Guernsey's countryside. Though particularly marked during the 15th. and 16th. centuries, this tendency also continued inexorably thereafter until by now the only Open Field system with component strips still to be seen is that adjoining la Rue du Chemin le Roi at Pleinmont (but see the note on page 332 at the end of this chapter).

The archetype of open-field cultivation, however, is provided by Alderney, with the system surviving to the present day. It is of great antiquity and was probably introduced as early as the Megalithic period on the plateau of rich soil in the centre and western end of the island, known as 'La Blaye' (from 'Blé' = 'corn' or 'wheat'). Because of this area's fertility fallow was rarely practised, *vraic* being spread on the ground to restore its vitality. The evidence of place-names indicates that the first locality to be brought into cultivation was in the centre of the Great Blaye, the limits of the arable zone being gradually extended until by the middle of the 15th. century the Blaye reached its present limits and was permanently enclosed.

The Blaye was divided into Riages — blocks of strips each with a total area of about 36 vergées, which were the property of the riagers. The riages ran north to south and at right-angles to each riage was a plot running east to west crossing it at the end and called a Vaindiff or Vaindivage, constituting a 'bout de riage', on which the riager could turn his plough when cultivating his land. Each vaindiff was three feet in width, forming a 'no-man's land' at the commencement of the neighbouring riage, which in its turn found another vaindiff on which it rested. A record of the vaindiffs was kept by the Douzaine (see Part III, Chapter Twelve) which operated as final arbiter in any dispute. Earthen banks kept cattle out of the Blaye as a whole while it was under cultivation, but at other times the animals were free to graze there, thus manuring the soil before spring sowing — an arrangement similar to the Banon period in Guernsey. In connection with this system of land tenure on the Blaye it is interesting to note that early in 1979 an action was taken in the Alderney Court by a riager against the chairman of the Building and Development Control Committee for permitting the adjoining owner to fence in the vaindiff to which he claimed lawful access. The action failed, not because the plaintiff lacked legal grounds for his submission, but because the court ruled that it was taken against the wrong defendant in that the legal right to which the plaintiff claimed entitlement was prejudiced not by the chairman or his committee, but by the person who obtained permission to erect the fence. In these circumstances the court advised the plaintiff to seek legal advice should he wish to pursue his suit in a further action.

Outside the arable Blaye the land was held in common by the entire community. These areas, known as Les Landes, Les Genêts and Le Giffoine (wastelands, furzelands, and hay areas) remained common land until 1831. In that year the economic distress which had prompted John Le Mesurier to surrender his 'Governorship' (see Part III, Chapter Twelve) — and which was exacerbated by the withdrawal of his household — led to a decision that all the common lands should be divided among island-born families, so as to provide them with a means of supporting themselves. For this purpose the common lands were divided into lots, which were classified into groups of 'good' and 'poor'; and the lots were allocated by ballot to the 52 qualified families, each receiving one 'good' and one 'poor' lot.

Alderney's original settlement of habitation was probably in the natural hollow adjoining the Marais area of St. Anne, where shelter was available from the strong winds, together with easy access to the Blaye and a supply of water in the stream which formerly flowed through the Marais area down to Platte Saline.

Until the Second World War, the 1,125 vergées of the Blaye was administered by the Douzaine, whose members inspected it twice yearly, not only settling disputes such as vaindiff entitlements, but also ensuring that gates and hedges were in good condition. The area of the Blaye available for agriculture was reduced in 1935 when Alderney's airport was carved out of its south-western corner. Despite some confusion after the Liberation arising from the removal of landmarks by the Germans, the strip system of holdings persists on the Blaye to the present day — though the strips are much smaller than originally because of subdivision among heirs of properties. The absence of hedges and boundaries creates a wide expanse of open land which is a unique feature of Alderney's landscape. The chief crop is carrots, which are exported to England.

Returning to Guernsey, the era of comparative tranquillity following the Hundred Years War encouraged a more settled agriculture — but living standards remained low until the end of the Tudor period. The richer folk shared with their livestock stone longhouses (consisting of a general living room plus byre) which initially were open to the roof. (The evolution of the Guernsey farmhouse is outlined in Appendix XV.) During the earlier periods living conditions were very simple, with sleeping provision consisting of a *lit d'fouaile* in one room, which in addition contained a large house-table actually built inside it. (The *lit d'fouaile* was a couch-like structure, consisting of a mattress stuffed with fern or *vraic*, housed in a wooden frame, which was built into the corner of a room. The present writer recalls one in his parents' kitchen during his infancy, though the last time he saw one was in a Torteval farmhouse in 1951 — unless one counts the Folk Museum in Saumarez Park). The surrounding land was ploughed by oxen for grain and parsnip cultivation. As these richer farmers enclosed wasteland to form extra fields, apple-orchards were planted and cider-making became an accessory occupation. As for the peasantry, they had their own smallholdings, manuring their fields with *vraic*, which also provided fuel for their living-room fires. In addition they fished, getting oil for their lamps from conger livers. To meet their humble needs they bartered their eggs and butter, there being little money apart from the small amount obtained from the sale of surplus corn in neighbouring Normandy.

During the 17th. century agriculture suffered considerable neglect, much labour being lost to the knitting trade (see Chapter Eight to follow). As a result, Guernsey was at times hardly able to support itself, and imported wheat from Sark, where the rich soil of the plateau yielded enough to meet the needs of the Serquiais and leave a surplus. A further blow to cereal cultivation came from cider becoming the staple drink of the islands, so that even more apple-orchards were added to those established in the previous century, each one enclosed by banks on which furze was grown for fuel. The local cider receives honourable mention in a pamphlet called *News from Sark*, written by a Londoner named F. Wearis, and published in 1671: 'And very well stored with fruit trees ... furnishing us with Syder not at all inferior to your Herefordshire Redstreak, and to render it the more wholesome 'tis general boyled with a little spice, which preserves it and gives it an incomparable Rellish'. In the occasional Guernsey farmstead one may yet come across a rather dilapidated 'Prinseux' (the building devoted to cider making) and therein the remains of a great wooden 'Emet' (Cider Press) while adjacent there stands a circular granite 'Tour' where the apples were crushed. Still to be found in this last year of the twentieth century (Anno Domini 2000) are a few islanders who, having survived into the very late evening of life, remember cider being thus produced in small quantities for family consumption: and during the inter-war period this pursuit was carried on to a much greater extent by the De La Salle Brothers at Les Vauxbelets — as is vividly recalled by the present writer who drank of it copiously and hence is nostalgically gratified to learn that Messrs. Michael Gallienne and James Meller of Les Fauxquets have started producing the beverage as a commercial venture, trading as the Guernsey Cider Company.

Guernsey's preoccupation with privateering and smuggling during the 18th. century brought farming to its nadir. Nevertheless, the century saw the invention (in Jersey) of La Grande Charrue for deep tilling. This enormous contrivance, hauled by 16 oxen and six horses, tended to be a communal implement, with neighbouring farmers pooling their resources and sharing in its use. The same century also saw the construction by the richer 'Chefs de Famille' of the solid granite farmhouses which still grace the Guernsey landscape.

Agricultural development on a much larger scale followed the end of the Napoleonic Wars. As previously, parsnips were a main crop, but wheat and potatoes were also becoming prominent. During the first half of the 19th. century the free entry of Guernsey produce into the United Kingdom enabled the farmers to profit from the exclusion of foreign grain ordained by the Corn Laws, so that a considerable export of wheat to England was a feature of these years. The repeal of the Corn Laws killed this trade, however, and thereafter wheat cultivation waned to such an extent that Guernsey has never again been self-supporting in grain. Later in the century, wheat cultivation also declined in Sark, whose farmers could not compete with the low-priced imports coming from North America. On the other hand, potato cultivation increased considerably, both to supply the needs of the distillers (who had developed a large export trade in potato spirit) and also to furnish exports of this vegetable to the English market — in competition with Jersey. In mid-century the onset of blight wrecked the potato trade, and by 1853 Guernsey was importing more than she exported. Although the cultivation of the crop subsequently recovered, it never regained a leading place, the fierce competition of Jersey finally killing the Guernsey potato as an export.

The inter-war years saw the potato (which was still an important crop for home consumption) threatened by the Colorado beetle — a threat which led the States to institute the spraying of crops. By now grass had become the main crop, taking up over half the cultivable area. About half of the grass was a rotation crop, permanent pasture being less common in the Bailiwick than in England. No special rotation is customary in Guernsey, however, with two crops a year often raised in the same field — early potatoes or broccoli being grown and cleared off the ground before the main root or grain crop. Grain cultivation, however, remained inconsiderable, so that in 1931, for example, only 933 vergées were under wheat, barley and oats combined.

In the years since the Second World War the mechanical

tractor with mounted implements has become a great boon to the Guernsey farmer, as the smallness of the fields presents special problems that are easily overcome by this handy machine. It can also be used on steep côtils which previously only saw the traditional Guernsey spade ('la Beque de Guernesi') with a wooden handle and a wooden heart-shaped blade tipped with iron. Tractors have been used extensively in Sark, too — where they also provide transport facilities. Indeed, since 1975, Harbour Hill has been provided with a 'bus' hauled by a tractor.

Despite its decline, the potato is still regarded as sufficiently important a crop for the States of Guernsey to have co-operated with the States of Jersey since the war in financing an anti-Colorado beetle campaign on the Cotentin Peninsula. The European Plant Protection Organisation eventually persuaded a reluctant France to shoulder part of the cost. It also set up a research institute to study the problems involved in collaboration with the Islands' own experts.

The forty years following the Second World War saw a dramatic resurgence of farming in Herm, thanks to the initiative and drive of Major 'Peter' Wood, who became the tenant in 1949. As a result the island supported nearly 100 head of cattle (at that time one of the largest herds in the Bailiwick), keeping it self-sufficient in milk even when summer tourists swelled its population to about 120. There was even a surplus for export to Guernsey — though in the winter this was used to fatten calves for veal. Potatoes, root crops, kale, wheat and barley were grown — and more than 1,000 rabbits per annum were trapped or shot for export to Guernsey. However, in the years 1989 and 1990 deficient rainfall with consequent silage shortage endangered the continuance of this agricultural profitability as it necessitated importing expensive fodder. To counter this threat 62 vergées were planted with New Zealand Brome Grass (capable of surviving in dry weather) to serve as cattle feed and a diversification project was launched, with more easily fed hens, sheep and pigs brought in to complement the dairy herd. Unfortunately this tactic proved unsuccessful, as did also the experiment of making the farm a tourist attraction, as too few visitors came forward to make it viable. Thus in the autumn of 1991 the supplementary animals were sent to Guernsey and Sark and the decision was taken to retain the dairy herd on an 'organic farming' basis, cutting out nitrate fertilizers and reducing herbicide spraying to a minimum. Sad to say, the summer of 1996 brought yet more trouble, with not only agriculture but also tourism and associated enterprises imperilled by a dire water shortage. The yield of the Belvoir Valley borehole fell from 10,000 to 2,000 gallons a day and it was additionally found that the island's water table had fallen by 40 feet. Drilling equipment was hastily imported with a view to sinking two new boreholes to a depth of 400 feet. Herm's entire economy was face to face with a major crisis, but this was mercifully averted thanks to the rapid success of the emergency drilling operations. This relief did not, however, alter the fact that a progressive decline in milk prices, coupled with the expense of complying with European Union hygiene requirements, rendered the maintenance of the dairy herd increasingly uneconomic, ultimately occasioning a piecemeal sale of the cows, the last batch of which was disposed of in October 1999, leaving a small number of beef cattle as the island's only surviving bovines — a sorry state of affairs.

Re the Open Field system at Pleinmont (page 326). When in Guernsey in October 2000 the present writer was appalled to find this site covered with piles of topsoil or of variegated refuse which obliterated the entire pattern of strips and intervening balks, leaving nothing to be seen of a unique agricultural relic — a deplorable occurrence, in the wake of which one can only cling to the faint hope that restoration may one day possibly be achieved.

Chapter Three

LIVESTOCK FARMING

EARLY IN THE REIGN OF GEORGE V a sustained attempt to trace the origins of the Guernsey Cow was made by the De La Salle Brothers operating the Agricultural College which then existed at Les Vauxbelets. Their investigations led them to conclude that in all probability the island owes its world-famous cattle to the monks of the Norman Period who seem to have introduced from France the Isigny breed of Normandy and the Froment du Léon strain of Brittany (where it is common around St. Pol du Léon), from the cross-fertilization of which they held that the 'Guernsey' developed. It has also been alleged — but not by the De La Salle Brothers — that during their occupancy of Herm from the late eleventh century onwards the Cherbourg Augustinians established cattle and sheep as livestock in that island as well. Mr. Nigel Jee, however, regards the Brothers' hypothesis with scepticism. While conceding the possibility that the eleventh and twelfth century monks may have brought their native kine with them, he is convinced that other cattle entering the island since then have added their contribution to local bovine evolution, thereby invalidating any theory postulating direct and uninterrupted descent from the monastic herds.

Whether introduced by the early monks or not, cattle cannot be said to have featured prominently in the island economy during the Middle Ages, only the odd cow being kept by a farmer as an adjunct to his subsistence farming — together with a few oxen as beasts of burden. Horses, too, were few, and the mainstay in livestock up to the end of the 16th. century consisted of sheep, which were let loose over winter pasture by right of common ('Banon') and provided meat, wool for clothing, and hides for footwear. Although discontinued from the First World War onwards, recent years have seen a modest revival of sheep farming in Guernsey — and even more so in Sark — but the experimental rearing of a hardy Shetland strain in Lihou Island proved unsuccessful and was abandoned.

No marked improvement in the breed of cattle was made until the 18th. century, when milk production rose and a small start was made in the export of beasts to Southampton — a development which eventuated in the earliest known written reference to island livestock in the form of a statement by Thomas Hale in a paper published in 1756 that, of all cattle in England 'the fine Kinds are the Dutch and Alderney Cows', to which he added 'but the Alderney Cow is preferable because it is hardier'. In similar vein, following the installation by George III ('Farmer George') over thirty years later of an island herd on his farm in Windsor Great Park, it became the practice in dairy farming contexts to sing the praises of the Alderney. It must, however, be borne in mind that for about a century and a half after the appearance of Hale's paper, usage in England indiscriminately designated as 'Alderney' cattle from any Channel Island; often with dishonest purpose, as was evidenced in 1810 by E.A.W. Martin's revelation in the *Manuscript History of Alderney* that 'about 1,500 Cows are Annually sent to England from Jersey and Guernsey under the name of Alderney Cows in order to enable the vendors to demand a greater price' — a tribute to the few which did come from that isle. It is also noteworthy that, innocent of any fraudulent intent, such confusion persisted as late as the inter-war years, with E.H. Shepherd's illustration accompanying A.A. Milne's poem suggesting that the animal whose drowsiness deprived the King of Butter for the Royal Slice of Bread must have come from Jersey! Deliberate falsity apart, the habit of naming Channel Island beasts generally as 'Alderney' largely arose from the fact that initially cattle circulated freely between the various parts of the archipelago, thereby acquiring many characteristics in common — and furthermore ships carrying island cattle for export frequently made Braye Harbour their last port of call *en route* for England, where they arrived 'from Alderney'. Subsequently, however, while selective breeding coupled with importation restrictions ultimately resulted in Jersey and Guernsey bovines becoming clearly differentiated, cross-breeding in Alderney between established indigenous bulls and cows imported from Guernsey eventually produced a distinctive animal which one learns from Mrs. Felicity Crump was remembered by the late Jurat T.X.H. Pantcheff as 'much paler than the Guernseys, somewhat smaller and with a different shaped head', while Mrs. Iris Godfray, writing in 1997, recalled a type with 'shorter fore-legs than the Guernsey cow and black markings on the head and a rounder body'. This species became a war casualty after the fall of France, when the evacuation of all livestock from the island brought the obliteration of the strain — if, indeed, it had survived that long, Messrs. Roger Venne and Geoffrey Allez averring in their *Alderney Annals* that 'the last calf of pure Alderney blood was born in 1927'.

During the second decade of the 19th. century the first of a series of rigorous enactments was made to preserve the purity of the local breed (1819). By these enactments a total prohibition was imposed on the importation of live cattle except for slaughter — hence the abattoir at the harbour. Not even the return to the island of Guernsey cows exhibited at English shows has been permitted. The result has been a unique animal completely free from tuberculosis, yielding a high-quality yellow-tinted milk, very rich in cream — and hence giving a golden-coloured butter. The quantity of the yield, however, has not proved to be exceptional, rarely exceeding 1,000 gallons per annum.

The growing importance of cattle farming at the end of the 18th. century stimulated the introduction of the Guernsey milk-can, which was first made in 1796 by J. Noel in his premises in Market Street. It was designed to give maximum capacity with the minimum use of metal, with the high neck stopping the milk from slopping over, and the tight lid keeping out the dust. Originally there were 15 sizes, the largest holding 40 pints, though nowadays none are made with a capacity exceeding 24 pints.

During the 19th. century the improvements in the breed were maintained largely thanks to the encouragement given by the first Agricultural Society founded in 1817 and the subsequent cattle fairs which it arranged. In 1811 Lord Braybrook imported the first entire Guernsey herd into England, while the first Guernseys entered the U.S.A. during the 1830s. Thereafter the cattle export trade thrived, averaging 600 animals annually, and rising to 1,044 head in 1913. In 1842 the pioneer society of 1817 was replaced by the Royal Guernsey Agricultural and Horticultural Society, founded to advise farmers in various branches of agriculture, particularly cattle breeding. Thus the Herd Book was instituted in 1881, with details of the best cattle, their ancestry, progeny, milk yield and butter fat. The custom also developed of tethering the cattle to economise on food supply and to make the fullest use of pasture, which was restricted by the small size of the fields and the wastage of land due to thick fossés and hedges.

In the early years of this century the reliability and regularity of communications encouraged farmers to depend more and more on imported foodstuffs for winter feeding — so that by 1938 over 3,500 tons of bran and cattle foods were being imported annually.

Despite the strong overseas demand for Guernseys during the inter-war years (when an average of 700 were shipped each year) the period saw a decline in the herd, which numbered only 4,864 in 1934. An enquiry commission discovered that the returns obtainable were no longer attractive enough to induce farmers to keep sufficient cattle to supply the island's milk needs. Several factors were invoked to explain the phenomenon, such as the fall in price obtainable for exported animals, the exodus of young farmers, the dearth of grassland, the increased cost of cattle food, and competition from imported butter and preserved milk. The root of the trouble, however, was the expansion of the 'growing' industry. Forsaking a mixture of farming and 'growing', many farmers sold off their cattle and specialized in tomato cultivation, instead of having one or two greenhouses as a sideline.

The German occupation having caused the annihilation of the Alderney herd and the decimation of that of Guernsey, strenuous efforts were needed to achieve recovery after the Liberation. At first progress was most promising. Guernsey cattle were sent to Alderney to rebuild that island's herd, and the advance was such that in 1947 the export overseas of Guernseys numbered eight hundred and thirty-five. By the 1960s, however, despite the facilities provided by the States Dairy as a useful marketing centre of milk, butter and cream, the herd had decreased, and exports became negligible. Pasture lost to building land is a major part of the trouble and has led to a situation where the import of milk has become a regular feature, while Guernsey butter has become a rarity.

An important recent trend has been the widespread use during the last 20 years or so of artificial insemination with semen specially tested by the States Dairy whereby the incidence of venereal disease has been virtually eliminated; while a revolutionary development has been the introduction of cross-breeding with the Charolais with a view to enhancing beef production.

This Charolais experiment marks Guernsey's first attempt to tackle beef production seriously, in place of a casual reliance on a few steers and the odd heifer that will not hold to service. Following an approach to the States Committee for Agriculture by the Guernsey Farmers' Association, the States approved the scheme in May 1971 in the hope that it would provide a second string for the island's cattle farming industry. As a result of this decision British Semen Exports Limited on September 25th., 1971 sent to Guernsey 100 doses of Charolais semen, collected from three 5½-year-old bulls, Clovis, Cypres and Chicago, all of which were top sires in the first team of Charolais bulls drawn from leading French herds to be progeny-tested in the United Kingdom under environmental and management conditions identical to those in France. The first cow was inseminated on September 28th., 1972, and the first live Charolais calf was born on July 14th., 1973. Within two years the herd was 40 in number, but the experiment was then rendered problematical by a fall in beef prices — on which the ultimate fate of the project obviously depends.

The Charolais-Guernsey cross beef was first tasted at the Guernsey Farmers' Association Dinner on February 6th., 1975. Speeches made at this function indicated the problems confronting the island's agriculture and referred specifically to the need to establish a balance between justice to the farmers and a fair price to the consumer in the context of continually rising prices for fodder and fertilizer; to the inadequate returns obtainable from milk production which has led to the economically questionable step of importing it, the experience of which underlined the need to increase yields so as to eliminate further imports; to the depletion of the farming community stemming from the growth in the size of farms resulting from amalgamations — a process which had reduced the number of individual holdings by two-thirds besides placing farming beyond the financial reach of many young people. As for the Charolais experiment, while its profitability and desirability were still unproven, the enterprise nevertheless demonstrated the willingness of the Guernsey farmer to accept new ideas — and it was to be hoped that this spirit of adaptability would eventually usher in better days.

A further adjunct to the livestock industry was developed in 1978, with Guernsey cheese being marketed for the first time. Initial results were encouraging, the demand of the housewife proving to be brisk.

Chapter Four

HORTICULTURE

AT THE TIME WHEN THE FIRST EDITION of this History was in preparation (late 1970s) the most casual glance out of the aircraft window by a holiday-maker coming to Guernsey for the first time would have sufficed to emphasise the pre-eminent place in the island's economy then occupied by horticulture; as even this would have been enough to reveal the multitude of greenhouses liberally distributed in all directions. The 'father' of this enterprise (which, alas, thrives no longer) was Peter Mourant, who in 1793 built in Candie Gardens a glasshouse (which still survives) to grow grapes and pineapples. The idea of the commercial exploitation of glasshouse products did not develop, however, until the years after Waterloo, when a start was made with the dispatch to England of choice specimens of the famous Guernsey lily.

Grapes rapidly became the main produce exported, and by 1841 many vineries (as such glasshouses were — and still are — called) were in operation, growing the Black Hamburg (which was especially successful in cold houses), the Muscat, and the Alicante — all table grapes. The advent of a regular steamer service stimulated the export of many hundreds of tons of grapes to the London market, as well as other delicate fruits which were grown as side-lines, such as melons (first raised under glass in 1803), peaches and figs.

In the 1860s the first 'love-apples' — so called because they were believed to have aphrodisiac properties — were grown. The seeds coming from America were cultivated in conservatories by a few farmers and horticulturists as a not particularly successful experiment, the fruit frequently remaining unsold (maybe, considering the alleged properties, being regarded as disreputable). By the 1870s, however, demand had increased, and more growers tried tomatoes as a 'catch crop' down the middle of the vinery, beneath the grapes and peaches.

In 1874 an export company was formed to foster the export of grapes, early potatoes, French beans, and the first experimental tomatoes. By 1889 several such companies were in existence. Furthermore, the decline in the shipbuilding industry had concurrently led to several ships' carpenters turning to building vineries. The modern glasshouse industry was born.

In 1884 J. Poat became the first person to grow tomatoes as a main crop. Others soon copied him, investing in glasshouses solely for tomatoes. Many of these were men of small means who used their savings to buy a plot of cheap land, then bought their own wood and glass, and by sheer hard work built up a small but thriving business.

Alongside the tomato industry grew up the flower and bulb business — which was also helped by the regular steamship service. Already in the 1850s Charles Smith had converted the old Andros estate of Normanville into the famous Caledonian Nursery. He started the flower export trade on a significant scale (as distinct from the few consignments of Guernsey lilies earlier in the century) in 1863 and 1864, sending camellias, daffodils and narcissi to Covent Garden. Others copied him — some sending their blooms in radish hampers in the hope of thereby evading customs duty — and the growth of the trade was such that in 1904 the value of flower exports was £40,000, and of bulb exports (mostly to Holland and the U.S.A.) £20,000.

The first half of the 20th. century saw 'growing' increase to the point where four men were engaged in it for every one in arable and pastoral farming combined. Already in 1894 the Guernsey Growers' Association had been founded to give advice to members and to arrange lectures for instruction and debate. The growth of the industry led to this being supplemented in the inter-war years by the Guernsey Growers' Mutual Improvement Association, instituted to grapple more closely with actual cultivation problems.

During the inter-war years tomatoes became the island's main economic activity, so that, by 1939, 2,240 vergées were under glasshouses of span construction, measuring 150ft. by 30ft., with frames of strong wood which were repainted white and puttied annually. A useful index of the progress of hothouse culture up to the Second World War is provided by the figures for anthracite imports, as follows:

Year	1913	1923	1932	1938
Tons imported	57,260	68,421	104,166	138,130

The ever-rising yields were encouraged by the use of artificial fertilizers which replaced stable manure, while soil steaming became the chief form of sterilisation, with steaming taking place one or two months before planting because of the steamed soil's need for a thorough soaking.

The 'tomato boom', with its ancillary flower and bulb industry, not only promoted an incessant search for plots leading to undesirable 'ribbon development' linking the ancient nucleated villages, but also attracted labour to the attendant carting, packing and box-making trades. Ships from the Baltic brought timber for greenhouse construction and also for the box factories, of which there were no less than eight producing baskets (or 'chips') taking 12 pounds of tomatoes each. An annual export of 30,000 tons needed more than 5½ million chips. The growth of the tomato export trade up to the Second World War was such that the quantity shipped in the last year of peace was nearly threefold that of the year preceding the First World War:

Year	1913	1928	1937	1939
Tons exported	13,517	25,069	31,639	35,038

This phenomenal rise of the tomato was accompanied by the decline of the grape, of which only 688 tons were exported in 1938 as against 1,737 tons in 1921. The fall in the fortunes of this fruit stemmed from adverse competition with grapes imported into England from foreign countries, plus the fact that the cultivation of grapes made greater demands on labour and skill than did that of the tomato. Labour made redundant by this decline found employment in the box factories — which also provided work for labour no longer required by the shrinking quarrying industry.

The inter-war years also saw the production by intensive horticulture of about 4,000 tons of flowers each year. Outdoor and glasshouse daffodils and narcissi were grown in January and February, followed by hothouse iris and tulips in March, and the same blooms grown in cold houses in April. May and June saw the cultivation of both indoor and outdoor gladioli, while the autumn was devoted to the chrysanthemum, which was grown outdoors in October and indoors in November and December. In addition about 400 tons of bulbs were exported annually despite the closure of the U.S.A. and Dutch markets during these years.

The large area under glass in Guernsey presented a special

problem of water supply. Some growers were able to provide water in their houses by the use of wind-driven pumps, which were a common feature of the inter-war Guernsey landscape. It was impossible for all requirements to be met in this way, and as domestic consumption was also increasing, the decision was taken in 1937 to construct the St. Saviour's reservoir with a capacity of 240 million gallons. The work (interrupted by the German occupation) was completed in 1946. As many growers who had previously obtained their own supplies neglected to replace their war-damaged plant after the Liberation, but instead drew on the reservoir, it has not fulfilled all the hopes originally placed in it, and water-shortage is an oft-recurring problem.

Although air raids, the concussion of A.A. gunfire, and unavoidable neglect reduced Guernsey's glasshouse area by some 300 vergées during the Occupation, the industry picked up again quickly after the war, its efficiency increased thanks to the help of the Experimental Station and the Advisory Service. Thus, although the decline in grapes continued, flower exports rose to two million boxes by the early 1960s, while by the end of the decade 5,000 tons of flowers, to the value of £3,350,000, were being exported annually. More recent years have seen remarkable developments in forced rose cultivation which, giving blooms throughout the year, enables Guernsey to supply the United Kingdom with 60 per cent. of its demand for this flower. Another development (of benefit both to island horticulture and to the Guernsey Post Office) has involved the dispatch of flowers by post in response to individual orders — where the 70,000 boxes sent when this venture started in 1982 had risen to 350,000 (a fivefold increase) by 1986, thereby demonstrating the success of an enterprise which has remained lucrative to this day.

Such achievements were, however, eclipsed by the remarkable post-war recovery staged in the case of the tomato, of which seven million 12-pound chips were already being exported annually by 1947. To deal with the controls imposed by the British Ministry of Food during this recovery period, the Tomato Marketing Board was established, and, as it seemed to work well, was set up on a permanent basis with statutory powers in 1951. It operated until the end of 1986, after which its functions were assumed by the Growers' Co-operative mentioned at the end of this chapter.

In 1961 a big step was taken in the rationalisation of the industry. Experiments having been carried out on the handling and bulk cartage of tomatoes, it was decided to replace the picturesque chips by shallow 12-pound trays which could fit on each other. These trays could be wired together in threes and then blocks of them could be stacked on a large flat tray to eliminate individual handling and help mechanical loading. This method, known as palletization, necessitated the building of the Tomato Board's Central Depot at Bulwer Avenue in St. Sampson's, to which the carters could bring the trays from the greenhouses, to be inspected, wired, covered with paper wrapping, and placed on pallets before being taken by lorry to St. Peter-Port harbour or La Villiaze airport.

Furthermore, there was also a marked improvement in the glasshouses themselves, modern metal-frame ones progressively replacing those of the traditional type, thereby enabling the latest technological, scientific and hygienic methods to be practised, incorporating thermostatic ventilation control, together with devices whereby the plants are automatically watered when thirsty and fed when hungry. A complementary development was the growing of the plants in peat modules instead of straight from the soil, which enabled a high standard of hygiene to be attained, with the modules discarded at the end of each season and replaced by new ones for the fresh planting. These advances between them made it possible to cultivate tomato plants which, thanks to a special method of training them, grow to a length of 30ft. and bear 28 to 30 trusses each, resulting in an increase of 43 per cent. in yield per glasshouse as compared with 1965. Thanks to these up-to-date methods the annual volume of tomatoes exported in the early 1980s averaged some 50,000 tons (obtained from a smaller area than that which produced 35,000 tons in 1939), with a market value of over £10,000,000. The total value of all horticultural exports combined was £35,200,000 in 1978.

In the early 1980s diversification in Guernsey horticulture was evidenced by experiments with peppers and aubergines, followed (with but transient success) by kiwi-fruit. These ventures were a by-product of the reduced profitability of tomato cultivation brought about by European Community regulations exposing Guernsey to competition from the Netherlands (where glasshouse heating costs receive a Government subsidy) and the Iberian Peninsula (where the climate renders such costs non-existent). As a consequence, growing this fruit, which in the 1950s accounted for 75% of the island's income and employment, only accounted for 10% thereof in 1987; the area devoted to the crop shrank from 2,000 vergées in the mid-1970s to 250 vergées in 1987; the computerized tomato nursery at Les Nicolles in Saint Sampson's, which had produced 200,000 trays of the fruit annually, closed in 1989 — and by 1993 only twenty growers still went in for tomato cultivation. Efforts to sustain the fruit's flagging fortunes led to the production of 'Tomato Wine', marketed under the trade name of 'Aztecato' — but with poor results. A more lucrative use for vineries was found with the launching in 1984 of 'Project Papillon', suggested by Mr. David Lowe and sponsored by the States' Labour and Welfare Department, which involved the breeding of butterflies in greenhouses in anticipation of demand from Parks, Stately Homes and National Trust properties in the United Kingdom. Originally breeding 20,000 of the five more common species (red admiral, painted lady, speckled wood, well brown and small tortoise-shell) the project at its outset aimed at the ultimate pupation of a greater variety of species totalling over 100,000 lepidoptera and selling for between 25 pence and 50 pence each after the first experimental year. This venture rapidly justified itself — so much so that after being confronted in 1987 with a level of demand such that over 3,000 requests for pupae could not be met, Carol Blackwell, as supervisor of the project, arranged for extra space to be made available for breeding in 1988 so as to ensure that all orders placed would be executed without fail. Yet another initiative came in 1987 with the cultivation of babacos, a fruit not previously grown in Guernsey, sales of which were started early that year by a group of growers trading as Channel Islands Exotics. Despite such individual successes, however, the standing of horticulture as a whole progressively waned throughout the 1980s, Conseiller Paul de Garis announcing early in 1993 that whereas ten years previously it had constituted 36% of the island's economic activity, by the time he spoke it only accounted for 5% thereof. Nevertheless it still yielded 6% of Guernsey's Gross Domestic Product and provided 10% of the employment available. For the year 1996 its 'impact on the island's economy' was assessed at £53.3 million.

Before leaving the subject of horticulture a few words need to be said on a topic which, although it caused a fair stir for a while, does not as yet appear to have come to anything of significance. In 1976, because of a feeling in some quarters that the Guernsey Growers' Association was too aloof an organisation to be of much help to rank-and-file practitioners, the formation of a Guernsey Growers' Union was recommended by the States' Horticultural Investigation Committee. Such a union was, in fact, eventually formed in 1977, but as a truly effective force proved to have been stillborn as a result of a refusal of the States to confirm its earlier provisional decision to authorise a levy on imported horticultural containers as a means of providing finance for the new body. As time went by the Guernsey Grower's Union showed no signs of rising like the Phoenix from the ashes of its early hopes — but early in 1987 fresh evidence of joint action by growers became manifest with the emergence of the Guernsey Grower's Co-operative, which replaced the defunct Tomato Marketing Board (abolished at the end of 1986) as the selling agency for island horticultural produce.

Chapter Five

VRAIC

SO CRUCIAL HAS IT BEEN to the insular economy throughout the ages that the local kelp deserves a chapter to itself — albeit a short one.

An invaluable 'harvest of the sea', *vraic* (French 'varech') is of two kinds. The first of these is *vraic venant* (or drift-weed), while the second category is *vraic scié*, which is attached to the rocks and cut off by billhooks or sickles — and considered to be worth two or three times as much as *vraic venant*. From time immemorial each variety, when spread over or ploughed deeply into the soil, has been a source of considerable fertility. Up to the time of the First World War it was also dried and used as fuel, giving a dull-red smouldering fire and leaving an ash which provided yet another good fertilizer, being rich in potash. In addition, it was sometimes used as stuffing for *lits d'fouaile*.

Its well-nigh indispensable contribution to agriculture has meant that *vraic* gathering has traditionally been regarded as a common right and never subject to feudal dues, though the exercise of the right has always been controlled by ordinances of the Court of Chief Pleas — and latterly of the States.

In olden times the first cutting of *vraic scié* began at the first full (or new, if this came earlier) moon after Candlemas (La Chandleur) and lasted until mid-March. Many ordinances limited this cutting to the manuring of the soil. The second cutting lasted from midsummer (La Saint Jean) until the end of August, but during the first moon the right was restricted to Les Pauvres. *Vraic venant* could be gathered all the year between sunrise and sunset, the period between sunset and sunrise being reserved for Les Pauvres. No *vraic*-gathering of any description was permitted on Sundays, and the use of boats, though not specifically forbidden, was frowned upon as making excessive inroads into a valuable crop which natural growth might not make good. The cuttings of *vraic scié* during the summer were often festive occasions, featuring youths and maidens, with garlands of flowers in their hair, wielding great rakes with heads two to three feet long, teeth of 14 ins. and sapling handles 12 to 18 ft. in length. Once the precious *vraic* had been gathered the youths and maidens bathed, while their elders prepared a feast including many varieties of *gâche*. Dancing followed for the rest of the evening.

When, in answer to the islanders' grievances, James I in 1607 sent over his Commissioners (see Part III, Chapter Six), they were particularly petitioned to perpetuate the ancient right of gathering *vraic*, being put in mind of the proverb — 'Point de vraic, point de hautgard' ('No *vraic*, no cornyard').

Although poaching by 'foreigners' was rare, a case did occur in 1830 when *vraic* was cut, loaded and carried away from the Bailiwick from the rocks off Herm (most likely to Jersey). This prompted an emergency ordinance instructing the constables to apprehend such criminals, coupled with a threat that not only would the Court confiscate the boats of such malefactors, but would also fine heavily each and every member of the crew.

H. D. Inglis in his book, *The Channel Islands*, published in 1834 (see Chapter Thirteen following) has this to say about *vraic*-gathering in Alderney in his day:

> The evening before that appointed for the vraic-gathering, the church-bells ring at six o'clock, which is the signal for all who are interested in vraic-gathering, i.e., all the inhabitants of the island who are owners of land, to assemble in the churchyard, and there the important point is discussed, whether all are ready to commence the next morning. Any sufficient cause that may prevent any one individual from joining in the vraic-gathering would be held a sufficient reason for postponing the day, because the liberty of gathering vraic is too valuable a privilege not to be equally enjoyed. If no one demurs, the day is considered to be fixed, and all retire, to prepare, by an early retirement to rest, for the labours of the next morning. It chanced to be vraic-gathering when I visited Alderney, and at high water, in the morning, the great bay fronting the south was lined with a dense semi-circle of eager islanders waiting the moment when the retreating tide should leave the rich prize within their reach.

The 1945 Liberation postal stamps showed a typical *vraicing* scene of the early 20th. century, with a horse-drawn *vraicing*-cart standing on the beach to which it had gained access by one of the granite slipways which are so characteristic a feature of the islands' coastlines. Such a nostalgic representation does not give a true picture of modern *vraic*-cutting, which has become a commercial enterprise, carried on mechanically with lorries in place of the traditional ox- or horse-drawn box carts — and permitted from July 15th. to the following April 15th. for *vraic scié*, with no restriction on *vraic venant*. During 1985 publicity was given to a technique evolved by Mr. Thomas le Prevost of Melrose, Castel, whereby *vraic venant* is picked up by tractor loaders and then tipped into side-flinger manure distributors which subsequently spread it over the fields. By these means as much as one hundred tons of vraic may be moved and strewn over farmland by two or three men in the course of a single day.

Chapter Six

FISHING

AS ONE WOULD EXPECT of islands on the Continental Shelf, fishing from the earliest times has been prominent among local occupations, so that, apart from agriculture, it is the oldest industry in the Bailiwick, and by the Middle Ages had become a mainstay of its livelihood: witness the excavation at Grandes Rocques in 1986 of the remains of an early 12th. century fishing village (with evidence also in situ of settlement much antecedent to this — going as far back indeed as 4,000 B.C.). Furthermore, by the beginning of the 13th. century its importance was such that King John, after his loss of Continental Normandy in 1204, included as a prominent feature of his measures to check links between the islands and the Norman mainland a prohibition on the export of catches thereto. That this calling (which was often carried on as an ancillary to their farming by the villeins) continued to be lucrative throughout the 13th. century is evidenced by the insistence of the kings on their Eperquirie rights and by the demand of Edward I in 1288 (already considered in Part II, Chapter Six) insisting on a cash payment in respect of catches other than those of conger.

From the 13th. to the 16th. century conger-eel, dried and smoked, was a valuable export to ports around the French coast as well as to England. The places where the fish were salted were known as 'saleries', the establishment of which was a feudal perquisite, controlled by the seigneurs. La Salerie in St. Peter-Port was foremost among these sites. During the Hundred Years War those participating in the conger-eel traffic often found themselves in difficulties, being subject to the accusation of trading with the king's enemies.

The profitability of Guernsey fishing received its first serious setback in the 16th. century when the decline in both the French and the English demand for salted conger and mackerel so threatened the islanders' means of livelihood as to drive those with more resources to branch out into overseas trade, while the more humble took to knitting woollen garments — as will be seen in a subsequent chapter.

In 1534/5 Guillaume de Guernezé sailed to the St. Lawrence with Jacques Cartier, and from the end of the same century onwards Jersey figured prominently in the Newfoundland cod fisheries, sending many ships across the Atlantic annually. The Bailiwick of Guernsey was also involved in this enterprise as many of the younger sons of Sark families took part in the trade in the first half of the 17th. century, their activities figuring prominently in the notebook of the minister, Elie Brévint. By the following century Guernseymen also participated in this venture, their involvement being instrumental in bringing Methodism to the island (see Part I, Chapter Twelve). Prominent among these was Elisha Tupper (1720–1802), the grandfather of the famous historian Ferdinand Brock Tupper, who played so extensive a part in these ventures as to evoke such admiration in the sister-island that a Jersey-built ship launched in 1789 was named *Tupper* in his honour. The trade, which lasted until the latter part of the 19th. century, was a three-way one. The boats were fitted out in the islands and sailed for the Newfoundland Banks, after which, the fishing completed and the catches sold to Roman Catholic countries for fast days, they headed for home with various cargoes which were either sold on the way or brought back to the islands.

Another fishing activity inspired by Jersey successes was in the case of oysters, where the prosperity accruing to Jersey from her exploiting the oyster beds north of Chausey from 1797 onwards encouraged the establishment in 1820 of a small oyster fishery in Guernsey, which lasted for a number of years. After a lapse of over a century, three years of experimentation by Mr. David Fletcher were crowned with success in 1984 when this enterprise was revived with the establishment at Grande Havre of beds yielding 90,000 molluscs in different stages of growth. Following this lead, two other concerns (Guernsey Sea Farms and Rocquaine Shellfish Ponds) also embarked on oyster farming, including the operation of onshore hatcheries.

Until 1978, when sea fisheries showed such a remarkable increase in the volume and value of all types of fish and shellfish caught that exports totalled £1,156,000, a serious decline had been feared in the economic significance of the fishing trade. This was ascribed to a shrinkage in plankton supplies caused by the main planktonic zone being moved north by a shift in climatic conditions, which reduced the availability of this staple food and hence of the fish population in the Bailiwick's waters. Fishing persisted, however, thanks to the good size of the local lobsters, as well as the crawfish and prawns, so that the trade is economically viable — though the original capital needed to set up in business under modern conditions is of substantial proportions. Unfortunately, however, the picturesque old-time pots made of willow are giving way to ugly contraptions made of wire netting. Also important is the fishing for the common crab, 'Cancer pagurus', which is carried to Guernsey waters in its free-swimming stage. In the winter the crabs migrate to deeper waters off the north-west coast of Guernsey, but they return in spring to the shallow seas around the island. Because of the great size to which they grow, these 'chancres' are prized as food, though the 'spider', 'Maia squinado', is considered a greater delicacy.

During the 1980s two areas in particular developed as vital fishing grounds for crab potters — one off Les Hanois and a more extensive one in mid-Channel north-west of Alderney. The exploitation of these areas came to be in jeopardy as a result of their 'invasion' by Belgian and United Kingdom trawlers, the fishing activities of which caused havoc by ripping through strings of pots with resultant losses so extensive as to imperil the survival of Guernsey's shellfish exports industry. In an effort to avert any such collapse a 'Gentlemen's Agreement' was negotiated in February 1984 in relation to the mid-Channel zone, where the Guernsey potters, whose backs, it was said, 'were up against the Hurd Deep — and there's no fish there', were allocated a somewhat more restricted area than that previously used in which to lay their gear, with the trawlers being permitted to fish through 'corridors' between the pots.

Far more dramatic incidents attended a dispute which arose nine years later, occasioned by French trawlermen infringing the Bailiwick's exclusion zone established in 1964 and 'poaching' the Alderney approaches to an extent exceeding the limited access thereto granted them in 1965 and 1992. An increasingly acrimonious confrontation (which initially involved first two Fisheries Committee officials and secondly three officers from *H.M.S. Brocklesbury* being 'shanghai-ed' and taken to the Cotentin) attracted world-wide attention when in late March thirty-nine French craft descended on the Town Harbour and over-awed their Guernsey counterparts into accepting an informal but distinctly pro-French 'agreement between fishermen'. This, however, was promptly repudiated both by the States and also by the British Government — and on April 2nd. the skipper of the French traveller *Calypso* was fined £3,750 for illegal fishing after arrest by *H.M.S. Jersey*. By way of reprisal the French naval vessel *Coriandre* in July 1993 confiscated a Guernsey fisherman's gear off Les Roches Douvres, normal Guernsey access to this area notwithstanding — but retaliation came in October when the skipper of the French craft *Melusine* was fined £10,000 for trespass in Bailiwick waters. Protests lodged with the French Government by the Bailiff's Office in February 1994 over the forcible exclusion of island boats from Cherbourg were followed in April by the same office submitting to the French Government claims for £45,000 compensation for losses arising from the dispute incurred by island fishermen.

A seemingly genuine misunderstanding led to a further confrontation late in June 1994 when, assured by their Government of their right to be there under 'L'Accord de la Baie de Granville' of 1839, several Granville trawlers (under naval protection) entered the scallop-rich 'Sark Box' north-east of Les Roches Douvres. H.M.S. *Guernsey* and the Sea Fisheries vessel *Access Challenger* made for the area, where the unfounded belief of the French skippers that a 'temporary relaxation of limits' had been negotiated earlier in the year possibly accounted for the 'aggressive posture' which the Secretary of the Fisheries Committee said had been adopted when he approached one of the boats to deliver a warning notice: and the experience convinced the Sea Fisheries President — Conseiller Ron le Moignan — that only by personal contacts between opposing officials could the discord be terminated.

The need for such a parley (possibly with both Bailiwicks involved) was emphasised in mid-July when, in protest against Jersey's announced intention of extending its territorial waters, the islets of Les Ecréhous were 'invaded' by demonstrators holding aloft the Banner of Normandy. In fact, however, while this was happening negotiations were already in progress and by an interim agreement — in essence a truce — concluded in August 1994 and valid for a twelvemonth as from September 12th. French vessels were permitted to fish Guernsey's six to twelve mile belt between the Guernsey/Jersey median line and the Etac de Sercq line (i.e. the 'Sark Box'), while Guernseymen were re-admitted to the six to twelve mile belt off Les Roches Douvres and to the Cap de la Hague approaches. As time went by, however, it became increasingly clear that this modus vivendi — although renewed in 1995 — was being honoured more in the breach than in the observance. Within hours of the compact's conclusion the Alderney boat *Royal Escape*, under menace of being set ablaze, was forced to abandon attempts to enter Cherbourg — and heavy fines imposed by the Royal Court on a sequence of French 'trespassers' not only failed to deter repeated illegal penetration into Bailiwick waters, but also provoked retaliatory intimidatory threats against Guernsey craft fishing around Les Roches Douvres. Indeed, one of the 'poachers' involved — M. Jean Pierre Leverrier — unrealistically complained to the European Commission, with the equally irrational declared intention (the Bailiwick's judicial autonomy notwithstanding) of taking subsequent action against Guernsey in the Queen's Bench Division in London, alleging unlawful Police detention and an illegal trial before the Magistrate's Court. His impressively apparelled French advocate, however, suffered the indignity of being refused admission to the Royal Court. Further 'talks between fishermen' in April 1996 having achieved nothing, the Sea Fisheries Committee envisaged the possibility of Guernsey's 258-strong fleet seeking sales beyond France (where 92% of its catch had normally been landed each year) and at the same time moving away from traditional fishing grounds to others further afield and nearer potential new markets.

In the wake of seemingly abortive discussions held in September 1996 between British and French Government officials, Guernsey's Sea Fisheries Committee and fishermen's representatives, Guernsey the following October 11th. gave notice that it would unilaterally terminate the 1994 accord with effect from the coming December 1st. As a consequence the position reverted to that which had obtained in 1992, giving the French limited access to the twelve-mile belt south, west and north of Guernsey, but excluding them from the seas east of the Bailiwick up to the Franco-British median line (part of which is the 'Haricot' area, rich in bream, sole, crab and lobster) and also from the Sark Box — the very arrangement the French infraction of which had originated the prolonged confrontation. Claiming that they were entitled by historical right to fish both in the 'Haricot' and in the Sark Box and in addition seeking an agreement on 'joint management' of all other seas around Guernsey; the French retaliated to Guernsey's action by debarring island craft from Les Roches Douvres and the waters off Cap de la Hague and threatened to defy their exclusion from the Sark Box and the 'Haricot' by sheer weight of numbers. In implementation of this threat French trawlers, with naval support, 'invaded' the Sark Box on December 2nd., behaving in an

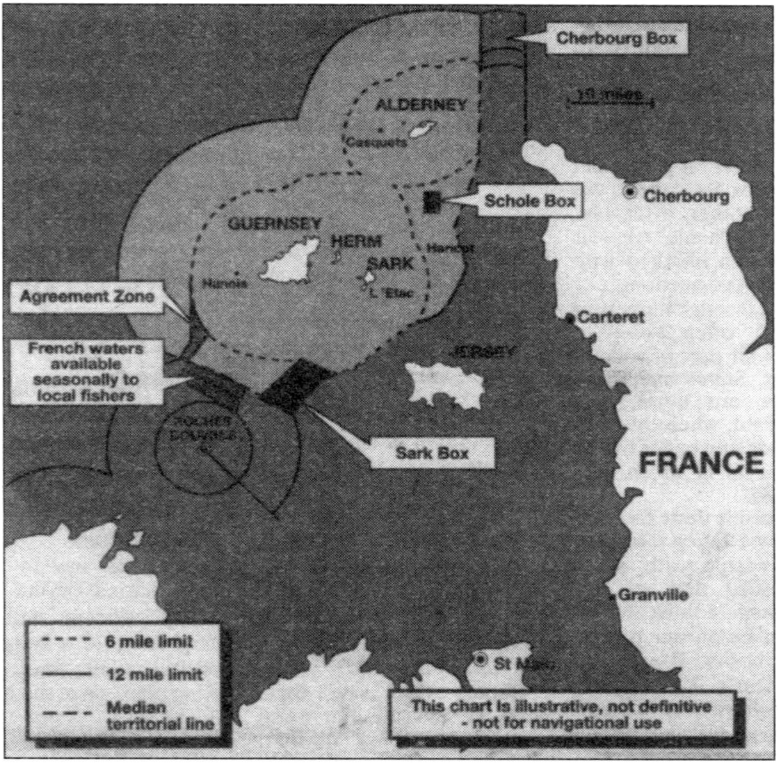

aggressive and provocative fashion and endangering the Sea Fisheries Inspection craft *Access Challenger* by closing in on it in contravention of the international code of conduct designed to prevent collisions. Moreover, these offences were compounded by the 'poachers' resisting attempts to inspect their catches and gear so as to ensure compliance with conservation regulations. Although the States had for over a decade shouldered the heavy upkeep costs of Alderney's breakwater as the Bailiwick's contribution to defence expenditure solicited by the Thatcher Administration in 1984 (see Part III, Chapter Eight) no effective defence against these bellicose intrusions was provided by the Royal Navy in December 1996 — and while an ensuing Parliamentary debate on Fisheries saw several Opposition Members (possibly spurred on by Guernsey demonstrators protesting outside the House) voicing marked disquiet over the course of events; the sole ministerial pronouncement merely deplored what was described as a widespread misrepresentation of the joint efforts to resolve the situation being made by the British and French Governments in consultation with Guernsey spokesmen.

Developments in this sorry business were obscured by a 'news blackout' from December 1996 to February 1998 when it emerged that the French had every intention of continuing to fish the Sark Box, claiming the right to do so by asserting it to be 'part of the Bay of Granville' and hence, in their view, open to them — and it furthermore transpired that representatives of the Norman fishermen, supported by the French Government Sea Fisheries Department, had asked both L'Assemblé Nationale and Le Sénat to arrange the renegotiation of the 1992 fishing agreement on the grounds that its terms were being interpreted differently by the opposing parties concerned. In addition, it was announced that Norman fishermen (plainly in contempt of the centuries-old autonomy of Guernsey's legal system which one of their leaders — Daniel Lefevre — derisively dismissed as 'mediaeval') had complained to the European Commission that the United Kingdom was breaking European Law by 'delegating its powers' to island courts, thereby enabling them to judge cases involving alleged offences in British waters. In this connection the French European Affairs Minister was reported as wishing to contact the United Kingdom Government for talks seeking the application of United Kingdom Law in Guernsey's seas and the grant to French lawyers of the right to plead in Guernsey's Courts. It was at this juncture that a Guernsey fisherman who feared that the entire Guernsey fishing industry was being driven into decline and who himself had been forced out of business by gear losses totalling £17,000 since December 1997 resulting from bellicose French behaviour complained that the Sea Fisheries Committee worked on a 'Monday to Friday 9 a.m. to 5 p.m.' basis, only taking action after the report of trouble; and that, while the French in the Sark Box were supported by their Government, their Navy, the European Union and financial subsidies, the protection afforded to Guernsey fishermen by the Royal Navy was woefully inadequate — possibly because of the Blair Administration's reluctance to become embroiled in any confrontation with a 'European Partner'. The month after that — March 1998 — Gallic intransigence was productive of yet further tension when the French naval authorities advised the master of the Granville trawler *Le Coelacanthe*, which had been arrested off Les Hanois suspected of fishing with illegal nets, to refuse to go to any port outside the European Union — though the skipper did eventually consent (under protest) to be escorted by H.M.S. *Lindisfarne* into Saint Peter-Port where he was later fined £1,500; a sanction which proved insufficiently severe to deter still another intrusion the following August when Cherbourg trawler *La Confiance* was detained off the west coast and conducted into the Town Harbour by the Sea Fisheries Patrol Boat *Leopardess*, assisted by H.M.S. *Bicester*. Shortly afterwards, eleven other French vessels sailed into the harbour to demonstrate their support for the detainee, while the French Sea Fisheries Minister lodged an official protest with the British Government.

This inconclusive and unsatisfactory state of affairs persisted — and cause for yet further disquiet arose the next year when in March 1999 there came the news that a draft agreement concluded between the United Kingdom, France and Jersey (but with Guernsey excluded from the negotiations) could, if enforced, deny to Guernsey fishermen access to 'La Mer Commune' — a 500 square mile belt stretching from the waters east of Les Roches Douvres to the area south of Les Minquiers and thence to that east of Les Ecréhous — wherein they had hitherto fished under the self-same 160-year-old 'Accord de la Baie de Granville' which the French themselves had invoked to justify their presence in the Haricot and the Sark Box. To make matters worse, the same agreement, if implemented, would restrict to thirty the number of Guernsey boats allowed to enter the 2,000 square miles of Jersey's territorial waters. It was thus a great relief to Guernsey's fishermen when in the wake of an assurance given early the following July to the Bailiff by the Home Office Minister Lord Williams that Guernsey's views would be considered before the United Kingdom decided whether or not to ratify this draft, there came an announcement by the President of the Sea Fisheries Committee that the ratification negotiations looked close to collapse. Prior to these welcome tidings, however, serious trouble had erupted in the April of 1999 when, following a fine of £4,000 imposed on the Cherbourg skipper Vincent Néel, a group of French trawlers dredging for scallops cut through the nets set out of the edge of the Sark Box by Messrs. Bud and Mark Blondel from their boat *Ceona-mara*, damaging between 3,000 and 5,000 metres of them and ruining their catch of spider crabs, with resultant losses amounting to £11,000. The protests and admonitions of the Sea Fisheries Officer Mr. Stephen Ozanne on board the protection vessel *Leopardess* were all ignored both by the French fishermen and by the French naval craft in attendance. To relieve this long-running tension the Guernsey Fishermen's Association in August 1999 proposed to the French the appointment of a neutral mediator (possibly Norwegian) commissioned to look at the problems with fresh eyes. Unfortunately the initial response to this proposal was hardly encouraging, consisting as it did of the detention later the same month of the Sea Fisheries Officer Mr. Roger Sendall on the French trawler which he had boarded to remonstrate about yet more 'poaching' and his enforced conveyance into French waters whence he was eventually airlifted and returned by helicopter.

Seven years after it had first made headline news this vexatious dispute over fishing rights clearly remained unresolved. Che sàrà sàrà.

Trials and tribulations such as these undoubtedly reduced the prosperity of Guernsey's fisherfolk which had previously been signalized by the construction between the Albert Marina and the Castle emplacement of a special wharf for their use — an undertaking incorporated in the general harbour development associated with the creation of the Elizabeth II Marina which was carried out between 1984 and 1989 (see Chapter Eighteen of this Part). Even then, however, no such happy state of affairs could be said to apply to Sark, where the concentration of economic activity on tourism following the opening of La Maseline harbour led to fishing by the Serquiais waning considerably. Alderney too experienced some decline, though its fleet nevertheless provided the island with a gross income of £753,000 in the year 1993.

The Bailiwick is in the northern extremity of the habitat of the Ormer, 'Oreille-de-mer', of the species 'Haliotis tuberculata' — a gastropod mollusc, often growing to four inches in length and from two to three inches wide, which is found clinging to the undersurface of rocks and under stones and boulders in the lowest tide zone. When removed from its mother-of-pearl shell, beaten, fried and stewed, it provides a mouth-watering delicacy. It is uncertain when the ormer first became valued as a food. Prehistoric kitchen middens, although yielding large quantities of limpets, very rarely contain ormers. However, F. Wearis, in his 1671 *News from Sark* (already referred to in Chapter Two of this Part) talks of 'a large shell-fish, taken plentifully at low tide, called an Ormond'; and he goes on to say that 'an epicure would think his pallat in paradice if he might but always gormandise on such delitious ambrosia'.

Anxieties regarding a diminishing supply were first felt during the 1870s and led to an ordinance of the Royal Court in 1876 regulating this fishery for the first time, forbidding the sale of ormers less than three inches in diameter, plus a complete prohibition from May 1st. to August 31st. A further ordinance in 1899 established a close season from April 7th. to December 1st. (altered to October 31st. in 1903).

These measures having had little effect, the Court appointed a study committee in 1922. On April 20th., 1923 this committee presented a Requête to the States seeking financial provision to enable Dr. T. A. Stephenson, D.Sc., an eminent zoologist, to pursue an investigation. Dr. Stephenson recommended that ormering be suspended for two years to allow the stocks to recover and that the situation be then re-investigated and suitable legislation formulated. At a meeting on February 24th., 1924 the States accepted these recommendations and the Royal Court passed an ordinance forbidding the collection of ormers until November 7th., 1926.

The ormer shortage persisted, however, and in 1962 the States commissioned Mr. G. R. Forster of the Marine Biological Association at Plymouth to carry out an investigation. Mr. Forster concluded that the beaches were grossly over-worked and that there was no justification for blaming aqua-lung divers for any shortage. Nevertheless, despite Mr. Forster's opinion, the States decided to prohibit the collection of ormers by diving except along the south coast. The increase in the ormer population along the west coast, reported in February 1975, seemed at the time to indicate that such precautions were justified.

In September 1974 a Japanese marine biologist, Ikuo Hayashi, arrived in Guernsey to take up a two-year appointment with the Sea Fisheries Committee on the recommendation of the Marine Biological Association of the United Kingdom. He set about investigating the problems of ormer breeding and of the conservation of supplies, based on his experience with the ormer's cousin — the abalone — in Japanese waters.

The shortage still persists, however, and the efforts of a total of 3,700 people on the two days permitted for ormering in January 1979 having been rewarded with the somewhat meagre average of 1.23 ormers each, allegations of illicit diving operations were made by some of the frustrated shore-gatherers. Determined efforts to improve matters were, however, begun in December 1982 with the launch of a scheme aimed at rearing imported baby ormers (originally incubated from Guernsey parents by Dr. John Mercer of Galway University's Shellfish Research Association, at his laboratory in Carna, County Galway, Republic of Ireland, and brought back to the island when 18 months old) which were placed in special 'hives' designed by Mr. John Lintell (the Sea Fisheries Officer) and set up at a number of sites in the hope of eventually creating a stable population of adults capable of unaided self-propagation. The 'first-fruits' of these efforts became apparent in December 1985 when, on the strength of a permit granted to Mr. Richard Tostevin's Rocquaine Shellfish Pond, two dozen 'farmed ormers' were sold at sixty pence each to people whose names had been on a waiting list for more than a year. Although boosting ormer stocks, however, the success of this experiment (which cost £40,000) was impaired by the 'invasion' of many 'hives' by crabs, constituting a marine equivalent of cuckoos in the nest! Removal of the 'hives' was begun in 1985. Nevertheless, undeterred by this setback yet another attempt to restore stocks was made in July 1999 when Mr. Richard Tostevin, aided by over eighty helpmeets, released nineteen million ormer larvae into coastal waters. The hope expressed that thumbnail size ormers would result by early 2001 was, however, accompanied by the warning that no 'ormer harvest' could be expected before the middle of the first decade of the twenty-first century.

In conclusion, it may be noted that the experience of the ormer famine had the effect of engendering an enhanced awareness of an alarming threat to animal and plant life generally in and around local waters. With this in mind, La Société Guernesiaise, with the blessing of the States' Sea Fisheries Committee, proposed early in 1987 the creation of a conservation area offshore from the littoral of Les Angulières. The hope was expressed that, progressively developing into an aquatic wilderness, this would in time provide an unspoilt habitat wherein, protected from interference by boat owners, potters, vraic gatherers, bait diggers and the population at large, rare species of marine life would be preserved.

Chapter Seven

PRIMITIVE INDUSTRY: THE STREAM THAT MADE ST. PETER-PORT

THIS WILL BE A MERE SNIPPET of a chapter — but worthwhile as giving a glimpse of the genesis of the Bailiwick's capital.

The growth of St. Peter-Port was fostered by early industrial development depending on a stream (now carried underground through storm water-sewers), which, formed by a confluence of three minor streams descending the valleys now occupied by Colborne Road, the Ruettes Brayes, and Prince Albert Road, flowed down the 'Vallée de la Misère' (now taken up by La Charroterie, the Bordage and Fountain Street).

At the confluence was a large reservoir, before entering which the water turned a mill at the Pont Renier, while at the foot of the Ruettes Brayes it formed a public lavoir. Below the reservoir it was dammed again and again to drive mills which ground corn or sawed timber, while in the vicinity of Park Street the blacksmiths (who were also farriers) used it for bonding wheels.

As the name suggests, the area of La Charroterie was given over to the building of carriages, and the box-carts used in *vraicing*, as well as the production of wooden ploughs and harrows and heavy wooden wheelbarrows.

In the Bordage the stream did service for bakers, brewers and other trades, while still lower, where the markets now stand, it not only turned more mills (of one of which Mill Street is evocative) but also provided a number of washing places for vegetables and clothes.

Near the present Market Steps the stream turned the Moulin du Milieu, and finally, flowing through the churchyard before entering the sea, it turned yet another mill mentioned as early as the 12th. century by Henry I in a deed confirming his father's gift of the church of Sancti Petri de Portu to the Abbey of Marmoutiers, where he refers to 'a certain water-mill in the churchyard of the same church'.

Chapter Eight

THE KNITTING INDUSTRY

THE MODERN HOLIDAY-MAKER on a visit to the islands who buys and wears one of the 'Guernseys' sold in considerable quantities to tourists is, in fact, patronising a local industry going back many centuries. Although at its peak in the first half of the 17th. century, the Bailiwick's knitting industry dates back to the beginning of the 16th. century — or even previous to that. As early as 1470 Thomas de Havilland obtained a royal grant to import wool and cloth from England and to re-export it to Normandy and Spain; while *c.* 1500 John Bonamy was importing raw wool and cotton yarn in his ship, *La Pitié*, and re-exporting it as knitted and woven goods, stockings and 'undergarments called Guernsey frocks'. The raw material supplied from England was subject to a quota, Guernsey being allowed 2,000 tods, Alderney 400, and Sark 200. Guernsey knitted goods were esteemed by royalty. Mary I had four waistcoats, four pairs of sleeves, and four pairs of hose, while Elizabeth I wore Guernsey stockings, and Mary Queen of Scots had six pairs of Guernsey gloves, besides three pairs of hose — one of which she wore at her execution.

This cottage industry, which reached its zenith in the 17th. century, involved first the women — who even risked the 'White Sheet of Penitence' treatment (mentioned in Part I, Chapter Seven) by knitting secretly on a Sunday in Calvinist Guernsey — and later on the men, to the detriment of agriculture. It was organised efficiently by the authorities, who appointed inspectors, confiscated goods of inferior quality, and petitioned the Crown for licences to import more wool. A booming export business was built up to England and France and (later in the same century) to America. Thus Peter Heylyn, who was in Guernsey in the reign of Charles I, noted: 'The principall commodity which they use to send abroad, are the works and labours of the poorer sort, as Wast-cotes, Stockins, and other manufactures made of wool, wherein they are exceeding cunning'.

The domestic manufacture of stockings became an important

source of income for Sark also in the early 17th. century, a leading rôle in the trade being played by the Le Gros family, who forged commercial links with the Le Pelleys of Guernsey (who were among the leading exporters of stockings to France and to England).

The industry was hard-hit by the Civil War, not only as a result of the blockade by Castle Cornet, but also because Anne of Austria (the Queen Regent of France during the minority of Louis XIV) forbade any trade from north-western France unless the trader had a pass signed by the Royalist Governor in the Castle. Inevitably, therefore, the trade was almost brought to a standstill.

Attempts at revival after the Restoration were impeded by French competition, by import restrictions imposed by Louis XIV, and by a cut in the import quota from England. Nevertheless, resourcefulness and determination eventually pulled the industry through. This is well exemplified in the case of Matthew de Sausmarez, another leading Guernsey merchant, who dealt with the knitters in their cottages through his wife, Bertranne, and had his brother, Michael, as his agent in Paris, besides other agents in St. Malo, Coutances, Rouen and Bordeaux. Through them he contrived, by sheer persistence, to sell his Bas à Hommes, his Rhingraves (petticoat breeches) and his Bas à Canon (thigh-length stockings).

The extent to which recovery had been achieved is well indicated by yet another passage in F. Wearis's 1671 *News from Sark*, alluding to 'the grand and almost only Manufacture of our Island being Knitting which our People perform with a wonderful dexterity both for Stockings, Gloves, Caps and Waste-coats, Men Women and Children being brought up to it'. Later he added: 'these commodities when finished we vend into England at the places aforesaid, having several small vessels for that purpose, and thence in return furnish our selves with necessaries'.

The decline of the cottage knitting industry followed its inability to compete with the factory products resulting from the Industrial Revolution, and it was moribund by the end of the 18th. century. Happily, however, there has latterly been a revival, thanks largely to the efforts of the Women's Institutes which have played a large part in resuscitating the manufacture of the traditional Guernsey, so that there are now several knitting businesses engaged in its production, the largest of which employs no fewer than 300 home knitters. Although the plain body and sleeves of the Guernseys are worked by machine for commercial purposes, the more complicated parts are still worked by hand. The Guernsey Federation of Women's Institutes issues its own pattern and trophies are presented annually for the best quality work submitted, expert judges ensuring that the traditional pattern is correct.

When the well-known Guernsey was first made is unknown. It may be Heylyn's 'waste-cote' — or it may stem from Bonamy's 'undergarments called Guernsey frocks'. Although the first date given by the O.E.D. for the use of the name 'guernsey' outside the island is 1851, such attire was commonplace in the Bailiwick long prior to that and in fact the suitability as an item of naval wear of what he called a 'Guernsey Jacket' was commented on by Lord Nelson on November 20th., 1804 (well before 1851) when, writing to the Commissioners of the Navy, he expressed the opinion that, while of 'most excellent' quality, it suffered from being 'too narrow and short' to be tucked snugly into a man's trousers but, if made 'three inches wider and six longer' (with 'ten inches or a foot' felt to 'be so much better'), this garment would then become 'the best and most valuable 'slops' (seamen's clothes) that ever were introduced into the service' and 'it would not be too many to send out one for every seaman in the fleet'. It may be described as a loose and long woollen vest with back and front identical, having knots to represent the knots in fishing-nets, a garter stitch for ripples on the shore, a two-by-two rib for ships' ladders, while a ship's rope is to be found on the shoulders.

Chapter Nine

SHIP-BUILDING

THE VIGOROUS ACTIVITY of Guernsey merchants in the early 19th. century, with their extensive operations in northern Europe, the Iberian Peninsula, the Mediterranean and South America, created the demand for a plentiful supply of ships — a demand swollen by the depletion of merchant fleets resulting from the Napoleonic Wars and which was even further increased a few years later by the growth of the granite trade (which will be dealt with in the next chapter).

As a result a ship-building industry came into existence, the first large ships being launched in 1815, followed by a rush in the 1830s which reached a peak in 1840 when 16 deep-sea traders were launched. The industry lasted on a large scale until the end of the 19th. century, while, in an attenuated form, it persists to the present day. As many as 13 yards grew up. The first yards were on the Galet Heaume, where more than 60 vessels were built before the site vanished under the esplanade to La Vallette built in 1862. Other yards were at La Tourgand (near the modern Weighbridge), Glategny, La Piette, the Longstore and Hougue à la Perre — but most of them were at St. Sampson's; building full-rigged ships, barques, schooners and cutters, and providing employment for carpenters, shipwrights, rope-makers, ships' chandlers, sail makers, caulkers, and timber merchants.

At first most ships were built for the deep-sea trades — swift schooners for fresh fruit cargoes from the Western Isles, as well as roomy brigs and brigantines for the South American and Spanish Main trades in sugar, rum, coffee, hides, tallow and hardwoods. Their quality was universally praised. When the *Costa Rica Packet* arrived in San Francisco after a record run from London, the shipping fraternity was so impressed that local ship-builders were advised to inspect her thoroughly and model their own work accordingly. She was built by Sebire of Hougue à la Perre — who constructed many ships for the Cape Horn run.

In 1864 the largest ship ever built and owned in Guernsey was launched — the 656-ton tea-clipper *Golden Spur*, coming from the yard of Peter Ogier in St. Sampson's.

Old tales of the sea appear to attach themselves to the building of ships as well, judging by the *Concordia* myth. The story goes that she stuck as she was launched and remained immovable for 3½ days. A bird flying continually over the vessel gave rise to suspicions of witchcraft, and a white wizard was therefore asked to help. This gentleman having scattered salt over the deck, the vessel immediately glided into the harbour.

The industry slowly wilted in face of the advent of iron ships driven by steam, despite its efforts to compete, signalised by the launching in 1874 of the wooden steamship S.S. *Commerce* — the first, indeed the only, Guernsey-built steamer. The last ship of consequence to be launched was the ketch *Sarnia* (also from Peter Ogier's yard) which was born to a sad destiny, being wrecked on the Ferrières, refloated and finally lost on the English coast.

During the shipyards' 19th.-century hey-day, nearly 300 hundred vessels were built in Guernsey, while a further 70 were lengthened and rebuilt. Island shipping during these years comprised ninety ships in the foreign trade which, in addition to a number sailing to the Mediterranean for dried fruit, featured outstandingly those (built mostly by James Sebire of Hougue à la Perre) owned and operated by the self-educated Captain William le Lacheur (1803–1863) who pioneered the Costa Rican coffee trade; combining these commercial activities with evangelistic work as an unpaid volunteer colporteur for the British and Foreign Bible Society which eventuated in the construction in Costa Rica (where many of his descendants still live) of the Church of the Good Shepherd wherein one finds a plaque commemorating this crusading merchant venturer 'by whose exertions public Protestant worship was established in this Republic'.

Although only two yards (Seaward Marine and Island Marine Craft) now remain, they perform honourable service. The former, specialising in small standardised 23 ft., 25 ft. and 29 ft. vessels ranging from £24,700 up to £110,000, produces about twenty craft a year and does regular business with Japan, while also selling to Finland, Denmark and Greece. The latter, by contrast, concentrates on cabin cruisers in the £9,900 to £90,000 price range and trades mostly with the U.K. and the European Union. In the case of each firm the sums quoted reflect 1995 values. In 1994 Seaward

Marine completed the magnificent new ambulance launch *Flying Christine III* and previous notable products from island yards have been her predecessor, *Flying Christine II* (built in 1964) and a launch designed to carry employees to Ford's factory across the river Thames.

Chapter Ten

QUARRYING

YACHTSMEN WHO MOOR THEIR VESSELS at La Beaucette Marina are taking advantage of a legacy of a major island industry in the 19th. century, as the anchorage was created by cutting a passage linking an empty granite quarry with the open sea, thereby flooding it for the accommodation of the craft.

The quarrying industry started early in the 19th. century when it was found that Guernsey granite, especially the diorite or blue granite quarried in the north-east of the island, was very durable — and a large outlet for this stone arose in London and south-east England for macadamising road surfaces, as well as for kerbs, granite setts and ornamental masonry. Thus much of the dressed stone on the Thames Embankment and the London bridges consists of Guernsey granite — and hundreds of tons were even sent to distant Odessa for building projects in that city.

From the quarries the stone was taken to St. Sampson's harbour (the growth of which was almost entirely attributable to this trade) to be crushed, and then tipped straight into the ships' holds. The loading was so co-ordinated and expert that a ship of 800 tons could be in and out the same day. The dramatic rise in the trade is well illustrated by the figures of tonnage exported, which increased from 2,000 tons in 1810 to 120,000 tons in 1854, and 458,000 in 1910. The traffic's steady expansion brought wealth and employment to the island and caused the population of the northern parishes to double in 30 years. Although the inter-war years saw a decline (from an export of 188,438 tons in 1928 to 110,737 tons in 1938) the industry nevertheless continued to make a substantial contribution to Guernsey's livelihood.

The post-war period saw the industry transferring itself from a labour-intensive to a capital-intensive basis. As a result, despite a reduction in the number of quarries operating to two — Chouet and Les Vardes — as against the 268 in 1933 listed on page 245 of *Peter Girard's Guernsey*, coupled with a decline in the labour force from 310 in 1935 to 76 in 1959, operating production, thanks to rationalisation and technical advance, remained much the same as pre-war. In 1963, for example, about 190,000 tons of stone were quarried, of which about 75,000 tons were exported. Local demand caused post-war exports to fluctuate. Thus the previous year (1962) saw only 44,000 tons exported, while the figure a decade before that (1953) was 102,000 tons.

The nature of post-war demand also altered, being almost entirely confined to that for crushed stone of very fine grades, to be used as an aggregate for concrete and for road macadamization. Little was produced by way of building stone as stone dressers were hard to find and demand was too small to warrant the high cost of mechanisation. Latterly local demand has absorbed the entire output, taking (*inter alia*) thousands of tons for the extensions to the Town Harbour from 1984 onwards (and thereby engendering a production peak of 227,000 tons in 1987 so that exports were discontinued, never to be re-commenced.) Indeed, a considerable quantity of stone was imported to facilitate the Longue Hougue Reclamation scheme launched in 1990. The closure of Chouet in April 1997 left Les Vardes (with dwindling reserves) as the island's sole working quarry — a state of affairs promoting the industry to embark on a recycling initiative, with a ready-mix plant near the Vale Castle producing concrete, using hard core which can be taken from building sites and road excavations. Such a search for salvation through diversification strongly suggests that as this book goes to press Guernsey's quarrying industry proper, in marked decline from its hey-day, could well be on its death-bed.

In Alderney the jetty, built at the end of the 19th. century to be capable of handling ships at all states of the tide, served as an outlet for the quarry industry from 1910 to 1940. This became the chief industrial enterprise of the island, on which 20 per cent. of the working population depended for its livelihood, the annual wages bill coming to £14,000. The industry was killed by the war, since when the output of the Mannez Quarry has been monopolised by the labour of Sisyphus involved in foreshoring the breakwater at Braye.

The stone trade even brought an industrial boom to little Herm, whose granite resources were first exploited on a systematic basis by Lieutenant-Colonel the Honourable John Lindsay, who bought the lease of the island from Pierre Mauger in 1815. Subsidized by his partner and prospective son-in-law, Jonathan Duncan, Lindsay undertook vast projects into which he sank every penny he had.

Not only did Lindsay build a harbour of a size capable of taking vessels up to 250 tons burthen, so that 600 tons of granite could be shipped daily; but he also bought shallow-draught sailing barges for shipping the stone and in addition installed quarrying machinery and stone chutes. Finally, broken by the venture, Lindsay approached the States of Guernsey for a £1,500 loan: only to find that the States, nettled by his persistent refusal to pay tax on the rum and gin consumed by his quarrymen, declined to accommodate him. The upshot was that Lindsay was driven into bankruptcy shortly before his death in 1826.

After his father-in-law's death, Duncan contrived to take the island on hire from the States, who held it *en saisi* owing to Lindsay's bankruptcy. He then reaped the benefit of Lindsay's capital outlay. Advertising widely, he obtained orders from far and wide, including the contractors for the construction of the Manchester Cotton Exchange and the Liverpool Liver Building. To meet his orders he imported a large number of labourers, to deal with whose drunkenness James Hooper was sworn in by St. Peter-Port Douzaine as Herm's constable, and the dome-shaped lock-up (still to be seen by the *White House* hotel) was erected.

In 1830 Duncan formed the Herm Granite Company, with Geoffrey Martin and Ebenezer Fernie as co-directors. Many Guernsey investors became shareholders, and business boomed sufficiently to warrant the installation of an iron tramway to convey stone to the harbour. The influx of labourers was such as to cause the population, which had stood at 37 in 1821, to rise to 191 by 1831, finally reaching 400 in 1839.

Then came the crash. In 1838 the Herm Granite Company was dissolved, and Duncan went bankrupt and withdrew, leaving creditors who had lost £12,000. Quarrying continued, however, as the Royal Court had granted the rest of the lease to the British Commercial Assurance Company — one of the main creditors. The year 1841 saw a resurgence. Ebenezer Fernie managed to raise some money, and, forming the Hayter Granite Company, continued to export stone until he relinquished the tenancy of the island in 1854 — when, however, the new tenants were required by the terms of the lease to respect the Hayter Company's quarrying rights.

In 1865 the States ordered that harbour dues be paid by all ships entering any harbour in the Bailiwick. This being opposed by the Hayter Granite Company, a compromise was reached whereby the dues paid by vessels entering Herm harbour to the extent of

£2,000 per annum were to be applied to defraying expenditure by the lessee on harbour improvement. Thanks to this concession, the waning fortunes of Herm's granite trade were once again revived, and the population, which had been steady at 50 from 1851 to 1861, rose to 92 in 1871.

This revival, however, proved to be a swan-song, and in the course of the 1870s, during the tenancy of Lieutenant-Colonel M. J. Fielden, the industry slowly died. This was partly due to the harbour being gradually destroyed by the battering of the sea (which makes one wonder what Fielden was doing with his £2,000 per annum) and the pool consequently became silted up so that ships could no longer berth — with the result that Herm was ill-equipped to compete with Guernsey and St. Sampson's deep-water harbour. This parlous position was exacerbated by the fact that the increased production of cement for concrete-making was killing the profit prospects of smaller stone traders. Thus the 1881 census saw the population down to thirty-two. The trade was dead — but it has an enduring monument in the steps from Carlton House Terrace to the Mall: a little bit of Herm in London.

An unfortunate by-product of Herm's granite era was the widespread vandalism whereby the quarrymen destroyed many cromlechs. Not only did Duncan order the removal of the Pierre aux Rats menhir to be dressed for export and shipped to London (see Part I, Chapter One), but the pioneer Guernsey archaeologist, Frederick Corbin Lukis, desperately attempting some archaeological salvage, was enraged that 'the workmen at Herm had orders to break up the surface rocks wherever they found them suitable for dressing as square blocks used in railway tunnels'.

By way of postscript it may be remarked that so intense was the granite hunger of the time that even Jethou and Crevichon were quarried in the first half of the 19th. century. There is a tradition that the steps of St. Paul's Cathedral are of Crevichon granite.

Chapter Eleven

MINING: A COSTLY FAILURE

A DEVELOPMENT which was destined to bring ruin to the Le Pelley family, followed by the loss of their seigneury of Sark, started in the year 1833 when John Hunt identified copper and silver lodes at Le Pot in Little Sark and asked permission of the seigneur (Peter Le Pelley) to open up a mine.

After receiving legal advice that his seigneurial rights gave him ownership of all mineral deposits in the Fief, Le Pelley granted Hunt a concession on October 17th., 1834, authorising him to sink shafts in Sark and Brecqhou for 31 years at an annual rental of £1 plus 6 per cent. of the ores or minerals raised. The very next day Hunt transferred this concession (together with another he had received in Guernsey) to the 'Guernsey and Sark Mining Company'. Two hundred shares of £5 each were issued to 66 shareholders, out of which Hunt held 30 and Le Pelley ten. By the articles of the company shareholders were bound to supply more capital if a General Meeting called for such.

After two disappointing years at Le Pot where, despite good indications, no metal in paying quantities was brought out, an accidental discovery revolutionised the situation. This arose from a sporting expedition in 1836 when a man sent by a huntsman to retrieve a shot rabbit which had fallen over the cliffs at Port Gorey returned with stones containing cassiterite ore. On examination, a lode was found exposed to the face of the cliff.

This lode was promptly named 'Sark's Hope'. The concession was extended to 39 years, the shareholders persuaded to put up a further £5,400, and work pressed ahead vigorously. In addition to the 70 to 80 Sercquiais who were employed in the venture (some as miners) 250 Cornish miners were imported, mostly housed in the barracks in Little Sark. Four shafts were sunk along the line of Sark's Hope, and from them eight galleries were driven out under the sea-bed. An engine house was built for a 120 h.p. steam engine to pump water from the workings, as well as an 18 h.p. engine for raising the cages in the shafts. In addition a crushing machine and a stamping mill were installed, a landing-place blasted out of the cliffs at Port Gorey, and a narrow-gauge railway laid. To publicise all these activities and attract support, Hunt opened an office at St. Peter-Port where he displayed a tea and coffee set made of Sark silver. Unfortunately it is not known what happened to this set later on.

On March 1st., 1839 Peter Le Pelley was drowned *en route* for Guernsey and was replaced as seigneur by his brother, Ernest, who came into his inheritance at a crucial moment, the mining company being obliged the following year (July 1840) to raise a loan of £1,000 from the Guernsey bank of Priaulx, Le Marchant, Rougier and Co. By 1844, however, it needed money yet again to install more powerful pumping equipment to cope with the deeper levels being worked, as another promising vein had been found 460 ft. below high-water mark. As by now £34,000 had been spent and only £4,000 worth of silver and lead obtained, the shareholders refused any further support — so that Le Pelley, desperate for money, was constrained to seek Crown permission to mortgage the fief and thereby raised £4,000 from Jean Allaire the privateer (whose exploits were mentioned in Part IV, Chapter Seven).

With this money the bank was repaid and a pumping machine of 230 h.p. installed. When a vein worth £600 per ton was struck at the deepest level, the miners were offered a bonus on output — but the vein rapidly proved to grow narrower and narrower as it was penetrated. Then nemesis struck. In 1845 the ceiling of the lowest gallery collapsed and the workings were flooded. No funds being available to install yet more powerful pumps, operations finally ceased in 1847.

Ernest Le Pelley died in 1849, and his son, Pierre Carey Le Pelley, being unable to meet the interest payments on the mortgage, Marie Allaire (heiress of Jean, who had died in 1846) foreclosed. Le Pelley obtained Crown permission to sell, and on December 4th., 1852 the fief was sold to Marie Collings (née Allaire) for £6,000, minus the £4,000 already advanced on mortgage and a further £616 overdue interest. Marie's son, the Reverend William Thomas Collings, succeeded his mother on her death the following summer, and thus established the present line of seigneurs.

Most of the silver mined in Sark was exported to France, where the best price was to be obtained. None of it was used to make Channel Isles plate as by the time the mines were opened, silver goods were no longer being manufactured locally. Previously, however, the islands' silversmiths had been highly skilled — some of them going to England, where they achieved considerable prosperity. Thus, for instance, the Guernseyman, Peter Perchard, Lord Mayor of London (1804–1805) was a successful silversmith who had learned his trade with his uncle, Matthew Perchard, a jeweller and goldsmith in Hatton Garden.

Besides his operations in Sark, John Hunt also initiated ventures in Guernsey and Herm. In Guernsey he obtained from the Crown Receiver in 1834 a 31-year concession to explore and work a copper vein on Fief Le Roi between Clarence Battery and Les Terres. Although he named it the Hope Copper Mine, nothing came of the project. There was rather more activity in Herm, where Hunt sank an experimental shaft for copper, lead and silver near Rosaire, and followed this by two more tunnels bored into the side of Valley Panto. Undeterred by the flooding of the workings and his lack of capital to purchase pumping equipment, Hunt went ahead and formed the Herm Mining Company in 1837 and in his offices in St. Peter-Port displayed ores of high metallic content which he claimed had been mined in Herm. With the counter-attractions of Sark, however, it proved impossible to raise sufficient capital, and operations petered out in 1838.

The year 1843 saw a *cause célèbre* arising out of a silver mining venture in Guernsey. Some time previously the Blanchelande Mining Corporation, with the blessing of Captain George Lefebvre, seigneur of the Fief de Blanchelande, had started mining for silver at Mount Durand in St. Martin's — but, unfortunately, its operations led to the drying up of wells, fountains and drinking troughs, not only in the immediate vicinity of Mount Durand, but also at La Bouvée and Les Courtes Falaises.

In these circumstances the Royal Court was approached on January 4th., 1843 with a request for an order closing the mine. The Court banned the exploitation of the mine for one month to allow all parties concerned time for full investigation. In the breathing space thus afforded, an indignant meeting of the Chefs de Famille of St. Martin's parish was held on January 17th., with the outcome that the constables and douzeniers were authorised to seek the intervention of other parishes and of the States — and, as a last resort, to sue the mining company for damages, the expenses of litigation to be raised by parochial taxation.

On May 3rd. the constables and douzeniers reported that legal proceedings had already been started, but in October the Chefs de Famille received a letter from the secretary of the Blanchelande

Mining Corporation, offering to abandon the rights granted by the seigneur of the Fief de Blanchelande and also to contribute £15 towards the cost of blocking up the mine, providing the parochial authorities undertook the work and withdrew all legal action against the Corporation. This was accompanied by another letter from George Lefebvre giving an undertaking not to exercise in future his right for research for precious metals in his fief except under sufficient securities given to the satisfaction of the parochial authorities. It being thus obvious that the seigneur and the Mining Corporation were anxious to rid themselves of a white elephant, plus the fact that the preservation of water supplies was safeguarded, a settlement was reached on the terms offered. The Mount Durand episode was closed.

Guernsey saw one last attempt to mine for silver when the Blanchelande Mining Corporation made a trial lateral boring at La Fosse — a creek on the St. Martin's side of Petit Bôt — thereby creating a tunnel which still exists. This venture also was fruitless.

Chapter Twelve

ENTERPRISES GREAT AND SMALL

NEWSPAPERS, playing cards, furniture and antiseptics make strange bedfellows — and yet they form the subject-matter of this chapter devoted to a miscellany of Guernsey business ventures.

Anyone taking refreshment in the public house in Pollet Street named after him cannot fail to be reminded by the décor of the Bailiwick's undoubted greatest entrepreneur — Thomas de la Rue, who was born in the Forest parish on March 24th., 1793.

In 1803, at the age of 10, young Thomas was apprenticed to a printer and publisher named Joseph Antoine Chevalier. In 1811, his apprenticeship completed, he was engaged by Thomas Greenslade as editor (at the age of 19) of a new newspaper called *Le Publiciste*, which was first issued in September 1812. In 1813 de la Rue left Greenslade to start his own newspaper, *Le Miroir Politique* — which he continued to issue after going into business in 1815 with his brother-in-law, publishing *La Liturgie*, illustrated with engravings on steel. Apart from *The Star* (Guernsey's first English language newspaper, which was first issued in 1813), all newspapers had been in French since the appearance of the very first, *La Gazette de L'île de Guernesey*, in 1789. There was now a proliferation of them, and de la Rue felt that the market was saturated. Commenting, 'C'est trop peut-être pour cette île', he sailed for England in 1816 to seek wider scope for his talents.

In London he first engaged in the manufacture of straw hats, as well as entering the stationery business with two partners, producing the first de la Rue playing cards in 1831. When straw hats went out of fashion in 1835, de la Rue's inventiveness led him to introduce bonnets of embossed paper, which were a great success for a time and led him into the ornamental paper trade. Thus arose the house of de la Rue and Sons. In 1838 the firm produced a special gold edition of *The Sun* newspaper to commemorate Queen Victoria's coronation, and the year 1851 saw de la Rue acting as deputy chairman to the Paper, Printing and Bookbinding Class in the Great Exhibition.

De la Rue's forebears had come to Guernsey as Huguenot refugees from France and, with this ancestry in mind, the French acknowledged his achievements by creating him Chevalier de la Légion d'Honneur in 1855. In the same year the firm secured the contract for printing the Great Britain fourpenny carmine postage stamp, following this up in 1859 with a further contract to print three denominations of currency notes for Mauritius. De la Rue introduced the extensive use of sulphate of barytes as a pigment, and the white enamel used on superior types of playing cards is a barytes white. Among his other innovations, de la Rue introduced several new printing inks and invented the embossing of bookbinders' cloths and paper-hangings. He also patented the fixing of iridescent films on paper.

At de la Rue's death on June 7th., 1866, the firm passed into the hands of his son, Warren de la Rue, who had been born in Guernsey in 1815.

An enterprise which, despite the excellence of its wares, was lilliputian in contrast to that of de la Rue, consisted of the manufacture of mahogany furniture. This industry was stimulated by the cargoes of mahogany brought back to the archipelago in ships returning from the Newfoundland fisheries, as a result of which a considerable amount of good quality mahogany furniture was made in Guernsey during the 18th. and 19th. centuries. A leading maker was Richard Guille of Pedvin Street, but as the furniture followed conventional designs, only experts are able to distinguish it from similar furniture made in the United Kingdom.

Another modest-sized industry involved the production of iodine, a number of small plants for the extraction of which existed in Guernsey during the 19th. and early 20th. centuries. One of these establishments, in St. Martin's, was responsible for the nickname, 'Steam Mill Lane', being given to Le Douit de la Porte. This little factory extracted its iodine from the ash of *vraic* which had been dried and burnt on Lihou Island, but, like others of its ilk, was unable to survive the competition of the large, efficient chemical works of the United Kingdom, with their access to cheaper sources of raw material.

A well-known name in connection with this product was that of Mr. Albert Best who, in conjunction with his Saint Martin's operations, also undertook the commercial extraction of iodine in the little factory adjoining his house on Lihou (of which islet he was the tenant) using *vraic* gathered on its shores. Although for a time Mr. Best supplied this disinfectant under contract to the British Army, the entire enterprise wilted and died in the early thirties in the face of subsidised exports from South America (especially Chile) which had long dominated the market. 'Guernsey iodine' was no more.

Chapter Thirteen

TOURISM AND LIGHT INDUSTRY

NOWADAYS assuredly one of the Bailiwick's major sources of income, the tourist industry dates back to slow beginnings which occurred in the years after Waterloo as a by-product of the arrival of a large number of retired naval and army officers, who, attracted by the low living costs, settled in the islands. They were visited by friends and relations, and this resulted in the archipelago becoming better known until eventually coming to be recognised as a group of tourist resorts in the late 1820s and early 1830s — a development which stimulated the appearance of guide books of which an outstanding example was *The Channel Islands*, by H. D. Inglis, published in 1834. The attraction of the islands was also enhanced by the fact that after 1815 crossing the Channel no longer involved the danger of attack by the enemy.

Another factor encouraging tourism was the development of communications with England and (to a lesser extent) with France. As sailing packets gave way to steam packets and paddle steamers, and later to steamships run by the railway companies, this improvement in communications, coupled with the cuts in fares resulting from fierce competition between rival steamship companies, led to the arrival of ever-increasing numbers of tourists, seeking not so much the joys of sea-bathing (which was not often indulged in at the time), as the beauty of the scenery and the pleasures of sight-seeing. The trend was further encouraged when the construction of St. Peter-Port's new harbour reached the point (on October 11th., 1858) where a temporary landing-place, enabling passengers to walk ashore over a gangway, eliminated the uncomfortable and annoying necessity of landing by tender.

Early in the 20th. century the economic potential of the tourist industry had become of sufficient consequence to prompt the Guernsey Chamber of Commerce to petition the States to set up a Committee to administer it. Accordingly the States Advertising Committee (from which the present States Tourist Committee — now Board — has developed) was constituted on November 22nd.,

1905, with a budget of £200. The increased publicity received by the Bailiwick as a result of the work of this committee led to a yet greater increase in tourist traffic until in 1913, the last complete year of peace, over 50,000 passengers arrived from England — not entirely tourists, of course; part of the number being accounted for by islanders returning from their own visits elsewhere.

During the inter-war years, when the advent of air travel made the Bailiwick even more easily accessible, the need to preserve Guernsey's attractiveness for tourists led to the creation of the States Natural Beauties Committee (forerunner of the Island Development Committee) with a mandate to prevent eye-sore developments. Thanks to these efforts Guernsey's annual intake of tourists during the '30s averaged 45,000, despite the prevalence of slump and unemployment.

The evacuation of 1940 and the 'curiosity value' of the subsequent enemy occupation had an enormous influence on post-war tourist traffic, which showed a tremendous increase. The States Tourist Committee set about judiciously advertising the islands, exploiting the charms of the coast scenery and the mildness of the climate. It also insisted, by legal enactments, on a high standard of space and comfort in hotels and guest houses. These efforts, coupled with the lure of cheap tobacco, wines and spirits (now, alas!, more cheaply acquired on the ships and aircraft) brought in no fewer than 67,000 tourists in 1947 — the first year after the lifting of post-Liberation travel restrictions. The long standing of the tourist industry means that several hotels date from the middle of the 19th. century and therefore have an established tradition of good service. This fact, coupled with the application of a system of compulsory grading and inspection of all hotels and boarding houses, turned the surge into a flood. In 1964 the tourist count was 180,000, while in 1978 it reached 331,596 — an increase of 25,710 on 1977.

Speaking at the Guernsey Hotels Association's annual banquet on February 13th., 1975, the Bailiff, Mr. J. H. Loveridge (later Sir John Loveridge) said that tourism had become the Bailiwick's second industry, accounting in 1974 for 30 per cent. of its export earnings (as against the United Kingdom, whose tourist industry accounted for only 5 per cent. of export earnings). He warned, however, that there is a limit to the number of tourists the island can take and therefore urged that the industry's prosperity should be sought along the path of quality rather than quantity, attracting wealthier visitors by a high standard of amenities. Evidence that this advice was heeded is furnished by the conversion of the *Vimiera De La Salle Novitiate* into the prestigious *Saint Pierre Park Hotel*; the erection of the large *Peninsula Hotel* at Les Dicqs; and the provision by several hitherto modest guest houses of *en suite* accommodation. Furthermore, to cater for the large numbers of visiting yachtsmen the creation of a marina at Beaucette Quarry in 1970 was followed by the appearance of the Victoria Marina at the Old Harbour in 1973 and that of the Albert Marina at the old Albert Dock in 1975, culminating in the construction of the capacious Elizabeth II Marina at the North Beach which was opened by H.M. the Queen in 1989 — a year in which the number of tourists rose to a peak of 460,000. Although, reflecting the ensuing widespread recession, this number had by 1993 fallen to 360,000, tourism remained Guernsey's second largest industry, bringing in no less than £100 million in 1992 — while by 1996 numbers were once again increasing, with that year's earnings amounting to £176 million, and with non-U.K. holiday makers (mostly French, German and Dutch) accounting for almost 25% of all visitors. Sad to say, this improvement was not sustained, the 1999 tourist influx giving rise to considerable disquiet and prompting an examination of the 'chicken and egg' relationship between the volume of tourist traffic and air service provision, with each seen as increasingly dependent on the other (see the penultimate paragraph of Chapter Nineteen of this Part). Furthermore, just as (if Dr. Samuel Johnson is to be believed) 'when a man is to be hanged in a fortnight, it concentrates his mind wonderfully'; so this unwelcome trend stimulated the realisation that, whereas the persistence of this decline would be serious enough for Guernsey, where of recent years 20% of all employment has arisen from the demands of holiday-makers, its consequences for the rest of the Bailiwick would be little short of catastrophic. In Alderney, where in 1998 one quarter of the population depended for its livelihood on the £4.4 million spent by visitors, this traffic generated 30% of all income — a level only surpassed by that derived from resident rentiers, yielding in the same year 50% thereof. Similarly, in 1998 two-thirds of the people of Sark earned their living from the tourist trade, which brought in 70% of the Fief Haubert's income; while in Herm reliance on this source of income was — as always — almost total, there being virtually no other.

Tourism in Sark may be said to date from the 1770s, when the practice of making up a party for a week-end trip to Sark became increasingly popular among Guernsey people. This early manifestation of tourist traffic was viewed askance by Chief Pleas, because of its accompanying drunkenness and rowdiness. Hence an ordinance of October 17th., 1771 banned violins in public houses because of the disturbance of the public peace by Guernsey trippers.

Hunt's efforts to get support for his mining ventures by arranging trips from his office in St. Peter-Port to inspect the silver mines laid the foundations of the modern tourist industry, and from the 1850s Sark's economy became ever more dependent on it. The landing tax was first imposed in 1859, and the income thus derived plus the increased receipts for Impôt duty resulting from the visitors' consumption of liquor, enabled the island to balance its budget without direct taxation.

In the winter of 1865/6 Creux Harbour breakwater was destroyed by gales, and the seigneur (Rev. W. T. Collings), realising the importance of the tourist trade, at once arranged with Mr. Agnew Giffard (who was in charge of the extension of St. Peter-Port harbour) to construct a new and improved harbour to be paid for by a tax on spirits. By the 1870s the *Bel Air* and *Dixcart* hotels were functioning, and many tenants lodged visitors as a sideline.

During the 1930s the late Dame de Sercq fostered the tourist traffic (which had by then become a major source of revenue) by lecture tours in the U.S.A., and by furthering the project for a deep-water harbour at La Maseline. Completed after the Liberation, this improved facility has led to a tremendous influx of tourists, 38,382 having paid the landing tax in 1967. Indeed, the fear has been growing during the recent past that Sark may have over-reached itself (especially as regards the hordes of day-trippers from Guernsey) and that the beauty of the island stands in jeopardy because of the inadequacy of its sanitary provision for such numbers, not to mention the mountains of litter deposited by these fleeting guests who, bringing their own packed lunches, spend but little in the local shops and hotels. To make matters worse, the danger is also felt of the ravages wrought by the day-trippers operating as a disincentive to the far more lucrative long-term clientele.

Alderney's remoteness and poor communications meant that tourists were rare before the Second World War, though there was a modest increase with the opening of the airport in 1935. Although frequent services by *Aurigny* and other airlines have in recent years made Alderney more accessible, this advantage has been partly offset by the high level of fares charged — a disincentive compounded by the costliness of the local hotels. Among steps taken or contemplated to increase the island's 'drawing power', the establishment of an electronic gambling system proved lucrative as from early 1998 when the States of Alderney licensed three companies (each paying £50,000 per annum for its franchise) to operate tax-free services enabling people all over the world to place bets by telephone, 'fax', 'e-mail' or the internet. The profitability of ventures of this nature became manifest in mid-May 1999 with the news that the shares in one of the operators concerned (NetBet) which had stood at 70 pence a month beforehand had by then reached 425 pence. While the planned opening of a casino was in the event postponed *sine die*, efforts were also made to improve the facilities for visiting yachtsmen and a suggestion was put forward that 'tax breaks' (i.e. tax concessions for new businesses) might well encourage developmental investment redounding to the benefit of the island.

The improvement of the facilities on Herm resulting from the energy and drive of Major 'Peter' Wood now attracts so many tourists to the *White House* hotel and the Camp Site that during the summer season they outnumber the local population by three to two. Furthermore, thanks to the ubiquity of sanitary provision and litter-bins, the island suffers far less from the day-tripper trade than does Sark.

The voracity of the average tourist's appetite for souvenirs has fostered the growth in the years since the war of a number of light industries in Guernsey catering for this demand. These include the manufacture of Guernsey milkcans and other copperware, the exquisite gold and silver creations of Bruce Russell (a Freeman of Goldsmiths' Hall) made in his attractive premises set in a nature reserve at Le Gron, plus also the production of clocks, ornamental candles and the local Eau de Cologne (an enterprise going back to pre-war days), as well as a pottery industry.

In the late 'fifties such an industry was also set up in Herm with the help of David Rawnsley of the Chelsea Pottery. It was conducted with particular flair and verve. The clay, taken from Hermetier beach, was washed in an old butter-churn, sieved and dried on plaster-of-Paris pads, and then thrown on a home-made potter's wheel to be fashioned into mugs, jugs and other vessels. After biscuit-firing (at 1,000 deg. Centigrade) had changed the clay's colour to a fetching honey-red, it was decorated, glazed, and re-fired at a higher temperature. The wares soon earned widespread esteem; but manpower shortage, by precluding efficient division of labour, made production costs ruinously high, so that the venture had to cease.

Paradoxically, however, the firm which for over thirty years was of outstanding importance among the light industries was in no way connected with the tourist trade. This was *Tektronix Guernsey Limited*, which was set up in September 1958 as the first overseas base of *Tektronix Incorporated* of Oregon, U.S.A. The main product was the oscilloscope and a staff of 700 was at one time employed (though this later dwindled to 220), many of them islanders who had undergone the necessary technical training. The products were carried to twenty different countries. Thus the decision reached in January 1990 to transfer the company's Guernsey-based production and marketing facilities the following May to a plant at Heernveen in Holland, as Guernsey's 'geographic location does not provide a presence of sufficient strength in the European market' administered a severe blow to the island's export earnings prospects, the extent of which may be deduced from the findings of an industrial census conducted by the Board of Trade and Industry at the end of 1986, showing that in the course of that year the Light Industrial Sector as a whole exported goods to the value of £80 million, with three-quarters of this total attributable to electronic firms. Hence the sober satisfaction occasioned by the subsequent announcement on the part of various other (though smaller) electronic and computer software concerns such as *Datalink*, *Dynatech* and *Eurotherm* of their intention to remain in the island, even though the first two withdrew twelve years later. Especially gratifying were four further developments during the 1990s. The first of these was the purchase in 1990 of *Eurotherm (Guernsey) Limited* from its parent company in the United Kingdom by the local management team, so as to insulate it from decisions made outside the island. Taking the name of *Offshore Electronics Limited*, this concern's turnover had increased six fold by 1998, when £10 million worth of sales was anticipated for the year 2000. The second was the move into the former Tektronix Factory at Saint Saviour's in 1994 of the *Specsavers Optical Group* which gave employment to a staff of 200 and in the previous year had made a profit of £5.2 million. The third was the dramatic rise of *Ribbon Revival*, manufacturers of office and computer printer consumables which, founded in a modest pied-à-terre in 1993 with two directors and two employees, was by 1995 established in large premises in Pitronnerie Road with a staff of 24, marketing its output through numerous outlets in the U.K. plus others in Ireland, Denmark, Malta, Mauritius, South Africa and the United Arab Emirates — and enhancing its prospects by entering into a partnership with Richard Branson's *Virgin Group* whereby it became the national distributor for all *Virgin Euromagnetic* products. The fourth development was in the realm of e-commerce (sometimes called e-business) which embraces any transaction or exchange of value made electronically, either to promote retailing, or — even more important — to facilitate the exchange of information between companies in each stage of production. As in such e-business tax is levied at the point where the electronic equipment is located, companies setting up web-based business operations in either Jersey or Guernsey make enormous savings by paying only island rates of tax. As a result, the *Daily Telegraph* of December 8th., 1998 reported that the archipelago as a whole was developing into 'Europe's Capital of e-commerce', with the firm of *Sun Microsystems* in association with *First Magellan* providing investors with a comprehensive package of e-commerce business.

Chapter Fourteen

'BUSINESS IN GREAT WATERS'

THE STRATEGIC POSITION of St. Peter-Port roadstead on the sea routes from southern Europe to Britain and the opposing Channel coasts has made Guernsey a key port of call throughout the centuries. The discovery by Mr. Richard Keen in November 1977 on the seabed near the Town harbour of late first-century amphorae of the type used for the conveyance of Garum (a fish sauce much prized by the Romans) from southern Spain to Britain strongly suggests that the island's commercial involvement is of considerable antiquity. This impression was reinforced by the same diver's further discovery on Christmas Day 1982 of the hull of a second century Roman ship about sixty-five feet long which enjoys the distinction of being the oldest craft ever found in British waters — and which was brought to the surface in 1985. (It was also established, incidentally, that yet another wreck of the same era awaits salvage near the Bréhon Tower.) Similar indications are provided by the excavations conducted at Jerbourg in early 1979 which, in the opinion of Dr. Barry Cunliffe, point to the area having been a fortified trading post on the route between St. Malo and Hengistbury in Dorset; possibly operated by refugees from Brittany who fled to Guernsey after an abortive rebellion against Julius Caesar in 56 B.C. and who obtained an income from tolls levied on visiting vessels. Such speculations apart, it is certain that the facilities for shelter and re-victualling provided by Guernsey on the route carrying the lucrative wine trade from Gascony to England was a prime consideration in motivating King John and his successors to make every effort to retain control of the archipelago after the loss of Continental Normandy. It is not surprising, therefore, that the islanders played a prominent part among those who 'go down to the sea in ships and occupy their business in great waters'. Indeed, geographical circumstances left them nowhere else to go.

The importance already attained by overseas trade at the end of the 13th. century is made evident by the vigorous insular reaction to Edward I's inauguration of his 'parva et nova custuma' in 1297. By this measure aliens paid on imports a customs rate 50 per cent. higher than that paid by native merchants on exports — and it classified island merchants as aliens. This threat by the king to a major source of island earnings, coming as it did a mere three years after a particularly savage onslaught by the king's enemies (the terrible raid of 1294), was seen by local merchants as adding insult to injury, and they vehemently protested that, although not English, neither were they aliens, and therefore should be exempt from the 50 per cent. surcharge. It was not, however, until the mid-14th. century that this argument was conceded, it being granted that, although not denizens, the status of the islanders was not that of aliens, but of 'reputed citizens'.

The point having been ultimately won, trade expanded, its extent by the middle of the 15th. century being indicated by a proclamation in 1459 by Henry IV of Castile, in which he granted a safe-conduct to Thomas de Sausmarez, Jean Dusson, Thomas Henry, and Guillaume Esstur to come and go for trade, ordering all his subjects to observe it.

The neutral status accorded to the islands by the 1480/1 Bull of Pope Sixtus IV gave a tremendous fillip to trade, misgivings about the continuance of which largely accounted for the leading islanders' initial opposition to Elizabeth I's religious changes, for fear that they would destroy the validity of the Bull (see Part I, Chapters Five and Six).

The Ile de Rhé campaign of 1627 had serious repercussions for the archipelago as it led Richelieu to forbid all trade with the islands. This setback provided yet another reason for disapproval of Charles I, and it is significant that Guernsey's leading 'Roundhead', Pierre de Beauvoir, was a prominent merchant having trade connections with Spain, Brittany and La Hague, exchanging wool, silk and velvet goods for French linen and laces, brandy and gloves, and Spanish wine.

The 18th. century was one of intense activity by Guernsey merchants, although their profits were menaced early in the century by the 1709 attempt of the Customs Commissioners to impose their rules on island trade. As seen in Part III, Chapter Seven, this attempt was successfully resisted, Guernsey obtaining confirmation of her ancient right to bring her produce freely into England.

The threat removed, Guernsey's merchants set out to exploit to the utmost the advantages of the island's geographical position and excellent roadstead. At first they tended to confine themselves to local trade, concentrating on Southampton and neighbouring French ports such as St. Malo, with the main cargoes consisting of cider, stone, lobsters, knitted goods, cattle and wine. As was also seen in Part III, Chapter Seven, Southampton merchants protested to no avail against these ventures. Later, however, Guernsey's traders extended their activities to the Atlantic and the Mediterranean, and a circular traffic was built up. A ship, for example, might sail with brandy to Madeira and barter it for wine, going on to the West Indies to change the wine for rum — which in its turn would be traded for fish in Newfoundland. The fish would be carried back for sale in Mediterranean ports. One of the main firms engaged in such traffic was Carteret Priaulx (founded 1712) which by the 1770s had business connections all over Europe and America.

The sale of wines and brandies captured from the French during the War of the League of Augsburg led to a most lucrative entrepôt trade in wines, based on the fact that St. Peter-Port was a free port, where English and French merchants could deposit their goods without the payment of duty until the favourable moment for a sale arrived. By a fortunate climatic freak, the temperature of the town's vaults was found to be ideal for the storage and maturing of wines and spirits. These vaults were dug out from the cliffs and the slopes of Mont Gibel; yet, despite their number, trade was at times so extensive that goods had to be stored in fields for want of anywhere else to put them. It was after the seven years' experience he gained as an apprentice in this trade with the house of Laurence Martin in Guernsey that the Jerseyman, Jean Martel (1684–1753), emigrated to France to found his world-famous cognac business.

In 1798 William Mooney, an English visitor, recorded in his diary: 'Guernsey is the Emporium of a Universal Trade and in 1796/7 the Exports from hence to England paid one million and a half into the Customs and Excise. This island is most conveniently situated for commerce with every part of Europe, and from its proximity to French ports, its merchants are enabled to take advantage of the state of their markets, as no others can'.

Although Napoleon had inaugurated his Continental System by the Berlin Decree of 1806, he was, in accordance with his dictum, 'France before all', inconsistent in its application, allowing relaxations from time to time to replenish his exchequer and even allowing the export of grain when there was a glut in 1809, well knowing that its ultimate destination would be Britain. Guernsey became the principal market for such interchanges, enabling her merchants to make useful profits by way of compensation for the diminution in the entrepôt trade brought about by the setting up of bonded warehouses in Britain.

With the coming of peace, Guernsey's merchants seized upon trade openings before foreign competitors, debilitated by the war, had had time to re-establish themselves. They sent out their ships to Spanish and Mediterranean ports for wine, then over to South America for coffee, sugar and hides, and finally either back to the island for another run or up to Antwerp or Hamburg for grain. It was this vigorous activity that stimulated the development of the ship-building industry. As the course of the 19th. century saw the island's economy come to be based more and more on her granite, her livestock, and her horticultural produce, so commerce lost its romantic far-flung scope and came to be associated almost completely with trade with Britain stemming from these local industries.

This is not, however, the end of the story, as a particularly lucrative type of commercial engagement, which has so far been denied mention, remains to be considered. The highly profitable venture concerned was smuggling, the floodgates for a vast volume of which had been opened by William III's repudiation of the archipelago's neutrality, outlawing as it did all legal trade with France. The smuggling era had dawned — and it was to last throughout the 18th. century. It is true that on a smaller scale activity of this nature had already been going on for some time — witness the unsuccessful attempts by the Customs Commissioners in 1681 to stop the smuggling between the Islands and West Country ports — but now, with no other type of Anglo/French trade possible, the islands' geographical position made them an ideal base of operations for breaking down bulk commodities into small portable packages for onward transmission, thus presenting opportunities which the islanders seized with both hands.

In time, dealing in contraband came to appear perfectly normal, so that by the mid-18th. century the island merchants saw trading, privateering and smuggling as no more than different aspects of a single attempt to win wealth from foreigners. The men of Guernsey, merchants, seamen and men with capital, taking advantage of their strategic location and good roadstead, worked together to exploit to the utmost the prospects opened up by this 'fair trading', the profits of which were making up for the progressive decline in the knitting industry. What is more, they were prepared to defend their participation in smuggling against the strictures of irritated British customs officials by arguing that their privileges conferred on them the right of a free port — and in any case, as the increased duties imposed by the British government had rendered smuggling inevitable, it was better that the profits should go to the Crown's subjects than to foreigners. Thus, after the 1709 rebuff, two plans by the Privy Council to suppress this underground commerce by establishing a Customs House in Guernsey (the first in 1717 and the second in 1720) collapsed in the face of vociferous objections by the islanders; who subsequently so opposed an actual British Customs presence in 1767 by what a later age was to call 'non-violent non-co-operation' as to render it fleeting. In yet another attempt to halt 'fair trading', Parliament in 1768 enacted legislation requiring all Channel Island vessels to be cleared from a British port. This was immediately seen as an infringement of the islands' charters, and hence was vigorously opposed. After a long struggle the measure was withdrawn and direct trade between the Islands and foreign ports was resumed.

The people of Alderney, whose energies had so profitably been directed to privateering during the Seven Years War, diverted them to smuggling once the war was over, to aid which the local population developed the specialised trade of making small kegs, so handy for use on a rocky cliff path in the dark. A lucrative period ensued, enabling John Le Mesurier, the 'Governor', to make many improvements in the island.

In 1807 came the day of reckoning. Despite vigorous protests from the States that any interference with 'fair trading' was an infringement of ancient privileges, the British government nevertheless extended the application of the British Smuggling Act to Channel Island waters, setting up local customs departments for its enforcement. The Guernsey authorities put as good a face as they could on the situation, founding in 1808 the local Chamber of Commerce to inhibit proscribed trading — and twelve years later one finds *The Star* newspaper making a virtue out of necessity, reporting primly in its issue of February 15th., 1820, that 'there is a permanent smuggling preventive service stationed at the entrance of our harbour, and a Registrar of Certificates' Office on shore, which renders it impossible, even were we so inclined, to attempt any illicit trade with our neighbours'. However, although appearances might have been saved, the cessation of the traffic in "Brandy for the Parson, 'Baccy for the Clerk; Laces for a Lady" proved to be a severe blow to the island's economy. In 1811 the Bank of Bishop, de Jersey and Company failed, as did also that of MacCullough, Allaire, Bonamy and Company. Guernsey thereafter had no bank of its own until the foundation in 1827 of the Bank of Priaulx, Le Marchant, Rougier and Company, known as the 'Guernsey Banking Company'.

The initial reaction of some Guernsey merchants at the outset of these developments was to transfer their activities to Alderney but in 1808 the customs officers established effective control over that island also — a fact which led to considerable distress. The results of an abrupt cessation of a great influx of money were disastrous. Building projects had to be abandoned and unemployment and poverty stared the Aurigniais in the face. The Bank of Alderney, which had its own note issue, crashed with heavy liabilities and a period of economic collapse set in which drove many islanders to emigrate; induced John Le Mesurier to relinquish his grant of the island (see Part III, Chapter Twelve); and, as was seen in Chapter Two of this Part, ultimately necessitated the distribution of common land in 'good' and 'poor' lots among the impoverished population. The only island in the Bailiwick not to suffer unduly was Sark, whose participation in the smuggling had been minimal and where, therefore, little dislocation was caused by its discontinuance.

These disruptions notwithstanding, control was obviously a *fait accompli* from which there was no escape and the eventual realization that its exercise by island officials would be preferable to that by appointees of the United Kingdom led to the States' Customs Department being established in 1858, at fist to facilitate the enforcement of the duties on imported goods (doubled that year after their initial imposition seven years previously) to help pay for the construction of the modern harbour which was then being undertaken — and thus (regardless of the continued presence in the island until 1973 of H.M. Customs and Excise for Ship Registry purposes) were appointed the original forerunners of the douaniers past whom present day travellers trundle their trolleys. Since 1973 the responsibilities of the Department employing these functionaries have steadily increased, commencing that year with its assumption of law enforcement activity. This was followed in 1975 by its absorption of the Immigration and Nationality Department, as a consequence of which it was renamed the States of Guernsey Customs and Immigration Department — and its subsequent expansion was such that in

1991 its law enforcement rôles regarding Investigation, Intelligence and Smuggling Prevention were separated, with each being entrusted to a specialist sub-division. So do great oaks from little acorns grow! That the oak needed to be of a considerable size were it to bear its burdens became appallingly evident late in 1998 with the alarming disclosure by Drug Concern that drug smuggling into the island had become international big business! More specifically, it was subsequently revealed (August 1999) that in the course of the self-same year of 1998 drugs valued at £200,000 had been confiscated by Guernsey Customs from 103 seizures and also that, thanks to advance detection, a further £1.5 million worth of drugs destined for the Channel Isles from overseas had been intercepted *en route* for the archipelago. This major evil of the *fin de siècle* period had certainly not left Guernsey unscathed.

One last thought. Looking back over this chapter prompts one to observe that the daring spirit which had animated the above mentioned 'fair-trading' adventures before they were brought to a halt is by no means dead, even if manifested nowadays in a more peaceful and legal guise: witness the achievement of Geoff Somers of Sark who in 1990 became the first Channel Islander to reach the South Pole.

Chapter Fifteen

FAIRS AND MARKETS

IN MOST ECONOMIES a characteristic feature of mediaeval commerce consisted of periodical fairs, providing more durable goods than the immediate necessities normally obtained in markets. Such was not the case in Guernsey, however, as the smallness of the island rendered the weekly market easily accessible to all, and led to the scope of its trading being wider than was the case with local markets in England or on the Continent. Nevertheless, it is true that to a limited extent Guernseymen made use of Norman and Bréton fairs for the purchase of horses and (initially) cattle. Thus the annual fair at Lessay in Normandy attracted some Guernsey buyers right up to the early years of the 20th. century.

Incidentally, the 19th.-century Castel fair, held in a field between the parish church and Le Préel, was, strictly speaking, a misnomer, partaking mostly of the nature of a cattle show, where premiums were distributed by the Agricultural Society (founded 1842) to the owners of the most promising heifers and finest bulls. It is nevertheless interesting to note that, despite its late establishment, its dates corresponded with those traditional for fairs in the Middle Ages — Easter, St. John the Baptist, and Michaelmas.

Apart from a mediaeval cattle staple which (if the nineteenth-century schoolmaster/poet Denys Corbet was right in so inferring from the locality's name) could possibly have been situate at Mont Marché in the Forest; Guernsey's original market was to be found in the district still known as Les Landes du Marché — an area so sited as to link a predominantly agricultural economy in the south of the island with one centred on fishing in the north. (It has been argued, incidentally, that the same focality also led to this location becoming in the early Middle Ages the venue of the emergent Court: hence, it is alleged, the name of Rue Cohu — Court Road — still attaching to the highway whereby one approaches this vicinage from the south-west.) During the late 13th. and early 14th. centuries the right to control this market by imposing weights and measures and receiving tolls was in dispute between the king and the seigneurs of Fief Le Comte and Fief St. Michel. Although the market's location was shortly to be moved despite the king's disapproval, he nevertheless won recognition of his rights of control.

In 1307 Edward II addressed a letter to Otto de Grandison:

> That having been informed that the market held at Les Landes has been transferred to a fief belonging to a private individual, to his prejudice, the Lord of the Isles was to order public proclamation to be made that it should be held there as usual, and nowhere else.

The 'fief belonging to a private individual' referred to the area of the Town, the growth of which from 1243 onwards had increasingly attracted trade away from Les Landes du Marché. Eventually, Edward II had to give way, reluctantly authorising in 1309 the market's transfer to a site (then rural) in the vicinity of the present-day War Memorial; but this location was soon abandoned in favour of that adjacent to the Town Church — though neither move impaired the King's right to market tolls or his control over weights and measures. Thus as late as 1813 when the States were first considering the purchase of the French Halles (effected in 1817) it was admitted that 'markets, by their very nature, arise from royal prerogative'. Furthermore, until recently market goods were still weighed on the Queen's Scales, using the queen's weights, in the building (completed in 1876 to the design of James Duquemin and now a café) bearing over its door the inscription, 'Poids de la Reine'.

After its removal to St. Peter-Port, the market was held for many centuries around every side of the Town church save that facing the sea — and as far up the High Street as the foot of Berthelot Street, as well as invading Cow Lane and Bull Lane (as la Rue Tanquerel of subsequent mention was often nicknamed). The location was, of course, in every way unsuitable, being overcrowded, malodorous and dirty — and yet it was used for four-and-a-half centuries. Meat and vegetables were exposed to all weathers, as well as to mud and flies, while Cow Lane and Bull Lane were so narrow that passers-by could not avoid brushing against the meat. It was indeed a mercy that the sea came half-way up Cow Lane at high tide and washed away the blood from the Friday slaughter — and the accumulated filth on all days.

The question of a covered market first arose in 1726, when a Committee of the States was appointed to select a site, but nothing was done until 1777, when a private syndicate took the matter in

MILITARY

29. Alderney: 'The Nunnery' — a Roman Fort of the Saxon Shore?

30. Mediaeval Fortification — Le Château de Rocquaine.

31. The Civil War: 'The Escape from Castle Cornet' (1643).

32. The Civil War: Castle Cornet – the gun-port whereby the Three Commissioners allegedly escaped (1643).

33. Fermain Bay, whence the Three Commissioners were abducted: also showing General Doyle's rampart (Napoleonic Wars) and 'Martello' Tower (War of American Independence).

34. The 'Gibraltar of the Channel': Alderney's massive Breakwater with Forts Grosnez and Tourgis in the background (Victorian era).

35. The Royal Guernsey Militia's last Inspection by Royalty (1935).

36. King's Birthday Parade (1936).

7. Second World War: Major H. W. Le Patourel winning the Victoria Cross–Tebourba, Tunisia, 3 December, 1942. (*Reproduced by courtesy of the Trustees of the Royal Hampshire Regiment*).

38. (*left*) Second World War: German Troops in Le Pollet (1940)

39. (*above*) Second World War: S.S. *St. Helier*, which brought last shipload of troops from Dunkirk, photographed in Guernsey, 1939.

40. (*below*) Second World War: Island of Burhou, showing the cottage which the Germans shelled out of existence

41. Second World War: Captain Fred Noyon, whose escape to Cherbourg alerted the Allies to the plight of the starving islanders.

42. Alderney: The Hammond Memorial to the Slave Workers who died during the German Occupation.

SOCIO/ECONOMIC

43. (*left*) Alderney: Old Churc
Tower and Gateway of
School provided by
John le Mesurier (1790)

44. (*below*) Cider making:
Apples being crushed in
Le Tour.

5. (*above*) Vraic gathering.

6. (*right*) The world's oldest surviving Pillar Box (1853).

47. (*above*) Guernsey's first tram (6 June 1879).

48. (*left*) L'Erée Aerodrome: Mr. Cecil Noel's 'Wee Mite' (1934).

49. (*right*) Guernsey can manufacture.

50. (*far right*) The finished article!

PEOPLE'S CAFÉ
WORKMAN'S HOME.
TEA
COFFEE
READING
ROOMS
2
TEAM TRAMWAY Co
GUERNSEY STEAM
TRAMWAY Co

51. The 19th-century fish market before its decline.

52. Les Poids de la Reine (mid-19th century).

53. Herm: The tourist industry and the crane from the mid-19th-century quarrying days.

54. The 1979 'Museum of the Year'.

55. Road Upkeep: Gathering of Pions at re-enactment of La Chevauchée de St Michel (1966).

hand. In that year a meat market company was formed and application made to the King-in-Council for permission to build a market. The very fact of such an application indicates the recognition of royal rights over St. Peter-Port's markets. The Order-in-Council authorising construction laid down that the company was to be allowed by the States certain duties on all cattle killed so long as it remained the proprietor of the market — but that the States were to have the option of taking over the market at any time, on payment of a sum equal to the company's original building costs.

Building started in 1780 in what had been the garden of the rectory, with the new assembly rooms (see Chapter Twenty-eight following) being erected on top to replace the old and cramped ones in the Pollet. The market was ready for the butchers in 1782 and they moved in from Cow Lane and Bull Lane. The vegetable and fruit sellers set up their stalls in the space in front of the new market (now La Place du Marché), but the fish vendors refused to move from the bottom of High Street. Not until 1812 did the fishmongers move — and then only to the bottom of Cornet Street (where some improvements had been made in 1778). They occupied an open space called 'dessous la grille' between the church and the Cimetière des Soeurs. Five years after this cautious move by the fishmongers — in 1817 — the States decided to exercise their purchase option and bought the market for £5,000, but the assembly rooms (which did not belong to the meat market company) remained in the hands of their proprietors until the States bought them in 1871 for £900.

In 1822 the meat market (designed by John Wilson) was built and the butchers moved in, leaving the 'old' market available to the vegetable sellers who, however, did not take to it, preferring La Place du Marché. Gradually it came to be used by vendors of eggs, butter, poultry, and fruit imported from Brittany, thus acquiring its present name of the French Halles. On the other side of La Place du Marché the States Arcade was completed in 1830 and set aside for the use of country people (not butchers) who brought in their own ready-dressed porkers and calves for sale. Hence the 10 divisions — one for each parish.

The vegetable market (associated with the Arcade and also designed by Wilson) followed the meat market between 1826 and 1830, being at the time allocated to fishmongers (at last weaned away from Cornet Street) and was therefore fitted with 40 marble-topped tables, which were later moved to a new fish market (designed by John Newton and completed in 1877) — the next building to go up. Last of all came the market halls with their renaissance-style central arch (erected between 1877 and 1879 at right-angles to the vegetable market and designed by Francis Chambers), beneath which is a large subterranean chamber with its monumental entrance and yet another Newton design, for many years used as a bond store, whose floor practically coincides with that of the ancient Vallée de la Misère, which, as seen in Chapter Seven of this Part, acted as the *accoucheur* of St. Peter-Port.

The method whereby the entire complex was financed from 1817 onwards is fascinating. The construction costs were paid for in States' notes, which were subsequently redeemed from the net revenue of the markets and of the shops and halls connected with the buildings. Thanks to the fact that Guernsey States' notes were not expected by the holders to be accepted as ordinary currency elsewhere, and also to the confidence of the people in the island government's credit, no difficulty arose. Thus a scheme of borrowing without interest was so successfully worked that the expedient was repeated to finance the building of roads, schools and public works in later years.

To complete the picture, it must be said that in addition to these installations there was also a pig market, which was held in a shed on the site later occupied by the 'bus terminus, and where farmers brought their pigs every Saturday. As pig-keeping declined, the pig market was closed shortly after the end of the First World War.

Sad to say, by the late 1990s a like fate had come to threaten the main complex, reduced as it was to a sickly ghost of the thriving *agora* of previous times, with its habitués amounting to 20% or less of the numbers frequenting the town's busy epicentre at Le Grand Carrefour. Initial suggestions for its revival envisaged forsaking the erstwhile meat-fish-vegetable tripartition in favour of establishing an 'anchor store' at the Mill Street end of the ensemble and supplementing this by further measures aimed at increasing the general appeal of the area. In due course — possibly because of the persuasive voice of Mammon proclaiming how lucrative a trade would flow from what was advocated and the consequent utter neglect of the warning that it profits a man nothing to gain the whole world if he thereby loses his soul — the above-mentioned 'further measures' eventualized in a proposed design deplored by many (including, to be frank, the present writer) as outrageously philistine — a repellent blot besmirching the face of the Bailiwick's capital and obliterating the aesthetic harmony in diversity of a hitherto highly esteemed architectural gem categorised by Sir Charles Brett in his prestigious *Parochial Survey* as a group of buildings within which every intrusion should be resisted. It was thus a source of pronounced gratification to the many protesters who on grounds of taste had deprecated the steps under consideration that on August 25th., 1998 the proposals relating thereto were rejected by the conjoint voice of the States' Heritage and Island Development Committees.

Although the developers the following Christmas submitted a revised plan (allegedly after discussion with the Island Development Committee) it was feared that not only would its implementation cause increased traffic problems, but also that the loss of a great deal of the historical and architectural integrity of the buildings would still be entailed — so that once again objections were registered with the Island Development and Heritage Committees.

Other plans (one hopes in better taste than those advanced for the markets) have been independently formulated for reversing the decline in the Mill Street/Mansell Street locality. Details are yet to be revealed. On verra ce qu'on verra.

No review of Guernsey's commercial provision would be complete without a mention of the commercial arcades, the remarkable creation of George Le Boutillier (1783–1867) to whom the island is also indebted for the first introduction of gaslight. A Jerseyman, Le Boutillier came to Guernsey in 1804 and set up a drapery business. During the 1830s this man of energy and vision embarked on the stupendous task of creating the commercial arcades by a stone and mortar invasion of Mont Gibel, involving a colossal excavation operation as well as the purchase of a cluster of houses in the High Street — an enormous financial burden — and also the Herculean task of quarrying away thousands of tons of gravel and stone. The extent of the endeavour undertaken by Le Boutillier may be appreciated by looking down on his achievement from the upper reaches of the arcade steps before reaching Clifton.

The work involved clearing some of the narrow alleys near the Town church so as to make way for the project, and it is likely that the steps opposite the church's north door constitute a relic of one of these — La Rue Tanquerel. The original intention was for the arcades to be covered with a glass roof, but this project was frustrated by the financial ruin which befell Le Boutillier as a result of his undertaking. After his bankruptcy George Le Boutillier emigrated to the U.S.A. in 1838, where he again became rich, returning to his native Jersey for his declining years.

Chapter Sixteen

LAND TRANSPORT

GUERNSEY'S OLDEST ROAD AUTHORITY was the Feudal Court of the Fief St. Michel (established mid-12th. century), on which devolved the duty of conducting an inspection of the king's highway. This inspection was an integral part of a colourful and elaborate ceremony known as La Chevauchée de St. Michel, the 13th.-century origins of which were of a religious nature, it being carried out annually at Trinity under a charter from the Bishop of Coutances with the object of ensuring that the highway was clear in readiness for the various parochial processions of the Blessed Sacrament held around the date of the Feast of Corpus Christi (the Thursday after Trinity) which was observed from 1264 onwards. There is, however, a strong possibility that the custom has much more ancient origins, harking back to vernal pagan perambulations designed to invoke the blessings of Ceres on the crops — an observance which was subsequently Christianised in the form of the blessing of the fields of Rogationtide.

In its composition La Chevauchée de St. Michel was made up of the Seneschal and Vavasseurs of the Fief Court, accompanied by the Crown Officers (H.M. Procureur, H.M. Comptroller, H.M. Greffier, H. M. Sergent, and the Prévôt du Roi) as well as the prévôts of other fiefs. All these personages were mounted and were attended by pions on foot, attired in black caps with a red ribbon behind, white shirts, white vests braided with red, long white breeches tied with red ribbon round the knee, and white stockings. Each of these attendants carried a wand bearing a red rosette. The Seneschal and the King's Officers were each allocated two pions as valets, though the vavasseurs were only allowed one each. A perquisite of the pions was their entitlement to kiss any woman they met *en route*, provided that no lady was kissed by more than one pion.

The Prévôt du Roi and the prévôts of the seigneurial fiefs took it in turn to carry a lance 11 ¼ feet long and any obstacle this lance encountered, such as stones of walls, branches of trees or projecting roots, had to be cleared away, and the proprietors of the land where the irregularities occurred were mulcted in a fine. Hence 'les grands chemins du roi' were kept in good trim.

Once the Fief St. Michel had been 'taken into the King's hand', the Fief Court (now consisting of crown appointees) was required every three years to see that the king's highway was kept open. After the Reformation the Popish associations of the ceremony were so repugnant to the Calvinist Colloque that the custom fell into desuetude. It was eventually revived in 1813 as a publicity exercise in connection with Sir John Doyle's road-making activities (see Part IV, Chapter Nine) and was carried out for the last time by the Fief Court (which was shortly afterwards abolished) on May 31st., 1837. The ceremony was, however, performed once more in 1966 to mark the ninth centenary of the conquest of England. Twenty-nine years later — in May 1995 — as part of the celebration of the Fiftieth Anniversary of the Liberation a further re-enactment was arranged by the Guernsey National Trust in conjunction with the G.A.D.O.C., the Horse Driving Society, the Riding and Hunt Club and the Pony Club.

An interesting reminder of La Chevauchée may be seen near Pleinmont Point in the form of La Table des Pions, a flat grassy mound with an encircling ring of stones, where the pions were served with refreshments while the horsemen were regaled at the nearby Château de Pezeries.

The actual maintenance of the roads, involving keeping the surface in repair and cutting back growth along the sides, was the responsibility of the owners of property bordering them, as they claimed that their properties did not end at the side of the road, but extended halfway across. Nevertheless, the general public enjoyed the ancient common-law right of free passage at all times. In return for their upkeep contributions the owners were exempted from parochial taxation or feudal dues in respect of their halves of the roads.

A 1534 ordinance by the Court of Chief Pleas required hedge growth to be cut back to allow free passage — a provision rendered especially necessary by the narrowness of the roads. This requirement was repeated in 1535 with instructions to the constables to ensure that property owners did, in fact, repair their sections of the roads. As these owners varied in skill and conscientiousness, the result was apt to be patchy and the road surface far from ideal, becoming extremely muddy in winter. The narrowness of the roads also made it necessary along particularly constricted stretches for 'gensages' (widened enclaves) to be provided on instructions from the constables and douzeniers to enable vehicles to meet and pass each other.

After the lapse of La Chevauchée, the constables of each parish, together with the 12 members of the douzaine and accompanied by three or four jurats, conducted a periodical *Visite des Chemins*, with a good deal of pomp and circumstance. A lance for measuring the height of overhanging branches was carried as in La Chevauchée, and fines were imposed on the proprietors of land whose hedges did not conform to the required standards.

A more frequent device, however, was to apply the principles of division of labour by making use of the sub-division of the parishes into vingtaines (later sometimes called cantons), three members of the parish douzaine being allotted to each vingtaine. St. Peter-Port had 11 vingtaines, St. Sampson's, Torteval, and the Forest three each, and the remaining parishes four. It was thus possible for *La Visite des Chemins* to be conducted vingtaine by vingtaine, being undertaken by the douzeniers allocated to the vingtaine in question, accompanied by the constables. After *La Visite* had been carried out a report was drawn up, signed by the constables and the douzeniers de la vingtaine, and presented to the full douzaine at the next parish meeting. After the reports had been considered by the douzaine, the constables would notify those whose sections of road or uncut hedges required attention, subsequently checking that the work had been done satisfactorily. Should any proprietor neglect to carry out the work required of him within the time allowed, the constables would arrange for it to be done by hired labour at the expense of the defaulter, who was also prosecuted for a fine.

During the mid-19th. century a new system was tried whereby, although individual responsibility for hedge-cutting was retained, each property owner became responsible for the whole width of the road over half his frontage, the width corresponding to the other half being the responsibility of the proprietor facing him. This arrangement not proving any great improvement on the previous one, the parishes decided to undertake to keep road surfaces usable, meeting the cost by a parochial levy on the owners of the property bordering the roads.

When, under the inspiration of Sir John Doyle, the States laid out the main roads in the early 19th. century, at the same time they shouldered the responsibility for their upkeep, defraying the cost by a tax called 'L'Equivalent' (i.e., the cash equivalent of erstwhile road-upkeep responsibilities of neighbouring property-owners). This tax was based on the length of each proprietor's frontage on the road, as recorded in the Cadastre, and was levied at the rate of two pence per running perch (seven yards). Collection of this tax (which was the forerunner of the modern occupiers' rate) was undertaken by the parish constables, who then handed over the proceeds to the supervisor.

Subsequent road construction was financed in a fashion similar to that employed in the case of the markets and towards the end of the 19th. century the States took over the care of *all* roads. The constables and douzaines, however, still retain residual highway responsibilities, in that inspections are made by each parish douzaine in June and September to ensure that all hedges have been trimmed, the constables of each parish reporting to the Michaelmas Chief Pleas that this has been done, and also that all quarries in their parishes are adequately fenced.

Sark's road system was inaugurated by Helier de Carteret soon after his colonisation of the island, as an adjunct to the defensive measures to which he was committed. Accordingly he set about the construction of Les Grands Chemins (or Chemins Royaux) — straight communicating roads with a width of 24 ft. to give easy access to any part of the island that might be threatened by attack. These were supplemented by minor roads of a width of 18 ft. leading off the main roads to the tenement clusters. The maintenance of this network was established as the direct responsibility of the tenants by an ordinance of October 1st., 1585, while Helier's son, Philippe was seigneur. Thus originated the Corvée obligations which, despite the protests of the tenants between 1803 and 1812 (already mentioned in Part II, Chapter Ten) persisted until 1951. Since 1951 road upkeep has been undertaken by hired labour, the cost being met by a household levy. Like Guernsey, Sark in the 18th. century was divided into vingtaines — two of them — for road inspection purposes.

Until the 18th. century the only vehicles using Guernsey's roads were various types of agricultural carts. The first closed carriage was very likely that of Lieutenant-Colonel P. A. Irving, who was the lieutenant-governor from 1770 to 1784. A horse-drawn omnibus service was in operation between St. Peter-Port and St. Sampson's as early as 1837 and in the 1870s these even attained double-decker status. A few were still running as late as the early inter-war years, when the present writer recalls travelling in one (single-decker) to Grandes Rocques. By this time the motor-bus was coming into its own and competition between several rival firms fostered an excellent service between the wars. The companies dwindled in number and, with the demise of the Watson 'Greys' concern in 1978, Guernsey came to be served by a monopoly in the form of the Guernsey Railway Company, which had absorbed Guernsey Motors Limited in 1974. This in its turn, however, was rendered unprofitable by the proliferation of the private motor-car and all services were halted on November 19th., 1980. A U.K. firm (Trafalgar Leisure International) was licensed to take over in January 1981, operating a monopoly undertaking as Guernseybus Limited. The troubles which had beset the Guernsey Railway Company continued, however, with demand deficiency leading to fare increases and service curtailments, thereby prompting yet more people to take to their cars — a vicious downward spiral reflected in the 1991 Census revelation that out of 30,162 work-bound islanders on the day of the count, only 401 (1.329%,) used public transport. After a long period of indecision the States of Deliberation in January 1995 reacted to this ever-worsening decline by adopting proposals put forward by the States' Traffic Committee involving the restriction of Guernseybus operations to the north and west of the island, while entrusting the routes covering Saint Martin's plus that to Pleinmont via the Airport to Island Coachways — a firm which had hitherto specialised in private hire business. It was also decided to incorporate into this system the control of fare levels by the States' Traffic Committee, while at the same time granting each operator a States' subsidy to help (*inter alia*) to finance improved services and the acquisition of comfortable modern vehicles — but subject to a maximum of £100,000 per annum in the case of Guernseybus and £150,000 per annum in the case of Island Coachways. This arrangement was planned to last for seven years with effect from September 15th., 1995, thus affording plentiful opportunities to compare the two concerns' performances with — it was hoped — a resultant mutual stimulus to greater efficiency. Furthermore it was felt that a septennium gave ample time to test the ability of an enhanced public transport provision charging controlled fares to wean islanders from their motor vehicles, 47,011 of which were recorded in 1997 as crowded into Guernsey's 24½ square miles. By mid-1998 the indicators were that this experiment had by then met with a modest success.

If one counts the short narrow-gauge lines laid to serve the Sark silver mines and the Herm quarries, all four major islands of the Bailiwick have had railways at some time, though the only survivor is that in Alderney dating from 1847 and connecting Mannez quarry with Braye breakwater for the purpose of carrying stone for fore-shoring operations. Thanks to the initiative of Mr. Roger Warren, passenger traffic on this line started at Easter 1980.

In Guernsey a light steam railway was opened between St. Peter-Port and St. Sampson's on June 6th., 1879, operated by the Guernsey Steam Tramway Company Ltd. After this company had been reconstituted as the Guernsey Railway Company Ltd. in 1889, the line was electrified in 1891 (becoming one of the first systems in the British Isles to have overhead current), and public service in this new guise began on February 20th., 1892, with the major power supply (it is interesting to note) coming from boiling water in a furnace wherein was burnt the island's refuse — the disposal of which was thereby achieved — and using the resultant steam to drive a generator running at 575 revolutions per minute and producing 500 volts at 85 kilowatts. Thus the paradox arose where a tramway company had run a train service, while a railway company ran a tramway. This company bought out the Guernsey Omnibus Company in 1895 — and survived until 1980. Because of the ferocity of competition from the 'buses, 55 years of railway operation came to an end when the trams ceased to run on June 9th., 1934 under an arrangement whereby, in return for assuming ownership of all the rails, sleepers and standards, the States met more than half the cost of lifting the rails and reinstating the roadway.

Within eight years Guernsey once more had a railway, as between the summer of 1942 and the late spring of 1943 the Germans laid a railway from St. Peter-Port around the east, north and west coasts as far as L'Erée to service their coastal fortifications. Only two concrete dates have been preserved — April 2nd., 1943, when the line was nearing Fort Richmond, and April 23rd., 1943, when it had reached Perelle — an advance of three-quarters of a mile in three weeks. The west coast section was dismantled towards the end of the same year (1943), but the rest remained until the Liberation, when all the lines were lifted.

Chapter Seventeen

SEA ROUTES

IT IS STRANGE TO REFLECT that, despite the outstanding importance of St. Peter-Port's roadstead making Guernsey a frequent port of call for shipping, no regularly-established service of sailings existed until the end of the 18th. century. Moreover, documentary evidence of island craft prior to this period is scanty, though the first Guernsey ship of which record exists goes as far back as the early 15th. century. This record is in the *Rotule Normandie*, where the *Mary* of Guernsey (Captain Capelle) is listed as one of the 286 ships that ferried Henry V's armies to France in 1415.

During the 18th. century a fleet of cutters provided the backbone of the island's trade with England. These heavily-built ships of 40 to 80 tons, with massive spars and the finest quality sails, ran when trade offered, and also plied between the island and such French ports as St. Malo, Binic, Cherbourg, Granville, and St. Brieux, carrying the farm produce of France to Guernsey, the same merchants going on them year after year to purchase fowls and eggs, vegetables, butter and meat.

The same single-masted craft were also the passenger ships of the cross-Channel trade, running to unfamiliar ports such as Hastings, Lyme Regis, Bridport, Brixham, Budleigh Salterton, and Sidmouth, often running up the beach on the flood tide, unloading when the tide went out and leaving again when next afloat. Although many had good accommodation, with separate saloons for ladies and gentlemen, the service was hit-and-miss, sailings depending on weather and cargoes. In 1788 a cutter on the Southampton trade was regarded as actively employed if she made eight round voyages within a year.

In 1794 the Post Office tired of such haphazard arrangements and put the 80-ton cutters *Chesterfield* and *Rover* on a regular service from Weymouth, sailing alternately on Saturday evenings and (if the wind stood fair) arriving in Guernsey on Sundays, thus scandalising the worshippers in the churches. In 1811 these ships were joined by the *Sir Francis Freeling*, and twice-weekly sailings were started, while in 1814 a service was inaugurated from Southampton with the 80-tonners *Aeolus*, *Diligent* and *Brilliant*. Of the many adventures which befell these cutters (running as they did throughout the Napoleonic Wars) two are especially noteworthy. The first of these involved the *Chesterfield*, which in 1811 was attacked by a French privateer, several passengers and crew being killed before she was finally captured and taken to Cherbourg. A happier outcome attended the *Brilliant*, when in 1814 she was taken by an American privateer. After her capture the prize-master headed for France, handing the wheel to a member of the regular crew when land was sighted. This seaman realised that the land was Alderney and took the ship into Braye harbour where the captors were captured.

A particularly historical moment was 6 a.m. on June 10th., 1823, as it was then that there arrived at St. Peter-Port the *Medina* (the first steamship ever to travel to the Channel Isles) which had been chartered by Colonel Fitzgerald to bring his family and himself, together with his furniture and household goods, to Guernsey. A paddle steamer, the *Medina* had been built in 1822 by Lynn Ratsey of Cowes at a cost of £7,000, with dimensions 85 ft. by 18 ft. 9 ins. by 9 ft. 10 ins. She carried a female figurehead and had auxiliary sail, being rigged as a two-masted schooner. Contemporary newspapers differ as to her tonnage (120 and 150), and also as to the time she took from Southampton (15 or 21 hours). The day following her arrival 132 Guernesiais took a trip on her to Jersey, accompanied by the Band of the town Regiment of the Militia. As 70 Jersiais decided to try the trip back, she returned to Guernsey with over 200 on board, the inter-island voyage taking four hours. This proved to be the *Medina*'s only visit, but although this little ship never returned to the islands, she plied for 58 years before being lost with all hands in the Irish Sea in 1880.

The mails, which had been brought from Weymouth since 1794, were first carried by steam packets in 1827 — and these government ships monopolised the steam service from that port from then until September 1839, when the Commercial Steam Packet Company allocated their ship, *Calpe*, to Weymouth for a service to Guernsey, Alderney and Cherbourg, connecting with the *Lady de Saumarez* at Guernsey for Jersey passengers.

Already in 1824, however, at the instigation of Sir John Milley Doyle (nephew of Guernsey's greatest lieutenant-governor, Sir

John Doyle) the steamship *Lord Beresford* had been launched from Scott's yard in Bristol, destined to operate a service between Portsmouth and the Islands. Of 160 tons and 70 h.p., she was a two-masted vessel 100 ft. long with a 25-ft. beam. Learning of this project, the merchants of Southampton, determined to stop Portsmouth from cornering a potentially profitable traffic, banded together and bought the steamship *Ariadne*, launched by Evans of Rotherhithe on May 1st., 1824. Of 197 tons and 72 h.p., she was a three-master, 117 ft. long. A race was on.

The first to make the crossing was the *Ariadne*, commanded by a Guernseyman, Captain Bazin, which arrived at St. Peter-Port on June 8th., 1824, with the rival *Lord Beresford* sailing directly to Jersey from Bristol on the 11th. In 1825 the *Lord Beresford* deserted Portsmouth for Southampton, and she and the *Ariadne* (which in the same year, on a day trip from Jersey, became the first steamship ever to call at Sark) each ran one round trip a week, both services arranging a wide choice of stage-coach connections between Southampton and London.

In 1835 a brief spate of competition with the *Liverpool* (which took to calling in at Southampton *en route* to Guernsey from London) led to the decision to introduce improved ships. Thus the *Lady de Saumarez* and the *Atlanta* were built, starting the long and ever-improving series of ships connecting Southampton with the Islands until 1961 when the *Isle of Guernsey* ran the last passenger voyage before all services were transferred to Weymouth.

In 1826 a steamship service was inaugurated from Plymouth, the P.S. *Sir Francis Drake* arriving at St. Peter-Port on June 9th. When in 1828 she was joined by the P.S. *Brunswick*, the Guernsey newspapers recorded that seven steamers now ran between Guernsey and England — three to Weymouth, two to Southampton, and two to Plymouth. The Plymouth service survived until the early years of the 20th. century.

A service between Guernsey and London that was to survive until the Second World War was started in 1831 by the *Lord of the Isles*, of 345 tons, which arrived in Guernsey on her maiden voyage on June 24th. As she called at Brighton, passengers could get to London in 21 hours if coach connections were good. In 1832 she left for war service in Portugal (the civil combat between Donna Maria and her uncle and rival claimant, Dom Miguel). In June 1835 this service was taken up by the *Liverpool* — the most luxurious ship yet seen in Guernsey. As she called at Southampton, she competed with the *Ariadne* and the *Lord Beresford* and a price-war ensued, bringing down Southampton-Guernsey fares to five shillings first class, and half-a-crown second class. At the end of August the *Liverpool* departed for service under the Queen of Spain, and fares reverted to 26 shillings first class, 15 shillings second class, and half a guinea deck class.

After the *Liverpool*'s departure, sailing schooners connected London with Guernsey until 1839 when, as already seen, the Commercial Steam Packet Company put the P.S. *Transit* (160 tons) on the run, with the P.S. *Calpe* (259 tons) as relief, both ships calling at Weymouth *en route*. It was the London service which in January 1850 provided Guernsey with its first sight of a screw steamship — the twin-masted cargo boat *Collier* (built of iron). Confined to cargo only prior to the German occupation, the service was not resumed after the Liberation.

Several other ports also sought to establish shipping lines with Guernsey, all of which proved to be ephemeral. While it lasted, however, the Littlehampton service ran the *Pera* — the first twin-screwed steamship to be seen in St. Peter-Port.

In 1848 the railway companies (which had already acquired interests in the steamship services to the archipelago) obtained powers to own and operate their own shipping services. Thus were the foundations laid for the long era of Great Western Railway ships running from Weymouth, in competition with those of the London and South Western (later Southern) Railway, running from Southampton. The determination of each of these two operators to out-perform the other led to dangerous racing in the second half of the 19th. century. The consequences of this proved disastrous on Maundy Thursday, March 30th., 1899, when the R.M.S. *Stella* of the L.S.W.R., eager to arrive in Guernsey ahead of the S.S. *Ibex* (her G.W.R. rival which was due there the same afternoon), pressed on at full speed despite the prevailing fog, struck La Roche Noire in Les Casquets at 19 knots and, her bottom ripped out, foundered with a loss of life given as 105 out of 217 souls thought to be on board in a Board of Trade Report of dubious accuracy dated June 2nd., 1899 — though more recently the meticulous researches undertaken by Mr. David Shayer (see Bibliography) prompted him to posit the overwhelming probability of the tragedy having resulted in 86 deaths out of a total ship's company of 199. The drowned included Mrs. Mary Rogers, born in Frome in Somerset, a stewardess whose heroic self-sacrifice in giving her lifebelt to a passenger and refusing a place in a lifeboat is commemorated in one of the windows honouring

'Noble Women' gracing Liverpool Cathedral's Lady Chapel. Sobered by this calamity, the services came to be operated in collaboration to such an extent that the absorption of both companies into British Railways on January 1st., 1948 brought no evident change until 1961 when, as a result of a rationalisation decision, all services were concentrated at Weymouth. Prior to railway nationalisation the Great Western vessel *St. Helier* (a mainstay of the Weymouth service during the 'thirties) achieved glory by limping home, badly crippled, with the last shipload of British soldiers from Dunkirk; her sailing from the East Mole at 2330 hours on June 2nd., 1940 occasioning the historic signal, 'To VA Dover from SNO Dunkirk BEF evacuated'. (The same action, incidentally, also saw the sinking of the *Lorina* — the 'star' Southern Railway ship of the 'twenties.) Also during the 'rival railways era' the first turbine-driven ships came into use on the run: the *Caesarea* and the *Sarnia* in 1910. The recent ships of the same names date from 1961, but the inauguration of 'roll-on, roll-off' facilities on June 27th., 1974 rendered them obsolete. After the withdrawal from service of the *Caesarea*, the *Sarnia* made her farewell sailing from Guernsey to Weymouth on September 5th., 1977. The same year saw Weymouth cease to be the only port serving the archipelago, car-ferry services being introduced from Portsmouth as well.

Supplemented from 1983 onwards by sailings from Torquay (calling at Alderney *en route*) provided in the summer months only by Torbay Seaways, the dual Weymouth/Portsmouth arrangement continued until 1985 — a year which saw radical changes stemming from the acquisition of the British Railways' 'Sealink' subsidiary by Sea Containers Limited, which, functioning as 'Sealink/British Ferries', inaugurated a luxury service from Portsmouth (via Cherbourg and Jersey) as a complement to the standard one from Weymouth. At the same time a local consortium, backed by Brittany Ferries, set up a rival concern (Channel Islands Ferries) making available a cheaper crossing from Portsmouth and thereby creaming off much of its competitor's potential custom. Eighteen months of mutual loss in the face of a demand insufficiency eventuated in a merger on September 30th., 1986, with the discontinuance without warning of the Weymouth run (save during the high season) and the formation of British Channel Island Ferries, pooling the two Portsmouth operations. An acrimonious divorce soon followed this autumnal *mariage de covenance*, each partner accusing the other of a failure to fulfil its commitments under the merger agreement. A lawsuit ensued, won by Channel Islands Ferries which (retaining the adjective 'British') thenceforth operated alone, supplying an additional ship to run the summer Weymouth service — though this did not last for long. In the wake of this estrangement Sealink/British Ferries announced in January 1987 its intention of preserving a residual presence in local waters by providing an experimental bi-weekly service between Guernsey and Cherbourg during the following July and August. In 1988 these sailings were extended from Cherbourg to Portsmouth and vice versa, thereby maintaining Guernsey's link with this port which B.C.I.F. the same year forsook in favour of Poole. Such sailings were, however, discontinued in 1990 — but the year 1992 saw the establishment of a fresh connection with the French mainland with the start of a bi-weekly Guernsey-Jersey-Granville service operated by the catamaran *Britannia* owned by the French company Channiland. In May 1994 this was supplemented by a direct Guernsey-Saint Malo service brought into operation by Emeraude Lines. Meanwhile, following the withdrawal of the main operators from Weymouth, Condor Limited in 1987 inaugurated from that port a hydrofoil service using a 450-seater wavepiercing catamaran making the crossing in 2¼ hours. In 1991 Torbay Seaways discontinued its sailings, while two years later Condor Limited enhanced its facilities by introducing car-carrying wavepiercers on its Weymouth route. These enhanced facilities provided B.C.I.F. with so formidable an adversary as to drive it out of business, with Condor buying up its competitor's passenger and freight services in January 1994, at the same time announcing its intention to continue running two of its defeated rival's ships — the first operating a night car-ferry service (forsaking Poole for Weymouth) as a supplement to the catamaran's daytime one and the second a freight service from Portsmouth.

In the event the night passenger service provided by traditional craft did not long survive, being discontinued in October 1996 and thereby leaving the catamarans as the sole shipping link with the United Kingdom — based once again on Poole rather than on Weymouth. Thereafter the catamarans' inability to maintain regular sailings in the face of the worst winter gales gave rise to much disquiet in 1997 — with the upshot that the first half of 1998 was given over to the consideration of tenders to run the U.K.-Channel Isles route which two other operators (P. & O. European Ferries and Hoverspeed) as well as Condor had submitted to the

Guernsey Transport Board and the Jersey Transport Authority. Because of the obvious impracticability of any arrangement issuing in the two Bailiwicks being served by different concerns, the Transport Board (which had initially preferred P. & O.) eventually decided somewhat reluctantly to advise the States to renew Condor's mandate — a course of action favoured by Jersey, to and from which island the bulk of the traffic flows.

As from the same time — early 1998 — twice-weekly winter and daily summer sailings from Weymouth supplemented those from spring to autumn out of Poole; while October 1999 saw the commencement of a year-round service from Portsmouth provided by the *Commodore Clipper*, a conventional ship owned by Condor's associated firm — Commodore Shipping Company — designed mainly for the carriage of freight but also with capacity for conveying up to 500 passengers (with *en suite* cabins available at an extra charge) and over 100 cars.

Shortly after the renewal of Condor's mandate came the injection of an element of cross-Channel competition with the introduction by another shipping firm, trading as Channel Hoppers, of a catamaran passenger link between the islands (including Sark plus — occasionally — Alderney) and Portsmouth, though without providing facilities for the transport of motor vehicles. Once started this service proved a great boon to Alderney, bringing more than 3,500 passengers to the island from the United Kingdom during 1998.

Before concluding this chapter, it would be appropriate briefly to consider the two major perils which confront shipping in the waters of the Bailiwick — the rocky islets of Les Casquets, seven miles to the west of Alderney, and the Hanois Reef, one mile to the west of Pleinmont.

A light existed on Les Casquets as early as 1726, but merely consisted of a coal-fire kept to a glow by the use of bellows. In 1790 three lighthouses were built (called St. Peter, St. Thomas and the Donjon), and a system of revolving lamps installed. These suffered considerable storm damage in 1823. In 1877 two of the lighthouses were demolished and the remaining one improved, providing the existing light giving three quick flashes every thirty seconds, at a height of 113 feet above high water.

Regarding the Hanois the States, spurred on by the forceful advocacy of Jurat H. Tupper, approached Trinity House, which in 1858 agreed to build a lighthouse on the reef providing Guernsey came within the jurisdiction of the Elder Brethren and paid the coasting rate instead of the overseas rate. In 1860, influenced by Tupper's arguments demonstrating that in 1858 the overseas rate had come to more than the coasting rate, Trinity House gave in. The foundation stone for the 100-ft. lighthouse was laid on August 15th., 1860 and the first light shone on December 8th., 1862. Until the advent of the helicopter ferry a century later, the little harbour at Portelet was the 'home port' for the lighthouse keepers.

In March 1986 Trinity House announced its intention of automating the archipelago's lighthouses, at the same time instituting a central control watch to check that the lights functioned as timed, while fog signals were to be operated from shore bases. This programme was completed with the automation of Alderney's Quesnard Lighthouse in 1997.

The whole point of building lighthouses is, of course, to prevent shipping disasters and although prevention is proverbially better than cure, yet cure is invaluable should distress fail to be averted — so that it is entirely meet to end this chapter by making reference to the work of the lifeboat service since its inception in 1803. Initially located at Saint Sampson's, the island's lifeboat base was permanently transferred to Saint Peter-Port following the move thither of the *John Lockett* in 1881. Before the advent of motorised craft, however, the sad fact is that the efforts of the service, while doubtless well-intentioned, were ineffectual. Over a period of one-and-a-quarter centuries (1803–1929) during which 260 wrecks occurred in local waters, the lifeboat was called out only seventeen times and only once (when five people were rescued from the schooner *Isabella Helen* in February 1885) were lives saved. Powered vessels date from October 27th., 1929, when the last of the 'pulling and sailing' boats (the *Arthur Lionel*, which had been launched on February 29th., 1912) was replaced by the petrol-engined *Queen Victoria*. Thenceforth unremitting endeavours to keep abreast of technological advance led to the employment of craft of ever-increasing sophistication, as evidenced in the Arun-type lifeboat officially named *Sir William Arnold* by H.R.H. the Duchess of Kent on May 23rd., 1974 and costing about £120,000, largely raised by public subscription — while even greater wizardry was forecast when in 1993 the provision in the near future was promised of a 25-knot Severn-type craft. Named *Spirit of Guernsey*, this vessel came into service in 1996.

The acquisition of the superb Arun boat occurred in the course of a particularly glorious era in the history of the service, marked by the magnificent career of Captain John Hubert Petit, who, when he retired from his post of Coxswain at the end of 1980 after twenty-eight years continuous service in the R.N.L.I. had become the most decorated lifeboat man in the Bailiwick's annals, holding a silver gallantry medal besides a bronze one with no less than three bars! His courage had also won his inclusion among the eleven 'Men of the Year' of 1978 — the year in which he was furthermore presented with the Maud Smith Award given annually to the person who has performed the bravest act of life-saving. He had been preceded by his Alderney-born father Hubert Ernest Petit (Coxswain 1948–1964 and himself awarded two gold gallantry medals — British and Norwegian — in 1963) so that the responsibility of leadership in this hazardous calling had been shouldered by the same family for well over thirty years. Becoming Harbour Master after ceasing to be Coxswain, Captain Petit finally retired in 1987 and was created M.B.E. in the 1988 New Year Honours. His successor (Coxswain Michael John Scales) in a short but brilliant career, proved himself amply worthy of his inheritance, his heroic exploits earning the award of a gold medal for gallantry in 1982, followed by a bronze one in 1984. Later the same year he resigned from the service on taking up an appointment as a yacht skipper in the Mediterranean. His departure, however, did not mean the end of the service's glorious traditions, the maintenance of which was once more in evidence on August 30th., 1992, when, beset by a force nine gale and fifteen to twenty foot seas, the rescue of a six-member crew was effected from a yacht north of the Hanois, Coxswain Peter Bisson thereby earning the R.N.L.I. Silver Gallantry Medal and also (as had Captain Petit before him) the Maud Smith Award.

Chapter Eighteen

'SAFE UNTO THE HAVEN'

ON THE OCCASION of his 1846 visit with his regal spouse, Albert Prince Consort ironically enquired why his islander hosts had their harbour on dry land. It is indeed true that at the time of this royal visit St. Peter-Port Harbour was still confined to two piers extending in an easterly direction from the Town Church and the North Pier Steps respectively (with the southern one — the present Albert Pier — curving round to the north) enclosing an area which the sea deserted entirely at low tide. The lighthouse at the tip of the southern pier was already in existence at the time of Victoria's and Albert's visit, having first shone on February 28th., 1832; but long before that a round-house — possibly a guard-house for prisoners *en route* for Castle Cornet — had stood on the spot, being referred to in an ordinance of the Chief Pleas of 1642 requiring that it should be rendered secure at public expense.

The genesis of Guernsey's main port is undoubtedly the pier which came to bear the name of the harbour's royal critic. It is certain that the south pier dates back to the 13th. century, as the record still exists of Edward I's authorisation of a duty of 12 sols tournois on all ships and of six sols tournois on all boats to defray reconstruction costs after the damage wrought by the French raiders in 1294 (the terrible incursion described in Part IV, Chapter Two). Although these duties were levied, their proceeds were misappropriated by the henchmen of Otto de Grandison, so that the pier remained in a sorry state — a condition which, sad to relate, persisted for over two-and-a-half centuries, as subsequent tolls were similarly persistently misapplied. It was not until the reign of Elizabeth I that firm steps at last put a stop to this malfeasance. In 1570 the bailiff and jurats were ordered to produce annually before the captain (Sir Thomas Leighton) an account of receipts and disbursements. It would seem, however, as if experience showed even more stringent measures to be necessary, as in 1580 the self-same bailiff and jurats were specifically directed to use *all* toll receipts for harbour works, with the result that, despite further intermittent fund malversation, the south pier was finally completed in 1590 — nearly 300 years after the French raid.

The north pier is of far more recent construction. Its building was ordered by the Court of Chief Pleas in 1694, but no work was started until about 1703, whereafter progress was delayed by wars, so that it was not completed until 1750.

The quays were built between 1775 and 1779, at last preventing the sea from running up to the houses, and even between them through the lanes and steps leading to the High Street. Nevertheless, the quay was narrow, rough and cobbled, the two piers were lower than they are today (consisting merely of huge boulders fitting roughly together) and streams and drains entered the harbour basin, causing a stench such as to make the houses in the High Street almost uninhabitable.

In 1815 Harbourmaster Deschamps built a causeway from the foot of the Truchot to a set of steps and a platform which had been constructed on the St. Julian Rocks (enabling passengers to be landed there when low tide rendered the harbour dry land), but no further developments occurred until 1830 when 187 merchants, shipowners and businessmen sent a petition to the States via the bailiff, Daniel de Lisle Brock, asking for harbour improvements. Brock, who favoured these projects, advocated a breakwater to Castle Cornet to protect the roadstead and the creation of a new harbour within this shield — as against current proposals merely to extend the south pier and to construct an arm going east and then south from the Truchot to meet it. Unfortunately the Court and the States did not respond to Brock's blandishments and refused to make any move until 1851 when, inspired by the persuasiveness of Jurat Henry Tupper (the future instigator of the Hanois lighthouse) approval was given to a plan prepared by a well-known engineer by the name of Rendel. The contract was assigned to Messrs. Le Gros and de la Mare and on August 24th., 1853, at the point where the Castle Walk now joins the mainland, the foundation stone was laid by the bailiff, Sir Peter Stafford Carey, in the presence of the States, the ceremony being placed on permanent record by the artist George Reynolds — whose work depicts, *inter alia*, a miscreant being disciplined by William Jesse, one of the four 'salaried assistant constables' for Saint Peter-Port who had just been appointed for the first time that year (see Part III, Chapter Eleven).

The breakwater connecting Castle Cornet with the mainland was finished in mid-1859, but already by the previous year work had progressed sufficiently to permit of a temporary landing place where passengers for the first time in history were enabled to walk ashore by gangway at all states of the tide. Storm experience having indicated the need for the Castle breakwater to be extended to the Tremies Rocks, the States approved this project in 1860. It being clear that protection from the north, too, was needed, the States in May 1862 authorised the construction of St. Julian's Pier as far as the extremity of the White Rock.

In 1864 Southampton packets began embarking passengers at the White Rock landing stage, and in 1867 the lighthouse on the Castle breakwater shone for the first time. The year 1886 saw the model yacht pond built at the instigation of the bailiff, Sir Edgar MacCulloch, while in 1892 the present Weighbridge was erected and the wharf used by London ships was constructed in 1899. Additions and adaptations effected during the 20th century include the New Jetty (a vast steel and concrete platform extending into the Pool) completed in 1929, the specially equipped containerisation wharf completed in 1972, and the car ferry ramp installed in 1974.

The entire harbour project was financed without any recourse to the London money market, nor were brokers' and underwriters' commissions incurred. The islanders were offered bonds carrying 3 per cent. interest and repayable on demand after reasonable notice, with accrued interest. The whole prime cost of £350,000 was raised in this way, and the bonds were redeemed from harbour revenues. This loan was extinguished before the end of the 19th. century, and the credit of the island backed by the splendid asset of the harbour stood very high.

Such an outlay came to appear puny in comparison with the £16 million cost of the vast project on which work began in January 1984, after authorisation by the States the previous month, aimed at reclaiming the North Beach area between La Salerie Corner and Saint Julian's Pier with a view to creating an additional marina and two extensive car parks whereby it was hoped — vainly, it later proved — to relieve congestion elsewhere in the Town. Officially opened by Her Majesty the Queen on May 23rd., 1989, this new feature was given the name of 'Queen Elizabeth II Marina'. Deepening the Pool of the existing harbour so as to facilitate the establishment of a further and steadier car ferry ramp to service larger ships was also undertaken, while yet other developments resulted in the creation of a new quay for Sark boats to the west of the New Jetty and of a special Fishing Wharf located between the Albert Marina and the Model Yacht Pond.

Although as a settlement and a haven St. Sampson's probably pre-dates St. Peter-Port, the present extensive St. Sampson's harbour was the joint result of the reclamation of the Braye du Valle and of the early 19th.-century quarry trade. The first step was taken in 1820 when the States voted £800 for the repair of the ancient breakwater on the Col du Mont Crevelt which had long given shelter to what was no more than a natural creek — and also for the construction of a quay on the north side of the creek. More work was undertaken between 1839 and 1841 when the north quay was extended as far as La Maisonette Rock, the south quay built, and the breakwater lengthened. Additional development followed in 1842 when the south quay was extended and a head built at right-angles to it, while in 1851 the Mont Crevelt breakwater was further lengthened and a quay provided on its north-east side. The next stage involved land reclamation. The old creek had contained two curving bays, one on the north and one on the south. In the late 1850s dry stone walls were built across their mouths, and the beaches behind infilled with ship's ballast and quarry rubbish. Then in 1862 the centre of the harbour was deepened and trenched, rocks inside the breakwater were removed, and the wall of the new north quay built. Finally in 1864 the west and south walls of the old north pier were rebuilt, the old bridge and south quay widened, and a careening hard constructed on the east side of the Crocq. No further development occurred until 1990 when work began on a £9.7 million land reclamation scheme south of the harbour mouth meant ultimately to facilitate an extension of berthing capacity. Unforeseen eventualities caused the completion of this project to be postponed, however, and as this book goes to press it is still not yet finalized.

The genesis of Alderney's harbour came in 1736 when the governor, Henry Le Mesurier, in an attempt to stimulate the island's trade, constructed a pier at Braye to replace the old harbour at Longy which silting had rendered progressively useless. This nucleus was enlarged beyond recognition by the British government's defence works started in 1847 (see Part IV, Chapter Ten), while the addition at the close of the 19th. century of a jetty projecting beyond the 'New' (or 'Little Crabby') Harbour enclosed by the Great Breakwater enabled ships to be handled at all states of the tide. When this work was finished Alderney's harbour was complete — apart from the eyesore of the metal jetty added by the Germans, the foundations of which by their stubborn defiance of the efforts of demolition contractors for long created a hazardous underwater obstruction.

Sark's original landing-place was at L'Eperquerie, but Helier de Carteret decided that a more convenient harbour could be made in La Baie de la Motte by piercing the cliff with a tunnel. This operation was not completed until 1588 — seven years after Helier's death — and remained Sark's only harbour provision until the mid-19th century. Severe damage to the old breakwater wrought by gales in the winter of 1865/6 led the seigneur (Rev. W. T. Collings) to arrange with Mr. Agnew Giffard, who was in charge of the St. Peter-Port extensions, to supervise the construction of a new and improved harbour-the present Creux harbour — financed by the imposition of a special tax on spirits. The work involved driving a second tunnel giving access to the new harbour (which was completed in 1868) and also cost poor Mr. Giffard his life, as he was drowned with four companions while returning to Guernsey on October 19th., 1868. The Pilcher Memorial above Havre Gosselin commemorates one of his fellows in misfortune.

During the 1930s the late Dame de Sercq enthusiastically advocated the creation of a deep-water harbour at La Maseline which (unlike Creux) would be accessible at all states of the tide. A fund was built up to finance the scheme, and work (which involved driving yet another tunnel) began in 1938, but was interrupted by the outbreak of war. The task was at last completed in 1947 and the new harbour was formally opened by H.R.H. the Duke of Edinburgh on the occasion of his visit to Sark in company with H.R.H. the Princess Elizabeth on June 23rd., 1949.

Herm's harbour (as has already been seen in Chapter Ten preceding) came into existence in the years after Waterloo as a by-product of the efforts of Lieutenant-Colonel Lindsay to develop the stone trade.

Chapter Nineteen

AIR TRAVEL

ALTHOUGH GUERNSEY entered the aviation scene with the establishment of a French seaplane base near Castle Cornet during the First World War, civil aviation dates from August 1923 when British Marine Air Aviation Limited started a passenger service employing a Sea Eagle flying-boat flown by Henri Biard (who later in life became a Guernsey resident). Initially landings took place in L'Ancresse Bay, but the service was soon transferred to St. Peter-Port, with the aircraft touching down in the Russel and coasting into the harbour. Henri Biard, incidentally, had been the winner of the 1922 Schneider Trophy Race.

In 1924 this service was taken over by Imperial Airways, who operated it every Friday. Of the two flying-boats employed, one was rammed by a ship in St. Peter-Port harbour and sank on January 10th., 1927, and in 1928 the Sea Eagle service was discontinued, to be briefly replaced in 1929 by Short Calcutta flying-boats before Imperial Airways withdrew its aircraft altogether, the service for the rest of that year being provided by a private concern. Thereafter Kirsten and Mace Limited provided a service from Woolston aerodrome, Southampton, with a 'Cutty Sark' amphibian which once again used St. Peter-Port harbour at the Guernsey end — but this operation was killed by the slump in 1930.

In 1931 a local group of aviation enthusiasts formed the Guernsey Aero Club and acquired a number of fields at L'Erée whose dividing hedges and walls were removed with the aim of creating an aerodrome. It was proposed to remove a hillock to the north of the area so as to enable the dimensions of the proposed airfield to be increased, but although demolition was started, the cost proved to be prohibitive, and this project was abandoned. Nevertheless, it is worth emphasising that it was here (and not in Alderney as is often but erroneously supposed) that the Bailiwick's initial aerodrome was brought into existence, from which the first flights of land-based aircraft took place. Guernsey's 'Orville Wright' was Mr. Cecil Noel, who flew his home-made aircraft 'The

Wee Mite' from this airfield in 1934, accompanied on one occasion by the present writer, who was eager to savour a joy-ride.

It was from this field also that in 1935 Sir Alan Cobham, with his 'Cobham Air Routes', ran the first land-based passenger service to operate from Guernsey. Flying to Bournemouth, the service was inaugurated on May 6th. (Silver Jubilee Day), but ended disastrously on July 3rd. when a crash of one of the Westland Wessex aircraft off Bournemouth resulted in the death of the pilot (Captain Ogden), though the one and only passenger was saved after a gruelling time in the sea. Thus the L'Erée service *ended* six weeks *before* the first aircraft landed in Alderney — as a subsequent paragraph will show.

In the meantime, on December 4th., 1933, Jersey Airways had started flying from St. Aubin's Bay, and on November 24th., 1934 Guernsey Airways Limited was registered in Guernsey as a wholly-owned subsidiary. On December 1st., 1934, Channel Islands Airways (in which the Southern and Great Western Railway Companies had large shareholdings) was registered in Jersey as a holding company to take over the two others.

On June 9th., 1935 a Saunders-Roe Windhover amphibian aircraft was brought into use by Guernsey Airways, flying from Jersey to St. Peter-Port harbour and — a few months later — going on to the new airport which Channel Island Airways had built in Alderney, where connections were made with De Havilland Rapides for flights to or from Southampton. The first 'plane landed in Alderney on August 15th., 1935, but the aerodrome was not granted a licence until October 11th. An attempt to make use of Sark (where Jersey Airways had obtained landing rights on some fields) was frustrated by the opposition of the Sercquiais, who petitioned the lieutenant-governor of Guernsey against any such development.

With L'Erée restricted in size and subject to flooding, these developments led to the need for adequate airport provision in Guernsey being increasingly voiced by the farther-seeing section of the community; and after a public meeting at St. George's Hall, addressed by Sir Alan Cobham, who gave it as his opinion that La Villiaze was the only possible site, the States, with much heart-searching (as good farmland was involved) finally decided on October 20th., 1935 to buy 315 vergées in this area. The land was duly acquired, and in May 1939 the airport was officially opened by Sir Kingsley Wood.

In 1947 Channel Island Airways came to an end. As it was not a United Kingdom company, but registered in Jersey, the States of both Jersey and Guernsey refused to assent to its incorporation into the nationalised British European Airways formed under the 1946 Civil Aviation Act of the United Kingdom parliament, arguing that such a course of action would be an infringement of the islands' privileges. However, the British government informed each Bailiwick that in view of the fact that Channel Islands Airways was not a foreign flag carrier, its aircraft would no longer be permitted to land at United Kingdom airports unless the company was absorbed into the B.E.A. *Force majeure* prevailed, and the incorporation took place on April 1st., 1947.

During the Occupation the Germans had enlarged the airport area, but had allowed the drainage system to deteriorate, so that after the Liberation it took some time to get the airport back into working order. Even so, La Villiaze remained prone to water-logging in winter, and after some hesitation for fear of letting in jet aircraft, a costly modernisation scheme was put in hand between 1958 and 1960, which by 1961 produced a hard runway of 4,800 feet, and also provided better-equipped terminal buildings.

The idea of separating nearly all flights to the islands, instead of calling at Guernsey *en route* for Jersey, took root in 1969. During the same year Alderney was faced with the possibility of having no air services as its airfield was too small for the larger aircraft coming into use. Thus Aurigny Air Services came into existence — a concern which, although running a Southampton-Alderney service as well, at first specialized predominantly in inter-island flights, initially employing Britten-Norman Islander 'planes operating every 15 minutes (60 minutes in winter) on a ''bus-stop' system. Trislander aircraft (later supplemented by yet more types) eventually replaced the Islander model and the airline subsequently extended its range of activities which, at the time of its acquisition by Close Brothers Private Equity in the spring of 2000, had come to include services to Stansted, Manchester and Amsterdam.

As for the little airport which spawned this thriving empyreal enterprise, the sad fact is that the regular flights therefrom (which, with shipping services considerably curtailed, make it Alderney's prime link with the outside world) do not automatically guarantee its financial viability. This became evident in April 1997 when the announcement of a £300,000 loss in 1995 was accompanied by a projected forecast of one of more than £350,000 for 1996 — and unfortunately failure to make a profit was still in evidence as this book went to print.

May 1963 saw the inauguration of cargo flights to and from Guernsey, providing an invaluable service to the flower trade and to the then flourishing tomato trade. Air services are now of incalculable value to the Bailiwick's communications — so essential indeed as to render dire the consequences of their withdrawal during the unprofitable winter months. To guard against such an eventuality the States' Transport Board — originally set up in 1987 to represent island interests in consultation with the British Civil Aviation Authority — was constituted the Bailiwick's Air Licensing Authority in the autumn of 1994, with a mandate to ensure the perpetuation of year-round services and their continuity from year to year; the provision of sufficient capacity to cater for tourism; and the maintenance of the lowest viable fare structure compatible with the highest possible frequency and standards of service. (One might observe that the last of these considerations is crucial, it being feared that fare levels might prove to be such as to deter tourists, on whose patronage the survival of services in general largely depends — witness the withdrawal of all K.L.M.–U.K. flights in 1998. The trouble seems to be that limited airport size, by ruling out the use of economical 'jumbo' craft, compels airlines to rely on smaller 'planes, the much higher running costs of which are reflected in the fares charged.)

One thing more. It would clearly be shameful to conclude this aeronautical survey without paying deserved tribute to the meritorious achievement of the intrepid Guernesiais airline pilot, Captain Peter ('Jerry') Girard, who by prompt and expert evasive action taken over western China on June 28th., 1999, when *en route* from Heathrow to Hong Kong avoided by a mere two hundred yards collision with an errant Korean aircraft, thereby saving the lives of his four hundred passengers, his crew and himself.

Chapter Twenty

POSTAL AND ELECTRONIC COMMUNICATIONS

NO REGULAR FACILITIES for the conveyance of mail were available to the people of the Bailiwick until 1794. Prior to that year an irregular system of privately-run post offices had grown up in the islands, operated by enterprising individuals who, for a fee, arranged with the captains of vessels sailing for England whereby these master-mariners would entrust letters to the post at the port of arrival. The fee charged was shared between the local postal entrepreneur and the ship's captain, the postal charges in England being paid by the addressee as was usual in the 18th. century.

In 1792, however, an investigation was conducted by a Post Office surveyor, and the contents of his report, together with the outbreak of war with revolutionary France the following year, prompted the British government to take action. The upshot was that in 1794 the Postmaster-General was ordered to establish a regular weekly packet service and two of the Dover packets (the 80-ton cutters *Chesterfield* and *Rover*) whose services were suspended because of the war, were transferred to Weymouth for the purpose, the Post Office requesting the Admiralty to assist in preventing the packets from 'being taken by the enemy'. At the same time the first official postmistress was appointed in Guernsey in the person of Mrs. Ann Watson, who was a relative of the Guernseyman, Paul Le Mesurier, Lord Mayor of London, 1793/4. Some years later — in 1811 — another cutter, the *Sir Francis Freeling*, joined the original two and twice-weekly sailings were started.

(Before pursuing this matter further, it is interesting to note that in addition to postal communications, supplementary arrangements were evolved within the archipelago during the Napoleonic Wars in the form of a visual telegraph devised in 1808 by Peter Andrew Mulgrave of Jersey who, by adapting for inter-island use the invention originated in France in 1792 by Claude Chappe, enabled messages to be signalled between Sark on the one hand and Alderney, Guernsey and Jersey on the other by the movement of semaphore arms, of which forty-two varied settings were available signifying numbers referable to a code book. Rapidly developed thanks to the patronage and encouragement of Philippe d'Auvergne in Jersey and Sir Peter de Havilland in Guernsey, this system — a memento of which remains in the cliff-top signalling tower after which is named the adjacent Telegraph Bay in Alderney — gave excellent service up to the conclusion of peace in 1814.)

After the coming of peace, the mail service was provided by the 80-tonners *Aeolus*, *Diligent* and *Brilliant* between 1824 and 1827. Then, following a feasibility investigation in 1826 by Mr. Freeling, Assistant Secretary of the G.P.O., steamships were put on the mail service, the first mail carried by steamer arriving in Guernsey on July 8th., 1827, on board the P.S. *Watersprite* of 162 tons and 60 h.p. In conjunction with the P.S. *Ivanhoe* (158 tons) this steamship provided a twice-weekly service until April 1828 when it was increased to thrice weekly with the advent of the P.S. *Meteor* of 190 tons (replaced, after she had been wrecked in 1830, by the *Flamer* — 165 tons and 60 h.p. — in 1831).

On January 1st., 1837 the Admiralty took over — an event signalised by the order that the ships' captains should wear cocked hats and swords and have the assistance of a master and pilot. In 1838 a ship built by the Admiralty especially for the Channel Islands mail service appeared in the form of the P.S. *Dasher* (275 tons and 100 h.p.) which could cover the distance from Weymouth in six hours if conditions were favourable.

In 1839 the mail-carrying monopoly of the government packets was broken when the Commercial Steam Packet Company obtained authorisation for one bag of mail per trip to be carried from Weymouth on the P.S. *Calpe* and another from London in the P.S. *Transit*. In the reverse direction the first mail from Guernsey to England by private steamer was dispatched by the *Lady de Saumarez*, sailing for Southampton on June 24th., 1840.

In 1844 it was decided that the mail packet station would be transferred to Southampton, the last Weymouth mail being carried by the government packet *Cuckoo* on April 23rd., 1845. The first official mails from Southampton arrived in Guernsey on April 26th., 1845 on the *Transit*. With this transference to Southampton, the contract for carrying mails was given to the South-Western Steam Packet Company (a subsidiary of the London and South Western Railway Company). Three years later (1848) the railway companies obtained power to own and operate boat services themselves (thus, thanks to train connections at Southampton, enabling mail from Guernsey to reach London the morning after dispatch) and railway steamers thereafter became the monopoly mail carriers for 90 years until this function also came to be performed by Channel Island Airways with the opening of La Villiaze airport in 1939.

During the 'Admiralty Era' the first post office was opened in Alderney (1843); while the 'railway era' saw the opening of Sark's post office in 1857 and that of Herm in 1925 — though it was closed again in 1938 because of lack of business. In addition, the 'railway era' saw three other important developments. The first of these featured the original pillar boxes. The brainchild of Anthony Trollope, the novelist, who was also a Post Office surveyor, the first experimental pillar boxes were set up in Jersey in 1852, followed by three in Guernsey in 1853. The box in Union Street survives and is now the oldest pillar box in the world still in use. The second development consisted of the institution (again thanks to the initiative of Jurat Henry Tupper) of the telegraph service via submarine cable between Guernsey and England on September 7th., 1858, when a message was delivered in London within 40 minutes of dispatch. Lastly came the significant development of the opening of the head post office in Smith Street in 1883.

The Bailiwick first attained a philatelic personality during the German Occupation when Guernsey for the first time printed its own stamps in denominations of ½d., 1d. and 2½d. After the Liberation these stamps were accepted as valid for postage anywhere in the world until April 1946, when they were demonetised. This did not mean the end of Bailiwick stamps, however, and the next 20 years may be nick-named the 'conveyance stamp era'. The departure of the post office from Herm in 1938 had meant that mail had to be handled by the Guernsey office, to which it was carried by motor boat. After the Liberation the tenant, Mr. A. G. Jefferies, in view of the considerable influx of tourists into the island, decided to charge a fee for the conveyance of the mails to Guernsey, issuing special stamps for the purpose. This practice was continued by Major 'Peter' Wood when he took over the tenancy in 1949 and the example was subsequently copied by the tenants of Brecqhou, Jethou and Lihou. Then, on October 1st., 1969, the Bailiwick became an independent postal authority in its own right, with its own special stamps. This development brought about the discontinuance of the 'conveyance stamps' from the smaller islands as constituting an infringement of the monopoly of the Guernsey Post Office.

From its inception the Bailiwick Postal Service, with its distinctive 'French Blue' livery, has proved most lucrative, its ever-increasing prosperity reflected in a profit of £450,000 on stamp sales to philatelists made in 1992, while the following year saw a revenue of £5.2 million yielding a surplus of £100,000 accruing to the postal side alone. A milestone was reached in 1983 when, in deference to feelings in that island, a Special Alderney Regional Issue was inaugurated. A further development occurred in 1993 when Postcodes, originally considered unnecessary, were introduced so as to facilitate mechanised sorting and to speed the passage through the U.K. system of mail destined for the Bailiwick.

On June 17th., 1896 the States, urged by Major-General Mainguy (a jurat) and advised by Mr. A. R. Bennett, a telephone engineer whose services General Mainguy had procured, appointed a Telephone Council to establish and operate a telephone system. On hearing of this, the National Telephone Company informed the States that they had the monopoly for the United Kingdom under the Post Office — to which Guernsey replied that, not being part of the United Kingdom, the company's monopoly was not applicable and its services could not be accepted. Thinking that a *fait accompli* would remove opposition, the response of the National Telephone Company was to erect a pole on Mont Gibel and run wires from it to sundry chimneys, walls and ridges. The constables of St. Peter-Port had the wires removed, whereupon the National Telephone Company brought an action against the constables, and the litigation was fought right through to the Judicial Committee of the Privy Council, which found in favour of the constables.

The next hurdle to be surmounted was provided by the Telegraph Acts, as the fact that they had been registered in Guernsey made it necessary to apply to the Postmaster-General for a licence to operate the proposed system. Here the Telephone Council ran into considerable difficulties, 18 months of reiterated representations being necessary to win the Postmaster-General's consent. The licence was eventually signed on December 31st., 1897, and the telephone department under the Telephone Council set about providing the island's service, going into operation at 8 a.m. on July 29th., 1898, with three exchanges, fifteen staff, seventy subscribers and six public telephones.

In 1909 Prince Blücher, tenant of Herm, enquired about the cost of establishing telephonic communication with Guernsey. He obviously considered the estimate he received as excessive, and in the event no cable was laid. During the tenancy of Mr. A. G. Jefferies a pigeon postal service was provided between Herm and Guernsey for urgent messages, and finally in 1950 the States Telephone Department provided a radio-telephone link with Guernsey. As a result Herm now possesses the smallest automatic public telephone exchange in the world.

On March 26th., 1931 Guernsey was first connected by submarine telephone cable with England (and hence ultimately with the rest of the world). At first, calls could only be made from the public call-box in St. John Street, adjoining the then telephone exchange. Prior to this a radio-telephone link from Guernsey to Alderney was opened on July 23rd., 1927.

In 1903, after a Guernsey-Sark telegraph cable had been laid, the General Post Office was asked to permit its use for telephonic communication, but the request was initially refused, possibly because of the bad blood arising from the earlier confrontation between the States of Guernsey and the Post Office's telephonic predecessors, the National Telephone Company. However, as a result of successful tests carried out in 1909 and ensuing protracted negotiations, a public telephone was installed in the Sark post office in 1915, followed by a switchboard in 1917, serving five subscribers. In 1925 a branch exchange of the Guernsey system was established, with 11 subscribers and two public telephones in service. In 1928 the telegraph cable was replaced by a telephone cable providing a trunk circuit between Guernsey and Sark, while in 1952 a V.H.F. radio link was inaugurated by La Dame calling Sir Ambrose Sherwill, Bailiff of Guernsey. In 1972 a U.H.F. link replaced the V.H.F., and since 1975 Sark's exchange has been extended and automated with a view to coping with an eventual 400 subscribers. Proof that this objective was achieved is provided by the 436 Sark numbers listed in the Telephone Directory for the year 2000.

Ownership of and responsibility for all trunk connections — with (in chronological sequence) Sark, Alderney, Jersey and the U.K. — initially attached to the United Kingdom's G.P.O., but both were jointly assumed in 1973 by the States Telecommunications Board and its Jersey counterpart, with the result that each thenceforth became a totally independent telecommunications authority.

There remains to be considered the electronic dissemination of news, views and entertainment. In this connection the Bailiwick acquired its own wireless station in 1982 with the opening on March 16th. of that year of Radio Guernsey, operated by the British Broadcasting Corporation under franchise from the States, the Broadcasting Committee of which was set up to act in a supervisory capacity. Ten years later — on October 15th., 1992 — a commercial station (likewise supervised by the States Broadcasting Committee 'went on the air', transmitting under the name of Island F.M. Nearly twenty years prior to the advent of Radio Guernsey local television transmissions (not exclusive to Guernsey but shared with Jersey) had commenced on September 1st., 1962, with the inauguration of Channel Television, functioning under the aegis of the Independent Television Authority — which, with the assumption of responsibility for sound programmes also, became as from July 12th., 1972, the Independent Broadcasting Authority; only to be metamorphosed yet again into the Independent Television Commission on January 1st., 1993, coincident with the discontinuance of its supervision of wireless transmissions.

Chapter Twenty-One

'OUTRAGEOUS FORTUNE'

THE DECAY OF THE OPEN-FIELD SYSTEM and the closure of land at the end of the 15th. and the beginning of the 16th. centuries led to poverty manifesting itself for the first time as a serious social evil in the Bailiwick. The inflation which affected the whole of Europe in the 16th. century made matters worse, and the problem was further exacerbated by the religious changes of the age. Up to the death of Henry VIII the sick, old and needy depended on the generosity of religious guilds (or Confraternities) of which there were several in each parish — though as far as sickness was concerned their munificence must have availed but little, bearing in mind the prevalence of the bubonic plague in the island which not only (as already mentioned in Part IV, Chapter Two) suffered cruelly from the Black Death between 1348 and 1350 but also repeatedly endured recurrences of this terrible pestilence during the 15th. and 16th. centuries. This support came under threat with the technical application to Guernsey of the Chantries Act of 1547 (a year, by the by, when a further outbreak of the plague which had started a twelvemonth earlier was still raging) but its impact was minimised by the Royal Court adopting a policy of dissimulation, making small token seizures from the Fraternities representing only a minute part of their revenues and by this apparent compliance with the Act's requirements so successfully avoiding any enforcement by Crown emissaries of the kind experienced in Jersey as to enable the charitable work of these bodies to be maintained until early in the reign of Elizabeth I, when the Huguenot triumph finally brought about their extinction. Thereafter the lot of 'Les Pauvres' was stark indeed, characterised by a hovel in which to live, with maybe a patch of furze on which a goat or two could browse, supplemented by whatever they could pick up to further their precarious existence, such as a few days' hire as labourers, or some rock-fishing, or service as seamen. These unfortunates had a precise legal status, laid down in the ordinances regulating *vraic*-gathering, where they were defined as those not subject to taxation and possessing neither cart nor draught beast who, forbidden to borrow carts or horses or even to make use of a barrow, were restricted to cutting the *vraic* and carrying it on their persons above high spring-tide mark — hence the expression, 'Varech à la poche'.

Even before the abolition of the Confraternities the problem posed by the impoverished was becoming serious and an ordinance of the Court of Chief Pleas of 1537 divided the poor into 'les pauvres indigènes' and 'les pauvres étrangers'. The latter, if they had not been in Guernsey for more than a year and a day, had to quit the island immediately, failing which they would be whipped and then handed over by the parish constables to the Prévôt, who would arrange for their deportation.

Concerning 'les pauvres indigènes' another ordinance of 1566 required that orphans and the children of those too poor to send them to England 'to learn a good trade' were to be found masters in their own parish to whom they might be apprenticed or, failing this, be sent to England as indentured apprentices by their parish constables at parish expense.

Yet a further ordinance, of 1588, ruled that the aged poor were to be subsidised from the alms of the church of their parish of residence and were therefore forbidden to beg save by special licence of the Royal Court. This reference to church alms indicates how the Presbyterian Establishment had adapted itself to provide assistance comparable to that formerly rendered by the Confraternities. Arrangements had been made whereby, in addition to their ecclesiastical duties, the elders ('anciens') in each parish also functioned as 'les Collecteurs du Trésor' while, working under their supervision, were a number of 'Trésoriers des Pauvres' (elected for three months, but frequently re-elected and usually serving for a year or more) who obtained 'poor money' from retirement collections every Sunday, supplemented by income from ratepayers who had been elected as Trésoriers, but who preferred to pay a fine to buy themselves out of this duty. These monies the Trésoriers disbursed to the poor. The number of Trésoriers in any parish corresponded to the number of vingtaines into which the parish was sub-divided, with each Trésorier responsible for the poor within one vingtaine.

Despite these measures, the persistence of the problem during the 17th. century led to an additional crop of ordinances during the 30 years preceding the outbreak of the Civil War. By an ordinance of 1611 an occasional *ad hoc* 'taxe des pauvres' was instituted, the constable and douzeniers of any parish where the Collecteur and Trésoriers had insufficient funds for poor relief being ordered to raise the tax at Easter and Michaelmas — but only if the need arose, and then only with specific authorisation from the Royal Court. A further ordinance, of 1622, prohibited begging on Midsummer's Eve and New Year's Day, while another of 1625 extended the prohibition to weddings and funerals, the custom of begging on all four occasions being regarded as undesirable legacies of Popery. Despite these restrictions, however, begging was frequent, and widespread, Peter Heylyn writing in 1628 (in which year, incidentally, yet another plague eruption intensified distress) that 'Children were continually crying alms of every stranger'. Lastly, an ordinance of 1632 made administrative readjustments, with the titles of Collecteur and Trésorier being changed over. Henceforth the elders ('anciens') were known as Trésoriers, while the deacons ('diacres') became 'les Collecteurs des Pauvres'.

The Civil War left such a legacy of destitution as to frighten the Royal Court into treating it as a crime, ordering that vagabonds should be apprehended and put in the stocks set up for the purpose in every parish churchyard. Indeed, during the reign of Charles II, distress in Alderney became so insupportable that Captain Nicholas Ling, the lieutenant-governor under Sir George Carteret, promulgated an ordinance to the effect that all poor children, who could not be supported by their parents, should be handed over for despatch to Sir George's colony of New Jersey, where they would be hired out for service. The Alderney Court approved this ordinance, which led to a steady decline in the island's population during the ensuing 30 years.

With the establishment of Anglicanism at the Restoration, the erstwhile Presbyterian elders became churchwardens with the title of 'Curateurs du Trésor'. The title of deacon ceased to be used (except of course for clergy not yet ordained as priests) but the previous 'diacres' continued to operate as Collecteurs des Pauvres. Later, with the decision to impose a general 'taxe des pauvres' in 1725, the churchwardens were relieved of their duties towards the poor by the institution of parochial officials with the title of 'Procureurs des Pauvres' in each parish, to whom the Collecteurs des Pauvres had to hand the 'taxe des pauvres' proceeds obtained from house-to-house collections in their respective vingtaines. As was seen in Part III, Chapter Eleven, the office of Procureur des Pauvres persists to the present day.

Under this secularised system of the 18th. century, for the purpose of administering relief the poor were divided into three categories. First came les pauvres indigènes, who received relief from their parishes by residential qualification, while the second type, les pauvres étrangers, received temporary assistance pending arrangements being made to send them back whence they came by the next available ship. Lastly there were les pauvres honteux, consisting of people of very small means (and who consequently did not qualify for relief in the ordinary way), but whose income was insufficient to sustain life. (This category is exemplified by a group of mendicant social outcasts at Le Hurel in Saint Martin's — popularly supposed to be practitioners of witchcraft — specifically referred to in 1847 by a Devonshire lady in an account of her visit to Guernsey in 1844.) They were helped partly by private legacies and gifts — and partly by 'assistance extraordinaire' from the Collecteurs des Pauvres.

In 1742 the Town Hospital (sometimes called La Maison de Charité) was founded by the ratepayers of St. Peter-Port for the poor of the town on land acquired in 1741, the institution being in use by 1743. The word 'hôpital', of course, designated a place where hospitality was dispensed, and not essentially medical treatment, though that also was provided when needed. It was largely financed by gifts from wealthy townsmen and, although upkeep devolved upon parochial taxation, the hospital was well endowed. Bearing in mind, however, that 1742 was in the middle of the privateering era (indeed the War of Jenkins' Ear was shading into that of the Austrian Succession at the time) and that the Hospital's inmates were set to work picking oakum (so useful in caulking ships' boards) and making ships' biscuits, it would seem that such endowment was not entirely disinterested, ensuring as it did a cheap source of two essential adjuncts to the island's corsairs' highly profitable ventures; so that the creation of this establishment exemplifies (as Mr. Richard Hocart has suggested) 'a splendid marriage of charity and self-interest'. Nevertheless, experience proved that herding the poor together and making them work did not solve all problems, as the inmates were inclined to sell to outsiders not only the product of their work, but also some of the hospital's property with which they had been supplied. Thus an ordinance of 1746 which forbade transactions with inmates was reiterated in 1793 together with a ban on the supply to any inmate of liquor — the usual 'currency' in such transactions.

Despite these difficulties the Town Hospital was sufficiently successful to prompt the country parishes to emulate it, seven of them banding together in 1751 to provide in the Castel the Country Hospital, run on similar lines for their necessitous aged and infirm, but with enough land attached to enable it to contribute to its own upkeep by being operated as a farm. The two country parishes which did not originally associate themselves with the project gradually came into the scheme — St. Pierre-du-Bois in 1798 and the Forest in 1826.

After the First World War full responsibility for the poor was assumed by the States, with the States' Public Assistance Board being set up to supplant parochial administration. As a result of this reform, the office of Collecteur des Pauvres was abolished and the Town and Country Hospitals were taken over, while the Procureurs des Pauvres (whose functions were transferred from the ecclesiastical to the secular side of parish business) came to be helped by newly-created Parochial Poor Law Boards with representation on the Public Assistance Board to which the Procureurs des Pauvres became responsible. This system persisted until the German Occupation, during which the Town Hospital alone became the Public Assistance Institution (part of the premises being converted after the Liberation into a home for the destitute); while the Country Hospital became an Emergency General Hospital (in the medical sense of the word) for the sick and injured.

In addition to parish (and later, States) provision, private benefactions have played a significant part in poor relief. The earliest of these dates from 1588 when Jurat Jean de la Court started the 'Bien des Pauvres Donataires de Monsieur Jean de la Court', with a gift of a house at Hauteville, two plots of land, and 15 quarters of wheat rente. Since then the fund (which is administered by the Royal Court) has been greatly increased by legacies and donations. In the early 17th. century Jurat Thomas de Lisle left a house at Les Islets as a 'Maison des Pauvres' for the poor of St. Pierre-du-Bois, as well as bequests for poor relief. A further fund 'for the benefit of the necessitious poor' was set up by Sir William Collings in 1849, while the Victoria Fund, created in 1897 to commemorate Queen Victoria's Diamond Jubilee, was designed 'to help all such deserving cases as are not provided for by the de la Court and Sir William Collings Funds'. The Diamond Jubilee year also saw the foundation of the Victoria Homes in Park Lane when Millbrook House was acquired John Bonamy Collings supported by William Mauger and Gervase Peek. This dwelling plus others nearby generously provided by the Fraser and Carey families in 1902, the Reverend Peter Thomas Mignot in 1930, the owners of the Carrington Shoe Shop in 1965, the Poat family in 1970 and the Kinross family in 1978, conjointly constitute a complex of 35 units of sheltered accommodation for the elderly, each fitted with an alarm bell whereby one of the two resident supervisors may be summoned in case of need. Finally, mention must be made of a highly specialised benefaction in the shape of the Priaulx Charity Fund, founded by John Priaulx in 1829, with the stipulation that it be used solely to provide surgical appliances for poor men suffering from hernia 'who do not belong to any of the hospitals of the island'.

The lot of Guernsey's poor over the years was also alleviated by the general prevalence of a patrician code whereby the richer inhabitants, with a commendable sense of social obligation, took *ad hoc* measures from time to time for the relief of distress as and when it arose. A particularly noteworthy example of such benevolence is seen in the generosity shown by the wealthy when cholera smote the island in 1832. Not only were several houses provided by their owners as havens of refuge from the risk of infection to which the poor of the Town Hospital could be moved, but a staggering total of more than £1,600 (at least £170,000 in 1996 terms) was contributed within 10 days of the launching by Lord de Saumarez of a fund to succour those widowed or orphaned as a consequence of the 103 deaths resulting from the epidemic.

The survival of this tradition was still in evidence in 1896 when in line with it there was founded a voluntary body originally called the Guernsey Rescue and Prevention Scheme which, enthusiastically encouraged by the Reverend Charles Guille, Rector of the Town Church, initially directed its efforts mainly towards the relief of 'fallen women'. Following several changes of title indicative of the widening scope of its activities this organisation, financed by donations from corporate and individual supporters, operates a century after its birth as the Guernsey Welfare Service, devoted to advising and/or helping anyone in need, ranging from unmarried mothers to discharged prisoners, the unemployed, drug addicts, indigent pensioners fallen into debt — and indeed anyone facing any difficulty of any kind with which he (or she) cannot cope. In addition, as far as the physically sick are concerned, it is gratifying to be able to record the persistence of such charitable benevolence right up to the present day — witness the provision, free of charge, for patients terminally ill with cancer-related or neurological diseases made at Les Bourgs Hospice in Saint Andrew's which since its establishment in 1991 has been financed solely by voluntary contributions.

Poor relief provision in Sark has remained substantially unchanged since the island's colonisation in the 16th. century. The system is financed by a local 'taxe des pauvres' (assessed on capital holdings) with each case being dealt with on its merits by the Court of Chief Pleas, whose decisions are implemented by the Overseers of the Poor, elected by Chief Pleas for a three-year term of office.

At the beginning of this chapter mention was made of the work of the mediaeval Confraternities in succouring the sick, old and needy. The case of the needy has now been dealt with, but the sick and the old remain to be considered. Apart from the indigent sick, who were cared for in the Town and Country Hospitals, and patients with infectious diseases who were served by the King Edward VII Sanatorium off Les Vieux Beaucamps (founded by Dr. Laurie Robinson in 1902), those of better financial standing who fell ill before the Second World War were treated either in private Nursing Homes or in the Victoria Cottage Hospital (founded by Doctor Laurie Robinson in 1888 and likewise a fee-paying establishment) where they received attention from their own family doctors. Prominent among the Nursing Homes were the Alexandra and the Ozanne, the former of which was founded by Agnes Priaulx in 1911 and closed by the Germans during the Occupation, with its ghost surviving in the form of a derelict building until its demolition in 1992 to make way for a modern specialist clinic also named after Edward VII's consort; while the latter — founded in 1922 and named after Lady Ozanne, wife of the Bailiff Sir Edward Ozanne — catered for maternity cases. This somewhat inadequate provision was greatly extended during the war by the conversion of the Country Hospital from its 'poor law' function to that of a general hospital.

The building adjoining the erstwhile Town Hospital which now provided flats for the elderly supplementing those at the Victoria Homes was a mental hospital until 1938 when the States acquired a site at Le Vauquiédor to provide more up-to-date treatment for the deranged. During the Occupation, however, the Germans took it over as a general hospital, and after the Liberation the States decided that this was, in fact, a better use for the premises. Accordingly the Country Hospital was adapted for the care of the mentally ill — a function which it still performs — while at the same time Le Vauquiédor House, refurbished and converted into a fine hospital, was on June 23rd., 1949, opened as the Princess Elizabeth Hospital by H.R.H. the Princess Elizabeth.

(Pausing while the cheers ring in the Princess's ears and harking back to the medical status quo ante-bellum, one is reminded that the Alexandra Nursing Home was not the sole victim of the Occupation, which also spelt the ultimate doom of the Victoria Cottage Hospital, left by the Germans in so poor a state as to preclude the resumption of its pre-war range of services. After lingering on as a Maternity Home operated in conjunction with the by then moribund Ozanne establishment, the transfer thence in 1973 of maternity cases to the Princess Elizabeth Hospital relegated the ex-Victoria — re-named the 'Island Maternity Hospital' — to providing for no more than post-natal convalescence and thereby further undermined its *raison d'être*, so that it finally closed in 1980.)

Alderney's first hospital — located in Victoria Street — owed its existence to the munificence of the Reverend Peter Thomas Mignot, C.B.E. (1863–1935), an indefatigable philanthropist (already mentioned in connection with the Victoria Homes) to whom Saint Stephen's and the Castel Churches are beholden for their organs and who also in the early 1930s paid for road construction at Le Val des Terres and also slum clearance in Cornet Street so as to give work to Guernsey's unemployed. In response to an appeal for a hospital in Alderney (his natal isle) this generous cleric bore the entire cost of building and equipping one in memory of his deceased wife Julie Le Messurier Mignot, after whom it was accordingly named when opened in September 1926. In addition the same donor provided an endowment fund to generate a contribution towards defraying running costs. All in all his gift amounted to £6,500 (£4,000 for the hospital and £2,500 for the fund) equivalent to nearly £200,000 as this book goes to print. Thirty years later, to cater for the post-war rise in Alderney's population, replacement premises were acquired at Crabby in 1958. Retaining the name 'Mignot Memorial Hospital', the new building was designed and paid for by the Nuffield Provincial Hospitals Trust, with quarters for the Matron being added later, generously provided by the island's ex-Judge, Brigadier F.G. French. One of the island's resident doctors is also Medical Officer of Health and under recent restructuring of health provision the hospital is now funded and administered by the States of Guernsey.

Sark, too, has a resident doctor, but no hospital provision. Seven years after the war, however, the *Flying Christine* ambulance launch came into service for the transport of urgent cases to the Princess Elizabeth Hospital in Guernsey from both Sark and Herm.

Mention of this vessel of mercy makes this an appropriate point at which to consider the fact that the existence in the Bailiwick of any ambulance service worthy of the name is due almost entirely to the courageous endeavours of Reginald Herbert Blanchford, O.B.E., G.M., O.St J., L.F.I.B.A. whose own gruesome experiences when involved in a near-fatal accident in 1930, impressing on him as they did the gross inadequacies of the ramshackle provision then made by the States, led to his joining the Saint John Ambulance Brigade Division established in Guernsey in 1934. After agitating until the division justified its title by acquiring a second-hand conveyance, Blanchford ran so efficient a service that in December 1939 (in anticipation of possible war-time casualties) the States handed over all ambulance responsibilities to the Brigade, promising to help with an annual grant as well as the purchase of new vehicles as and when necessary.

Having kept the service intact throughout the Occupation by an audacious series of improvisations, Blanchford turned his attention after Liberation to improving the island's blood-transfusion arrangements and to setting up air ambulance facilities for taking emergency cases to England. He then launched a campaign for the installation of a radio-controlled ambulance system, successfully overcoming the reluctance of the Postmaster-General to grant a licence for such an operation. On March 6th., 1947 Lieutenant-General Sir Philip Neame, V.C., the lieutenant-governor, formally opened the new radio-equipped ambulance station — the first in the world.

Convinced of the dire need for a marine ambulance to facilitate cliff-rescue work as well as to ferry urgent cases from the smaller islands, and undaunted by the disapproval both of the States and of the Saint John Council, Blanchford followed up his radio success by appealing to the public through the Round Table Association to finance such a venture. The initial response permitted the acquisition in 1952 of a launch (the above-mentioned *Flying Christine*) which was fitted out appropriately and performed sterling service in the ensuing years. Finance, however, remained a perennial problem, the States in 1951 having already cavilled at fulfilling the 1939 pledge to replace road vehicles, and it was not until the summer of 1956 that a report on the Guernsey service drawn up by Harold T. Ferrier, Director of Ambulances of the Joint Committee of the Red Cross and Saint John in London, ultimately prodded the States into assuming the fully supportive rôle which has since been maintained.

This financial support enabled the service in 1992 to improve the facilities which it provides by acquiring for the first time in the person of Mr. Jon Beausire (and at a training cost of between £3,000 and £4,000 met by the Board of Health) a paramedic specialist capable of performing at the scene of an incident life-saving techniques previously only carried out by doctors on arrival at hospital — and thereby eliminating an erstwhile delay beset with potentially fatal consequences.

Reginald Blanchford, who had been granted the rank of M.B.E. (later raised to O.B.E.) in 1951 in recognition of his services, was accorded the Queen's Commendation in February 1957 for a daring cliff rescue the previous summer. This was followed in June of the same year by the Order of Saint John presenting him with its Life-saving Medal in gold. Finally, in November 1958 at an Investiture in Buckingham Palace H.M. the Queen awarded this gallant islander the George Medal for his great bravery and endurance. Mr. Blanchford retired in 1977. He was, however, in attendance on November 28th., 1994, at the ceremony where H.R.H. the Duke of Gloucester (to whom he was presented) named *Flying Christine III* which, described as 'The world's most advanced marine ambulance' is — like her predecessor *Flying Christine II* — a purpose designed craft, specially constructed to facilitate the high-speed provision of medical and life-saving aid at sea.

Although Guernsey has no complete social security system, yet no charge is made for beds or food in the Princess Elizabeth Hospital, and some years ago a scheme was introduced whereby medicines may be obtained on prescription from chemists at a nominal charge much as in the United Kingdom. The services of doctors, dentists and opticians have, however, to be paid for by those receiving them. On January 1st., 1965 a comprehensive system of social insurance came into force, to which everyone must contribute, with employed persons paying just over half the contribution. Benefits include retirement pensions, widows' pensions, and sickness payments. Under a reciprocal arrangement with the British government, free medical attention to U.K. residents visiting the Bailiwick was available until 1998, in which year the discontinuance of this facility was made inevitable by the Blair Administration's insistence on the reimbursement of expenses incurred in treating Bailiwick residents visiting the United Kingdom to the extent that they exceeded the cost of treating U.K. visitors incurred by the Bailiwick.

In July 1995 the States voted in favour of a plan to come into effect on January 1st., 1996, and giving the Bailiwick more extensive health provision than ever before known. Already in January 1994 the decision reached in 1992 to impose hospital and out-patient charges had been rescinded and by this further development a system was established giving all Bailiwick residents (save those of Sark) cover for specialist acute care, consultations, treatment and operations undertaken by the Medical Specialist Group at its Alexandra House Clinic, in hospitals and at Les Bourgs Hospice. To fund such provision, every adult (unless exempted on grounds of insufficient means) became required to make contributions shared equally between employee and employer and calculated at 1% of the employee's earnings (with no account taken of unearned income) but not exceeding a joint payment equivalent to £4.26 per week — though with liability for the entire sum devolving on pensioners who by definition have no employers to share the burden. General Practice was excluded from the scheme, though in regard thereto the health benefit grants initially approved in 1988 and implemented in January 1991 were retained, amounting to £8 per attendance at a G.P.'s surgery or £4 for a nurse consultation — in addition to which existing private health insurance arrangements (possibly adapted to cover primary care only) could naturally be continued if desired.

A less welcome development in medical provision has been seen, however, in the lack of local nursing staff constraining the Board of Health to seek further afield, recruiting for the Princess Elizabeth Hospital twenty-nine Filipino nurses (with Spanish as their primary language) between November 1999 and March 2000, with the intention to obtain a further thirty being announced in May 2000; in which month it also emerged that in the fields of psychiatric and geriatric care there was a shortage of thirty-five nurses in the Castel and King Edward VII Hospitals.

Before concluding this chapter, mention must be made of provision for geriatric infirmity, the earliest example of which consists of the Victoria Homes considered above — and supplementary whereto accommodation of like nature has in the more recent past been made available at the ex-asylum in Hospital Lane of previous incidental mention. In 1938, on the death of the third Lord de Saumarez, the States bought his residence of Saumarez Park from the fourth lord, who wished to dispose of it — and in 1945 opened the house as a hostel, run by a warden and matron, accepting up to 55 elderly men and women as residents. The hostel is administered by a Board of Management, who depend on voluntary contributions and any payments the residents themselves are able to make for the enjoyment of this spacious house, together with the beautiful surrounding grounds maintained by the States as a public park. Yet further assistance for those of advanced years was envisaged in November 1998 when a compulsory long-term insurance scheme was proposed with the aim of extending help to the aged in need of residential care, whose contributions would be limited to £100 per week, with the balance (up to as much as £400 per week) being paid by the scheme. Whereas hitherto the scale of help had been linked to the assets of the person needing care and hence frequently resulting in the loss of these assets built up over a lifetime, the new scheme would help to safeguard what had so thriftily been accumulated. It was suggested that the implementation of these proposals would be financed by an income-geared levy not exceeding £5 a week payable by all islanders except children, people on benefit and those already in long-term care.

Geriatric provision has also been made on a voluntary basis since 1919 by the Hospitaller Sisters of the Sacred Heart in their Home at Le Platon, St. Peter-Port (see Part I, Chapter Twelve). Lastly, in 1964 the King Edward VII Hospital in the Castel was turned into a geriatric hospital, having originally been built as a sanatorium for infectious diseases. It operates in conjunction with the residential homes of Longue Rue, Maison Maritaine and Duchess of Kent, to which the old folk are transferred after a course of therapeutic treatment.

Within the context of the entire complex of post Second World War medical arrangements the need for the Town Hospital progressively waned and in November 1983 the Board of Health announced its intention to vacate it completely when the extension then being made to the Duchess of Kent House was completed, centralizing all accommodation for elderly patients on the King Edward VII/Castel Hospital site. In pursuance of this policy — and in defiance of the vociferous disapproval of the island's doctors — the 244-year life of La Maison de Charité was finally brought to an end on October 1st., 1986, the twelve men patients still remaining at the time of closure being transferred to the Princess Elizabeth Hospital while the fourteen women went to the Castel. In April 1993, after extensive adaptation costing £5 million and preserving the façade, the building was re-opened as a replacement Police Station (though now styled Police Headquarters) for that in St James' Street, which the requirements of the age had rendered inadequate.

Chapter Twenty-Two

'FILTHY LUCRE'

THE OLDER GENERATION of islanders will recall that when, as children, they were given a penny to spend — capable in those pre-inflationary days of buying something — the coin received bore on its obverse the arms of the Bailiwick, together with the word 'Guernesey' spelt in the French fashion, while the reverse carried the minting date and the inscription, '8 Doubles', which could be understood as 'Huit Doubles' or 'Eight Doubles' according to taste. Behind this design lies the fascinating tale of the Bailiwick's numismatic history, the vicissitudes of which stem from the persistence of the idea that, despite their attachment to the English (and subsequently British) Crown as from John's loss of Continental Normandy in 1204, the islanders were nevertheless obliged to employ the same currency 'dont usent les hommes de Normandie' — with the result that French money was used to the exclusion of English until after the Napoleonic Wars.

The basic unit of the French currency system was the livre tournois (which became the universal currency of France in 1667). This was divided into 20 sous — or sols — which in their turn consisted of either 12 deniers or four liards. The last-named coin took its name from Guigues Liard, who is said to have originated it in Dauphiné in the year 1430. At the same time there also existed a coin called the double, as it corresponded to two deniers (i.e., six to the sou). This ancient coin was an established piece by the 16th. century, the word 'double' to indicate a monetary unit of small value being employed by Thomas Bowes in his translation of de la Primaudaye's 'French Academie' in the volume published in 1589. With the double comprising two deniers and the liard three a certain amount of confusion arose, so that the liard was at times referred to as the double — as in the Royal Court ordinance of 1623 regulating against the displacement of good doubles (meaning liards) by worthless deniers emanating from mainland Normandy. It is, incidentally, interesting to note that in one respect the ghost of these long obsolete units is still with us, in that the livre tournois continues to be used for the purpose of calculating rentes, with one livre tournois having the equivalence of 6.8p (on the basis — confirmed by H.M. Greffier in November 1995 — of 14 livres tournois being valued at 19s.-0½d. — i.e. 95.2 pence — in pre-decimal days).

In France itself the purchasing power of the liard declined until it was worth far less than 25 per cent. of a sou — but its value was preserved in the islands. This fact led mainland Norman traders to enhance their profits by making payment to islanders entirely in liards, with the result that enormous quantities of these coins were accumulated in the Bailiwick, where hoards of them were thriftily stacked away in caches which still come to light from time to time. Gresham's Law was working with a vengeance. In an attempt to cope with this flood the States of Guernsey in the mid-18th. century stabilised the liard at eight to the sou — which, although far in excess of its value on the French mainland, was a necessary level because of its frequent use in the payment of feudal dues.

For many years the livre tournois had been nicknamed the 'franc' — a name which had stemmed from a gold coin minted in 1360 by John II bearing the legend 'Johannes D. G. Franc. R.' ('Johannes Dei gratia Francorum Rex'). In 1799 the Directorate determined to decimalise the currency and decided to make 'franc' the official name for the main unit, which was divided into 10 decimos (later to fall out of use) and 100 centimes. As a consequence the livre tournois was phased out, though it continued to circulate until 1834 at a rate of 81 livres tournois to 80 francs — while in Guernsey in 1830 its mind-boggling notional value against sterling was quoted by John Jacob as 'one shilling and one-sixth of a fourteenth part'. The sou also survived under the guise of five centimes, but the importance of this reform for the Channel Isles was the utter disappearance of the liard. Even at its Guernsey valuation, five-eighths of a centime obviously did not make sense, while at its French valuation the resulting fraction of a centime was ludicrous.

Guernsey reacted to this new development in accordance with the ancient tradition that insular Normandy had to use the same money as mainland Normandy. Thus, on November 8th., 1799, a Royal Court proposal was placed before the States to the effect that that body should have a copper coinage struck. There was a precedent for the assumption of coinage rights by the Guernsey States in that in 1533 a certain Collas Guillemotte had been appointed, with the approval of the governor representing the

Crown (Sir Francis Weston) to design and mint coins known as fréluques, which remained in circulation for over a century.

Although the Court's proposal was accepted, nothing was done to implement it until 1813, when the encumbrances to trade and to the settlement of feudal dues arising from the ever-increasing shortage of liards provoked the States to seek an Order-in-Council confirming a Projet de Loi authorising a local currency issue. Even so, it was not until 1830 that the issue was finally struck by the Birmingham firm of Boulton, in defiance of the requirement accompanying the Order-in-Council that the coins should be made by the Royal Mint. Nobody could accuse the Guernesiais of being over-hasty or impetuous.

The basis of the Guernsey coinage which now saw the light of day was the double, which in effect corresponded to the old liard restored to its original value of a quarter of a sou. The first issue consisted of one and four double pieces, with two and eight double pieces following later.

For transactions of *small* value these coins circulated interchangeably with the United Kingdom money brought in by the British garrison, and by the English settlers who started to come over in the years after Waterloo. Thus eight doubles was regarded as one penny, four as a halfpenny, and two as a farthing — as had been stipulated in an Order of October 1st., 1821, made by that year's Michaelmas Chief Pleas during the interim between the authorization of an island coinage and its actual minting; pending which there functioned as the Double a bewildering miscellany of metal tokens, embracing British and foreign small change and even including old buttons beaten flat! For transactions of *large* value, however, this equivalence did not work, as the silver coinage in Guernsey consisted of the French one-, two- and five-franc pieces, with 80 doubles being equal to a franc (= four to a sou — the old value of the liard). As the rate of exchange between France and the United Kingdom throughout the 19th. century was 25.2 francs to the pound, then obviously 2,016 (= 25.2 x 80) doubles made up one pound sterling. This was the same as 252 eight-double pieces. An English rentier settling in Guernsey could consequently get 252 'penny equivalents' for each sovereign — as against 240 British pennies. His income was automatically increased by five per cent. So over they came, bringing their money with them and augmenting the yield of local taxes.

After the First World War the erosion in the value of the franc resulting from the conflict led to the decision to discard the French connection entirely and to adopt a complete affinity between local and United Kingdom currency. In line with this decision, the value of the double was rearranged at 1,920 to the pound (very appropriately, as the alteration took place in the year 1920), and thus an eight-double piece became identical with an English penny. However, it was not until 1956 that the English spelling of Guernsey was employed on the coinage — the first time, incidentally, that it was struck by the Royal Mint.

During the years preceding decimalisation the avidity of souvenir-hunting tourists led to the virtual disappearance of eight-, four-, two- and one-double pieces. In 1956 a Guernsey threepenny bit was issued and in 1966 Guernsey anticipated the United Kingdom in having a coin instead of a note for half of a pound, issuing a square ten shilling coin to mark the ninth centenary of the conquest of England.

The Bailiwick 'went decimal' on February 15th., 1971, at the same time as the United Kingdom, with its own issue of 50p, 10p, 5p, 2p, 1p and ½p coins. A One Pound piece followed in December 1980 — in advance of its English counterpart — but it proved very unpopular, so that the Guernsey One Pound Note remained in circulation long after the corresponding Bank of England issue had been demonetized. It is, indeed, still used throughout the Bailiwick at the time of writing. A further minting put into circulation in 1985 included a special £2 coin struck to commemorate the fortieth anniversary of the Liberation. It also made numismatic history because of the appearance for the very first time on Guernsey coinage of the Monarch's Head — borne on the obverse together with the Bailiwick Seal. The occasion was additionally marked by the announcement of plans thenceforth to issue fresh sets of coins every five years. Yet another development ensued in 1989 when, coinciding with the visit to that island of H.M. the Queen, a distinctive Alderney specie appeared for the first time, taking the form of a further £2 piece designed to mark this auspicious event. Although of distinct design, the similarity of these coins in size, shape and weight to the United Kingdom issue enables the returning tourist to dispose of them, illegally, in slot machines back home. Moreover, tourists who are philatelists as well will also be reminded of the 'double' coins of yesteryear when surveying their collections, as these were featured in the definitive issue of Guernsey postage stamps between 1979 and 1985.

The delay between concept and execution in the minting of the Bailiwick's coins meant that their appearance was, in fact, preceded by that of Guernsey notes, the first issue of which took place in 1816, when it was specifically devoted to financing the projects for improved marketing facilities — as seen in Chapter 15 of this Part. Further issues were authorised by the States between 1816 and 1834 for other specific purposes, such as laying roads, improving schools, and paying off the floating debt.

All these early issues were scrupulously redeemed by the States in 'real' money (i.e., French franc coins), but in the later 1830s the practice of earmarking issues for particular ends was discontinued. A paper currency had been launched.

Almost immediately the States had to contend with competition in the form of note issue by two banks (the Old Bank and the Commercial Bank). As the three issues between them threatened to flood the island with paper money, the bailiff, Daniel de Lisle Brock, called a States meeting to halt the incipient inflation by asserting the States' monopoly right to issue notes. Shortly afterwards, by a self-denying ordinance, the States' issue was limited to £40,000 — a limitation that was observed until the First World War. Five-pound notes were discontinued, and the issue was confined to one-pound and ten-shilling notes.

Nowadays the States issue as many notes (ranging from one pound to fifty pounds) as they can get into circulation — with the 1994 figure amounting to £46,194,500 consisting of £11,517,000 in new notes and £34,677,500 in used ones re-issued. The aim is still that of obtaining interest-free money, as the States are providing themselves with purchasing power to the extent of the issue. Difficulties arise, however, from a much more formidable competitor than the small early 19th.-century local banks, in the form of the English notes brought over by tourists, refusal to accept which would undermine one of the Bailiwick's main attractions to the British holiday-maker: the absence of currency problems. Against this competition Guernsey notes have to hold their own so as not to be driven out of circulation by a perverted variant of Gresham's Law — 'good' money being driven out by 'better'.

The battle is waged through the banking system. The banks credit the States' accounts according to the requirements of the Finance and Advisory Committee and if any individual bank branch acquires a surplus of English notes, it sends this excess back to England — or returns a comparable value in Guernsey notes to the States, debiting their account accordingly. In an effort to avoid this latter (and undesirable) eventuality, the population is exhorted to pay wages and cash cheques in Guernsey notes — which will ultimately find their way back to the banks again as a counterweight to the English ones.

A further monetary problem which has become increasingly evident of recent years has been that associated with the growing circulation in the Bailiwick of notes and coins from Jersey, together with a smaller number of notes issued in Scotland, Northern Ireland and the Isle of Man. In a statement pursuant to a query on the part of a correspondent published in the *Guernsey Weekly Press* of July 12th., 1985, Conseiller (as he then was) Roydon Falla (the President of the States' Advisory and Finance Committee at the time) indicated that legal tender in the Bailiwick is confined to notes and coins issued by the States of Guernsey plus notes issued by the Bank of England and coins which are legal tender in the United Kingdom as well. Consequently, 'Jersey, Scottish, Northern Irish and Isle of Man currency is not legal tender in Guernsey, nor is the currency of any other territory'. The Conseiller went on to explain, however, that such monies are nevertheless normally accepted by islanders, thanks to a widespread confidence within the community that they may be used to settle debts, despite the fact that in strict legality creditors are entitled to refuse them.

Chapter Twenty-Three

FEATURES FISCAL AND FINANCIAL

THE MEDIAEVAL THEORY in western Europe was that 'the King should live of his own' — i.e., meet the expenses of government from his income as a feudal magnate. This applied as much to Guernsey as anywhere else, the warden being expected to defray the costs of administration from the feudal revenues farmed out to him. Thus the need for income from taxation was felt predominantly by the individual parishes, as a means of financing the miscellany of administrative responsibilities which fell upon their shoulders.

The traditional basis of the direct taxation on which the parishes relied — a basis persisting up to the present century — was real estate, the capital value of which was assessed in quarters of wheat rente (notionally £25), taxes being levied at such percentage thereof as circumstances required. The franchise for the election of douzeniers (and hence for the douzaine delegates who attended the States) was restricted to such owners of real estate, who were known as Chefs de Famille.

Fundamental to the system was (and still is) the register of the value of real property known as the Cadastre, which is kept, in duplicate, by the individual parishes and by the Cadastre Department of the States. The taxation to provide for parochial outlay on such items as road upkeep and poor relief (such as the 'Taxe des Pauvres' instituted in 1725 and referred to in Chapter Twenty-One preceding) was calculated on the basis of the Cadastre.

After the First World War the capital value of property ceased to be the basis of taxation, being replaced by a rateable value theoretically associated with the annual rent which a property would normally command. Furthermore, parochial taxation (save in Saint Sampson's) was transferred from a levy on the owners of property to one on the occupiers — hence the name of 'Occupiers' Rate'. This rate (which partly defrays ecclesiastical expenses) may only be levied after a Remède has been granted by the Royal

Court. Additional parochial income has been obtained from the issue of licences, such as those for dogs and shot-guns and (until a few years ago) for bicycles.

The progressive decline in the power exercised by the wardens and its assumption by the bailiff and the Royal Court, meant that the new masters stood in need of tax income to meet their expenses, as the Crown remained the recipient of feudal dues until after the Second World War. The money required for such purposes tended at first to be obtained from tolls on shipping, an early example of which was that imposed in 1305 to finance the repair of St. Peter-Port mole (see Part III, Chapter Four). Thus taxation imposed by the island government was now added to that levied by the parishes.

It has already been seen (Part III, Chapter Six) that at the time of their first emergence one of the main functions of the States arose 'quand il est question de lever quelque argent pour la necessité publique'. Although the method whereby they might proceed 'de lever quelque argent' included direct taxation of property-owners, it has just been noted above that this was primarily a parochial source of revenue, and it was therefore more usual to raise money by impôts on various commodities, especially wines and tobacco) as well as the aforementioned shipping tolls, which became a major source of income with the proliferation of shipping coming to the island in the 19th. century. When, however, any rare and exceptional contingency arose involving expenditure beyond the yield of such duties, recourse was had to the island-wide taxation of property owners mentioned in the last sentence, but employing in its imposition a quota system whereby the taxpayers of Saint Peter-Port contributed one-third of the sum to be raised and those of the Castel, Saint Saviour's and Saint Pierre-du-Bois one-ninth each, with a further one-eleventh coming from Saint Martin's, one thirteenth from the Vale, one-sixteenth from Saint Andrew's, one-twenty-fifth from the Forest and one-thirtieth each from Saint Sampson's and Torteval. It was in the early 19th. century also that the States for the first time embarked on the taxation of property-owners on a regular basis, with the imposition of the 'equivalent' to meet the cost of road upkeep — as was seen in Chapter Sixteen of this Part. When it was proposed to follow this up with a general levy on property owners throughout the island in place of the quota system, such was the consternation engendered among the taxpayers of Saint Peter-Port (who stood thereby to pay much more than hitherto) as eventually to usher in the States' Reform of 1844 referred to in Part III Chapter Eight. (It may, however, be remarked parenthetically that the fears of the townsfolk were to prove somewhat premature as, although the general levy was officially authorized at the same time as the States' Reform Law was enacted, no tax of this nature was in fact imposed until the First World War and, moreover, was discontinued permanently thereafter — though it is true that its lineal descendent survives in the form of an island-wide tax based on rateable values which is levied by the States on owners of property in addition to the rate required of occupiers by their respective parishes.)

Income Tax was not introduced until after the First World War. At its outset envisaged in 1918 as a device to help raise a contribution from Guernsey of £100,000 towards the Empire's war expenses, it was somewhat belatedly authorized by a Projet de Loi of July 1919 confirmed by Order-in-Council the following December, with a levy at its inception of 2.925% (or 7d. in the £) and, although retained after the disappearance of its initial *raison d'être*, remained very moderate right up to the Second World War, never amounting to more than 4.375% (or 10½d. in the £). Even at its present level of 20% it compares favourably with the basic rate charged in the United Kingdom. Originally taxpayers were individually responsible for settling periodic demands calculated on the basis of declarations of income which they were legally obliged to submit. Under a system introduced in 1980, however, each person's assessment came to be founded on his or her declared previous year's earnings with the tax thus arrived at deducted by employers under the Employees' Tax Instalment scheme, popularly known as 'E.T.I.' As this book was being prepared for publication consideration was being given to replacing this arrangement by one similar to that called 'Pay-as-you-earn' ('P.A.Y.E.') in the United Kingdom, with assessments based on current income levels rather than those of the past.

During and immediately after the Second World War the States levied a sales tax on all goods at 8½ per cent, but this experiment in a generalised indirect taxation was discontinued after a short while.

A subsidiary source of income for many years consisted of stamp duties, States of Guernsey revenue stamps having to be affixed to legal documents and also to receipts.

Of recent years feudal dues have once again become part of the income of Guernsey's government, with the arrangement since 1947 whereby the revenues of Fief le Roi accrue to the States in consideration of that body paying the salary of the Lieutenant-Governor and associated disbursements. During the early 1980s this source of revenue was progressively augmented, first by the partial and then by the full implementation of the policy mentioned in Part II, Chapter Nine, under which all Congé payments formerly made to the Seigneurs and Dames of private fiefs are diverted to the States via the Crown.

In Alderney reliance was placed entirely on impôts and property tax until after the Second World War when, on Guernsey's assumption of responsibility for the stricken island, its inhabitants came under the Guernsey tax system and so paid income tax for the first time. Of late years, however, Alderney's duties on spirits and tobacco have at times diverged from those of Guernsey.

Although Sark did not emulate Guernsey in introducing Income Tax in 1922, preferring to continue reliance on the traditional standby of a property tax at a level fixed annually by Chief Pleas, the replacement of this arrangement by the hitherto resisted Income Tax was warily advocated in July 2000 (as has already been seen in Part III, Chapter Thirteen), thereby precipitating a furore in Chief Pleas. Originating as an adjunct of the historical property tax is the 'Taxe des Pauvres' mentioned in Chapter Twenty-One preceding, but far more lucrative are the impôts levied on goods such as tobacco and alcohol. Lastly, there is the landing tax, and the associated tax on the tonnage of ships using Sark's harbours, both of which date from 1859 and by means of which tourists help to finance the upkeep of the lovely isle from which they derive so much pleasure.

Attention now needs to be turned to an outstandingly important by-product of the tax system. Thanks to its comparatively low rates of income tax, together with the absence of surtax, value added tax, and capital gains and transfer taxes, in a geographical location near the United Kingdom, the Bailiwick has from the late 1950s onwards developed a 'finance industry' which has become its major source of income, generating in 1999 60% of the island's export earnings and with 6,000 employees who between them contributed in the same year over 50% of Guernsey's Income Tax Revenue.

Oversight of these highly profitable operations is exercised by the Guernsey Financial Services Commission under a Director-General with direct responsibility to the States' Advisory and Finance Committee and consisting of three divisions (Banking, Investment Fund Business and Insurance — each with its own

Superintendent) corresponding to the three main manifestations of this lucrative sphere of activity which have developed. Firstly, starting with the establishment of a branch in Guernsey by Kleinwort Benson, there has been a proliferation of merchant and other banking business, in which field a plethora of British and foreign houses is now represented, the international nature of whose business is highlighted by the fact that 65% of all deposits are in currencies other than sterling. Secondly, a widespread development of investment and unit trust funds operating from the Bailiwick followed rapidly on the setting up of the first such organisation in 1959 in the shape of the Investment Trust of Guernsey which rapidly acquired vast net assets. A number of these funds now specialise in European and North American investments. Thirdly, a major expansion ensued in the field of insurance, with the *Review* of the Guernsey Society reporting in mid-1987 that the position had been reached where the island had become internationally recognised as a leading insurance centre, handling a large proportion of the world's aviation insurance business, covering thousands of millions of dollars worth of aircraft and other risks. Yet another development in this field was that of 'captive' insurance, the growth of which was such that by the beginning of 1992 Mr. S.W. Butterworth, Superintendent of Insurance, announced that Guernsey had become the biggest captive insurance centre in Europe — to which one might add that by 1995 in the whole world only Bermuda and the Cayman Islands were bigger centres. (It should perhaps be explained that the expression 'captive insurance — coined by Frederick Reiss in 1953 — originally designated an insurance concern set up and owned by a parent company to cover it and its subsidiary enterprises against losses affecting their earnings per share and their book value per share — with the corollary that such business was non-competitive, with ascertained and restricted liability. The meaning of the term was, however, subsequently extended to embrace not only single parent ownership but also traditional association business, jointly owned insurance ventures and even insurance purchasing groups and risk retention groups.) All in all, by 1999 the position had been reached whereby over 300 institutions of the three types mentioned above had been established in the island, 75 of which were banks holding funds in deposit totalling £56,581 million — and in the same year the prospect arose of a still further favourable opening, with Guernsey's anticipated emergence as the world's second market (the only other being New York) for

Financial Guarantee Insurance business. Early 1998 saw the dawn of yet another aspect of financial activity when preliminary steps were taken towards creating the Channel Islands Stock Exchange to be based in Saint Peter-Port and advocated by the Guernsey Financial Services Commission's Director-General, Mr. Peter Crook. Trading in fact started late in October of the same year. Furthermore, since the late 1950s there has been a considerable influx into the Bailiwick of 'tax refugees' from the United Kingdom — all of whom are only too happy to swell local coffers by paying Guernsey's modest levels of income tax, occupiers' rate and impôt duties. Although this wave of immigration was partly stemmed, it was by no means halted as a result of the British government's decision in 1974 that capital transfer tax would henceforth be levied on United Kingdom residents settling in the Channel Isles, thereby making it more difficult for such people to dispose of their assets — particularly real estate — in an advantageous way. Even the income tax element may be avoided by any newcomer judicious enough to settle in Sark — witness the millionaire, Mr. Leonard Matcham (1911–1987), who for many years directed his empire of multifarious business activities from his base in Brecqhou.

A less agreeable side to the 'finance industry' has, however, been seen in the distortion of the real estate market resulting from massive increase in demand for housing accompanying the arrival of 'tax refugees'. In an effort to prevent the swamping of this market the States instituted a system whereby those without domiciliary entitlement could only occupy premises bought on the 'open market' confined to houses of high rateable value. The phenomenal prices commanded by such properties have, however, driven marginal native demand for this type of accommodation 'down market' so that the prices in the 'local' range have risen also, to the detriment of the interests of indigenous Guernsey folk which the system was designed to protect.

To make matters worse, the property boom's reflection in soaring site values provides a standing temptation to farmers and growers to forsake their pursuits, lured by the quick and rich rewards to be had from land sales. There has been an ominous trend of late years for greenhouses deliberately to be neglected in the hope that their eventual derelict condition, by rendering the land they occupy 'unproductive', will result in their owners obtaining permission to 'develop'. The potential social disaster implicit in such courses of action is terrifyingly obvious.

Finally, a particularly scandalous side effect of the 'finance industry' is the injustice perpetrated by the fact that the definition of what constitutes the right to occupy 'local market' premises is such as to exclude expatriate islanders from returning to their birthplace unless they are wealthy enough to acquire a residence in the fabulously expensive 'open' bracket.

These undesirable adjuncts of the Bailiwick's development as a financial centre brought into existence — in 1976 — the Guernsey Association, formed with the five-fold objective of promoting and protecting the quality of life of Guernsey people; facilitating the return of expatriate islanders; protecting and conserving the use of land; promoting fuller utilisation of existing dwellings so as to provide more housing for Guernsey people; and urging physical immigration control in preference to the manipulation of the property market.

Although this organisation's crusading activities came to an end with its dissolution in December 1993, circumstances arising since its formation had been such as to encourage concrete proposals for several measures akin to those which it had advocated. While the Association at its demise claimed that the election of Conseillers by popular vote had been instituted thanks largely to the climate of opinion which it had fostered; this ginger group was also instrumental in nurturing an attitude of mind favouring the limitation of immigration by direct controls rather than by relying solely on manipulating the property market. A workforce scarcity brought about by the growth in economic activity generated by the Finance Industry so stimulated labour immigration as to produce a population increase of 2,169 between the 1981 and 1986 censuses, with later developments indicating a most disquieting demographic trend occasioning a fear that it might at any time exceed 60,000 (the actual 1996 Census figure was 58,681) — a level verging on the intolerable. The threat to the island's basic social structure and environmental stability implicit in this alarming prospect prompted the Advisory and Finance Committee in July 1987 to recommend a much more rigorous implementation of housing regulations, supplemented by the introduction of employment controls, involving a work permit system designed to ensure that the annual average of 3,000 seasonal workers arriving each summer would in fact leave in the autumn, rather than staying on and infiltrating the resident population.

Chapter Twenty-Four

THE BAILIWICK AND THE EUROPEAN COMMUNITY*

THE BRITISH GOVERNMENT'S original application to join the European Community gave rise to marked consternation in the Bailiwick — where attachment to Albion's commercial coat-tails had already proved costly, with British adhesion to the European Free Trade Association (by ending the preferential duty on imported raw leaf) forcing the Guernsey Tobacco Company in 1965 to abandon its hitherto lucrative cigarette production. Perturbation now arose from the fear that should the United Kingdom gain Common Market entry, the Bailiwick (its autonomy notwithstanding) would have to follow suit, as Article 227–4 of the Treaty of Rome lays down that its provisions 'shall apply to any European territories for whose external relations a member state is responsible'. The situation thus tended to confirm the islands' somewhat wary attitude towards London's governmental apparatus, summed up later by the then Deputy Cecil de Sausmarez, as a very strong feeling towards Windsor, combined with a desire to keep away from Westminster and to remain on friendly terms with Whitehall, but never to have a love affair with it.

The islanders' misgivings were not greatly allayed by the British government's announcement that if they wished the islands could elect to assume complete independence and hence stay outside the Community as no longer being territories for whose external relations the United Kingdom was responsible. The trouble was that such an ability to 'opt out' did not remove the dilemma that the consequences likely to ensue from staying out were as daunting as those implicit in entering — hence the local anxiety accompanying the years of negotiation.

*Even though since November 1st., 1993 the official title of the European Organisation has been 'Union' the term 'Community' is retained in this chapter — and with justification, as in strict legality neither our Bailiwick nor that of Jersey forms part of the European Union, the official status of each Bailiwick remaining that of an associate member of the Community.

Entering the Community seemed to involve several unattractive prospects, of which six were especially worrying. In the first place, as the Bailiwick had no purchase taxes, the introduction of value added tax would have meant that prices rose by the full amount of the tax — to the detriment of the tourist industry as well as of domestic living standards. Secondly, as the Bailiwick's visible imports (£23,655,000 in 1969) considerably exceeded its visible exports (£18,306,000 in 1969) much alarm was aroused by the possibility of the enforcement of the origin system (whereby taxes on goods are paid to their source of origin anywhere within the Community) as this would mean that the Bailiwick would be making considerable net tax payments to foreign governments — a serious matter for a society whose foreign exchange earnings were negligible. Thirdly, harmonised excise duties were also dreaded as the abolition of the differential between United Kingdom and Guernsey prices would reduce the Bailiwick's attractions as a tourist resort, as well as depriving Guernsey of the tax revenue derived from the purchase of British customs allowance by tourists. In the fourth place, the harmonisation of *direct* tax provisions was even more feared, both as an increased tax burden for the inhabitants and also as a threat to the lucrative finance industry attracted to the Bailiwick by low direct taxes. The fifth apprehension was that the policy of free movement of labour would pose practically insoluble problems for small islands whose resources were already strained by massive immigration, despite strict controls over the entry of aliens and even stricter ones over house-occupation by non-islanders. Last, but not least, the consequences for horticulture flowing from Continental produce sharing the free entry to the United Kingdom markets hitherto enjoyed only by the islands, whose advantages would thereby be eroded, were particularly alarming for Guernsey, whose horticultural produce accounted for 80 per cent. of her visible exports.

As against the six-headed Scylla menacing entry, there were the perils of Charybdis to consider should the Bailiwick stay outside the European Community. To begin with, if the Bailiwick stayed outside, the United Kingdom would be compelled to levy the Common External Tariff against its exports. This deterrent to the British purchase of island horticultural produce, compounded by the duty-free availability in Great Britain of Continental produce, would have been disastrous for what was then Guernsey's premier industry. On top of that, the maintenance of the Bailiwick's monetary union with the United Kingdom would eventually be put at risk by European monetary integration — again to the detriment of the tourist trade and the finance industry.

Confronted with these unenviable alternatives, the islands of the Bailiwick reacted in different ways. Because of her considerable reliance at that time on horticulture, Guernsey felt that, on balance, the maintenance of the British connection was of prime importance, concluding that 'we cannot live if we are excluded from our present and potential markets for horticultural produce, or any other exports'. Guernsey therefore accepted that she would probably have to go into the Community, but hoped that special arrangements could be made in respect of taxation, agriculture, horticulture and immigration.

The likelihood of such 'special arrangements' being arrived at was not, however, by any means certain, as in 1967 a United Kingdom government statement had described the possibility of modifications to Article 227–4 as 'remote'. This uncertainty caused particular consternation in Alderney which, bereft of visible exports (and hence denied any potential benefit from a wider market) derives her income almost exclusively from tourists and 'tax refugees', both attracted by low levels of taxation. Hence Alderney at one point even toyed with the idea of emulating Anguilla's attitude to St. Kitts-Nevis, and in the island's submission to the Commission on the Constitution (see Part III, Chapter Ten) urged 'that the constitutional relationship between the United Kingdom and Alderney should be so altered that Alderney's inclusion in certain international treaties, which affect her financial and domestic affairs, should be dependent upon the concurrence of the States of Alderney'.

Sark also felt apprehensive about the fate of her special fiscal status (including a complete absence of income tax) and of the possible associated repercussions on her tourist trade (made even more lucrative by landing tax revenue) as well as on her attraction to 'tax refugees'. Thus a petition in October 1967, submitted by La Dame de Sercq to the Queen-in-Council, asked 'that the island should be excluded from any provisions resulting from the membership of the United Kingdom of the European Economic Community, and that the ancient privileges and rights re-affirmed by Her Majesty the Queen in person in July 1957, should continue in force without change or alteration'.

In the event the dark cloud turned out to have a very silvery lining indeed. An announcement was made in November 1971 that agreement had been reached regarding 'arrangements short of full membership which would provide for an exchange of reciprocal rights and obligations between the Community and the Islands'. The main features of these terms were later embodied in Article 227–5 of the Treaty of Rome. They were five in number. Firstly, free trade in industrial goods would be established between the Islands and the Community and the Islands would apply the Common External Tariff. Secondly, for agricultural goods there would also be free trade and the system of levies on imports from outside countries would be applied. By the third of the terms, however, the Islands would be exempt from all other Community regulations except those necessary to apply free industrial and agricultural trade. By the fourth provision the rights of Islanders in the United Kingdom would be protected, but the Islands would not be permitted to discriminate between British residents and visitors and the nationals of other Community countries — i.e., the same regulations for admission should apply to all. Lastly, it was provided that any unforeseen problems could be dealt with under a safeguard clause.

Addressing a special meeting of the States attended also by Sark and Alderney delegations, the late Lord Rippon (at that time the Right Honourable Geoffrey Rippon) gave an assurance of continued freedom to maintain the features distinguishing island life from that of the United Kingdom, as well as a guaranteed preservation of fiscal autonomy. Although in regard to the terms Mr. Rippon expressed his 'firm belief that they could not have been better', he nevertheless made it clear that the decision now rested with the insular authorities whether to accept them or to opt for complete independence. Such an option, however, would carry four main implications. In the first place, a new constitutional relationship with the British Crown would have to be negotiated and the Bailiwick would have to assume responsibility for conducting its own external affairs and for defence. Secondly, all exports to the Community, including the United Kingdom, would be subject to the Common External Tariff and other levies. Thirdly, the Bailiwick would cease to come under United Kingdom arrangements for exchange control purposes — and lastly, the islanders would lose their preferential rights of access to work in the United Kingdom.

The case for accepting the terms was obviously overwhelming and the Advisory and Finance Committee recommended such a course of action — a recommendation which was approved unanimously by the States. Hence on January 1st., 1973 the

Bailiwick joined the European Community with the status of 'in but half out', in accordance with the provisions of Article 277–5 of the Treaty of Rome as implemented by Protocol 3 of the United Kingdom's Treaty of Accession.

Despite the favourable nature of the terms under which the Bailiwick entered the Community, several problems of adaptation are likely to persist for some time. As was virtually inevitable, the Bailiwick's farmers and growers have had to face much stiffer competition in the United Kingdom market because of the reduction of tariff barriers against its Continental competitors — a situation which has eventuated in the need for ever-increasing subsidisation of horticultural exports by the States since the autumn of 1979, despite which the tomato trade has been brought to the verge of extinction. The possibility also has to be faced of additional inflationary effects resulting from British entry into the European Community reducing the Bailiwick's competitiveness as a tourist resort. Although the depreciation of the pound at first partially operated as an off-setting factor, it is nevertheless true that a 'package deal' holiday in Spain can prove to be cheaper to a Londoner than one in the islands. Further difficulties are possible should any further harmonisation of excise duties bring a reduction in the United Kingdom's alcohol and tobacco duties, as this would reduce the differential between Island and United Kingdom prices, making the Bailiwick less attractive as a tourist resort and also reducing the revenue from the purchase of these goods in the Islands by visitors. It is also true that any direct action by the Community against 'tax havens' could have adverse effects — but this would be difficult to implement as fiscal autonomy has been guaranteed. On the other hand, were economic and monetary union ever to be achieved, this would work to the advantage of the Bailiwick as a financial centre. What's to come is still unsure.

This uncertainty became apparent when a by-product of the 1973 arrangements not anticipated at the time manifested itself with the advent of European Passports in 1992, those issued to Guernesiais or Guernesiaises carrying the endorsement, 'Holder is not entitled to benefit from E.C. provisions relating to employment or establishment'; thereby denying to native islanders the right to live or work permanently anywhere in the European Community — save only the United Kingdom, whither ancient charters guarantee access.

It might further — and perhaps more portentously — be added

that while at the time of writing (1998) the Bailiwick's relationship with the European Union is still in strict legality confined to the 'arrangements short of full membership' provided for by Article 227–5 of the Treaty of Rome; in practice a somewhat closer association has evolved since the first appearance of this History arising from the fact that, although by the terms of Protocol 3 (the progeny, as has been seen, of Article 227–5) Guernsey need not submit to any attempted imposition of Euro-regulations, it has nevertheless occasionally been felt that to refuse compliance therewith would be imprudent. With this trend in mind, a report in the *Sunday Telegraph* of May 4th., 1997 assumed a distinctly disturbing significance, revealing as it did that among a set of maps of 'Euro-regions' prepared in Brussels there is one showing the Channel Isles in the same colour as the adjacent French mainland, suggesting an envisaged future incorporation of the archipelago into the European Union as part of the 'Basse Normandie Euro-region'. If this map be indeed the harbinger of things to come, the situation thereby established would indubitably be a very far cry from that accepted by the States in 1973 on the basis of the assurances given by Lord Rippon — though remarkably similar to the status planned by the Third Reich for application to Alderney in the wake of Germany's victory! Nor was this all! Indeed, it was not long before one urgently-felt foreboding in particular augmented the misgivings over future prospects in general engendered by these cartographical inferences. This serious qualm became known the next December with the news that dread of a seemingly imminent threat to insular autonomy had led 61% of Sark's adult population to sign a petition to the European Commission seeking that their island's feudal way of life be left undisturbed and altered by none save the Serquiais themselves should they at any time so desire. On any rational assessment it appeared hard to understand how the Commission could possibly be considered entitled to interfere as feared by the petitioners in the internal affairs of a territory protected by the provisions of Protocol 3 of the United Kingdom's Treaty of Accession and also by those of Article 227–5 of the Treaty of Rome — unless, of course, one invokes the old adage that Might is Right!

The fear of such an identification of Might with Right being indeed the coming trend was expressed in September 1998 by Mr. Brian Walden, whose assessment led him to be apprehensive that Guernsey could well be 'sacrificed for the greater good of Europe', with the United Kingdom Government 'reacting to pressure from

Europe by chipping away at the independence of the Channel Islands through interference and the imposition of irksome regulations'. In this connection one might add that such a prospect, though hardly pleasing, could be inferred from the openness to rescission of Protocol 3 (widely disliked by the Continental members of the European Union) should a unanimous vote be cast against it in the European Commission; so that from the 1993 Maastricht Treaty onwards it had only escaped repeal because of the United Kingdom's adhesion to it precluding any such unanimity — and here it is pertinent to observe that Mr. Walden's remarks clearly reflected a degree of uncertainty attending the continuance of this adhesion by a British Government whose attitude to the Channel Isles since taking office in May 1997 has not been a particularly friendly one (see Chapter Eleven of Part III).

Chapter Twenty-Five

'TRUSTEES OF POSTERITY': CHILD EDUCATION

IF IT BE TRUE that a community's most rewarding investment is in the education of its children — the 'trustees of posterity' in the words of Benjamin Disraeli — then it is also true that for the greater part of the Bailiwick's history its people were so blind to the profits thus to be gained that right up to the last 150 years the provision made in this respect even by Guernsey's leading Alma Mater — Elizabeth College — was, as will be seen, little short of farcical. Indeed, the fact of the matter is that the present-day educational system in the islands is predominantly a creation of the 19th. century in that, although several schools existed previously, their educational value was minimal, such perfunctory efforts as they made tending to be vitiated by a prevailing atmosphere of indifference verging on hostility. Consequently, the tale to be told regarding earlier times is not a particularly flattering one.

The first school of whose foundation a record exists dates from 1513. In that year Thomas Le Marquant and his wife, Jannette Thelry, made a gift to St. Peter-Port of a house and garden on the north side of the chapel of St. Julien for use as the parish school. They also bestowed two quarters of annual wheat rente upon the schoolmaster who was to repeat with his charges daily an anthem of Our Lady, with a De Profundis and an Ave Maria, for the souls of the donors, of their friends, and for all souls in general. This school eventually came to be known as La Petite Ecole de la Ville, to distinguish it from Elizabeth College (founded 50 years later) which was referred to as 'La Grande Ecole'. La Petite Ecole de la Ville was rebuilt in the early 19th. century, standing near the point where the modern St. Julian's Avenue debouches upon the esplanade. After its demolition resulting from the creation of this thoroughfare, it was replaced early in the present century by Vauvert School, which is thus its lineal descendant. In addition, there continues to this day a nostalgic evocation of this ancient foundation's educational contribution in that the income deriving from the 'Petit Ecole de la Ville Fund' is still applied to the purchase of textbooks for island schools generally.

The Elizabeth College register shows that in 1563 when Elizabeth I founded it, she also gave an endowment to La Petite Ecole de la Ville and, in addition, endowed schools at St. Pierre-du-Bois and St. Martin's. Thus at least three parish schools existed by the time the Calvinists captured the Guernsey ecclesiastical establishment in 1565 (see Part I, Chapter Six). To the credit of these disciples of Geneva stands the fact that they accompanied the more savage aspects of their witch-hunting activities by an attempt to counter the spread of ignorant superstition by education. Thus, in addition to the catechism classes held weekly in the churches, they fostered the establishment of schools in some of the parishes still lacking them. It is evident, for example, that the Vale School must have existed by 1615 as a record is extant of one Samuel Bonamy being ordered to be flogged there for stealing. It was, however, after the Restoration and the imposition of Anglicanism (see Part I, Chapter Eight) that the Castel School was founded in 1675 at St. George's Chapel, being moved to its present site in 1735. Similarly, St. Saviour's School was founded in 1736 after the failure of a previous venture initiated by the rector, the Rev. Alexandre de Soulies, in 1687. Rudimentary though their educational provision undoubtedly was these schools were nevertheless the ancestors of the parish schools of the 20th. century.

As in England, the religious bodies took the lead in educational provision in the early 19th. century. The Anglicans set up one of their National schools in the building erected on Mont Gibel, which later came to be known as the Central Hall and was finally destroyed by fire in 1984, while the Nonconformists established a 'British School' in New Place, the pupils paying a small weekly sum for their instruction. At the end of the century this was fourpence a week, payable each Monday. Under the stimulus of these examples the various parish schools were aroused from their lethargy in the decade after Waterloo, while in 1883 and 1895 two Intermediate Schools (one for each sex) were founded to provide what may be called a grammar school course without a sixth form. It was not, however, until 1900 that school attendance became compulsory in the island. A particularly praiseworthy contribution towards improving nineteenth century educational facilities was made by Mr. — later Jurat — Peter Roussel (1815–1879) of whom *The Star* remarked at the time of his death that 'by his untiring exertions the educational standard in our parochial schools has been raised to a high position' — and that, for this cause, 'he laboured unceasingly ... devoting not only his time and great intellectual powers, but also his purse and his influence with lavish liberality'. An extract from his *Notre Pays* faces the title page of this book. Yet another benefactor was Admiral Sir James Saumarez, Bart. (as he then was) who during Mr. Roussel's boyhood gave generous support to the parish schools of Le Castel, Saint Pierre-du-Bois and Saint Andrew's, as well as founding a four-year exhibition to be awarded to the best classical and theological student at Elizabeth College.

It is now necessary to go back to the 16th. century in order to trace the development of Guernsey's only public school. In 1563, when the island was in a state of some religious confusion with a 'grass-roots' Calvinism opposed by anti-Calvinist jurats (see Part I, Chapter Six) Queen Elizabeth I founded Elizabeth College, perhaps in the hope that it would exert a pro-Anglican influence. Here again, however, she was confronted by the language difficulties which constrained her to accept a Calvinist ecclesiastical establishment two years later, and hence had to acquiesce in the appointment as first master of the Flemish Calvinist refugee, Dr. Adrian Saravia. To accommodate her foundation, Elizabeth granted the land adjoining La Rue des Frères, previously held by the Franciscans whose house had been dissolved under Henry VIII (see Part I, Chapter Three), adding a further 10 vergées in 1568, when the entire property was handed over to the States of Guernsey, who have been its landlords ever since. The area thus formed was bounded by the Grange, Upland Road, La Rue des Frères and College Street — though today the land occupied by the College is far more restricted. For the support of the master, Elizabeth I granted 80 quarters of wheat rente out of the royal revenues.

Originally no pupil paid for tuition, but at New Year made a gift of one guinea to the master, and one shilling to the servant, in addition to contributing two shillings and sixpence towards the cost of coals. (It should be explained that these sums are based on an arbitrary identification of the sol tournois with the English shilling.) Dr. Saravia did not for long receive his annual guinea per pupil, as in 1568 he left in disgust at the ignorance and inertia of the islanders.

Still hoping to use the foundation as an Anglican influence Charles I in 1635, at the instance of Archbishop Laud, founded three scholarships — at Exeter, Jesus, and Pembroke colleges,

Oxford — for Channel Islanders (see Part I, Chapter Eight). Pupils at Elizabeth College still seek the advantages of these 'Charles I scholarships'. In 1678, after the Anglican Church had at last been established in Guernsey, Bishop Morley of Winchester founded five further scholarships at Pembroke. Again the primary object was to recruit Anglican clergy — the scholars being expected to return, preferably in Holy Orders, after graduation.

Despite these encouragements the career of Elizabeth College continued to be a disappointing one. The islanders were uninterested, pupils were lacking, and the master's position became a complete sinecure — indeed at times there was no master at all. The States kept the fabric in repair, but the intentions of the foundress were never fully carried out, land was stolen, and some of the endowments were misappropriated. So rudimentary were the facilities offered by the school that during the 18th. century the sons of better-off families tended to be sent to England for a year or two, to make good their educational deficiencies, widen their outlook and improve their English. By 1799 Elizabeth College had only one pupil.

By 1821 George Le Boutillier of Arcade fame (see Chapter Fifteen of this Part), fearful for his own sons' education prospects, became so critical of the state of affairs that he approached the lieutenant-governor, Sir John Colborne, about the matter. Colborne appealed to the dean in his capacity as Visitor to the College, but in vain. This was hardly surprising as the dean (Daniel Durand) was also the master, having been appointed in 1795, since when he had seen fit to sequester the revenues into the hands of the churchwardens of the Town church — despite the fact that the college was not a church benefice and the master was not even required to be a clergyman.

Faced with this obduracy Colborne in 1824, in alliance with the bailiff, Daniel de Lisle Brock, managed to get rid of Durand by an arrangement between him and the States whereby he abandoned his rights to the buildings, land and rentes, in return for an annual pension of £60. This done, Colborne, Le Boutillier and Brock obtained the appointment of a Committee of Inquiry in 1825. This enquiry revealed that much of the land had, in fact, been alienated, that at Durand's retirement there were only 16 pupils (and never since 1563 had there been more than 25) and finally that Durand had felt no obligation to teach anybody anything.

In the meanwhile a temporary building had been obtained where on October 11th., 1824 classes were started under the Rev.

Charles William Stocker, who rapidly made a name for himself as an enthusiastic flogger. His tenure of office was not for long, as he left shortly before the present building was completed.

On October 19th., 1826 the foundation stone of the present school was laid by Sir John Colborne. In Tudor Gothic style and covered with brown stucco, the building, designed by John Wilson, was handed over to the Rev. G. W. Stocker's successor, Dr. Procter, on August 20th., 1829. In the new school the first two names on the roll were those of Sir John Colborne's two sons, while the next three were the sons of George Le Boutillier. Apart from its enforced sojourn at Buxton in Derbyshire during the Occupation, the college has provided Guernsey with an excellent public school ever since.

By contrast with the royal foundation of its male counterpart, the Ladies' College owes its existence to the efforts of Mrs. F. Mann and the Rev. T. W. Sidebotham, joint secretaries of the Guernsey Ladies' Educational Association — an enterprise formed by the issue of 200 shares of £5 each, which wished to set up a girls' school comparable to the Ladies' College at Cheltenham. Thus financed, the College opened at the top of the Grange in a pair of houses (later known as 'Ladymead' and the Carouselle Hotel) on October 10th., 1872 with 16 pupils (which had increased to 70 by the end of the first year of operation). In 1878 moving downhill to 'Detroit' (originally owned by the brother of Sir Isaac Brock, in honour of whose exploits it was named) this prestigious girls' seminary continued to be run by the Association until ownership was vested in the States by Order-in-Council in 1962 — three years before it forsook 'Detroit' (which became the Island Education Office) for its present home at 'Melrose' in Les Gravées.

Because of the desire to emulate Cheltenham, Miss Dorothea Beale, the headmistress of that school, was consulted, with the result that she supplied from her staff the new college's first principal, Miss Susan Eaton. Two subsequent principals also came from Cheltenham in the persons of Miss Laura Eaton, and Miss A. Mellish.

The college spent the war years at Denbigh in Wales, taking in girls from other evacuated Guernsey schools. During the exile pupils numbered between 60 and 70: they now amount to about four hundred and fifty. With the admission in July 1981 of its principal (Miss Josette Honey) to membership of the Girls' School Association, the college attained public school status.

The conclusion of successful negotiations to effect an innovative educational development was made public in July 1999 when Mr. David Toze, Principal of Elizabeth College, having emphasized that without a strong Sixth Form the future of neither school was secure, announced that an agreement had been reached between the Ladies' College and his own for joint courses to be offered as from the following September in a merged 'truly academic independent colleges' Sixth Form' providing a 'mature mixed environment for students that will prepare them for university'; and operating as a 'genuine partnership' whereby each college would be 'strengthened immeasurably'.

Before the Second World War the parish schools operated as elementary schools and were attended for the most part by children who on leaving would enter the ranks of hired labour, while the two Colleges provided grammar school courses for those seeking admission to the universities or entry to the professions. The Intermediate Schools, as their name implied, were midway between these two extremes, being primarily designed to prepare children to undertake commercial and industrial careers. The more able or affluent pupils at the parish elementary schools went on to the Intermediate Schools or the Colleges at about 11 years of age, the former by scholarship, the latter on a fee-paying basis. During the '30s the parish schools were reorganised in geographical districts as specialist schools for juniors or seniors respectively. After the Liberation, the senior elementary schools became secondary schools — comparable to secondary modern schools in England — and their number was eventually increased with the opening of Beaucamps School by H.R.H. the Princess Margaret on May 4th., 1959, Saint Peter-Port School by H.R.H. The Princess Alexandra on October 10th., 1968, and La Mare de Carteret Schools (Primary as well as Secondary) by H.M. Queen Elizabeth the Queen Mother on May 28th., 1975. In the field of primary education 1976 saw the school at Mare de Carteret acquiring a companion with the opening by Jurat S.W. Gavey, O.B.E., on November 19th., of another school at La Hougette, designed (with more adequate provision in mind) to replace the former parish schools of Saint Pierre-du-Bois and Saint Saviour's. Signs of yet further improvement became apparent in 1996 when work began on a £3 million development at the hitherto modest Hautes Capelles School, which on completion emerged as one of the finest schools in the island. Meanwhile the two Intermediate Schools — now renamed Grammar Schools — started to provide a full Grammar School course, differentiated from the two colleges only in not being regarded as public schools. In 1985 they were combined into a unified co-educational establishment housed in new premises at La Rue des Varendes in Saint Andrew's which on May 8th. of that year were opened by H.R.H. the Duchess of Kent.

It is sobering to reflect, however, that Guernsey's educational provision is bedevilled by difficulties in obtaining staff, many teachers being recruited from United Kingdom agencies and frequently only staying in the island for a relatively short time before returning whence they came, thereby depriving the schools' pupils of the confidence which derives from a rapport developing between them and well-known long-serving mentors.

Valuable educational facilities have also been provided since the early years of the present century by a number of schools run by various Roman Catholic religious orders, the most noteworthy of which have been Les Vauxbelets for boys and Blanchelande for girls — as already noted in Part I, Chapter Twelve.

Alderney had to thank the lucrative privateering ventures of the late 18th. century for its first school, which was provided by the 'hereditary governor' from the profits that he had reaped. Hence the inscription still to be seen above the old school gate:

> Ecole Publique bâtie et fondée par Jean Le Mesurier,
> Ecuyer, Gouverneur de cette isle, A.D. 1790.

This foundation, catering for boys, was later supplemented by another for girls, set up by Major-General John le Mesurier's wife Martha Perchard in a room at Government House. Writing in 1830, John Jacob records that about sixty pupils received tuition at each of these establishments — but it was not until 1924 that compulsory education was introduced in the island (the last place in the British Isles to take this step) and the present all-age (4 to 16 years) school of Saint Anne, dating from 1966 and staffed by a headmaster and six assistants, is attended by about 200 pupils, for whom further educational facilities are available in Guernsey.

Mr. F. Wearis, in his *News from Sark*, printed in 1671 (and already noted in Chapter Two of this Part) referring to Elie Brévint, says, 'The present Minister ... hath lately begun Teach Grammar to the Children with Writing and Arithmetick, erecting a School for that purpose, so that who knows to what prodigious Learning we may here one day arrive?' What Brévint had in fact done was to build on a room to the outhouse at Le Manoir which did duty as a church — and this had to suffice until Pierre Le Pelley, seigneur 1820–39, set about providing improved facilities. With a loan from the States of Guernsey and the co-operation of the National Schools Society, a new school was built on a site he donated north of the church, building being started in 1829.

In his will made in 1837, still thinking that the silver-mining operations would at any moment make Sark an El Dorado, Pierre donated a site near Le Manoir for a further island school for 30 pupils. After Pierre was drowned in 1839 his brother and heir, Ernest Le Pelley, carried out these wishes. The site was given to the island, and the junior school built on it. Both schools still operate, but, as in the case of Alderney, Sark children have to go to Guernsey for secondary education.

During the quarrying boom on Herm, the Reverend Henry Benwall, with financial assistance from the townsfolk of St. Peter-Port, established an island school in 1838. The rough quarrymen, however, who had no wish for their children to receive any education, refused to make any contribution. An approach to the States of Guernsey asking for the diversion of part of the impôt on spirits to help support the school was also unsuccessful. The upshot was that although 40 children were in attendance, this little school was forced to close in 1840. After the Second World War, however, a new school was established in the 'castle keep' part of the Manor House. A schoolmistress was appointed in 1956, and children are taught up to the age of 14 after which they go to Guernsey for further education.

Chapter Twenty-Six

'INGREDERE UT PROFICIAS'

THE SAD TRUTH that 'a prophet is not without honour, save in his own country' (until, possibly, after his death) is well illustrated in the careers of Thomas Guille and his colleague, Frederick Mansell Allès. Born in the Forest parish in 1817, Thomas Guille emigrated at the age of 14 to the U.S.A., where (first as apprentice to and later as partner of an elder Guernsey immigrant named Daniel Mauger) he not only thrived as a house-painter and decorator, but also educated himself, accumulating several hundred volumes of standard works by the age of twenty. While still a young man he became an associate (again in the painting and decorating business) of his boyhood friend and fellow emigré, Frederick Mansell Allès, to such purpose that they prospered exceedingly and became wealthy men.

Visiting Guernsey in 1851, Guille advocated the formation of parish libraries in a series of newspaper articles, but nothing definite was done until a second visit in 1855, when the Guille Library Committee was formed and Guille's book collection divided into five sections placed in charge of friends with the idea of the sections being exchanged in rotation — but this was not in fact done.

In 1867 Guille returned to Guernsey for good and brought all the books to a central depot in St. Peter-Port, save for a reading room in St. Martin's, which he personally superintended for three years, after which he concentrated upon the central establishment. This proved to be a thankless task, as his fellow-islanders evinced little desire to avail themselves of his services. Prospects improved, however, when Guille's old friend Allès came to his aid in 1881. Between them they bought from the States for £900 the old assembly rooms for conversion into a public subscription library in 1883, better access being provided by the creation in 1886 of the present Market Street entrance designed by James Charles Torode (1851–1896) whose work may also be seen in the De Beauvoir Terrace downhill from Saint Stephen's Church.

The Guille-Allès Library had been born, but neither Guille nor Allès felt that they had attained their main objective. Over the entrance they had placed the combined motto and exhortation, 'Ingredere ut proficias' ('Enter that thou mayest profit'). Far from profiting, however, the working-class, whom Guille and Allès, as self-made men, hoped would be the main beneficiaries of their efforts, could not even be prevailed upon to enter.

In an effort to attract proletarian patronage and on the assumption that a middle-class milieu acted as a deterrent, Guille, in the year of Allès' death (1895) founded the Artisans' Institute in a building adjoining Les Poids de la Reine given by the States for the purpose. Because of his own death the following year (1896) Guille was spared the realisation that this venture, too, was doomed to a mediocre fate. It dragged on with indifferent success until the Second World War when it was finally killed by the persistent apathy of those for whom it had been designed.

As for the library, the subscription system was replaced by a free lending service jointly financed by the Guille-Allès Council and the States in 1981, after the premises had been extensively refurbished thanks to the generosity of Sir Charles and Lady Hayward of Jethou. These measures reacted favourably on the popularity of the Library, which by 1995 attracted an average of 22,000 users annually.

On the floor above their library Guille and Allès established a museum (largely inherited from the Mechanics' Institution — of which more in the next chapter), but this, too, attracted little interest, with much the same, unfortunately, applying to the archaeological museum bequeathed to the Island in 1907 by Captain Francis du Bois Lukis, the son of Frederick Corbin Lukis (1788–1871) and housed in his residence in the Grange, which the legacy also made available for a nominal sum.

In 1889 Osmond de Beauvoir Priaulx left his property of Candie, including his house, his large personal library and his gardens, as a bequest to the people of Guernsey. The admirable Reference Library is administered by the Priaulx Council, and although freely available to all persons over 18 years of age, shares the fate of the Guille-Allès Library in being predominantly utilised by the middle classes.

In the adjacent Candie Gardens a new building, opened in 1978, houses the combined Guille-Allès, Lukis and Candie Museums (the last-named consisting of a collection of ceramics, prints and pictures, left to the Island in 1928 by Wilfred Carey of

Candie in the Castel) which since 1937 had been located in the deconsecrated church of St. Barnabas. It is pleasant to be able to record that — thanks largely to tourist patronage — this attractively-sited and imaginatively-arranged museum (which incorporates a, café in the erstwhile Victorian Bandstand and in 1979 won the coveted 'Museum of the Year' award) has attracted much more interest than the adjacent library. A comparable success has also been enjoyed by yet another museum opened in 1975 at Le Château de Rocquaine (Fort Grey) which, after extensive refurbishing, was converted for the display of maritime exhibits.

Chapter Twenty-Seven

SEDULOUS SEEKERS AND SAVANTS

NOTWITHSTANDING THE LACK OF RESPONSE accorded to the efforts of Thomas Guille and Frederick Allès, there is nevertheless always a nucleus of young people who resemble the co-founders of Guernsey's Library in being anxious for self-improvement. It was to cater for such that in the year 1832 (when Thomas Guille was 15) the Mechanics' Institution was founded, designed to provide facilities for advancement for skilled craftsmen, be they employers, self-employed or employees, who desired to make good the inadequacies of such boyhood schooling as they might or might not have obtained in the parish schools where attendance at that time was in any case optional. Very appropriately, the president of the new institution was Frederick Corbin Lukis (1788–1871), who in his own person had based his life's work on self-instruction, justly earning fame in the realm of archaeology. His interest in this field of study had been aroused in 1811 when he shared, together with the eminent botanist and artist, Joshua Gosselin, in the discovery of the cromlech at La Varde.

This experience having fired his enthusiasm, he set about devoting his life to the excavation and examination of dolmens in the Bailiwick, saving many from destruction and preserving their contents for posterity in the museum which is now in the possession of the island and newly displayed in Candie Gardens. Refusing to accept current assumptions without further verification, it was he who established, contrary to popular belief, that dolmens were tombs and not 'Druids' Altars'. The difficulties involved in disseminating knowledge may be appreciated when one recalls that during the inter-war period (about 60 years after the death of Lukis) a notice board near the Vale church pointing towards La Varde still bore the legend, 'To the Druids' Altar'.

In its early days the institution provided lessons in La Petite Ecole de la Ville after school hours, and, although this policy was discontinued in 1833, it was revived in 1835 when Mr. W. B. Moullin became secretary, with 40 pupils among the junior members receiving one-and-a-half hour's instruction from the senior members every weekday evening except Saturdays. French, English and arithmetic were taught, while the drawing class was superintended by no less a person than the famous local artist, Paul Naftel.

The institution, which was housed originally in a room in the National Schools and subsequently in a room in the States' Arcade balcony, subscribed to all local and Jersey newspapers and also to informed periodicals such as the *Saturday Magazine*, the *Penny Encyclopaedia* and *Chambers' Edinburgh Journal* — as well as building up a library which eventually totalled nearly 4,000 books. After September 1836 the instruction classes dwindled and the institution concentrated more on engaging visiting lecturers to deliver discourses often above the understanding of the membership which, not surprisingly, fell in numbers.

After Jurat Edgar MacCulloch (later Sir Edgar MacCulloch, bailiff) became president in October 1850, a report recommended that the changed nature of the organisation should be recognised in its title and constitution. Accordingly, after some heart-searching, the name was changed to the Mechanics' Institution and Literary Society, while the clause to the effect that two-thirds of the committee was to consist of master or journeymen mechanics was amended to a requirement that one-half of the committee should be so composed. Thereafter the institution carried on mainly as a lecture society and museum, supplemented by a library and reading room. Interest declined, and by December 1881 such serious financial difficulties had arisen that the offer of Thomas Guille and Frederick Allès to take over everything, including debts, was accepted, and the institution was wound up. Its museum became the nucleus of the museum established by Guille and Allès, while its library made a significant addition to their own, which was opened the following month (January 1882).

The leading members of the defunct institution met together on October 10th., 1882 and formed the Guernsey Natural Science Society. This name was soon changed to the Guernsey Society of Natural Science, with Jurat Edgar MacCulloch as president: and yet again to the Guernsey Society of Natural Science and Local Research. So it remained until 1922 when, on the recommendation of the late Miss Edith Carey, the eminent local historian, it became 'La Société Guernesiaise'.

La Société Guernesiaise has now become the Island's foremost learned society, studying the archaeology, history, folklore, language, geography, geology, fauna and flora of the Bailiwick.

It arranges lectures and holds meetings for reading and discussing papers, as well as arranging exhibitions and visits to places of interest. Its *Transactions*, published annually, knowledgeably investigates a variety of island matters and provides the student with an invaluable storehouse of information. Rendered homeless in 1981 by the refurbishment of the Guille-Allès Library robbing it of the premises which had served as its centre of operations since its foundation, La Société immediately launched an appeal whereby the funds were raised to finance the creation of new Headquarters in Candie Gardens opened on April 12th., 1986, by Sir Charles Frossard, Bailiff of Guernsey — who later the same day delivered the inaugural address in the new building.

La Société's companion organisation, the Guernsey Society, was founded in the United Kingdom in 1943 by Sir Donald Banks, Air Commodore Henry Brock, and Colonel G. D. Ozanne, originally to give help to refugees from the Bailiwick. It persists as a society consisting mostly, but not entirely, of expatriates, which seeks to promote the welfare of Guernsey and its people. Its publication, *The Review*, which appears three times a year, contains articles of academic, cultural and nostalgic interest which, however, do not aspire to the depth or detail of the studies characterising its senior counterpart's *Transactions*.

Whereas the Second World War, by posing an immediate refugee problem, had prompted the establishment of the Guernsey Society, its aftermath revealed an unwelcome circumstance which led to the creation of yet another body operating in the educational field. In the wake of the euphoria of the Liberation a culturally disastrous legacy of the conflict became apparent when thousands of child evacuees concluded a fire-year sojourn in Great Britain by returning to their birthplace as English monoglots, thereby bringing the island's ancient variant of the Langue d'Oil under threat of extinction. To counter (and, if possible, to reverse) this trend L'Assembllaïe d'Guernesiais was constituted in 1956 with the aim of fostering the study and preservation of Guernsey's linguistic heritage. This organization's Dictionary Committee collaborated with Mrs. Marie de Garis in the compilation of her Dictiounnaire Angllais-Guernesiais, published initially by La Société Guernesiaise in 1967 (with a supplement appearing in 1973) and subsequently extensively revised and enlarged so as to embrace a Guernesiais-English Section in the edition published by Phillimore in 1982 to mark the centenary of La Société — ever a staunch ally of L'Assembllaïe.

Chapter Twenty-Eight

CULTURAL LIFE AND THE ARTS

ONE ONLY HAS TO CONTEMPLATE the frivolities of Mardi Gras reduced to the austerity of a pancake on crossing the Channel to become acutely aware of the less endearing attributes of Protestantism, embodying a severity which today would be countenanced by few who employ this term to designate their religious affinity. Thanks to the Via Media of the Elizabethan church settlement, England was spared the more extreme rigours of Reformed canons of conduct, so that survival was assured for such traditional jollifications as Morris dancing and May Day revels, enshrining the culture of the common people. Guernsey, however, was far less fortunate in this respect, the kill-joy régime of the Calvinists from 1565 to 1660 not only obliterating the colourful practices of La Chévauchée, but also leading to the almost complete disappearance of such traditional dances as La Violette, La Bébèe and La Bérouaise.

The fate of Guernsey makes it gratifying to be able to say that the Puritanical gloom of Geneva seems to have made less impact in Alderney, whose people struck Inglis (see Chapter Thirteen of this Part) as being as improvident and carefree as the Guernesiais were thrifty, and where the dance, 'Mon beau Laurier' survived well into the 19th. century. Bundles of flowers were strung up across the roadway, around which a rhythmic hand-in-hand dance would be taken up to the strains of 'A mon beau Laurier qui danse', ending with embraces between partners.

Another dance which survived in Alderney until the mid-19th. century, despite the efforts to suppress it of Governor John Le Mesurier (1744–1793) was 'Les Brandons', which took place on the first Sunday in Lent. A circular dance involving repeated kissing, it reached its climax with the lighting of firebrands ('Brandons') which were waved to and fro to the great peril of the thatched cottages.

One more custom associated with revelry persists in Alderney to the present time, in the form of 'Milk-a-Punch' Sunday (the first

Sunday in May) when the public houses serve rum punch free of charge to all comers in memory of the previous tradition whereby one was at liberty to milk the first cow within reach, gather eggs from the first hen in sight, add rum and make punch.

In Guernsey the increased prosperity of the 18th. century, coupled with the presence of a garrison in the Bailiwick, led to regular ballroom dances (or 'assemblies' as they were called) being held. These functions took place in the Assembly Rooms, built in 1780 by 20 of the ruling families in the Island over the new meat market, to replace the incommodious accommodation in the Pollet hitherto utilised for such gatherings. The rules for admittance were very strict, limiting the entrée to about 60 local families, as well as the officers of the garrison and eligible officials in the governor's entourage. This exclusiveness enraged the privateering *nouveaux riches*, whose aspirations to social recognition were thereby thwarted — and great bitterness was engendered between the 'Forties', as the parvenus were called, and the accepted and established 'Sixties'.

The social needs supplied by the Assembly Rooms having declined as the 19th. century advanced, the States bought the premises in 1870, whereupon they became a venue for public entertainments until they were sold to Guille and Allès for their library in 1882.

Guernsey's first theatre was *La Comédie*, regarding which F.B. Tupper in his *History of Guernsey* records that about 1775 'a theatre was fitted out in a store near the Hospital', and in relation to which handbills for the season 1783/4 are preserved at the Priaulx Library. It was followed by the more substantial *Theatre Royal* which was built in 1793/4 on a site in la Rue Marguerite (New Street) — and which in 1798 became the *mise en scène* of an altercation between William Tupper (the historian's uncle) and Lieutenant Charles Thompson of the Garrison Regiment, leading to Tupper being mortally wounded in the ensuing duel. During its life of over a century the most famous actor to tread its boards was Edmund Kean. Early in the 20th. century it was demolished to make room for an extension to the Royal Court. By then St. Peter-Port had another theatre. St. Julian's Avenue had been opened in 1870 and the hall destined to become *St. Julian's Theatre* was erected in this new thoroughfare. This continued in use as a theatre (stage plays in the last decade of its life being interspersed with film performances) until 1931 when the entire building was re-equipped and converted into the *Gaumont Palace* cinema.

The inter-war period was the great era of the cinema, in Guernsey as elsewhere. The island's original 'Picture Palaces' — established before the First World War as the *Electric* at Rectory House, Market Square (now the Co-Operative Stores) and as the *Empire* at Mont Crevelt (now the All Island Carpet Company) — had by then closed their doors, but one after another three cinemas replaced them, to be joined by a fourth shortly before World War Two. Of these, the *Gaumont Palace* (which — initially as the *Oddfellows' Hall* and subsequently as *Saint Julian's Theatre* — had provided varied thespian and musical fare since 1876, with the supplementary attractions first of occasional displays of 'animated pictures' as from 1896 and later of cinematographic presentations starting in 1914) acquired its final name — as already mentioned — when opened after refurbishment in 1931; the *Lyric* (a converted Nonconformist Chapel) screened films from 1923 onwards; and the *North Cinema* (another converted Chapel) from 1929. To this trio was added in 1937 the *Regal* (in 1948 re-named the *Odeon*), a luxurious purpose-built cinema, notable for its Compton Organ and unique in boasting a car park. This proliferation of cinemas left the rather unprepossessing *Palace* theatre at the foot of la Rue des Frères (the erstwhile *Hippodrome* and affectionately known as 'Billy Bartlett's' as from 1911, when it was taken over by that worthy) as the last bastion of the legitimate stage, with a repertory company in constant session during the 1930s.

The provision of the *Palace* theatre was supplemented from time to time by very fine amateur dramatic performances which were staged by the Guernsey Amateur Dramatic and Operatic Company at either *St. George's Hall* or the *Central Hall* — whose post-war career as the *Little Theatre* was thereby foreshadowed. Unfortunately, this career was abruptly terminated in March 1984 by a disastrous fire which gutted the entire building. In a wider context, Guernsey made a significant contribution to the theatre in the inter-war years in providing the stage with the fine actor Barry Jones, while the post-war period has seen another Guernseyman achieving theatrical fame in the person of Roy Dotrice. Furthermore, Olivia de Havilland who before and after the Second World War achieved fame in Hollywood films, was born of island stock, her father Walter, the son of the Reverend Charles de Havilland, Vicar of Saint Matthew's Cobo, having been educated at Elizabeth College. Frequently visiting Guernsey after the Second World War, in 1966 this renowned actress played the rôle of her great-great-grandmother while leading la Chevauchée around the island during the celebrations of the ninth centenary of the conquest of England. The dress which she then wore is now in the possession of the National Trust of Guernsey.

Sad to say, the *Palace*, a war casualty, had finally disappeared by 1951 and the post-war period saw the island's cinemas suffer a comparable fate in the face of declining attendances, the last survivor (the *Gaumont Palace*) closing to make way for the Bank of Bermuda in 1985. Films continued to be shown, however, at the *Beau Séjour Leisure Centre* and at the *Mallard Hotel* in the Forest — while in the case of the stage a pleasing development has been the presentation of Shakespearean productions at Castle Cornet.

In 1908 the Channel Islands Eisteddfodau were instituted in Jersey by Dean Samuel Falle, thanks to whose drive and enthusiasm a venture which started as a few simple competitions developed into a festival of music and arts where prominent adjudicators were engaged in each subject, and which ran for well over a fortnight each autumn. Falle's initiative evoked no response beyond his native shores until after the First World War, when on November 21st., 1921, the Eisteddfod Society was founded by the Reverend Frederick Paine (the Methodist Minister at Ebenezer Chapel) and Mrs. Edith Noel with the object of promoting a comparable bardic occasion in Guernsey — and its efforts came to fruition a year later when at an inaugural session on October 31st., 1922, the Guernsey Eisteddfod was formally declared open by His Excellency the Lieutenant-Governor, Major-General Sir John Edward Capper, K.C.B., K.C.V.O. This project rapidly achieved a success commensurate with that of its predecessor in the sister isle and as Guernsey's Eisteddfod was arranged so as to avoid coinciding with Jersey's, inter-insular competition developed and became a powerful stimulus to a high standard of achievement.

Another valuable cultural contribution was made by the Guille-Allès Choral and Orchestral Association which, by its regular performances at *St. George's Hall* of great oratorios and secular musical compositions, did much to sustain an interest in, and a love for, the best in music for a period of more than 30 years until the Association died out in the years preceding the Second World War.

Performance by string orchestras (notably that under the baton of Domenico Santangelo) and military bands (the Garrison Regiment and the Militia) also attracted widespread support during the '30s, and this led to the conversion of the bandstand in

Candie Gardens into the concert auditorium which, unfortunately, came to be regarded as failing to meet safety requirements, so that it was closed in 1969. To safeguard future provision in this field the States, after toying with the idea of converting the deconsecrated church of Saint James the Less into a Police Station, came in November 1983 to an accommodation with the 'Friends of Saint James Association' which resulted in renovation work being put in hand in July 1984 and the building being opened as a Concert Hall and Cultural Centre by H.R.H. the Duke of Kent on July 5th., 1985. It was initially envisaged that while the States would maintain the structure's fabric and exterior decoration, the 'Friends' would rent the building and bear all administrative and running costs — but the resources at their command proved insufficient to meet this obligation in toto, necessitating an annual subsidy from the States to enable Saint James to remain open. At the same time, testimony to the Bailiwick's musical traditions being alive and well was provided in the career of David Le Page who, subsequent to winning the Yehudi Menuhin International Violin Competition in 1985 and acquiring further experience with various chamber orchestras, obtained teaching posts both at Warwick University and at the Gloucester Music Centre, combining these commitments with European tours as a member of the Kreutzer Quartet. Yet further evidence of the survival of these traditions may be seen in the pianist Martyn Dorey, who in the autumn of 1994 was invited by the Speaker of the House of Commons to entertain her guests at a banquet in the Speaker's House.

In December 1976 the Bailiff of Guernsey, Sir John Loveridge, opened the *Beau Séjour Leisure Centre* which embodies a theatre cum cinema and concert hall, a swimming pool, a restaurant, bar, and provision for dancing, and a wide variety of games and sporting activities. Besides entailing the loss of an attractive Georgian house and a secluded woodland pleasance, the implementation of this project (the opponents of which feared would prove to be nothing but a ruinously expensive and grotesque white elephant) involved a heavy financial burden in construction costs, which considerably exceeded the original estimate of £2,000,000. When the States in 1972 voted in favour of developing this complex, the decision was made to devote the bulk of the proceeds of the States' Lottery (which had been instituted the previous year) towards financing the scheme. At the time of its opening £500,000 was transferred from the funds of what had become the Channel Islands' Lottery (the Guernsey and Jersey Lotteries having been combined in 1973) to the aid of the new centre so as to give it initial working capital. Besides catering for tourists, the leisure centre also aims at attracting the conference trade. It was here that was convened the extraordinary meeting of the Court of Chief Pleas on the occasion of the visit to the Bailiwick of Queen Elizabeth II in 1978.

The sacrifice of Beau Séjour House (given an 'A' rating — signifying 'a building of the highest merit to be preserved at all costs' — by Sir Charles Brett in his 1974 survey of Saint Peter-Port) so as to facilitate the establishment of this Leisure Centre, highlights the threat to the community's environmental heritage which, in Guernsey as elsewhere, is unfortunately a frequent bedfellow of 'progress'. Some years earlier an acute awareness of such dangers on the part of a group of public-spirited islanders had led to the foundation on December 7th., 1960, of the National Trust of Guernsey, the objects of which were specified as being to arouse and stir public opinion in an endeavour to preserve the remaining natural beauty of the island; to prevent the further desecration of houses and properties of historic and architectural merit; and to create machinery to acquire and hold in perpetuity on behalf of the island all manner of real property which, in the opinion of the Trust Council, should be preserved in its natural condition and/or state. The Trust's first property — Le Vaux de Monel at Pleinmont — was donated to it the following June by Miss M.G. Bonamy Collings, a founder member, and thereafter acquisitions steadily multiplied, with September 28th., 1987, seeing the triumphal culmination of four years of effort when Sir Charles Frossard, Bailiff of Guernsey, declared open the fine seventeenth century property of Number 26, Cornet Street (familiar to the present writer in his youth as the home of part of his family — and designated by Mr. John McCormack, author of *The Guernsey House* as the earliest complete building of any age within the putative walls of Saint Peter-Port) which the Trust, as an act of faith, had refurbished after purchasing it in a derelict state in November 1983 with a view to using it as its Headquarters.

Among its other activities, the National Trust also donated £10,000 to the previously-mentioned Friends of Saint James Association after its foundation on November 28th., 1981, and thenceforth gave that body unswerving support in its efforts to preserve a fine example of Neo-Classical architecture as a Cultural Centre, not only for Concerts, but as a home for the Arts generally. Specifically to foster and encourage the Arts within the Bailiwick yet another organisation — the Arts Council of the Bailiwick of Guernsey — was founded in May 1981 at the instigation of Messrs. Malcolm Reynard, H. C. Timewell and Reuben Dorey, as well as Mrs. Joan Ozanne, with Mr. Hardwick Nichols (who in April 1987 became its first Honorary President) as Chairman. The initial Patrons included His Excellency the Lieutenant-Governor, Miss Olivia de Havilland, Roy Dotrice and Sir High Casson. Financed by an annual block grant from the States, supplemented by subscriptions from its two hundred members plus donations from well-wishers together with occasional sponsorship of individual events, the Council not only presents exhibitions and musical recitals but also produces a bi-monthly *Diary of Events* and a Bulletin entitled *Artefact*, each of which is made available free of charge to the general public. The Arts Council has a close compeer in the Guernsey Community Arts Association which concentrates on efforts to establish — and subsequently, it hopes, to administer — a Bailiwick Arts Centre.

The Bailiwick has provided inspiration for Joseph Mallord William Turner, R.A. (1771–1851), who immortalised La Coupée in Sark, and also for the great impressionist Auguste Renoir (1841–1919), who visited Guernsey in 1883 and whose pictures painted locally, including 'La Baie de Moulin Huet' and 'Femme Assise au Bord de la Mer', were a few years ago reproduced in a postage-stamp issue. Another worthy of note is Thomas Whitcombe (1752–1824) with his paintings of Castle Cornet beset by stormy seas. In addition, however, it has not been lacking in artists of its own.

The first of these in chronological order of birth is Joshua Gosselin (1739–1813), who distinguished himself as botanist and antiquarian as well as acquiring fame for his superb water colours, over 200 of which are still in existence. Especially noteworthy are his study of St. Peter-Port as seen from Castle Cornet (1793) and that of Castle Cornet and the adjacent islands, which he painted from his home in Glategny Esplanade in 1775. As a botanist, Gosselin made a splendid collection of over 600 Guernsey wild plants. Many of these he pressed, thanks to which they remain to this day almost as fresh as when gathered. Lastly, it was the plans and records of the island's dolmens made by Gosselin early in the 19th. century which initially stimulated Lukis's study of Guernsey's archaeology.

Peter Le Liévre (1812–1871) was born in Guernsey and became

a wine merchant by profession, and a geologist by inclination — but his fame stems above all from his drawings which, although the work of an amateur, are worthy to take him into the first rank. He loved to draw maritime scenes with a wealth of detail, and his drawings generally are of outstanding artistry and rich in variety, agreeably portraying the spirit of his times.

Paul Naftel (1817–1891) came of a Quaker clock-making family of St. Saviour's, whose 'Grandfathers' inscribed 'Thomas André Naftel à Guernesey' are much esteemed, being as reliable now as when new. Paul, however, took no interest in the family business, and, taking the post of drawing master at Elizabeth College, distinguished himself by his drawings of the Bailiwick — among which that of the quay at St. Peter-Port is his masterpiece. Also much prized are his pictures of the Lake District and other parts of northern England.

An acquaintance of Naftel, Arnold Helcke, who was by profession a chemist engaged in the manufacture of gunpowder, came to the Bailiwick as a small child in the mid-1840s and remained until he left for England in the mid-1870s. Although an amateur, his paintings are nevertheless remarkable for the way in which they capture so perfectly many of the views around Guernsey.

William Toplis (1857–1942) became a Serquiais by adoption, remaining in the island with which he fell in love until his death there during the German Occupation. He set up a studio at Maison Rouge and was often to be seen about the cliffs and bays painting the scenes which captivated him. In collaboration with John Oxenham, he brought out a sumptuous *Book of Sark* which, embellished by his most celebrated paintings, now fetches a very high price when one of the rare copies is available.

Also deserving of mention are the gifted artist Peter Monamy (1681–1749), whose ancestor's inscription — 'Le Paix de Dieu soit ceans, fait le 18 Octobre 1578 de part André Monamy' — adorns the T.S.B. premises in High Street; Mathais Finucane, famed for his droll picture of the 1811 Market Place crowded with caricatures of island notables; George Reynolds, who recorded in oils the ceremony of laying the Foundation Stone of the Town Harbour in 1853; Ethel Sophia Cheesewright (1874–1977) whose many paintings of Sark included that of La Grande Grève which for many years adorned the mailboat *Isle of Sark*; and Edouard Le Poidevin (1880–1972) whose landscapes of Guernsey and Sark are remarkable for the meticulous accuracy with which the rocks and plants are therein reproduced in the bright colours of the island's shorelines. To these one may add Sarah Louise Kilpack (1839–1909) with her oil paintings of coastal scenes featuring notably Le Château de Rocquaine and the Vale Castle; Sheila Elizabeth Noble, whose paintings include impressive studies of Bordeaux Harbour and of Petit Port; Pamela Dorey with her emphasis on the portrayal of light and whose works have been sold as far afield as Japan; and especially William John Caparne (1856–1940) who in his tram-car studio at Bon Port painted not only sundry beautiful island scenes but also several floral studies, mainly featuring irises, in the cultivation of which he was an expert. Finally, by contrast one thinks of the achievement on a more mundane plane of the Guernseyman Herbert Tourtel (1874–1931) who, together with his wife Mary (1874–1948) in credited with the creation in 1920 of the popular children's cartoon character Rupert the Bear.

The praises of the Bailiwick have been sung in verse by Michael Drayton (1563–1631) and by Algernon Charles Swinburne (1837–1909). In addition, first Herm and then Jethou provided both home and inspiration for Sir Edward Montague Compton Mackenzie, O.B.E. (1883–1974) whose *Fairy Gold* has a local setting (with Herm and Jethou discreetly disguised as Roon and Carrackoon — off-shore islands 'across the Sound from Penzawn in Lyonnesse': and with Sir Percival Perry — the author's successor as Herm's tenant — deftly caricatured as Sir Caleb Fuller); Sark became the residence of John Oxenham — born William Arthur Dunkerley (1861–1941) — who made it the locale of several novels, the foremost of which is perhaps *Carette of Sark*; while Alderney was 'adopted' by Terence Hanbury White (1906–1964) of *Once and Future King* fame.

As for Guernsey, besides its great Victorian poet-cum-lexicographer of the Patois idiom — George Métivier (1790–1881) — and his bardic disciple Denys Corbet (1826–1910); the island may more recently boast a native-born littérateur of top-rate calibre in Gerald Basil Edwards (1899–1976) whose novel, *The Book of Ebenezer Le Page* (written throughout in 'Guernsey English' and published posthumously in 1981) is acclaimed by the eminent author, John Fowles, as 'a portrait and memorial that must surely become a classic of the island'. Worthy too of note is Victor Hubert Coysh (1906–1994) — the author of the original Foreword to this history — who, with a far more extensive knowledge of the entire Bailiwick than that of any of his contemporaries, widened his fellow-islanders' horizons through a stream of informative newspaper articles during his career as a journalist as well as enlightening them by his many books, foremost among which are *Alderney*, *Channel Islets* and *A Visitor's Guide to Guernsey, Alderney and Sark* — culminating in a quartet of historically evocative illustrated surveys produced jointly with his friend Carel Toms. Furthermore, Guernsey also had the distinction of providing a sanctuary for the greatest literary lion ever to reside in the archipelago in the person of Victor Marie Hugo (1802–1885) who from 1855 to 1870, as a political exile from the Second Empire, lived in Hauteville House (donated in 1927 to the city of Paris) which, as a skilful and practical craftsman in all forms of woodwork and with a passion for bric à brac, he transformed into a veritable museum of treasures. His mistress, Juliette Drouet, lived a few doors down the road, and guests at select dinner parties were presented to 'Madame la mère de mes enfants' and 'Madame mon amie'.

Asylum was granted by Guernsey to Hugo despite the hostile attitude of Palmerston, who, after becoming prime minister in February 1855, so objected to refugees of his ilk engaging in political activity (such as the publication of the Republican newspaper *L'Homme* in Jersey) as to press for their extradition to the United Kingdom. He wrote in this connection to Sir George Grey (the Home Secretary) on October 12th. of the same year that 'we are not doing justice to our faithful and zealous Ally the Emperor of the French, by allowing a knot of his mortal Enemies to be plotting within an hour's sail or row of his shores'.

In the study at the top of his house of refuge, through a window of which he could see his beloved France, Hugo stood at a plain shelf of black walnut, writing *Les Misérables, L'Homme Qui Rit* and *Les Travailleurs de la Mer* (set in Guernsey) the dedication of which, inscribed on his statue in Candie Gardens, will serve as a fitting conclusion to this book:

Au rocher d'hospitalité et de liberté, à ce coin de vielle terre normande où vit
le noble petit peuple de la mer, à l'Ile de Guernesey, sévère et douce.

FINIS

APPENDIX I

Lords of the Isles, Wardens, and Sub-Wardens

(Richard Coeur de Lion — Henry VII)

KEY

BLOCK CAPITALS	=	LORDS OF THE ISLES
Italics	=	Wardens, 'Governors', etc.
No embellishment	=	Sub-Wardens, 'Lieutenants', etc.
* after an entry	=	See note at the end of the list.
(S/H)	=	'Captain of Guernsey', but subordinate to Sir Richard Harliston as 'Captain-in-Chief' of the whole archipelago

1198–1199	JOHN, COUNT OF MORTAIN (later King John)
1200–1204	PIERRE DE PREAUX
1203–1206	Gregory Balizan
1206–1207	*Geoffrey de Lucy*
1207–1220	*Philippe d'Aubigny* (uncle)
1220–1223	*Philippe d'Aubigny* (nephew)
1223–1226	*Geoffrey de Lucy*
1226–1227	*Richard, Baron Grey of Codnor*
1227–1229	*Guillaume de St. Jean*
1229–1230	*Richard, Baron Grey of Codnor*
	John de Grey (brother) (joint)
1230–1232	*Henry de Trubleville*
1232–1234	*Philip de Carteret*
	Amaury de St. Amand (joint)
1232–1234	Guillaume de St. Jean
	Philippe d'Aubigny (nephew) (joint)
1234–1240	HENRY DE TRUBLEVILLE
1234–1235	Nicholas de Meules
1235	Gerard de Lampersand
	Guillaume de Dampierre
	William Blom (joint)
1235–1240	Drew de Barentin

1240–1241	*William de Boeles*
1241–1252	*Drew de Barentin*
1252–1254	*Richard, Baron Grey of Codnor*
1254–1272	THE PRINCE EDWARD (later Edward I)
1258–1260	*Drew de Barentin* (during Edward's disgrace after siding with de Montfort)
1262–1267	Sir Gilbert Talbot
	Thomas Boulton (joint)
1267–1269	William de Barentin
1269–1270	Hugh de Trubleville
1270–1274	*Richard, King of the Romans* (Edward on Crusade: succeeded to throne 1272 while away)
1271–1274	Arnaud Jean, de Contivo
1274	Jean Wyger
1275–1277	*Sir Otto de Grandison*
1275–1276	Raoul de Broughton
1276–1278	Philippe Burnel
1277–1294	SIR OTTO DE GRANDISON
1278–1281	Guillaume de St. Remi
	Denis de Tilbury (joint)
1282–1288	Renaut d'Ashwell
1284–1290	Sir Stephen Wallard
1290–1293	Guillaume de St. Remi
1294	Sir William de Grandison
	Henri de Bonvillars (Prior of Wenlock) (joint)
1294–1297	*Henry de Cobham*
1294	*Sir Nicholas de Cheney* (during Cobham's illness)
1297–1298	*Sir Nicholas de Cheney*
1298–1328	SIR OTTO DE GRANDISON
1298	Henri de Bonvillars (Prior of Wenlock)
1299–1302	Denis de Tilbury
	Guillaume de Cosignton (joint)
1302–1307	John de Newent
1304	Pierre Le Marchant (also bailiff)
1306–1309	John de Ditton
1309	Massey de la Court (also bailiff)
1309–1319	Drew de Barentin
	Sir Pierre de Petitfeu (joint)
	(In 1318 Prince Edward — later Edward III — was appointed Lord of the Isles in the belief that Otto de Grandison had died. The mistake was quickly realised and the appointment nullified.)

1319–1321	Pierre de Balmes
1321–1324	Sir Gerard d'Oron
1324–1326	Jean de Clyvedon
1326–1327	Raoul Basset de Drayton
	Jean de Roches (joint)
1327–1328	Jean de Roches
	Robert de Norton (joint)
1328–1330	*Jean de Roches*
1330–1331	*Pierre Bernard de Pynesole*
	Laurens de Gaillard (joint)
1331	*Sir William de Cheney* (month of August only)
1331–1333	*Thomas, Baron Wake of Liddell*
1333	*Henry, Lord de Ferrars of Groby*
1334–1337	*Henry, Lord de Ferrars of Groby*
	William, Baron Montacute (joint)
1334–1336	Walter de Weston
1337–1340	*Sir Thomas de Ferrars*
1338	Walter de Weston
1340	Walter de Weston (after driving out French)
1341–1343	*Thomas de Hampton*
1343	*Sir William de Cheney*
1343–1347	*Sir Thomas de Ferrars*
1343–1347	Walter de Weston
1347–1348	Sir Ralph de Harmesthorpe
1348–1349	*Robert Wyville*
	Thomas de Clifford (joint)
1349–1354	*John, Baron Mautravers*
1353	Ralph de Horsey
1354–1356	*William Strury*
1356–1357	*Sir Thomas de Holland*
1356	Sir Otto de Holland
1357–1358	*Sir Otto de Holland*
1357	Thomas de Langhurst
1358–1366	*Sir Edmund de Cheney*
1363	William de Birketon
1364	John Le Marchant (also bailiff)
1365	Nicholas de Cheney
1367–1372	*Walter Hewet*
1368–1371	William de Asthorp
1371	John Coke
1372–1374	*Sir Edmund Rose*
1372–1373	Sir Ralph de Harmesthorpe

1374	*William de Asthorp*
1374	John Coke
1374–1376	*Thomas de Beauchamp, Earl of Warwick*
1376–1393	*Sir Hugh de Calverley*
1378	Jacques de Calverley
1378–1382	Henry Ryther
1384–1385	Roger Walden
1393	Jacques de Golafre
1393–1396	*Sir John de Golafre of Langley*
1396–1405	*Edward, Earl of Rutland* (became Duke of York, 1401)
1405	*Sir John de Lisle*
1405	John Peraunt
1406–1415	*Edward, Duke of York* (killed at Agincourt)
1409–1412	Richard, Earl of Cambridge
1415–1435	JOHN, DUKE OF BEDFORD (Regent of France)
1416	Henry Mulso
1436–1442	*Sir John Bernard*
1437–1447	HUMPHREY, DUKE OF GLOUCESTER
1444	Sir John Bernard
	(In 1445 Henry Beauchamp, Duke of Warwick, was granted the Lordship of the Isles in reversion, but he died before Gloucester.)
1447–1449	LADY ANNE DE BEAUCHAMP*
1447	*John, Viscount Beaumont*
	Ralph Botiller, Lord Sudeley (joint) (Anne a minor)
1448	*William de la Pole, Duke of Suffolk*
1448	William Bertram
1449–1459	RICHARD NEVILLE, EARL OF WARWICK*
1453–1455	John Nanfan
1456	Colin Otis
1457	John Nanfan
1460–1461	*John Nanfan* (Neville in eclipse after defeat at Ludford and flight to Calais.)
1460	Druet Le Marchant
1461–1471	RICHARD NEVILLE, EARL OF WARWICK*
1466	Thomas de la Court (also bailiff)
1468	Geoffrey Wallish
1471–1487	LADY ANNE BEAUCHAMP, COUNTESS OF WARWICK* (Assumed title after Neville's death at Barnet; last to hold it.)

1473–1486	*Sir Richard Harliston ('Captain-in-Chief of the Islands of Jersey, Guernsey, Sark and Alderney')*
1476	Edward de Courtney
1476–1477	James Norris
1477	William de Courtney
1478–1484	Sir John Dichefield (S/H)
1482–1484	Sir Edward Brampton (S/H)
1484	Thomas Rydley (S/H)
1485	Edmund Weston (S/H)
	Thomas de St. Martin's (S/H) (joint)
1485	David Philip (S/H)
	Mathew Baker (S/H) (joint)

*Because he pre-deceased the Duke of Gloucester, Henry de Beauchamp, Duke of Warwick, never assumed the Lordship of the Isles granted to him in reversion in 1445. In these circumstances Lady Anne de Beauchamp, the infant daughter of the Duke of Warwick, inherited the title of Lady of the Isles on the death of Humphrey, Duke of Gloucester, in 1447. Keepers were appointed to look after the islands as she was a minor. She died in 1449, and her aunt, Lady Anne de Beauchamp, sister of the infant Lady Anne's father, inherited the title of Lady of the Isles. Lady Anne was married to Richard Neville, Earl of Warwick (the King Maker), who now took the title of Lord of the Isles in the right of his wife. Richard Neville was in eclipse between 1459 and 1461, after his defeat at Ludford and flight to Calais. He resumed the Lordship of the Isles after the Yorkist victory at Towton in 1461 and (despite his later adhesion to the Lancastrian cause) retained the office until his death at the Battle of Barnet in 1471. His widow now assumed the title in her own right until she relinquished it in 1487.

APPENDIX II

GOVERNORS and Lieutenant-Governors of GUERNSEY

(Henry VII — Victoria)

KEY

BLOCK CAPITALS	=	GOVERNORS
Roman type	=	Lieutenant-Governors
(K)	=	Royalist appointment
(P)	=	Parliamentary appointment

1486–1509	EDMUND WESTON
1488–1490	John Apris

1503	David Philip
1509–1522	SIR RICHARD WESTON
1509–1522	Oliver Oglander
1522–1533	Thomas Oglander
1533–1541	SIR FRANCIS WESTON
1541–1545	SIR RICHARD LONG
1545–1553	SIR PETER MEWTIS
1551–1570	Thomas Compton (also bailiff, 1562–1570)
1553–1561	SIR LEONARD CHAMBERLAIN
1561–1570	SIR FRANCIS CHAMBERLAIN
1570–1609	SIR THOMAS LEIGHTON
1580	Thomas Wigmore (also bailiff, 1581, deposed 1588)
1591	George Paulet
1600	Lord Zouche
1605–1608	Peter Carey
1610–1621	GEORGE, LORD CAREW OF CLOPTON, EARL OF TOTNES
1610–1629	Sir Amias de Carteret
1620	Thomas Andros
1621–1644	HENRY, LORD DANVERS, EARL OF DANBY
1621–1644	Sir Peter Osborne
1625	Captain Nathaniel Darrell (deputy to Osborne)
1643–1649	ROBERT, EARL OF WARWICK (P)
1643–1649	Colonel Robert Russel (P)
1644–1649	SIR PETER OSBORNE (K)
1644–1646	Captain Nathaniel Darrell (K)
1646–1649	Sir Baldwin Wake (K)
1647–1651	Major James Harrison (P)
1649–1651	HENRY, LORD PERCY (K)
1649–1651	Colonel Sir Roger Burgess (K)
1649–1650	COLONEL ALBAN COXE (P)
1650	Colonel Henry Sharp (P)
1651–1660	COLONEL JOHN BINGHAM (P)
1653	John Clark (P)
1654–1658	Captain Charles Waterhouse (P)
1659	Colonel John Weaver (P)
1660	MAJOR HENRY WANSEYE (P)
1660	Captain Sharp (P)
	(Restoration of the Monarchy — May 1660)
1660–1662	SIR HUGH POLLARD
1661–1664	Captain Nathaniel Darrell (son of previous Captain Darrell)

1662–1665	CHRISTOPHER, FIRST BARON HATTON OF KIRBY
1664–1680	Captain William Sheldon
1665–1670	COLONEL SIR JONATHAN ATKINS
1670–1706	CHRISTOPHER, FIRST VISCOUNT HATTON OF GRETTON
1681	Captain George Lyttleton
1684	Captain The Honourable Charles Hatton
1685	Charles Macarty
1687	Colonel John Legge
1688	Captain Godolphin
1689–1703	Lieutenant Bernard Ellis
1697	Captain Henry Mordaunt
1704–1706	Sir Edmund Andros (also bailiff)
1706–1711	GENERAL CHARLES CHURCHILL
1707	Oliver Hetherington
1711–1726	Giles Spicer
1715–1732	LIEUTENANT-GENERAL DANIEL LORD HARVEY
1726–1735	Louis Dollon
1732	THE RIGHT HONOURABLE GEORGE, EARL OF CHOLMONDLEY
1735–1737	MAJOR-GENERAL RICHARD SUTTON
1735–1745	John Graham
1737–1739	FIELD MARSHAL FRANCIS, MARQUIS DE MONTANDRE
1742	ALGERNON, LORD PERCY, EARL OF NORTHUMBER-LAND AND DUKE OF SOMERSET
1745–1756	Charles Strahan
1750–1752	FIELD MARSHAL SIR JOHN LIGONIER, K.B.
1752–1766	GENERAL JOHN, EARL DE LA WARR
1756–1776	Captain Sir John Mylne
1766	SIR RICHARD LYTTLETON
1770–1794	FIELD MARSHAL SIR JEFFERY AMHERST, K.B., (later Lord Amherst)
1770–1783	Lieutenant-Colonel Paulus Aemilius Irving
1784–1793	Lieutenant-Colonel William Brown
1793	Major-General Thomas Dundas (later knighted)
1793	Colonel James Henry Craig
1793–1796	Major-General John Small
1796–1802	Lieutenant-General Sir Hew Dalrymple

1797	GENERAL CHARLES, EARL GREY OF HOWICK, K.B.
1803–1816	Lieutenant-General Sir John Doyle, Baronet, G.C.B., K.C.
1807–1827	LIEUTENANT-GENERAL GEORGE, EARL OF PEMBROKE
1816–1821	Major-General Henry Bailey
1821–1828	Major-General Sir John Colborne, K.C.B.
1827–1834	SIR WILLIAM KEPPEL, G.C.B. (last Appointment)
1828–1837	Major-General John Dawes Ross

(In 1835 the office of governor was abolished, so that Major-General Ross, for the rest of his term of office, became the first lieutenant-governor to be the direct representative of the Crown. Thereafter only lieutenant-governors were appointed.)

APPENDIX III

Lieutenant-Governors of Guernsey

(Victoria — Elizabeth II)

1837	General Sir James Douglas, K.C.B.
1842	Major-General Sir William Francis Patrick Napier, K.C.B.
1848	Lieutenant-General Sir John Bell, K.C.B.
1854	Lieutenant-General William Thomas Knollys
1856	Lieutenant-General George Judd Harding, C.B.
1859	Lieutenant-General Sir Marcus John Slade
1864	Lieutenant-General Charles Rochfort Scott
1869	Lieutenant-General Edward Frome
1874	Lieutenant-General The Honourable St. George Gerald Foley, C.B.
1879	Lieutenant-General Alexander Abercrombie Nelson, C.B.
1883	Lieutenant-General Henry Andrew Sarel, C.B.
1885	Lieutenant-General John Henry Ford Elkington, C.B.
1889	Lieutenant-General Sir Edward Bulwer, K.C.B.
1894	General Nathaniel Stevenson
1899	Major-General Michael Henry Saward

1903 Major-General Barrington Bulk Douglas Campbell,
C.B., C.V.O.
1908 Major-General Robert Auld, C.B.
1911 Major-General Sir Edward Owen Fisher Hamilton, K.C.B.
1914 Major-General Henry Merrick Lawson, C.B.
1914 General Sir Reginald Clare Hart, V.C., K.C.B., K.C.V.O.
1918 Lieutenant-General Sir Lancelot Edward Kiggell,
K.C.B., K.C.M.G.
1920 Major-General Sir John Edward Capper, K.C.B., K.C.V.O.
1925 Major-General Charles, The Lord Sackville,
K.B.E., C.B., C.M.G.
1929 Major-General Walter Patrick, The Lord Ruthven,
C.B., D.S.O.
1934 Major-General Sir Edward Broadbent,
K.C.B., C.B., C.M.G., D.S.O.
1939 Major-General Alexander Telfer-Smollott,
C.B., D.S.O., M.C.
1940 Major-General John Minshull-Ford, C.B., D.S.O., M.C.
1940 Victor Gosselin Carey, Esq. (later knighted)
1945 Lieutenant-General Sir Philip Neame,
V.C., K.B.E., C.B., D.S.O.
1953 Air Marshal Sir Thomas Elmhirst, K.B.E., C.B., A.F.C.
1958 Vice Admiral Sir Geoffrey Robson,
K.B.E., C.B., D.S.O., D.S.C.
1963 Lieutenant-General Sir Charles Coleman,
K.C.B., C.M.G., D.S.O.
1969 Vice Admiral Sir Charles Mills, K.C.B., C.B.E., D.S.C.
1974 Vice Admiral Sir John Martin, K.C.B., D.S.C., M.N.I.
1979 Air Chief Marshal Sir Peter de Lacey Le Cheminant,
G.B.E., K.C.B., D.F.C.

(Sir Peter is a Guernseyman. Although the office of lieutenant-governor had been held by Guernseymen previously, they have usually been bailiffs as well, so that Sir Peter has the distinction of being the first Guernseyman, other than a bailiff, to be the lieutenant-governor since Thomas Andros held the office in 1620.)

1985 Lieutenant-General Sir Alexander Crawford Simpson
Boswell, K.C.B., C.B.E.
1990 Lieutenant-General Sir Michael Wilkins, K.C.B., O.B.E.
1994 Vice Admiral Sir John Coward, K.C.B., D.S.O.
2000 Lieutenant-General Sir John Foley,
K.C.B., O.B.E., M.C.

APPENDIX IV

Bailiffs of Guernsey

KEY

(W) = Also Warden of the Isles
(L/G) = Also Sub-Warden, Lieutenant-Governor, or similar

1270	Hugh de Trubleville (L/G 1269/70)
1278	Guillaume de St. Remi (L/G 1278/81)
1282	Renaut de Ashwell (L/G)
1288/9	Guillaume de St. Remi
1292	Guillaume de St. Remi — slain in 1294 French raid
1297	Sir Nicholas de Cheney (W 1297)
1298	Pierre Le Marchant
1299	Radulphus De Gand
1300	Robert Comberwell
1301	Radulph de Haverland
1302	John de Newent (L/G 1302/7)
1303	Radulphus Gaultier
1304	Pierre Le Marchant (L/G 1304)
1305	Massey de la Court (L/G 1309)
1310	James de Vinchelez
1311	Robert Le Gay
1313	Gaultier de la Hogue
1315	Massey de la Court
1317	Pierre Le Marchant
1318	Massey de la Court
1319	Robert Le Gay
1320	Radulphus Gaultier
1321	John Le Marchant
1322	James de Vinchelez
1323	William Le Petit
1324	Guillaume de Souslemont
1325	William Le Petit
1325/6	Pierre de Garis
1327	Henry de St. Martin
1328	Radulphus Le Gay
1329	Radulphus Cokerel
1330	Geoffrey de la Hogue
1331	Thomas d'Esterfield
1331/2	Radulphus Le Gay

1340	Jean de la Lande
1347	Jean de la Lande (tenure uncertain: still bailiff 1353)
1357	John Le Marchant (L/G 1364)
1384	John Nicholas (or Nicolle)
1387	Gervais de Clermont
1412	James Coquerel
1433	Thomas de la Court
1446	John Henry
1447	Guillaume Cartier
1466	Thomas de la Court (L/G 1465/6)
1470	Pierre de Beauvoir
1480	Edmund de Cheney
1481	Nicholas Fouaschin
1483	John Blondel
1499	John Martin
1511	James Guille
1538	Thomas Compton
1545	John Haryvell
1549	Helier Gosselin (deposed 1562)
1562	Thomas Compton (L/G 1552/70)
1571	Guillaume de Beauvoir
1581	Thomas Wigmore (L/G 1580: deposed 1588)
1588	Louis de Vic
1601	Amice de Carteret (L/G 1610/20)
1631	Jean de Quetteville (suspended as a royalist by the States 1643)
1644	Pierre de Beauvoir (parliamentary appointment by Earl of Warwick)
1647	Pierre de Beauvoir suspended and reinstated by Colonel Russell
1651	Pierre de Beauvoir deposed by parliament
1652	Pierre de Beauvoir reappointed
1653	Pierre de Beauvoir removed by parliament, which ordered that office of bailiff should be held by each of the jurats for a month at a time.
1656	Pierre de Beauvoir reappointed (retired at Restoration, 1660)
1661	Amias Andros
1674	Sir Edmund Andros (L/G 1704/6)
1714	Jean de Sausmarez
1728	Josué Le Marchant
1752	Eleazar Le Marchant

1758 Samuel Bonamy
1771 William Le Marchant
1800 Robert Porrett Le Marchant
1810 Sir Peter de Havilland
1821 Daniel de Lisle Brock
1843 Jean Guille
1845 Sir Peter Stafford Carey
1883 John de Havilland Utermarck
1884 Sir Edgar MacCulloch
1895 Sir Thomas Godfray Carey
1902 Sir Henry A. Giffard
1908 Sir William Carey
1915 Sir Edward Chepmell Ozanne
1922 Sir Havilland Walter de Sausmarez, Baronet
1929 Arthur William Bell
1935 Sir Victor Gosselin Carey (L/G 1940/45)
1946 Sir Ambrose J. Sherwill
1959 Sir William H. Arnold
1973 Sir John Loveridge
1982 Sir Charles Frossard
1992 Sir Graham Dorey
1999 de Vic G. Carey, Esq.

APPENDIX V

Deans of Guernsey

1295 Nicholas Merienne
1354 Simon de St. Martin
(There is a gap in the records until 1469)
1469 Guillaume Le Feyvre
1497 Pierre Houssaye
1499 Jean Le Feyvre
1507 James Olivier
1509 George Elys
1546 Pierre Charles
1547 Jacques Amy
1563 John After
(During the Presbyterian period there were no deans)
1662 John de Sausmarez

1697 Nicholas Le Mesurier
1716 John Bonamy
1739 John le Mesurier
1759 John Hemming
1765 Elie Crespin
1796 Daniel Francis Durand
1832 Nicholas Carey
1862 William Guille
1869 Carey Brock
1892 Thomas Bell
1917 John B. V. Penfold
1922 Douglas Falkland Carey
1931 Agnew Walter Giles Giffard
1947 Edward Louis Frossard
1967 Frederick Walter Cogman
1978 John William Foster, B.E.M.
1989 Jeffrey Robert Fenwick
1995 Frederick Marc Trickey

APPENDIX VI

'Hereditary Governors' of Alderney

1660 Edward and James de Carteret and Clement Le Couteur granted Alderney by Charles II.
1660 Sir George Carteret had grant transferred to him by the above. (Captain Nicholas Ling as resident lieutenant-governor.)
1679 Lady de Carteret (widow of Sir George).
1682 Sir Edmund Andros acquired grant from Lady de Carteret. (Thomas Le Mesurier as resident lieutenant-governor.)
1713 George Andros.
1714 John Le Mesurier, on behalf of the daughters of George Andros, whose uncle he was by marriage.
1721 Anne Le Mesurier (née Andros) wife of John Le Mesurier.
1729 Henry Le Mesurier.
1744 John Le Mesurier (Peter Le Mesurier, lieutenant-governor, 1773–1793).
1793 Peter Le Mesurier.
1803 John Le Mesurier.

1825 Patent sold to the Crown by John Le Mesurier, whereupon the Governor of Guernsey took Alderney within his charge.

APPENDIX VII

Judges of Alderney

1612 Pierre Herivel
1637 Edouard Gauvain
1641 Pierre Le Cocq
1653 Richard Le Cocq
1683 Nicholas Le Cocq
1702 Nicole Duplain
1703 Thomas Le Cocq (suspended from office 1738, but retained appointment)
1760 Jean Simon
1769 Jean Gauvain
1803 Jean Ollivier
1807 Pierre Gauvain
1837 Jean Gaudion
1856 Thomas Clucas
1876 Thomas Nicholson Barbenson
1893 J. A. Le Cocq
1898 N. P. L. C. Barbenson
1913 Major R. W. Mellish
1938 Brigadier Frederick G. French
1947 Sir Frank Wiltshire
1949 Office of judge abolished.

APPENDIX VIII

Presidents of the States of Alderney

1949 Sydney Peck Herivel
1970 George William Baron
1976 Jon Kay-Mouat
1994 George William Baron
1996 Jon Kay-Mouat

APPENDIX IX

Seigneurs and Dames of Sark

1565 Helier de Carteret
1581 Philippe de Carteret
1594 Sir Philippe de Carteret
1643 Sir Philippe de Carteret, Baronet
1663 Sir Philippe de Carteret, Baronet
1693 Sir Charles de Carteret, Baronet
1715 Lord John Carteret
1720 Colonel John Johnson, who bought the fief from Lord John Carteret
1723 James Milner, who bought the fief on the death of Colonel Johnson
1730 Joseph Wilcock, Bishop of Gloucester (Executor of James Milner)
1730 Susanne Le Pelley, who bought the fief from the Bishop of Gloucester
1733 Nicholas Le Pelley
1742 Daniel Le Pelley
1752 Pierre Le Pelley
1778 Pierre Le Pelley
1820 Pierre Le Pelley
1839 Ernest Le Pelley
1849 Peter Carey Le Pelley
1852 Marie Collings, who bought the fief from Peter Carey le Pelley
1853 Reverend William Thomas Collings
1882 William Frederick Collings
1927 Sibyl Mary Hathaway (previously Beaumont: née Collings) (Robert Hathaway technically Seigneur from 1929 to 1954)
1974 John Michael Beaumont

APPENDIX X

Tenants of Herm

1717 Charles Nowall
1737 Peter Carey I
1766 Peter Carey II

1770 Caroline Carey
1774 Peter John and Thomas de Jersey
1779 John de Jersey
1800 Pierre Mauger
1815 Lieutenant-Colonel The Honourable John Lindsay
1826 *en saisi* by States of Guernsey
1830 Jonathan Duncan
1836 British Commercial Assurance Company
1842 Ebenezer Fernie
1854 Job Henry & Steven Touzeau-Martin (conjointly)
1860 Thomas Bartlett
1862 Thomas Hyde
1867 Lieutenant-Colonel M. J. Fielden
1877 James Considine
1878 Arthur Maxwell
1881 James Considine
1882 Carthusian Order
1884 James Stern Linklater and Company
1889 West Bank Leignitz of Silesia
1891 Prince Blücher von Wahlstatt
1917 Wheadon and Company
1920 Sir Edward Montague Compton Mackenzie, O.B.E.
1923 Sir Percival Lea Perry
1946 Mr. Alfred Graham Jefferies
1949 Major Alexander Gough ('Peter') Wood
1987 'Wood of Herm Island' (a company owned entirely by members of the Wood family and holding the island on a lease extended to 2049, with Adrian Heyworth Esq. — son-in-law of Major 'Peter' Wood — as Chairman and Island Manager)

APPENDIX XI

Tenants of Jethou

1717 Charles Nowall
1737 Charles Mauger
1758 Thomas Guille and Thomas Le Marchant (jointly)
1779 Henry de Jersey (père)
1781 Henry de Jersey (fils)

1800 Phillip de Quesnel
1821 Edward Falla, Peter Le Cocq, Nicholas Le Feuvre and Peter de Lisle
1822 Jean Allaire
1846 Marie Collings (née Allaire)
1852 Island taken over by the States of Guernsey for quarrying
1856 George Charles Gee
1863 Messrs. Giffard, Lindell and Perry (jointly)
1867 Lieutenant-Colonel Montague Fielden
1877 Island in the hands of caretakers on behalf of the Crown
1880 W. H. B. Moullin, Esq.
1885 Crown caretakers
1890 Sir Henry Austin Lee, K.C.M.G., C.B. (sub-let to Mr. F. J. Guy, 1899–1910)
1918 Crown caretakers
1920 Sir Edward Montague Compton Mackenzie, O.B.E.
1934 Harold Fortington
1944 Mrs. Fortington (widow of Harold)
(Mr. and Mrs. George MacDonald left in charge during the Second World War)
1948 Lieutenant-Colonel William Gill Withycombe
1955 Philip S. Watkins
1957 Herman Stockey
1958 Group Captain W. Hedley Cliff, D.S.O.
1964 Susan Faed
1971 Sir Charles Hayward, C.B.E.
1984 Anthony Duckworth Esq.
1991 Messrs. Peter Ogden and Philip Hulme
1995 States of Guernsey as 'Head Tenant', with Messrs. Peter Ogden and Philip Hulme (enjoying a guaranteed tenure until 2007) as Sub-Tenants.

APPENDIX XII

Menhirs

Guernsey

La Longue Rocque, Les Paysans, St. Pierre-du-Bois.

La Pierre de l'Essart, Le Crocq, St. Saviour's (with accompanying small menhir).

Le Perron du Roi, Le Bourg, Forest.
The 'Christianized' menhir, St. Saviour's church gateway.
Recumbent 'Christianized' menhir, L 'Ancresse Common.
La Pierre Sainte, La Moye, Vale.
Standing stone at Route St. Clair, St. Sampson's.
'Sous l'Eglise', St. Stephen's Lane, St. Peter-Port.
(possibly) Daniel de Lisle Brock memorial, St. Sampson's.
Christianized menhir outside Vale Church.

Jethou

Menhir at centre of Cannon Field.
Menhir to north of Fairy Wood.

Statue-Menhirs

'La Gran'mère du Chimquière', St. Martin's graveyard.
Female figure in Castel churchyard.
(possibly) Shouldered-form megalith 750 yards south of La Vaurocque crossroads, Sark.

APPENDIX XIII

Dolmens

Guernsey

Le Déhus dolmen (named after Teus or Theus, a nocturnal spectre said to haunt it) — Paradis, Vale.
La Rocque qui Sonne — Vale schoolyard.
La Varde dolmen — L'Ancresse Common.
L'Autel des Landes — L'Ancresse Common.
La Mare es Maures cysts — L'Ancresse Common.
The 'Cyst in the Circle' — Sandy Hook, L'Islet.
Sandy Lane cyst — L'Islet.
Le Creux es Fées — L'Erée.
Le Catioroc dolmen — Perelle.
Delancey dolmen (in a poor state) — Delancey Park.
Ruined dolmen outside Vale Church.

N.B. — In 1981 excavations at a site on L'Ancresse Common named Les Fouaillages, which had been commenced in 1979, revealed a tomb dated on pottery evidence *c.* 4500 B.C., and thought to be the oldest man-made structure in Europe.

Alderney

Les Pourciaux, Longy.

(Before the Second World War, two dolmens stood at this site, but they were obliterated by the Germans. One of them, however, came to light once more during building operations in 1968 — though reduced to a heap of small stones and a depression.)

Cyst near Fort Tourgis.

Sark

Cyst above Clouet Bay.
Cyst above Vermandaie Bay.

Herm

Dolmen at Oyster Point (largely buried by sand-drift).
Tomb at Robert's Cross.
Slab-lined cyst on the Common.
Cyst on Le Petit Monceau.
Le Grand Monceau — two passage-graves and a cyst (obscured by brambles).

Jethou

Slab-lined pit near Gibbet site (damaged by quarrymen during 1850s) is possibly a cyst with capstone missing.

APPENDIX XIV

Feudal Courts

N.B: This Appendix lists only those Feudal Courts whose meeting places are physically in evidence. Consequently it does not include courts such as (for example) Massy Gros (whose assembly point is the roadway opposite the entrance to Sausmarez Manor) or (to give another example) Le Franc Fief de St. Martin, which traditionally convenes on the site of Le Pont Archon, at the foot of Fountain Street, near the Town Church. Map references (both here and in Appendix XV) are to *Perry's Guide Maps of Guernsey*.

INDOOR COURTS

Court of Chief Pleas (H.M. The Queen's Feudal Court)
Royal Court House, Rue du Manoir, St. Peter-Port (17 F5)

Fief Le Comte
Building near St. George's Gateway, Les Deslisles, Castel (15 E3)

Fief de Sausmarez
Building adjoining main gates, Sausmarez Manor, Sausmarez Road, St. Martin's (31 El)

COURTS MEETING IN HOUSES

Fief Anneville et Fauville
Anneville Manor House, Ruette des Annevilles, St. Sampson's (9 F3)*

Fief de Blanchelande
La Barberie, Saints Bay Road, Saint Martin's (30 B3)†

Fief Groignet
Le Groignet Manor House, Rue à l'Eau, King's Mills, Castel (14 D5)‡

OPEN-AIR COURTS

Fief Beuval (or Des Espèces)
On greensward fronting Les Sages, Route des Sages, St. Pierre-du-Bois (26 Dl)

Fief de Janin Besnard
Forecourt of Le Colombier Farmhouse, Rue du Colombier, Torteval (27 E2)‡

Fief de la Court
Junction of Les Pelleys and Le Frie Plaidy, Castel (15 F5)

Fief de la Rue Frairie
Junction of Rue des Buttes and Les Hunquets, St. Andrew's (23 G5)

Fief Jean du Gaillard
Head of lane by south exit of churchyard, St. Saviour's church (22 A3)

Fief des Gohiers
Camp de l'Eglise, St. Saviour's (22 A2)

Fief des Longues
La Rue Fevresse, St. Saviour's (22 A5)

Fief de St. Michel
Low stone bench at foot of statue-menhir in graveyard, Castel Church (15 H4)

Fief Suart
Route de Lihou, facing down La Rue de Longfrie, St. Pierre-du-Bois (27 Fl)

Fief Robert de Vicq
Gable end of house, cul-de-sac off La Rue des Simons, Torteval (26 D3)

Explanations of Symbols

* There is also a fief seat in the house porch.

† The Seigneur de Blanchelande, under a Deed of Covenant of May 21st., 1649, enjoys the right — albeit not exercised of late — to hold his Court annually in this house which occupies the site of the ancient Priory of Martinvast and was given its present name in the last decade of the 17th. century by the then owner (Edouard Mauger) in memory of the pre-ransom period of slavery which he endured after his capture by Barbary pirates. The distinct texture of part of the building's wall reveals where the entrance to a special court chamber was once located.

‡ Each of these locations has a pigeonnier, while in addition the latter boasts a colombier dating back to 1330. It fell into decay but was restored in the years 1956 and 1957 thanks to the initiative of Advocate Walter Langlois, whose wife Elsie May was La Dame du Fief Janin Besnard. Only at Le Groignet, however, are doves to be seen.

APPENDIX XV

An Outline of the Evolution of the Guernsey Farmhouse

Stage 1 — The Early Middle Ages

The One-Storey 'Two-Part' Longhouse, consisting of two compartments of unequal length, open to the roof. The larger compartment, with a fireplace, provided a living and sleeping room, while the smaller (the byre) served as a shelter for the farmer's cattle.

Example: Le Petit Jardin, Le Variouf, Forest (Perry 29 E4).

Stage 1a — Late 14th. and early 15th. centuries

The One-Storey Longhouse improved. The larger compartment (the kitchen) protected from draughts by the erection of a screen across it, thereby creating a passageway from the front door (Le Grand Huis) to the back one (Le Petit Huis). Ceilings also inserted so as to provide a loft.

Example: La Coquerie, Rue de la Terre Norgiot, St. Saviour's (Perry 13 FS).

Stage 1b — Late 15th. century

Greater privacy in sleeping accommodation obtained by the construction within the loft of an upstairs room (the solar) over the byre, with access provided by a circular stair-well (La Tourelle) attached to the back of the house — or by a ladder or internal stairs from the passageway.

Example: La Couture House, Collings Road, St. Peter-Port (Perry 16 D3).

Stage 2 — Early 16th. century

The Partial Two-Storey House, created by building up the bedroom end of the longhouse to two storeys, the cross-wall forming a gable-end against which the lower roof of the loft abutted. The byre (sometimes replaced by a parlour) was beneath the bedroom, while the kitchen-living room remained one-storey.

Example: L'Epinel, Rue de L'Epinel, Forest (Perry 28 C4).

Stage 3 — Mid-16th. to mid-17th. centuries

The Seven-Window Two-Storey House, consisting of parlour and kitchen separated by a passageway downstairs, with upstairs three or four bedrooms lit by four windows — while on the ground floor the front door is flanked by two windows on the kitchen side and one on the parlour side. Also known as the 'small parlour' or 'Guernsey' House. (Of similar appearance are longhouses of variety lb, adapted to include an extra bedroom above the kitchen, with the byre converted into a parlour — e.g., Les Merriennes Cottage, Rue de L'Eglise, St. Martin's: Perry 24 D5).

Example: La Fosse, Les Jehans, Torteval (Perry 27 F3).

Stage 4 — Mid-17th. century to late 18th. century

The Nine-Window Two-Storey House, also known as the 'large parlour' or 'Jersey' house (after the island where it was originally developed). This is a larger variant of the 'Guernsey' house, with five upstairs windows and two either side of the front door downstairs. (The preceding parenthetic remarks regarding long-house adaptation apply here, too — e.g., Les Picques, Route des Picques, St. Saviour's: Perry 22 B4).

Example: Les Grandes Mielles, Grandes Mielles Lane, Vale (Perry 8 C2).

N.B. (1) Dates give the main construction periods of the various types. Many buildings with similar features are of subsequent erection.

(2) Many surviving farmhouses of all types have attached to them by way of annexe a 'Dower House' or 'Widow's Third', provided for the accommodation of the late owner's relict when the house proper was inherited by his heir. (Example: Le Bourg, Forest, home of Thomas de la Rue of playing-card fame — Perry 29 E2.)

(3) Under the influence of the Huguenot influx after the Reformation, farmhouses of the period 1570 to 1650 are often characterised by doorways topped by semi-circular arches consisting of two *Voussoirs* (semi-circular rows of stones) which are shoulderless. (Example: La Maison de Haut, Rue des Messuriers, St. Pierre-du-Bois [Perry 27 G1].) The 'Jersey' variant has but one Voussoir, with the springer stones having L-shaped shoulders. (Example: gateway to the erstwhile Town Hospital, transferred thither from L'Hyvreuse [Perry 17 F5].)

APPENDIX XVI

Format of a Typical Letter of Marque

'[Name of Monarch], by the Grace of God [etc., etc.].

'Whereas our said Commissioners for executing the office of our High Admiral have thought [name of privateer] fitly qualified who hath equipped, furnished and victualled a ship called [name of the ship], privateer, of the burthen of about . . . tons, whereof the said [name of privateer] is Commander. Know ye therefore, that we do by these presents grant Commission to, and do license and authorize the said [name of privateer] to set forth in warlike manner the said ship called [name of ship], privateer, and by his own command and with force of arms to apprehend, seize and take the ships, vessels and goods belonging to France and other our enemies, their vessels and subjects or other inhabiting within any of their countries, territories or dominions.

'Provided always that the said [name of privateer] keep an exact journal of his providings, and therein particularly take notion of all Prizes which shall be taken by him.

'And we pray and desire all Kings, Princes, Potentates, Estates and Republics, being our friends and allies, to give the said [name of privateer] all aid, assistance and succour in their ports with his said ship.

'Given at London ... day of [month] [year].'

APPENDIX XVII

For Valour: The Exploit at the Tebourba Gap

December 3rd., 1942 was the fourth and final day of the Battle for the control of the Tebourba Gap (20 miles to the west of Tunis) which had started at dawn on November 30th. At 1000 hours on that day enemy parachute troops of the Sturmgruppe 'Koch' started to attack the whole of the positions held by the much depleted Second Battalion of the Royal Hampshire Regiment. Most of the fire was directed at the Battalion's left flank. After about an hour the Officer Commanding 'Z' Company, Major H. W. Le Patourel, reported that enemy forces had established themselves, after a furious battle, on positions lately occupied by a company from another unit and were bringing heavy machine gun and mortar fire to bear on his left-hand section post on Point 186. Assault detachments from 'Z' Company were despatched and succeeded in reaching the top but were unable to retain the position owing to heavy casualties from enemy fire.

In the course of a desperate attempt to clear the enemy from the high ground on the Battalion's left Major Le Patourel displayed the heroism that earned him the Victoria Cross. The citation accompanying the award reads — 'This officer then personally led four volunteers under very heavy fire to the top in a last attempt to dislodge several enemy machine guns. The party was heavily engaged by machine gun fire and Major Le Patourel rallied his men several times and engaged the enemy, silencing several machine gun posts. Finally when the remainder of his party were all killed or wounded, he went forward alone with a pistol and some grenades to attack enemy machine guns at close quarters and from this action he did not return ... Major Le Patourel's most gallant conduct and self-sacrifice, his brilliant leadership and tenacious devotion to duty in the face of a determined enemy were beyond praise'.

It was believed that Major Le Patourel was killed — and indeed his Victoria Cross was awarded posthumously. It was discovered later that he had been seriously wounded and taken prisoner.

APPENDIX XVIII

Typical Notification of Application for a Rémède authorizing Parochial Taxation to cover Ecclesiastical and Secular Expenditure

LA GAZETTE OFFICIELLE

REMEDE
CASTEL PARISH

The Constables of the Castel Parish hereby notify the Electors and Ratepayers of the said Parish that they will apply to the Royal Court at 10.45 a.m. on THURSDAY, 12th May, 1988 to obtain the Rémède to levy by means of Occupiers' Rate the sum of £79,089,06, Seventy-nine thousand and eighty-nine pounds and six pence, at the rate of 36p in the pound as per Cadastre Rateable Value of all properties in the Cadastre in accordance with the deliberations of the said Electors and Ratepayers at their meeting held on the 21st day of April 1988, namely:

ECCLESIASTICAL NEEDS

	£
Ordinary Repairs to the Parish Church	1,000.00
Extra ordinary repair to Parochial Cemetery including re-surfacing paths and cemetery car park	8,120.86
Ordinary Repairs to Rectory	500.00
Ordinary upkeep of Parochial Cemetery	8,803.00
Insurance of Parish Church and Rectory	1,544.00
Half cost of cleaning Parish Church	300.00
Rateable Value Tax on Rectory and Lands belonging to the Cure	160.00
Repairs and upkeep of Parish Church clock	100.00
Upkeep of Bells and remuneration to Ringers on Public Occasions	30.00
Cost of Publications and Sundries	150.00
	£20,707.86

SECULAR NEEDS

Cost of Publications and Parochial Notices	1,100.00
Parochial Administration including Clerical Expenses	15,115.20
Street Lighting	2,401.00
Road Signs and Parish Seats	300.00
Household Refuse Collection and Disposal	35,225.00
Troughs	65.00
Penstocks: Albecq and Grand Marais	200.00
Contribution to St Matthew's Church	1,800.00
Library Castel Primary School	450.00
Library Les Beaucamps Secondary School	120.00
Library La Mare de Carteret Primary School	225.00
Library La Mare de Carteret Secondary School	120.00
Grant Mont Varouf School	60.00
Miscellaneous Expenses including Cadastre Expenses	950.00
Cobo Car/Boat Park	250.00
	£79,089.06

April 22nd 1988
M. J. DE JERSEY
C. R. BICHARD
Constables (1953/5/7)

APPENDIX XIX

Chronological Table

Before Christ

Circa	6000	onwards — Seasonal visits to island by nomads hunting seals etc. (Opinion of Dr. Patton)
Circa	5500	Hunting Tribe at L'Ancresse } Evidence of Les Fouaillages Excavations
Circa	4500	Island's oldest tomb erected } Evidence of Les Fouaillages Excavations
		Farming village at L'Ancresse } Evidence of Les Fouaillages Excavations
Pre	4000	Le Déhus Dolmen and other Passage Graves
Circa	3000	Statue Menhir in Castel Graveyard
		La Gran'mère du Chimquière
Circa	1800	Possible depopulation of Guernsey as a result of merciless raids by migrants from Eastern Europe
	56	Refugee rebels against Julius Caesar in Gaul set up a trading post at Jerbourg. (Opinion of Dr. Cunliffe.)

Annis Domini

Circa	100	Roman galley carrying amphorae of Garum founders in roadstead
Circa	360	Kendrick's estimate of construction of nunnery in Alderney
Pre	396	Possible inclusion of islands in evangelistic campaign of St. Martin de Tours
Circa	500	Visigoths in Sark
Circa	530	Guernsey converted by St. Sampson
	565	St. Magloire lands in Sark (traditional date)
	575	Conversion of Alderney by St. Vignal
	586	Reputed death of St. Magloire
	709	Tidal wave inundates Vazon forest and cuts off Hanois Rocks
Circa	850	Massacre of Sark monks by Norsemen under Jarl Hasting
Circa	890	Jarl Godefroy (Geoffroi le Grand Sarrazin) said to have built castle on the site of the Castel church
	911	Rollo becomes first Duke of Normandy (Treaty of St. Clair sur Epte)
Circa	925	Islands and Cotentin subjugated by pagan Norsemen
	933	Victory of William Longsword over Brétons adds archipelago to the Duchy of Normandy

	996	Accession of Duke Richard II, who established effective ducal control over the Islands
	1020	Duke Richard II divides Guernsey between Vicomtes of Bessin and Cotentin
Circa	1030	Charter of Duke Robert I provides first mention of several Guernsey churches
		Duke Robert I establishes Benedictines in Herm
	1042	Duke William II restores western Guernsey to Vicomte du Bessin after it had been held by Mont St. Michel
Circa	1048	Duke William II grants four fiefs in St. Andrew's to Church
	1049	Geoffroi de Montbrai appointed to the See of Coutances and establishes effective ecclesiastical control over islands
	1054	Alderney church granted to church of Ste. Marie in Cherbourg
Circa	1055	Restauld donates Jethou to Mont St. Michel
	1057	Duke William II grants Alderney and Sark to Geoffroi de Montbrai
Circa	1062	Duke William II transfers Herm to Augustinians of Cherbourg
	1066	Duke William II conquers England
	1087	Accession of Duke Robert II
	1093	English Crown claims Sark and half of Alderney (Geoffroi de Montbrai in revolt against William Rufus to whom Duke Robert had mortgaged Normandy)
	1106	Duke Robert II defeated at Tenchebrai. Henry I seizes Duchy
	1107	William de Vernon becomes Seigneur of Sark
	1120	Fief du Bessin becomes known as Fief Le Comte when Vicomte du Bessin becomes Earl of Chester
	1134	Charter mentions Alderney church as dedicated to Ste. Marie
	1144	Geoffrey of Anjou becomes Duke of Normandy
	1150	Duke Henry II crowned
	1150–1178	Papal Bulls indicate recovery of Guernsey holdings by Mont St. Michel
	1156	Pope Adrian IV confirms Lihou Priory to Mont St. Michel

1160 Land in Sark donated by William de Vernon to the Abbot of Montebourg, who maintains a solitary monk on the island

1190 Crown grants Alderney in Fief to Guillaume l'Ingeniour

1198 John, Lord of the Isles, grants land near Saints to the Abbey of Blanchelande

1200 Pierre de Preaux appointed Lord of the Isles

1204 John loses Continental Normandy

1206 First depredations of Eustace the Monk
Building of Castle Cornet started

1212 Eustace the Monk seizes Sark

1214 Philippe d'Aubigny regains Sark which John seizes after de Vernon's support of Philip Augustus

1217 Eustace the Monk killed at Sandwich
Treaty of Lambeth — French recognise Henry III's title to the Isles

Circa 1236 Document 'Status Insulae de Aurineo' indicates Alderney Court as already established

1238 Sons of Guillaume l'Ingeniour sell Alderney back to Crown

1244 First documentary mention of Château des Marais

1248 Drew de Barentin ordered to record islands' legal usages

1254 Henry III annexes archipelago to the Crown

1259 Henry III drops title of Duke of Normandy, but islands continue to be administered as though he still were Duke

1275 Edward I appoints Otto de Grandison as Warden

1277 Otto de Grandison becomes Lord of the Isles

1278 Edward I sends common seal to Bailiffs of Jersey and Guernsey

1288 Edward I settles Eperquerie dispute — villeins to pay two deniers for every 100 fish caught between Easter and Michaelmas

1291 Ralph, son of Odo, temporarily becomes 'Bailiff of Sark and Alderney'

1294 Savage French raid kills 25 per cent of population and despoils two of Guernsey's churches

1299 First General Eyre. Bailiff emerges as a purely judicial officer

1304 Second General Eyre

1304 Edward I issues separate seals to Bailiffs of Jersey and Guernsey
1305 Earliest known example of local legislation (petition to levy toll on shipping to pay for harbour repairs)
1307 Transfer of market from Les Landes du Marché to Town church area referred to in letter of Edward II
1309 Third General Eyre
Royal permission to transfer market from Les Landes du Marché to St. Peter-Port
Construction of Jerbourg Castle started
1320 Fourth General Eyre — execution of Gautier de la Salle
1321 Gerard d'Oron appointed sub-warden and imprisoned by bailiff
1323 Otto de Grandison visits islands
Fifth General Eyre
1328 Death of Otto de Grandison
1331 Seigneur du Fief de Sausmarez becomes ex officio Chatelain of Jerbourg Castle
Sixth (and last) General Eyre — hostile demonstration by Guernseymen
1333 Petition contesting validity of English statutes in islands
1335 Jean de Roches ordered to 'array the men of the islands' — possibly birth of Militia
1336 David Bruce raids Islands
1337 Sporadic French raids
1338–1340 Bailiwick occupied by the French
1340 Walter de Weston regains islands from the French
1341 Charter of Edward III confirms insular privileges
1343 Brother John Duraunt petitions Edward III not to seize Sark Priory. Sark later occupied by the French
1345 Castle Cornet re-taken from the French
1347 French driven from Sark
1356 French again take Castle Cornet
1357 Castle Cornet regained
La Tour Beauregard built
1360 Treaty of Brétigny — French abandon claims to Islands in return for English recognition of Bishop of Coutances
1363 Le Marchant family of Guernsey acquire Brecqhou

1369 Abbots assign to Church Trésors certain rentes in perpetuity in lieu of contributions towards upkeep
1370 Edward III orders islanders to prepare to defend themselves
1372 La Déscente des Aragousais
1373 Sark temporarily abandoned after devastation by Bertrand de Guesclin
1378 Papal Schism — Islands under Urbanite Bishop of Nantes
1380 French under Admiral de Vienne temporarily occupy Castle Cornet
1392 Nicholas Henry seeks perrnission of Abbé de Mont St. Michel to build Ste. Appoline
1394 Charter of Richard II authorises building of Ste. Appoline
1406 Sub-warden utilises timber from derelict Benedictine Priory in the Vale for repairs to Castle Cornet
1414 Alien priories taken into the king's hand (Henry V)
1415 First mention of a Guernsey ship — *Mary* (Captain Capelle) helps to ferry Henry V's armies to France
1417 End of papal schism — islands return to See of Coutances
1425 Guernsey ships take part in blockade of Mont St. Michel
1429 Assembly of embryonic States prototype of uncertain composition
1454 Paston letter mentions repulse of large-scale French attack
1459 Henry IV of Castile grants safe conduct to Guernsey traders in his domains
Earl of March (later Edward IV) takes refuge in Guernsey after Rout of Ludford
1463 Margaret of Anjou offers islands to Louis XI in return for aid to Lancastrains
1468 Guernseymen help to expel French from Jersey, thus earning Charter from Edward IV confirming the island's liberties
1470 Start of knitting industry — Thomas de Havilland obtains royal grant to import wool
1478 Sir John Dichefield becomes first Governor of

Guernsey separately — but subordinate to Sir Richard Harliston as 'Captain-in-Chief' of the entire archipelago

1480/1 Bull of Sixtus IV grants neutrality to archipelago

1481 Earliest States' Meeting of which records survive

1486 Edmund Weston becomes Guernsey's first governor directly under Crown

1494 Writ of the Privy Seal } Henry VII's

1495 Order-in-Council } Governmental Code

1496 Pope Alexander VI transfers Islands to Diocese of Salisbury

1499 Islands re-transferred to the See of Winchester — but remain de facto under Coutances

1500 John Bonamy exports 'undergarments called Guernsey frocks'

1513 Thomas Le Marquant endows Petite Ecole de la Vilie

1532 Last Prior of Lihou (Jacques Tournier) finally resigns

1533 Fréluques minted locally by Collas Guillemotte

1534 Ordinance requires hedges cut back to avoid impeding roads

1536 Governor reports departure of Franciscans and forfeiture of their land (future Elizabeth College site) to Henry VIII

1545 Sir Peter Mewtis adds to defences of Castle Cornet

1546 Oldest surviving Ordinance relating to Guernsey Militia

1547–1563 Jacques Amy in office as dean

1549 French occupy Sark

1550 Order-in-Council confirms ecclesiastical jurisdiction of Bishop of Coutances

1553 Edward VI's Second Prayer Book translated into French

French expelled from Sark by Adrian Crole (Flemish corsair)

1556 Burning of Catherine Cauchés, daughters and grandson

1558 French under Captain Malesart despoil Alderney

1560 Charter of Elizabeth I (first Charter to be addressed to Guernsey specifically)

1560–1562 Occupation of Sark by Seigneur of Glatigny

1562 Sir Francis Chamberlain informs Cecil of religious disaffection

1562 Helier Gosselin (burner of Cauchés family) dismissed as bailiff
1563 Nicholas Baudouin obtains governor's permission to form a Calvinist Consistory in St. Peter-Port
Provisional grant of Sark by Queen's Commissioners to Helier de Carteret
Elizabeth I founds Elizabeth College and endows schools in St. Pierre-du-Bois and St Martin's
1564 Anti-Huguenot riot in St. Peter-Port
1565 Adrian de Saravia reports anti-Huguenot riots to Cecil — jurats summoned to Privy Council and seven dismissed
Order-in-Council sanctions Calvinist Consistory in St. Peter-Port only, but also requires that dues shall continue to be paid to the Bishop of Coutances
Helier de Carteret settles in Sark with Letters Patent from Elizabeth I
Cosmé Brévint appointed as Sark minister
1569 Order-in-Council regulates relations between governor and bailiff
Elizabeth I places Islands definitively under See of Winchester
Synod draws up 'Police et Discipline Ecclesiastique'
1570 Brévint's prestige results in Sark becoming venue for Fifth Synod
1572 Elizabeth I creates Sark a Fief Haubert in its own right
1575 Discontinuance of institution to livings by the Bishop of Winchester (offensive to Calvinist susceptibilities)
1576 'Police et Discipline Ecclesiastique' officially adopted by the Synod
1578 Popular disturbances — bailiff and jurats flee to Castle Cornet
1579 Sark Chief Pleas instituted
1581 Sir Thomas Leighton triumphs in confrontation with bailiff, who resigns
Privy Council calls for report on Guernsey's legal usages
Bishop of Winchester appoints Procureur (Louis de Vic) as his Commissary

1582 Enraged Calvinist ministers bring charges against de Vic who, supported by Leighton, is exonerated by Walsingham

L'Approbation des Lois

1583 Nicholas Baudouin (founder of local Calvinism) leaves for England

Clameur de Haro abolished in Continental Normandy but retained in Islands

Order-in-Council separates legislative functions of Sark Chief Pleas from judicial functions of Sark Court

1584 John Chamberlain granted Alderney in fief by the Crown

1585 Ordinance imposes Corvée obligations in Sark (two days a year)

1588 Ordinance that aged poor be subsidised by Church alms

Tunnel completed to Sark harbour in Baie de la Motte

1590 Completion of South Pier of Old Harbour

1591 John Chamberlain sells his Alderney rights to the Earl of Essex

1598 First privateering venture — Elizabeth I gives Jean Briard (commanding *The Dove)* Letters of Marque to attack French

1601 Cosmé Brévint censured by Guernsey Colloque

1604 Petition to James I for strengthening bailiff and States *vis-à-vis* governor

1605 Death of Cosmé Brévint

1606 Ordinance restricting Sark Chief Pleas membership to Quarantaine holders

1607 Petition for a Provincial States General and the institution of an Appeal Court

Dispute between Aurigniais and William Chamberlain settled — Simon Maçon takes up Alderney living

1608 Order-in-Council restricts governor's powers, obliging him to consult Royal Court

Amice de Carteret introduces division of jurats into three quartets

1611 Occasional *ad hoc* 'taxe des pauvres' instituted

Letters Patent from James I *re* Sark Holdings

1612 Guernsey Colloque appoints Elie Brévint to Sark living

1612 Title of 'Judge' given to erstwhile Prévôt in Alderney
1613 Letter from King-in-Council states James I's determination to introduce Anglicanism
1614 On representations of De La Marche James decides to tolerate Presbyterianism in Guernsey
1620 Earl of Essex makes over Alderney to Sir William Essex (no relation)
Jean Nicole of La Sablonerie banished from Sark for practising the Black Art
1621 Ordinance restricts office of douzenier to property owners — Franchise likewise restricted
1627 Sir Peter Osborne repels French attack on Alderney
Rachel Alexandre of Sark burnt as a sorceress
1635 Laud establishes Oxford fellowships for Channel Islanders in theological training
1636 Laud prepares to order an episcopal visitation
1637 Laud cancels episcopal visitation on advice of governor (Lord Danby)
1642 Death of Sir William Essex — Alderney reverts to Earl of Essex
Guernsey declares for parliament in Civil War
Parliament confiscates Fief of Sark from Sir Philippe de Carteret
1643 Jean de Quetteville (royalist bailiff) deposed Puritan leaders captured by royalists — subsequently escape from Castle Cornet
1644 Abortive royalist attack on Sark
1646 Earl of Essex dies without issue — Alderney holding lapses
Sir Baldwin Wake replaces Sir Peter Osborne as royalist lieutenant-governor at Castle Cornet
1647 de Quetteville returns from England and contests Pierre de Beauvoir's assumption of office of bailiff, which is, however, later confirmed by parliament
1651 Surrender of Castle Cornet (last royalist stronghold)
1653 Parliament orders that jurats should each act as bailiff for a month at a time
1656 Pierre de Beauvoir reinstated as permanent bailiff
1660 Restoration — Pierre de Beauvoir resigns as bailiff
Royal Court of Guernsey reinstates de Carterets in Sark

1660 Alderney's government divorced from that of Guernsey — Sir George Carteret becomes its governor
1661 Amais Andros assumes office as royalist bailiff
1662 B.C.P. translated into French by Rev. John Durell
Rev. Elie Picot reappointed in Alderney as Anglican incumbent
1663 Anglicanism officially established — Bishop of Winchester appoints John de Sausmarez as Dean
1667 John Tupper conducts privateering operations against Dutch
1672 Explosion obliges governor to quit Castle Cornet for town
1674 Death of Elie Brévint — final disappearance of Calvinism — Moise Benoist appointed as Anglican incumbent in Sark
1675 First meeting of Sark Court in its present form — office of Seneschal instituted
1681 British customs fail in attempt to stop smuggling between Islands and the West Country
Dame Rachel le Marchant renounces Brechou in favour of the Seigneur of Sark
1687 James II appoints Colonel John Legge as Roman Catholic lieutenant-governor
1688 Protestant coup — Legge taken into custody — William and Mary acknowledged
1689 William III terminates archipelago's neutral status
1690 Complaint of Guernseymen over billeting of troops
1691 Order-in-Council regulates billeting procedure
1692 Start of main privateering era — John Tupper takes part in battle of Cap La Hogue
1700 'Barriere de la Ville' stones erected
1709 Frustrated attempt by British customs to control island trade
1717 Abolition of Banon
1719 Army garrison withdrawn — defence of island devolves on Militia
1721 Beginning of Le Mesurier dynasty in Alderney
1725 Establishment of Procureurs des Pauvres in each parish
1726 Primitive coal-fire light on Les Casquets
1730 Sark Militia emerges from Quarantaine Defence Force

1736 Braye Harbour founded by Henry Le Mesurier
1737 'Fee farm' system of land holdings established
1738 Thomas Le Cocq (in dispute with Alderney governor) suspended from office as Judge
1740 Philip and Thomas de Sausmarez set out with Anson to circumnavigate globe
1742 Foundation of Town hospital for poor of St. Peter-Port
1744 Service in Sark Militia made compulsory between ages of 16 and 60
1747 Philip de Saumarez, commanding H.M.S. *Nottingham*, killed off Brest
1750 Completion of North Pier of Old Harbour
1751 Country hospital for poor established in the Castel
1752 Dismissal of incumbent (Pierre Levrier) by Dame of Sark
1755 Seigneur (Pierre Le Pelley) invites rector of Vale to officiate in Sark — Levrier raises Clameur de Haro
1756 Senseschal expels Levrier for causing public mischief
Lucrative privateering operations started from Alderney
1757 Cayeux Deschamps an acceptable appointment to Sark living
1761 New Ground (now Cambridge Park) acquired for drilling Town regiment of Militia
1763 First of series of enactments to preserve purity of cattle
1765 Birth of General John Gaspard Le Marchant
1768 Successful opposition to Act of Parliament requiring Channel Isles vessels to be cleared from a British port
1769 Birth of Sir Isaac Brock
1770 Alderney's first Court House built
James Saumarez enters Navy
1773 Guernsey's first fire brigade (part-time amateurs)
1775 Guernsey's first theatre (*La Comédie*) opened
1778 Ordinance limits constables' term of office to three years maximum, one year minimum
France enters American Independence War — construction of 'Martello' towers put in hand
Governor of Cherbourg refers to Channel Island privateers as the 'despair of France'
1779 Completion of old harbour quays

1780 Construction of Fort George commenced
1782 British government undertakes to supply Militia clothing
Meat market (now French Halles) and assembly rooms completed
1783 Mutiny of 10th. Regiment at Fort George quelled
1785 Jean de Quetteville brings Methodism to Guernsey
1787 William Gardiner produces six-inch map of Guernsey
Adam Clarke introduces Methodism to Alderney
John Wesley visits the Bailiwick
1788 Birth of Frederick Corbin Lukis
1789 Building of Holy Trinity church
First Methodist chapel built in Rue Le Marchant
Publication of first Guernsey newspaper (*La Gazette*)
1790 Alderney governor endows school in St. Anne
First Methodist chapel opened in Alderney
Three lighthouses built on Les Casquets
1792 French clerics seek refuge from Jacobins — party includes Chateaubriand
Roman Catholic chapel established in Le Bordage
1793 Birth of Thomas la Rue
Captain James Saumarez brings 10 transports of Roman Catholic refugees from France to Guernsey
Peter Mourant builds first glasshouse (for grapes and pineapples) in Candie
1794 James Saumarez eludes capture in action off Vazon
First regular mail service established
Guernsey's first purpose-built theatre opened (*Theatre Royal*)
1796 J. Noel makes first Guernsey milkcan
First Methodist chapel opened in Sark
Thomas de Carteret of La Forge challenges Sark Seigneur's Droit de Multure
1797 Arson of Sark seigneur's mill
1798 Sunday Militia parades abolished because of Methodist opposition
1799 Building of Royal Court House
Tension with Russian troops quartered at Delancey
1801 One constable per parish required to attend Chief Pleas
1802 General John Gaspard Le Marchant founds Royal Military College

1803 Rear-Admiral Saumarez assumes command in Guernsey waters
Sir John Doyle embarks on extensive fortifications
1806 Doyle commences reclamation of Braye du Valle and later drives roads to Vazon and L'Erée
1807 British Smuggling Act applied to Islands despite protest
1810 Granite export started
1811 Lukis and Gosselin excavate La Varde Dolmen
Start of cattle export (Lord Braybrook imports first Guernsey herd into England)
1812 Deaths in action of General John Gaspard Le Marchant and Sir Isaac Brock
Disgruntled tenants consent to Corvée service on La Coupée on condition of seigneur contributing to cost
1813 Publication of first English-language newspaper (*Star*)
1815 Building of Guernsey prison completed
Start of shipbuilding industry
First exploitation of granite on Herm
1816 First issue of local currency notes (to finance market scheme)
1817 Seigneur (Pierre le Pelley) obtains grant from Church Building Society for new Sark church (St. Peter's)
Foundation of first Agricultural Society
States buy meat market (French Halles)
1818 Rebuilding of Torteval church
First visit to archipelago by Anglican Bishop (Salisbury)
Bishop consecrates St. James The Less as Anglican Church with services in English
1821 St. Peter's (Sark) licensed for divine service
1822 Building of present meat market
1823 Arrival of *Medina* (first steamship to travel to Channel Isles)
1825 John Le Mesurier surrenders Alderney to Crown — island placed under jurisdiction of Lieutenant-Governor of Guernsey
1827 'Guernsey Banking Company' set up
Mails first brought by steamship
1829 First visit to Bailiwick of Bishop of Winchester

1829 St. Peter's (Sark) consecrated
Sark's first school built
Present Elizabeth College building completed
Notre Dame de Rosaire opened as Guernsey's first Roman Catholic church
1830 First local coinage struck, based on the double (80 to franc)
1831 Island Militias designated 'Royal'
1832 Foundation of Mechanics' Institution
Daniel de Lisle Brock successfully resists attempt by St. Pancras Council to prosecute Guernsey Sheriff in England
1834 Silver mining starts in Sark
The Channel Islands (D. H. Inglis) — first Tourist Guide Book
Death of last governor (Sir William Keppell)
1835 Sark seigneur acquires quarantaine holding of La Moinerie de Haut
Office of governor abolished — lieutenant-governors become the direct representatives of the Crown
1836 Erection of St. John's church
Death of Admiral Lord de Saumarez
1837 Horse 'bus service started (Town to St. Sampson's)
1838 Emigration to U.S.A. of George Le Boutillier, bankrupted by excavation of Arcades
Rev. Benwall, chaplain on Herm — St. Tugual's restored
1840 Official boundaries of Town extended (area without Préciput)
1841 Franchise extended to include taxpayers (i.e., property owners)
1843 Opening of Alderney post office
1844 Douzaine delegates replace constables as States members
Cantonal douzaines established in St. Peter-Port (abolished 1948)
Sir William Napier lands forces 'to quell insurrection'
Circa 1845 Pusey inaugurates use of surplices in Sark church
1846 Visit of Victoria and Albert
1847 End of silver mining in Sark
Construction of naval base and forts started in Alderney

1848 First Roman Catholic church established in Alderney
Victoria Tower built
Railway company shipping services started
1850 S.S. *Collier* becomes the first screw steamer to visit Guernsey
Consecration of St. Anne's, Alderney
1851 St. Joseph's Roman Catholic church opened
1852 St. Matthew's (Cobo) opened
Present Methodist church opened in Alderney
1853 World's first pillar boxes (that in Union Street survives)
Paid policemen first recruited in St. Peter-Port
Seigneur obtains appointment of quartermaster for Sark Militia
1854 Victoria and Albert visit Alderney
1855 Arrival of Victor Hugo (stayed until 1870)
1856 Construction of Bréhon tower
1857 Sark post office opened
Second visit of Victoria and Albert to Alderney
1858 Passengers able to land by gangway for the first time
Telegraph service inaugurated
Guernsey Customs established
1859 Sark Landing Tax inaugurated
Second visit of Victoria and Albert
1862 Hanois lighthouse commences operation
1863 Charles Smith starts flower export trade
1864 Opening of St. Stephen's church
Completion of modern harbour — first passengers land at White Rock
Final completion of St. Sampson's harbour
Launching of *Golden Spur* — Guernsey's largest ship
1865 States impose dues for use of any harbour in Bailiwick
Circa 1865 First 'love apples' (tomatoes) grown
1868 Creux harbour completed in Sark
Arrival of Sisters of Mercy
1870 Departure of Victor Hugo
1871 Death of Frederick Corbin Lukis
1872 British government reluctantly agrees to maintain Alderney breakwater
Ladies' College opened
1874 Opening of St. Barnabas's church

1874 Arrival of Sisters of Mercy in Alderney
Sisters of Notre Dame des Chênes open schools in Burnt Lane
Launching of S.S. *Commerce* — only Guernsey-built steamer
First Fruit Export Company set up
1876 First ordinance controlling ormer fishery
1877 Two Casquets lighthouses demolished — third (existing one) improved
1879 Light steam railway opened between Town and St. Sampson's
1881 Herd Book for local cattle instituted
1882 Guernsey Society for Natural Science founded (forerunner of Société Guernesiaise)
Carthusians take up residence in Herm — plant Montery pines
1883 Smith Street post office opened
Opening of Guille-Allès Library
Boys' Intermediate School founded
1884 Carthusians leave Herm
Tomatoes grown for first time as main crop by J. Poat
1889 Osmond Priaulx leaves his library to the island
1892 Electric tramway replaces steam railway
1894 Guernsey Growers' Association founded
1895 Thomas Guille founds Artisans' Institute
Girls' Intermediate School opened
1898 Telephone service established
1899 Pym mutiny in Militia
Deputés du Peuple added to States
George Nurse wins V.C. at Colenso
1900 End of Sark Militia
Lewis Halliday wins V.C. in China Boxer Rising
1901 Channel Fleet uses Alderney base during manoeuvres.
1902 Sisters of Sacred Heart of Jesus set up Blanchelande College
1904 Les Soeurs de la Présentation establish schools at Les Côtils and La Chaumière
De La Salle Brothers acquire Les Vauxbelets and Vimiera
1905 States Advisory Committee (forerunner of Tourist Committee) constituted

1905 Inter-Island 'Muratti' football competition started
1908 Dean Samuel Falle institutes Channel Isles Eisteddfodau
1914 Last witchcraft trial in Guernsey — Mrs. Lake: eight days for disorderly conduct
1915 Sark telephone service inaugurated
1917 Royal Guernsey Light Infantry commended for Cambrai action
1918 R.G.L.I. cut to pieces on the Lys — only 100 survive
1919 Hospitaller Sisters of the Sacred Heart set up Le Platon Home
1920 Affinity established between Guernsey and U.K. currency with 1,920 doubles to the £
Island police force constituted
Number of deputies in States increased
Suffrage made theoretically universal — but with special application for registration required of non-ratepayers
1921 Visit of George V and Queen Mary
1922 Sark Reform Law adds 12 People's deputies to Chief Pleas
Income tax introduced in Guernsey for the first time
Natural Science Society re-named Société Guernesiaise
Inauguration of Guernsey Eisteddfod
1923 People's deputies introduced in Alderney
Dispute with U.K. government over Imperial Defence payment
Inauguration of air service from England (flying boat)
Brother Déodat starts building Les Vauxbelets little chapel
1925 Herm post office opened (closed 1938)
Present Methodist church opened in Sark
Original Mignot Memorial Hospital opened in Alderney
1927 Imperial contribution dispute settled: U.K. Treasury accepts 'once-for-all gift'
Hauteville House donated to the city of Paris
Guernsey-Alderney radio-telephone link established
1928 U.K. government withdraws financial support for Militia
1929 Dame de Sercq gives to tenant of Brechou Chief Pleas seat attached to La Moinerie de Haut

1929 Completion of New Jetty
Royal Alderney Militia Artillery abolished
1931 Telephone link with England established
1934 Cecil Noel flies 'Wee Mite' from L'Erée
Tramway service discontinued
1935 First land-based air service to England — Cobham Air Routes from L'Erée
Visit of Prince of Wales. Militia inspected by royalty for the last time
Alderney airstrip opened
1937 Work started on St. Saviour's reservoir
1939 Opening of La Villaize airport — air mail started
Garrison withdrawn — defence devolves on Militia
1940 Royal Guernsey Militia disbanded — members join British army
Archipelago declared an open town — evacuation
Air raid on Town harbour
Start of German Occupation — Graf von Schmettow C.-in-C.
Ambrose Sherwill President of Controlling Committee
Sherwill deposed for helping Nicolle and Symes — replaced by Jurat John Leale
1941 Hitler orders fortification of Islands
1942 Start of deportations
Commando raid on Sark and 'chained prisoners' allegations
Major Wallace Le Patourel wins V.C. at Tebourba, Tunisia, December 3rd.
1943 Charybdis funeral
Guernsey Society founded in U. K. — originally to help refugees
1944 R.C.A.F. attack neutralises Fort George
Arrest of Machon and Falla — death of Machon from ill-treatment
Arrival of *Vega* averts starvation
1945 Huffmeier replaces von Schmettow
Liberation — Visit of George VI and Queen Elizabeth
1946 Herm ceases to be a Crown holding — purchased by States
1947 Completion of La Maseline harbour in Sark
Crown relinquishes revenues of Fief Le Roi to States who henceforth pay salary of lieutenant-governor

1948 British Nationality Act defines national status of Channel Islanders
Guernsey Reform Law } Courts unable
Government of Alderney Law } to legislate
Jurats debarred from States of Deliberation — replaced by Conseillers
Increased number of deputies in States
Douzaine representatives replace delegates
Universal Franchise introduced
Cantonal douzaines in St. Peter-Port abolished
President of States replaces Judge in Alderney
1949 Visit of H.R.H. Princess Elizabeth — Princess Elizabeth hospital opened
Alderney Land and Property Law by implication disallows préciput in Alderney
1951 Death of Bro. Déodat, builder of Les Vauxbelets little chapel
Corvée in Sark abolished in favour of household levy for road upkeep
Sark Chief Pleas enabled to pass an ordinance over head of seigneur
Decision taken against re-establishment of Guernsey Militia
Tomato Marketing Board set up as a permanent institution
1954 Préciput abolished in Guernsey
1955 Rev. Frank Drake has mental vision of church in chicken-run
1957 Chapel of Christ the Healer dedicated by Bishop of Winchester
Visit of Queen Elizabeth II — Ceremony of Homage enacted in both Guernsey and Sark
1958 Establishment of Tektronix (start of light industry)
Mignot Memorial Hospital reborn in Alderney and re-sited at Crabby
1959 Formation of Investment Trust of Guernsey — Birth of 'Finance Industry'
Visit to Bailiwick by H.R.H. Princess Margaret
1961 Tomato chips replaced by trays
Bailiwick Court of Appeal instituted
1962 Inaugural transmission by Channel Television
1963 Air cargo service inaugurated

1964 Bailiff becomes sole judge of law (Order of Royal Court)
1965 Comprehensive social security system instituted
1966 Special coinage struck and Chevauchée re-enacted to mark ninth centenary of conquest of England
1969 Bailiwick becomes an independent postal authority — so that 'conveyance stamps' from smaller islands discontinued
1970 Guernsey's first marina opened at Beaucette Quarry
1971 States accept special terms for Bailiwick's membership of E.E.C. — effective from January 1st., 1973
1972 Completion of containerization wharf at harbour
1973 Report of Commission on Constitution recommends creation of a 'Council for the Islands'
Birth of first crossbred Charolais/Guernsey calf
1974 Installation of 'roll-on', 'roll-off' facilities at harbour
1975 Full legal rights granted to Sark married women
Alderney jurats debarred from membership of States
Maritime museum opened at Château de Rocquaine (Fort Grey)
1976 States vote in favour of abolishing Congé
Parish rectors excluded from States of Election (for Conseillers)
Formation of Guernsey Association
Opening of Beau Séjour Leisure Centre
1977 States approve Projet de Loi to abolish feudal dues
Farewell sailing of S.S. *Sarnia* last non-car-ferry ship
Sark acknowledges divorce, except where it affects inheritance rights
Mr. Richard Keen discovers late first-century amphorae of Garum near Town harbour
1978 Second visit of Elizabeth II
Guernsey cheese marketed for the first time
Island museum opened in Candie Gardens
1979 Privy Council refers back to the States the 1977 Projet de Loi concerning feudal dues
States subsequently decide to retain these dues, with all income from private fiefs being diverted to the Crown
'Museum of the Year' award won by the New Museum in Candie Gardens
1980 Alderney railway opened to passenger traffic

1980 All omnibus services discontinued with bankruptcy of Guernsey Railway Company
States vote to convert church of St. James The Less to a police station
Coin for £1 introduced
1981 'Guernseybus Limited' re-commences omnibus service
Europe's oldest tomb (*c.* 4500 B.C.) unearthed at Les Fouaillages
New Nationality Bill obfuscates status of Channel Islanders
Ladies' College attains public school status
Subscription system replaced by free lending service at Guille-Allès library
1982 Mr. Richard Keen discovers hull of second century Roman ship in Town harbour
Radio Guernsey starts broadcasting
1983 Start of scheme attempting to reverse former decline
Earliest surviving complete building in Town (26, Cornet Street) acquired by National Trust of Guernsey
States agree with 'Friends of St James' Association' to convert ex-church into a Concert Hall instead of a Police Station
Alderney Regional Postage Stamp issue inaugurated
1984 North Beach extension to Town Harbour commenced
Oyster fishery re-established after a century's lapse
Extensive restoration of Le Château des Marais
Remains of Roman houses discovered at La Plaiderie
Little Theatre (Central Hall) gutted by fire
Visit of H.M. Queen Elizabeth the Queen Mother
'Project Papillon' launched in disused vineries
British Government suggests annual contribution to its Exchequer with imponderable implications for future Island/United Kingdom relationships
Remains of Roman hypocaust found under Castel Church
1985 New Guernsey Flag flown for first time
Centenary of Hugo's death: French President visits island incognito and inspects Hauteville House
H.R.H. the Duchess of Kent visits Bailiwick for 40th. anniversary of Liberation: also opens new co-educational Grammar School

1985 H.R.H. the Duke of Kent opens St. James Cultural Centre
New coinage issue carries Monarch's Head for the first time
Island loses its last cinema: Gaumont Palace sold to provide site for Bank of Bermuda building
Second century Roman ship in Town Harbour brought to surface
Thomas Owen's 'Guernsey Falcon' of 1550 re-mounted in Mewtis Bulwark
Mrs. Dorothy Winifred le Pelley becomes first woman Jurat
1986 Reginald Blanchford mentioned in Guinness Book of Records as holder of highest number of awards for gallantry ever granted to a civilian
Trinity House announces plans to automate all its lighthouses in the Bailiwick, beginning in 1989
Ruins of fishing village *c.* 1110 (and Neolithic evidences too) excavated at Grandes Rocques adjoining Port des Malades
Defence Contribution dispute resolved by British Government's acceptance of Guernsey's offer to maintain Alderney Breakwater
Two-day visit to Bailiwick by H.R.H. the Princess Anne
States approve construction of special fishing wharf between Castle Emplacement and Albert Marina
Island visited by H.R.H. the Prince Edward
Town hospital closed
Sealink/British Ferries & Channel Islands Ferries merge — but soon divorce. Services to Weymouth discontinued
1987 Guernsey Growers' Co-Operative replaces Tomato Marketing Board as agency for selling produce
La Société Guernesiaise proposes creation of a marine conservation area offshore from Les Angulières
Institution of a Review Board to hear complaints against States' Departments
Work Permit system advocated by Advisory & Finance Committee
Following extensive refurbishment, 26, Cornet Street opened by Bailiff as National Trust Headquarters

1988 Bailiwick sponsors Earls Court Boat Show, exhibiting (*inter alia*) a display featuring the Town Harbour which dominated the function

Royal Assent given to law requiring candidates for election as Conseiller to have at least 30 months' experience in the States

Plans announced for massive extension to St. Sampson's Harbour

States' Ordinance enforces seat belts in front seats of cars

1989 Bailiwick visited by H.M. Queen Elizabeth II

Distinctive Alderney coinage minted for the first time

Islander Martine Le Moignan becomes first-ever British winner of Women's World Squash Racquets Championship

Earl Ferrers opens new prison at Les Nicolles

New Weights and Measures Law ordains use of metric units of weight and capacity, but retains traditional Dry Capacity Measures for Rentes calculations and Vergées and Perches for land transfer purposes. This law does apply to Sark.

1990 Bailiwick visited by H.R.H. the Princess Alexandria

Perelle Battery destroyed by gales but promptly reconstructed

Work begun on a £9.7 million land reclamation scheme south of St. Sampson's Harbour

Sark 'invaded' by a Frenchman (André Jean Pierre Marie Gardes) who, armed with a semi-automatic gun, claimed to be the rightful Siegneur. He was fined £200 and jailed for seven days.

Threat to export earnings posed by departure of Tektronix Ltd.

1991 Petit Port steps badly damaged by landslide

Liza Opie wins the British Open Squash Racquets Championship

1992 Bailiwick visited by H.R.H. the Duchess of Gloucester, who opened an extension to the Princess Elizabeth Hospital

Ambulance Service acquires its fist paramedic specialist (Mr. Jon Beausire)

News released of discovery of Elizabethan ship off Alderney

1992 Elizabeth College admits girls for the first time in its history — but only as VI Formers

1993 Fearing a threat to Sark's autonomy, Chief Pleas denies ratification to three Projets de Loi implementing European Community legislation

Alderney constitutional reform: half membership of States to be elected biennially in future

Town Hospital, extensively adapted, becomes Island Police Station

Guernsey Association dissolved

States approve constitutional revision instituting election of Conseillers by popular vote

Start of prolonged dispute with French over fishing rights in island waters and around Roches Douvres

Alderney's armorial bearings registered by College of Arms

1994 Conseillers elected by popular vote for first time

British Channel Island Ferries bought out by Condor Ltd. All passenger services centred on Weymouth and freight ones on Portsmouth

Association Football: Matthew Le Tissier becomes the first Guernseyman to win a full England Cap

Death in office of Lieutenant-General Sir Michael Wilkins, K.C.B., O.B.E.: first death since 1911 of Lieutenant-Governor while still in office

Establishment of Guernsey's own Air Licensing Authority

States acquire fee-farm lease of Lihou Island

Liza Opie awarded M.B.E.

H.R.H. the Duke of Gloucester names *Flying Christine III*

1995 Inauguration of States-subsidised 'bus service

Viral infection at Castel Hospital causes five deaths

Visits of H.R.H. the Prince of Wales and H.R.H. the Duchess of Kent

Rôle of Head Tenant of Jethou assumed by States

1996 Roman artefacts indicating a possible second century Gallo-Roman site unearthed beneath Bonded Store in Church Square

Inauguration of compulsory 'specialist' health service

Visit of H.R.H. the Princess Royal

1996 Mrs. Linda Le Vasseur becomes the first Guernsey-woman to go through a form of ordination to the priesthood

Traditional craft taken out of shipping service

Sark's title to Brecqhou disputed in court action brought by David and Frederick Barclay, the islet's joint tenants

1997 Shipping passenger services again based on Poole

Visit of H.R.H. the Princess Margaret

First ever 'Women's Muratti' played, with Guernsey winning

Considerable extensions made to the Alderney Society Museum

Serquiais petition European Human Rights Commission against change being imposed on their island

John van Katwyk & Geoff Gavey become the first Guernseymen to row across the Atlantic Ocean

1998 Guernsey/United Kingdom constitutional relationships impaired by latter initiating a review of financial regulations without accustomed prior consultation

Prosperity of fishing industry menaced by aggressiveness of French, who also sought discontinuance of the Bailiwick's judicial autonomy

States vote for abolition of office of Conseiller as from April 2000

After considering tenders from rivals States renew Condor's mandate to operate the Guernsey-U.K. sea route

Deanery Synod votes in favour of women being eligible for appointment to island livings

Death of Major A. G. ('Peter') Wood of Herm

1999 Sark's inheritance laws modified to comply with Human Rights requirements

Joint Elizabeth/Ladies' College Sixth Form established

Guernsey/U.K. dispute over method of appointing Lieutenant-Governor

By his expertise Captain Peter ('Jerry') Girard avoids catastrophic air collision over China

Blanchelande College established at Les Vauxbelets.

INDEX

N.B. — In the compilation of this Index all prefixes have been ignored. Thus (for example) 'Le Pelley' will be found under 'P' instead of 'L', while 'De Sausmarez' comes under 'S' rather than 'D'.

POSTSCRIPT: TWO AFTERTHOUGHTS

In the hope that he might thereby partly expiate his textual sins of omission the author would like to draw attention to the following:

(1) It is interesting to note that the self-same Geoffroi de Montbrai, Bishop of Coutances, who is featured on page 13 as making effective his see's erstwhile nominal episcopal control over our archipelago, officiated on Christmas Day 1066 at the coronation of William the Conqueror in Westminster Abbey.

(2) Grateful thanks are due to Mr. R. E. Le Bargy for his reminder of the cogent assertion of Guernsey's position vis-à-vis the U.K. (see Part III, Chapter Eleven) made by Jurat Laurent Carey in his "Essai sur les Institutions, Lois et Coutumes de l'Ile de Guernesey" (1889) wherein he put forward a powerful contention which, translated into English, reads –

> "We can see clearly by what has been said and which is founded on authenticated and incontestable facts, that the English Kings became our sovereigns only because William the Conqueror subjugated England, uniting its government and that of the province of Normandy under the same head. But this island did not become thereby a dependency of the Kingdom of England. It is not one of her conquests and has never been formally or tacitly united with her. It has always remained a residue of the lands which the Conqueror possessed in Normandy when he conquered England, so it cannot be part of that Kingdom because Normandy never became an English province. On the contrary, in all truth, England is the country which has been conquered. The Normans, our ancient compatriots, have more right to command there than have the English to command in Normandy."

Airbnb Beginner's Guide to Hosting

How to set up and run your own Airbnb business

4th edition

Lauren Coats

Art by Danielle O'Malley

introduction

Know that you can and will accomplish your dreams. It all begins with believing in yourself and knowing that it is going to happen. Then you'll need hard work, dedication, ignited passion, focus, humbleness, and honorable intentions. Believe in yourself, even if no one else does.

For interactive guidance in setting up your new vacation rental and creating a business plan, check out my video course ***Airbnb Express: Start Hosting in 14 Days*** on the Teachable platform.

https://lauren-coats-s-school.teachable.com/p/airbnb

You'll get $40 in free Airbnb travel credit as a new host when you use my Airbnb brand ambassador referral link. Please consider supporting me in this way! I'll get a bonus after you welcome your first guest.

www.airbnb.com/r/laurencoats

My intention in writing and publishing this book is to empower and enable seekers of financial independence with the best tips they need to become successful on the Airbnb platform quickly, while simultaneously creating and honoring positive experiences for the travelers they host.

contents

chapter 1
the golden key

welcome superstar!

I've written this book specifically for brand new Airbnb entrepreneurial hosts seeking financial independence who will manage between 1-10 vacation rentals, primarily by themselves, or train employees to be reliable and available to support the guests and business operations. You will learn how to make decisions to create your Airbnb's brand, decoration, furnishing, vibe, how to navigate pricing, get 5-star reviews, and become an efficient, relaxed host naturally. I intend to offer valuable insights to make your hosting journey smooth, confident, profitable, and successful from day 1 and to minimize your frustrations and failures due to lack of experience.

the golden key

Managing your guest expectations is the #1 secret to creating a successful vacation rental business. Your primary work as a host is to identify, manage, and follow through on meeting and exceeding your guest's expectations. This is how you're going to be able to ask your guests to leave you 5-star reviews directly! *It's much easier than it sounds.*

Airbnb's review system allows users to choose between 1 and 5 stars, and receiving 4 stars is technically a negative score according to the review system because it shows that you failed to fulfill your guest's expectations. How often your Airbnb listing will show up in the search results depends on your score. The higher it is, the more often you'll appear = more bookings = a more profitable business. It's ALL about 5-stars.

so how do you get 5-star reviews?

First step, truly offer a great guest experience. I believe in you! What kind of service would you want to receive on your vacation? A smooth check in, accuracy of the listing, and having your expectations met. Essentially, feeling like you got what you were expecting at a good value for how much you paid.

Your guests want your house to look like it does in the photos. If you haven't correctly represented your space and have posted inaccurate photos, Airbnb may give them a refund without your consent. Don't claim it to be "spacious" when it is a tiny studio. A guest will leave you 5 stars if they received what they expected to receive.

This is VERY achievable! They are not leaving you a review that says your place is a 5-star resort, 5 stars simply means their expectations were fulfilled.

Another primary guest expectation is that you will be available to receive communication from your guests when they need something, last minute, late, urgently, or somewhat immediately. If you work a full-time job with your phone on silent all day and go offline for days at a time, you may be brewing some potentially harmful future reviews, big refunds, and costly cancellations. I recommend to check your phone every few hours when hosting guests. As Airbnb listings succeed based on their review scores and written reviews, one of your top priorities is setting your guest's expectations accurately. We can break this down into three steps.

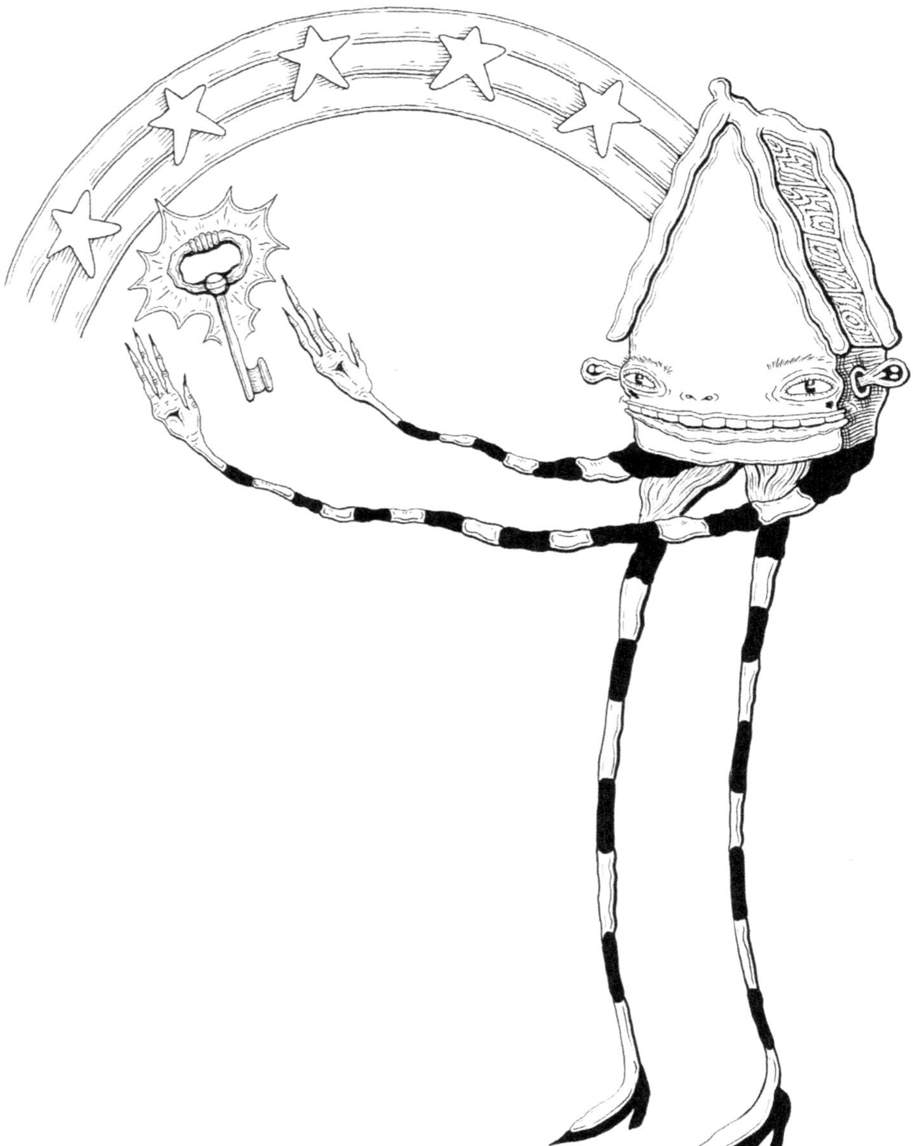

Step 1. Accurately describe your space on your listing, don't inauthentically exaggerate. Share any negative features of your space on your listing that guests will definitely notice and have to deal with. They don't want to be surprised by loud noises of a highway or the construction site next door, mold on the ceiling, no hot water, no cooking supplies, no shampoo, no towels, or any other situation that can interrupt their smooth, peaceful travel and enjoyment.

Step 2. Use photos that show the true reality of your home. We definitely want to glamorize your listing with professional photos. But if your photos do not accurately reflect what you are offering and you choose to hide parts of your home that are ugly or less than perfect, you are sure to get 1-3 star reviews consistently.

Step 3. If you will not be available to help your guests 24/7, be sure to set that expectation on your listing. Guests will automatically expect that anytime they write to you with an urgent concern, you'll be available. If you know that you are not online often or have other responsibilities, you can share this on your listing in the "interactions with guests" section to property set the expectation.

the golden key philosophy

Your guests are super excited about their trip! They worked hard to save money for this vacation, and if you haven't truly represented yourself or your service, you may fail to meet their expectations. What your guests think they are getting should be delivered, or you can count on very low review scores, some hate mail, and/or Airbnb automatically processing them a refund.

Use all your energy to make your space great and ready to gently exceed their expectations. Have something awesome in the home that surprises your guests! This could be a small welcome gift, personalized note, a few drinks in the fridge, nice luxurious towels, soft sheets - a small detail that wasn't expressed in the listing, but your guests are sure to appreciate, notice, and will make them think, "wow! It's even better than I thought it was going to be!" That's the host's golden key, the art of earning 5-star reviews and obtaining Super Host status (explained later).

to be or not to be?

1. can I commit to a 24/7 online lifestyle?

You will be playing a vacation rental property management role, which is usually a 24/7 commitment. As a responsible host, you or your co--host will be available to your guests last minute and semi-around the clock. Sometimes guests will lock themselves out at 11pm and request you come over right away with a spare key, or one afternoon a hot water heater may break and you will spend the whole day meeting handymen and handling the repair. When an urgent request arises, you can also reply to your guests with your soonest availability and try to accommodate them ASAP according to your schedule.

Depending on the issue, they could receive a refund from Airbnb due to any delay in your response or having their trip ruined by your unavailability. Some requests may need to be handled immediately, so the best practice is to always have someone available to speak with guests. I have been at social events having a great time, only to have to leave for an Airbnb emergency. To have designated off-hours, you'll need to hire a co-host to be on duty when you're offline.

In general, guests want to be well cared for and feel that your top priority is their comfort. When hosting, I look at my phone every 3-4 hours to ensure an Airbnb situation hasn't gotten out of control out of nowhere. Week-long, disconnected, offline camping trips will happen after my Airbnb host career ends or I hire an unbelievably proficient co-host. You can definitely hire someone to run your Airbnb App and take phone calls. Still, every detail and nuance of protocol for particular issues is hard to train someone on, especially if you have multiple rentals with different property owners or in different locations.

There is a sensitivity to handle everything correctly to ensure positive guest reviews and positive client, owner, landlord relations. Can you trust your friend, employee, or co-host to handle every situation with maximum hospitality and problem-solving skills? To follow all of your detailed instructions accurately? If you are the property owner, it will be much easier to train your co-host to provide excellent service to your guests when you go offline. Just know, you are most likely committing to being available or managing someone to be online 24/7, unless you are going to block the calendar when you choose to be offline.

2. do I want to commit to be an amazing host?

To be a fantastic host, and therefore make fantastic money, you must have the hosting trifecta. Excellent communication skills + incredible cleaning team + a smooth check-in/check-out process for your guests. Responding to guest questions, concerns, and extra requests with speed, care, and detailed accuracy is essential, and making sure the guests have checked in without delay or frustration are important communication responsibilities. Lockboxes for check-in are a host's best friend. You will need cleaners that are reliable, make themselves available to you, have excellent attention to detail, and are able to follow your instructions.

3. do I have the time and finances to invest in this?

If you set up an Airbnb from scratch in an empty house, you have quite a task ahead of you. Depending on your budget, availability, and the team you have to assist you, it could take a month from start to finish. Buying all the supplies, furnishing the home, decorating, photographing, making your listing, and doing competition research to price your home accordingly, it is a long list of tasks.

In general, it will cost a minimum of $2,000-$10,000 to set up an Airbnb from scratch in the USA, I´m talking an empty house or apartment. It could be the first month's rent + security deposit, purchasing all the necessary items and furniture, paying workers to help move furniture and utility bills. Bedding alone can easily cost $500+. Be aware it could take a few months to make back your initial investment.

Suppose the market is good for Airbnb rentals in your area, and you have made the basic calculations of your expenses, time investment, financial investment, the achievable price per night, occupancy rate, and profit margin. In that case, you could have just started an amazing small business with plenty of room for growth. If the price per night and monthly income from your bookings will not cover your expenses, you need to re-think your new Airbnb project.

chapter 2
setting up your new space

how exciting!

You've found a space where the local government, owner, and/or landlord has given you permission to do Airbnb legally. Maybe you've just bought a new investment property or you'll be welcoming guests into your own home. Now it's time to set it up!

What is the vibe or feeling you want your space to have? What is your budget for all the supplies, furniture, and decorations? Do you have an SUV or truck for picking up furniture? With this information, you will develop a buying strategy for your new supplies.

what is a buying strategy?

It is the method of using retail shops and online forums to buy your supplies according to your timeline and budget. Ikea, Amazon, Craigslist, Wayfair.com, Overstock.com, second-hand shops/thrift stores, Big Lots, Home Goods, dollar stores, Goodwill, Marshalls, and Wal-Mart are great economical resources for furnishing your new Airbnb. Many of these recommendations are American over-stock retail stores, selling brand new, brand names for 40-60% less than department stores. You may have an equivalent available in your country.

What is your timeline and budget? Depending on your answer, you will buy things quicker for convenience or have more time to shop around for better prices and designs. Maybe you will need to hire someone and rent a truck for moving furniture, coordinating your furniture buying/moving on those days.

developing your buying strategy

Make a list of all the items you need to buy. You can reference the supply list I have provided in the following chapter to have an overview of everything you may need for each room. High-quality bedding can be purchased quickly through Amazon. For all other items, first, go to the stores you like best and buy the cooler, nicer, design items at an affordable cost. You can peruse second-hand shops, Home Goods, Big Lots, Marshalls, Ikea, etc for these items, or any discount retail store.

If you don't find what you love and what's affordable during these exploring trips, head over to Wal-Mart as your last stop to buy everything you couldn't find elsewhere. If you don't find it there, go back to Amazon for convenience and speed. An Amazon prime membership will come in handy throughout your hosting career if your in the USA.

purchasing furniture

There are many different places to buy furniture. Free Craigslist (a classified advertisement website), paid Craigslist, yard sales, Amazon, Alibaba.com, Ikea, thrift shops, second-hand furniture shops, Overstock.com, NextDoor App, Letgo.com, Goodwill, Offerup.com, any second-hand websites. Many items you can also buy new from discount stores like Wal-Mart or Big Lots.

assembling furniture

I resist furnishing the entire home with Ikea goods, as I don't have the patience for assembly and following the detailed instructions. I usually hire a friend to do it, but at $15+/hour, it takes my friends so long that I usually could have bought something I liked better with the money I paid for them to put it together. I created a job, this is positive, but Ikea furniture can be mega-intense if you are using it in the entire place. Keep assembly time in mind.

furniture positions

Move around your couch, carpets, chairs, dining table, coffee table, and armoires for best decorative value and spacious living. Try more than one set up, take photos and ask your friends what they think. If you have an aesthetically sensitive friend with good taste, invite them over and have them critique your furniture position ideas. Just because your friend, partner, or family member suggests a particular furniture set up, do what feels right to you. You can also view the photographs and make decisions based on how they look and feel. If you have the budget for an interior designer, I highly recommend hiring one.

decorating the space

The home décor areas of Ikea, Wal-Mart, Costco, Ross, Marshalls, Amazon, Home Goods, World Market, and your local dollar store are great places to find decorations. I like to use succulents or a few little cactus plants in a cute pot as they are low maintenance, candle sets (whi-ch is a controversial move due to the risk of fire), high-quality artificial plants in beautiful pots, little statues, colorful books, antiques, baskets, and rocks and shells. A decorative mirror in each room is a great way to fill up wall space and is easy to match to your furniture and artwork.

décor goals

When you look at the furniture you have, the location of your property and the amenities you offer, you can think about what your goals are for

VINCENT
LIVE
80° & SUNNY
LOS ANGELES
DIVAS
ALIENS
TRAVEL

the space. What are the best attributes and how can you enhance them? Do you have an awesome patio? Fill it with plants and a relaxing patio table and chairs, photograph it, and then highlight it in your listing as a zen morning coffee space or romantic evening wine table. Great view? You could highlight that in your featured photo and decorate the space around it. Mountain cabin? You can decorate your place to accent the marketable, unique features you have and let them shine.

theme

Is your home beach-y, neutral, family-friendly, clean and minimal, modern and elegant, bohemian, kitschy, eclectic, or a hotel-style, business friendly place? What kind of environment and experience do you want to create? What design and aesthetics do you want to have? Do you want to cater to business people, couples, large families, millennials? All these groups, or maybe 2 or 3? Setting goals and thinking about the style you want your space to have will guide your purchases along the way. Maybe you are on a very tight budget and will be using free or available second-hand furniture, no problem! See what you can piece together by buying artwork or decorative pillows to tie your odds and ends together.

feel

How do you want your space to feel? Cozy and homey, modern and chic, minimal and grey, colorful and artistic, relaxing and zen, spacious and neutral? You must ask yourself what is the feel of your home, as this will guide your purchasing, decorating and also help you to describe your space when you create your Airbnb listing.

artwork

Artwork can be a very expensive and a subjective topic. I always recommend one or two paintings in each room that work well together and a large decorative mirror on the other wall. I first buy artwork that goes with the furniture, then complementary decorative mirrors, and lastly, the items for coffee tables, counters, bedside tables, and bathroom vanities. I use mirrors between 1.5'-2.5' x 2'-3'. You can also hang it on top of a dresser for a vanity feel in the bedrooms. You can start to purchase your art and design items in any order, just know that at some point you'll need to tie it all together so it doesn't feel chaotic or random.

home décor items

There are many elegant, simple, and chic items you can place on coffee tables, bedside tables, kitchen shelves, bathroom shelves, to add a homey feeling and 'fill out' the space. Little statues, succulent plants, small boxes, picture frames with lovely nature photos, and used books are a few examples. In general, people choose Airbnb for the "home" feeling (also the kitchen!), so if your furnishing an empty place, be sure to start collecting knick-knacks, books, and fun carpets where you can.

Without home décor items, your place could feel barren and not lived in. I like to use upscale and tasteful artificial plants. They are not easy to find. You may find a lot of plastic, rubber-looking ones, which I don´t recommend. Buying inexpensive books at Goodwill, thrift stores or second-hand shops for fifty cents to $2 will fill up a bookshelf, coffee table, or bedroom shelves.

Goodwill, the Salvation Army, and second-hand shops are a great place to pick up inexpensive or unique decorative items for the home. You can also choose stylish and elegant pots for some house plants, just be sure to select plants that only need water once a week or less. It´s not a great idea to ask your guests to water the plants… they want to chill.

chapter 3
purchasing supplies

what kind of bedding should I purchase?

I suggest buying microfiber linens online. They resist stains, lint, and wrinkles. Wrinkles are a huge issue with bedding – you will not want to be paying your cleaner extra time to iron all your sheets and duvets. I buy mostly from Amazon, they have an incredible assortment of micro-fiber options, and in-store bedding can be much more expensive. I prefer to use medium shades as they show fewer stains and lint. Light colors will stain easily and you cannot bleach them, and dark colors will show lint dramatically. Practical, long-lasting color choices would be medium grey, medium blue, teal, and purple colors.

Your bedding choice is also going to depend on the level of luxury you are offering. If this is an expensive upscale listing, I recommend going with white, as it is the standard sign of a luxury hotel. But know your cleaner will need to bleach them regularly and you can expect to replace your bedding much more often due to stains. As a traveler, I prefer white, but as a host, it is the more expensive choice.

Heavy duty and ribbed towels are recommended, as your towels will be washed an incredible amount and little threads may come loose and pull, destroying the towel for future reservation. Ribbed towels hide these imperfections. I recommend stocking at least one extra towel for guests. For example, if you have four guests, provide five towels. You can also provide the same amount of towels every time, regardless of your guest count, to keep track of your bedding inventory easily. This will assist you in charging guests for missing towels, but know that most guests will use every towel you give them, so this choice will require more laundry time. If you live near a beach, river, lake, or other swimming areas, I suggest providing separate beach/outdoor towels, as your guests will take your bath towels there if you don't provide an alternative.

the stained bedding challenge

When your guest checks out, and you (or your cleaner) discover a stain, you will want to charge them the $40-$80 you spent on the sheet set. They may then retaliate by leaving you a 1-star review and/or detailing everything in their review that was not 100% perfect about their stay as a kind of revenge. It's even possible they lie in the review as a catharsis for their frustration of this unexpected extra fee.

Asking a guest for a 5-star review while simultaneously charging them $60 to replace your sheets from a small mascara stain is not ideal. There is a delicate, sensitive way to approach this, such as sending a photo and asking if they can pay the replacement, but then you won't want to suggest that they leave you a review. If this is your first, second or third guest and you are desperate for positive reviews to get the business going, I would suggest eating the cost in exchange for a potentially high-quality review!

kitchen supplies

There are quite a few essentials for the kitchen, but how stocked you want to be is up to you. You will need a decent quality set of pots and pans (they will quickly be destroyed if they are very low quality), cooking utensils, eating utensils, plates, bowls, and cups for a few extra people. For example, if you offer a space for three guests, you should have eating utensils for at least four to five people.

A microwave, coffee maker, dish soap, hand soap, trash bags, a clean sponge, knives, cutting board, cookie sheet, oven mitts, and cooking essentials like oil, salt, pepper, spices, coffee, powdered creamer, and sugar are the basics. Adding additional cooking supplies like a toaster, grater, and whisk are up to you. I like to fill out the kitchen the best I can, as many guests choose Airbnb instead of a hotel so they can cook. I recommend Ikea, dollar stores, Amazon, and Wal-Mart for these items.

bathroom supplies

A sparkling clean bathroom is so important for running a successful Airbnb. As there are very few items going into the bathroom, each one is very important. A decorative, refillable hand soap dispenser, good quality shampoo, conditioner, body wash, non-damaged bath mats, a mold-free shower curtain, and color-coordinated hand towels are the main items. A decorative item on the bathroom sink is a nice touch.

I like to use bath mats from Ikea. They have grey and beige options, among a few other colors. It is a soft, velvety shag mat, washes very easily with towels and is very durable and long-lasting. They make large and small rectangle sizes. The large size is called "Toftbo" and the small size is called "Badaren." If you choose to use bath mats with a rubber bottom, the rubber will deteriorate after a few laundry cycles and spread to your other bedding.

You can purchase large, pump-style shampoo and conditioner bottles at Costco (wholesale superstore) or online. We used Trésemme as it has a salon-style bottle, a decent reputation, comes in a large size and is affordable and available at Costco in bulk. Using a large, pump-style body wash is also a great option instead of giving a new bar soap to each guest which will be thrown away after their short stay at your place. You can also buy decorative, refillable pump bottles for your shampoos, label them, and then refill them as necessary.

To summarize, I like to have a colorful hand soap dispenser, a colorful hand towel and then neutral bath mats and neutral shower curtains. Having a super clean and decorative bathroom will add a lot of comfort to your guests, as we all enjoy relaxing in a clean shower. I recommend Ikea, Amazon, and Wal-Mart for these items.

cleaning supplies

Your method for purchasing cleaning supplies and stocking cleaning supplies is up to you, but it is recommended to have a set for your cleaners locked away in the supply closet, as well as some available for your guests. The basics would be a broom and dustpan, all-purpose cleaner, rubber gloves, glass cleaner, cleaning rags, a washable microfiber mop, and vacuum if you have carpets or not.

Guests will often use these supplies to clean up after themselves during long-term stays and before checking out because they also desire to receive a 5-star review from you. You could require your cleaners to bring their own supplies if you prefer not to stock lots of extra supplies. I use Mrs. Meyers's natural cleaners and advertise that I use non-toxic, chemical-free supplies where available. This is a personal choice and also a marketing tool for chemically-conscious guests and families. I recommend Wal-Mart, Amazon, and dollar stores for these items. Consider having a small vacuum for guests to use, and a larger one for you in your supply closet. Vacuums pick up a lot of hair, a super important thing to get rid of.

setting up a locked supply closet

You will need an area to designate as your locked 'supply closet.' Here you will store extra toilet paper, paper towels, dish soap refill bottles,

hand soap refill bottles, shampoos, conditioners, soaps, bedding sets, refill coffee, oil, salt, pepper, trash bags, cleaning supplies, kitchen sponges, pillows, air mattresses, and anything else you use to refill the supplies for your guests. I highly recommend choosing a closet, large cabinet, garage (if stored here, place all items in plastic bins with tight lids for protection), or storage area accessible only to the cleaning team.

If you do not lock this supply area, you can expect your guests to go through it, use whatever they like, and take some of it with them. Especially in American culture, traveling to a hotel or going on vacation puts us in the mindset of luxury and abundance, and we like to use all the towels we can and look through the cabinets for free extra things to enjoy. I use a lock with numbers/letters so any cleaner can access it without needing a key. It is also recommended to keep an extra set of clean bedding here, in case your bedding is damaged there is a clean, spare set on-site.

Set Up Supply Lists

This list is for homes with queen-size beds, a bathroom, kitchen, patio, BBQ area and a living room sleeping option like a pull-out couch, air mattress, folding bed or cot. Edit this list to fit your space!

living room furniture

Sleeper couch
Coffee table
Mirror, paintings
End tables
Lamps
Carpets
TV, cable, Roku, Netflix
TV stand

Air mattress
Folding bed or cot

bedroom furniture

Queen mattresses
Mattress protectors
Queen bed frames
Bedside tables
Lamps
Decorations, candles, plants, books
TV's
Mirrors, paintings, artwork
Hangers for closet
Dressers
Alarm clocks

general furniture

Dining table
Dining chairs
Desk
Desk chair
Desk ornaments
Carpets
Doormats
Patio furniture
BBQ
2 lockboxes
Ironing board
Iron
Twin-size folding bed
Large laundry bags
Laundry basket

Heaters
A/C units

decorations

Decorative candle sets
Artificial plants
Used books
Succulent and cactus plants
Paintings
Large mirrors
Real plants for the entrance, patio and house

kitchen supplies

Hot water kettle
Microwave
Coffee maker
Toaster
Wooden spoon, spatula, whisk, kitchen utensil set
Fork, spoon and knife set for 10 people
Knife and scissor block set
Ziplock bags, aluminum foil, saran wrap, wax paper
Mixing bowls
Dish drying rack
Cookie sheets and bakeware
Oven mits
Dishrags
Kitchen sponges
Dish soap
Dishwasher tabs
Large and small trash bags
Large coffee refill
Coffee

Powdered coffee creamer
White and brown sugar
Coffee filters
Cooking oils
Salt and pepper
Basic spice set
Set of 8-10 plates, cups, bowls, coffee cups, glasses, wine glasses
Wine bottle opener
BBQ grill, lighter fluid, long lighter, grill tongs, charcoal
Large dish soap refill
Tea
Large trash can
Placemats for table
Coasters

one bathroom

2 large shampoo, conditioner, body wash
1 bubble bath if you have a tub
Shower curtain
Shower curtain rings
Decorative refillable soap holder
Decorations, fake plants, statues, succulents, books
Toilet brush
Plunger
Small trash can
Hairdryer

cleaning supplies

Mop, I suggest washable microfiber
Bucket
All-purpose cleaners
Vacuum

Cleaning rags
Gloves
Glass cleaner
Spray bathroom cleaners
Broom and dustpan
Scrub brush/cleaning sponges
Large lint rollers
Laundry detergent

refill supplies

Toilet paper
Paper towels
Trash bags small and large
Coffee, oil, coffee filters, shampoos
Laundry detergent

linens for a queen 1 bedroom + twin bed + 1 bathroom

This list includes one extra bedding set, and one piece per item as a spare.

7-10 bath towels
4-6 hand towels
7 beach towels
3-5 bathmats
3-5 queen sheet sets
3 duvet covers
4 pillows
Extra blankets, throws for the couch, decorative pillows
7-9 washcloths
1 queen comforter
1 twin comforter
Twin bed linens, 2 twin sheets sets, 2 duvets, pillowcases

linens for queen 2 bedroom + queen pull out + twin bed + 2 bathrooms

This list includes one extra bedding set and one piece per item as a spare.

18-20 bath towels
8 hand towels
18 beach towels
5 bathmats
7 queen sheet sets, fitted sheet, flat sheet, 2 pillowcases
7 duvet covers that come with 2 pillowcases
8 pillows
Extra blankets, throws for the couch, alternative style blankets
Decorative pillows for the couch
18-20 washcloths
3 queen comforters
1 twin comforter
Twin bed linens, 2 twin sheets sets, 2 duvets, pillowcases

www.airbnb.com/r/Laurencoats
I WANT YOU
to get 40$ travel credit when you use Lauren's new host referral link

chapter 4
creating the listing

*If you are a brand-new host to Airbnb, you will get $40 in free travel credit when you use my new host referral link to create your first listing as a host! **www.airbnb.com/r/laurencoats**

photography

Hiring a professional or semi-professional photographer with a fisheye/ wide-angle lens is the best investment you will make for your Airbnb's success by far. Cell phones and regular digital SLR lenses do not capture the entire space in the photo. These photos can make a space look small, unattractive and unprofessional. Blurry or dimly lit photos will not get you the results you are working so hard for. Please do not underestimate the importance of this mandatory step for your success.

Achieving a highly-priced nightly rate for your rental is a direct reflection of the quality of your photos. New iPhones using the .05x setting will capture quite a bit of the space and produce high-quality images, although hiring a professional photographer with a wide-angle lens is still recommended.

When doing your photoshoot, make sure the home is super clean and that everything is staged and set up beautifully. The hand towels are folded nicely in the bathroom, duvet covers are on and stretched flat on the bed, the kitchen is clean and not cluttered, bathrooms are spotless and have something decorative or colorful (empty grey bathrooms don't feel very welcoming). Open all the windows or curtains, turn on every light, and do the photoshoot on a sunny day around mid-day. Doing it in the evening will not give your space a bright, warm feeling. Using a flash on your camera as the main method of illuminating your space is not recommended. Add some fruit on the kitchen table, a book on the coffee table, and small touches that stage the home to look lived in.

To find a photographer, you can put an ad online for a photo student or a real estate photographer to come with a wide-angle/fisheye lens. The cost to professionally photograph an Airbnb space is usually between $100-$350. The photographer will do the shoot and then a basic edit of the images for you. No need for studio lights as you'd like your photos to look realistic and accurate.

Airbnb also offers a professional photography service on their website in select areas where they have contracted photographers working with them. I have worked with one in Los Angeles, California, and had a positive experience. Airbnb's price is around $150-$350 depending on your homes size. You can get a free quote on their website for your listing, although from the time of the request for a photoshoot until they photograph it and load the images into your Airbnb listing, it could take 3-5 weeks.

photo editing

When selecting photos and uploading them onto your listing, you want to present the four strongest, most beautiful, most telling photos you have first. These are going to be the photos that people see when they are cruising Airbnb for potential homes. After those first four initial photos, you´ll want to give them a visual tour of the home. Start with the living room, the sunroom if you have one, the bedrooms, the kit-

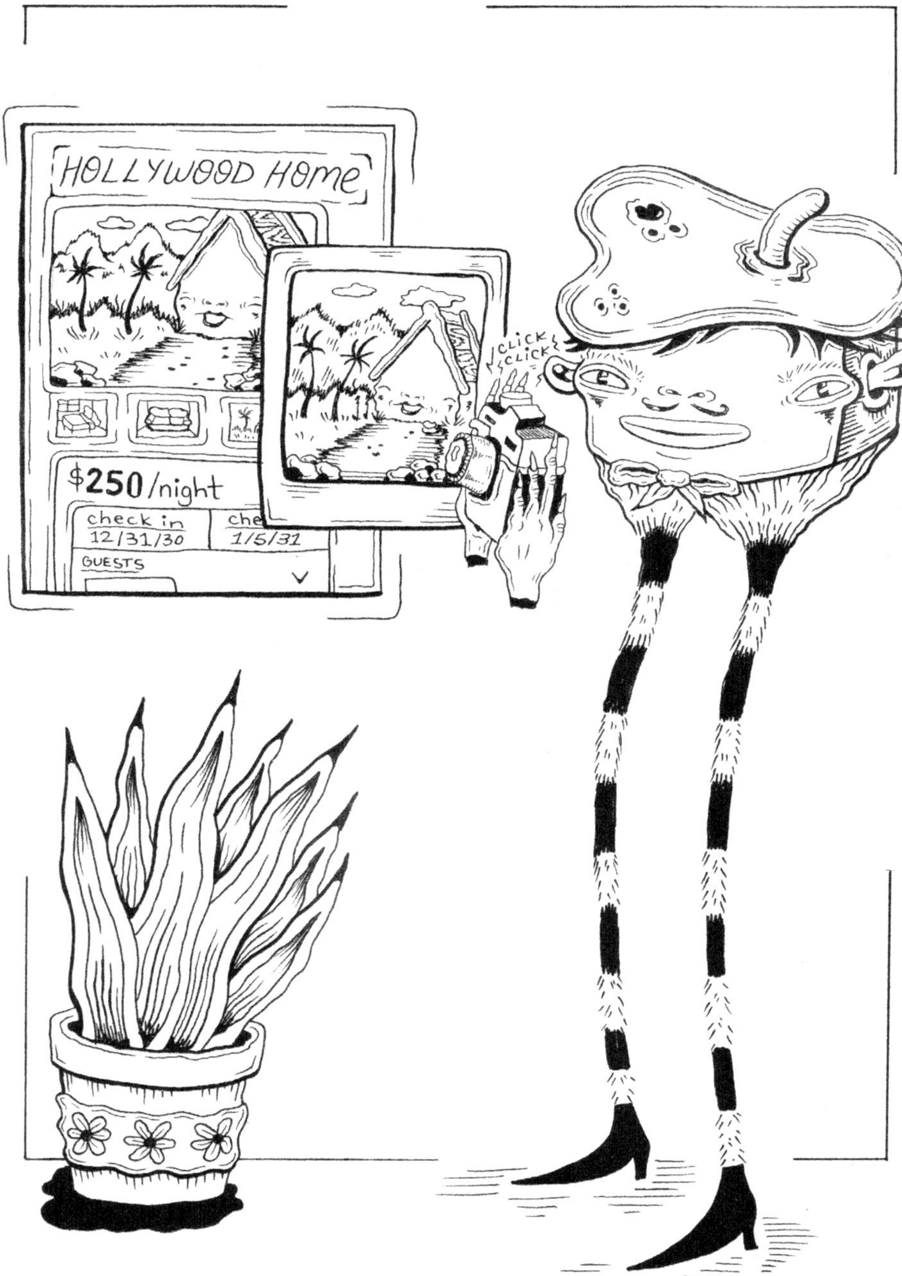
HOLLYWOOD HOME
$250/night
check in
12/31/30
che
1/5/31
GUESTS
CLICK
CLICK

chen, the bathroom, the outdoor/patio area, and then the exterior if you wish to show it.

Between 12-22 photos are all you need. Do not put more! If you have a massive property or mansion, you can extend this to 24-25 photos. If you put too many photos, especially repetitive photos of the same areas, you are declaring that you are an unprofessional host who is going to waste their time and provide an immature service. Your professional presentation here with a clear, well-lit, visual storytelling sequence of photos is sharing so much about your professional ability to take care of them as a guest. As they walk from room to room through your photo selection, their imagination is going to light up, the fantasy of what their experience could be will flood their veins, dopamine is released.... An emotional bond has been made. They will pay whatever it costs, they want your house!

title

The title for your Airbnb listing should accentuate its best qualities. Do you have an ocean view? Very easy – your title should shout Ocean View. A sought-after, popular local neighborhood? Put it in the title. Quiet and private, cozy and sunny, spacious, antique, or retro? Highlight the best amenities and unique features in your title. Airbnb's search results algorithm favors longer titles, so add a + sign and include "+ Huge Patio" or "+ High Ceilings" - write the longest title you can. Some hosts believe adding an emoji like a heart or star catches the eye and leads to more bookings. You can do experiments with your title formatting throughout the hosting journey and see what brings more inquiries.

My Airbnb's in Hollywood had every title start with "Hollywood" which was the hottest feature to sell. Location, vibe, stand-out qualities, amenities, major benefits (like quiet, large, cozy, comfortable), or even something unique you offer. You can try out more eccentric titles and see how it goes. You may want to appeal to the masses or a niche group, both are valuable strategies depending on your location. An important part of host marketing is doing experiments with your listing's design - trying different titles, descriptions, photo orders, etc. You may choose to change these a few times as to see what is attracting the most clicks.

copy

Write an inviting description about your place, highlighting the best aspects of your home, neighborhood, and its unique characteristics. Central location, near specific tourist attractions, peaceful and quiet or isolated, large and spacious, cozy or sunny, private or a busy area, any attractive adjectives and statements you can use to describe your place are welcome here.

In "The Space" area of the Airbnb listing, you can create a story about what it's like to stay at your home. "You enter into our large and spacious, cozy living room with a large wrap-around couch and a large flat-screen TV, great for enjoying a movie with friends. The open and fully stocked kitchen is great for preparing your family meals, and our sunny and beautifully decorated bedrooms have comfortable beds to relax in and have a peaceful rest." You describe the attribute first, then suggest the benefit, painting a picture of how the guest could enjoy it during their stay. This will, once again, spark their imagination, create a fantasy in their mind, and seal that emotional bond we are looking for to consistently bring in top dollar bookings. The more demand your rental receives, the higher your pricing can go!

interactions with guests

In this section of your listing, you can customize your hosting lifestyle by setting guest communication and host availability expectations. If you choose to be more hands-off, an example for this section of your listing would be, "My full-time job and family schedule keep me very busy. I will try to make myself available to you when needed, but I have other obligations as well." This may deter people from booking your place, which will hurt your occupancy rate, but at least you have correctly set the expectation. I say, "I am on Airbnb messenger a few times a day, but texts to my cell are the quickest way to reach me." Managing many properties without a co-host is a full-time job requiring you to constantly be online and available.

setting guest policies and the house rules

As the host, you will be designing your operating system and the guest experience. If you are managing the Airbnb property for a client/ homeowner, or simply creating rules for your own place, you will need to specify in your listing what your policies are. No noise after 10pm? Specific quiet hours? No parties, events, or pets? No late check-in? Late check-in allowed, but you will not be available to help them after 11pm if they have an issue? Clearly setting the policies will ensure your guests have correct expectations. As discussed in chapter 1, when guest expectations are not met, they are likely to leave bad reviews, which will cost you.

chapter 5
hosting 101

What am I going to be doing as a host? What are my responsibilities?

guest communications

This includes answering questions, confirming reservations, sending guests the house manual and instructions before their arrival, giving local dining and activity recommendations, and receiving phone calls and text messages.

monitoring the calendar

The calendar is one of my favorite places on the Airbnb App. When you have launched your properties online, you can see day by day who is checking in and who is checking out displayed as a daily feed. You can also click on each properties calendar, set your prices by night, view your payouts, message guests, stay up to date with your guest's arrivals and departures, adjust the pricing for vacant nights, and review your progress and success with occupancy rates.

managing cleanings

Discussed in detail in the following chapter, cleaning is a complicated

Our local favorite, Chez Paris, is to die for!

system if you have many rentals. Hiring and training excellent cleaners is your first step. From there, you will be creating their schedule. The date, name of the property, and guest count should be included so the cleaner knows how many guests to set up for, such as extra beds, towels, and bedding. Knowing the location of your cleaner's washer and dryer, as well as its speed per load, will help you manage it.

keeping track of the bedding inventory

Guests will sometimes destroy or steal a washcloth, hand towels, or bath towels. My cleaner always leaves the same number of towels so we know if some are missing, regardless of the guest count. I have her inspect the bedding while taking it off the bed, looking for stains due to oil, permanent marker, make-up, adhesive, or burn holes. Bedding is costly because you need a lot of it, so staying on top of the inventory is important. Otherwise, you will be paying out of pocket regularly to replace unseen, damaged, or missing bedding.

managing supplies, re-stocking, re-ordering

Depending on your space, you may have many supplies and materials to purchase regularly. Training your cleaners to alert you on re-stocking needs is a great plan. Buying toilet paper, paper towels, cleaning supplies, trash bags, and laundry detergent in bulk and then stocking it in the locked supply closet is recommended. You should be able to trust that your cleaner is not going to take supplies for themselves. You may also have to re-order bedding or furniture if things are damaged or broken. You could also have your supplies delivered to your cleaner's home, which they will bring with them the next time they clean.

managing expenses and recurring bills

You may be running an Airbnb for a property-owning client, at your own house, or in an apartment building. When setting up an Airbnb, the main expenses are the monthly rent, supplies, furniture, and then purchasing the recurring supplies. This can be an initial investment of anywhere from $500-$10,000 depending on your style, what you already have, and the property's rent/mortgage. Then you will need to pay for home repairs and the recurring expenses like utilities and guest supplies. Gas, electric, trash, internet, TV, Netflix, gardener, toilet paper, paper towels, laundry detergent, coffee, kitchen supplies, and cleaning supplies are your main recurring expenses.

organizing repairs

If your space is in an apartment building, this may involve calling the property manager or super to arrange a convenient time for both the handyman and the guest to make the repair. You may need to go on-site depending on the repair and the comfort level of your guests. If you are hosting a personally owned home or condo, you will need to curate a list of local, trustworthy, talented handymen and plumbers. Meeting, employing, training them on the units and where things are is vital for a self-sustaining Airbnb. If your handyman knows your place and can be trusted to have the extra lockbox code, it simplifies your job to call him and send him over (after checking with your guests first of course) to make quick, last-minute emergency repairs.

hiring gardeners and managing trash day

If you manage Airbnb's in personal homes, the grass and landscaping will need regular maintenance. If you are not cutting the grass yourself, you may need to hire a gardener to work independently, coming by every week or two weeks to tidy the yard. You may also choose to hire a neighbor, the gardener, or someone to stop by on trash days to put the cans in the street and bring them back in.

My gardener comes on the day the bins go to the street, and he does this for me. I then have my cleaner bring the bins back in on her next clean there. I write on her schedule which days she needs to bring the trash bins in, so she doesn't forget. If you find yourself in a bind, you can always ask your guests to take the bins out for you. I cannot recommend this, as most guests would prefer no maintenance responsibilities during their stay.

communicating with Airbnb customer service

You will probably experience a guest issue where you're unsure what to do or how to handle the situation. One great thing about Airbnb is the call center, you can chat with a live person 24/7 about your issues. These days, the standard Airbnb phone operator has limited knowledge.

If you are requesting something they say they cannot do, ask to be transferred to a 'case manager.' These are senior agents who know the website's details, rules and can go into a reservation, make necessary changes for you, or call your guest and get things done for you. The live support agent may deny your request to speak to a case manager, which is okay. You can always hang up and call back to get another agent who may have more knowledge and experience to assist you.

At the beginning of my Airbnb career, everyone I spoke to knew everything I asked. Since 2018, the company has grown tremendously, and I think they've hired a new fleet of less knowledgeable, scripted phone operators. I try to keep my patience as they claim things 'can't be done' or 'don't exist' – because I know they do, I've done it before.

Always be polite! This is your business, your cash flow, your daily bread, and the Airbnb customer service representative is the "boss," they have power over your business. Simply ask for a case manager, and be even more polite and grateful towards them. They can help you. Yelling at an Airbnb employee is a quick way not to get what you want.

managing resolution center claims

The 'resolution center' is where you or your guest can make a claim for some kind of payment or refund request related to an issue or complaint. You can view this section in your Airbnb App or on the website. As a host, you are responsible for addressing your guest's claims and complaints here and also publishing your own damage reports and requests for additional payments.

making damage reports

If your place is damaged in any way, you will want to immediately upload photos of the damage and make a claim in the Airbnb resolution center. This must be done by the main host's account/the admin account, as a co-host cannot request or send money. If you are not the admin and cannot reach your main host or do not have their log-in details to immediately report it yourself through their account, call Airbnb customer service to alert them of the damage.

In the past, it was required to report and claim damage before the next guest arrived. This could be 3 pm the same day, and maybe you received photos from your cleaner of the damage at noon. You were on a three-hour time race to contact the necessary parties and claim the damage before it was too late. Airbnb wanted to make the correct guest responsible, to be done before another guest checks in.

Nowadays with 'aircover,' Airbnb's new, free insurance policy, they say that hosts have 14 days to make a claim. I have not tested this new policy, but as a general rule, the sooner you make the damage claim and provide evidence, the smoother your claim is likely to be. It doesn't make much sense to claim something 10 days later when you've already had 3 more guests stay at the property. How can you really prove who it was?

upgrading the space

After you've had your Airbnb for a while, you may receive valuable guest feedback or raise enough funds to take your space to the next level of luxury or comfort. You may want to add a fantastic BBQ and patio furniture set, get new art for the walls, add decorative chairs or carpets, or get more upscale bedding. There are endless possibilities for upgrading. You will also want to photograph the upgrades immediately, post them on your listing, and up your pricing accordingly!

use 'insights' to adjust your marketing techniques

Airbnb has added a section called 'insights' on your dashboard. As you begin your hosting career, this is where you are going to be able to do an in-depth review and evaluation of your business. Here you will find tabs such as performance evaluator, opportunities, quality, occupancy and rates, conversion stats, earning stats (income), Super Host evaluation and requirements, as well as a very detailed cleaning section for guidance on keeping your place tip top.

Using this information, you'll be inspired to convert more visitors to guests, see how often you appear in search results (which is an expression of how well you are doing in the Airbnb algorithm), and understand your performance over the past months. Don't get too hung up as a newbie, just keep being an awesome host, keeping your place clean and organized, and communicating in a timely fashion with good vibes. A good product and service will begin to shine and really pull in 5-star reviews over time.

chapter 6
vip communication techniques

pre-written quick reply messages

In the "quick replies" message area of the Airbnb App for hosts or desktop browser window, you can pre-write any helpful messages that you send all the time. I love this feature and highly recommend the time investment for writing informative, caring, clear, and universal messages to improve your speed, thoroughness, and communication capabilities with your guests.

This could be directions, parking instructions, the local coffee shop or breakfast joint recommendation, the wifi details, your early check-in policy, check-out protocol, asking for a 5-star review, you name it! Especially if you have more than one Airbnb, you are going to get tired of typing the same things over and over from scratch constantly. Go for a hike or spend some time petting your dog instead of madly poking away at your cell phone the wifi username and password…again!

for example...

I often get early check-in requests, but my cleaning team needs about 3 hours to clean, so the earliest check-in I offer is 2 pm instead of 3 pm. I have a pre-written, quick reply message I send to my guests when they request an early check-in. "Hello! I'm so sorry, my cleaning team will not have the apartment ready until 2 pm at the earliest. When they finish, I will contact you right away so you can check in. Feel free to come by and drop your luggage off any time after 11:30 am. Just be sure to leave the keys in the lockbox so the cleaners can enter. Thanks!"

The same goes for review requests. "Hey! I hope you had a great stay at my place! Would you be up leaving a review about your experience? I will also leave a 5-star for you right now! Thanks!" You can also send a pre-written message when checking on your guests, "Hey! How is your stay going?" or when your guest makes a reservation, "We will be very happy to host you, thanks for booking with us! I'll send more details about check-in and parking details closer to the date. Thanks!" With a touch of a few buttons, you can automate your common responses. I recommend you take the time to write these so they sound personal from you, not robotic or cold, automatic or absent of sentiment.

hands-off hosting

You can create an electronic guidebook, local guide binder and house manual that will do your job for you. Compile a list of all the best local grocery stores, restaurants, activities, and nearby shopping centers and put it in a word document. Assemble all the house instructions like how to use the TV and thermostat, where the towels and alarm clocks are, or how to use the BBQ. Your guests can then be pretty self-sufficient and don't need to bother you for this information. They will be grateful to have the information at their fingertips and you will have more free time.

house manual

The house manual is a pre-written message that you send to your guests as instructions for their stay. I like to send it approximately 7-14 days before their arrival, but you could send it 3 days before if you prefer.

Some guests get nervous if they have not received it a week in advance, and some will not check it until the day of arrival. The address, lockbox code, parking instructions, location of extra bedding/towels, how to use the TV or coffee maker, how to change the temperature, the wifi details, where to find the alarm clocks, and details about the laundry machines if needed are common things to explain in your house manual. You can also request information from them, like their estimated check-in/check-out times. It's worth investing the time to make a thorough house manual as it will dramatically reduce the number of questions you need to answer while your guests are staying.

for example...

You have not included TV instructions in your house manual, and you have an elderly couple staying in your place, desperate for the nightly news. You may have to give them a tutorial on the phone for half an hour, only to head over in person to get the TV on for them. If you wrote detailed TV instructions in your house manual, you can kindly refer them to the manual for the instructions, and let them know if they still have questions or concerns to contact you right away and you will do your best to sort out the problem for them as soon as possible.

The same goes for any details or questions the guest is asking for. Where do I park? Where is the lockbox? I can't find it. Any and all guest questions can be covered and soothed with a detailed house manual.

The pre-written house manual is available in the "quick replies" area of your message center, simply click on a guest message in your inbox and you will see an icon that looks like pieces of paper with lines/text on it. Click on this, and you will find your library of "quick replies," pre-written messages and responses, and the option to edit or create new messages. You will also include a copy of this in the back of your "local guide" binder, or display this information interactively with a Hostfully electronic guidebook (more details on that later).

House Manual Example

Hey! Here is some helpful information for your stay.

LOCATION
The address is xx Avenue, xx, xx. The lockbox code is xxx, and it is on the front gate to the right of the pedestrian gate entrance. When you leave, please lock the doors and return the keys to the lockbox.

INTERNET
The internet network name is Welcome and the password is Freedom144

LAUNDRY
You will see the laundry machines on the back patio in the left corner. If you'd like to use them, there is laundry soap under the kitchen sink.

COFFEE
You will find ground coffee with a pour-over, pour-over filters, sugar, and powdered creamer to the left of the microwave. There is also instant coffee and a traditional coffee maker.

YOGA STUDIO
Walk around to the back of the house near the outdoor dining table and you will find the shaded yoga area.

PARKING
I'm very sorry, but there is only street parking. Please do not park in the driveway as that is only for the neighboring tenants.

ELECTRONICS
The TV can be turned on with the large remote, be sure it is in HDMI 2 input mode. The small remote controls the Roku, where you can find

Netflix and many other entertainment channels.

The thermostat can be found in the hallway near the kitchen door entrance. Here you can adjust the central air to the temperature.
We have an outdoor stereo system. You will find the controller outside on the patio to the left of the patio door. Bluetooth your phone or use the auxiliary cord to play tunes in the backyard.

CHECK-IN/AMENITIES
Check-in is after 3 pm and check-out is by 11am. If you already know around what time you will be checking in and out, please send me a message and let me know. I can coordinate early check in's and late check out's for you and other guests with this information!

Extra blankets, pillows and towels are in the hallway linen closet. The black garbage cans (in the driveway) are for regular garbage. Recycling goes in the blue can.

THANK YOU!
If you have any issues or concerns during your stay, please contact me immediately. I am a dedicated host and want to ensure you have a wonderful holiday and experience.

I'm on Airbnb messenger a few times a day, but texts/calls to xxx-xxx--xxxx is the best way to get an immediate response.

Enjoy your stay! Lauren

Hostfully's free electronic guidebook

There is a new and outstanding, free electronic guidebook software platform available for Airbnb hosts by a company called Hostfully. If you have ever traveled with a Lonely Planet guidebook, you'll know how incredible it is to have a guidebook with multiple categories when visiting a new city, highlighting popular trendy restaurants, activities, convenience services, and more.

Hostfully offers one free electronic guidebook for hosts and offers affordable rates for hosts wishing to create more than one guidebook ($4-$10 monthly subscription fee per guidebook). Google automatically populates each recommendation's data, so you can quickly add your favorite local restaurants, shops, activities, local experiences, parks, sightseeing, even holistic suggestions like yoga studios, spas, or healing centers.

Guests can click the guidebook links, start navigation to the destination, call the business, or go to their website directly within the guidebook. It is very interactive, fluid, and completely integrated with a smart phone. It also has a map feature, which allows guests to create an itinerary based on your suggestions and by location.

The software is very easy to use. Simply go to Hostfully.com and sign up for one free guidebook, or choose a plan for how many guidebooks you would like to create. You then populate the guidebook with your Airbnb rentals address, photo, check-in information, your contact details, and select from their menu of guest check-out instructions (turn off all the lights, lock the door, leave the keys in the lockbox, etc).

Then, you will enter your favorite local suggestions by category. If your suggestion has registered their business with Google, all of the information will automatically populate, such as photos, the address, phone number, website, operation hours, etc. You can also choose their 'wizard' function which will populate all this information for you. Chosen by AI, it may not be the places you would recommend, so I prefer to do it manually.

There is also an area to create instructional cards for your amenities. For example, you can fill in the instructions for using the washing machine,

Mom's
BAKERY
Local Stores
Bakery-867-5309
COFFEE-330-8004
Museums
MOMA-882-4431
KIDS-992-5581
CHEZ Paris
Restaurants
ChezParis-311-2211
ITALIAN-835-1113
Local Parks
CENTRAL-223 MAIN ST
SUNSET-85 B'WAY

dishwasher, thermostat, the location of the first aid kit, laundry closet, the location of the cleaning supplies, and how to use the TV. All the information and instructions a guest could ever want is available at their fingertips, on-demand. I'm all about it!

automatic your customer service

I made an electronic guidebook for my Airbnb in less than 3 hours, and I made an extensive list of suggestions. As Hostfully has integrated with Google directly, I saved so many hours of research. The best benefit of making an electronic guidebook is that it allows for "hands-off hosting." This means that once you set up this automated tool, you have eliminated 90% of your guest's questions.

As my guidebook has all my local suggestions, as well as all of the check-in/check-out details, the wifi details, lockbox code, instructions for how to use the A/C, etc, my guests never need to call or write me for information. They have everything they need to maximize their time in the local area and use the house with ease. This is a 5-star experience.

Creating an electronic guidebook may sound like a daunting task, but trust me, this is the second wisest investment you will make for your business, just behind professional photography. Let's say you are managing eight apartments, and each guest asks you around three standard questions per day. That's thirty-two questions.

The real treat of having an electronic guidebook is the amount of incredible 5-star reviews you will get. Guests will be overjoyed having all this information at their fingertips, as it really gives them the chance to explore the local area confidently, guided by your local expertise. You'll be sure to receive deep gratitude, as this local resource will totally change their experience.

let it work *for* you

Better reviews = higher-priced bookings = a more profitable business. Meanwhile, you're busy with your hands-off hosting lifestyle. Once you have a local team of maids, handymen, and two trusted contacts who can address emergencies on-site, you're ready to go remote, traveling the world, or your country, as a remote Airbnb host!

The guidebook also has more advanced features like selling late check--outs, experiences, or optional items directly through the guidebook's Marketplace area. You'll link your bank account and guests can purchase things from you directly, outside of Airbnb. If you own a local tourism company or want to partner with local businesses, you can sell their services and take a commission for advertising them. You can also have guests sign documents, agree to rules, provide their passport number and other rental related business functions.

3 formats – link, book and QR

Instead of sending your guests a pre-written house manual, you'll send them a link to your guidebook or they can use the QR code. Hostfully also offers a PDF version, so once your guidebook is complete, you can print it out and have it available in book format for your guests to enjoy while relaxing in the home. The guest does not need an App to use it, it's simply a link that opens in their internet browser.

location guide and binder

This is a binder or booklet you keep on the living room coffee table for your Airbnb guests to use as a local resource. It has a list of all the close by and walking distance attractions, the local grocery stores, and the popular, highly recommended, amazing dining options around. I recommend taking the time to create a Hostfully electronic guidebook and printing the PDF version to keep in the home for guests, but if you prefer to make a recommendation list manually instead, find my tips below!

If I'm not a long-time local in the area, I type in the property's location on Google Maps and search 'food' and then "popular." Here, you will find all the popular local eateries. I then assemble these tips into a word document, organizing them by categories (fast, casual, fine-dining, coffee, etc.) and write a short description, the address, the distance from the house, and the phone number. You can also do this with attractions, surfboard rentals, the library, hot air ballooning, popular tourist streets and neighborhoods, or shopping areas. The more, the merrier! Guests will instantly feel how much you care about their trip and comfort.

If you are a true local to the neighborhood, compile an extensive guide for them! It can easily make their trip 100 times more special. This will also assist your mission of getting amazing, 5-star reviews. On the last page of this binder, include a version of the house manual with instructions on how to use everything in the house.

When a guest writes you with a question that you have answered in your binder, you can kindly reply, "Hello! Please check the last page of the local guide binder on the coffee table near the television. We have detailed instructions written there for your convenience. Please let me know if you have any additional questions or concerns with it. Thanks!" You have saved yourself an extensive tutorial with your guest on how to do something in the home.

Hollywood Local Guide

Enter your address here

Grocery Stores

PAVILIONS

*slightly more expensive than the average grocery store.
Supermarket chain with standard groceries plus deli items.
Organic products · Produce, Sushi
727 N Vine St, Los Angeles, CA 90038
local.pavilions.com
(323) 461-4167

RALPHS

*average grocery store.
Standard Grocery Store · Produce, Meats
1233 N La Brea Ave, West Hollywood, CA 90038
ralphs.com
(323) 876-8790

SPROUTS

*upscale, health food, organic, vegetarian-friendly.
Specialty grocery store chain.
915 N La Brea Ave, Los Angeles, CA 90038
sprouts.com
(323) 217-1642

TRADER JOE'S

*tropical-themed, healthy grocery store with unique items.
Grocery chain with a variety of organics, dairy, wine & beer.
7310 Santa Monica Blvd, West Hollywood, CA 90046
traderjoes.com
(323) 969-8048

Coffee Shops

STIR CRAZY COFFEE SHOP
Coffee spot with local art, sandwiches, pastries, & free Wi-Fi.
Quick bite · Fast service · Hip
6903 Melrose Ave, Los Angeles, CA 90038
(323) 934-4656

STARBUCKS
Coffeehouse chain known for its roasts, snacks, & free Wi-Fi.
Quick bite · Fast service · Hip
859 N Highland Ave, Los Angeles, CA 90038
starbucks.com
(323) 493-1868

Bakery

DELICIOUS COOKIES AND MILK
Unassuming bakery known for its specialty cookies.
829 N Highland Ave, Los Angeles, CA 90038
delusciouscookies.com
(323) 460-2370

Gourmet Sandwiches

MENDOCINO FARMS
Creative sandwiches, soups, salads, & seasonal ingredients.
Comfort food · Quick bite · Healthy options
7100 Santa Monica Blvd #195, West Hollywood, CA 90046
Located in: West Hollywood Gateway
mendocinofarms.com
(323) 512-2700

Café's

CALIFORNIA CHICKEN CAFE
Menu of rotisserie chicken, wraps and salads plus sides.
Comfort food · Quick bite · Fast service
6805 Melrose Ave, Los Angeles, CA 90038
(323) 935-5877

CAFÉ GRATITUDE LARCHMONT
Vegan organic fare and smoothies, hippie-inspired names.
Comfort food · Small plates · Quick bite
639 N Larchmont Blvd, Los Angeles, CA 90004
cafegratitude.com
(323) 580-6383

BLU JAM CAFÉ
American cafe for Euro-accented breakfast served all day.
Comfort food · Healthy options · Hip
7371 Melrose Ave, Los Angeles, CA 90046
(323) 951-9191

Pizza

PIZZERIA MOZZA
*Popular and well-known gourmet pizza restaurant.
Acclaimed wood-burning-oven pizzas & antipasti in busy digs.
Late-night food · Comfort food · Small plates
641 N Highland Ave, Los Angeles, CA 90036
la.pizzeriamozza.com // (323) 297-0101

Restaurants

GRUB
Quirky brunch & American comfort fare served in a 1920s bungalow.

Comfort food · Quick bite · Hip
911 Seward St, Los Angeles, CA 90038
grub-la.com
(323) 461-3663

LALA'S ARGENTINIAN GRILL
Argentine-style meats, salads and pastas with ambience.
Late-night food · Happy hour drinks · Comfort food
7229 Melrose Ave, Los Angeles, CA 90046
lalasgrillonline.com
(323) 934-6838

THE CAT AND THE FIDDLE RESTAURANT AND PUB
Classic pub grub in a punk rock-influenced British bar.
Happy hour food · Late-night food · Happy hour drinks
742 N Highland Ave, Los Angeles, CA 90038
thecatandfiddle.com
(323) 468-3800

PETIT TROIS
Cozy spot with Parisian fare & full bar.
Late-night food · Comfort food · Small plates
718 N Highland Ave, Los Angeles, CA 90038
(323) 468-8916

Quick Bites

TA-EEM GRILL
*Great Kosher Mediterranean food, plates are enough for two.
Offers buffet style falafel, shawarma and glatt kosher dishes.
Late-night food · Small plates · Quick bite
7422 Melrose Ave, Los Angeles, CA 90046
ta-eemgrillinc.com
(323) 944-0013

PINKS HOT DOGS
*Can be quick or a long wait – iconic LA hot dog stand.
Creatively topped dogs draw long lines at this roadside spot.
Late-night food · Comfort food · Quick bite
709 N La Brea Ave, Los Angeles, CA 90038
pinkshollywood.com // (323) 931-4223

Upscale Dining

PROVIDENCE
Chef Michael Cimarusti's fine dining with innovative dishes.
Hip · Quiet · Great dessert
5955 Melrose Ave, Los Angeles, CA 90038
(323) 460-4170

RAO'S HOLLYWOOD
Replica of the New York eatery, upscale homestyle Italian fare.
Comfort food · Hip · Great dessert
1006 Seward St, Los Angeles, CA 90038
raosrestaurants.com
(323) 962-7267

House Manual and Practical Information

TV Instructions

The TV can be turned on with the large remote, be sure it is in HDMI 2 input mode. The small remote controls Roku and Netflix.

Thermostat Information

The thermostat can be found in the hallway near the kitchen door entrance. Here you can adjust the central air temperature.

Internet
Network Name: Welcome
Password: Freedom144

Alarm Clocks
Alarm clocks are available in the top drawer of the dressers.

Bath Towels, Extra Bedding, Twin Folding Bed
There are bath towels, extra blankets, and pillows in the linen closet at the end of the hallway. There is a twin-sized folding bed in the dining room closet with clean bedding next to it on the shelf. Feel free to set it up wherever you like, in the living room or one of the bedrooms.

Outdoor Yoga Studio
Walk around to the back of the house near the outdoor dining table, and you will find the shaded yoga area.

Trash Cans
The black garbage cans are for regular garbage, blue is for recycling.

chapter 7

I need a break! co-hosts

Do you feel ready to take some time off the App? Don´t want to answer another question or critique your maid's work until you have a little me-time? The 24/7 life eating you up inside? Let´s prep a proficient co-host to take some weight off your shoulders.

how to depend on a co-host

Now that you have your property all set up, it's time to train some friends, dependable employees, co-workers, or a backup person in the event you are unavailable to do your hosting duties or have an emergency. The co-host should know everything about the properties and the system you have created. For example, where the supply closet is, what goes inside, who are the cleaners, what are their schedules for this month and contact information, what does the listing say and promise to the guests? Which handyman should they call for which repairs, how to use the lockboxes, the location of the emergency backup lockbox, where and what is the bedding, how are the beds made and where do the towels go? They should also be trained on how to clean the apartment themselves if there is a cleaner issue and there are no cleaners available.

You can also train them on the Airbnb App. What is the inbox/messaging system, how does the calendar work, what is your average pricing, how to write messages or use quick replies, how to make a claim, and how to accept reservation alterations.

This is a lot of information, so you may want to make a reference manual for your co-hosts so they know what to do and what to say in the event of an issue. Sometimes I ask friends to cover for me by taking phone calls, and I alert my guests of the temporary change via Airbnb messenger. "Hello! I am going hiking on Tuesday and Wednesday and may be in an out-of-service area. If you have any pressing concerns, please call my local co-host Tom at ## and he will assist you. I'll be back online on Thursday! Thanks so much, and sorry for the inconvenience. Can you confirm that you've seen this message? Best, Lauren."

It is important to confirm that the guest has received the message. Otherwise, they may be calling you over and over while you are offline, and when you return online there is a disturbing situation. They didn't see your message that they should have called Tom! Some guests are not tech-savvy, new to the platform, or simply don't read all the information you share with them.

Once you have confirmed with your guests that Tom will be temporarily taking care of them, Tom should check the App every so often, accept/decline guest reservations, address any guest messages that look urgent/emergency, and then take phone calls if guests have immediate issues. A lot of messages could wait 48 hours until you are back online. You can even ask Tom to write to your guests, "Hi! Lauren is hiking, and I am covering for her until Thursday. I'm not sure the answer to your question, but I will have her get back to you right away Thursday morning! Sorry for the inconvenience! Best, Tom."

check-in days

You may not want to go offline if you have check-in and check-outs on these days, as there are many variables for your substitute-host Tom to

Good Morning!
LAUREN IS AWAY FOR THE DAY. MY NAME IS TOM AND I WILL BE HAPPY TO HELP!

handle. For example, something is broken, the guest arrived early and didn't tell anyone and they need to be politely asked to leave and come back later, something is lost or a damage claim needs to be filed, bedding is missing and the cleaners don't have extra so new bedding needs to be immediately purchased, etc. Tom may not remember, know what to do or who to contact, and it could be a mess for your guests checking in. He would also have to be on top of the cleaners, making sure they showed up and set up the house correctly, or go and clean himself if they didn't show up.

With reservation requests, you have 24 hours to respond, or you are penalized in your "response rate" score and your Super Host status is threatened. So technically, you can go offline for 23 hours without incurring a penalty for being an unresponsive Host. Another option is to train Tom to peek into the inbox every 23 hours and accept/decline requests based on your guest policies. For example, a potential guest has made a request and wants to have a birthday party at your place, but you say on your listing no parties or events. Tom would have to decline that for you.

I mostly do Instant Booking and accept most inquiries unless there is a red flag in their message or in their reviews. I am able to do this because I host pretty basic, cute apartments that are set up just for Airbnb guests. They are not my personal home, are not filled with my personal sentimental furniture, and they are not luxury spaces. If any of these conditions apply to you, you can check the potential guest out by reading through all their reviews and asking them personal questions like why are they coming and what are their planned local activities. You can ask them whatever you like within reason to feel more comfortable with their reservation and to confirm that they are not going having a party. Be aware that the more invasive your questioning, the less likely they will want to book with you. Privacy is epic with Airbnb guests, as a lot of them are already skeptical about your professionality and quality of service compared to a hotel.

Accepting guest reservations is completely up to you, and you should be comfortable and personally confident about each new guest you approve to host. This will vary greatly depending on the quality and value of your home. For example, your place is a luxury Malibu beach house with $100,000 worth of furnishings. With such an investment, you'll want to screen your guests much more in-depth than if you are offering a riverside campsite for $25/night.

keep in mind..

It is crucial to have someone with extensive knowledge of your rentals and protocols if you want to go offline or be hands-off regularly. I've managed many Airbnb units, all owned by different clients, and each rentals protocol was unique. Therefore, it was very challenging for me to train someone on every detail of my client's sensitivities, preferences, expectations, pet peeves, and the specific protocol for each guest issue or repair.

My strategy is to go offline for 23 hours at a time when I have no check-outs/check-ins and pay my co-host Tom $20 an hour to take phone calls and handle pressing guest issues while I'm out of the picture. I don't ask him to go into my Airbnb App or messenger, I handle that every 23 hours, but let him do the on-site, emergency tasks for my guests via receiving phone calls. I personally find it more stressful to trust Tom to do everything correctly while I'm offline and risk him making a wrong move, which could cause me to lose my clients or get a bad review from a frustrated guest.

I personally choose to alert my guests to call Tom with emergencies and check my Airbnb messenger every 23 hours. I am a one-man show except for my cleaners and handymen, but there may be an easy way in your business structure to share the reigns with another so you can disconnect in a stress-free way. You will have to over-communicate to make sure the other is always up to date. If you are the property owner, you can relax much more, as you don't need to worry about losing your clients, just losing future guests to a bad review that was left because your co-host Tom made a wrong move.

Note that this is my personal opinion and choice while managing six or seven Airbnb rentals at once. If you have 2 or 3, especially if you are the property owner, depending on a co-host may be much easier. I highly recommend training at least one trusted friend or loved one on the details of your business, you never know when you are going to need back up.

Another great option would be having a business partner and manage everything together. You'll be splitting the profit, but you'll have flexibility in your personal life to take vacations, attend social events out of town, turn your phone off for more than 23 hours, or simply focus on other passions.

chapter 8

how to set the pricing

step 1: competition research

It's time to check out your local competition and see how you can maximize your listing to compete and succeed.

The first step will be to look for rentals and listings in your area that are similar in guest count, amenities, space, and comfort. Type in your neighborhood or city into Airbnb's "traveling" platform. Here you will enter your guest count, home type, how many beds, your amenities, facilities, neighborhood, and I would slide the price filter down to under $300 if applicable, as you don't want to search through the luxury mansion versions of your guest count. Do not fill in specific dates as you will not be able to see all the available listings around you.

After filling in the filters, click search and see what places come up. You can also view the map version to check out your neighbors' listings. Takes some notes about what they are charging, how many are rentals are available, what amenities they don't have that you have, etc. Next, do this search with only your guest count, so you can see the wider range of competition in your area.

Depending on your location, many listings will come up, and you can now review their marketing copy. How do they highlight the nei-

$425
$275
$2,000
$195
$300
$1,125

ghborhood? Go through their listing and see how they describe the benefits of the location, take notes and use these insights to highlight your location on your listing.

Some listings will appear to be luxurious versions of your place and some under furnished or unattractive. You will want to check out the listings that offer the same number of bedrooms, bed count, and amenities. Check what amenities they offer, read their reviews, and learn what's going on with your competition. For example, a review like: "It's so messed up there is no map to the bus stop, it's so hard to find!"

If you are also advising your guests to use that bus line, have a map in your home for guests to reference. You can learn a lot about what guests want and need by looking at your competition's reviews. Suppose your competition has a glorious backyard and personal laundry room, and you are offering an apartment with no yard and no laundry facilities. In that case, you may reduce the price of your place. By checking on your neighbors, you can evaluate the market around you.

Then you will want to check out your competition's calendar by clicking "check availability." Here you will see how they manage their pricing. By moving your cursor over the calendar's available days, you can see how the nightly prices differ. Informed hosts will fluctuate their pricing for weekends, weekdays, holidays, and local events. Have the Super Bowl around the corner from you? Double or triple the price of those nights. You will see that your local competition is adjusting and changing their nightly price based on season, month, day, holidays, and the local events calendar.

After reviewing the listings close to you that have similar amenities, you can choose to price your place lower to win over new reservations, in the same range, or slightly higher and glam up your listing with high-quality photos and décor to outshine the local option. You can gain inspiration by studying the listings around you that are succeeding. Success can be evaluated by high review scores, positive written reviews, and a fully booked calendar. Note that some people live in their space part-time, so their availability may not accurately reflect their success. Look at what these hosts are doing on their listing, what guests are asking for, and what you could provide that they can't. What is the niche you can fill?

the airbnb smart pricing feature

This is an optional feature and algorithm of Airbnb that will automatically set or show a suggested price for your listing based on similar listings around you, the amenities you offer, your ratings/review scores, and the supply/demand for each date. If you are the last listing available and ten people are searching, the price will automatically go up because there is no supply and lots of demand. If there is no one searching your area for a few days, Airbnb will drop it to the lowest minimum price you have specified to try to attract bookings for you.

I look to smart pricing for insight into supply and demand but don't use it often or live by it, as its suggestions are not reliable. If you choose to use it, you'll need to set minimum and maximum amounts, as sometimes it will suggest $42/night, and sometimes $188/night for the same home. It is a computer recommendation, so it may not factor in your incredible decorations or your place's special feeling. It gives a rough market value for your space based on demand.

When in your "calendar" you can click on a series of days and then click on "see price tips" located under the smart pricing box. Here you will see what they are recommending for each day. If you set the price within 5% of their recommendation, they claim to advertise your listing more and that you are more likely to get booked. Sometimes it is way too low or high for my comfort, so I choose my prices based on my knowledge of the price points that have gotten me booked quickly in the past, and the price points I set that didn't attract anyone.

AirDNA

This is an independent, online data portal of all Airbnb and VRBO (HomeAway) vacation rentals in your area. This will give priceless insight into the pricing trends of your local market. AirDNA typically charges $40 for access to your area's data for a month. You will see the top percentile and lower percentile ranges of all comparable listings in categories such as occupancy rate, price per night, and general market trends of your area's vacation rentals. It has filter options for finding comparable homes, such as three bedroom/two bath, etc. I highly recommend signing up for a one-month subscription. You can review this data and find out what the top, mid-range, and lowest comparable rentals are receiving per night, as well as how fully booked they have been over the last few seasons.

Remember, the prices shown on AirDNA include the cleaning fee, so you will need to calculate a slightly lower rate unless you do not charge a cleaning fee and you include cleaning for free in your nightly rate. If you are looking to buy a property to invest in and set up as a vacation rental, AirDNA also offers services for researching that. This is a top-notch, professional tool for dedicated, serious, and thorough hosts who seek to be successful long-term. The data is presented in a visually compelling way with graphs and charts, and very easy to use and understand, I love it. Visit them at www.airdna.co

pricing experiments

Pricing is a game and flow of experimentation. You'll get personal experience with which rates quickly attract renters, which seasons require lower prices, and have a better understanding of your local market by regularly checking in with smart pricing suggestions. I review my calendar to change my pricing twice a week, seeing which days were booked and what gaps/available windows those bookings created, and I adjust my pricing accordingly. For example, I receive a new booking that creates a one-night availability on each side. Because I have a high cleaning fee, I will dramatically lower the price of those two nights, to help them get booked and still be affordable.

my beginning price, why so low?

Pricing is an intricate game that you will catch onto with time. For your first week/weeks of rental, you will want to make the price lower than usual to attract more people to book. This is because your home and listing do not have any reviews yet. Airbnb listings live and die by reviews. Each guest you host can leave a public review on your page and rate you by stars in a few categories, so you will want to do everything in your power to honestly represent your space in the listing. Remember, they even have a category for guests to review that says "accuracy of listing." It's all about the expectation management!

At first, you will lower the price, get some guests to book, and share with them that they will be your first guests. For example, "Hello Emily! We are so happy to host you. Indeed you will be our first guest (or you will be one of our first guests!), and we are looking forward to your feedback and tips on how we could make our space and guest experience even better. Please be in touch if you have any questions or issues, as we want to guarantee you have a 5-star experience in our home."

Emily will probably be understanding and feel special for being first, and glad that you care about her opinion and comfort. Once Emily's been in for a day or two, ask her how it's going. Once her reservation goes well and she has checked out, you can write her a message to ask how her stay was. If she says "great!" then you can ask, "So glad to hear that Emily! Would you be up to leaving us a nice review about your experience? As you are our first guest, it would add so much to our listing and new business. I will also leave you a 5-star right now! It was a pleasure to host you, come back anytime! All the best, Lauren."

extra person fee

In your listing, you have the option to add an 'extra fee' for extra guests. For example, you rent your place for $100 per night for up to three guests. After three guests, you charge $10 per person, per night. If they have six guests, you will be receiving $130 per night during their stay. This allows you to cover additional utility costs and deep cleaning because the place will probably be messier. You will have to use more bedding and towels, set up more beds, and purchase a folding bed or air mattress, which are all additional costs for you. These small details can add up quickly, as you have many people staying in your space and using the facilities.

cleaning fee

Setting the cleaning fee is up to you. You can charge exactly what you pay your cleaner, slightly more to receive more income or cover the cost of your cleaning supplies, or less and cover the cleaner's fee in the nightly booking price. You could also choose to have a higher price per night and no cleaning fee, paying the cleaner out of pocket. Do some basic calculations and see what's best for you.

security deposit

Setting this amount on your listing is up to you. It may seem intimidating to guests if there is a $400 security deposit. They may assume that amount will be held on their card upon booking and released after their check-out. In reality, Airbnb does not charge this at the time of booking, they only charge this if you make a damage claim in the resolution center, and the guest agrees to it, or Airbnb rules the "resolution case" in your favor.

for example...

I make a claim for $200 because the guest broke my coffee table and TV, and I alert the guest about it. Airbnb accepts and validates my claim, and they charge the guest $200 because this $400 security deposit allows Airbnb to do so. I personally choose to put a $150 security deposit in the USA, as it's not too high and not too low for either host or guest.

Aircover

Airbnb has recently started offering 'aircover' which is free insurance coverage for your rental automatically. This includes $1 million in liability insurance, $1 damage protection, pet damage protection, deep cleaning protection, income loss protection if you need to cancel confirmed bookings due to damage, and they offer a 14-day filing window for damage claims. They are also promising quick reimbursements, typically within 2 weeks and a fast-track for Super Hosts with a dedicated line of support specialists.

This is a new policy that I did not have access to while running my business and I can see the huge gap it is filling. It used to be extremely challenging to get Airbnb's help if you had a guest do severe damage in your place and didn't have the original receipts of every item purchased, with proof that it was part of your Airbnb unit, such as in-unit photos.

I imagine you will still need all the documentation and receipts for everything you've purchased showing the value if you want to use aircover. I would not rely too heavily on this promise, as the terms and conditions are written as an insurance policy and it does not cover things deemed as wear and tear, acts of nature, etc.

There are also affordable short-term rental insurances you can buy for peace of mind from a private insurance company. In my experience hosting more than 4000 travelers over a few years, I have made maybe ten damage reports, mostly for damaged sheets or missing plates/cups. I recommend doing your due diligence by screening renters as I have advised in previous chapters, and deny bookings that feel sketchy to you, following your intuition about a reservation is a great way to minimize risk.

chapter 9

your cleaners and the logistics

Having a super clean space shares the #1 spot for the most important hosting duty, just alongside your excellent photography, brilliant communication skills and smooth as silk check-in/check-out process.

bedding sets and cleaning times

Bedding management is a crucial aspect of running your Airbnb smoothly. There are complicated logistics to be worked out here depending on how many properties you have. As standard check-out/check-in times give about a four-hour window for the cleaners to prepare the home (11 am check out, 3 pm check-in), your cleaning team may be done cleaning in one or two hours. They will not have enough time to do all the laundry on-site (2-3 loads = 3-4 hours). If you have one cleaner coming in to clean, it may take them 2-3 hours to clean, but you will have to pay them to wait for the laundry to be ready (upwards of 3.5-4 hours for everything to dry and be ready). If you have 2-4 check-outs in one day, doing all the laundry on-site is impossible.

creating bedding sets

This is an extra, clean, full bedding set for the entire home: Fitted sheets, flat sheets, duvet covers, pillowcases, towels, hand towels, washcloths, and bathmats. With extra bedding sets, the cleaners can enter, clean, change the bedding, and move on to the next apartment or finish quickly. They could also start the laundry while cleaning and keep that going at each rental. Wash a load at one home, take it with them wet and dry it at the next. Cleaners will then do the rest of the dirty laundry at home on their own time. I buy high-quality, large square plastic bags with zippered tops for these sets, as everything fits in one place and retains its folded shape. You will often see cheap Chinese versions of these bags with a blue, black and red pinstripe design.

The amount of time needed to do three laundry loads is an average of 3 hours (depending on your machines). If a cleaning team needs to clean three apartments in four hours, and it takes three hours to do all the laundry per place, that's twelve hours of laundry. You will have to work out the payment arrangement (a flat fee per job or hourly) for your cleaner to incorporate doing the laundry at home. Sometimes one cleaner will pick up the laundry from each rental, go to the Laundromat, and then return each clean set to each apartment. This will be two to four hours of work, plus the cost of the Laundromat.

I don't recommend this system. It is an expensive investment to order duplicate bedding sets, but you will save time and money in the long term by allowing your cleaners to do laundry at home in their off-time. You will want your cleaning team to have a car and laundry machines at home so they can safely transport and do the laundry easily without visiting Laundromats.

bedding set logistics

My best recommendation is to purchase enough extra bedding 'sets' so the cleaner can move quickly and turn over all needed apartments without being delayed by the laundry. You will also want to consider having universal bedding/towels for all your places, so the bedding is the same and interchangeable for all your Airbnb's. If you choose to do home-specific bedding, you may need to have more than one duplicate bedding set, as different cleaners may be cleaning on different days. For example, Molly cleans apartment 1 on Tuesday. On Thursday, Mary is set to clean apartment 1. Will she have to drive across town to pick up the clean bedding from Molly? This will add one to two hours to her cleaning process, therefore costing you more money.

I also recommend having spares for all your bedding in the supply closet. In case of damage, you have replacements on hand and can avoid having to re-order/re-stock one of all your bedding supplies. The most common causes of bedding damages are oil stains, makeup stains, and burn holes.

When you make a damage claim in Airbnb's "Resolution Center," you will have to select the price of the replacement, and if you have it on hand, it is an easy way to get reimbursed quickly for the damage, and it saves the headache of re-ordering one of everything.

washing style

I recommend washing all the sheets and duvets together, and then the towels and bathmats together, so it's best to choose colors that can be washed together. If you mix towels with sheets, you can expect a fair amount of lint on your sheets. If this happens, re-wash your sheets with detergent and baking soda, and then dry them with a few dryer sheets to help release the lint. As a last resort, you will use a lint roller.

hiring cleaners

This may or may not be the biggest challenge with your Airbnb business. I have divided this section into two parts. 1. For the single host who has only one place. 2. For the multi-unit host, running 2-10+ Airbnb's.

1. single unit cleaner's strategy

If you are a single unit host, you may be offering your backyard backhouse, a room in your own home, or a nearby place that is easy to manage yourself. You will be cleaning yourself or employing a friend, partner, relative, or local cleaning professionals to help you out. Your needs are pretty manageable, as you'll have 1-3 cleans per week depending on your guest's length of stay.

I recommend you train a few friends and a few local cleaners on how to prepare your place if you are unavailable or choose to be a remote host for one unit. Your trained cleaners should know how to set up the bedding, where to put the towels, what supplies to check and refill, where the storage closet is, how to check for damages and what items to check to make sure they weren't stolen.

It is important to schedule your cleaners the best you can in advance. As you are not providing a full-time job for your cleaners, you can expect that they may not always be available or totally reliable as they have other responsibilities and employment. Therefore you will want to train multiple part-time cleaners who can fill in at the last minute if needed. Oftentimes, you may get a last-minute booking, and if you are unavailable, it could be stressful to find someone last minute to clean and prepare the place for your next guests.

Typical cleaning hours are between 11 am-3 pm, so your cleaners should be available during those hours, seven days a week. Experienced, professional, detailed cleaners are recommended - not everyone knows how to properly 'clean.' Fresh, clean bedding and a super clean bathroom are the most important focuses. You may want to have an extra bedding 'set' for each cleaner you are regularly using, so your cleaners can do the laundry on their off-time at home.

for example...

Perhaps it takes the cleaner 1.5 hours to clean and prepare your place, but it takes them 3 hours to clean and do two laundry loads on-site (one load of bedding, one load of towels). Will you pay them $18/hour for 3 hours, a total of $54 to clean your place, and hang around to wait for the laundry? Or will you pay them $27 for cleaning ($18/hour x 1.5 hours) and then $10 to do the laundry at home on their own time (total of $37)?

They will probably enjoy doing laundry at home while cooking dinner or watching TV and getting paid for it, I know I did! You could choose to pay a flat fee per clean and have them hang around and wait for the laundry to be ready so you don't have to buy duplicate bedding sets, but this is not the most efficient route. You would save money in the long run by investing in extra bedding sets from the beginning ($54 versus $37 over and over, this will add up).

managing your cleaners, single unit

If you are always using different cleaners, it is recommended to give each of them a bedding set because you will save money in the long run. It is more likely they can make themselves available last minute for 1-2 hours to clean, instead of 3-4 hours to do the laundry on-site as well. You also have the option of doing the laundry yourself and preparing it for them. They could pick up the clean bedding set from your home when they are on their way to clean and drop off the dirty laundry when they finish. You could also drop it off to them or have it ready in the supply closet. There are many options here for saving money by doing the laundry yourself.

Cleaners usually work independently. They arrive and clean without seeing you or you checking their work before the guest's check-in, so it is vital to train them properly and give them a detailed cleaning checklist

ECO

so they don't forget anything. I check my new cleaners' work for the first 3-5 cleans, and if I find many errors and see that they are not able to follow the cleaning checklist properly, I search for a new cleaner. I have included a cleaning checklist template in this book.

cleaner communication protocols, single unit

When the cleaner first arrives, they check for the keys and then text you that they have the keys. Secondly, have them scan for stolen items and damages. You have a limited time window to report damages/missing items to Airbnb, so you will want to get photos from your cleaners and upload them right away to the "resolution center" in the Airbnb App so that you can be reimbursed by the guest with Airbnb's help. Then the cleaner will start the laundry, or not if they will be doing it all at home, and clean everything, with the final step of texting you when they leave so you know it's done, and you can offer the next guest an early check-in since the place is ready!

2. multi-unit cleaning strategy, running 2-10+ units

This is my specialty. I have been running 3-7 Airbnb's simultaneously since I began my hosting journey and have discovered a million ways not to run the cleaning system.

my best recommendation

Assuming that your Airbnb's are in the same city or similar neighborhood, you will want to hire a professional cleaner with a staff of their own. My "head cleaner" has four or five workers she has trained, and she brings one or two of them with her depending on how many cleanings she has for the day. I require her to train them at least five to eight times on a home before I allow her to send them to clean a rental alone without her. She works as a head maid, managing her own team of cleaners, managing all the laundry and bedding sets, and paying them all individually from what I pay her. This is really, really, really the best way to run multi-units in the same area. It eliminates the need to schedule and communicate with many cleaners and organize replacements if a cleaner does not show up.

your cleaner is a property manager too

Your cleaner is more than a cleaner. They do many other property management tasks. They check for damages, take photos and send them to you immediately, look for stolen items (hairdryer, iron, ironing board), check for lost keys, inspect the bedding for damages and send photos, pick up trash around the property, alert you when supplies are low so you can re-stock, manage your supply closet, refill the supplies in the home, alert you when something is broken, they make the beds look hotel style, they set up extra air mattresses or couch beds when needed, alert you when the gardener or trashman didn't come, they might even meet handymen and show them around for you if they are there cleaning anyway. You need cleaners with the ability to do more than just clean, they should be able to follow your instructions as well.

benefits of a head cleaner system

I have experimented with hiring cleaning companies for all my places or for individual apartments, hiring and training specific cleaners for specific apartments, training many cleaners on many apartments, using professional Airbnb cleaning services, paying my friends or acquaintances to work independently with my cleaning checklist or with me supervising.

My take away from years of success and failure with cleaners is to hire a head cleaner. Let the head cleaner employ workers, train them, manage them, schedule them, and be responsible for them. If you can give them enough jobs, they will make themselves available for you, and reliability is sorted because many trained backup cleaners want work from you.

They have now made their own little cleaning company with many employees that depend on this relationship with you. They don't want to lose your business, so they will make things happen for you.

I use universal bedding (the same for every place) for all my Airbnb rentals, so I give my head cleaner three full bedding sets for six apartments, and she cycles them through and does all the laundry herself at home. Your head cleaner and some cleaners must have a car (for carrying lots of dirty bedding and cleaning supplies) and laundry machines at home. If they are paying to do laundry at a Laundromat, they are losing money and 2-3 hours just to do your laundry.

some tips about other cleaning systems

If you hire an Airbnb-specific cleaning company or cleaning team, know that they are doing many other cleans between 11 am-3 pm and may breeze through your place without checking details or being thorough. They may tick all the boxes on the to-do list but may cut corners because they are on a super limited time frame.

My "professional Airbnb cleaners" left towels wet, beds unchanged, were relatively unavailable, and 'forgot' to check for damages as they were racing to clean many rentals (not all mine) in just four hours. If you can find a reliable and top-notch Airbnb cleaning service, congrats! You have alleviated a large responsibility from your plate.

managing multiple cleaner's yourself

If you choose to hire multiple cleaners that work separately, you will constantly be chasing them for availability. For example, Susan is free Thursdays and Fridays, Ellen only Wednesday-Friday, Sammy is free Sundays and Tuesdays, etc. You will be balancing many people's limited availabilities and chasing to book them and map out your cleaning schedule.

What if Ellen doesn't show up due to a personal emergency, and the others aren't free, and you are out of town? It happens. You may have to cancel the next reservation, potentially ruining someone's hard-earned vacation plans and lose your Super Host status. What if your guest extends their stay for an additional day, and you need to rework Ellen's schedule last minute, but no one is free on such short notice? You're in a bind.

cleaning crew availability and training

You want to have a cohesive team of cleaners working together to cover for each other. By using the "head cleaner" system, you are eliminating a ton of work for yourself, creating jobs, and allowing someone else to handle details, schedules, stress, and the availability puzzle for you. You're also letting them be the boss and run their own business inside your business, potentially maximizing profits for themselves and allowing them to create jobs for their friends or family.

Your cleaning crew will need to be available seven days a week, between 11 am-3 pm, or whatever your check-out/check-in window of time is. I like to hire cleaners and check their work the first few times they clean, evaluating their natural inclination for detail. I have hired and let go so many cleaners because they do not clean to the standard I need to ensure my guests are happy.

Believe it or not, everyone does not know how to clean in a detailed manner, and you will want an experienced cleaner with an impeccable eye for detail. I give my cleaners a cleaning checklist and require them to initial after every task is done. See the template in the book following this chapter.

reliable cleaners + lockboxes = the best system

Hopefully, after the initial hiring and training of your cleaners, you have secured a team of super talented and trustworthy cleaners that work independently. If not, your full-time job is interviewing, training, and checking on your cleaners in training.

If you have a lockbox, then check-in and check-outs can be very simple. First, you text your cleaner or have them text you, letting you know that they have arrived and started cleaning (their arrival will also let you know that the previous guest checked out and left the keys in the lockbox). A bit later, you receive a text that they have finished cleaning and the place is ready. Now you can text your next guest and offer them an early check-in if they desire since the home is ready. Later, you will message your new guest and confirm that they figured out the lockbox and have checked into your place ok.

This system is deleting the two hours that some Hosts put in driving to the property to check their cleaner's work and then waiting around for the guest to arrive at the supposed "arrival time" to hand off the keys. With the lockbox system in place, I sit on my patio, drink tea, text away while my cleaners do the dirty work, and my lockboxes do my Host check-in duties for me.

cleaning review scores

Your cleaner's attention to detail will make your Airbnb succeed with fantastic cleaning review scores or make your Airbnb fail with a few bad cleaning reviews. "There was hair in the tub! Hair on the sink! Ew, gross!" Your cleaner can potentially destroy your business in one day if the guest leaves a bad enough review. You can definitely bounce back but most likely, you will feel a large dent in your pocket from this situation.

In the emergency situation that the guest is disgusted by the status of your place, you can usually offer your guest a partial or full refund in exchange for them not leaving you a review. Sometimes, this may be

STOP
HAVE YOU SIGNED UP USING LAUREN'S new host referral link?

worth it and necessary. Once, I had a guest find a used deodorant stick in the bed after my new "Professional Airbnb Cleaning Service" did not change the beds, just made them up. I gave the guest a full refund in exchange for her not leaving me a review.

Refunds saved the day! The guest does have fourteen days to leave a review, so you will have to tell them that you will issue the refund after the fourteen-day window is over. Since you have written this promise to them on Airbnb messenger, they should feel confident that they will definitely get the refund after fourteen days because Airbnb can hold you responsible for your promise. I can't say that Airbnb loves this system, but so far they haven't commented or complained about it.

Your cleaners need to know and understand Airbnb's cleaning review score system, be extremely reliable, and understand that if they mess up and a guest leaves a bad review, they may have lost their job and messed up your business. They have to really understand Airbnb's review system to take care of your business for you properly. I treat my cleaners with the utmost respect and appreciation because my business is literally in their hands.

If you want to drive over and check every home after every clean, then you are taking the responsibility out of the cleaner's hands. But if you have many Airbnb´s, logistically, this could be impossible so having trustworthy, incredible cleaners is a preferable way to run your show. If you want to go do another job during the day or relax at home with your dog and cook Italian food from scratch, you will need a good cleaner that works independently.

cleaner communications

Another important quality in your cleaner is their communication abilities. Does your cleaner take instructions and follow them? Can they stay in contact and keep you updated on their arrival, departure, supply needs, re-stocking needs, damages, issues at the house? They must write you these details ASAP and keep you in the loop, promptly sending photos of issues and problems. Otherwise, your guests will be the ones to tell you something is broken or missing, and it will be too late to charge the previous guest.

If you find that your cleaner is not communicating, and your reviews and scores are going down because of the issues that could have been avoided if she would have communicated better, you can design a detailed communication protocol for her to follow. Your other choice is to jump back into the full-time sea of hiring and training (and firing) cleaners, which can last weeks or months.

cleaners, bedding sets and laundry

I have spoken extensively about laundry already, but it cannot be pronounced loudly enough that you should invest in duplicate bedding sets and have your cleaners do the laundry at their house. This is a smooth, no-hassle, proven system. You do not want to limit yourself by having a cleaner hang around for four hours waiting for laundry to be ready. They could have gone and cleaned another apartment for the same price.

Instead, you had one cleaner hanging around for four hours at one apartment and had to hunt down another available cleaner to clean and hang around at another apartment, and you paid them all double to wait for the towels to dry. You do have the option of only providing a duplicate set of towels, hand towels, and bath mats, having them wash all the sheets, duvets, and pillowcases on-site which is easily accomplished in a two-hour window.

It's best to maximize your cleaning team's speed and efficiency because availability and your cleaners' cost are important factors when managing your Airbnb's cleaning needs and your profit margin. The less cleaners you have, the more jobs you can give them, so the more they will want to make themselves available to you. There are fewer people to manage, train and depend on, and you can develop a great communication system between you and your cleaners if you are working together regularly.

cleaner payments and appreciation

As for payment, I like to pay per job. I experimented with hourly but found that sometimes it's a quick clean, and sometimes it's a more extensive clean or set up, but it always balances out the same for the cleaner over time, and I don't have to worry about cleaners hanging around to get paid more. If I pay a flat rate of $60 to clean a one-bedroom and do the laundry at home, sometimes it will take her 1.5 hours to clean and then an hour of laundry at home, sometimes it might take 3 hours to clean and set up, and one hour of laundry at home, in general, she is always making $15-$25 per hour.

The only issue here is that they may try to rush through the job since it's a flat rate, so you have to keep your standards high and perhaps regularly check their work, have them send you photos, and keep them responsible for errors. I charge my cleaners between $5-$10 per mistake I find when I check, although I rarely charge unless it's an obvious mistake like not leaving any bath mats or not cleaning out the refrigerator. Therefore, my cleaners are financially responsible for their quality of work.

I also choose to pay my cleaners very well so they don't want to lose the job, they follow my instructions, stay reliable and make themselves available. It's a win-win, mutually beneficial relationship. I don't like the thought of spending another two months interviewing, hiring, training, inspecting, and firing cleaners who don't care about their work or my self-built business.

My head cleaner is an amazing woman that I respect, so I treat her with an attitude of deep appreciation. When she makes mistakes, I am pretty easy on her, as I need her commitment, reliability, high standard of work, fantastic communication skills, and incredible cleaner management abilities. My world would be so much harder without her, so if she forgets something, I ask nicely to remember to do it in the future, and she does. If she didn't, I would have to take measures to ensure the house is cleaned properly for my guests.

This may mean hiring a new cleaner, inflicting large financial penalties, or lowering her payment and paying a third party (usually a friend) $20 to go over and check her work. It will take them 10-15 minutes to check everything, but I pay them for their driving time, etc. Remember, no one is perfect, but when you give your cleaning team a checklist and ask them to do a final check, they are responsible for making sure that everything is done correctly 95%-100% of the time. The success of your business depends on it.

In the past, I have had to train and fire so many cleaners for so many reasons, it was emotionally exhausting and too much drama. Finding a hard-working, reliable, highly detailed, intelligent, adaptable person who is great at following specific instructions and makes themselves available is a miracle. I wish you the best for finding yours! Shout out to my #1 Mrs. Erica, words can't express my love and gratitude for how she changed my life.

When you have found one, your job responsibility gets cut in half. Show them appreciation, respect, spoil them, treat them like queens and kings! They are the foundation of your business operations, besides you. Please don't treat them badly or look down on them, they are keeping your business profitable by showing up and doing a great job.

paying the cleaners

It is essential to set up a payment system with your cleaner, what day they will send their invoice, and what day you will pay them. I have my cleaner send the invoice Sunday night, and I leave her a check in my mailbox before Monday night. I also do PayPal and Venmo for her when I am out of town. Sometimes the schedule you made for the cleaner does not reflect exactly what cleans were done.

Let's say you received two new reservations in the middle of the week and added those cleans to her schedule with a casual text, or the guest extended their stay one night and now the dates on the schedule are not accurate. It can be challenging to keep up with what you owe if you are running five apartments, and you had three different cleaners do a total of eighteen cleans, many last minute or with date changes. Creating a manageable invoicing and payment system with your cleaners will erase a lot of stress and money mismanagement.

chapter 10

review system & Super Host

Positive 5-star reviews are the #1 determining factor in making you a profitable business. Therefore, getting them and improving your rating towards Super Host status may be a top goal for you, depending if this is a side hustle or your main stream of income.

asking for a review

First and foremost, if your guest had an issue during their stay (bug in the bed, sink not working, broken dining table, door handle fell off, not enough towels), any issue at all, even tiny, I recommend you DO NOT ask them or mention anything about leaving a review. Chances are, they will mention the problem, exaggerate it, and maybe even try to get a partial refund for their 'inconvenience.' I have a straightforward, pretty fool-proof method.

problematic guests

If your guest experienced any kind of issue during their stay, leave it alone. They are not your review target. No review is a MILLION times better than a negative review. Guests who didn't have their expectations met can be ruthless, and they probably don't understand what it's like to run a business that lives or dies by reviews. They may not comprehend the number of variables you are juggling and could slam you hard. They could be having a bad day and vent their misplaced anger into your review. They may even have the personality of always searching for something to complain about, an unconscious negative thinking process that must point out other people's failures. They may feel deep satisfaction retaliating against you for something that was beyond your control. Don't underestimate who you're dealing with.

very happy guests

For guests that are ecstatic at checkout, "Hi! We just checked out and had the best trip ever! Thanks so much for opening your lovely home! We will definitely come back and stay with you again!," you will simply say "Thanks so much! I'm so happy you had a great time. Would you be up to leaving us a review about your experience? I will also leave you a 5-star review right now. Come back anytime! Thanks so much, and safe travels." I ask them to review me and gently let them know that I will be leaving them a 5-star review, hinting that that is what I'd like to receive also.

unknown guests

After a non-problematic guest checks out, I always write them, "Hey! How was your stay with us?" In my experience, about 50-60% of people answer back. Many people check out, sign off Airbnb, and forget about you. If they do write back, "It was incredible, we loved it!" – Follow the protocol for Very Happy Guests. If they say, "Oh, it was fine," you could investigate further, but I recommend you only do so if you are VERY needy for more reviews. In this case, you would respond, "Oh ok! Did you have a good time exploring (insert your city name here)? Did you like the decorations of the house? Was it comfortable for you?"

This is a bit risky because they could just jump to leaving all their 'helpful' or obnoxious criticisms as a review instead of writing you back personally. But they may reply, "Oh, the house wasn't so great, it was ok" or "It was an excellent house, just my grandma got sick, so the trip wasn't as we had hoped." Here you will gain insight into their experience and be able to guess if they had a good enough time to ask them to leave you a positive review.

You are aiming for 5-stars for every review, 4-stars is not actually a positive review. You only want enthusiastic, highly pleased guests to review you. Guests who had an ok good time will probably feel generous giving you 4-stars, which will drag down your average and put you towards the bottom of the Airbnb search algorithm.

host review wisdom

If a guest had an ok or underwhelming trip, don't ask for a review. One bad review can temporarily close down your listing's success or deter all future guests from booking. I recommend only asking for a review of their experience if they clearly stated that they loved the place.

I once had a group of Grandmas on a girl's week trip at my place, and after their stay, they praised me and thanked me sincerely for a fantastic holiday. I then reached out and asked for a review, only to find they made a laundry list of every tiny detail of the place that wasn't perfect, in an exaggerated way. "The tub was so hard to enter! It's too tall! They desperately need a railing and handlebar to step into the tub! It is not safe to bathe here!"

I was so upset but was able to empathize with their senior-perspective complaints. I had personally met them, given them a tour, sat with them for an hour chatting and giving recommendations, they told me they loved the house, why would they jeopardize the business I worked so

SUPERHOST

hard to take care of and to build? Unless you are a homeowner or small business owner, sometimes guests have no idea how hard it is to upkeep a property and run/manage your own small business and are merciless with their criticism. Some people see the world as a cup half empty, and inviting them to share their opinion is a risky game.

Super Host status

Super Host status is a profound place to be as an Airbnb host. You will attract more reservations, benefit from a significant increase in earnings, you'll be featured higher in the Airbnb algorithm search results, and will be included in promotional emails. A Super Host is an Airbnb host who has met certain credentials, so guests know they will receive superb hospitality.

what is required to be a Super Host?

A 4.8 overall rating for your listings over the past year, <1% cancellation rate (which means you can basically never cancel on a guest), you host a minimum number of reservations per quarter, and you have a 90% response rate, which means you respond to guest messages within 24 hours at least 90% of the time. There is a filter for guests to search only for Super Host listings, and you will receive a special badge on the corner of your photo as a promotion tool. If you call Airbnb directly and offer an understandable reason why you need cancel, often they will waive the penalty so you can keep your Super Host status or eligibility.

When I travel with Airbnb, I always go for a Super Host listing if it's available and economical. As Airbnb is a home-sharing platform with little regulation besides reviews, this badge creates a deep sense of trust in travelers, and is worthwhile to pursue. An evaluation takes place every three months to re-certify your status.

chapter II

importance of traveling & hosting

A wise man travels to discover himself, to travel is to take a journey into yourself, travel far enough you meet yourself, to travel the world is to meet your soul, travel is the only thing you buy that makes you richer...

Traveling is a heart and mind-expanding activity, whether you are a Western person visiting a third world country for the first time or just a curious explorer flying into a new city. Each new culture, new experience, new exploration takes us one step closer to getting to know who we are beyond our conditioning, cultural programming, everyday routine and stressors.

We start to see our natural passions express themselves, we discover new things that deeply resonate with us, it is true that traveling in a new environment can bring priceless self-awareness. As you travel into new cultures, you have the ability to observe your behavior through a new lens, and a deeper level of your true essence is revealed to you.

When we host travelers, we are giving the ultimate gift. We are honoring another human being that has sacrificed and worked hard for this opportunity to travel and live their dreams. This can be a time of self-healing and life-changing experiences, and it should be respected with grand importance. Your guest has the ability to enjoy life without the stress and burdens of everyday life's responsibilities. They have the

possibility to reset, re-charge, re-connect and gain inspiration for their life path. They may be seeking a cure for a hopeless depression they can't shake. It is a precious moment.

I encourage you to host intentionally, consciously, responsibly, and provide a truly beautiful service and experience. You are offering a secure place to rest in an unknown and sometimes intimidating new place, and sometimes you are unknowingly providing emotional support to a weary, fearful traveler. With this deeper understanding, you now have the opportunity to achieve a new level of fulfillment with your work, as every ounce of energy spent making your space comfortable, beautiful, clean, and ready is not lost. It is an investment in someone else's happiness. Oftentimes positive reviews and gratitude-filled messages confirm this. Tired travelers are the norm, so be prepared, patient, understanding, and hospitable! It is your responsibility.

By hosting your own Airbnb, you are working for yourself. You are your own boss. You decide your lifestyle, schedule, work hours, employee's, the design, essence, and energy of the space and experience. This is personal power and freedom. You also create jobs for others (your cleaner, handyman, co-hosts), a precious gift and contribution to your community. You can be the boss you always wanted to have and be independent of the 9-5 system. You are creating a space for people to travel comfortably and be inspired by new experiences in a new place. Your work can positively change lives or destroy the $1000's of dollars investment your guest made for their well-deserved vacation.

I love to take care of guests and be friendly, check on them, upgrade the spaces with nicer art, decorations, and appliances as possible. I care that they enjoy their stay, that they can relax there and seek the inspirational experiences they crave.

chapter 12

thank you!

Check out my step-by-step video course for more interactive guidance ***Airbnb Express: Start Hosting in 14 days*** on Teachable.

https://lauren-coats-s-school.teachable.com/p/airbnb

If you are a brand-new host to Airbnb, you will receive $40 in Airbnb travel credit by signing up with my new host referral link to create your first listing as a host. Thank you for your support!

www.airbnb.com/r/laurencoats

I offer wealth-building coaching and business developement consulting for Airbnb hosts, vacation rentals and property rentals in general, nowadays you have many options beyond Airbnb. Contact me for a 1:1 and let's discover how I can help.

Schedule on Calendly: **www.calendly.com/laurencoats144**

May you thrive in your Airbnb hosting career, meet beautiful new people through your business, host wonderful travelers, impact lives in a positive way, get rich and enjoy the process. *With love, Lauren*

about the author

I hosted over 4000 travelers in California while running my own Airbnb management company. I'm a self-taught, all-in-one DIY Airbnb host, property manager, and official Airbnb brand ambassador.

Traveling to more than 30 countries as a truth seeker, I come to the hosting business with a deep understanding of what a traveler needs to be comforted and relaxed on the road. I know what a welcoming home away from home really feels like, and what is does to harmonize my body chemistry so I have the power to keep exploring. Connect with me on Instagram **@Freedomjoy144** or by email lauren@laurencoats.com.

How about the amazing illustrations and cover design by my friend and artist Danielle O'Malley! What a spectacular creator and radiant goddess. Check out her Instagram **@danielleomalleeey** and website **www.danielleardenomalley.net/shop**

Book Design: Lauren Coats
www.laurencoats.com/airbnb
Cover Art & Illustrations: Danielle O'Malley
www.daniellear denomalley.net/shop

Printed in Great Britain
by Amazon

60327154R00061